The American Civil War

The
American
Civil War

Timothy H. Donovan, Jr.
Roy K. Flint
Arthur V. Grant, Jr.
Gerald P. Stadler

Thomas E. Griess
Series Editor

DEPARTMENT OF HISTORY
UNITED STATES MILITARY ACADEMY
WEST POINT, NEW YORK

AVERY PUBLISHING GROUP INC.
Wayne, New Jersey

Illustration Credits

The publisher would like to thank Dr. George Lankevich for the use of his historical library collection, which was the source of much illustrative material. All original artwork was produced by Edward J. Krasnoborski.

Painting on page 235 done by Tom Lovell, copyrighted by the National Geographic Society. Reprinted by permission.

Series Editor, Thomas E. Griess
In-House Editor, Joanne Abrams
Cover design by Martin Hochberg

Library of Congress Cataloging in Publication Data

The American Civil War.

    Bibliography: p.
    Includes index.
    1. United States--History--Civil War, 1861-1865--
Campaigns. I. Donovan, Timothy H. II. United States
Military Academy. Dept. of History.
E470.A45 1986   973.7'3   86-20626
ISBN 0-89529-318-8
ISBN 0-89529-272-6 (pbk.)

Contents

To the former members of the Department of History who have found a "soldier's resting place beneath a soldier's blow."

Illustrations

Acknowledgements

The completion of this textbook was made possible by the professional dedication of many people. Colonel Thomas E. Griess' guidance and firm mastery of the subject material insured that the important issues were addressed. Mr. Edward J. Krasnoborski's unique cartographical abilities are evident in the maps that accompany the text. Mr. Michael P. Musick of the Old Military Records Branch, National Archives, was very helpful in making available the records of the Army of the Potomac and Headquarters of the Army. The officers of the Department of History, who first used these chapters to teach the course entitled History of the Military Art, offered critical judgments of our interpretations and helped find the errors in our style. Major Paul Renschen, Major Jack Mountcastle, and Captain James Johnson were particularly helpful; we appreciate their interest, and after careful consideration of their suggestions, we have altered the text in some cases to reflect their ideas. Mr. Bob Schnare and Mrs. Marie Capps of the United States Military Academy Archives provided valuable assistance in locating many of the photographs used in the text. Mr. Jacob Sheads of the National Park Service guided the authors on a unique tour of the Gettysburg battlefield. His continued interest in the faculty of the Department of History is greatly appreciated.

Mrs. Sally French and Mrs. Sharen Pacenza worked diligently to insure that critical deadlines were met and that the typed material was of the highest quality. Their cheerful attitude in times of stress was especially helpful.

Finally, all of our families had to suffer through the whine of minie balls and the rattle of musketry that we took home with us each night. Their unwavering support was a welcome salve to the wounds of the day.

Timothy H. Donovan, Jr.
Roy K. Flint
Arthur V. Grant, Jr.
Gerald P. Stadler

West Point, New York

Foreword

For over a century, cadets at the United States Military Academy have studied the military campaigns of the American Civil War in varying degrees of detail. It was not until 1938, however, that T. Dodson Stamps, professor and head of the Department of Military Art and Engineering, introduced an atlas of battle maps to support that study; that atlas was specially devised to accompany the text then in use, Matthew Forney Steele's *American Campaigns*. The concept of a closely integrated narrative and graphical portrayal has been a feature of the course entitled History of the Military Art since that time.

In 1959, Vincent J. Esposito, Stamps' successor as head of the Department of Military Art and Engineering, adopted for cadet use the unique two-volume *West Point Atlas of American Wars*, which Esposito had edited. It served its purpose well. In 1967, however, changes in the course in the History of the Military Art required the development of a new text. Course-long themes, a broader treatment of military history, and less emphasis on operational detail were among the changes that dictated new textual and teaching approaches.

The American Civil War was conceived as a text that would present developments in the military art in the 1860s, using the war's campaigns as the primary instructional vehicle, but encompassing broader themes than the purely operational ones. The text was also designed to stress the totality of the war and to show the relationship between events unfolding in the Eastern and Western Theaters of Operations. Finally, the pivotal 1863 Vicksburg Campaign was selected for treatment in more detail in order to provide cadets with the opportunity to study one aspect of the war in greater depth.

Four faculty members of the Department of History at the United States Military Academy shared in the writing of this text. After Roy K. Flint introduces the major issues of the war and sets the stage for the intense conflict of sectional interests, Gerald P. Stadler takes the reader from the initial blunders at First Bull Run through the turn of the tide in the West at Vicksburg. In Chapter 7, Timothy H. Donovan, Jr. describes Lee's splendid victories at Fredericksburg and Chancellorsville. The final chapters by Arthur V. Grant, Jr. recount the turn of the tide in the East at Gettysburg and follow the rise of Grant from his resounding victory at Chattanooga to the final drama at Appomattox.

Utilizing some primary source materials and many sound secondary sources, these authors have written a thoughtful and stimulating narrative that examines the military lessons of the war critically and combines operational and institutional treatments of military history. The Department of History and a large number of students are indebted to them for their efforts, which were made under the pressure of time and with minimal resources.

Gerald Stadler and Arthur Grant, relying in part but not solely upon the Esposito atlas, designed the maps that appear in the supporting campaign atlas. The Department of History is indebted to Mr. Edward J. Krasnoborski, who supervised the entire map-drafting effort and brilliantly performed most of the cartographic work.

The present edition of *The American Civil War* is essentially the text that was published at the Military Academy in 1977. As editor, I have attempted to clarify certain passages for the general reader, amplify purely military terminology, and improve the evenness of the narrative. The editor is grateful for the advice and suggestions rendered by Rudy Shur and Joanne Abrams of Avery Publishing Group, Inc. Their assistance was timely and helpful. Ms. Abrams immeasurably improved the narrative through her painstaking editing, corrections of lapses in syntax, and penetrating questions related to clarity of expression.

Thomas E. Griess
Series Editor

Introduction

America's Civil War may well have been the last romantic war. Images of sweaty, trail-hardened soldiers, inured to the rigors of seemingly endless marches, led by aristocratic officers, and pitted against each other in great battles of flashing brilliance, fill the minds of many who live in the automobile age of the twentieth century. Somehow, perceptions of that war are dominated by visions of gallant heroes mounted on bigger-than-life horses caught up in a tragic struggle. Southerners, some still rankled by defeat, glory in the exploits of Robert E. Lee, "Stonewall" Jackson, and "Jeb" Stuart; northerners find ample evidence of a strong union and vigorous economic system in the determination and innovativeness of Lincoln, Grant, Sherman, and Sheridan, and the wartime productivity of the North. Both points of view are bolstered by the justness of each side's cause. So compelling is the charm of the war that serious scholars and laymen for over a hundred years have joined together to perpetuate its history—and its mythology—in endless study, in popular novels and films, and in regular meetings of countless Civil War Round Tables spread throughout the United States and the world. Perhaps more than any other event in American history, the Civil War has become a part of our national folklore, our truly common experience, affecting Anglo-Americans, European immigrants, and blacks alike. In this regard, it is unique. To serious students of the military art, the war is unique in other ways as well.

In the pages of this text, the reader will still find the heroes, the villains, the explosive violence, the brilliant successes, and the monumental blunders, for one cannot write about the Civil War without capturing some of the excitement that enthralls us all. The romantic mythology and folklore, however, have been set aside when possible in favor of a view of the war as part of the long sweep of military history and the evolution of the military art. From these pages, there emerges a picture of a populous democracy that was split by intense and competitive nationalistic fervor, determined not to compromise on the issues, armed with mass-produced weapons, supplied by ever-expanding supply bases, fighting over great distances, and led in battle by an emerging elite of professional officers. In short, the authors have illuminated the evolutionary meaning of a war that was fought roughly midway between the Napoleonic and World War I periods, during the great transformation from muskets to machineguns. It is in these terms that the reader should view the Civil War. If in the process the heroes lose some of their luster, the purposes of education will have been served.

The Nation Divided   1

In the history of the military art, the American Civil War shares a place of distinction with the French Revolution and the Napoleonic wars. In each of these two periods, social, political, economic, technological, and military factors came together to transform warfare, so that those who survived from the onset were fighting in a wholly new style by the end of the conflict. After experiencing initial success against the undisciplined French Revolutionary armies, the small, highly disciplined formations, arranged according to the practice of Frederick the Great, reeled back from the disciplined fury of the corps of Napoleon. Thereafter, mass armies, spurred on by nationalist zeal and organized and led to achieve the greatest possible offensive power, dominated the battlefields of Europe. By the time General Bonaparte had become Emperor Napoleon I, he had harnessed the potential of French nationalism and converted it into military power to be used for the destruction of his nation's enemies. The democratization of war was to change the nature of war and international relations forever after.

Similarly, the American Civil War profoundly changed warfare. Exploiting equally intense nationalist fervor, rival governments raised mass armies to fight for a victory that in the end would mean the destruction of either the Union or the Confederacy. But whereas Napoleon's armies fought with weapons little different from those used by Gustavus Adolphus, Marlborough, and Frederick, American armies carried rifles and artillery of greater, though still imperfect, effect. Mass armies armed with mass-produced weapons of vastly increased lethality crippled each other at long range until they finally had to dig themselves into the ground to escape complete destruction. Although overlooked by a number of observers at the time, the offensive power that was so efficiently developed by Napoleon, and later emulated by Federal forces at Bull Run and Confederate forces at Shiloh, was stymied by the heavy firepower that technology had made possible. Warfare had entered a new era, one in which the production of rapid-fire weapons made the defensive force behind entrenchments ascendant over the enemy force maneuvering toward it in the open. Nor was this the only change in tactical relationships.

The American Civil War illustrates an even more fundamental change in the nature of war caused by democratization and the Industrial Revolution. As Walter Millis has pointed out, war was losing its one redeeming virtue: the ability to reach a rapid decision.[1] At his best, Napoleon humbled Prussia and her army in just over seven weeks; it took Union forces four years to reach a similar point in the Civil War. During that time, each side increased its commitment, and while the opposing peoples grew discouraged, they refused to quit. Time after time, the armies hurled themselves at each other, recoiled to resupply themselves with more men and machines, and struck again. It was only when the Confederacy could send no more men and machines that the issue was finally settled. While there were technical military reasons for the failure to reach a Napoleonic decision, part of the explanation lay in the nature of the American people. Of great importance, too, were the physical characteristics of the land over which the war was fought.

The Theaters of War

By European standards, America was a vast and primitive land. *(See Atlas Map No. 2.)* Its most striking feature was the immensity of the territory that lay within the nation's borders. The two main theaters of war—northern Virginia and the valley of the Mississippi River—were about 700 miles apart at the northern ends. In 1861, General Albert Sidney Johnston, commanding the Confederate defenses between the Appalachian Mountains and the Mississippi River, tried to cover a front 400 miles long. When penetrating that line during his two-year campaign from Paducah, Kentucky to Vicksburg, Mississippi, Major General Ulysses S. Grant faced a march greater in distance than that from Berlin to Warsaw. One of the military ironies of the war is that with all of the geographical space available, the Confederacy chose to sacrifice the protection that distance offered by moving its capital from Montgomery, Alabama to Richmond, Virginia, which was situated only 100 miles south of the national capital in Washington, D.C.

Complicating problems born of the great distances were obstacles to the movement of armies. Mountains and high hills covered much of the area, forming a natural division between what came to be known as the Eastern and Western Theaters of Operations. The Appalachian Mountain chain ran all the way from Pennsylvania through Maryland, Virginia, the Carolinas, northern Georgia, and Alabama. With few passes for either railroad or foot movement, the huge barrier forced the belligerents to create two fronts and, in many ways, to fight two wars.

In the East, Federal and Confederate forces opposed each other in the 100-mile stretch of land between Washington and Richmond that was bounded by the Chesapeake Bay to the east and the Allegheny and Blue Ridge Mountains to the west. Because the mountain barrier ran in a northeasterly-to-southwesterly direction, the width of the Eastern Theater narrowed in northern Virginia. In the low country, the land was forested where not cleared for farming. Even the farms were relatively small. According to one observer, space could rarely be found for employing more than six or seven artillery batteries in Virginia. Similarly, the scarcity of large open areas normally prevented the maneuvering of cavalry in the traditional charge of opposing lines.[2] Obstacles to movement were also created by large forests. The most notable of these was the Wilderness of central Virginia, which became the scene of heavy fighting in 1863 and 1864. On the western flank, the Shenandoah Valley, lying between the Allegheny and Blue Ridge Mountains, provided the Confederacy with a rich source of food as well as a friendly and well concealed avenue of approach into Maryland and Pennsylvania. On the eastern flank, the waters of the Chesapeake Bay and the Atlantic Ocean provided the Union Navy with easy movement along the coast and up the major rivers that flowed into the bay. These rivers—the Potomac, the Rappahannock, the York, and the James—ran from the western mountains to the east and, along with their swampy tangled tributaries, formed obstacles to north-south movement, thereby confining crossings to well known and easily observed fords. Generally, then, the terrain east of the Appalachian Mountain barrier favored defense on land and naval operations along the eastern seaboard.

West of the Appalachian barrier, the nature of the major terrain features radically altered the strategic situation. There,

the wooded mountain ridges plunged far south to their foothills between Birmingham, Alabama and Atlanta, Georgia. Although cut by a few narrow passes to the north, the rugged mountains were broken in an east-west direction only by the valley of the Tennessee River at Chattanooga, Tennessee. In order for major armies to reach the lower Confederacy and to link the Eastern and Western Theaters, control of a line between Chattanooga and Atlanta was necessary to skirt the southern end of the Appalachian barrier. West of the mountains, three major rivers trisected the theater. The Cumberland River, the easternmost, drained northern Tennessee and southern Kentucky, dropped south to Nashville, Tennessee, and then flowed north to the Ohio River at Smithland, Kentucky. Just a few miles to the west, at Paducah, was the mouth of the Tennessee River, which followed a lengthy course from the mountains of east Tennessee through Knoxville, Chattanooga, Huntsville, and Florence, Alabama, finally winding north to the Ohio River. The last of the great western rivers was the Mississippi, which flowed south through St. Louis, was joined by the Ohio at Cairo, Illinois, and then meandered south to New Orleans and the Gulf of Mexico. Rather than serving as barriers to north-south movement, as did the eastern rivers, the Cumberland, Tennessee, and Mississippi served as highways for the side that could dominate them. Further, the Mississippi separated Texas, Louisiana, and Arkansas from the rest of the Confederacy, serving as a significant hindrance to east-west movement. Because of the river system, the terrain in the West favored offensive operations in either a northerly or southerly direction.

Transport and Mobility

To circumvent the geographic obstacles and to traverse the great distances, the combatants had to be able to exploit existing transportation systems. In this capability, Federal forces far exceeded the Confederates. River craft of all sorts were pressed into service as transports and gunboats. During the war, newly designed iron-clad boats—with colorful names such as the "Pook Turtle"—enabled the Federal command to employ combined ground and naval forces along the rivers, deep in the southernmost regions of the Confederacy. Because of superior industrial capacity, the North was also able to exploit the nation's railroad systems.

On the eve of the Civil War, there were three principal railroad systems in the United States. *(See Atlas Map No. 2.)* The first was an east-west system of multiple railroad lines running north of the Ohio River and connecting the old Northwest Territory and the trans-Mississippi West with the east. This system was retained intact by the North and, along with the northern rivers, the canals, and the Great Lakes, provided

A Union Gunboat

The Construction of Railroad Bridges Becomes an Important Adjunct to Strategic Mobility

a high-capacity transportation network that greatly speeded the movement of armies and supplies between theaters. It also provided the principal means of transporting western produce to eastern markets, a profitable spinoff of secession that led to midwestern demands to reopen the Mississippi River to less costly transportation. The second system lay along the eastern seaboard and connected, however inefficiently, Chattanooga, Atlanta, and Richmond. Prewar lines between Richmond and Washington, as well as east-west lines throughout Virginia, aided both sides in the struggle that occurred in the area between the two capitals. The third system ran parallel to the Mississippi River, through the state of Mississippi. This system aided armies operating in the Mississippi Valley. Few east-west lines connected the southern systems, and only one line ran through the mountain barrier, connecting Richmond with Chattanooga and the Mississippi River at Memphis. Further, southern railroad systems were built of different gauges, necessitating the unloading and reloading of cargo while it was enroute to its destination. Even so, before hostilities were underway, Confederate military analysts concluded that the southern railroad system, however sparse and nonstandard, provided better lateral communications than that possessed by the North, and thus accorded to the Confederacy the advantage of interior lines.*

Although both armies were regularly to move over great distances by utilizing steampower, once at their destinations, mobility was once again reduced to that of walking men and horses. There was no improvement in tactical transportation comparable to that in the strategic arena. Roads were still narrow, dusty, and restricted in dry weather. Rain frequently reduced them to mud. River crossings, wet or dry, presented major logistical problems. In actuality, the most common means of conveyance was the horse.

Social and Political Issues

Populating the vast country were vigorous and industrious people who had somehow decided that only war could solve their fundamental problems. From a population of about 4 million during the American Revolution, the country had grown to over 31 million by 1860.[3] Most of this growth was a result of the creation of large families. About 4 million people, however, had come by way of immigration in the 20 years before the breakout of the war. A good deal of the rapid expansion in population was centered west of the Appalachian

chain. Significantly, most of the increase had taken place in the northern states, and was concomitant to the growth of towns and cities. By 1860, New York City had a population of over a half-million and was followed in size by Philadelphia, Boston, and Baltimore on the east coast, and Cincinnati, St. Louis, and Chicago in the West. By 1861, the expanding population west of the Appalachians had led to a predictable phenomenon: the Union had grown from 13 to 33 states. The political implications are clear when one realizes that the expansion in northern population was accompanied by the creation of more and more states with northern attitudes and sentiments. In 1861, this meant anti-slavery sentiment.

Slavery and its part in bringing on secession and the Civil War are complex issues that cannot be dealt with either traditionally or simplistically. Causes of the war are also tied to the growth of America's population, urban migration, religious revivalism and reforming zeal, racism, constitutional questions, and perhaps most of all, territorial expansion.[4]

As the United States grew politically, its leaders dealt with political problems by compromising on practical issues. Usually, these compromises were struck by the two political parties that represented the majority of Americans. This proved to be an effective way to resolve questions of tariffs, internal improvements, banking, and other such issues. By maintaining a balance between the interests of the North, the South, and the West, political issues could be settled relatively easily within the framework of the Constitution and by a crisscrossing of economic, social, and sectional divisions. Stability was reinforced because a vast majority of the population shared a common heritage, experience, and ideals. Further, most people lived independently, without any direct contact with their government. The conflict became more emotional, however, as the nation grew and the imbalance in population increased the political power of the North—and those western states that were offshoots of the North—at the expense of the South. Changing attitudes among the fast growing northern population, buttressed by prosperity, fostered a northern nationalism. There was a newly awakened spirit of participation in this sectional growth that demanded more than just a vote; it demanded the freedom to change those things that were seen as being wrong. More importantly, northern nationalism insisted upon majority rule.

In the South, cotton and slavery had become the bedrock of the economic, social, and political structure of the section. Although cotton was a minor crop and slavery was virtually moribund by 1800, interest revived after the invention of the cotton gin by Eli Whitney. Thereafter, the growth of the cotton economy and the South's dependence upon it was dramatic. In 1800, the cotton crop had been but 70,000 bales; in 1860, it amounted to 4,000,000 bales.[5] As cotton production came

*Interior lines is a term that describes the condition of a force that can reinforce its separated units more rapidly than separated opposing units can reinforce each other. The condition exists when the force occupies a central position relative to its enemy, or when it possesses superior lateral communications.

New York City, the Most Highly Populated Northern City in 1860

A Typical Southern City in 1856

to rely on the use of slave labor, the two became interdependent. As a result, southern cotton growers invested much capital in slaves; eventually, not only agriculture, but the entire social system, depended upon slavery.

As this process cemented itself into the "southern way of life," northern reformers began to attack slavery on grounds of immorality. Defenders of slavery, eschewing apology, created arguments for the preservation of the "peculiar institution," for behind the economic importance of slavery was its role in the social system. In 1860, out of a population of 9 million in the slave states, there were 3.5 million slaves, and only 383,000 white slaveowners. Half of the owners held fewer than 5 slaves, and only 48,000 owned 20 or more slaves.[6] From these figures, it is clear that the social and economic system for which a million white southerners fought was one created for a small minority of slaveowning farmers and planters. Slavery, then, must have meant a great deal even to those white men who owned no slaves at all. To explain this sentiment, some scholars suggest that the existence of slavery provided social status to all white men, no matter how low their station, and that slaveownership was a way to improve one's position within one's community.

Regardless of personal reasons for fighting for a slave system, the combined forces of northern criticism, political pressure, and defensiveness set southerners more and more apart from northerners and westerners. By the eve of the Civil War, the South had developed its own nationalism, which was based on a sense of distinctiveness. It was agrarian, aristocratic, and scornful of the competitive and materialistic culture of the North. Southern politicians fought against the growing strength of the northern states by constructing a strong senatorial block in Congress that more often than not won its point by compromise. As a strategy for ultimate victory—that is, the avoidance of defeat—these politicians exploited the national obsession with Manifest Destiny, seeking to increase the number of slaveholding states by winning constitutional support for the extension of slavery into the western territories. After the Missouri Compromise of 1820 prohibited slavery north of the 36°30′ latitudinal meridian, southerners looked to Texas, the territories acquired from Mexico, Cuba, and finally the Kansas-Nebraska territories for congressional reinforcement. By the 1850s, the question of slavery had become a political issue and a subject of popular debate, and therefore was all the more dangerous.[7] In the end, the new political forces that had grown in the North would no longer compromise with the defenders of slavery. The issue upon which they made a stand was the extension of slavery to the territories, and the medium through which their views were expressed was the Republican Party. According to Peter J. Parish:

The slavery issue burst through this effective but limited piece of political machinery. It blew to pieces the party system, and the normal pattern of bargain and compromise. It destroyed the Whig party, split the Democratic party wide open, and created a new party, the Republicans, sectional rather than national. . . .[8]

Based on a platform representing northern viewpoints, Abraham Lincoln's election as President on the Republican ticket in 1860 was the explosive element that finally caused secession. With a Republican in the White House, southern nationalists saw no hope within the Union. They decided to go their own way.

Secession and Fort Sumter

On December 20, 1860, South Carolina became the first state to secede from the Union. In a little over a month, it was followed by Mississippi, Florida, Alabama, Georgia, Louisiana, and Texas. Not waiting for Lincoln's inauguration, on February 4, delegates of the seceded states met at Montgomery, Alabama to draw up a constitution and establish a government. Even after his inauguration on March 4, 1861, President Lincoln patiently bided his time, hoping for a reconciliation with the seceded states. In this hope he was to suffer disappointment, for a series of explosive events was occurring too quickly to permit the luxury of delay.

During the months following secession, most Federal administrative responsibilities passed peacefully from the control of the national government to that of the seceded state governments. States quietly undertook delivery of the mails, operated arsenals, took over military posts, and assumed other Federal functions whenever it was clear to Federal authorities that resistance was impossible. The transfer of coastal fortifications was, however, a different matter, for the Federal Government retained its ability to defend them by using the Navy. The two most important posts remaining under Federal control in the South were Fort Pickens at Pensacola, Florida and Fort Sumter at Charleston, South Carolina. Of the two, Fort Sumter, located in the heart of the secessionist stronghold, attracted the greatest interest and promised to provoke a test of wills between the new President and the leaders of the secession movement.

Although opposed by some of his advisers—including Lieutenant General Winfield Scott, still serving as the Commanding General of the Army—Lincoln decided to go to the aid of the garrison in Fort Sumter rather than avoid a showdown. After receiving word from Major Robert Anderson, commander of Fort Sumter, that he could hold out for only six more weeks, Lincoln considered the options. Military

CHARLESTON

MERCURY

EXTRA:

Passed unanimously at 1.15 o'clock, P. M. December 20th, 1860.

AN ORDINANCE

To dissolve the Union between the State of South Carolina and other States united with her under the compact entitled " The Constitution of the United States of America."

We, the People of the State of South Carolina, in Convention assembled, do declare and ordain, and it is hereby declared and ordained,

That the Ordinance adopted by us in Convention, on the twenty-third day of May, in the year of our Lord one thousand seven hundred and eighty-eight, whereby the Constitution of the United States of America was ratified, and also, all Acts and parts of Acts of the General Assembly of this State, ratifying amendments of the said Constitution, are hereby repealed; and that the union now subsisting between South Carolina and other States, under the name of " The United States of America," is hereby dissolved.

THE

UNION

IS

DISSOLVED!

Announcement of South Carolina's Secession From the Union, December 20, 1860

The Inauguration of Abraham Lincoln, March 4, 1861

advice was discouraging—overcautious and unaggressive—until a retired naval officer, Gustavus Vasa Fox, proposed that a fleet of fast tugs run supplies to Sumter under the cover of darkness. After careful and lengthy deliberation, Lincoln directed that a relief force be prepared to move on order. During the first week of April, the President informed Fox, Anderson, and the Governor of South Carolina that he intended to send provisions to the fort; military force was to be used only if the relief expedition met resistance or if the fort were attacked. In this way, Lincoln shifted responsibility to the secessionists for firing the first shot. Jefferson Davis, the newly designated President of the Confederacy, responded by ordering Brigadier

Fort Sumter, South Carolina, 1861

General Pierre Gustave Toutant Beauregard, the Confederate commander in Charleston, to demand the surrender of the garrison before the relief expedition could arrive. After unsuccessful negotiations, Anderson rejected the ultimatum and prepared to resist should he be fired upon.

At about 4:30 a.m. on April 12, Confederate forces surrounding Fort Sumter fired the first shots of the bombardment. For 30 hours, Anderson and his small command fought back. Although there were no casualties, damage to the fort was heavy. The relief expedition, dispersed by a storm at sea and unable to intervene, began to assemble off Charleston harbor in time to witness the closing action. As supplies of ammunition and food dwindled, Anderson decided that he must surrender the battered fort. Striking the colors, he embarked his men aboard Fox's ships and sailed north.

As the first violent act, the bombardment of Fort Sumter had a dramatic effect on both the North and the South. Northern opinion swung strongly against the secessionist cause, and northerners shared the conviction that action had to be taken to restore the Union. In the South, secessionist spirits soared now that all ties with the Union seemed to have been severed. In those states of the upper South that had not yet decided to secede, the effect of Sumter was decisive. When they realized that force would be used against the seceded states, Virginia, North Carolina, Tennessee, and Arkansas followed their southern brethren into the Confederacy. Of the slaveholding states, only Delaware, Maryland, Kentucky, and Missouri remained in the Union—at least for the moment.

Once Fort Sumter had been fired upon, leaders on both sides seemed to assume that the next logicial step would be a military confrontation—in the North to force the seceded states to recognize the indestructibility of the Union, and in the South to achieve independence. Although Lincoln and the northern people had not sought a war, the Fort Sumter incident showed that the South intended to back up secession with military force. On the other hand, Lincoln's decision to risk a showdown over Sumter indicated his belief that as President of the United States he had to protect United States property, and that as the leader of the Republican Party he had to stand firm against the proponents of slavery. Jefferson Davis and the Confederate Congress faced equally strong pressures to take a resolute stand against coercion by the Federal Government. Many southerners were ready for a fight and believed that war was inevitable. Some, less realistically perhaps, had honestly believed that independence could be achieved peacefully. The firing on Fort Sumter removed the ambiguities and

On April 14, 1861, the Flag of the Confederate States of America Is Raised Over Fort Sumter

destroyed much of the optimism. Thereafter, Lincoln found himself pledged to re-establish the Union, while Davis was equally determined to dissolve it. There was no maneuver room left, so the nation chose civil war to resolve its differences.

Strategy

War between the North and the South dictated fundamental strategies. To restore the Union, northern armies would have to enter the South and force compliance with the laws of the nation. The South had only to keep those armies out. The problem was how best to gain those ends. Each side immediately began laying plans to achieve its military objectives.

Weakness in the southern economy was to influence northern strategy throughout the war. From the very first decision to establish a naval blockade of southern ports, the dependence of the Confederacy upon outside aid was the target. Other than foodstuffs—bread, meat, sugar, and a little salt—the South had few resources for waging war. Since the Union retained control of nearly all of the ships and crews in the United States Navy—a total of 69 vessels scattered on distant stations—a blockade was not only feasible, but also promised success. Concurrent with the blockade, Union diplomacy aimed at isolating the South and preventing recognition of the Confederacy as a legitimate government, or even as a belligerent.

A major strategic goal of the Union was to maintain, by whatever means necessary, the loyalty of the four slaveholding border states* that had not seceded by April 1861. According to Lincoln, the loss of Missouri, Kentucky, and Maryland would create a problem too great for solution. Delaware proved to have too small a pro-slavery sentiment to present a problem, but this was not true of Maryland. Trouble had erupted in Maryland even before Lincoln's inauguration, and later, as blue-clad Federal recruits marched through Baltimore, violence threatened to split the state. For a while, Washington was virtually isolated as Lincoln and the Governor of Maryland maneuvered to insure the loyalty of the state. When Union troops finally found their way into Washington by way of the Chesapeake Bay and Annapolis, pro-Union sentiment asserted itself. By early summer, the state, even though sharply divided, was firmly in the Union camp.

Kentucky tried to maintain a precarious neutrality after her leaders had sought a compromise following the bombardment

*The reader will recall that Maryland and Virginia surround Washington, D.C. Along with Missouri, Kentucky, and Delaware, these states were known as the border states. They were so called because, although southern by tradition, they were divided on the slavery issue, and their economic ties were with the North.

of Fort Sumter. During the summer of 1861, the Governor leaned toward the Confederacy, but was restrained by strong Unionist sentiment. Finally, in early September, the state's neutrality was violated by Confederate forces which occupied Columbus on the Mississippi River. Brigadier General Ulysses S. Grant immediately moved into Paducah and seized the mouth of the Tennessee River. Reflecting strong Unionist influence, the Kentucky Legislature ordered the withdrawal of the Confederate troops, but by that time the Confederates were busy constructing a defensive line through the southern portion of the state. Thereafter, the traditional Kentucky Government counted itself in the Union camp, while a rival state government represented Kentucky in the Confederacy.

Missouri fought its own civil war within the larger conflict as it tried to resolve its allegiance. In the end, the state remained divided by a number of factions: pro-slavery and anti-slavery, Union and Confederate, native American and immigrant German, and others. For the remainder of the war, the Union cause was dominant in Missouri by virtue of the presence of Federal troops and Union control of the Mississippi River. For most Missourians, the war was a tragedy of internal strife and lawlessness that took on all of the evils of guerrilla warfare.

By the fall of 1861, the Union had *de jure* authority, if not complete control, over the border states, and a kind of frontline emerged between the North and South. Northern military strategy then concentrated on the attainment of two main goals: the capture of Richmond and the control of the Mississippi River.

At first, Winfield Scott, the Commanding General, outlined a two-pronged scheme: a Federal naval blockade of all Confederate ports, and a complementary offensive to seize control of the Mississippi River, thereby splitting the Confederacy. He believed that these actions would force the South's collapse. Dubbed the "Anaconda Plan" for its resemblance to strangulation by the snake, Scott's proposal was judged to be too slow, and was certainly unsuitable in light of the optimism and enthusiasm of the times. More importantly, it failed to recognize the fact that Union forces would have to occupy the entire South in order to reimpose law and order. The situation demanded aggressive offensive action, and military critics, particularly in northern newspapers, called for an advance on Richmond to end the war.

Thus, in time, two great contending armies would be created and used to contest the ground between the two capitals throughout the war, while more troops would struggle for control of the Mississippi Valley and the "heartland" that lay between the great river and the Appalachian barrier. *(See Atlas Map No. 1.)* As the struggle progressed, the eastern war became a sporadic seesaw contest that seemed at times to be relatively indecisive, locking the huge armies of General

Lieutenant General Winfield Scott

Robert E. Lee and his successive opponents in a ponderous wrestling match. By contrast, the western war, despite brief and intermittent diversions, demonstrated purpose, direction, and a clear sense of objective, as Federal troops seized central and western Tennessee and drove south to Vicksburg, north from New Orleans, east to Chattanooga, south to Atlanta around the great mountain barrier, and—ultimately—north to link up with the eastern armies.

As the war went on, Lincoln saw that there was no way to coax, intimidate, or convince the Confederate States to return to the Union other than by military conquest. When the full impact of this fact had been absorbed, the President accepted the idea of total war. Beginning soon after the Union defeat at Bull Run, Lincoln not only mobilized the northern war effort to its fullest capacity, but also looked for more far-reaching ways to diminish the capabilities of the South. He turned again to the issue of slavery, not as a social or political point of dispute, but as a weapon of total war. Fully understanding the social, political, and economic importance of slavery to southern society, Lincoln proposed to abolish the institution, thus unleashing what would become a complete revolution in the Confederacy. Delaying the implementation of the Emancipation Proclamation until January 1, 1863, the President offered one last chance for peaceful reunion. In fact, the proclamation was ultimately to free only those slaves who were in Confederate-controlled territory. Neither the slaveholding border states nor Confederate territory under Federal control was affected; slavery in those excluded areas was to be abolished by constitutional amendment. In the short term, Lincoln hoped to deliver a psychological blow to the South, cripple its economy, and increase the internal security

problem behind Confederate lines. Throughout the summer and fall of 1862, the President awaited a significant northern military victory that would provide an opportunity to issue his proclamation, which would serve to plunge the divided nation further into the abyss of total war.

Jefferson Davis faced what seemed at first to be an easier strategic task: to defend the South simply by holding Union armies at bay. In practice, this became impossible because of Union superiority in numbers and the great expanse of territory that had to be defended.

Davis enjoyed great success in the East because he had excellent military commanders available, a relatively narrow front, terrain that favored the defense, and, until Grant took command, opponents who practiced inferior generalship. In the West, however, war had to be waged far differently to prevent Union armies from penetrating the South. Even the terrain worked to thwart southern plans. The rivers and railroad systems favored the advancing Union armies, particularly astride the Mississippi corridor. In the central Tennessee sector, the Tennessee and Cumberland Rivers led the Union armies quickly to the few lateral railroad lines that southern generals claimed provided the advantage of interior lines. Lightly defended because of the unmanageably long front, the line crumbled, permitting the Union armies to break the lateral transportation system and, consequently, to force the Confederates to surrender Kentucky and central and western Tennessee and to withdraw into northern Mississippi and Alabama. Grant's victorious ground and naval campaign against Forts Henry and Donelson gave him the strategic advantage of interior lines once he broke the railroad line between Bowling Green, Kentucky and Memphis, Tennessee. From that point on, Union control of the major rivers and supporting railroads accorded the blue-clad armies greater mobility than their enemies.

But what were Davis and his western general to do? Historian Thomas L. Connelly points out that the problem was to decide what could be sacrificed. Regardless of the production

Union Gunboats Insure Control of the Southern Rivers

attributed to the Tredegar Iron Works in Richmond, the Tennessee-Alabama-Georgia area was the economic heartland of the Confederacy. Before Grant swept through Tennessee, the state produced most of the South's iron for all military and industrial purposes, and much of its gunpowder, percussion caps, rifles, artillery, and other essential materiel, including locomotives. The early loss of Tennessee forced the relocation of these factories and the creation of new ones in Alabama and Georgia at Columbus, Augusta, Macon, Atlanta, Selma, Birmingham, Tuscalossa, and numerous other small towns and villages. Davis' quandary was very real, for if he gave up any part of the West, the Confederate war effort would suffer.[9] Further, southern governors and local politicians insisted that their states be defended. Political influence was largely responsible for the defense of the northern Mississippi Valley long after it was prudent to give it up in light of the military situation. For both military and political reasons, therefore, Davis' solution was to try to maintain control over the entire area. His strategic decision was easy to criticize, but difficult to avoid—given the decision to go to war in the first place.

In execution, the South's defensive strategy included several offensive thrusts into the North. In 1862, Lee and Braxton Bragg mounted an action that was closely akin to a coordinated offensive when Lee invaded Maryland and Bragg drove almost as far as the Ohio River in Kentucky. In 1863, Lee once again struck northward into Pennsylvania, all the way to the outskirts of Harrisburg, the state capital. Occasionally, large southern raiding parties—led first by John Hunt Morgan and later by Lieutenant General Jubal Early—crossed west and east of the mountain barrier to terrorize the northern populations. Generally, however, the South defended, delayed, and withdrew to defend again in a four-year war that ended in 1865. At that point, two exhausted southern armies under the command of Joseph E. Johnston and Lee were positioned virtually back-to-back in the areas of Durham Station, North Carolina and Appomattox. Virginia, a little over 100 miles apart. There, the eastern and western wars ended in Confederate surrender.

Resources

The South's failure to gain foreign support for the Confederate cause was very damaging to its aspirations. From the beginning of the war, southern leaders believed that cotton was of such great importance to the northern economy that the disruption of trade with New York and New England would result in a demand for a resumption of normal relations. Similarly, because the southern states supplied more than four-fifths of the cotton used in British and Western European mills, Confederate leaders banked on intervention and assistance from Great Britain and France to maintain an uninterrupted flow

of cotton. Surely, they reasoned, the Europeans would not stand by and watch the South subjugated when mere diplomatic recognition would virtually assure southern independence. They were wrong on both counts. Northern industrialists suffered somewhat from the loss of trade, but not enough to force an end to the war. The British Government chose to pull back from intervention, partly because of domestic pressure, and partly because it found ample cotton elsewhere. The South was left to cope with the blockade using only its own resources, and to confront the larger invading Union forces across the long frontier with armies supplied by a hastily organized industrial effort. Surprisingly, no battle fought in either the East or West was decided by a shortage of guns and ammunition.

The South's ability to survive four years of war without help is all the more remarkable considering the disparity in resources between the two sides in 1861. By almost every quantitative comparison, the Union's capability was vastly superior to that of the Confederacy. The northern population, not counting the border states, numbered almost 19 million. The western territories and the border states added another 3.8 million, for a total of almost 23 million. Southern states had a total population of 9 million, of which 3.5 million were slaves. While the slaves released white men from the labor force to fight, they represented a potential internal security problem, particularly after the issuance of the Emancipation Proclamation in September 1862. Thousands of these blacks eventually served in the Union Army against their former masters.

As intimated earlier, the North's industrial power was more intimidating than its manpower. Even after southern industry expanded following the loss of Tennessee, the entire South was easily outproduced by New York *or* Pennsylvania *or* Massachusetts.[10] When Colonel Josiah Gorgas, the brilliant organizer of Confederate ordnance supplies, evaluated the stocks of guns and munitions in the Confederacy, he was shocked by how little materiel was on hand. He could find only 159,010 small arms. About 1,000 cannon of all types, including many obsolete models, had been captured at the Norfolk Navy Yard and in the forts along the southern coasts. Until 1863, most of the weapons used by Confederate armies were run through the blockade or captured from Union armies; only about 10 percent were produced in the Confederacy. In an effort to decrease southern dependence upon blockade-running, Gorgas established a number of armories to manufacture weapons. This proved to bne particularly difficult, owing to the lack of skilled labor and machinery. Nevertheless, cannon foundries were organized in the three Georgia communities of Macon, Columbus, and Augusta. Powder production also was transferred to Augusta; a new iron manufacturing center grew in Selma, Alabama; and shot and shell were manufactured in Salisbury, Virginia and Montgomery, Alabama. By 1864, Gorgas was able to say, "Where three years ago we were not making a gun, a pistol, nor a sabre, no shot nor shell (except at the Tredegar Works)—a pound of powder—we now make all these in quantities to meet the demands of our large armies."[11] So remarkable were these efforts that the southern historian Clement Eaton concluded that Confederate armies were at times better armed than their enemies.

Confederate accomplishments were all the more remarkable considering the paucity of existing industrial plants upon which the South could build. Only one powder factory existed near Nashville, and it was lost early in the war. The mainstay of the production of Confederate cannon was the Tredegar Iron Works in Richmond, which remained in southern hands until the end of the war. Much of the iron ore and other metals necessary to war production were lost when most of Tennessee fell. As a result, new iron and coal fields had to be developed, leading to the growth of the steel industry in the vicinity of Birmingham, Alabama.[12] Still, copper, mercury, and lead had to be supplied for the most part by blockade-runners. If the northern blockade had a direct effect, it was in the curtailment of the supply of metals other than iron.

Although the North began the war with an existing manufacturing capability, it did not possess a plethora of weapons. A little more than 446,000 rifles and muskets of varying quality were in northern arsenals at the outset of the war. Only 8 out of every 100 of these shoulder arms were rifled, and close to 50 percent had been converted from the flintlock to the percussion system. Many soldiers who received these converted weapons considered them next to worthless. Like the South, the North turned to Europe to compensate for the shortfall in weapons. In June 1861, Colonel George L. Schuyler of New York was directed to buy 100,000 rifled muskets, 20,000 cavalry sabers, 10,000 revolvers, and 10,000 carbines from abroad. His efforts produced small arms that were not known for their outstanding quality. Some soldiers stated that it took two or three pulls of the trigger to get one discharge from the Austrian model. The German states, then in the process of converting to the needle gun, also unloaded most of their outdated models. Subsequent purchasing trips yielded weapons of similar quality. "In short, the refuse of all Europe passed into the hands of the American volunteers."[13] Gradually, government arsenals and private contractors began to meet the high demand for small arms.

The equipping of artillery units did not pose as great a problem. In the same period of time that over 4,000,000 small arms had to be provided, only 7,892 cannon were required. These were produced by firms that followed manufacturing techniques pioneered by men like Robert P. Parrott, John A. Dahlgren, and Thomas J. Rodman. As a result, cannon production was not a major problem for the Federal Army.

Nowhere was the economic superiority of the North more evident than in its system of transportation. Of the 31,000 miles of railroad that existed in 1860, only 9,000 miles were in the states of the Confederacy. *(See Atlas Map No. 2.)* Northern railroads were designed to speed communication between the East and West; in the South, however, many miles of railroad ran from inland terminals to seaports such as Richmond, Wilmington, Charleston, and Savannah—without any substantial and coordinated means of interconnection. Shortages of railroad lines, rolling stock, and poor maintenance therefore doomed the South to the evils of poor distribution, even when industrial production finally made much needed supplies available. Further, in a nation dependent upon outside aid and facing the dangers of blockade, the lack of naval and merchant shipping was fatal. The success of the few Confederate commerce raiders that were at sea indicates that even a modest navy would have made a significant difference. About all that the Confederacy could do was to feed and clothe itself—with difficulty—and to rush the development of an industrial base in the relative security of the lower South.

The task of simultaneously managing mobilization and directing the war was one of monumental proportions for both sides; it was made even more difficult by the democratic nature of the two opposing governments. In this regard, the North clearly had the strongest organization.

Governing in Wartime

Northern strength lay in the continuity of the institutions of the Federal Government. As a generalization, one can say that the President and the executive branch, the Congress, and the judiciary continued to perform their traditional functions. In practice, some normal governmental procedures were altered or abandoned as war powers increased at the expense of rule by law. According to James G. Randall and David Donald, the "line was blurred between state and federal functions, between executive, legislative, and judicial authority, and between civil and military spheres."[14]

Lincoln probably increased presidential power more than any other president before or since the Civil War. He virtually declared war independently of Congress when he proclaimed an insurrection on April 15, 1861. Moreover, he enlarged the Army, appropriated money, and then, after the fact, asked Congress to endorse his actions. Lincoln thereafter tended to assume more and more authority rather than seek legislation to gain the powers that he wanted. For the most part, Congress cooperated with the President, but by building a monopoly on emergency power, he was to alienate many politicians. Opposition increased as the war progressed, but the President yielded only when forced to do so, ignoring his critics

President Abraham Lincoln

Lincoln justified his actions on the grounds that secession was an illegal act of rebellion rather than a war, as understood by the international community. In order to obstruct southern negotiations with foreign powers, Lincoln believed that it was necessary to avoid any suggestion that the Federal Government recognized a legitimate rival in the South. To approach Congress requesting a declaration of war, as the Constitution demanded, would have accorded the Confederacy the status of belligerency and even of legitimacy. He therefore refused to negotiate with representatives of the Confederacy, thus officially ignoring its existence. In theory, then, Lincoln assumed powers, that might be better called police powers, in order to restore law and order in a disrupted land. Naturally, he could not ignore the existence of a full-scale war, and policies emerged that were inconsistent with the image he sought to project. In addition to raising a multi-million-man "police force," the Government blockaded the southern coasts and ports, a measure that normally signified a state of belligerency in international law. It recognized and enforced the rights of prisoners of war, treating them with humanity rather than as criminals, and it respected the rights and property of southerners who did not support the war.

Wider emergency powers meant that, on occasion, the President practiced a mild form of despotism, particularly when constitutional rule of law came into conflict with military necessity. He was severely criticized for his handling of dissension. Too often, detractors claimed, the Government's definition of "disloyalty" seemed more closely tied to domestic

whenever possible.[15] Congress responded indirectly by creating the Committee on the Conduct of the War, a watchdog body that oversaw executive policy, the performance of generals, and sundry other functions that often found committee members meddling in military and other executive affairs.

Wartime Washington

political opposition aimed at defeating the Republican Party than to the provision of aid and assistance to the enemy. Moreover, the discontent of midwesterners, farmers, and their political leaders with the economic gouging practiced by northeastern industrialists and railroad men often brought the Government under criticism, fairly or unfairly, dependent upon the degree to which one support the form of populist sentiment that surfaced sporadically.[16]

The most famous cases of governmental suppression were those involving the secret societies* that were created to defeat Lincoln. Adoptingg colorful names such as Knights of the Golden Circle, Order of American Knights, and Sons of Liberty, the societies were thought to have memberships numbering in the hundreds of thousands. Further, members were accused of being in communication with the enemy, working for the defeat of the Federal armies, aiding desertion, and discouraging enlistment. Whether they were guilty of these charges or not, the existence of the secret societies created uncertainty, fear, and overreaction. Consequently, Lincoln took drastic steps to curtail their activities. Concluding that the laws were inadequate and the courts incapable of dealing with the problem, he suspended *habeas corpus* and, in complete disregard of the Constitution and the judicial organization, authorized summary arrest on executive authority. Later, he even proclaimed that anyone charged with a "disloyal" act was subject to trial by military court-martial. Although these actions were subsequently judged to be unconstitutional, wholly or in part, some 13,000 such arrests were recorded during the course of the war, and in all probability there were many more that were never reported.[17] Naturally, the President's disregard of constitutional rights was widely protested, and the whole Union war effort was examined critically by the press.

Dealing with a free press in a total war proved to be a unique experience. For the first time, American newspapers abandoned their role as advocates of a particular cause and met the needs of the people by providing news about the fathers, sons, and husbands fighting on widely scattered battlefields. Additionally, with such a large percentage of the population directly and indirectly involved in the war, the policies of the Government were of greater interest to the general reader. Usually, the Government did not control the news or impose censorship. Lincoln's main concern was with the success of military operations. Many newspapers that were critical, or even abusive, escaped punishment. But when the administration detected editorial policy that it believed to be prejudicial to military success, it was quick to close the offending newspaper. The New York *World*, the Louisville *Courier*, the New Orleans *Crescent*, the Baltimore *Gazette*,

*The members of these societies were known as "Copperheads."

and the Philadelphia *Evening Journal* all were closed at one time or another during the war. Still, Lincoln moderated the actions of his generals. When Ambrose E. Burnside—a politically minded general—closed the Chicago *Times* for disloyal and incendiary sentiments, Lincoln was unconvinced of the need and revoked the order.[18]

Newspaper reporters, seeking news of the war in the field, clashed with those soldiers who saw the journalists' efforts as meddlesome, troublesome, and, when uncomplimentary, downright disloyal. As a result, newspapermen received almost no support in some military commands.[19] George B. McClellan imposed strict censorship, and eventually kept reporters away from the front; George Gordon Meade ordered a correspondent of the Philadelphia *Inquirer* to be paraded wearing a sign that said "Libeller of the Press"; Henry Halleck physically evicted correspondents; and William T. Sherman court-martialed those who accompanied the Yazoo expedition against his orders. Admittedly, these were extreme cases, and some generals—Grant, George Thomas, Philip Sheridan, and Lee—understood the important connection between keeping the public informed and maintaining support of the war effort. In their commands, relations were cooperative if not cordial.[20] On balance, then, the Lincoln administration took harsh steps in mobilizing and running the war when the President thought it was necessary, but tempered its actions with leniency.

In the South, the Davis administration had to deal with different and far more difficult problems than those facing the Union. Morover, it had to do so without the benefit of those political advantages enjoyed by the North. The Confederacy was created by a convention assembled at Montgomery, Alabama on February 4, 1861 to construct an independent government. The convention became the successor to the Federal Government, and quickly chose Jefferson Davis as the President; selected the "Stars and Bars" as a flag; began to negotiate with foreign governments, the border states, and even the government in Washington; and set about drawing up a constitution for the seceded territory.

The Confederacy was founded on the "right of secession," a controversial constitutional interpretation dating from the early days of the Republic. According to politicians of "states rights" persuasion, the people of the several states had created the Federal Government and had accepted Federal supremacy in certain matters as long as Federal power operated within accepted limits. Therefore, sovereignty lay in the hands of the people, and the people, acting through their states, could alter any arrangement that they had made. When Federal supremacy exceeded the parameters accepted by the people, the states could terminate their association with the Federal Government by seceding from the Union. In spite of the dangers of further fragmentation inherent in such a philosophy of

Montgomery, Alabama: The First Confederate Capital

government, the Confederate constitution reflected a strong commitment to states rights.

As written, the Confederate constitution did not greatly differ from the Constitution of the United States.[21] Its preamble enjoined each state to act in "its sovereign and independent character" to form a permanent Federal Government rather than a "more perfect union." It permitted state governments to impeach officers of the Confederacy who were acting wholly within the state; enabled the people to "recall" by amendment and, by inference, to secede if necessary; and prevented the Confederate Government from interfering with the ownership of slaves. The operation of the central government, however, changed somewhat. Congress had to pass appropriation bills by a two-thirds vote in both houses; the President could veto portions of a bill without vetoing the entire measure; the constitutional amendment process was simplified; heads of executive departments were permitted to speak before either house of Congress; and the President was to be elected for a single six-year term.[22] Upon this constitutional basis, the Confederate Government confronted the problems of waging war. Not surprisingly, President Davis' main difficulties were significantly different from those faced by Lincoln.

Most vexing was the financing of the war. The South had always been an agricultural area with few banks or commercial houses, and little currency. So little was there that the Secretary of Treasury, Christopher G. Memminger, used his own funds to furnish his office. To establish a treasury, Memminger borrowed money from the State of Alabama and from banks in New Orleans. Thereafter, the Confederacy financed the war by an uneven combination of taxation, loans, and paper money.

Taxation was never a major source of income in the Confederacy. Since import and export duties were curtailed by the blockade, the Government resorted to taxing the states. The states in turn issued paper money to pay the taxes. In 1863, the Confederate Congress finally passed a direct tax on the people, but it was so unpopular that subsequent legislation seriously weakened the measure. In all, taxes accounted for only one percent of the South's income. Nor was there enough specie to permit borrowing on a large scale. The Government was able to borrow $15 million from the New Orleans banks; $100 million from planters and farmers, much of which was paid in paper money and produce; and $15 million from the European banking house of Emile Erlanger & Company. Ultimately, the South received only about $3 million from this

President Jefferson Davis

last source, while subscribers to the loan lost most of their investment. In all, loans accounted for 39 percent of the South's income and amounted to only $712 million by the end of the war.[23]

Although the issuance of paper money was initially avoided by Confederate leaders, the failure of taxation and loans eventually forced them to the printing press. By the end of the war, $1.5 billion in paper had been issued. Since productivity had declined during wartime, prices soared in response to the flood of paper. Inflation brought great suffering—particularly to the families and widows of soldiers, who had to exist on the low pay of their sponsors. By the end of the war, although privates' pay was only $18 per month, boots cost $200, coats $350, pants $100, bacon $9 a pound, and flour $1,000 a barrel in Richmond.[24] Financing the war was such a difficult problem that it is remarkable that the Confederacy lasted as long as it did, and understandable that economic suffering created a schism in the South.

While Lincoln labored to some extent under the pressures of dissent during the war, Davis also had a burden to bear. Southern unionists dissented throughout the war, but they were in such a minority that their actions were serious problems only in limited areas, particularly in east Tennessee and other mountainous regions of Appalachia. In many areas, small farmers saw the war as a slaveholder's plot to preserve slavery, and this dissent occasionally resulted in guerrilla activity. Sizable Confederate military forces had to patrol parts of Tennessee and Alabama.[25] To cope with lawlessness and acts of disloyalty, Davis, like Lincoln, suspended *habeas cor-*

pus. Some of the states, however, reacted by releasing prisoners. The Georgia Legislature even "nullified" Davis' act by declaring it unconstitutional.[26] Predictably, states rights turned out to be a major evil in a nation trying to organize itself for war.

Often as a result of issues involving states rights, newspapers were consistently critical of the Confederate Government. Davis fared reasonably well in the press until the late winter of 1861–1862, when Grant broke the western line at Forts Henry and Donelson. Thereafter, the Richmond *Examiner,* the Charleston *Mercury,* and a number of other influential southern papers denounced the President regularly. The Augusta *Chronicle & Sentinel* was purchased by a group of Davis' political enemies, including the Governor of Georgia, for the express purpose of attacking the President. He was accused of incompetence, favoritism, and despotism, and was vilified for suspending *habeas corpus.* Ironically, the actions of the Davis administration were mild when compared with those of Lincoln's agents in regard to handling the press and protecting civil liberties. Relatively few newspapers were suppressed, and even though it was a crime to publish details of military strengths and movements, military news went uncensored. An anti-sedition law aimed at the press was introduced in the Congress in 1863, but failed to pass. Still, newspaper correspondents in the field suffered in much the same way as their northern brethren in the Fourth Estate. Generals Earl Van Dorn and Braxton Bragg threatened to close newspapers printing anything that might undermine confidence in a commanding officer. In January 1862, all correspondents were banished from the Army of Northern Virginia. So critical were southern newspapers of Confederate military commanders and their campaigns that Lee once said that the only military geniuses in the South were newspaper editors. In fairness, however, it should be pointed out that with the notable exceptions mentioned, most southern newspapers cooperated with the Davis administration regarding military information, if not political support.[27]

Without doubt, issues arising from strong states rights sentiments did much to hamper Davis' efforts. It was not uncommon for state governments to obstruct tax collection and to interfere with the process of conscription for constitutional reasons. Davis' two greatest antagonists were Governors Joseph E. Brown of Georgia and Zebulon Vance of North Carolina. Brown believed that Georgia should defend herself, raise her own funds, develop her own industry, and even conduct her own foreign policy. In the course of the war, Brown sent diplomatic envoys abroad, attempted to keep Confederate tax collectors out of the state, and even contemplated a separate peace when it appeared certain the Union would win the war. Vance never varied in his loyalty to the South, but proved to be a prickly adversary as he protected the sovereignty of North Carolina and its people.[28] Under these conditions, Davis was never able to exercise wartime powers in the Confederate presidency such as those that Lincoln was able to wield in the North. Nevertheless, the South began the war with some advantages, among which the quality of her army was most prominent.

Manpower Mobilization

The two governments raised their armies in remarkably similar ways. Each initially relied upon the state governments to recruit and equip soldiers, virtually without centralized control.[29] In the South, this was a manifestation of strong states rights attitudes; in the North, it was the easiest way to raise large numbers of troops quickly. At first, the response was so enthusiastic that the states were asked to slow their efforts. As the war progressed and enthusiasm waned, however, both sides realized that greater centralized control of manpower, production of war materiel, and distribution of supplies were needed. Eventually, conscription was used by both governments. In the beginning, however, the states were crucial to the mobilization efforts.

The South was the first side to begin raising troops. As soon as it seceded, each state took steps to mobilize military forces, relying on traditional militia and volunteer organizations. Late in February 1861, the Confederate Congress authorized President Davis to take charge of military operations, to receive property confiscated from the United States, and to accept into service military units offered by the states. On March 6, the Congress further authorized Davis to call out the militia for six months' service and to accept 100,000 volunteers for one year. On the same day, Congress created a regular army of about 10,000 men. The response to these first calls was enthusiastic, and the spring and summer saw recruiting goals exceeded, particularly after the Confederate victory at Bull Run in July. Optimism was high because most people believed that this was to be a short and glorious war. Showing a clear understanding of the true situation, on August 8, Congress called for another 400,000 volunteers for up to three years' service in response to further mobilization in the North after Bull Run.

By the spring of 1862, the war had begun to go badly for the South. Forts Henry and Donelson had fallen, New Orleans was being threatened, the battle at Shiloh had resulted in heavy casualties, and the Union armies of the West had advanced almost into the lower South. In the East, George B. McClellan had begun his Peninsular Campaign against Richmond. As the fortunes of war ran against the South, recruiting diminished and the 12-month men prepared to go home. Once again basing its actions on reality rather than political ideology, the Confederate Congress turned to conscription to bolster its manpower supply. The President was authorized to draft white men between the ages of 18 and 35 for three years' service. Subsequent legislation widened the age limits to 17 and 45, provided for exemptions, and, near the end of the war, authorized the use of slaves in labor units (February 1864) and as soldiers (March 1865). Confederate records are incomplete, but it is estimated that a total of one million southerners served during the war.

The Federal Government waited until after the bombardment of Fort Sumter to begin preparations. It, too, had to resort to extraordinary measures, for the small Regular Army was unable to cope with rebellion on such a large scale. About 1,100 officers and over 15,000 enlisted men were organized into 19 infantry, artillery, cavalry, and mounted riflemen regiments. While 313 of its officers "went south," most of the enlisted men remained loyal to their government. Of the 198 companies in the Regular Army, 183 were stationed in 79 posts along the frontier. Even after Fort Sumter, the Army could not abandon the frontier until trained replacements could come to its relief. Tied down to their frontier posts, over 1,000 troops became prisoners of war before they could even be withdrawn from Texas. Nevertheless, the regular establishment provided some advantages. It had a structure and a chain of command upon which a wartime organization could be built. As Commander-in-Chief, President Lincoln worked through his Secretary of War, Simon Cameron (and later the able Edwin M. Stanton), and the Commanding General, Winfield Scott. Also in being were the bureaus that served as the army staff. Concerned primarily with procurement matters, these staff divisions constituted the machinery through which mobilization was to be directed. Headed by aging career soldiers of limited vision, the bureaus often impeded rather than expedited necessary measures. In spite of the efforts of General Henry W. Halleck, it was not until Grant took command of the Army in 1864 that a reasonably effective coordinating staff was assembled on an *ad hoc* basis under Halleck's able direction as its chief. As with the South, the Federal Government had to rely initially upon the states to provide manpower for the Union.

No plans existed in the North for the mobilization of manpower or for the waging of war. The only legal basis for the President's expansion of the armed forces was the Militia Act of 1792, which authorized the President to use the militia to suppress insurrection. The day after Fort Sumter surrendered, Lincoln exercised this authority by calling for 75,000 militia. Quotas were assigned to the states with instructions to muster the troops at various locations on May 20. After Virginia and the other states of the upper South seceded, the President

VOLUNTEERS WANTED!

AN ATTACK UPON WASHINGTON ANTICIPATED ! !

THE COUNTRY TO THE RESCUE!

A REGIMENT FOR SERVICE

UNDER THE FLAG OF THE UNITED STATES

IS BEING FORMED   IN JEFFERSON COUNTY.

☞ NOW IS THE TIME TO BE ENROLLED !

Patriotism and love of Country alike demand a ready response from every man capable of bearing arms in this trying hour, to sustain not merely the existence of the Government, but to vindicate the honor of that Flag so ruthlessly torn by traitor hands from the walls of Sumter.

RECRUITING RENDEZVOUS

Are open in the village of WATERTOWN, and at all the principal villages in the County, for the formatiom of Companies, or parts of Companies.   ☞ Officers to be immediately elected by those enrolled.

WATERTOWN, APRIL 20, 1861.   WM. C. BROWNE, Col. Comd'g 35th Regiment.

Ingalls, Brockway & Beebee, Printers, Reformer Office, Watertown.

Union Recruiting Poster, April 20, 1861

decided that he could not wait for Congress to convene. Consequently, he issued another proclamation, increasing the size of the Regular Army by almost 23,000 men, calling for 42,000 volunteers for three years, and asking for 18,000 seamen for the Navy. When Congress met on July 4, it approved the President's actions and authorized him to call for an additional 500,000 volunteers to serve from six months to three years, at his discretion. The act defined the status of volunteers, equalizing pay with that of the Regulars, prescribing the organization of volunteer regiments, and giving the President the right to appoint general officers while empowering state governors to appoint other officers. As the war progressed, more volunteers were called from the states, and, frequently, regiments were raised by the governors and private individuals without a quota. Competition between militia, state volunteers, and regular units created confusion that was not eliminated until order was restored in the fall of 1861.

As the war expanded in 1862, there was an increased need for replacements and for additional men to guard the lengthening lines of communication. As in the South, the North's enthusiasm for war had waned by 1862, and the response to calls for volunteers fell off. A new system had to be employed, and that system was conscription. At first, conscription was to be managed within the states by the governors. All men between the ages of 18 and 45 were subject to call, but exemptions and substitutions were permitted. The draft of 1862 was never implemented; the states' drive for—and payment of—volunteers proved to be sufficient. As a result, it was not until 1863 that a Federal draft was enacted by Congress. The Enrollment Act was a Federal statute that bypassed states and for the first time centralized the mobilization machinery in the Federal Government. Thus, a fundamental change in the relationship between the Central Government and the states was quietly enacted by a willing Congress. The draft proved to be an inefficient mechanism, however; of the 292,441 men called, 164,395 were exempted, 26,002 provided substitutes, and another 52,288 paid a commutation that released them from service. The net gain was 35,883 men enrolled at a cost of $15,686,400. To fill the never-ending need for replacements, the Government continued to call for volunteers, and the Federal draft was postponed. By the end of the war, only 6 percent of the total Union manpower had been raised by conscription. Its greatest contribution seems to have been the encouragement of volunteer enlistments.

Blacks were first accepted for military service by an act passed in July 1862. The first recruitment of blacks took place in the occupied areas of the South. Although some states organized a few black regiments, the organization of black manpower was undertaken by the Bureau for Colored Troops, an agency of the Federal Government. Recruiting was accelerated in the spring of 1863 and continued until the end of the war. In all, over 186,000 black soldiers served in 120 infantry regiments, 13 artillery regiments, and 7 cavalry regiments during the war.

Training and Tactical Doctrine

Once the armies began to assemble, questions of training and doctrine arose, but they were never systematically dealt with by the rival governments. Whatever training and discipline the troops were to receive resulted from the efforts of individual commanders rather than established doctrine. Perhaps it was best for the soldiers on both sides that there was no uniform doctrine. At Bull Run, Sherman sent his battalions into battle one by one; when one was ineffective, another took its place.[30] Sherman and his fellow officers learned much as the war progressed. Most importantly, they realized that modern firepower had reached such a high degree of lethality that the experiences of the Mexican War were no longer reliable guidelines. It would be at least two years, however, before that truism became apparent to officers and men alike. Until then, infantry tactics were designed in accordance with prewar rules and concepts.

From its earliest days, the United States Army had modeled its tactics on European practices. At times, it followed the French example; at other times, the British. But always its infantry was trained to attack in close-ordered linear formations behind a screen of skirmishers, to exploit disciplined volleys of musket fire, and to deliver the final assault with the bayonet. In this pattern of musketry there was an implicit assumption that the bayonet would ultimately decide the issue between opposing lines.[31] Early in the war, therefore, offensive formations were arranged with the intent of deciding the outcome of battle with a bayonet charge. At the time of Bull Run, the weapon in the hands of many units on both sides was still the short-range musket, and it was possible to line up at a hundred yards, blaze away, and then hope to close the interval at a rush.

As the war progressed, however, new weapons were distributed to both armies—often by capture—with a dramatic effect on tactics. The firepower of the modern rifled musket made the formations in which infantry had previously attacked obsolete. This change was a direct result of the significant technological improvement of the rifle.

The evolution of an efficient rifled musket began in the eighteenth century with the replacement of the flintlock firing mechanism with a fulminate of mercury percussion cap.[32] When this cap received a sharp blow from the hammer, a flame ran through the touchhole to ignite the powder in the chamber of the musket. The next step in the evolution of the rifle was the development of a cylindrical bullet with a conoidal shape. The bullet fit loosely in the barrel and was made of relatively soft lead. In its base was a hollowed area. When the powder exploded in the chamber, gas pressure forced the thin walls of the base of the bullet to expand and seal the bore. Rifling in the bore caused the bullet to spin as it left the muzzle, a factor that stabilized the flight of the bullet and increased its effective range. The new rifled weapons were deadly accurate at ranges beyond 200 yards, and could kill at up to 1,000 yards. The bullet, invented in 1823 by an Englishman named Norton, was introduced to the French Army by Captain Claude E. Minié, after whom it was named. By 1855, the United States Army had adopted the percussion cap and had begun to rifle its muskets to fire the Minié ball. By 1861, United States arsenals were producing a standard muzzle-loading rifle for the Regular Army.

Compared with that of earlier muskets, the operation of the rifled musket was simple. Each soldier carried paper cartridges in which were sealed powder and a Minié ball. To load, the soldier bit through the paper, poured powder and ball down the barrel, wadded the paper and dropped it down the barrel, and struck the contents several times with a ramrod. He then fitted the percussion cap over the small nipple near the base of the hammer, cocked the hammer, and took aim. A practiced soldier could fire two or three rounds a minute from the standing position. When prone, the soldier found his task to be far more slow and difficult. He was then compelled to lie on his back, contorted and perhaps inadvertently exposed to enemy fire. The solution to this problem came with the development of breech-loading weapons.

Breech-loading shoulder arms had long been known, and, in fact, had been adopted by the United States Army in 1819. However, these early weapons were technically unsatisfactory because gas and flame escaped from the breech. The first good American breech-loader was developed at Harpers Ferry and was known as the Sharps. It was a single-shot rifle, and a carbine version was used extensively by the cavalry after its perfection in 1859. Once the problem of sealing the gas was solved, repeating rifles began to appear. The 16-shot Henry and the 7-shot Spencer both made their appearance in the Civil War, primarily as cavalry carbines. Popular as these weapons were, they still constituted only a small percentage of the total individual weapons produced. Many conventional soldiers of the day, including Robert E. Lee, considered the breech-loaders untested and wasteful of ammunition, and therefore discouraged their adoption.[33]

The rifled musket had a profound impact on infantry tactics. Greater accuracy of rifle fire forced men in battlelines to move apart in order to present the smallest possible targets for enemy fire. As individuals dispersed, the density of men on the battlefield decreased. Because of increased ranges, armies tended to form for battle farther apart, thus increasing the distance that the infantrymen had to traverse to reach the enemy line and prolonging their exposure to accurate fire. Armies reacted to the increased lethality of the weapons by deciding battles more often by firepower than by shock action. In the end, battles took longer to fight, and commanders gradually began to lose their ability to reach a clear decision on a single battlefield.[34]

Artillery tactics, also, were affected as the war progressed. At first, artillery fire was poorly coordinated, whether between artillery units or between artillery and infantry units. Gradually, however, both Union and Confederate officers learned how to improve this operational technique. With increasing frequency, guns were massed to gain their maximum effect.[35] Still, no technological development similar to the invention of the infantry rifled musket affected the guns themselves. Rifled artillery was developed, and demonstrated much greater range and accuracy than anything employed before the war; but it was never the gun upon which the armies relied, as heavy forests prevented exploitation of the greater ranges. Both sides preferred direct support from the old smoothbore 12-pounder Napoleons. The smoothbore gun fired exploding shells to a range of 1,200 yards, grapeshot to 400 yards, and canister to 200 yards.* The popularity of the smoothbore rested on the deadly effects of the latter two types of projectiles on attacking infantry. Although Civil War artillery was strong in the defense, it had serious limitations when supporting its own infantry in the attack. Forced to fire from a position some distance behind the lines, smoothbore artillery had neither the range nor accuracy to cover the ground between the lines of combatants. It could not fire effectively into the area immediately in front of the enemy lines to prepare for the assault. As a result, attacking infantry was vulnerable to the grapeshot and canister of artillery in a defensive position.[36] Even when artillery tried to accompany the infantry in the attack, either it was overwhelmed by the massed guns in the defensive position, or the gunners were driven from their pieces by accurate rifle fire.

The ultimate effect of the increased lethality of arms was to restrict maneuver by infantry and to cause armies to dig field fortifications whenever they halted. From the Battle of Fredericksburg to the end of the war, entrenchments became more and more important for survival. Attacking infantry might be stopped short of their objective, but within a short time after halting they had dug elaborate fortifications only a few yards from the enemy trench. In the age of the rifleman, the defense had become ascendant over the advancing formations of Napoleonic origin.

---

*Canister and grapeshot were both antipersonnel projectiles. The former consisted of many small missiles encased in a can; the can burst upon leaving the muzzle, thereby scattering the smaller missiles. Grapeshot consisted of smaller missiles held together by rods, wires, or plates.

The cavalry provided the only glimmer of hope for restoring mobility to the battlefield. However much they may have been romanticized, cavalrymen no longer attacked their enemy in the boot-to-boot charge of bygone days. Civil War cavalry filled its primary role in reconnaissance, covering and screening the movements of armies and performing other essential security missions. When forced to fight against infantry, cavalrymen dismounted and fought as infantry. Very rarely did cavalry attack infantry while mounted, and then only under the most desperate circumstances and never against infantry dug in with artillery. In reality, cavalrymen on both sides were dragoons, riding to the battlefield with great speed and then fighting on foot. Late in the war, when armed with repeating rifles, Union cavalry units in particular could be as formidable as many infantry units.[37]

Leadership

Effective coordination of the combined-arms team required strong leadership. Some southerners felt that this was not going to be a problem: not only were southern gentlemen natural leaders, but southern boys were born soldiers who possessed great resourcefulness and vast courage. As one southern elementary school textbook asked: "If one Confederate soldier can whip 7 Yankees, how many soldiers can whip 49 Yankees?" Professional soldiers and political leaders in the South, however, were less sanguine about the innate superiority of the Confederate private, and therefore scoured the countryside to provide him with good leaders. Essentially, there were four sources that could be tapped to produce commissioned officers. The most important of these was the officer corps of the United States Army. Men such as Robert E. Lee of Virginia were eminently qualified to fill positions of responsibility in the fledgling Confederate Army. Graduates of the United States Military Academy, who had retired or resigned from the old army before the war, also were valued for their leadership potential. Additionally, men who had served in the volunteer organizations during the Mexican War could bring valuable leadership experience to the ranks of the Confederate officer corps. Finally, various military academies in the South, including such noteworthy institutions as the Virginia Military Institute and the South Carolina Military Academy (The Citadel), could be counted on to provide capable men.

In the Eastern Theater, southern optimism appeared to be well-founded. The leadership of the Army of Northern Virginia seemed to outshine its northern counterpart on every occasion. But the war was not selective in its choice of victims, and as the casualty lists lengthened, the availability of qualified officer replacements diminished. By war's end, the Confederate Army was suffering from a paucity of good leaders.[38]

On the other hand, the North appeared to begin the war with less able military leaders. Part of the reason for this was the widespread practice of commissioning officers to curry political favor. Lincoln often has been criticized for appointing men like Benjamin F. Butler to the rank of general officer. Butler's appointment clearly was designed to align the Massachusetts Democrats behind the war effort. With the states seceding in rapid succession, however, Lincoln had to gather as much political support for the Federal effort as was humanly possible. Appointments to important positions within the Army were an effective means of gaining the necessary support. In the final analysis, the North had the same sources of leadership as the South. West Pointers who remained with the Union Army outnumbered those who resigned to serve with the South by almost 2 to 1. In addition, the United States Military Academy continued to provide a small but qualified group of regular officers throughout the war. Still, many generalships were distributed on the basis of political considerations.

In contrast to the poor showing in the East, the leadership of the Federal forces in the West moved inexorably towards victory. Brief setbacks occurred in many of the campaigns, but these were rapidly overcome. The South was powerless to stop the blue tide that gradually eroded the Confederate West.[39]

A comparison of the high-level leadership of the opposing armies is difficult to make, because the problems each side faced were markedly different. For example, there is a strong temptation to try to imagine the course the war would have taken if Robert E. Lee had commanded the Union Army instead of the Army of Northern Virginia. Based on Lee's brilliant performance at the head of the army in Virginia, it would seem logical that the North would have fared much better if Lee had chosen to remain within the Union. The outcome, however, is not quite as clear as it would first seem. Lee's use of nineteenth century strategic concepts—which kept the Confederates in Virginia, fending off Federal thrusts towards the southern capital—were ideally suited to the task that faced him. But as already has been mentioned, warfare had changed drastically, and this type of Napoleonic strategy was not suitable for the attacker. As long as the North's generals conducted almost classic Napoleonic campaigns, Lee was successful. Once Ulysses S. Grant took command, however, the situation became radically different. No longer was the war viewed in northern eyes as a series of campaigns that culminated in giant setpiece battles around the enemy's capital. Grant set all of the Federal armies in motion simultaneously and fought a single, lengthy campaign that eventually destroyed both the South's armies and its resources. A modern war of attrition had developed, and Grant was its creator. The ghost of Napoleon now had a slightly different cast.

Notes

[1]Walter Millis, *Arms and Men* (New York, 1956), pp. 124–125.

[2]G.F.R. Henderson, *The Civil War: A Soldier's View*, ed. by Jay Luvaas (Chicago, 1958), pp. 191, 203.

[3]Peter J. Parish, *The American Civil War* (New York, 1975), pp. 20–21. Much of the discussion of political philosophies, events leading to the war, comparative capabilities, and the nature of the opposing governments was taken from this excellent study of the war. The older but still reliable work by James G. Randall and David Donald, *The Civil War and Reconstruction*, 2nd edition (Boston, 1961) was also used.

[4]The discussion of slavery and the causes of the war was taken from William H. Cartwright and Richard L. Watson, Jr. (eds.), *The Reinterpretation of American History and Culture* (Washington, 1973), pp. 329–336, and Parish, *The American Civil War*, pp. 23–33.

[5]Parish, *The American Civil War*, p. 28.

[6]*Ibid.*, p. 29.

[7]Cartwright and Watson, *Reinterpretation*, p. 343.

[8]Parish, *The American Civil War*, p. 26.

[9]Thomas L. Connelly, "The Other Civil War," *American History Illustrated*, VIII (November, 1973), 29.

[10]Parish, *The American Civil War*, p. 110.

[11]Clement Eaton, *A History of the Southern Confederacy* (New York, 1965), p. 134. Chapter Seven of Eaton's work is the basis for the discussion of Confederate logistical capabilities at the onset of the war.

[12]*Ibid.*, pp. 134–138.

[13]Fred A. Shannon, *The Organization and Administration of the Union Army, 1861–1865* (2 vols.; Gloucester, 1965), I, 110–119; Comte de Paris, *History of the Civil War in America* (4 vols.; Philadelphia, 1875), I, 299.

[14]Randall and Donald, *Civil War and Reconstruction*, p. 293.

[15]*Ibid.*, pp. 293, 295–297.

[16]*Ibid.*, pp. 297–299.

[17]*Ibid.*, pp. 299–301.

[18]*Ibid.*, pp. 307–308.

[19]Bruce Catton, "Tribute to Civil War Newsmen," *Army Information Digest*, XVI (August, 1961), 82–83.

[20]John M. Virden, "Correspondents Cover the Battle," *Army Information Digest*, XVI (August, 1961), 85, 88.

[21]Eaton, *The Southern Confederacy*, p. 51.

[22]*Ibid.*, pp. 51–52; Randall and Donald, *Civil War and Reconstruction*, pp. 157–159.

[23]Eaton, *The Southern Confederacy*, pp. 227–228; Randall and Donald, *Civil War and Reconstruction*, pp. 257–260.

[24]Randall and Donald, *Civil War and Reconstruction*, pp. 262–263.

[25]Connelly, "The Other Civil War," p. 28.

[26]Randall and Donald, *Civil War and Reconstruction*, pp. 269–270.

[27]Eaton, *The Southern Confederacy*, pp. 222–224.

[28]Randall and Donald, *Civil War and Reconstruction*, pp. 267–268.

[29]The following discussion of manpower mobilization relies upon Chapter IV of the excellent study by Lieutenant Colonel Marvin A. Kreidberg and First Lieutenant Merton G. Henry, *History of Military Mobilization in the United States Army, 1775–1945* (Washington, D.C., 1955).

[30]Henderson, *The Civil War: A Soldier's View*, p. 208.

[31]John K. Mahon, "Civil War Infantry Assault Tactics," *Military Affairs*, XXV (Summer, 1961), 60.

[32]The information on the technical evolution of the rifle was derived from Bernard and Fawn M. Brodie, *From Crossbow to H-bomb* (Bloomington, 1973), pp. 131–139.

[33]Mahon, "Civil War Infantry Assault Tactics," pp. 57–58.

[34]*Ibid.*, p. 59.

[35]Henderson, *The Civil War: A Soldier's View*, p. 203.

[36]Mahon, "Civil War Infantry Assault Tactics," p. 66.

[37]Henderson, *The Civil War: A Soldier's View*, pp. 211–212.

[38]E. Merton Coulter, *The Confederate States of America* (Baton Rouge, La., 1950) pp. 518, 331–332; Douglas Southall Freeman, *Lee's Lieutenants: A Study in Command* (3 vols.; New York, 1942), I, 711; Eaton, *The Southern Confederacy*, pp. 112–113.

[39]T. Harry Williams, *Lincoln and His Generals* (New York, 1952), pp. 10–11; Eaton, *The Southern Confederacy*, p. 112

Early Trials: Bull Run and Shiloh

2

The opening major engagement between southern and northern armies—the First Battle of Bull Run in July 1861—exposed to the view of layman and professional, private and general, the unpreparedness of American armies to fight successful major battles. This revelation should have come as no surprise. That the public and private sector of the country expected more, reflected not only a lack of appreciation of what was required to build an army and formulate a strategy, but also an almost brazen confidence that once the American Government and people decided to do something, they could not be deterred by mere practical problems.

War was a reality, and the transformation of the masses of men and equipment that began to accumulate in April 1861 into an effective army demanded prime consideration in both Richmond and Washington. The leadership of the armies lacked the training and experience needed for the scale of management necessary in the Civil War. The leaders would have to learn quickly. The Mexican War that had ended 13 years earlier provided no useful precedent, either in scope or in the changes in tactics introduced by the rifled musket. The strength of the Regular Army at the beginning of the Civil War (17,113 officers and men) was further diluted by the operational demands that scattered over two-thirds of the forces along the western frontiers and in western territories that were not yet states.[1] The size of that army in and of itself, however, was not the heart of the problem, even though the numbers of trained professionals and experienced veterans who would be available as leaven for the volunteer ranks was a consideration. Being small, the United States Army thought small. An officer who had been a captain for 15 years and then was suddenly promoted to the rank of brigadier general could be expected to have difficulty making the transition to the command of a substantially larger number of men. Too often he reverted to the comfortable habits of the company commander. It happened at First Bull Run and afterward. The weaknesses in the scope and depth of training necessary to

expand the Army for larger conflict revealed itself in other ways. Lieutenant General Winfield Scott, commander of one of the two invading armies in the Mexican War (1846–1848), neither had nor acquired a functional staff as Commander-in-Chief at the beginning of the Civil War. Senior officers in the field did no better, quickly adding personal and special staff officers, but leaving vacant such critical posts as chief of staff, operations officer, and intelligence officer.

A productive staff section, such as the one that emerged in Europe and evolved in the United States decades later, was by no means a common organizational fact of armies belonging to the major powers of 1861. Nevertheless, even what was known or what had proven to be essential in previous European wars or in the American experience in Mexico had seemingly been forgotten. The lack of an adequately appointed and organized staff impeded rapid preparation and direction of the armies. Field commanders could provide neither staff supervision nor personal supervision for the training and drilling of green troops and officers. In addition, the business of attending to daily operations of a routine nature too often robbed commanders of the time needed to make long-range plans.

The same maladies plagued the mushrooming armies of both North and South, but the increasing pressure to take action left little time to reflect on weaknesses. The commander of the southern forces around Richmond, General Pierre Gustave Toutant Beauregard, was operating under the watchful eyes of authorities in Richmond; his, however, was primarily a defensive role. On the other hand, Brigadier General Irvin McDowell, commanding the growing Federal forces around Washington, was under pressure to take the initiative and give the Rebels a drubbing. Public and congressional sentiment—but, most important, presidential inclination—urged McDowell to attack. The General-in-Chief, Winfield Scott, attempted to dissuade the President and Cabinet from pressing for an attack. He was not successful. One compelling argu-

Brigadier General Irvin McDowell

ment for a prompt offensive was the keen interest in obtaining battle service from the three-month volunteers before their terms expired. Consequently, McDowell prepared a plan of action that would carry the attack to the Confederates. His plan was sound, but complicated. It demanded from McDowell's green army substantially more than it possessed in troop training, habits of coordination, or the sinews of a seasoned headquarters—staff experience.

First Bull Run

McDowell planned to make his main attack an envelopment by two divisions advancing in column. *(See inset, Atlas Map No. 3.)* At the same time, two feints were to be executed. The main attack aimed to strike at right angles to the army's route of march. However, there was no provision for the use of cavalry; moreover, the mounted arm was not organized to adequately serve the army command. It was, instead, responsive to subordinate commanders. In fact, the entire organization of McDowell's army betrayed the weaknesses of hasty, thoughtless assembly. The regiments of the northern army were grouped into 13 brigades and further organized into 5 divisions. These relationships were neither habitual nor practiced, however, since the organization became effective only a few days before the movement toward the battlefield.[2] The foregoing is not necessarily an indictment of McDowell's unpreparedness or incapacity of high command. Prior to the Civil War, his command experience had been as a lieutenant in the field artillery. In addition, subordinates and seniors alike either failed to see or attached little importance to the

flaws in McDowell's planning or organization prior to the battle. Men were spoiling for a fight; ironically, not all who were, wore uniforms.

On the Confederate side, the general who commanded the troops that stood between McDowell and his target (Richmond) was the same officer who in April had given the order to fire on Fort Sumter—P.G.T. Beauregard. As late as June 23, 1861, he described his plan for the anticipated battle in terms of a Confederate defensive stance, but in late June he began to articulate a bolder, more offensive attitude.[3] To meet the invading Yankee army, Beauregard considered the additional force of Joseph E. Johnston (deployed to the northwest near Winchester) essential to his offensive scheme. *(See Atlas Map No. 3.)* But Johnston, a newly-appointed full general, occupied a vital role in overall Confederate defense by pinning 18,000 Federal troops in position with his own force of 12,000. Nevertheless, when a Federal probe at Blackburn's Ford turned into a minor skirmish, thereby revealing the seriousness of Yankee intentions, Confederate authorities in Richmond ordered Johnston to join Beauregard. A skillful withdrawal and confused Union orders permitted Johnston to join Beauregard without a similar move being made by the Federal force that had been watching Johnston.[4] Together, Johnston and Beauregard could muster over 34,000 troops to oppose the estimated 35,000 serving under McDowell. Beauregard explained to Johnston, who arrived on July 20,

Brigadier General Pierre Gustave Toutant Beauregard

that the enemy was presumably at Centreville. Beauregard proposed to gather all the forces within the twists and turns of the small stream named Bull Run, and then strike the Federals at Centreville. Johnston, the senior of the two, listened as Beauregard explained. He was unfamiliar with the terrain, and had too little daylight left to examine in person the untidy expanse of small hills cut by ravines and valleys that would become the next day's battlefield. Johnston approved Beauregard's plan and delegated to him the battlefield direction of it.[5]

Movement to Contact

In the meantime, on July 16 McDowell had begun to move his army from the vicinity of Washington in the general direction of Centreville. At that time, he contemplated a turning movement of the enemy's right flank, but his own reconnaissance led him to examine the other flank of the deployed Confederate forces for a place to maneuver. Hence, the development of the plan described above grew out of McDowell's intent to turn the left flank of the Confederates.[6]

McDowell was forced to delay his attack for a number of reasons. For one thing, his inexperienced staff had trouble coping with the complex plan and issuing implementing orders. The greenness of the troops also led to a loose organization and slowness in marching. Finally, time was wasted cooking rations. McDowell chose July 21 for his attack. He made the decision on July 20, as the usefulness of his three-month volunteers slipped away and the gathering of the Confederate Congress in Richmond increased the pressure for positive action. The delay in launching the attack was costly. As soon as the Federal forces began to move, authorities in Richmond ordered Johnston's force to reinforce Beauregard. On July 19, the lead elements of Brigadier General Thomas Jonathan Jackson's brigade joined Beauregard. *(See Atlas Map No. 3.)* General Johnston himself and the bulk of his force arrived the next day, while the Federal troops under Major General Robert Patterson remained pinned in the Shenandoah Valley, unaware that Johnston had eluded them.[7]

That Saturday, on July 20, 1861, the two armies faced each other. Each prepared to attack the other in what many contemporary observers expected would be the battle that would end the war. Each side was composed of green troops and leaders who were untried at the levels of command to which they had recently been elevated. Each army drew from identical sources for tactics and doctrine. There is little to indicate a significant difference in the quality of leadership or soldiery on either side. Probably the only factor that stood out as a difference between the two armies was the number of 90-day volunteers under McDowell's command—many composing

entire companies or batteries—who stood on the verge of discharge as the summer wore on. The Confederacy had no three-month volunteers.

In his attack on July 21, McDowell expected to pin Confederate forces in position with a secondary effort at Stone Bridge and a feint at Blackburn's Ford, while his main effort struck the Confederate left flank in a dawn assault at Sudley Springs. *(See inset, Atlas Map No. 3.)* Mismanagement, delays, and inexperience combined to wreck McDowell's timetable and dilute the strength of his efforts. Brigadier General Daniel Tyler's division started too late to reach the positions from which it was to launch the secondary attack and feint. By moving late, his troops inadvertently impeded the progress of other Federal forces by choking the road network around Centreville. The two divisions of Colonels David Hunter and Samuel B. Heintzelman stood on the turnpike between their camps and the town, waiting two or three hours before moving to the position for the main attack. The troops had been aroused from sleep shortly after midnight. Richardson's brigade of Tyler's division, in making the feint at Blackburn's Ford at daybreak, alerted Beauregard to the fact that McDowell might be seizing the initiative. At the same time, Beauregard learned of the Federal advance toward Stone Bridge by the remainder of Tyler's division. *(Neither movement shown on map.)* Although Beauregard did order a westward shifting of the brigades of Brigadier General Barnard E. Bee, Brigadier General Thomas J. Jackson, and Colonel Francis S. Bartow *(movement not shown on map)*, he nevertheless began issuing orders for the previously planned Confederate attack toward Centreville. Meanwhile, Colonel Nathan G. Evans was not deceived by Tyler's weakly forged secondary attack at Stone Bridge, and began shifting his force to the northwest to oppose the main Federal assault at Sudley Springs.[8] *(Movement not shown on map.)*

The coordination between Tyler's attack and the main attack was ineffective. Consequently, the separate assaults occurred several hours apart. Moreover, the delay of the two divisions that were moving circuitously to Sudley Springs permitted discovery by alert Confederates. All was not lost, certainly, but the errors and delays made McDowell's work substantially more difficult.

The Battle of Bull Run

The Federal main attack developed quickly once the troops had crossed the ford at Sudley Springs and forced back the determined Confederate defenders. Hunter's division opened the Federal assault. On the high ground north of Young's Branch, Evans' brigade had been joined by the brigades of Bee and Bartow, and this trio of Confederate commanders

Bull Run Creek, 1861

urged their troops to hold and dispute the growing Federal attack. *(This first attack not shown on map.)* At 11:30 a.m., the Confederate infantry finally withdrew across the Warrenton Turnpike and re-formed along a strong line across Henry House Hill, anchored on Jackson's brigade.[9]

Thus far, the battle on the Confederate side had been fought by subordinate commanders. Evans' initiative had placed him astride the line of advance of the main Federal attack. The brigades of Bee, Bartow, and Jackson had been ordered to the Confederate left by Beauregard to respond to the early morning action reported there. The Confederate commander, however, was still determined to launch troops from his right and center in an attack on Centreville, where he believed the major part of the Union army was located. Not until 9:00 a.m. had either Beauregard or Johnston recognized that McDowell had definitely stolen the initiative from them, and that two of his divisions were already crossing Bull Run. At that time, it was still not clear to the Confederate commanders that what was unfolding on the left was in fact the main Union effort.

Beauregard and Johnston remained on a low hill to the rear of Mitchell's Ford, awaiting the development of the Confederate attack. Finally—the precise time is not entirely clear—Beauregard could no longer ignore the growing roar of musketry and cannon on the left, as well as the clouds of dust climbing skyward, betraying the movement of major Federal forces. In addition, Beauregard discovered that Confederate troops aroused at 4:00 a.m. had still not crossed Bull Run for the attack. Confusion, unsent orders, discretionary orders, and inexperience removed the last hope of a Confederate attack; Beauregard reluctantly issued the canceling orders. To assuage Johnston's growing concern over what appeared to be a major battle on the Confederate left, Beauregard sent a staff officer to ascertain the situation. At 11:00 a.m., there was still no information. Earlier, Johnston had given to Beauregard the task of conducting the battle, but Beauregard could restrain himself no longer. He announced: ''The battle is there. I am going.'' At that moment, while many elements of the Confederate Army were fiercely engaged in the battle, the Army as a whole lacked anything resembling unity. Beauregard hurriedly issued brief orders and galloped after Johnston. The scene they encountered as they neared the fighting was a disquieting one of large numbers of straggling, demoralized, and, in many cases, wounded men.[10]

South of Sudley Springs, the troops making McDowell's main effort had increased the pressure on the improvised Confederate defense. As previously noted, the Federal divisions had driven the brigades of Evans, Bee, and Bartow back to Henry House Hill, where they joined Jackson's brigade at about 11:30 a.m. Colonel William T. Sherman's brigade, having crossed Bull Run north of Stone Bridge, had helped precipitate the Confederate withdrawal. *(Sherman's movement not shown on map.)* Now able to threaten the Confederates on Henry House Hill from two directions and to add previously uncommitted brigades to the weight of his attack, McDowell seemed to be on the verge of caving in Beauregard's left flank and winning the battle.

The undoing of the Federal attack, however, was already in progress. The problem was rooted in the command and control arrangements at McDowell's headquarters. His staff was simply too inexperienced to control the scattered units under his command. As a result, McDowell made decisions and exercised control only over what he could see or immediately influence. Consequently, he failed to bring into the battle the full weight of those troop units available to him. Because he was on the offensive, this deficiency was more damaging to his cause than the same failure was to that of his Confederate opponent. Under these circumstances, McDowell's brigades, often without coordinating direction, attacked and re-attacked across the open plateau on which the Henry House stood. *(See inset, Atlas Map No. 3.)* Confederate units were hurried from other sections of the battlefield to reinforce the strongpoint that was built around the brigade of "Stonewall" Jackson, southeast of the Henry House.[11]

Confederate artillery, entirely smoothbore, held its own against the mixed smoothbore and rifled Federal guns. The close range of the contest negated the advantage of range of the rifled cannon. To the right of the Federal position, two Regular Army batteries anchored the southern end of the Union line and delivered a punishing fire on the Confederate defenders, ripping the lines of infantry and destroying artillery pieces. To increase the effectiveness of their fire, McDowell had earlier moved the two Federal batteries, commanded by Captains Charles Griffin and James B. Ricketts, closer to the Confederate position. Now, a regiment of infantry, mistakenly identified as Federal, emerged from the nearby woods and produced a deadly volley that cut down cannoneer and horse alike. The hapless batteries never recovered. As the battle raged back and forth across the hilltop, the guns could no longer be manned. The Federal line wavered. What caused the first withdrawal of Federal troops from their line is not clear, but the withdrawal began—to a degree, as a result of increased pressure exerted by southern reinforcements—in an orderly fashion.[12]

The raw Union troops behaved well in the attack and the give-and-take fighting on Henry House Hill. The orderly withdrawal, however, quickly degenerated into a rout as the Confederate defenders continued to pour musket fire into the retreating Federal troops that crowded the roads to Sudley Springs and Stone Bridge. *(Federal withdrawal not shown on map.)* Exhausted, hungry, and demoralized, the troops did not even stop at Centreville, but trudged 20 miles more to the safety of the Potomac River. The most strenuous efforts of leaders at all levels could not re-form the retreating stream of disillusioned soldiers. A rear guard was formed, using elements of Colonel Dixon S. Miles' division as its nucleus.[13]

The Confederates did not pursue. Confusion and disorganization in Confederate ranks at the moment of success delayed an effective pursuit when it would have caught the Federal column at its most vulnerable time. Soon the opportunity slipped away. The first significant contest of the war was a Confederate victory of major proportions.

A War On Rivers

The war in the West was largely a war of river lines. Many of the obscure towns and way stations located on these rivers became landmarks as the fighting around them focused attention on them. Other towns never saw a pitched battle, but were important because of location. Such a town was Cairo, Illinois, at the confluence of the Ohio and Mississippi Rivers. *(See Atlas Map No. 4.)* The Union needed to gain control of the town; it would be dangerous in Confederate hands. Moreover, in the first year of the war, Cairo was under the command of a previously unknown brigadier general who would fight that war of river lines to its successful conclusion. His name was Ulysses S. Grant.

Grant reached Cairo on September 4, 1861. His troops, most of whom had preceded him, were finding the oppressive humidity uncomfortable and demoralizing. The populace of the southern Illinois town was not entirely friendly. Nor were the dock rats and mosquitos. Dysentery, malaria, and fever

Cairo, Illinois

Brigadier General Ulysses S. Grant

structure would persist for many months before a more practicable arrangement evolved. President Lincoln pressed his military commanders to produce a coherent, mutually supportive strategy, but, despite energetic and liberal telegraphic exchanges of messages, the trio of McClellan, Buell, and Halleck could not agree upon the best course to be followed in the West. The fundamental line of agreement was that the initiative must be carried by the Federal side. After all, the Confederate States had seceded, and sought no additional territory by conquest. To the South went the defensive mission. What the Union commanders could not decide was how that defense should be broken.[15]

The southern commander in the West, General Albert Sidney Johnston, felt that he had too much territory to defend and too few troops with which to defend it. He was right. Taking command in mid-September 1861, Johnston was ranked as one of the outstanding soldiers of the Confederacy. The fact that he was on the defensive allowed him to economize his resources; but the Union forces arrayed against him were far superior in numbers and better equipped, giving him cause to look carefully for points of potential Federal penetration. Halleck, commanding the Department of Missouri, was in charge of over 90,000 troops by early 1862,

were silent and deadly companions of the soldiers who fought along the river lines. Grant's commander, Major General John C. Frémont, anxious to extend Federal penetration deeper into southwestern Missouri, sent Grant toward Belmont to make a demonstration. Taking along an armored gunboat, the new brigadier set out on November 6, proceeded ashore on the seventh, was routed the same day, and managed to extricate his small command with no less than 600 casualties. Grant and his forces survived the ordeal. In his memoirs, he soberly recorded his perception that audacity needs to be tempered with a generous measure of sound judgment.[14]

The command of the Federal effort between the Blue Ridge Mountains and the Mississippi River Valley was shared by two leaders, Major Generals Don Carlos Buell and Henry W. Halleck (who replaced Frémont shortly after Grant's excursion into Missouri). *(See Atlas Map No. 4.)* Overall command of the Union armies fell upon the shoulders of Major General George B. McClellan, who also directly commanded the forces in and around Washington. This defect of the command

Major General Don Carlos Buell

although some were committed to point defenses. To the east, Buell's Department of the Ohio contained approximately 45,000 troops. To defend against both, Johnston could muster only 43,000. His pleas to Richmond for more troops competed with similar insistent demands from other corners of the Confederacy. Initially, however, time would favor the Confederates as they increased their numbers and fortified weak points. The Union commanders had to choose a scheme for the Western Theater quickly—or face a task that grew more difficult by the week.[16]

The Federal military commanders continued to search for a concerted strategy with which the war could be prosecuted. Months had passed since the first shots had been fired at Fort Sumter in the Carolina waters. Lieutenant General Winfield Scott, venerable head of the Union military effort at the beginning of the war, had proposed a strategic scheme designed to pressure the Confederacy from all sides, by land and sea. But the plan, nicknamed by some the "Anaconda Plan," gained little support. One of the supposed defects of Scott's strategy was that it assumed a war of long duration, whereas most contemporary military critics felt that the war would be won quickly by a dramatic series of lightning strokes. At any rate,

Major General Henry W. Halleck

Scott retired and stepped down, to be replaced by McClellan. In early 1862, President Lincoln exhorted his field commanders to action. On January 27, 1862, he issued the rather extraordinary War Order Number One, which directed all naval and land forces to ready themselves to move against the Confederacy on February 22. The President was impatient. *(See Atlas Map No. 4.)* In response to Lincoln's order, McClellan submitted a plan that not only described what his own Army of the Potomac would do, but also advanced the idea of coordinated thrusts along the Cumberland and Tennessee Rivers by forces under Buell and Halleck.[17]

Halleck had already given considerable thought to operations that would strike the vulnerable spot at which the two rivers crossed the Kentucky-Tennessee boundary. Grant, also, had given his assessment that the uncompleted forts guarding the rivers could be wrested from Confederate control. Flag Officer Andrew Foote, with whom Grant had discussed the project, agreed. Finally, Halleck authorized the venture.[18]

Grant's troops—23 regiments comprising 15,000 men—began to move on February 2, 1862. *(See Atlas Map No. 5.)* Because transports were in short supply, the troops had to be shuttled to the area of Fort Henry, a movement that was completed on February 6. Near flood conditions on the Tennessee River did not help the Confederates. Fort Henry was poorly positioned on low ground, and was partly under water. Confederate efforts had been devoted to completing Fort Heiman, which was situated across the river on a string of hills. Construction, however, had barely started on that work, so the new fort offered no help to the defense of Fort Henry.

Fort Henry fell quickly. Grant made his preparations on February 5, even as troops were still arriving. Although he intended to attack the next day, muddy roads were slowing the occupation of attack positions. Flag Officer Foote correctly noted that the low position of the fort placed its guns at a distinct disadvantage: they had to fire up at the armored prows of his gunboats. Without waiting for the infantry, Foote attacked the fort with his gunboats. Though the attacking fleet sustained 59 hits, no serious damage resulted, and the cannon of the gunboats tore up their Confederate opposite numbers in the fort, as well as the protecting earthworks. After evacuating most of his force, the Confederate commander surrendered later the same day with less than 100 effectives.[19]

Grant's next target was Fort Donelson on the Cumberland River, only a short cross-country march away. As soon as Fort Henry had been taken, a force was sent south along the Tennessee River to destroy the Memphis and Ohio Railroad bridge there. Loss of that rail link would compound the difficulties of the Confederate defenders. Grant informed Halleck that he expected to attack Fort Donelson on February 8, but was unable to implement this plan because the rain continued to

Federal Gunboats Attack Fort Henry, February 1862

fall, turning the linking roads into quagmires. However, preparations continued, and Grant was ready to march his two lead divisions, commanded by Charles F. Smith and John A. McClernand, on February 12. *(See Atlas Map No. 5.)* Although there was no direct or formal command link between Grant and Foote, the two continued to work together in a highly cooperative fashion. Grant's target was not only Fort Donelson, but, equally important, the vital east-west Confederate railway link that crossed the Cumberland River at Clarksville. Prior to February 12, Foote had already started north on the Tennessee River with three gunboats. While enroute, Foote planned to pick up another gunboat, as well as transports jammed with reinforcements for Grant. He and Grant intended to link up near Fort Donelson for a joint effort.[20]

In many respects, the army that Grant moved to Fort Donelson was a green organization. Troops had been elated and surprised by the easy victory at Fort Henry. Unseasonably warm weather caused many inexperienced soldiers to discard overcoats and blankets recklessly, and equally inexperienced or reticent leaders did not stop them. By the evening of the twelfth, both divisions were within two miles of Fort Donelson.

Grant's plan followed the pattern already established at Fort Henry. There, however, the bulk of the garrison had escaped because Grant's forces had not been in position before Foote began his bombardment. At Fort Donelson, he intended to encircle the Confederate strongpoint completely to prevent any forces from escaping. Foote would then attack the water batteries with his gunboats and defeat them, and the completed investment would force the defenders to surrender. Grant believed that he would have to move quickly before local Confederate reinforcements strengthened the garrison of the fort or arrived to test his encirclement. What Grant did not know was that some reinforcements had already arrived.[21]

Albert Sidney Johnston's dilemma was that virtually any choice he could make would be wrong. The primary question had been which way he wanted to be wrong. The loss of Fort Henry had signaled impending danger to Fort Donelson and Clarksville, both vital points along the Cumberland River. *(See Atlas Map No. 4.)* Worse yet, the garrison at Bowling Green was extremely vulnerable, and would be severely jeopardized if Fort Donelson and Clarksville were to fall. Buell was holding a Union force of greater strength at Louisville, and if the Union plan succeeded, the smaller Confederate contingent at Bowling Green would be caught in a vise. Most important, and probably most upsetting to the Confederate commanders in the West, was the emerging fact that Federal strategy had taken on an offensive nature and was posing a serious threat to the South. Johnston had evaluated both his task and his resources. He had also conferred with his second in command, P.G.T. Beauregard (recently transferred from Virginia), as well as the commander at Bowling Green. Finally, he had decided to withdraw the force under Major General William J. Hardee from Bowling Green to Nashville,

General Albert Sidney Johnston

rived to renew the attack the next day. Light infantry skirmishes of little consequence marked the thirteenth. Of more importance to all troops was the weather: the temperature dropped to freezing, bringing in a wind-driven rain that turned into a snowstorm. Overcoats and blankets thrown away the preceding day were sorely missed.[23]

The highlight of February 14 was the resounding Confederate success in defeating Foote's gunboats. Many factors caused the reversal of the experience at Fort Henry. When Foote had his gunboats close to less than 500 yards, his crews and weapons took a terrific pounding from the lighter batteries of the fort. In addition, the elevation of the fort's guns caused the gunboats to incorrectly estimate the distance to the fort. Little ground contact occurred on the fourteenth, but the mauling of Foote's fleet not only rendered his gunboats unable to resume the attack the next day, but also raised serious questions

and to send 12,000 reinforcements to Fort Donelson to oppose Grant.[22]

On the morning of February 13, Grant was in no position to do anything with his ground forces. He faced over 18,000 Confederates in the fort and its entrenchments—more than his own strength, because he had left part of his force behind at Fort Henry to attend to captured equipment and the defense of the fort. Grant had not only msicalculated the size of the garrison, but had also underestimated the strength of the Fort Donelson river defenses. In addition, the alertness and readiness of the encircling force left something to be desired, a deficiency that would exist under Grant's command again a couple of months later. Yet the mark of the productive commander is not based on the number or size of errors he commits as much as the speed and success with which he corrects them. Grant's record became stronger with each test.

On the thirteenth, Grant continued to extend his lengthy lines of investment while Foote's gunboats bombarded the fort. *(See inset, Atlas Map No. 5.)* Union troops continued to arrive, yet the land investment of the fort was still far from complete, partly due to the swampy nature of the surrounding ground and the sheer length of the investing line. But the biggest disappointment was the ineffectiveness of the naval gunboat, the *Carondelet,* against the cannon of the fort. That night, Grant received the welcome news that the other three gunboats—the *Pittsburgh, Louisville,* and *St. Louis*—had ar-

Commodore Andrew H. Foote

about their effectiveness against well-emplaced shore batteries. *(See inset, Atlas Map No. 5.)* On the fifteenth, while
Grant conferred with Foote aboard his flagship, a stunning
message reached the Federal general. McClernand had received a surprise attack against his position on the right of
the Union investment, and the strength of the attack threatened
a Confederate breakout. Grant rode immediately to the spot.

In the Confederate camp, the success of the batteries against
the Union gunboats was cause for cheer, but the Confederate
commanders also realized that the only way to prevent capture
of the encircled army was to break through the Union lines
and retreat to join the Confederate forces at Nashville. John
B. Floyd, senior of the four Confederate generals in the fort,
had ordered Brigadier General Gideon J. Pillow to breach
McClernand's part of the line. Once the Federal encirclement
had been broken, Brigadier General Simon B. Buckner would
pull his troops out of the trenches and follow through the gap.
Even though the breach was made, some unknown factor
caused Pillow to order Buckner and his forces back into the
trenches. Floyd, after some vacillation, concurred in the order.
The gains of the successful attack were thus virtually thrown
away. At the same time, Grant arrived on the scene, received
the grim reports of the breakthrough at the height of the
Confederate success, and judged that the Confederates had
exhausted their energy and resources. Grant reacted quickly
and decisively. He told McClernand that the position must
be retaken by counterattack. Lew Wallace, on McClernand's
left, was directed to support the counterattack. Expecting that
the Confederates had thinned other parts of the line for the
attack, Grant ordered C.F. Smith to attack and capture the
trenches to his front. *(See inset, Atlas Map No. 5.)* To Foote,
Grant sent word that his damaged gunboats must reopen the
river attack. Ultimately, the Confederate attack was soundly
defeated, while the Federal lines, shaken and in some places
pushed back, held the encircled enemy.[24]

Colonel Nathan Bedford Forrest refused to spend his Confederate cavalry in an action that he was certain would end
in surrender. He therefore slipped out through the Federal
right during the night. So did Generals Floyd and Pillow,
leaving the junior general, Simon B. Buckner, in command.
His message to Grant at 3:00 a.m. on February 16, requesting
an armistice and the consideration of terms of surrender, drew
from Grant this laconic dispatch:

> Sir: Yours of this date proposing Armistice and appoint-
> ment of Commissioners to settle terms of Capitulation
> is just received. No terms except unconditional and
> immediate surrender can be accepted. I propose to move
> immediately upon your works, I am sir, very respectfully
>
> > Your obt. svt.
> > U.S. Grant
> > Brig. Gen.[25]

Brigadier General Simon Bolivar Buckner

Buckner surrendered 11,500 men, over 40 cannon, and
many small arms, heavy guns, and horses. Most importantly, he surrendered an army. Ulysses S. Grant was no
longer an obscure general from Illinois.

Grant at Shiloh

The fall of Fort Donelson ruptured the northern defensive line
of the Confederacy in the Western Theater of Operations. *(See
Atlas Map No. 6.)* The capture of the two forts led to the
permanent cutting of the important east-west rail link between
Nashville and Memphis. Ominously, Federal troops were
poised on both the Cumberland and Tennessee Rivers, ready
to drive the penetration farther southward. The coming battle
at Shiloh would deepen that penetration and carry the Union
standard nearly to the southern boundary of Tennessee. Yet
the battle would almost be a Federal disaster, and would
provide another important step in the military education of
Ulysses S. Grant.

Opposing Strategies

After the losses of Forts Henry and Donelson, the Confederate
commander, Albert Sidney Johnston, had no intention of waiting to see what the next Federal move would be. Therefore,
he promptly abandoned Bowling Green, Kentucky and
Nashville, Tennessee, and focused his attention on the major
weakness of the Confederate deployment in the West—the
dispersion of forces. Too few troops were being compelled

to defend widely-scattered points, exposing the separated elements of the Confederate forces to defeat in detail.* Johnston was not alone in recognizing the vulnerability of the Confederate forces in the West. Both his subordinates and his superiors in Richmond reacted. Coastal defenses lost their higher priority, and 5,000 troops left New Orleans for Corinth, Mississippi. Major General Braxton Bragg and his force of 10,000 men moved immediately from Mobile, Alabama to Corinth. Johnston's aim was to assemble an army at Corinth rapidly and defeat the growing Federal force that was collecting at Pittsburg Landing, no more than 20 miles away. *(See Atlas Map No. 7.)* Relying upon his intelligence sources, Johnston correctly judged that the Federal force under Buell, enroute from Nashville, had been directed to reinforce the Union army already assembling on the Tennessee River. He must strike soon.[26]

Without a doubt, there would be an army for Johnston to fight once he assembled his forces at Corinth. Who would be commanding it, however, was somewhat in doubt early in March of 1862. Misunderstandings and the vagaries of an imperfect telegraph system helped to create a serious disruption between Major General Henry Halleck and his most successful subordinate, Grant. For a period of several days, Halleck virtually stripped Grant of the authority to command, although Halleck did not in fact relieve him. Consequently, in early March the speed and smoothness of the Federal effort left something to be desired. In addition, Buell's force of 50,000, ordered south from Nashville by Halleck, consumed nearly two weeks as it moved overland to Columbia. *(See Atlas Map No. 7.)* Buell's march was slowed both by his own lethargy and by the bridges that had been destroyed by retreating Confederates. As a result, he would not join forces with Grant until the first day of the Battle of Shiloh. The storm between Halleck and Grant blew over in the middle of March, about the same time that Halleck was given sole, unrestricted command of the Union war effort from the eastern edge of Tennessee to the Missouri River. By this time, the division of C.F. Smith had already moved south along the Tennessee River. On March 18, the difficulties between Halleck and Grant having been smoothed out, Grant himself moved to Savannah, a few miles north of Pittsburg Landing. His aim was to trigger action with the growing number of Confederate troops in the area. Halleck wanted Grant's troops to cut the railroad connection at Corinth, thereby rendering it useless to the Confederates, and Grant intended to use that mission as a springboard to bring on a battle with the Confederate army assembling at Corinth. Halleck sensed this from Grant's

telegrams, and cautioned against it until Buell could join with Grant: "Don't let the enemy draw you into an engagement now. Wait until you are properly fortified and receive orders." Sufficient Confederate troops had arrived in Corinth by March 18—mainly from Mobile and New Orleans—to prevent Union forces from cutting the railroad without a fight. The senior Federal commander, Halleck, was not ready to let Grant bring on an engagement until he was reinforced, and could not or would not hurry Buell. In the meantime, Albert Sidney Johnston continued to receive information about the growing size of Grant's force at Pittsburg Landing, as well as the slow but unrelenting movement of Buell's army to join Grant. Johnston determined to attack.[27]

By early April, approximately 40,000 Confederate soldiers had been gathered in and around Corinth. On April 3, Johnston issued the order to his three corps commanders to be ready to march by 6:00 a.m. that same day. Johnston's address to his troops exhorted: "The fire should be low, always at a distinct mark. It is expected that much and effective work will be done with the bayonet." And so it would. Johnston intended to attack early on the morning of Saturday, April 5, 1862. However, because his recently assembled army did not yet plan and march like veterans and professionals, there would be no attack on April 5. Grant said as much in his dispatches to Halleck: the southern force gathering at Corinth was low in spirit and morale, not possessed of the same patriotic zeal as northern soldiers, and—in the last analysis—vulnerable to attack and ripe for defeat. The first week of April would teach him to judge his future opponents more carefully.

The Confederate army was not without problems. Its units had not worked together as an army and had been hurriedly assembled. Staff and command personnel were in many cases inexperienced and relatively untrained. Staff preparation for the march to meet the enemy was patently poor. In fact, the march and the organization of the Confederate force was so haphazard on the day preceding the attack that Beauregard proposed to postpone the effort. Johnston prevailed, however, knowing that his chance would be gone once Buell joined Grant. In his battle order, the Confederate commander sacrificed one important factor, seriously impairing the fighting power of the southern force. Apparently, he had abandoned his original plan to attack with left, center, and right wings (in fact, corps) and a reserve. Instead, he permitted Beauregard, second in command, to attack in three parallel lines, or waves, which became predictably and hopelessly intermixed and confused once the normal give-and-take of the typical Civil War battlefield began. The change reduced the combat power available at the front as well as significantly increasing the difficulty of effective command and control.[28]

---

*Defeat in detail occurs when one force defeats part of an enemy force before the other part of the enemy force can come to the assistance of the first part.

The Confederate Attack at Shiloh

The Confederate army that attacked on Sunday morning, April 6, achieved remarkable surprise. *(See Atlas Map No. 8.)* Food still in cookpots, simmering over fires, fell into the hands of the first wave of Confederate soldiers. Some Union troops were still in their sleeping rolls. The Federal forces, five divisions, evidently had camped wherever they could among the forest and tangled brush adjacent to Pittsburg Landing. Streams and swamps added to the fragmentation of the bivouac site. Yet the serious lack of fundamental security is inexplicable, especially in light of warnings of nearby troop concentrations by subordinate commanders and more than occasional contact between Federal soldiers and what appeared to be pickets during the two-day period preceding the Sunday attack. A further complication was the lack of coordination between Buell and Grant. Even though the lead division—that of Brigadier General William Nelson—of Buell's force reached Savannah on April 3 and 4, it stayed there to await Buell's arrival. Grant kept his own headquarters at Savannah in order to meet Buell when the latter arrived, thus removing himself nine miles from his own command. Entrenchments around an encampment were considered neither desirable nor essential at this stage of the war. No small number of the Union commanders felt that entrenchments were counterproductive, as they discouraged inexperienced troops from leaving the entrenchments to launch an attack. In summary, the Federal command, from private to general, was neither mentally nor physically prepared for the Confederate attack. The weight of the initial attack fell on Sherman's and Prentiss' divisions, which were holding the right-center of the Union position. Prentiss' division was driven back on the equally unprepared division of Stephen Hurlbut, while Sherman's troops were pushed back into the bivouac of McClernand's division, giving up, in the process, a small building near Owl Creek called Shiloh Church.[29]

Johnston intended to hit the Federal left with his main attack, pushing the Union divisons in a wheeling motion against Owl and Snake Creeks and away from Pittsburg Landing. The attacking formation of corps in column with divisions on line, however, did not provide the Confederate right with the necessary concentration of combat power. Consequently, a frontal attack resulted. Beauregard, managing reinforcements and the reserve in the rear, ordered the corps of Major General Leonidas Polk and Brigadier General John C. Breckinridge respectively to the left and to the right early in the day, extending the Confederate line and removing any opportunity to later influence action with a fresh reserve. This action merely extended the length of the frontal attack in progress. Johnston moved directly to the front, leaving the conduct of

Brigadier General William Tecumseh Sherman

the battle, for all practical purposes, in the hands of his second in command.[30]

At his headquarters, aboard the steamer *Tigress* docked at Savannah, Grant heard the boom of the cannonade at about 6:00 a.m., indicating that more than a skirmish was in progress. He disembarked at Pittsburg Landing between 7:00 a.m. and 7:30 a.m., the signs of the fight being already evident as his horse stepped ashore at the landing. Stragglers were crowding around the landing and under the bluffs. Weaponless, often hatless, and usually breathless, they were sullen in their determination not to return to the fight. Normally, they would already be starting to scatter over the countryside. At Shiloh, though, the landing drew them like a magnet. Grant rode by the stragglers and moved toward the sound of the guns.[31]

Prior to leaving Savannah, Grant had sent two messages, one directing Nelson to bring his division to Pittsburg Landing, and the other advising Buell of the ongoing battle. At the battlefield, his forward divisions had already taken a solid pounding. Moving quickly, Grant spoke with W.H.L. Wallace, whose division was not yet engaged, and with Prentiss and Sherman. Grant gave his staff the tasks of immediately organizing ammunition trains for the frontline divisions and of collecting and organizing the stragglers. The nature of the Confederate attack and the compartmentalized Federal encampment produced a series of individual battles at the outset, rather than a single battlefront. This situation demanded that Grant step in positively to control it. Prentiss, hit hard, fell back to the northwest and regrouped what was left of his division in a pocket between the divisions of W.H.L. Wallace and Stephen Hurlbut. That pocket, later nicknamed the "Hornet's Nest" *(see Atlas Map No. 8.)*, would cost Prentiss' division dearly before the day was over, but would also be one of the primary factors denying the Confederates victory on April 6. When Prentiss pulled his division back under heavy pressure, he exposed the left flank of McClernand's division, but the prewar Democratic politician stubbornly faced in two directions and held his ground. At about 10:30 a.m., Sherman, hit in the flank by cavalry, was also forced to withdraw under the attack from Hardee's corps. Consequently, McClernand, now with both flanks exposed, was finally compelled to fall back. Despite repeated messages and the exertions of his staff, Grant could not get his reserve, under Lew Wallace, to the front. Moreover, none of Buell's divisions was able to join in the battle. Grant did receive some offshore fire support from gunboats later in the day, but the result of the day's fighting would, for the most part, ride on the shoulders of his five division commanders and their 33,000 men.[32]

Morning gave way to afternoon, and Grant continued to make the rounds, personally directing troops and exhorting his commanders to stave off disaster. To Prentiss, whose division held the salient called the Hornet's Nest, Grant's instructions were simple and clear: hold your ground at all costs. Soldiers and officers who saw Grant that day agreed that his face displayed anxiety, but not defeat. By noon, the divisions of Sherman and McClernand, already forced back to the road just west of Shiloh Church, withdrew again under the relentless attack of Hardee's and Polk's corps. Elsewhere along the Union line, Grant was still unable to establish a cohesive line or a mutually supporting defense. By 4:00 p.m., the continuous attacks of the Confederate corps of Breckinridge and Bragg had driven back the divisions of Hurlbut and W.H.L. Wallace, and Prentiss' division in the Hornet's Nest created an even more prominent salient than before. The last time that Grant visited the division in its exposed position, he told one fellow Illinoisan who commanded a regiment that the Confederates had expended their major effort for the day. In fact, throughout the afternoon, Grant stubbornly refused to admit defeat or plan for retreat, despite the fact that his divisions continued to fall back under pressure and his reinforcements failed to arrive. Grant's attitude, transmitted to his subordinates, and his frequent personal direction at critical

junctures of the battle may have been the most significant contributions the general made that day.[33]

In mid-afternoon, the Confederate Army lost its leader. Johnston fell after leading a charge by a brigade of Breckinridge's corps, victim of a bullet wound in the leg that cut an artery and proved fatal. But the Confederate Army was plagued by more than the loss of its commanding general. While Grant's forces were being forced back, position by position, hour by hour, the attacking Confederate corps had nearly expended their energy. By late afternoon, critical shortages of ammunition had begun to affect the brigades. Nor was there any appreciable reserve with which Beauregard, now the commander, could finish the work his soldiers had so heroically carried on all day. Having prepared and marched for two days prior to the battle, the Confederate soldiers were near exhaustion. Significantly, the most strenuous efforts of the Confederate attackers had achieved neither a breakthrough nor an overwhelming defeat against any portion of the Federal line. Southern casualties were heavy. Stragglers abounded as the tired, hungry Confederates paused to take advantage of ample Union rations in overrun camps. The dedicated defense by the Federal division of Prentiss in the Hornet's Nest was not contained and bypassed by the advancing Confederate corps, but rather attracted an inordinate amount of the Confederate infantry, who attacked from three sides. Prentiss finally surrendered his division at around 5:30 p.m., but by that time the remaining Federal divisions had formed a strong line along the Hamburg-Savannah Road and its northward extension to Pittsburg Landing. *(See Atlas Map No. 8.)* In addition, Grant's chief of staff, Colonel Joseph A. Webster, had assembled a battery of 50 cannon to bolster the Union left near the Tennessee River. Located just north of Dill's Branch, it delivered a punishing fire into the infantry of Hardee and Bragg.[34]

The Union line along the Hamburg-Savannah Road held. Although Grant met Buell late in the afternoon, reinforcements from the latter's divisions did not make a significant contribution to the battle on April 6. Lew Wallace's division of Grant's army did not reach the battlefield until 7:15 p.m. Realizing that he could not fight to a successful conclusion that day, Beauregard suspended the attack at 6:00 p.m. However, Bragg, who had not received the order, launched one more attack, with one brigade advancing with the bayonet because it had run entirely out of ammunition. The attack failed, signaling the end of the Confederate offensive.[35]

The Advantage Shifts to the Union Forces

On April 7, the Federal effort still lacked a coordinated command, but for a different reason. Halleck, the overall commander, was not on the scene. Although Grant was senior to

Buell, he was apparently reluctant to exercise command over Buell's forces. As a result, the independent attacks launched by Grant's and Buell's forces at 5:00 a.m. drove the Confederates from the ground gained the previous day, but did not produce a coordinated cohesive attack. *(See Atlas Map No. 9.)* The fight of the seventh was not an easy one. The Confederates resisted stubbornly, surrendering ground unwillingly—through steadily—until about noon, when Beauregard judged that a retreat was in order. He organized a rear guard to cover the withdrawal of his battered army to Corinth. Grant did not launch a pursuit, believing that his troops were too weary for an effective chase. Buell, too, chose not to pursue. With Halleck not present, and no other authority to direct a pursuit, the Confederates retired unmolested. Braxton Bragg gave a candid estimate of the missed Federal opportunity when he wrote to Beauregard the day after the battle: "Our condition is horrible. Troops utterly disorganized. Road almost impassable. No provisions and no forage . . . . Our artillery is being left all along the road by its officers; indeed, I find but few officers with their men." Later, he added, "If we are pursued by a vigorous force we will lose all in our rear. The whole road presents the scene of a rout, and no mortal power could restrain it."[36] The Union losses in missing, wounded, and killed were nearly 14,000. The Confederates lost just less than 11,000 soldiers. Shiloh quickly captured the headlines,

overshadowing another Confederate defeat on April 7—the fall of Island Number 10 in the Mississippi River to a siege directed by Major General John Pope.

The war along river lines in the West promised to gain momentum. Actions along the Tennessee, Cumberland, and Mississippi Rivers carried the brunt of the war into southern territory and threatened multiple penetrations. Professionals conceded that there would probably be no quick end to the war, no dramatic lightning strokes to crush the Confederacy. Grant himself had learned a great deal at Shiloh—not the least important of which was the tenacity and dedication of the Confederate soldier.

Having occurred nine months apart and at a great distance from each other, the Battles of First Bull Run and Shiloh may seem like an uncommon pair for study. Perhaps the most important single factor that links the two distinctly different battles and demands their joint consideration is the pattern of the errors committed in each. The military body of neither North nor South was ready professionally when the war began. Shiloh and First Bull Run underline the lack of preparedness that characterized every army in every theater of operation, Confederate and Union alike, during the first year of war. This would change. The training of privates, sergeants, company officers, staffs, and generals was to continue.

Notes

[1]John G. Nicolay and John Hay, *Abraham Lincoln: A History* (10 vols.; New York, 1890), IV, 65. Additional information concerning the locations of the scattered parts of the Army in 1861 are in Francis Paul Prucha, "Distribution of Regular Troops Before the Civil War," *Military Affairs*, XVI (1952), 169–173; and William A. Ganoe, *History of the United States Army* (New York, 1924), pp. 243–246.

[2]*The War of the Rebellion: A Compilation of the Official Records of the Union and Confederate Armies* (130 vols.; Washington, 1880–1901), Series I, II, 67, 303–305, 314–315, 324. (Hereinafter cited as *OR*. Unless otherwise indicated, subsequent references to the *OR* are to Series I.) See also Kenneth P. Williams, *Lincoln Finds a General* (5 vols.; New York, 1949–1959), I, 67, concerning special and regular staffs. James B. Fry, who was on McDowell's staff at the First Battle of Bull Run, describes the organization of the Union force in his article in *Battles and Leaders of the Civil War*, ed. by Robert Underwood Johnson and Clarence Clough Buel (4 vols.; New York, 1884–1888), I, 171–176. (Hereinafter cited as *B&L*.)

[3]*OR*, II, 486, 504ff. An excellent analysis of Beauregard's shift from defensive to offensive thinking is contained in Douglas Southall Freeman, *Lee's Lieutenants: A Study in Command* (3 vols.; New York, 1942), I, 39–40, 42–43.

[4]*OR*, II, 172, 475.

[5]*B&L*, I, 245–247 (Joseph E. Johnston's article); Freeman, *Lee's Lieutenants*, I, 47–52.

[6]*OR*, II, 308, 317, 324 (McDowell's report).

[7]*OR*, II, 169–170, 172.

[8]Freeman, *Lee's Lieutenants*, I, 63–64.

[9]*OR*, II, 480–481 (Jackson's report); see also 474, 487, 566.

[10]E. Porter Alexander, *Military Memoirs of a Confederate*, with introduction and notes by T. Harry Williams (Bloomington, Ind., 1962), p. 34; Joseph E. Johnston, *Narrative of Military Operations, Directed During the Late War Between the States* (New York, 1874), p. 47.

[11]*OR*, II, 492, 493, 495; Johnston, *Narrative*, p. 48.

[12]*OR*, II, 320, 347, 394, 402, 406, 407, 481, 494; *B&L*, I, 188–191.

[13]*OR*, II, 372–376, 482, 747, 748.

[14]Ulysses S. Grant, *Personal Memoirs of U.S. Grant*, (2 vols.; New York, 1885), I, 272–276; see also *B&L*, I, 348–349 (Polk's article).

[15]*OR*, Series II, I, 849, 853, 859, 891; Series I, VII, 443–444, 521, 524, 526, 527, 528–529, 530–531, 533–534, 535, 537–538, 543, 544, 547.

[16]Johnston's difficulty is examined in *B&L*, 546–548 (William P. Johnston's article).

[17]*OR*, V, 41; K.P. Williams, *Lincoln Finds a General*, III, 187–188.

[18]*OR*, VII, 121, is Grant's January 28, 1862 announcement of intent to Halleck to proceed against Fort Henry. See the same source for Halleck's authorizing reply of January 30, 1862.

[19]*OR*, VII, 124–126 (Grant's report), 136–144 (Report of Confederate commander, Tilghman); *B&L*, I, 368–372.

[20]*OR*, VII, 124 (Grant's report to Halleck, ending with: "I shall take and destroy Fort Donelson on the 8th and return to Fort Henry.").

[21]*OR*, VII, 161–164.

[22]*B&L*, I, 400–403, (Article by Lew Wallace, one of Grant's commanders).

[23]*B&L*, I, 410; *OR*, VII, 174 (McClernand's report).

[24]Grant, *Personal Memoirs*, I, 305–307; *B&L*, I, 413–421 (Lew Wallace's article); *OR*, VII, 166, 188, 190, 194, 201, 215, 613–614, 618.

[25]*OR*, VII, 160–161.

[26]Stanley Horn, *The Army of Tennessee* (Indianapolis, 1941), pp. 107–115; *OR*, VII, 899–900, and VI, 398.

[27]*B&L*, I, 555. For exchange between Halleck and Grant, and Halleck's cautionary dispatch to Grant, see *OR*, X, Pt. 1, 32, 41, and Pt. 2, 46, 49, 51, 52, 55, 62.

[28]*B&L*, I, 454–460 (Article by General Johnston's son, William P. Johnston).

[29]*OR*, X, Pt. 1, 119, 133, 186, 259, 263, 278, 288.

[30]Thomas Jordan, "Notes of a Confederate Staff Officer at Shiloh," in *B&L*, I, 599–603.

[31]Bruce Catton, *Grant Moves South* (Boston, 1960), pp. 225–226; Grant, *Personal Memoirs*, I, 340–352.

[32]*OR*, X, Pt. 1, 112, 248, 249–250, 288, 396, 573, 577–578; Grant, *Personal Memoirs*, I, 340.

[33]Bruce Catton, *U.S. Grant and the American Military Tradition* (New York, 1954), pp. 83–87, 106.

[34]Joseph W. Rich, *The Battle of Shiloh* (Iowa City, 1911), p. 78; Manning F. Force, *From Fort Henry to Corinth* (New York, 1882), p. 155.

[35]*B&L*, I, 602; *OR*, X, Pt. 1, 551, 555.

[36]*OR*, X, Pt. 2, 94, 96–97, 98, 398, 400; Grant, *Personal Memoirs*, I, 354–355; *B&L*, I, 603.

Challenge and Response in the East, 1862

3

The Union disaster at the First Battle of Bull Run jolted Federal authorities in Washington and brought them to the realization that their armed forces were not prepared for war, despite the large numbers of volunteers who were flocking to the colors. At the same time, the unexpected setback led to a profound change in the Federal means of directing the war in the East—a change that would influence the campaigns in and around Virginia for over a year. President Lincoln reached the conclusion that Irvin McDowell was not the man to direct the efforts of Union forces against Davis' surprisingly capable and resilient armies in Virginia. Despite the fact that both public and political opinion had goaded McDowell into an early advance to Manassas, the President could not continue to support a man who had not brought the victory that the uninformed northern public and press had glibly expected.

The day after the First Battle of Bull Run, Major General George B. McClellan was summoned to Washington and given command of all forces in the vicinity—forces that were destined to become the Army of the Potomac. The new commander seemed to have those qualifications that would insure success. An 1846 West Point graduate who had had experience in the Mexican War, McClellan had also served in a position of unique prestige before the Civil War as a member of a three-man commission that traveled to Europe and observed the Crimean War, as well as the armies of the leading powers of Europe. During the 1850s, McClellan left the Army and built a reputation in civilian life as a railroad president. Early in the Civil War, like many other Academy graduates who had left the Army, he volunteered his services and quickly secured an appointment as a general of volunteers. Victories in West Virginia, though small in scale, brought McClellan national prominence and led Lincoln to charge him with the task of building an army out of the disorganized and untrained assortment of troops in and around Washington. More importantly, Lincoln urgently needed a commander who could lead that army to victory over the Confederates. McClellan's brash

confidence and formidable reputation gave Lincoln cause to believe that the victor of West Virginia was equal to the more demanding tasks in Virginia.

A New Commander Tries His Hand

The organizing and training of the Army of the Potomac occupied McClellan's immediate attention. From the recruits that poured into Washington—100,000 men had arrived by mid-October as a result of Congress' decision to call 500,000 volunteers—he created an excellent fighting force that would bear the imprint of his organizational genius and skillful direction of training throughout the rest of the war.[1] When General Winfield Scott retired in November, exhausted and chagrined by McClellan's undermining efforts, the latter succeeded him as Commander-in-Chief of all ground forces of the Union. The dual role of Commander-in-Chief and army commander would have taxed the most capable general, and McClellan's failure to devise a suitable strategy for Halleck and Buell in the West* suggests that McClellan was less than successful in discharging the burden of both responsibilities. More immediately pertinent to our present narrative, however, is the manner in which McClellan's forces performed in the East.

After the rout of Federal forces at Bull Run, a Confederate army under the command of Joseph E. Johnston remained in the area of Centreville. In addition, the Confederates boldly established batteries to command the lower part of the Potomac River and thereby seal off Washington from the sea. An abortive and badly mismanaged attempt to challenge the Confederates at Ball's Bluff, near Leesburg (see Atlas Map No. 3), resulted in the loss of the commander and most of

---

*See Chapter 2 for a discussion of this point.

Major General George B. McClellan

the force. These three factors—the unchallenged presence of Johnston's army, the closing of the Potomac, and the Ball's Bluff affair—eroded the Government's confidence in McClellan. There was a definite stirring in Congress and the administration. The press also demanded action—the Rebels must be punished.

At first, McClellan contemplated an advance against Johnston's army, which the growing force under his command outnumbered nearly 2 to 1. Lincoln favored that direct approach. By the end of November, however, McClellan had shifted his attention to Richmond. He had devised a plan that would take the Confederate capital and, by so doing, deal a crushing blow to Confederate morale. To accomplish this aim, McClellan intended to move his army by sea, undetected, near to the mouth of the Rappahannock River, advance rapidly up the Peninsula, and finally capture Richmond before Johnston's force at Centreville could react and interpose itself between McClellan and the Confederate capital. A steady improvement of the fortifications of Washington gave McClellan the confidence to leave a small force to defend the Union capital while he moved the major portion of his force against Richmond. But Lincoln and his advisers opposed any plan that would remove the Army of the Potomac from a position between Johnston's army and Washington.[2]

Several factors conspired to delay the action until February 1862, when an exasperated President finally issued the first of a series of war orders directing McClellan to move against Johnston. Among these factors were the onset of winter with

its rains and McClellan's bout with typhoid fever. More important, though, was the inability of Lincoln and McClellan to reach an agreement on the strategy to be employed. The Union commander resisted the pressure from all quarters, however, and by early march he secured approval to move his army to the Peninsula, as orginally proposed.[3]

The Confederates were having little difficulty anticipating what McClellan would do, thanks to a steady flow of intelligence issued from within Federal lines. This flow was undoubtedly assisted by southern sympathizers, who were difficult if not impossible to weed out of Washington during the major portion of the war. Anticipating McClellan's seaborne approach, Johnston withdrew south of the Rappahannock early in March, removing an important element of McClellan's initial calculation that Johnston would not be able to reach Richmond before the assault of the Federal forces. Soon after Johnston's army withdrew, McClellan moved his army to Centreville on a "shakedown" march designed to test the performance of the newly trained troops. President Lincoln used the opportunity to remove McClellan from overall command, restricting his authority to the Army of the Potomac, which would require his full attention during the coming campaign. When McClellan's army finally began its voyage to the Peninsula, the landing site was shifted to Fortress Monroe rather than Urbana, since the former was in Union hands and could not be challenged as easily as a landing site closer to the new location of Johnston's army.[4]

Jackson in the Valley

When Thomas J. "Stonewall" Jackson was promoted to Major General after the First Battle of Bull Run and assigned to command the Valley District (essentially the Shenandoah Valley) in November 1861, he took over a small body of militia that would form the nucleus of what would become one of the most effective secondary efforts in the history of the war. The activity of "Stonewall" Jackson in his famous Valley Campaign had a profound effect on the major struggle between McClellan's and Johnston's armies on the Peninsula, and also serves as an instructive model of the superb use of maneuver and economy of force.

Jackson's Mission and Initial Operations

Initially, Jackson's two-fold purpose was to watch the enemy forces in the vicinity of the Valley and to be prepared to reinforce Johnston. But by the end of the year, when reinforcements had increased his strength to around 10,000, Confederate leaders* gradually enlarged the role of Jackson's force and authorized him to undertake diversionary operations that would pin Federal forces in the Valley. Jackson made his headquarters at Winchester, in the northern part of the Valley. By November, he had already grown impatient with the inactivity imposed upon him by the size of his force and the passive nature of his mission. Accordingly, he submitted a plan that was aimed at forcing a reaction from McClellan's still green troops around Washington. The War Department approved his plan soon after the reinforcements mentioned above joined his force in December. Characteristically, Jackson told neither his commanders nor his staff what he had in mind.[5]

On January 1, 1862, Jackson struck out northwestward toward Bath *(see Atlas Map No. 10)* in an attempt to engage the small Union force stationed there. By the night of January 3, a shift from unusually balmy weather to bitter cold made the march a miserable one for those numerous men who had unwisely left their winter coats behind. Thirty-six miles were covered in three days—a rate of march that Jackson regarded as being far from satisfactory. Finding that the alerted force

*Robert E. Lee, then serving as Jefferson Davis' military adviser, was one of these leaders. His role in planning the use of Jackson's force was substantial.

Thomas Jonathan "Stonewall" Jackson.

at Bath had withdrawn before his arrival, Jackson still hoped to engage another Union force at Romney, to the southwest. He therefore turned his column of cold, grumbling men in that direction. Several days of snow and sleet made the going extremely slow over the mountain roads. The horses, which had not been adequately shod, were spattered to the knees with frozen blood. When his little army dragged into Romney on January 14, much the worse for wear, it again found that the Union forces had withdrawn. Some consolation could be drawn from the discovery of Union stores and equipment left behind. Disappointed, Jackson began the return trip to Winchester, taking one brigade (his old "Stonewall" brigade, commanded by Brigadier General Richard B. Garnett) with him, and leaving the remaining force under Major General William W. Loring at Romney. He arrived at Winchester on January 24.[6] As far as the mission of the expedition was concerned, the venture had been a failure. In addition, he had exposed troops and animals to an ordeal they would not soon forget. To Jackson, the venture had also brought a stern reminder that training, discipline, and staff work were below the standard he must achieve if he expected his force to respond to the type of operations that he intended to undertake.

Loring and his command were so thoroughly disgusted with the whole operation that the directive by Jackson to remain remotely isolated in Romney was regarded as an unacceptable capstone to a pointless campaign. Appealing directly to the Secretary of War, Loring received permission to return to Winchester with his force. Jackson complied with the countermand to his order, but, viewing the Secretary's action as interference in his command, submitted his resignation. The episode undoubtedly taught the Secretary of War, Judah Benjamin, something about command channels and the personality of Jackson. Only the urgings of General Johnston and Governor Hatcher of Virginia persuaded Jackson to withdraw his resignation. Not coincidentally, Loring was transferred out of the Valley District.[7]

When Joseph E. Johnston received word of McClellan's intended landing on the Peninsula and withdrew south of the Rappahannock, he also re-called Brigadier General Ambrose Powell Hill and his detachment from Leesburg, leaving Jackson in an exposed position in the northern part of the Valley. *(See Atlas Map No. 10, Hill's movement not shown.)* There, across the Potomac near Harper's Ferry, he faced a force of approximately 23,000 Union troops under Major General Nathaniel P. Banks. Between March 12 and March 17, Jackson withdrew southward to Strasburg. From this time until the conclusion of the Valley Campaign, Jackson's deliberate provocation of the forces in and around the Valley played directly on the fears of Lincoln and other authorities in Washington for the safety of the capital, and in turn influenced McClellan's advance toward Richmond.

Bank's Initial Advance

At the end of February, Banks set in motion a chain of events that would lead to a clash with Jackson. Using ponton bridges to cross the Potomac River near Harper's Ferry, he moved the lead elements of his corps into Winchester on March 12. Discovering that Jackson had retreated to the south, Banks sent a division under Brigadier General James Shields in pursuit on March 17. Under pressure from the larger force, Jackson continued to move southward, covering his retreat with the cavalry of Lieutenant Colonel Turner Ashby. While Jackson withdrew to Mt. Jackson, Shields moved south to Strasburg, sending his cavalry on ahead to maintain contact with Ashby. Ashby covered Jackson's withdrawal well, for Shields' cavalry returned to rejoin the division on March 19, reporting that Jackson had fled from the Valley and left only a small covering force under Ashby behind. Deciding to leave Shields at Winchester, Banks thereupon moved his main force toward the east side of the Blue Ridge Mountains to assist McClellan.[8] This was exactly what Jackson was supposed to prevent from happening.

In order to prevent the reinforcement of McClellan, Johnston's instructions directed Jackson to occupy the attention of Union forces in the Valley. He was expected to do this, however, without becoming involved in a decisive engagement that would permit Jackson's smaller force to be destroyed.[9] On March 21, Ashby advised Jackson of the withdrawal of Banks' force. The next day, Ashby attacked the outpost of Shields' division just south of Winchester as Jackson hurried north to deliver a stronger attack that would attract Banks' attention. In a day and a half, Jackson's force of 3,500 marched 36 miles, attacking Shields' division (9,000 to 10,000 strong) at Kernstown shortly after noon on March 23. The Confederates were soundly defeated in a battle that lasted the afternoon. Disappointed, and apparently feeling that he had failed to carry out Johnston's orders, Jackson retreated. But his tactical defeat brought strategic results of far-reaching effect, for Shields concluded that Jackson would not attack a far superior force unless he was expecting aid from nearby forces. This belief was reported to Banks. Soon, another division of Banks' corps was on the way to reinforce Shields, followed by the remainder of Banks' corps. Jackson's attack not only halted the march of Banks' corps to assist McClellan, but also prompted Lincoln to withhold one of McClellan's other four corps—McDowell's—even as McClellan was setting out for Fortress Monroe. As the fear of Jackson's threat to Washington grew with the rumors of his activity in the Valley, another division of 10,000 men was diverted from McClellan to assist Major General John C. Frémont on the western side of the Valley. The loss to McClellan was significant, reducing his invading force from 155,000

to 92,000. Far from failing, then, the audacious Valley commander had succeeded well beyond his or Johnston's expectations. But he had to maintain the pressure.[10]

For the time being, Jackson could do little to oppose the sizable forces gathering against him. After the affair at Kernstown, which had triggered the return of Banks' corps and the dispatch of McDowell's corps, Jackson withdrew up the entire length of the Valley, not stopping until he reached the vicinity of Swift Run Gap. *(See Atlas Map No. 10.)* At that location, his force totaled about 8,000 men. Major General Richard S. Ewell, who commanded another 8,000 at Gordonsville, could cooperate with him if necessary. In addition, another 3,000 under the command of Edward Johnson were stationed near Staunton. After Jackson had withdrawn up the Valley, Banks followed at a respectable distance, finally halting near Harrisonburg at the end of April. Under his command were approximately 15,000 men. To the west was the Federal Mountain Department, commanded by Frémont, with another 8,000 men. McDowell's corps remained east of the Blue Ridge Mountains, approximately 30,000 strong. It was apparent to Jackson that these forces might be hesitant to attack him. However, he also realized that unless he again gained their attention, he could not keep them pinned in position near the Valley and thus unavailable to reinforce McClellan.

A Bold Diversionary March Forces Banks to Withdraw

On April 29, Jackson proposed an audacious plan to Lee.* Jackson could not accept the risk of attacking Banks frontally or trying to get around behind his rear as long as the southernmost elements of Frémont's forces—particularly Brigadier General Robert H. Milroy's brigade at McDowell—threatened his own flank and rear. Jackson therefore intended to march by a circuitous route to join Major General Edward Johnson's force at Westview, attack and drive back the southern wing of Frémont's force, and then return to the vicinity of Harrisonburg, where he could join Ewell's division for a combined attack against Banks. Part of the success of the plan depended on the concurrent inactivity of Banks. In this respect, the Federal redistribution of forces would help. Lee approved the plan, leaving the details of execution to Jackson.[11]

Because neither the campaign in the Valley nor that on the Peninsula can be fully understood without noting the relation of one to the other, it is necessary to momentarily shift attention to the major event in the theater—the landing of McClel-

---

*Although Jackson's force was a part of Johnston's army, Jackson secured approval for most of his plans from Lee, who was still Davis' military adviser. Lee, in turn, advised Johnston of what Jackson was doing.

Federal Siege Mortars in Front of Yorktown

lan's force below Richmond. By April 2, McClellan had accumulated nearly 50,000 troops at Fortress Monroe and was ready to proceed up the Peninsula. A Confederate council of war in Richmond had debated the wisdom of trying to hold Yorktown. *(See Atlas Map No. 11.)* Despite Joseph E. Johnston's objections, it was decided that Major General John B. Magruder would defend the town and attempt to delay McClellan as long as possible. It was a wise decision, although the Confederate commanders could not have known at the time just how long it would detain McClellan. McClellan attacked the Yorktown defenses frontally for two reasons. First, erroneous intelligence reports misled him; second, the Federal Navy was unable to send a sizable force up either the York or James Rivers—an action that would have allowed McClellan to outflank the town. Skillfully extending the entrenchments of Yorktown all the way across the Peninsula and rapidly shifting forces from one part of the line to another, Magruder played on McClellan's misconception that the Confederate force was vastly superior to his own. The Union commander's misjudgment was reinforced by his abominable intelligence system, which was run by the civilian Pinkerton agency. Accordingly convinced that he must conduct a virtual siege operation, McClellan permitted the Confederates to delay him on the tip of the Peninsula until early May. When it became apparent to Johnston that McClellan had gathered an overwhelming combination of troops and artillery in front of Yorktown, the Confederate commander secured permission to evacuate the position; on May 3, Magruder began pulling out. The skillful rear-guard action of Brigadier General J.E.B. Stuart's cavalry and the delaying action fought by the force under Major General James Longstreet permitted Magruder

to extricate his entire force, as well as most of his baggage and stores.[12] Yorktown was in Federal hands, but the Confederate defense had delayed McClellan a vital month—at just the time that Jackson was about to implement the plan that would engage the forces of Frémont and Banks in the Valley. It is worth noting that when Lincoln had relieved McClellan of the command of all Union ground forces, McClellan became a co-equal commander in the Eastern Theater with Frémont and Banks; overall command remained in Washington, in the hands of Lincoln and Secretary of War Edwin McMasters Stanton. Coordination of the principal eastern armies would be essential to insure success in the Valley and the Peninsula.

While McClellan was slowly overcoming the Yorktown defensive line, Jackson prepared his small command for a new assault in the Valley. No one in Jackson's command knew all the components of his plan—except for the taciturn "Stonewall" himself. As Jackson's troops marched southward toward Port Republic, Ewell attempted to deceive Banks and threaten his flank by moving through Swift Run Gap to occupy the camps abandoned by Jackson's men. *(See Atlas Map No. 10.)* To further deceive Banks and to cover Jackson's departure, Ashby's cavalrymen pushed forward toward Harrisonburg in what appeared to be a reconnaissance in force. Jackson began to move on April 30. Plagued that day and the next by heavy rains that turned roads into quagmires, the impatient Jackson could cover only five miles a day. Passing through Brown's Gap and then turning west when he reached the railroad near Mechum's River Station, Jackson was favored by better weather, and was able to reach Staunton on May 4. Giving his troops a day and a half for rest, he was on the road again, reinforced by Johnson's troops, which brought the total of his striking force to about 10,000. Outnumbered in the Valley, he could still concentrate superior combat power against the outposts of Frémont if he hurried.

When skirmishing began on May 7, Milroy's brigade offered stiff resistance at McDowell, 25 miles from Staunton. The Federals fought a stubborn defense through the next day, hoping that the nearby brigade at Franklin, commanded by Major General Robert C. Schenck, could reinforce them with its 6,000 men. But by the night of the eighth, no help had arrived, and Milroy was forced to retreat northward. Jackson was still having trouble getting his command to respond in the manner he desired, and, although Ashby's cavalry started in pursuit on May 9, the infantry was slow in following. Unable to regain contact with the retreating Federals, Jackson abandoned the pursuit on May 12, just short of Franklin. This phase of the operation had achieved its goal: to prevent Frémont's forces from interfering when Jackson turned his attention to Banks. Retracing his steps, the Confederate commander now headed for Harrisonburg and a junction with Ewell.[13]

But not all was going well for the Confederates back in the southern end of the Valley. The complicated command arrangement under which Jackson was operating was beginning to show strain, and Ewell was caught in the middle. "Old Baldy," as his troops called him, found himself responding, or attempting to respond, to orders from Joseph E. Johnston, Lee, and Jackson. Part of the problem resulted from Banks' withdrawal from Ewell's front; this move became necessary when Banks' corps was weakened by the loss of one division, which had been sent to join McDowell on the other side of the Blue Ridge Mountains. Although Jackson had ordered Ewell to watch Banks, he had made no provision for what Ewell should do if Banks withdrew. When Jackson returned, he quickly set aside Ewell's doubts: Jackson, with the main body, followed the withdrawal northward on the west side of Massanutten Mountain while Ewell followed the road up the east side of Massanutten Mountain, paralleling Jackson's force. When Jackson reached New Market and Ewell reached Luray on the other side of the mountain, Ashby's cavalry was already pressing close to Banks' lines where he had stopped his withdrawal near Strasburg.

On May 20, disquieting news reached Jackson at New Market. Ewell had forwarded him a copy of a dispatch from Johnston, ordering Ewell back to the east and vetoing an attack on Banks. Pondering the opportunity that was about to slip out of his hands, Jackson asked Ewell to delay the execution of Johnston's order until he received an answer to a dispatch of his own. Hastily, he had decided to go over Johnston's head and request permission directly from Lee to retain Ewell and continue with his plan. When Lee's approval reached Jackson, there was no tarrying as he embarked on a deceptive march that caught Banks completely by surprise.[14] Moving his own force through Luray Gap to the east while Ashby's screen occupied Banks' attention at Strasburg, Jackson combined his own 10,000 with Ewell's 6,000 and marched as rapidly as possible up the east side of the Massanutten. *(See Atlas Map No. 10.)* In effect, Jackson was using the mountain as a giant screen drawn between him and his enemy.

When Jackson's troops emerged from the east side of Luray Gap, neither they nor their commanders knew exactly what the secretive Jackson had in mind for his next move. Once on the east side of the Massanutten Mountain, he could turn southward, which was unlikely but possible; move northward; or strike eastward across the Blue Ridge Mountains toward the Federal forces gathered there under McDowell. On the morning of May 22, Jackson turned his column north toward Front Royal, still intent on coming to grips with Banks, but hoping to fall on his flank or rear by approaching from the east. That night, Jackson's force camped within ten miles of Front Royal. The next morning, he was able to move within less than two miles of Front Royal before his force was de-

tected. He quickly overwhelmed the 1,000-man garrison early in the afternoon.

Through careful planning and swift marching, Jackson had made every effort to insure that the garrison at Front Royal was cut off from outside assistance and could not send timely warnings to Banks near Strasburg. Early the next morning, Ashby and his cavalry pushed on toward Strasburg. Meanwhile, several columns of infantry moved along the roads to Winchester in an effort to determine what Banks would do, and, hopefully, to prevent Banks' further withdrawal to the north. Despite the vague rumors that reached Banks, it was after midnight before he interpreted Jackson's attack at Front Royal as more than a raid, and it was morning before he made up his mind to avoid what appeared to be a trap. Only when the evidence revealed the extent of Jackson's northward movement did Banks recognize that Jackson was not far to the south, where he had been last reported. Finally aware of the true situation, the Federal commander started north toward Winchester.[15]

Jackson's subordinates were still not meeting his high standards, and caused him no end of frustration and anxiety as they almost upset this vital phase of his operation. The inability to move his infantry brigades forward rapidly at Front Royal grew out of an error in staff work, and was compounded by the unexplained failure of the artillery to come forward rapidly when contact was first made. Only Jackson's personal intervention in sending an available cavalry force into action prevented the escape of at least part of the outnumbered Federal garrison. The errors did not cease as he turned his attention to Banks during the Union retreat from Strasburg. The slowness of the Confederate advance toward Winchester prevented Jackson from trapping Banks' force. In addition, Ashby's pursuing cavalrymen, striking Banks' abandoned trains, paused to loot them until Jackson angrily ordered the cavalry commander to regroup his force and resume the pursuit. Banks decided to make a stand at Winchester on May 25, but when it became evident that Jackson would overpower him there, he withdrew farther northward toward Martinsburg and crossed the Potomac River that night.

The last chance to trap Banks' retreating contingent was lost in an odd way. Demonstrating admirable initiative, Ashby led his cavalry toward Harper's Ferry in an attempt to cut off what appeared to be part of Banks' force trying to make an escape in that direction. Accordingly, Jackson logically turned to the cavalry commander of Ewell's division, Colonel George H. "Maryland" Steuart, and directed him to take over the direct pursuit of Banks' retreating Federal troops. Steuart, schooled in the tradition of the old Army and a stickler for proper channels, refused to obey the order, as it did not come from his direct superior, Ewell. (The order reached Steuart in the hands of one of Jackson's aides.) Eventually, a "proper" order was issued, and Steuart joined in the pursuit. However, valuable time had been lost, and Banks made good his withdrawal over the Potomac.[16]

The student of Jackson's Valley Campaign should not conclude from the incidents cited above that his tiny army was plagued with errors in performance or incompetent staff work. Quite the contrary, Jackson's steady improvement of the responsiveness of his command as well as his unceasing efforts to turn the infantry into "foot cavalry" produced the magnificent marching and skillful maneuvers that had thus far marked the campaign. Jackson's uncompromisingly high standards of performance and his stern, rigorous discipline, however, were only beginning to be fully appreciated by the cavalrymen, artillerymen, and infantrymen serving under him. The former Virginia Military Institute professor was an uncanny tactician and strategist whose demands upon himself, his subordinate commanders, and his men required a caliber of performance that was probably not achieved in any other command in either northern or southern armies at this relatively early stage of the war. Nevertheless, in the summer of 1862, even as well trained and well led a command as Jackson's still had room for improvement.

The success of Jackson's aggressive actions, which threw back Frémont's advance elements near the southern end of the Valley and culminated in his spectacular drive against Banks, stirred understandably deep concern and swift reactions in the Federal capital of Washington. Jackson's actions in the Valley also affected McClellan's operations on the Peninsula.

Timidity and Bungling on the Peninsula

Part of the success of McClellan's operations on the Peninsula depended on the support provided by the Federal Navy, which ranged the York and James Rivers. Early in March 1862, the Confederates completed work on an ironclad, the *Virginia* (known in the North as the *Merrimac*), in the James River. On March 8, the *Virginia* sank two wooden Union warships on a sortie into Hampton Roads. *(See Atlas Map No. 11.)* On the following day, the appearance of the Federal ironclad, the *Monitor,* in Hampton Roads, provoked the first contest between two ironclads in naval history. Although the fighting between the two warships was inconclusive, the *Virginia* was damaged and withdrew up the river, remaining, however, a constant threat to Federal shipping near the mouth of the James and a positive deterrent to Union use of the James River. After Yorktown fell into Federal hands in early May, the Confederate ironclad became a liability, for its deep draft

prohibited its withdrawal farther up the river, and it was not sufficiently seaworthy to escape to the open sea. Consequently, she was scuttled in mid-May to prevent her from falling into Federal hands. (The *Monitor* did not survive the war either, sinking while trying to reach Charleston, South Carolina in December of 1862.) More importantly, the intentional sinking of the *Virginia* gave the Federal Navy use of the James River, an important contribution to the succeeding campaign.[17]

The advance of McClellan up the Peninsula beyond the defensive lines at Yorktown proceeded at an amazingly slow pace, influenced to no small degree by McClellan's erroneous impression of the relative strengths of the two opposing armies. As long as President Lincoln kept a string on McDowell's corps to respond to what he regarded as a threat to Washington, McClellan was convinced that his expedition against Richmond was compromised by the shortage of troops he believed critical to the success of his operations. What compounded the problem was the unique intelligence apparatus, the Pinkerton agency, upon which McClellan relied for information regarding the enemy army. Pinkerton had agents operating behind Confederate lines and in Richmond, and had apparently gathered rather substantial amounts of reliable information. However, for some reason, he chose to give McClellan inflated reports of the size of Johnston's army that only served to slow down the chronically cautious McClellan. Despite the fact that Johnston opposed McClellan's 105,000 with no more than 60,000 Confederate troops of all types, Pinkerton's estimates, accepted at face value by McClellan, attributed to Johnston the staggering total of somewhere between 150,000 and 200,000 troops. Consequently, McClellan had advanced only as far as White House by May 17 *(see Atlas Map No. 11)*, and only another 12 miles to the Chickahominy River by May 20. By the twenty-fifth, McClellan had crossed two of his corps (Major Generals Samuel P. Heintzelman and Erasmus D. Keyes) over the river. He kept the other three corps (Major Generals Fitz-John Porter, William B. Franklin, and Edwin V. Sumner) on the north side of the river to link up with McDowell, who, it was anticipated, would come down from the north to join McClellan's army.[18]

Joseph E. Johnston fully recognized the seriousness of what would face him once McDowell's corps joined McClellan's army. Thus he was particularly sensitive to the report that McDowell, reinforced by Shields' division, had begun to move to join McClellan on May 26. Johnston hastily assessed the situation and planned an attack that would capitalize on the separation of McClellan's command on the two sides of the Chickahominy River. He intended to attack on the twenty-ninth, concentrating against Porter's corps, which formed the extreme right of McClellan's line. At that point, however, the impact of Jackson's Valley Campaign intervened. Not knowing how large a Confederate force Jackson might have behind him or what his next move would be, a nervous President Lincoln and a careful Secretary of War Stanton halted the southward movement of McDowell's corps and directed him to move instead to the relief of Banks, who was then battling Jackson in the Valley. *(See inset, Atlas Map No. 10.)* Frémont, also, was directed to join in the concentration against Jackson. No matter that McDowell proetested that the combination of Frémont and Banks was more than adequate to handle Jackson's smaller force, and that it would take him several days to move into a position to threaten Jackson, while he was only a three–days' march from McClellan. The order stood.[19]

The Battle of Fair Oaks

As soon as Johnston learned of the re-call of McDowell, he was able to relax momentarily and review the possibility of selecting an alternate place to attack McClellan. Originally, he had intended to attack the northernmost part of the Federal line, which would require a difficult assault across the Chickahominy River. Instead, Johnston decided to concentrate against the two corps that McClellan had stationed on the south side of the river. The current high water level made the new plan particularly attractive, as it would make it difficult for the Federal commander to move reinforcements quickly across the river to aid the threatened corps. In a well-conceived plan, Johnston proposed to use as many as eight available divisions to attack simultaneously along the entire front of the two Federal corps. *(See Atlas Map No. 11.)* Lacking a formal corps organization, he improvised by giving his senior division commanders (Magruder, Longstreet, and Gustavus W. Smith) the control of more than their own divisions, but this expedient and the work of not yet fully experienced staffs combined to frustrate the excellent scheme that Johnston had devised.

The Battle of Fair Oaks, or Seven Pines, opened on the morning of May 31, with the coordination of the several Confederate divisions failing from start to finish. Even the individual brigades of the same division attacked separately as the battle continued throughout the day. When nightfall ended the fighting, the Confederates had lost 6,134 men. Union losses amounted to 5,031. It was the first major offensive battle for the Confederate forces in Virginia since the clash at the First Battle of Bull Run nearly a year earlier, and the outcome suggested that a degree of complacency had permeated the Confederate command since the easy victory over McDowell the previous year. E. Porter Alexander, a Confederate officer who fought almost the entire war in the Virginia theater, offered these comments on the problems within the Confederate ranks:

> The fighting qualities of the troops engaged proved excellent, but the trouble was in our organization which could not handle the available force effectively. That was due partly to our lack of staff officers trained to military routine, partly to the unwieldy structure of our army into large divisions, instead of into corps and partly to the personal peculiarities of our commander whose impatience of detail appears in the misunderstanding between himself and Longstreet [Longstreet's division took a wrong road, meant for use by another division, providing the initial cause of lack of coordination among the attacks], and in the lack of written orders to officers charged with carrying into effect important plans.
>
> Perhaps our greatest deficiency at this period was in the artillery service. None of our batteries were combined into battalions, but each infantry brigade had a battery attached to it. There were no field officers of artillery, charged with combining batteries and massing them to concentrate heavy fire upon important points. . . .
>
> We had no lack of batteries. The roads were full of them, but there was no organization to make them effective. Both roads and open fields were in a very miry condition, and all movements would have been slow, but a competent officer by doubling teams could have brought up guns with little delay.[20]

Perhaps the most significant outcome of the battle occurred as a result of the two wounds that Joseph E. Johnston suffered near the end of the day. He was sufficiently immobilized to cause Jefferson Davis to appoint a new commander for the army: his own military adviser, Robert E. Lee. The quiet, unpretentious Virginian took command of Johnston's forces on June 1, the first step in the beginning of a career that was to become a legend in the history of the Civil War.

Lee Assumes Command

Having taken command of the forces around Richmond after observing the contest between Johnston and McClellan for several weeks, Lee could not have failed to draw his own conclusions concerning the best method to repel McClellan's forces and the character of his opponent. However, even if Lee entertained ideas of offensive movements against the Federal forces north and east of Richmond, his first priority had to be the defense of the Confederate capital. Moreover, the disappointing results of the Battle of Fair Oaks had served to demoralize the Confederate soldiers, and Lee knew that he must reverse that attitude. With the energy and vigor that would become characteristic of his command, Lee turned

General Robert E. Lee

temporarily to the shovel, directing his subordinate commanders to improve and strengthen the entrenchments that guarded the eastern approaches to Richmond. As the days passed with no apparent preparation for offensive action on the part of the Confederate forces, politicians and journalists in the Confederate capital began to display impatience with Lee's emphasis on defense. His troops, unaccustomed to the digging that would become routine later in the war, nicknamed Lee the "King of Spades." But Lee would not stand on the defensive long. His attention was already centered on finding a way to strike McClellan's army and drive it away from the Confederate capital.[21]

For that task, Lee decided that he would need the additional force commanded by Jackson in the Valley. As previously noted, Jackson's presence there had already served to divert McDowell's corps from McClellan. How Jackson continued to deprive McClellan of additional reinforcements and eventually joined Lee forms the concluding chapter to his remarkable campaign in the Valley. For that account, it is necessary to return to the northern end of the Shenandoah Valley at the end of May. There, Jackson, having driven Banks across the Potomac River, faced the converging forces of Frémont, Banks, and McDowell, which were moving to cut him off and destroy his small army of less than 20,000 men.

Hard Marching and Thunder in the Valley

After having successfully forced Banks north of the Potomac, "Stonewall" Jackson had no intention of keeping his foot cavalry in their exposed position in the vicinity of Harper's Ferry. *(See inset, Atlas Map No. 10.)* His mission was to divert forces from the Union campaign on the Peninsula, but not to engage his small command uselessly in a decisive campaign with superior Federal forces. With his command concentrated at Halltown, Jackson learned on May 29 that Frémont was moving to cut him off south of his position. On the next day, Jackson received information concerning the movement of part of McDowell's corps, and consequently decided to withdraw his command from the vulnerable position near the Potomac River.[22]

A Potential Trap at Strasburg

On the surface, Union prospects for trapping Jackson appeared good. Shields' division of McDowell's corps, marching ahead of the remainder of the corps, moved through Thoroughfare Gap of the Blue Ridge Mountains toward Front Royal, and was closer to Strasburg, the focal point of the Federal trap, than was Jackson's command. On the other side of the Shenandoah Valley and at the head of 15,000 troops, Frémont moved through Wardensville toward Strasburg from the other direction. After Jackson began his withdrawal to the south on May 30, Banks recrossed the Potomac at the head of approximately 11,000 men. Thus the three converging Union forces totaled over 35,000 men.[23]

But three elements were working in Jackson's favor. In the first place, the activities of the three Union forces were being controlled and coordinated not by a local commander, but by the Secretary of War in Washington. Lincoln and Stanton may have been fully justified in removing the authority of overall command from George McClellan when he demonstrated his unfitness to handle that position prior to his embarkation for the Peninsula. However, their failure to designate an overall commander for the forces in and around the vicinity of the Valley and Washington was a grievous error, and produced a serious lack of coordination among the Federal commanders now engaged in an attempt to execute a maneuver that required close cooperation and unity of effort. Then there was the reputation and stature that was already attached to "Stonewall" Jackson as a result of his exploits in the Valley. It was probably worth an incalculable additional number of troops to him, as he hurried southward to avoid the trap. Frémont advanced cautiously, and Shields, without specific instructions from McDowell to reach Strasburg before Jackson, made no effort to push forward to that town, even though he could have reached it before the lead elements of Jackson's main body. Neither, apparently, relished the idea of tackling Jackson without assistance. In addition to the uncoordinated Federal command arrangement and the formidable reputation that Jackson had already built, the Confederate commander had a third asset working for him. Painstakingly, he had developed in his command the hardiness and discipline needed to march rapidly over long distances. Legends had already sprung up within his command about the peculiarities of Jackson that manifested themselves in detailed instructions regarding the methods by which a march was to be conducted. By experimentation, he had determined that his troops could cover more ground over a sustained period of time if he marched them for 50 minutes and then imposed a 10-minute rest break. Nor was the style of the break overlooked. Jackson insisted that the men lie down during the breaks—not stand around or sit on the ground—for he was convinced that in this way the troops would derive the most benefit from the regular breaks that he prescribed.[24]

These and other idiosyncrasies of the stern Confederate commander paid rich dividends as he pushed his men day and night on May 30 and 31, racing to reach Strasburg before his command could be cut off. The success of the race, however, was not left to the speed and durability of his foot cavalry. Ashby's cavalry dashed ahead and turned to the west to delay Frémont's advance. A brigade of infantry moved ahead of Jackson's column to turn east at Strasburg and challenge the advance of Shields, who, in addition to his own 10,000 troops, had 10,000 of McDowell's men on the road behind him. When the main column of Jackson's army reached Strasburg on May 31, he was only halfway out of the trap; his trains followed the column, and they also had to be cleared through Strasburg. Since Frémont's troops were closest to reaching Strasburg, Jackson shuffled his command again, sending Ewell with his division to assist Ashby in holding the western Federal force in check long enough for the Confederate trains to pass through the town. By the night of the thirty-first, Jackson had escaped from the trap. One brigade had covered 36 miles in a day. When McDowell reached Front Royal on the evening of May 31, he sent his cavalry forward to Strasburg, but Ewell doubled back from his position in front of Frémont and repulsed the inquisitive Federal horsemen as they approached the town. Bringing up the rear guard of Jackson's force was the weary but reliable Stonewall Brigade.[25]

When the Stonewall Brigade passed through Strasburg on June 1, Frémont's lead elements fell in on the road behind it, skirmishing with Jackson's rear guard, but keeping a respectable distance. McDowell, in the meantime turned Shields'

division south to try to cut Jackson off at Luray Gap. *(See Atlas Map No. 10.)* Behind Frémont, Banks, also, was in pursuit, bringing the total of Union forces engaged in trying to trap the elusive Confederate to approximately 50,000 troops. But Jackson anticipated the Federal commanders and sent Ashby ahead to prevent Shields from using Luray Gap, a task that was executed by burning the bridge over which Shields would have to pass. At the same time, Jackson's rear guard destroyed bridges and threw up hasty obstacles in the path of Frémont. Unable to cross at Luray Gap, Shields pushed southward toward Conrad's Store, where he could cross to the west and meet the head of Jackson's column at Harrisonburg. As he advanced, he could hear the cannon fire on the other side of Massanutten Mountain, signaling the constant skirmishes between Frémont's lead elements and Jackson's rear guard. But the redoubtable Ashby was a step ahead again, racing to destroy the bridge over the South Fork before Shields could claim it. On June 5, Jackson reached Harrisonburg, where he turned southeast to cross the bridge over the South Fork at Port Republic. He had won the race, but he paid a heavy price when General Ashby, in a stiff rear-guard action on June 6, was killed. A civilian turned soldier at the beginning of the war, Ashby was mourned by the entire command, and must be considered an indispensable element in the successful escape of Jackson from the converging forces that had harried his troops for nearly a week as he pushed southward up the Valley.[26]

Final Battles in the Valley Campaign

Jackson rested his command for two days near Cross Keys while his cavalry, positioned on both sides of Massanutten Mountain, watched Frémont's troops, stationed in Harrisonburg, and Shields' troops, advancing slowly from the east. *(See Atlas Map No. 10.)* Jackson was still capable of escaping to the southeast, toward Richmond. Nevertheless, on the night of June 7, before the two Federal forces could unite against him, he boldly formed an offensive plan to deal with each enemy force in turn. The plan was to hold Frémont at Cross Keys with Ewell's division while he turned against Shields with his main body. Once Shields was overwhelmed, he would throw his entire command against Frémont, the stronger of the two Federal forces. It was a design for a classic defeat in detail. Jackson never fully realized his ambition, however, as Frémont did not wait, but attacked Ewell's division on June 8, thinking he was attacking the main part of Jackson's army. Nevertheless, Frémont's hesitancy resulted in a piecemeal attack, which Ewell successfully contained.* Part of Fré-

*A piecemeal attack is an attack in which the subordinate units of a force are committed to the assault as they become available, on an attack in which the timing breaks down and the subordinate units are committed in an uncoordinated manner.

mont's caution grew from his uncertainty concerning the whereabouts and status of Shields. The following morning, Jackson moved out to engage Shields' force, meeting the two advance brigades under Tyler two miles north of Port Republic. By now, Jackson had abandoned his plan to attack Frémont after dispensing with Shields' force, so he called Ewell's division to reinforce the attack against Shields. With the help of Ewell, Shields' advance elements were pushed back to the north after four or five hours of fierce fighting. However, as the Union troops retreated toward Conrad's Store, they were reinforced by the remainder of Shields' force, and were thus able to halt the Confederate pursuit just before nightfall.[27]

Jackson withdrew, and by midnight of June 9 was back in the area of Brown's Gap, bringing the Valley Campaign to an end. When the record of his operations is reviewed, it is readily apparent that he lost as many battles as he won. Yet, far more important in an evaluation of the campaign is the strategic impact of Jackson's bold and swift operations on the contest between the major armies on the Peninsula. Jackson's force of less than 20,000 men was the key element in the struggle to balance the difference between the contending Union and Confederate armies in the vicinity of Washington and Richmond. Between Jackson and Lee (earlier, Johnston), the Confederates could boast a total strength slightly above 100,000. In the vicinity of Washington, Richmond, and the Valley, the combined forces of McClellan, Banks, McDowell, Frémont, and the garrison of Washington totaled more than 200,000 troops, the impact of which was effectively diluted by the remarkable series of operations that Jackson launched from March through the beginning of June. Even as Jackson was buffeting the Federal troops in the battles of Cross Keys and Port Republic, Lee was developing a scheme for attacking McClellan in the vicinity of Richmond. His plans would include the redoubtable Valley army.

McClellan Turned Back

Lee's first concern was to remove, or at least neutralize, the threat of McClellan's army near Richmond. As long as Jackson kept the Federal forces in and near the Valley occupied, Lee could feel fairly certain that McClellan would not receive substantial reinforcements. But Jackson's presence in the Valley would serve to pin down the forces under Frémont, Banks, and McDowell for only so long. Even as Jackson's battles at Cross Keys and Port Republic were occurring, part of McDowell's corps was earmarked for dispatch to McClellan's army on the Peninsula. Despite the urging and prodding that McClellan was receiving from Washington, Lee could neither ascertain when the Union commander intended to attack nor

detect any signs of a Federal withdrawal. Therefore, with an audacity that would become one of his best-known characteristics, the Confederate leader decided to move offensively against McClellan.

The Federal army was still split by the Chickahominy River, although the effect of that barrier was partially overcome as bridges were built across it. The more logical position from which to initiate offensive operations against the defenses of Richmond was the south side of the Chickahominy, which explains the presence of the larger portion of McClellan's army in that location. However, because his base for supplies and reinforcements was at White House, which was accessible via the Pamunkey and York Rivers, McClellan kept Porter's corps on the north side of the Chickahominy to protect that base. *(See Atlas Map No. 11.)* Lee chose Porter's corps as his first target, hoping to overwhelm it before McClellan could send assistance north of the river. On June 11, he sent Brigadier General William Henry Chase Whiting's division north by rail to Staunton to create the impression of a renewed offensive by Jackson in the Valley. At the same time, with the help of about 17,000 reinforcements that he had received from Georgia and the Carolinas, Lee prepared to move against Porter.[28] To gain additional information, he sent Stuart out around the left flank of the Federal position to reconnoiter the flank and rear of the enemy forces. Unfortunately, the orders that Lee gave to Stuart were sufficiently permissive to allow the flamboyant cavalry commander to interpret them in the broadest fashion and turn the reconnaissance into a far-ranging raid that carried his horsemen entirely around McClellan's army on June 12-15. It was a magnificent grandstand play that appealed to Stuart's love of dash and adventure, but it alerted McClellan to the vulnerability of his rear and his supply base on the Pamunkey River. Even before Lee attacked Porter's corps, McClellan had started to shift his base from the old location to a more secure site at Harrison's Landing on the James River. Stuart, although an excellent cavalry commander, was impetuous at times. However, the real fault for the inadvertent disclosure must rest with Lee, whose flexible order permitted the untimely and largely unproductive raid.[29]

To launch an effective attack against Porter's corps, Lee would have to assemble as much of his army on the north side of the Chickahominy as possible, while leaving a thin defense between Richmond and the bulk of his army on the north bank. He began to do this quietly in the third week of June. In the meantime, Jackson, now joined by Whiting's division, moved secretly to link forces with Lee so that he could cooperate in the attack in the vicinity of Richmond. By June 24, McClellan and the authorities in Washington had concluded that Jackson was moving to join Lee. But so well did he conceal his withdrawal from the southern end of the Valley that he was 15 miles from Richmond, at Ashland's

Station, on June 25. McClellan's slowness and caution, although not elements upon which Lee could depend, were nevertheless important factors in clearing the way for Lee's offensive.

A quick survey of the numbers of troops involved on each side of the Chickahominy illustrates the boldness of Lee's plan and the opportunity that awaited McClellan. Counting Jackson's men, Lee had approximately 65,000 troops north of the Chickahominy to attack Porter's corps of 30,000. Magruder's and Major General Benjamin Huger's divisions, which totaled only 25,000, constituted the only force standing between Richmond and McClellan's four corps of 60,000. But the excellent scheme conceived by Lee miscarried. For some inexplicable reason, Jackson halted and went into bivouac instead of joining in the attack against Porter on June 26. A.P. Hill, growing impatient because his assault was to be coordinated with Jackson's arrival, advanced alone and without orders, only to be repulsed in a bloody fight. Longstreet and Daniel H. Hill did not even get into the fight. Although the spoiling attack by Magruder and Huger south of the river convinced McClellan not to launch an assault in that location, Lee's intended envelopment of Porter by Jackson and the anticipated defeat of Porter's corps were never realized. On the twenty-seventh, Porter, still facing the bulk of Lee's army, began a skillful withdrawal toward the south side of the Chickahominy, and McClellan ordered the shift of his base to the James River. Then, much against the advice and urgings of his subordinate commanders, McClellan yielded to inflated estimates of the size of the Confederate army and Lee's demonstrated initiative and ordered the withdrawal of his entire army to the James River![30]

What followed was a series of battles, called the Seven Days' Battles, that lasted through July 1, as McClellan's retreating corps were attacked in flank and rear by Lee. *(See Atlas Map No. 11.)* Curiously, McClellan was rarely present at the front to supervise the conduct of his corps. The conduct of McClellan's corps commanders, however, produced skillful rear-guard actions and counterattacks, demonstrating that the Army of the Potomac had the potential to be a first-rate fighting force if only properly led at the highest level. McClellan evidently was not the man to do it.

The problems of the Confederate force were different. Relying heavily on Jackson, for whom he had gained a great deal of respect as a result of the Valley Campaign, Lee was disappointed by the performance of his subordinate. Unlike any period before the Seven Days' Battles or any period afterward, Jackson was as much of a hindrance as he was an asset. After his failure to attack on time on June 26, he failed to respond promptly to Lee's plans on three more occasions during the week's fighting around Richmond. However, Jackson's lethargy was only a part of Lee's problem. Repeatedly, Lee was the victim of poor staff work, which wrecked excellent plans as he attempted to isolate and defeat in detail the corps of McClellan's army. Other factors, too, complicated Lee's operations, including the cumbersome organization of the Confederate Army, which included as yet no organization larger than the division. In addition, it should be noted that Lee demanded a great deal from his subordinate commanders by devising plans that required the concentration of his forces on the battlefield—a difficult maneuver even for the best trained fighting force. Nor should the fact be overlooked that Lee himself was new to high-level command. Lee was learning, and so was his army. The final lesson would be a sobering one.[31]

After five days of hard marching and heavy losses, the Confederates faced McClellan's army where it had gathered on a low but prominent two-mile-wide mound called Malvern Hill, located adjacent to the James River. Although the position could not be flanked, Lee recognized that it was his last opportunity to destroy the Union army, and therefore launched an attack against the position on July 1. The combination of poor staff coordination and the inability to bring more than a fraction of the Confederate artillery up to support the piecemeal attacks of Lee's divisions produced a predictable repulse. Porter, commanding the united corps at Malvern Hill—McClellan was absent, having left for Harrison's Landing—conducted a skillful defense, assisted by the excellent opportunities offered by the terrain and the outstanding collection and direction of the Federal artillery under Colonel Henry J. Hunt.[32]

For all practical purposes, the campaign was over, although McClellan's army remained at Harrison's Landing until August. Lee's army had demonstrated the need for reorganization and improved staff work; but the new commander had successfully blunted the threat to Richmond. Union casualties during the Seven Days' Battles numbered about 16,000, while Lee, attacking with a smaller army, had sustained nearly 20,000 casualties.

Lee Against Pope

Reorganization in Both Armies

Dismayed by the ineffectiveness of Federal efforts to trap and destroy Jackson's forces in the Valley, Lincoln ordered another organizational change. He summoned Major General John Pope from the Western Theater, where Pope had demonstrated a commendable degree of success, to command the newly formed Army of Virginia—a collection of the corps of Banks, Frémont (who soon resigned), and McDowell, as well as

The Federal Defense of Malvern Hill, July 1862

some lesser forces.[33] He also called Major General Henry W. Halleck from the West in mid-July to become the General-in-Chief of all Federal ground forces. McClellan meanwhile continued to appeal for reinforcements to assist in the capture of Richmond, but the administration in Washington—and Lincoln in particular—was beginning to suspect that no infusion of reinforcements would revive the stalled offensive of "Little Mac." After visiting McClellan and his army of 90,000 on the James River and listening to the general's insistence that Lee had 200,000 opposing him, Halleck confirmed the administration's resolve to send no more troops to that area.[34]

All the while, the Federal high command was still having difficulty devising useful orders with which to direct its armies in the field. Pope's Army of Virginia was given a three-fold mission that, under close scrutiny, nearly defied compliance. With his army, Pope was directed to "cover the City of Washington from any attack from the direction of Richmond; to make such dispositions as were necessary to assure the safety of the Valley of the Shenandoah; and at the same time so to operate on the enemy's lines of communication in the direction of Gordonsville and Charlottesville as to draw off if possible a considerable force of the enemy from Richmond, and thus relieve the operations against that city of the Army of the Potomac."[35] Pope did not smooth the way for his assumption of command when he issued a bold and presump-

tuous order to his troops, criticizing their past performance. dated July 14 and issued from his "Headquarters in the Saddle"—an unfortunate choice of words that gave pundits no small source of ammunition for ridicule—Pope pompously told his men that he wanted to hear no more of "taking strong positions and holding them" or "lines of retreat" or "bases of supplies." "Let us discard such ideas," he wrote, adding, "Let us study the probable lines of retreat of our opponents and leave our own to take care of themselves. . . . Success and glory are in the advance. Disaster and shame lurk in the rear. . . ."[36] Unfortunately for the Union, Lee would measure the generalship of Pope more reliably than would any address that general might issue to his troops.

The Army of Northern Virginia took a much needed rest after the conclusion of the Seven Days' Battles. However, there was much work to be done even if there was to be no major fighting for a few weeks. A corps organization had not yet been introduced into the southern army, but, anticipating this, Lee did the next best thing. Although Longstreet and Jackson were not promoted to the rank of lieutenant general, Lee designated a right wing and a left wing of his army and placed the divisions in these wings under the command of the two generals. Moreover, to improve the efficiency of the artillery, Lee authorized the grouping of batteries into battalions. (A year would pass before a similar change was made in the Federal armies.) Improvements also appeared in the weapons and equipment of the artillery and infantry as captured items from the Seven Days' Battles were issued to Confederate troops. These weapons and equipment would prove an important addition to Confederate stocks throughout nearly the first two years of the war. Finally, Lee supervised the energetic construction of additional entrenchments and fortifications to guard the eastern approaches to Richmond. This last step was a necesary one if he was to be able to move his army away from the Confederate capital on offensive operations and leave behind a reduced force for the protection of the city.[37]

Jackson at Cedar Mountain

In the middle of July, Lee sent two divisions, numbering 12,000, north to the vicinity of Gordonsville. Led by Jackson, this force was to guard against any approach by Pope's army, which numbered approximately 47,000. *(See Atlas Map No. 12; Jackson's move not shown.)* Jackson wanted to launch offensive operations against Pope, but found that the size of his force was inadequate for the job. Appealing to Lee for additional troops, Jackson had to wait until the end of July while Lee carefully watched McClellan to determine if the Union commander intended another attempt against Richmond. But McClellan had no intention of attacking what he still believed to be a much superior force, and, on July 27, Lee sent the division of A.P. Hill, 12,000 strong, to join Jackson at Gordonsville. *(See Atlas Map No. 12; Hill's move not shown.)* In the meantime, having already decided that no further purpose could be served by keeping McClellan's army in its present position, Halleck had ordered Pope to move south across the Rappahannock to attract Lee's attention so that the Confederate forces around Richmond would not interfere with McClellan's withdrawal.[38]

As Pope's force was crossing the Rappahannock on August 6, Jackson saw an excellent opportunity to defeat part of Pope's force on the south side of the river, where it was separated from the rest of his army. Though the plan was an excellent one, the intense, humid heat so slowed the marching rate of Jackson's newly collected command that a sizable portion of Pope's army had crossed the river before Jackson met them on August 9 in the Battle of Cedar Mountain. *(Movement not shown on map.)* Poor staff work still persisted in the Confederate organization, and the blunders and errors that occurred delayed the divisions of Jackson's force from being ready until well after noon. Misunderstanding Pope's orders, Banks, who commanded the lead Federal corps, attacked Jackson, completely upsetting Jackson's planned attack. But with the help of A.P. Hill's division, Jackson drove Banks' corps back and continued the pursuit until after dark.

Finally, Banks' corps received support from the lead elements of two additional corps of Pope's army, and Jackson's pursuit was halted. Then the two armies watched each other for two days. Finally, Jackson withdrew to Gordonsville while Pope pulled back to the Rapidan River. The battle, which resulted in approximately 1,300 Federal casualties and over 2,300 Confederate casualties, gained little—tactically or strategically—for either side. But the result convinced Lee that Jackson alone could not handle Pope, and on August 13, after being informed of the plans to withdraw McClellan from the Peninsula, Lee sent Longstreet's wing northward to join Jackson.[39]

With Longstreet and Jackson united south of the Rapidan by August 17, Lee had 55,000 troops to oppose approximately the same number under Pope. *(See Situation 17 August 1862, Atlas Map No. 12.)* But after a week of maneuvering, he was unable to turn either flank of the position that Pope held on the north side of the river or to entice Pope into an attack against the Confederate position. Moreover, reinforcements were beginning to reach Pope, and the main body of McClellan's army was already disembarking at Alexandria, south of Washington, after having withdrawn from the Peninsula. It was apparent to Lee that within a few more days Pope's numbers could swell to such a size that Lee could no longer strike him. If Lee was going to move, he would have to do so quickly. In the meantime, Pope had withdrawn behind the Rappahannock.[40]

Major General John Pope

The Second Battle of Bull Run

On August 24, Lee and Jackson discussed a bold plan to force a reaction from Pope and maneuver him into a position more favorable for a Confederate attack.[41] The next morning, Jackson moved north around the southern end of the Bull Run Mountains. Turning east at Salem, a small town that was located on the railroad that ran from Manassas through Thoroughfare Gap, Jackson pushed his troops hard and reached Bristoe Station in time to go into bivouac for the night. *(See Situation 24 August 1862, Atlas Map No. 12.)* He was squarely on Pope's line of communication. An empty Federal train passed through Jackson's position and, although fired upon, was not stopped. Thus, it was able to proceed to Manassas, seven miles away, and give warning of Jackson's force. After dark, however, Jackson sent out two regiments that successfully captured the important rail junction and Federal supply depot there at about midnight.[42] Now, leaving a small screen of active artillery and infantry in front of Pope, Lee set Longstreet in motion to follow Jackson's route. By the twenty-sixth, Pope was aware both of Jackson's force at Manassas and of Longstreet's movement northward.[43]

The boldness of Lee's maneuver gave Pope a unique opportunity to engage and defeat first one and then the other wing of the Confederate army before the two could be reunited. First, however, he had to find and fight Jackson. It is difficult to understand Pope's thinking and the movements of his units as he tried to trap Jackson with his approximately 75,000 troops.[44] The Union difficulties had apparent roots. Without evaluating the competence of Pope himself as a general, two factors should be understood that seriously impaired his ability to cope with Lee's fast-moving and more responsive army. First, Pope had no cavalry under his direct control with which to perform the critical role of reconnaissance. It was distributed among the corps of his command, posted on picket duty, guarding vital installations, or performing as couriers. Not yet had the Federal Army learned how to organize and use its cavalry to best effect. In contrast, Lee had placed his cavalry entirely under the command of Major General J.E.B. Stuart, who traveled with Jackson, and the colorful Stuart, despite his sometimes counterproductive impetuosity, was a capable and aggressive commander of the mounted arm. At the same time, Pope's command suffered from another weakness: the lack of a good working relationship between Pope and his subordinates. Pope's bombastic address to his troops, cited earlier, probably contributed to the strained relations. Nor did the fact that he was junior to all of his corps commanders help. Most damaging was the inability of the subordinate commanders to place full confidence in their as yet untried commander, despite his favorable record in the West. Being unaccustomed to Pope, they misunderstood his orders.

Moreover, certain information available to subordinate commanders did not find its way to Pope, and errors of omission by Pope were always brought to his attention. Therefore, the atmosphere that permeated the Army of Virginia was certainly not the best one in which to respond to a rapidly changing tactical development; side by side with excellent opportunities for success were the seeds of disaster. In short, Pope's army, and perhaps the commander himself, was simply unable to cope with Lee.[45]

On August 27, Pope disposed his corps in an attempt to close a trap around Jackson at Manassas and prevent the junction of Jackson and Longstreet. *(See The Concentration 27–29 August, 1862, Atlas Map No. 12.)* Jackson, however, did not tarry long at Manassas Junction after taking what he could and destroying the rest. In addition, the corps that Pope sent in the direction of Thoroughfare Gap had not been told how to deal with Longstreet. Without the assistance of cavalry, Pope lost track of Jackson, who moved northwest, to an area near Sudley Springs, even though elements of one Federal corps skirmished with his troops before they left Manassas. As Pope was rapidly losing control of the situation, Jackson took up a strong position on Stony Ridge, hoping to encourage Pope to attack him so that he could hold Pope in position until Lee arrived with Longstreet's corps. When a division of McDowell's command passed in front of Jackson's concealed wing on August 28, Jackson attacked it to draw attention to his location. Alerted, Pope directed the concentration of his

Manassas Junction After the Departure of the Confederates, August 27, 1862

army against Jackson, apparently forgetting or ignoring Longstreet in his haste to deal with Jackson. Consequently, on August 29, Longstreet, after pushing aside the lone division left judiciously by McDowell to guard the pass, was able to move through Thoroughfare Gap.

A careful reading of the orders that Pope now issued to his corps discloses that Pope was not even aware of the location of all of his units, a consequence of his subordinates' failure to keep him fully informed of their movements and Pope's own inability to contend with what was admittedly a confusing situation.[46] The attack against Jackson on August 29 was delivered piecemeal and frontally. Consequently, despite fierce fighting that pushed Jackson's outnumbered wing to the limits of endurance, Pope was unable to dislodge him from his position. Although Longstreet arrived on Jackson's right on the twenty-ninth, he persuaded Lee to allow him to delay his attack until the next day. This was perhaps the only serious error that Lee committed in the campaign, for the weight of Longstreet's corps against the unsuspecting flank of Pope's army on August 29 would have dealt the Union army a devastating blow. Misinterpreting the effect of his attack against Jackson that same day, Pope presumed that the Confederates were withdrawing on the thirtieth. He ordered a pursuit. With the combined force of both Longstreet's and Jackson's wings, to which was added the effective fire of the Confederate artillery, Lee succeeded in driving Pope back to Henry House Hill near Bull Run by the night of August 30. Some fighting persisted as Pope continued to withdraw to the east through September 1. Lee tried to pin Pope in position or prevent his withdrawal to Washington. But his best opportunity had been on August 29, and on September 3 he had to content himself with watching Pope and his army withdraw inside the defenses of Washington.[47]

The Second Bull Run Campaign was over, and Lee, with an army of 55,000, was within 20 miles of the Federal capital. Although a variety of conditions contributed to Lee's success against Pope, the one that stands out in sharp contrast to others is the fact that Pope had been outgeneraled. A marked improvement in the organization of Lee's Army of Northern Virginia, the better responsiveness of that army, and Lee's demonstrated skill in handling it established the Confederate army as a much more formidable combat force than it had been when it turned McClellan back before Richmond in the Seven Days' Battles. Lee had been in command for exactly three months, at the head of an army that had never totaled more than 85,000 troops; yet he had outmaneuvered and outfought an opposing array of Union troops that numbered close to 200,000. Keenly aware of the momentum that his latest campaign had generated and buoyed by the confidence of his troops and subordinate commanders, Lee turned his attention to a continuation of further offensive operations.

The Antietam Campaign

September 7, 1862 (?)

To Genl. R.E. Lee, Comdg &c, Genl. B. Bragg, Comdg. &c, Genl. E.K. Smith, Comdg. &c

Sirs:

It is deemed proper that you should in accordance with established usage announce by proclamation to the people of _____ the motives and purposes of your presence among them at the head of an invading army, and you are instructed in such proclamation to make known,

That the Confederate Government is waging this war solely for self-defence, that it has no design of conquest or any other purpose than to secure peace and the abandonment by the United States of its pretensions to govern a people who have never been their subjects and who prefer self-government to a Union with them. . . .

That among the pretexts urged for continuance of the War is the assertion that the Confederate Government desires to deprive the United States of the free navigation of the Western Rivers although the truth is that the Confederate Congress by public act, prior to the commencement of the War, enacted that ''the peaceful navigation of the Mississippi River is hereby declared free to the citizens of the States upon its borders, or upon the borders of its navigable tributaries''—a declaration to which this Government has always been and is still ready to adhere.

That now at a juncture when our arms have been successful, we restrict ourselves to the same just and moderate demand, that we made at the darkest period of our reverses, the simple demand that the people of the United States should cease to war upon us and permit us to pursue our own path to happiness, while they in peace pursue theirs.

That we are debarred from the renewal of formal proposals for peace by having no reason to expect that they would be received with the respect mutually due by nations in their intercourse, whether in peace or in war. . . .

That the Confederate army therefore comes to occupy the territory of their enemies and to make it the theatre of hostilities. That with the people of _____ themselves rests the power to put an end to this invasion of their homes, for if unable to prevail on the Government of the United States to conclude a general peace, their own State Government in the exercise of its sovereignty can secure immunity from the desolating effects of warfare on the soil of the State by a separate treaty of peace which this government will ever be ready to conclude on the most just and liberal basis.

That the responsibility thus rests on the people of _____ of continuing an unjust and aggressive warfare upon the Confederate States, a warfare which can never end in any other manner than that now proposed. With them is the option of preserving the blessings of peace, by the simple abandonment of the design of subjugating a people over whom no right of dominion has ever been conferred either by God or man.

JEFFN. DAVIS[48]

As the armies of E. Kirby Smith and Braxton Bragg prepared to drive northward into eastern Tennessee and Kentucky, Lee set his sights on an invasion of Maryland. *(See Atlas Map No. 1.)* The star of the Confederacy was definitely in the ascendant, and, in both the Eastern and Western Theaters, Confederate commanders and the government in Richmond alike hoped to capitalize on the momentum of previous successes and the anticipated sympathy that smoldered in the border states. The operations west of the Allegheny Mountains will be examined in a later phase that considers the war in the West, although those operations paralleled Lee's invasion in the East.

In the letter of September 7 to three of his army commanders in the field, Jefferson Davis set the tone for the next phase of Confederate operations — offensive thrusts into the territory of the United States as part of an overall defensive posture of the Confederacy. The merits of that particular strategic philosophy depended to a degree on the specific goals each of the army commanders set for himself, and the chances for successfully achieving those aims. In the case of Lee and his contemplated invasion of Maryland, it was not a foregone conclusion that the Army of Northern Virginia, notwithstanding its past successes, was capable of producing the intended results in its drive northward. To President Davis, Lee wrote, "The army is not properly equipped for an invasion of an enemy's territory. It lacks much of the material of war, is feeble in transportation . . . and the men are poorly provided with clothes, and, in thousands of instances, are destitute of shoes."[49] Yet the army that Lee led was a mobile army, not because of any material assets, but because Lee understood and had to date demonstrated better than any general the advantage of a commander who uses his mobility to surprise, upset, and unbalance his opponents. In the same letter to Davis, Lee declared, ". . . we cannot afford to be idle, and though weaker than our opponents in men and military equipments, must endeavor to harass if we cannot destroy them."[50] Lee's skill and audacity led Yankee soldiers to joke sourly that Lee not only commanded his own Army of Northern Virginia, but the Union Army of the Potomac as well!

Yet even as Lee was reminding his superiors of his deplorable state of supplies, he was preparing his army for its first venture into Union territory. Several considerations influenced his decision to make a thrust northward into Maryland. Morale was exceedingly high in the Army of Northern Virginia after it humiliated the larger Army of Virginia under its pompous commander, John Pope. Lee's veterans were capably led by two of the best corps commanders in the Confederacy: James

"Old Pete" Longstreet and "Stonewall" Jackson. (Neither Longstreet nor Jackson yet held the title of "corps commander".) As different as any two men could be, Longstreet and Jackson were nevertheless skillful tacticians, tough fighters, and inspirations to the men they led. An invading army could be the deciding factor in the struggle to sway Confederate sympathy and inspire Maryland to break away from the Union and join the Confederacy. This fact loomed large in the calculations of Lee and Jefferson Davis. Lee also viewed his expedition as a way of shifting the fighting away from his beloved and battle-weary Virginia, not only for sentimental reasons, although they may have influenced him, but also because such mundane items as soldiers' food and animals' forage were becoming increasingly scarce in war-ravaged Virginia. Finally, another decisive victory over a Union army, coupled with the presence of a large southern army on Union soil, might impress European governments, notably England and France, and lead them to recognize the Confederate Government. Such an act would bring material and moral support.[51] Potentially, enormous possibilities depended on the success of Lee's invasion. But he would have to move swiftly.

Crossing the Potomac River near Leesburg, Lee finished assembling his army around Frederick, Maryland by September 7, 1862. *(See Atlas Map No. 13a.)* In accordance with the attitude expressed by Jefferson Davis, Lee issued a proclamation to the people of Maryland the next day, declaring that the Confederate States stood ready to help the Marylanders.[52] However, in a letter written to President Davis a short time later, he confided, ". . . I do not anticipate any general rising of the people on our behalf."[53] That part of the anticipated fruits of the invasion would not be realized.

More pressing was the movement of Federal troops toward Lee's army. After seeing the sorry spectacle of Pope's Army of Virginia streaming back into the defenses of Washington, Lincoln quietly removed him from command and incorporated his army into the Army of the Potomac. But who was to command the only army that could challenge Lee and stand between him and the Federal capital? McClellan was still the commander of that army, but he had already demonstrated that his intelligence gathering apparatus had not improved since his departure from the Peninsula. When McClellan was at Alexandria, Halleck had directed that he send troops to assist Pope while Jackson's wing of 25,000 was looting and burning Union stores at Manassas Junction. McClellan declined to send the requested troops, informing Halleck that Jackson's force of 100,000 (McClellan's estimate) was too serious a threat to Washington. After his timid execution of a well-conceived plan on the Peninsula, Lincoln, Halleck, and a growing body of critics in Washington were dubious of McClellan's ability to fight, even though few doubted his organizational skill or the hat-throwing, cheering devotion of the troops of the Army of the Potomac. Finally, Lincoln reluctantly consented to retain McClellan in command. Apparently no one else had the credentials for the job. The deciding factor, though, was the continued widespread confidence that troops and most subordinate commanders had in McClellan.[54]

On September 9, Confederate informers and cavalry told Lee that four corps of the Army of the Potomac were moving against him and were presently north and northwest of Washington.[55] Characteristically, Lee pushed northward.

Confusion and frenzied activity grew in Union headquarters as excited reports poured in about Lee's daring thrust. Lee's movements mystified McClellan as the latter moved cautiously toward the eastern edge of the Catoctin Mountains. With five corps and two separate divisions, the Union army numbered approximately 84,000 troops, not counting the two corps, one division, and other troops left behind for the defense of the Federal capital. McClellan now repeated the error that he had made during earlier operations: he grasped at inflated reports of Lee's strength and wired Washington that he faced a force of ''120,000 men or more.''[56] In fact, Lee's strength never exceeded 60,000. But in that curious blend of caution and boldness that persisted in his dispatches, McClellan optimistically informed the President: ''As soon as I find out where to strike, I will be after them without an hour's delay.''[57]

Lee's direction no doubt added to the growing nervousness at McClellan's headquarters. While the Shenandoah Valley, farther west, would have offerd the Confederate army a concealed route into Maryland, Lee chose a more exposed path east of the Blue Ridge Mountains to force an early Union reaction. Once across the Potomac, he intended to shift his line of communication west into the more secure Shenandoah Valley. But this move required that he eliminate the threat of 12,000 Union troops at Harper's Ferry. ''Stonewall'' Jackson drew the assignment and was sent south by Lee to capture Harper's Ferry, not only to neutralize the flanking position on the Confederate line of communication from the Valley, but also to take possession of the vital small arms, artillery weapons, and ammunition stored there.[58] By September 9, therefore, Lee had audaciously split his army, and events began to move more rapidly. By the evening of the thirteenth, he had divided his army again, this time in response to a rumor that Pennsylvania militia threatened his army from the north. Lee sent Longstreet's corps minus three divisions to Hagerstown to turn back this force.[59] (It never appeared.) The only forces that remained on McClellan's front were the thin line of three divisions (Richard Anderson, Lafayette McLaws, and D.H. Hill) that Lee retained plus the cavalry screen of Jeb Stuart in the gaps of South Mountain, which was already being probed by the Union cavalry under Alfred Pleasonton. *(See Atlas Map No. 13b.)*

At this point, fate intervened on McClellan's behalf. A copy of an order from Lee to his subordinate commanders, wrapped around three cigars, fell into McClellan's hands. Dated September 9, the order outlined Confederate movements for the next several days and gave McClellan a clear picture of the dispersion of Lee's army.[60] McClellan received the message late on the thirteenth and telegraphed Lincoln: ''I have all the plans of the rebels, and will catch them in their own trap if my men are equal to the emergency.''[61] Moving quickly, he could attack and defeat the separated, weaker parts of the Army of Northern Virginia, one by one. Carelessly, McClellan discussed the implications of his tremendous stroke of luck within the hearing of a southern sympathizer. By evening, Lee had learned of McClellan's discovery.[62] At that point, his forces were scattered from Harper's Ferry to Hagerstown.

The reactions of the two commanders were characteristic. Lee considered the vulnerability of his scattered forces and re-called Longstreet's corps to the vicinity of Boonsboro, but left Jackson to complete what Lee still considered to be a vital mission at Harper's Ferry. McClellan allowed 16 precious hours to slip by before he even put his forces in motion toward the passes through South Mountain.[63] Stubborn fighting there by D.H. Hill's division bought more hours for Lee and delayed McClellan another important day. Stuart's cavalry provided a vital assist. McClellan, aware of Jackson's effort to reduce Harper's Ferry, sent Franklin's corps to force Crampton's Gap and relieve the Federal garrison at the Ferry. After fighting throughout the afternoon of the fourteenth, Franklin succeeded in overcoming McLaw's division and was able to pass through the Gap.

When Jackson arrived in the vicinity of Harper's Ferry, an area with which he was intimately familiar, he at once perceived that he could capture the Federal garrison if he could gain command of the three hill masses surrounding Harper's Ferry—Bolivar Heights, Maryland Heights, and Loudoun Heights—for his artillery. *(See inset, Atlas Map No. 13b.)* By the afternoon of the fourteenth, he was in possession of the three hills, and was thereby able to bombard the Federal garrison from all three positions. When he resumed the bombardment the next morning, the Federal commander, seeing that his cause was hopeless, surrendered at 9:00 a.m. Jackson hurried north to join Lee, leaving behind A.P. Hill's division to accept the Union surrender and gather together the supplies, ammunition, and weapons of the depot. ''By a severe night's march,'' Jackson reported, ''we reached the vicinity of Sharpsburg on the morning of the 16th''—simple but eloquent testimony to the mobility and determination of Lee's army and his subordinate commanders. Longstreet, having returned from his mission to the north, rejoined Lee near Sharpsburg.[64]

''It had been hoped to engage the enemy during the 15th,''[65] McClellan reported. Nevertheless, he used up the fifteenth *and* sixteenth directing the placement of batteries, indicating the bivouacs for the different corps, and making changes in the positions of subordinate elements of corps—all activities that needed supervision, but that could have been managed by competent subordinates. Lee used the time to unite his army along the high ground that surrounded the town of Sharpsburg just east of the Potomac River. *(See Atlas Map No. 14a.)* To his front ran the Antietam Creek, an obstacle of limited value since four bridges along Lee's front crossed the creek and were supplemented by various fording sites. While the position that Lee chose for his defensive battle may have had tactical merit, it invited disaster as a strategic selection. To his rear was the Potomac River, which was neraly unfordable along the entire length of the Confederate position. Only one site—Boteler's Ford, behind the right of Lee's line—provided a possible exit from the position. If McClellan's forces were able to reach the ford, the Confederates would be pinned against the river with no way out.[66]

McClellan's plan of attack is difficult to reconstruct since he apparently issued no written orders to his subordinate commanders. Instead, in his report after the battle, he described his intent "to make the main attack upon the enemy's left—at least to create a diversion in favor of the main attack, with the hope of something more, by assailing the enemy's right—and, as soon as one or both of the flank movements were fully successful, to attack with any reserve I might then have in hand."[67] Though this concept was somewhat vague and indistinct, the superiority in combat power that McClellan possessed—over 80,000 troops available for the assaults opposed to Lee's 55,000, plus a marked advantage in quality and quantity of artillery—gave him the ability to overwhelm Lee if he could concentrate his forces. To add to the Confederates' difficulties, by the selection of his position for defense, Lee had given to the Federal artillery the advantage of being able to place their longer-range weapons on the dominating hill mass east of Antietam Creek, a circumstance that took a heavy toll of Confederate infantry and artillery during the battle.[68]

McClellan opened the action early on September 17. An all-day piecemeal Union attack followed—or, more accurately, five separate attacks—permitting Lee to shift reserves from one part of the threatened line to another. Major elements of two of McClellan's six corps (Franklin and Porter) hardly participated in the battle, diluting the advantage that McClellan had enjoyed at the start.[69] Instead of a coordinated attack, the assaults of the corps rippled from north to south during the day, beginning with Joseph Hooker's corps. In the south, Ambrose E. Burnside, who was to deliver the diversion that McClellan wrote of in his report after the battle, was deploying his corps for attack at 7:00 a.m., but received no order to attack until three hours later. When he did try to force a crossing over Burnside Bridge on Antietam Creek, shortly after noon, he was repulsed twice in savage fighting. More thorough reconnaissance beforehand would have revealed what Burnside's troops discovered in the afternoon: that the creek was fordable only a short distance from the bridge. Using the fords, Burnside had his corps across by 3:00 p.m. and began pushing the Confederate right wing back. If he reached the Potomac, he would cut off Lee's line of retreat via Boteler's Ford. But A.P. Hill had completed his work at Harper's Ferry and, urged on by couriers from Lee and Jackson, came boiling up on the Confederate right late in the day. After a punishing 17-mile march, Hill threw his exhausted, sweating infantrymen into the flank of Burnside's attacking corps, without so much as breaking step. *(See Atlas Map No. 14b.)* It was enough to tip the balance, and Burnside's stubbornly fighting infantry were driven back step by step across Antietam Creek. The repulse of Burnside in the south stopped the last serious Union penetration.[70]

The Battle of Antietam was over. Both armies bivouacked in position during the night, and watched each other throughout the next day. McClellan continued to receive reinforcements and had available in his own command nearly 24,000 troops (Franklin's and Porter's corps) who had taken little part in the fighting. In contrast, Lee had lost nearly a quarter of his command in dead and wounded. Nevertheless, McClellan declined to attack. Lee began his withdrawal on the night of

Burnside Bridge

"Bloody Lane" During the Battle of Antietam, September, 1862

the eighteenth, using Boteler's Ford; it continued unmolested, with the exception of timid probing by Porter's corps.

With no more than 55,000 men, Lee had successfully beaten back Union attacks by a force consisting of just under 90,000 men. Yet the Confederate invasion had been a failure. Marylanders did not rally to the Confederate banner. Foreign recognition never materialized. Lee's hard-pressed veterans failed to cripple the Army of the Potomac, even though Antietam claimed the bloodiest single day of fighting in the war: over 22,000 casualties on both sides. President Lincoln joined McClellan in declaring Antietam a Union victory and used the opportunity to issue his Emancipation Proclamation—a political device of far-reaching implications, both domesti-

cally and in foreign capitals. Soon after, he relieved McClellan, and the paradoxical Union general passed from the military scene of the war.

Despite the failure of the invasion to achieve any of its intended aims, Lee emerged as an even more impressive and respected commander. Outnumbered and poorly equipped, Lee's veterans could hold their heads high. Lee would demonstrate several more times that his army was more responsive, more cohesive, and more mobile than the numerically superior and better equipped Federal forces. Although in Jackson and Longstreet—and particularly the fiery and brilliant ex-VMI professor—he had extremely capable subordinates, the major difference was Robert E. Lee himself.

Notes

[1]Matthew Forney Steele, *American Campaigns* (Washington, 1951), p. 93; Kenneth P. Williams, *Lincoln Finds a General* (5 vols.; New York, 1949–1959), I, 122–130; George B. McClellan, *McClellan's Own Story* (New York, 1887), pp. 84, 172–173.

[2]T. Harry Williams, *Lincoln and His Generals* (New York, 1952), pp. 29–31, 51; K.P. Williams, *Lincoln Finds a General*, I, 132–134; *The War of the Rebellion: A Compilation of the Official Records of the Union and Confederate Armies* (130 vols.; Washington, 1880–1901), Series I, V, 6–8; X, Pt. 3, 3–34. (Hereinafter cited as *OR*. Unless otherwise indicated, all subsequent references to the *OR* are to Series I.)

[3]*OR*, V, 41 (McClellan's report); McClellan, *Own Story*, pp. 195–196, 228–229; *OR*, V, 45–46, 49–50.

[4]T. Harry Williams, *Lincoln and His Generals*, pp. 70–74.

[5]*OR*, V, 926–937, 938–940, 944, 946.

[6]Frank E. Vandiver, *Mighty Stonewall* (New York, 1957) pp. 180–190; *OR*, V, 965–969, 393–394, 1034, 1039; Douglas Southall Freeman, *Lee's Lieutenants: A Study in Command* (3 vols.; New York, 1942), I, 122–124.

[7]Freeman, *Lee's Lieutenants*, I, 123–129; Vandiver, *Mighty Stonewall*, pp. 190–195; *OR*, V, 1040–1041, 1050–1051, 1063, 1065–1066, 1070.

[8]*OR*, V, 1088, 1092, 1095; G.F.R. Henderson, *Stonewall Jackson and the American Civil War* (New York, 1949), pp. 175–179; Vandiver, *Mighty Stonewall*, pp. 198–203; Freeman, *Lee's Lieutenants*, I, 306.

[9]Joseph E. Johnston, *Narrative of Military Operations Directed During the Late War Between the States* (New York, 1874), pp. 106–107.

[10]*OR*, XII, Pt. 3, 380–383, 384, 836; Freeman, *Lee's Lieutenants*, I, 312–317.

[11]*OR*, XII, Pt. 3, 371–372; Freeman, *Lee's Lieutenants*, I, 328–346.

[12]*OR*, V, 54, 59–61; XI, Pt. 1, 14, 15, 71; XI, Pt. 3, 74–77; K.P. Williams, *Lincoln Finds a General*, I, 159–167.

[13]E. Porter Alexander, *Military Memoirs of a Confederate*, with introduction and notes by T. Harry Williams (Bloomington, Ind., 1962), pp. 95–97; Freeman, *Lee's Lieutenants*, I, 347–361.

[14]*OR*, XII, Pt. 3, 896–898.

[15]Henderson, *Stonewall Jackson*, pp. 267–270, 288.

[16]*OR*, XII, Pt. 1, 556–565, 702, 725; Pt. 3, 895; Freeman, *Lee's Lieutenants*, I, 374–382, 403–407.

[17]For detailed accounts of the building of the two ironclads as well as the contrast between the two, see the series of articles in *Battles and Leaders of the Civil War*, ed. by Robert Underwood Johnson and Clarence Clough Buel (4 vols.; New York, 1884–1888), I, 692–750. (Hereinafter cited as *B&L*.)

[18]*OR*, XI, Pt. 3, 134, 143, 148–149; Pt. 1 (McClellan's report), 28–30.

[19]*OR*, XII, Pt. 4, 219, 220–221, 226; K.P. Williams, *Lincoln Finds a General*, I, 172–176.

[20]Alexander, *Military Memoirs of a Confederate*, p. 90. For a detailed description of the battle and the preparation leading to it, see Freeman, *Lee's Lieutenants*, I, 219–263.

[21]Alexander, *Military Memoirs of a Confederate*, pp. 109–113.

[22]Freeman, *Lee's Lieutenants*, I, 418–419; Vandiver, *Mighty Stonewall*, p. 262.

[23]*OR*, XII, Pt. 1, 11–12, 643–648; Pt. 3, 627.

[24]Freeman, *Lee's Lieutenants*, I, 370; Vandiver, *Mighty Stonewall*, pp. 232–233.

[25]*OR*, XII, Pt. 1, 14, 708; William Allan, "Jackson's Valley Campaign," *Southern Historical Society Papers*, XLIII (1920), 246–255; Vandiver, *Mighty Stonewall*, pp. 263–267.

[26]Henderson, *Stonewall Jackson*, pp. 265–270; *OR*, XII, Pt. 1, 16, 750–751; Pt. 3, 314–315.

[27]*OR*, XII, Pt. 1, 714–782, 784–785, 818; Freeman, *Lee's Lieutenants*, I, 435–463.

[28]*OR*, XI, Pt. 2, 490; Freeman, *Lee's Lieutenants*, I, 494–502; Douglas Southall Freeman, *R.E. Lee: A Biography* (4 vols.; New York, 1934), II, 110–121.

[29]Steele, *American Campaigns*, p. 99; Alexander, *Military Memoirs of a Confederate*, pp. 113–114.

[30]*OR*, XII, Pt. 1, 283, 677, 682–683; Pt. 4, 314. See also K.P. Williams, *Lincoln Finds a General*, I, 219–225; William Swinton, *Campaigns of the Army of the Potomac* (New York, 1866), pp. 140–146.

[31]Freeman's account in *Lee's Lieutenants*, I, 503–587 is probably the best available of the Seven Days' Battles. See also K.P. Williams, *Lincoln Finds a General*, I, 224–241, and Alexander, *Military Memoirs of a Confederate*, pp. 115–155.

[32]Two excellent articles by opposing generals at Malvern Hill (D.H. Hill and Porter) provide a useful perspective of the battle. *B&L*, II, 383–395, 406–426.

[33]Swinton, *Campaigns of the Army of the Potomac*, pp. 168–169.

[34]*OR*, XI, Pt. 3, 281, 286, 291–292, 294, 298–299, 301–303. See also the excellent summary of the unproductive exchange between McClellan and his superiors in Washington regarding the strength of McClellan's army and his steady bombardment of Washington with incomprehensible statistics in K.P. Williams, *Lincoln Finds a General*, I, 242–256, and valuable information in Williams' endnotes, pp. 419–422.

[35]Steele, *American Campaigns*, p. 117.

[36]Alexander, *Military Memoirs of a Confederate*, p. 176.

[37]*Ibid.*, pp. 175–176.

[38]Swinton, *Campaigns of the Army of the Potomac*, pp. 172–175.

[39]Freeman, *Lee's Lieutenants*, II, 10–53.

[40]T. Harry Williams, *Lincoln and His Generals*, pp. 148–150; Alexander, *Military Memoirs of a Confederate*, pp. 185–190.

[41]Freeman, *Lee's Lieutenants*, II, 82–83.

[42]W.B. Taliaferro, "Jackson's Raid Against Pope," in *B&L*, II, 501–504. Taliaferro, a general in Jackson's command, testified to Jackson's continued secretiveness when he wrote: "No man save one in that corps, whatever may have been his rank, knew our destination." Taliaferro, like others of Jackson's subordinates, groused about their commander's reluctance to communicate his plans.

[43]James Longstreet, "Our March Against Pope" in *B&L*, II, 516–517; *OR*, XII, Pt. 4, 653–657.

[44]See Pope's article in *B&L*, "The Second Battle of Bull Run," II, 456–462, for Pope's evaluation of Lee's actions.

[45]K.P. Williams, *Lincoln Finds a General*, I, 295–302.

[46]Henderson, *Stonewall Jackson*, p. 443; K.P. Williams, *Lincoln Finds a General*, I, 309–317; *OR*, XII, Pt. 2, 34–35, 70–71; Pt. 4, 627, 675, 685, 688, 702.

[47]Freeman, *Lee's Lieutenants*, II, 87–143. See also Pope's article in *B&L*, II, 467–490.

[48]*OR*, XIX, Pt. 2, 598–599.

[49]*Ibid.*

[50]*Ibid.*, 590–591.

[51]Freeman, *R.E. Lee,* II, 350–361.

[52]*OR,* XIX, Pt. 2, 601–602.

[53]*Ibid.*, 596.

[54]K.P. Williams, *Lincoln Finds a General,* I, 356–361.

[55]Alexander, *Military Memoirs of a Confederate,* pp. 222–228.

[56]*OR,* XIX, Pt. 2, 281.

[57]*Ibid.*, 211.

[58]*B&L,* II, 604–606 (J.G. Walker's account).

[59]*OR,* XIX, Pt. 1, 145, 839; Alexander, *Military Memoirs of a Confederate,* p. 228.

[60]Freeman, *Lee's Lieutenants,* II, 173, 715–723.

[61]*OR,* XIX, Pt. 2, 281.

[62]Freeman, *Lee's Lieutenants,* II, 173.

[63]Swinton, *Campaigns of the Army of the Potomac,* pp. 201–202; *OR,* XIX, Pt. 2, 608.

[64]Steele, *American Campaigns,* pp. 129–131; *OR,* XIX, Pt. 1, 955; Pt. 2, 610.

[65]*OR,* XIX, Pt. 1, 53.

[66]Swinton, *Campaigns of the Army of the Potomac,* pp. 209–210.

[67]Steel, *American Campaigns,* p. 131.

[68]K.P. Williams, *Lincoln Finds a General,* II, 446–450.

[69]*OR,* XIX, Pt. 1, 149–150.

[70]*OR,* XIX, Pt. 1, 981; Freeman, *Lee's Lieutenants,* II, 203–225.

Vicksburg Under Attack

After the bloody repulse of the southern army at the Battle of Shiloh, the western door to the Confederacy stood ajar for a deeper Federal penetration. Although the soldiers of Don Carlos Buell and Ulysses S. Grant held the battlefield, the desperate fighting at Shiloh could hardly be called a resounding Union victory. Pierre G.T. Beauregard's army—A.S. Johnston, it will be recalled, fell mortally wounded on the first day of the battle—withdrew in good order to the security of Corinth, southwest of Shiloh. To turn the repulse of Beauregard's army into a great victory, the Union commanders had to press their advantage, come to grips with the sizable Confederate army (estimated at about 70,000), and maintain the momentum of offensive operations in the Western Theater.

Prelude in Tennessee

The responsibility for an energetic prosecution of the next phase of Federal operations in the West fell squarely on the shoulders of Major General Henry W. Halleck, the commander of the Department of the Mississippi. This department stretched all the way from the Mississippi River to a north-south line that ran approximately through Chattanooga. In the latter part of July 1862, Union officials added the Army of the Mississippi, commanded by Major General John Pope, to Halleck's command. Pope had recently won a small but valuable victory in capturing Island No. 10, below Cairo, Illinois, on the Mississippi. *(See Atlas Map No. 15.)* Buell continued to command the Army of the Ohio, while Major General George H. Thomas took command of the Army of

the Tennessee. Continuing the reorganization of the armies of his department, Halleck assigned Major General John McClernand to command the reserve, which was composed of McClernand's division and the division of Major General Lew Wallace. Halleck then rearranged his army into three wings: the right wing, under Thomas; the center, under Buell; and the left, under Pope. The reorganization included the shift of Grant to the position of deputy commander, directly under Halleck, but separated from the command of troops. The unpreparedness of Grant's army on the first day of the Battle of Shiloh had apparently shaken Halleck's confidence in him. In the newspapers, stories reported that Grant's army had suffered because of improper security and the lack of entrenchments. Although Halleck chose not to add to these stories, either publicly or in his reports to the War Department, he made his feelings known to Grant on April 11 when he wrote: "Your army is not now in condition to resist an attack. It must be made so without delay."[1] In private correspondence to a friend in Washington, Halleck penned an even sharper criticism of Grant on April 18: "Brave & able on the field he has no idea of how to regulate & organize his forces before a battle or how to conduct the operations of a campaign."[2] In addition to the impact that Halleck's judgment had on Grant's career, it had the negative effect of depriving Halleck of an aggressive commander of troops when he needed one most. As deputy commander, Grant could have provided Halleck with the means to regulate the movements of his large force. However, Halleck chose not to utilize Grant as such. In his *Memoirs,* Grant summed up his role in the terse statement: "For myself I was little more than an observer."[3]

Federal Caution at Corinth

The failure of Grant's troops to entrench and the subsequent surprise at the Shiloh battlefield produced an even more profound effect on Halleck and, consequently, on the course of the war. He was determined not to allow his troops to be surprised again. After preparations for the advance against Corinth were completed in the weeks following the Battle of Shiloh, Halleck began his advance on April 30. Cautiously entrenching each day, the Union armies inched toward Corinth, their objective, only 20 miles from the Shiloh battlefield. *(See Atlas Map No. 15.)* In what Grant described as "a siege from the start to the close,"[4] the movement occupied all of the month of May.

As the Federal armies advanced toward Corinth, Beauregard entrenched the town against the anticipated assault. Finally, choosing retreat rather than encirclement and capture, Beauregard gave the order for evacuation and slipped out of Corinth, following the railroad line south to Tupelo. On May 30, Halleck moved into Corinth, telegraphing his superiors in Washington: "General Beauregard evidently distrusts his army, or he would have defended so strong a position. His troops are generally much discouraged and demoralized. For the last few days their resistance has been slight."[5] Corinth, however, was a hollow victory for the Federal forces, because an entire month of prime campaigning season had been absorbed moving a little over 20 miles against negligible resistance. Beauregard's army had escaped. A pursuit was attempted by Pope's army, but was canceled on June 9.

It is difficult to evaluate the Union's strategy at this time in the Western Theater of War. Apparently, Halleck proposed to deepen the Federal penetration of the South, but the pace of his operations was slow enough to permit the initiative to pass into Confederate hands. The hostile population of most of Tennessee certainly compounded his problem of rear area security and maintenance of supply lines, dictating vigilance and the use of troops to protect vital areas already taken. During the month of April, one division of Buell's Army of the Ohio, commanded by Major General Ormsby M. Mitchel, moved south from Murfreesboro in Tennessee to Shelbyville, Fayetteville, and finally northern Georgia, thus achieving the deepest Union penetration of the South to date. *(See Atlas Maps No. 15 and 16, Mitchel's April move not shown.)* Mitchel, however, could not persuade either his superior (Buell) or Halleck to reinforce him so that he could move against Chattanooga. Failing this, he was compelled to pull back from his exposed position, astride the railroad between Tuscumbia and Huntsville, to a more defensible line.

Halleck was also trying to conform his movements to what he perceived the strategic policy of his Union superiors in Washington to be at the time. Having missed one chance to strike at Chattanooga by reinforcing Mitchel in April, he sent Buell's army east in June, instructing it to advance along the Memphis and Charleston railroad with Chattanooga as the target. The direction of Buell's advance reflected President Lincoln's wish to have a Union force drive into eastern Tennessee for the protection and encouragement of the pro-Union element there. But Buell's progress was slow. A great deal of time was consumed in keeping the railroad repaired so that it could serve as a supply line. Such repairs were necessitated by both previous damage to the line and ongoing Confederate raids.

Federal Dispersal of Forces

During the second week of June, Pope answered a summons from Washington to go east to command the newly created Army of Virginia, whereupon Major General William S. Rosecrans took command of the Army of the Mississippi. Further reorganization returned Thomas to the command of his old division, while Grant resumed command of the Army of the Tennessee. Sherman, now a major general, led his own division and that of Major General Stephen A. Hurlbut in a march toward Memphis. McClernand and his "reserve" turned west toward Bolivar and Memphis. The formidable army that Halleck had at his disposal was being fragmented, and, thus, any hope for a decisive strategy in the West was temporarily swept aside. In his *Memoirs,* Sherman observed: "Had he held his force as a unit he could have gone to Mobile, or Vicksburg or anywhere in that region, which would by one move have solved the whole Mississippi problem. . . ."[6] In explanation of Halleck's dilemma, Sherman added: ". . . from what he told me, I believe he intended such a campaign, but was overruled from Washington." An examination of Halleck's correspondence with the War Department confirms Sherman's suggestion that Halleck proposed an advance toward Mobile. However, it does not appear that he gave serious consideration to any major effort toward Vicksburg at the time. Possibly, this omission resulted from Lincoln's hope that naval efforts already underway would remove Vicksburg from Confederate control. For whatever reason, the Union effort in the West lacked a unified and positive direction, and the Confederates were not long in capitalizing on this deficiency.

In an effort to provide a focal point for the formulation of national military strategy and coordinated direction of the war, President Lincoln summoned Halleck to Washington to act as the General-in-Chief on July 11. No overall commander in the Western Theater replaced him. Instead, Grant assumed responsibility for the western portion of Tennessee and that part of Kentucky west of the Cumberland River, besides the area under control of his Army of the Tennessee. Buell's Army of the Ohio remained an independent command, an unfortunate arrangement that would contribute to the continued drift of Union western strategy for several months.

Confederate Seizure of the Initiative

Unintimidated by the number of troops available to Grant and Buell—they totaled well over 100,000—and inspired by the news of the repulse of Major General George McClellan's army in front of Richmond, the Confederates deveoped an offensive scheme for the Western Theater. As soon as Beauregard ascertained that the Union pursuit had been abandoned after the Confederate withdrawal from Corinth, he turned over his command to General Braxton Bragg. (Beauregard, who suffered from poor health, retired to Mobile to rest.) Shortly thereafter, President Davis assigned Bragg to command of the Western Department, which stretched all the way from Virginia to the Mississippi River. On July 18, Bragg decided to move the bulk of his forces to Chattanooga. *(See Atlas Map No. 15.)* Before the end of July, troops of the western part of Bragg's command began to move by rail from Tupelo to Montgomery along the long route that led to Chattanooga. Some elements moved overland through Rome, Georgia. In a dispatch to Richmond on July 23, Bragg outlined his intended operations:

> I have concluded . . . to reduce this position [Tupelo] . . . to the defensive, move my spare force rapidly to East Tennessee, and there endeavor to frustrate [the enemy's] lines and assail him in the rear. . . . Major General Van Dorn, with about 16,000 effectives, will hold the line of the Mississippi. Major General Price with a similar force, will face the enemy on this frontier. . . . With the balance of the forces, some 35,000 effectives, I hope, in conjunction with Major General Smith, to strike an effective blow through Middle Tennessee, gaining the enemy's rear, cutting off his supplies and dividing his forces, so as to encounter him in detail. In any event much will be accomplished in simply preserving our line and preventing a descent into Georgia.[7]

Bragg's scheme snatched the initiative from the combined Union forces under Grant and Buell. The Union commanders had no clear idea of where the next Confederate blow would fall. On the same day that Bragg revealed the outline of his plans to Richmond, Grant telegraphed Halleck in Washington:

> Since you have left here the greatest vigilance has been kept up by our cavalry to the front, but nothing absolutely certain of the movements of the enemy has been learned. It is certain, however, that a movement has taken place from Tupelo, in what direction or for what purpose is not so certain.[8]

In a few days, Major General E. Kirby Smith, who was stationed around Knoxville, Tennessee with a Confederate army of about 18,000, would give Grant and Buell the first clear indication of southern intentions.

By July 30, Grant had been able to sift through the mass of rumors and determine that Bragg had moved the majority of his forces and his headquarters to northern Georgia.[9] Buell, commanding the Army of the Ohio, kept his attention focused on Chattanooga, having been urged by the War Department to reach that place in force before Bragg could do so. In the middle of August, the design of the Confederate attack against Tennessee and Kentucky began to unfold as Kirby Smith moved northward from Knoxville, bypassing the Cumberland Gap to the west. *(See Atlas Map No. 16.)* By September 2, Smith had brushed aside a weak opposing force at Richmond, Kentucky, and gained control of Lexington, farther north, where he established his headquarters. Clearly, Buell's plans to reach Chattanooga would have to be temporarily set aside, as he turned his attention to the flanking position* of Smith in Kentucky. Adjusting accordingly, Buell fell back toward Murfreesboro from northern Alabama in the latter part of August. He continued his northward movement—first to Nashville, and then to Bowling Green, Kentucky—as the full impact of Kirby Smith's bold penetration of eastern Tennessee and Kentucky became apparent. His appeal to Grant for reinforcements brought two divisions from Rosecrans' Army of the Mississippi, as Grant stripped the less vital portions of his command to assist Buell. In all, the imaginative plan of Bragg was threatening the Federal position in three separate areas of the Western Theater as he concentrated on bringing Tennessee and Kentucky under Confederate control. *(See Atlas Map No. 16.)* The Confederate armies of Major General Earl Van Dorn and Major General Sterling Price threatened Corinth from the south and west, directly on Grant's front. The growing strength of Bragg's force in the vicinity of Chattanooga made possible a Confederate strike in force into the middle of Tennessee, as well as the more dangerous long-term linkup with Kirby Smith in Kentucky.

The potential disaster facing Union forces was not limited to the Western Theater. On August 29 and 30, Robert E. Lee handed Pope a staggering defeat at the Second Battle of Bull Run, while McClellan, whose Peninsula Campaign had failed, was in the process of withdrawing from his position in front of Richmond. Not content to have shattered Pope's army, Lee was already planning his invasion of Maryland with an eye toward liberating that state for the Confederacy, handing another Federal army a defeat, and enhancing the South's

---

*A force that occupies a flanking position is one that is located to the left or right of an advancing enemy force. From such a position, it can threaten the advancing force, thereby causing that advancing force either to detach elements to screen the flanking force or to cease advancing in order to attack the flanking force.

drive for foreign recognition. The period of July–September 1862 must have brought cheer throughout the Confederacy and caused President Lincoln to ponder how he was to salvage victory from the dispiriting developments in the Eastern and Western Theaters of War.

The threat to middle Tennessee became a reality when Bragg crossed the Cumberland Plateau and finished establishing his headquarters at Sparta, Tennessee by September 5. On the same day, Buell completed concentrating his army at Murfreesboro to cover Nashville. When Buell learned that Kirby Smith was already in eastern Kentucky, he realized that the most dangerous immediate threat was the juncture of Bragg's and Smith's invading forces. Consequently, Buell left a covering force at Nashville and withdrew to Bowling Green. Still one step ahead, Bragg was already at Glasgow, just east of Bowling Green. By the seventeenth, Bragg had overpowered the 4,000-man garrison at Munfordville. The governors of Ohio and Kentucky were busy trying to curb the panic in Cincinnati and Louisville, where the citizens feared an attack by the combined armies of Bragg and Smith. On September 14, Buell telegraphed Washington that his major concern was the prevention of a union between Bragg's and Smith's forces. Moreover, he advised the commander in Cincinnati that he intended to move his army against Bragg on September 16.[10]

From the middle of April until the middle of September 1862, the war in the West had been largely a war of maneuver, with the Confederates maintaining the initiative from the time that Halleck broke off the pursuit of Beauregard's army near Corinth. *(See Atlas Map No. 16.)* In part, the successes of both Kirby Smith and Braxton Bragg stemmed from the excellence of their cavalry. The skill of the Confederate mounted arm emerged in the three classic uses of that arm: screening the movements of the armies; producing timely intelligence through aggressive reconnaissance; and raiding enemy railroads, supply depots, and isolated outposts. The performances of Brigadier Generals Nathan Bedford Forrest and Joseph Wheeler were the most notable. The quality and quantity of Union cavalry suffered by comparison, giving Bragg and Smith a decided advantage as they moved north. By the middle of September, however, the pace of operations produced a telling effect among the Confederate cavalry forces. A message from Forrest to his commander on September 22, in response to further orders for raiding and demonstrations, is revealing, especially in view of the aggressive nature of its author: ''It will be impossible for me to carry out your orders on account of the condition that my horses are in.''[11] What Forrest described was just one of several ominous signs that the momentum and energy of the Confederate attempt to liberate Kentucky were nearly spent. At the same time, fighting began to erupt in both Grant's and Buell's sectors, as the

The Railroad Depot in Nashville, Tennessee

Confederate invasion reached its high tide in Kentucky and stubbornly receded.

The Battles of Iuka and Corinth

To further his theater-wide strategy, Bragg wanted to prevent Grant and Buell from reinforcing each other. Accordingly, he directed Price and Van Dorn to pin down Grant's force by creating a diversion on the east side of the Mississippi River. As has already been noted, Grant had sent two divisions of Rosecrans' army to Buell in early September, when Bragg had begun his drive northward into Kentucky. Later, Grant would send a third division to strengthen the Army of the Ohio. At the same time, Bragg optimistically saw an opportunity for Price to penetrate Grant's weakened defenses in the vicinity of Corinth and strike northward to join Bragg's and Smith's forces in the area of Nashville. However, Grant's skillful concentration of his limited forces foiled that attempt when he moved Rosecrans' reduced army and his only reserve division against Price at Iuka on September 19. *(See Atlas Map No. 16.)* Only the failure of Rosecrans to close the trap by covering all exits from Iuka saved Price from encirclement and capture.

As Price withdrew his army, he abandoned his plans to reach Nashville and there effect a linkup with Bragg's forces. Instead, he moved west to join Van Dorn for another attempt to defeat the taciturn Grant. Van Dorn, being the senior, commanded the thrust against the Union forces. Corinth was Van Dorn's target, for he hoped to defeat the two divisions of Rosecrans' army that were reported to be there before Grant could unite other forces at that place. If successful, not only would he be on his way to defeating Grant's forces in detail, but he also would open a breach in Grant's thin southern defense line. In the latter part of September, incomplete intelligence and an error in judgment on Grant's part led him to mistakenly believe that the next Confederate effort would be launched in the direction of the Mississippi River.[12] As continued intelligence poured in from the strategically placed division of Stephen A. Hurlbut at Bolivar, however, Grant revised his estimate and telegraphed Halleck in Washington on October 1:

> For several days there has been a movement of the rebels south of my front, which left it in doubt whether Bolivar or Corinth was to be the point of attack. It is now clear that Corinth is to be the point, and that from the west or southwest. . . . My position is precarious, but hope to get out of it all right.[13]

To Halleck, as well as Secretary of War Stanton and President Lincoln, it must have been a refreshing change to hear from a general who was about to be attacked, but intended to make do with what he had.*

With three divisions totaling approximately 22,000 men, the combined forces of Price and Van Dorn struck Corinth at 7:30 a.m. on October 3. Although Van Dorn drove in the pickets and outer line of defense of Rosecrans' divisions, the roughly equal number of Union defenders resisted every attempt by the Confederates to penetrate the inner defenses. The entrenchments, built by Beauregard and strengthened over the months by Union troops, served Rosecrans well. As soon as Grant was convinced that a major battle was in progress, he simultaneously hurried two regiments from Jackson toward Corinth and started Hurlbut's division on its way from Bolivar, 46 miles away. Not content to repulse Van Dorn, Grant wanted to trap and defeat the Confederate army. Early the next morning, Van Dorn resumed the attack after opening with his artillery. But the Union lines held, even though pushed back in several sectors. From the right of the Union line, Major General Charles S. Hamilton broke the back of the last Confederate assault with the fire of his artillery. Before noon on the fourth, Van Dorn began his withdrawal. However, the trap that Grant had hoped for never materialized. Delay in starting the pursuit, the impediment to movement caused by the presence of four divisions on one road, misunderstood orders, and a variety of other miscues left an opening to the south, enabling Van Dorn to extricate his command and elude his pursuers. On October 6, Grant decided to break off the pursuit, since Van Dorn had for all practical purposes outdis-

tanced Rosecrans before he could straighten out the tangle that had permitted the Confederates to escape. Grant certainly had expected more from the battles of Iuka and Corinth. Nevertheless, he had prevented a Confederate penetration of west Tennessee, notwithstanding the dispatch of reinforcements to Buell, and had denied Price and Van Dorn the chance to move to Nashville and bolster Bragg's army.

Bragg's Fight for Control of Kentucky and Tennessee

As noted earlier, at about the same time that the Battle of Iuka was being fought (September 19), Buell was preparing to attack Bragg and thus prevent him from joining forces with Kirby Smith. This, in fact, was what Bragg wanted. Like Smith, Bragg viewed Buell's army as the single most formidable obstacle that stood in the way of establishing southern control in central and eastern Kentucky. To force a fight between the two armies, Bragg remained at Munfordville for several days, hoping that Buell would attack him. Bragg's army numbered somewhere between 30,000 and 35,000; Buell commanded about 46,000 at Bowling Green. But Buell would not attack, and, on September 21, Bragg began to move toward Bardstown in order to combine his force with the 18,000 men under Kirby Smith, still at Lexington. As soon as Bragg uncovered Munfordville, Buell promptly moved to Louisville. *(See Atlas Map No. 16.)* On the last day of September, Bragg joined Smith and elements of Smith's force at Frankfort, Kentucky, to inaugurate a secessionist governor. Although Lee's Army of Northern Virginia had been turned back in Maryland during the third week of September, the establishment of a secessionist government in eastern Kentucky increased Washington's dissatisfaction with Buell. The anticipated support for the Confederate cause among eastern Kentuckians failed to materialize, however. On September 14, Major General John P. McCown had relayed to Richmond an optimistic estimate of potential recruiting strength in eastern Kentucky: "General E.K. Smith calls for arms for the Kentuckians flocking to his standard. Could arm 20,000 men if he had arms."[14] On September 25, Bragg wired a gloomier appraisal to Richmond:

> I regret to say we are sadly disappointed at the want of action by our friends in Kentucky. We have so far received no accession to this army. General Smith has secured about a brigade—not half our losses by casualties of different kinds. We have 15,000 stand of arms and no one to use them. Unless a change occurs soon we must abandon the garden spot of Kentucky to its cupidity.[15]

The armies of Buell and Bragg clashed near Perryville on October 7 in what can most accurately be described as a

---

*This attitude contrasted sharply with the pleas for reinforcements that McClellan and Buell had been sending to Washington.

meeting engagement.* Bragg apparently did not realize that he faced the bulk of Buell's force, twice the size of his own—over 36,000 against 16,000—and attacked the next day. A Confederate tactical success against the left of the Union line failed to carry the day for the southerners, and the battle was a draw, with over 3,000 casualties on both sides. Bragg withdrew to Harrodsburg, where he was joined by Kirby Smith's force on the tenth. Buell's pursuit lacked vigor, and was effectively disputed by the excellent rear-guard performance of Wheeler's cavalry. Unenthusiastic about continuing his pursuit into the more difficult and mountainous terrain of eastern Tennessee, Buell broke it off on October 12 and withdrew his forces to Glasgow and Bowling Green. Bragg continued his retirement in a southeasterly direction, moving to Morristown, Tennessee. For the administration in Washington, Buell's failure to destroy Bragg's army was further evidence of the lack of energy with which Buell had challenged the invasion by Smith's and Bragg's forces. Accordingly, on October 25, Rosecrans was designated to replace Buell as army commander. In addition, he was appointed to head the newly created Department of the Cumberland.

The western commanders had not yet seen the last of Bragg and his design to wrest Tennessee from Union control. Transferring his army by way of Knoxville and Chattanooga, Bragg began to concentrate it around Murfreesboro in early November. His plan was to launch another northward advance. *(See Atlas Map No. 17.)* In the meantime, Rosecrans assembled his forces in the area of Nashville. He used the respite to gather supplies at Nashville and to revitalize his cavalry through reorganization and the selection of a new commander. Despite urgings from Washington, Rosecrans was determined not to move against Bragg until he was satisfied that his army was ready. In this, he was more successful than McDowell had been earlier. On December 26, his army began to move south. On that same day, Confederate cavalry under Brigadier General John H. Morgan broke the railway between Louisville and Nashville, underlining the wisdom of Rosecrans' preparatory efforts to stockpile supplies at a forward base rather than rely upon the railroad for resupply.

Rosecrans' army marched over several routes, one for each of his three corps, which were commanded by Thomas, Alexander M. McCook, and Thomas L. Crittenden. Effective delaying tactics by Wheeler's cavalry slowed the Union advance and gave ample warning to Bragg of Rosecrans' approach. Pulling his scattered forces in from around Murfreesboro, Bragg concentrated his 38,000 troops north and northwest of that town to fight Rosecrans. By the evening of the thirtieth, both forces were deployed, and faced each other northwest of Murfreesboro. By odd coincidence, the two commanders

*A meeting engagement occurs when opposing forces are moving toward each other and engage before either can adequately plan to attack or defend.

had developed nearly identical attack plans, each intending to hold with his right and attack with his left. Rosecrans had the numerical edge, outnumbering Bragg by approximately 47,000. Nevertheless, the advantage would belong to the side that attacked first. At dawn on December 31, Bragg struck.

Initially, the Federal right was driven back, recoiling under the weight of the attack by the Confederate corps of Hardee and Polk. A timely counterattack by an alert division commander, Major General Philip Sheridan, and Rosecrans' calm but resolute control of his battered units arrested Polk's and Hardee's forward progress and stabilized the battle shortly before noon. Rosecrans' new cavalry chief, Brigadier General David S. Stanley, hurried forward to the Union right flank and stopped Wheeler's attempt to turn that flank. So far, Bragg's right wing, under Breckinridge, had not taken part in the attack. Bragg correctly judged that Rosecrans must have weakened the left of his line in an effort to reinforce the embattled right flank. Consequently, Bragg ordered Breckinridge to join Polk's corps in order to strengthen Polk for an attack of the Union left. But this second effort by Bragg met with no success. Rosecrans maintained his position and reorganized for a better defense, while Bragg tried again on January 2 and 3 to dislodge the Federal force from its position anchored to the Stones River. Finally, on January 3, Bragg began his withdrawal to Tullahoma, 36 miles to the south.

The Battle of Stones River marked the last chapter of Bragg's ambitious but unsuccessful invasion of Tennessee. Rosecrans occupied Murfreesboro after the withdrawal of Bragg's army, but chose not to pursue. Yet it was a Union triumph, heartening to superiors in Washington who two months earlier had despaired when eastern Tennessee and Kentucky seemed lost. Of the battle, one historian writes: ". . . more than most other battles of the war, this was a conflict between the wills of the opposing commanders. Rosecrans . . . would not admit himself beaten and so—in the end—won a victory of sorts."[16]

A Naval Attempt: Farragut and New Orleans

During March and April of 1862, the Federal Navy tightened its blockade and continued to close southern ports on the Atlantic coast and in the Gulf of Mexico. The capture of Fort Pulaski at the mouth of the Savannah River closed Savannah in April. *(See Atlas Map No. 18.)* Along the Florida Gulf coast, Federal fleet elements closed Apalachicola in April 1862 and Pensacola in May 1862. Biloxi, Mississippi had already been captured. The only useful ports available to the South after the first year of the war were Wilmington, North Carolina;

Rear Admiral David Glasgow Farragut

two major obstacles—other than the forts—that lay in his path: a heavy boom constructed by the Confederate defenders, and a host of fire rafts that the Confederates planned to float down the river with the current into the oncoming Federal warships.[19]

At 2:00 a.m. on April 24, 1862, Farragut began his run. The thoroughness of his preparations paid off as the boom was successfuly broken and swept aside. Dodging the fire rafts in the treacherous channel was an intricate task, but within three hours the flotilla had scattered or destroyed the dozen Confederate vessels that formed the last line of seaborne defense between Farragut and New Orleans.[20] Cut off from New Orleans, Forts Jackson and St. Philip soon surrendered. On the last day of the month, Butler's troops marched into the city. Farragut was already making plans for a deeper penetration of the river.[21]

In early May, Captain Farragut started up the Mississippi. Baton Rouge fell as quickly as New Orleans, and the state government of Louisiana fled inland. Natchez fell next without resistance. But at Vicksburg, in mid-May, Farragut found that he could no longer rely on the presence of his formidable fleet to intimidate the defenders of the Mississippi towns. Moreover, Farragut's guns could not be sufficiently elevated to challenge the Confederate cannon emplaced on Vicksburg's tall bluffs. Rumors that 20,000 Confederate reinforcements had been dispatched from nearby Jackson persuaded Farragut to backtrack to New Orleans until more substantial ground support developed.[22]

Mobile, Alabama; New Orleans, Louisiana; and, of lesser importance, Galveston, Texas.

As Union troops and the inland Navy on the upper Mississippi River worked their way southward in early 1862, Commander David Porter, leading the Gulf Blockade Squadron, proposed to Secretary of the Navy Gideon Welles that a naval expedition be assembled to assault and capture New Orleans.[17] While Welles cared little for Porter, he liked the idea. President Lincoln concurred. The man selected to command the expedition was a veteran of 50 years' service, having received his baptism of fire as a 9-year-old acting midshipman during the War of 1812. His name was Captain David Glasgow Farragut.

With a force of 18 warships supported by 20 schooners mounting mortars and commanded by Porter, Farragut had refueled, refitted, sailed, and reached the mouth of the Mississippi by mid-March. Linking up with Major General Ben Butler's force of 18,000 troops, Farragut was ready to launch the attack by the middle of April. On April 18, Porter's mortar boats began firing the first of over 16,000 shells into Forts Jackson and St. Philip (*see Atlas Map No. 18*), defending the main channel up the Mississippi, 75 miles below New Orleans.[18] After five days, the results were disappointing. Farragut lost patience with the ineffective bombardment and proposed to bypass the forts for a direct run to New Orleans. Over Porter's protests, Farragut prepared his flotilla for the

The Deck of One of Porter's Mortar Schooners

Strategic Gropings and Haphazard Coordination

Mud and water had been the constant and disagreeable companions of the soldiers of Major General John A. McClernand's XIII Corps for weeks on the west side of the Mississippi River. At daybreak on the morning of April 30, 1863, the corps stepped aboard the transports of Porter's fleet and began to cross the great tawny waterway. Having been chosen to spearhead Grant's forthcoming attack of Vicksburg, they were on the verge of salvaging a campaign that had dragged on for months and was marked by repeated failures. To understand the development of the scheme that Grant set in motion in April, the student of Grant's masterpiece of planning and execution must retrace the muddy steps of these Union soldiers along the maze of paths that had begun several months earlier, in 1862. Although full of frustration and initially fraught with failure, the campaign to reach Vicksburg ranks as one of the most instructive and ultimately successful ones of the American Civil War. It began in Memphis in November of 1862.

Corinth had belonged to Union forces since May of 1862, when Beauregard evacuated it under increasing Union pressure. Loss of the important east-west railroad link from Corinth to Memphis and the ominous presence of a Federal navy flotilla above Memphis on the Mississippi River convinced the defenders at Fort Pillow *(see Atlas Map No. 19a)* to evacuate that northern Confederate outpost during June 3-5. On June 6, the citizens of Memphis grimly watched as their last hope for defense disappeared. The strong Federal force of five ironclads and four rams under Commodore Charles Davis wrecked the makeshift Confederate flotilla of eight improvised gunboats. Only one Confederate gunboat survived the two hours of ramming and close-quarter fighting under the bluffs of Memphis. Before noon, the mayor of Memphis surrendered the city.

As already noted, the Mississippi River was also under attack from the south, by virtue of Farragut's seizure of Baton Rouge and Natchez, as well as his unsuccessful sortie against Vicksburg. After New Orleans fell, a drive was launched from the south by Major General Nathaniel P. Banks (Butler's successor), clearing the river up to the southern boundary of the State of Mississippi. The part of the river that remained under Confederate control was that part adjacent to the southern half of the State of Mississippi. It was guarded by two remaining strongholds at Vicksburg and Port Hudson. Vicksburg would be the next target.

In sharpening his professional skills, Major General Ulysses S. Grant had come a long way since his quiet, unheralded entry into the service as a colonel of Illinois volunteers in 1861. He was the hero of the capture of Forts Henry and Donelson in early 1862—a victory that revealed a resourcefulness and energy in leadership that contrasted sharply with the previous operations in that part of the Western Theater. Grant's experience at Shiloh in April of 1862 undoubtedly added to his own understanding of how the war should be fought in the West. The obvious and well-publicized errors and confusion that brought Grant's command so close to disaster tarnished his reputation and reminded him and his critics that he, like so many other rising commanders in armies of North and South alike, had not yet fully mastered the art of contemporary warfare. But Grant was learning, and the fortunate and well-placed confidence of Lincoln led the President to defend Grant against the formidable array of critics who clamored for his relief before and during the campaign against Vicksburg.

The task of capturing Vicksburg and eliminating organized Confederate resistance in Mississippi depended on Grant's ability to surmount an amazingly varied set of obstacles, only one of which was the enemy force facing him. Before the campaign against the Mississippi River strongpoint was over, Grant would contend not only with Confederate divisions, but also with an independent-minded and ambitious subordinate, as well as the increasing numbers of contrabands (self-liberated slaves) who flocked to the advancing Union armies.

The immediate opposition facing Grant consisted of approximately 35,000 Confederate troops scattered throughout the State of Mississippi and adjoining territory. Most of these men had been under the command of Lieutenant General John C. Pemberton since the third week of October 1862. Earlier, in July, Grant had considered a move against Vicksburg, even as he was preparing to send reinforcements to Buell in Tennessee and Kentucky. In a letter to Elihu Washburne, representative to Congress from Illinois and friend of Grant, the Union commander outlined what he thought he could do when his troop level ws raised to a strength commensurate with the task.[23] At the same time, other aspects of the western war demanded Grant's attention. After Van Dorn's troops were repulsed during the first week of October, Grant considered the possibility of another Confederate attempt to pierce his thin defensive line in the south. In addition, he advised Halleck of his concern for the apparent absence of a comprehensive strategy for operations in the West:

> You have never suggested to me any plan of operations in this department, and as I do not know anything of those of commanders to my right or left I have none therefore that is not independent of all other forces than those under my immediate command.

> As situated now, with no more troops, I can do nothing but defend my positions, and do not feel at liberty to abandon any of them without first consulting you.[24]

Grant's Overland Advance on Vicksburg

Evidently, the strategy of the Federal armies in the West was far from being fully developed. Looking ahead to a time when troop strength would permit a resumption of offensive operations in his part of the Western Theater, Grant suggested to Halleck that both sides of the Mississippi River be placed under one commander, a request that Washington pondered and eventually fulfilled.[25] In late October, Grant may have sensed the change of direction and momentum of the war as Confederate invasions failed east and west of the Appalachian Mountains. The welcome news that Washington intended to send substantial reinforcements to bolster the approximately 48,000 troops he commanded provided the positive indication for which Grant had been waiting.

Without waiting for all of the reinforcements he was scheduled to receive—10 regiments were on the way from Illinois, as well as additional troops from Wisconsin and Minnesota—Grant set his plan in motion. On November 2, Grant advanced from Corinth toward Holly Springs. He informed Halleck of his operation in progress and identified Grenada as a likely intermediate objective in the southward drive through Mississippi. The General-in-Chief promptly telegraphed his approval of Grant's scheme, advising him that "a large force will ascend the river from New Orleans."[26]

The Mississippi Central Railroad, originating in Grand Junction, Tennessee, formed the logistical artery for the Federal advance into Mississippi and influenced the route of Grant's operations, thus underlining the vital and growing importance of railroads in this era of warfare. Although maintaining the railroad would cost the Federal force troops both to guard and repair the line, Grant saw no need to depart from a conventional advance in November of 1862. When the army renewed its move on November 4, two wings of the Army of the Tennessee concentrated around Grand Junction while Sherman's corps—the right wing of the army—remained at Memphis awaiting Grant's further orders. Hurlbut's troops occupied western Tennessee to protect the northward extension of Grant's line of communication to Columbus, Kentucky and to retain control of other important points in that area. On November 13, Grant's main force of 37,000 troops reached Holly Springs, where Grant immediately established an advance supply base. *(See Atlas Map No. 19a.)* The Confederate defenders fell back in the face of Grant's advance, establishing a strong defensive position on the south side of the Tallahatchie River. In an attempt to avoid a costly assault against the Confederate position at the river, Grant asked for help from the Union troops stationed at Helena, Arkansas, across the Mississippi. Even though these troops did not fall under Grant's authority, the local commander, Brigadier General Cadwallader C. Washburn, responded promptly. On Novem-

ber 27, a 2,000-man strike force under Washburn's command crossed the Mississippi River to threaten the flank and rear of Pemberton's defensive position on the Tallahatchie. Washburn's raid was only partially successful, being stubbornly blunted by a smaller cavalry force that guarded the flank of the Confederate position. But Washburn's sortie scared Pemberton enough to persuade him to withdraw his force from behind the Tallahatchie, southward to the Yalabusha. This gave Grant the chance to push his forces over the Tallahatchie, and encouraged the Union commander to direct Sherman to bring his troops from Memphis and join him south of the river.[27]

Unfortunately, the Confederates were not the only opponent that Grant faced. Wars and campaigns are rarely tidy affairs in which each commander can devote his undivided attention to his enemy, and, in this respect, the Civil War was no different. Within the Union ranks, Grant had an opponent as stubborn and aggressive as the gray-clad Rebels who stood between him and the opening of the Mississippi River.

The McClernand Diversion

Far away in Washington, a situation had been developing since the early fall of 1862 with profound implications for Grant's operations against Vicksburg. John A. McClernand had been a Democratic congressman from Illinois before being appointed a major general of volunteers in March 1862. Five months later, he temporarily left the Army and returned to his home state to assist in recruiting. An able recruiter he

Major General John A. McClernand

was, for McClernand had played a key role in inspiring the 30-day volunteers of the 21st Illinois Regiment to enlist for three years back in June of 1861.[28] But in the summer and fall of 1862, McClernand was concerned with something far more ambitious than mere recruiting. On September 28, he sent a long letter to President Lincoln proposing that an expedition of 60,000 men drive down the Mississippi River, carry the war into the heart of the rebellion, and reopen that waterway for the Union.[29] In a later exchange of letters with Secretary of War Edwin M. Stanton, the size of the force was reduced to 20,000, but one element of the general's plan remained unchanged—McClernand would command the expedition.

To Lincoln, certain aspects of the rather unorthodox proposition had merit. McClernand was a Democrat, while Lincoln's administration was Republican. The value of having an influential Democrat promote a major military operation, as well as actively recruit thousands of volunteers in Illinois and neighboring states, could not be easily ignored by the President. Active support for the war was indeed welcome, if not essential, during the middle of 1862, when Union reverses produced a marked drop in the number of volunteers. The apathy was especially acute in the Midwest, where McClernand intended to raise the army that he proposed to take down the river. On October 20, McClernand received a secret order from Stanton, endorsed by Lincoln, that gave McClernand the authority he desired. The wording of the order was significant. It authorized McClernand:

> . . . to proceed to the States of Indiana, Illinois, and Iowa, to organize the troops remaining in those States and to be raised by volunteering or draft, and forward them with all despatch to Memphis, Cairo, or such other points as may hereafter be designated by the general-in-chief, to the end that, when a sufficient force not required by the operations of General Grant's command shall be raised, an expedition may be organized under General McClernand's command against Vicksburg and to clear the Mississippi River and open navigation to New Orleans.[30]

The implications of this order would create confusion and uncertainty at Grant's headquarters since he was unaware of the operation that was developing within the territory that he commanded. Nor would he be aware of the contents of the secret order until nearly two months later. A final sentence added a twist that apparently escaped McClernand's notice at the time: ''The forces so organized will remain subject to the designation of the general-in-chief, and be employed according to such exigencies as the service in his judgment may require.''

Although Grant was unaware of the contents of McClernand's directive, he could not fail to hear the rumors that

began to circulate about the impending operation for which McClernand was industriously raising troops.[31] The regiments were beginning to appear in Memphis and Helena, where Sherman had busily outfitted and trained them to take part in active operations. Regardless of what personal rivalry there may have been between McClernand and Grant, they had already served together, and the association convinced Grant that McClernand was a poor choice to head the expedition down the river. In a message to Halleck in early December, Grant suggested that Sherman would be a far better choice.[32] But events and the friction of war were about to take the matter out of Grant's hands temporarily. The Confederates opposing Grant were not content to slow down the tempo of operations while Grant tried to sort out the role that McClernand was to play, either within his command or as an independent commander.

Taking advantage of his growing strength, Grant changed his mind in early December. Ordering Sherman back to Memphis to prepare for a move down the river, Grant kept Pemberton's forces occupied with the threat of his overland advance. Sherman left two of his divisions with Grant's army south of Holly Springs, returned to Memphis, and gathered together a force that would ultimately number 32,000. In fact, many of the troops that Sherman would take were those recruited by McClernand to be a part of *his* pet project to open the Mississippi. Whether by design or necessity, Grant was redirecting McClernand's army out from under him. McClernand was back in Springfield, Illinois, convinced that he had done all he could do in the way of raising troops. Impatient, he bombarded Washington with messages asking that he be sent south to Memphis to take command of his troops.[33] On December 8, Grant advised Halleck of his plan to send Sherman down the river. Sherman left Memphis with three divisions on December 20, intending to assault Vicksburg from a toehold that he would establish on the east side of the river above Vicksburg with the help of the naval flotilla accompanying him. An important element in Grant's calculations was the success that he would have in diverting Pemberton's attention from Sherman's activity so that the Confederate commander could not bring the bulk of his forces against Sherman's assaulting divisions. Then the roof fell in on Grant's overland venture.

Confederate Raids and Sherman's Abortive Assault

Nathan Bedford Forrest, the audacious and capable Confederate cavalry commander who had already done so much to harass and frustrate the efforts of Buell and Rosecrans, ripped apart the Federal line of communication in western Tennessee. Crossing the Tennessee River on December 18, Forrest wrecked the important rail junction at Jackson, Tennessee on

Major General Nathan Bedford Forrest

the twentieth, breaking the telegraph communications as well. Ironically, it was during Forrest's raid that Grant finally received specific orders from Halleck in Washington to order McClernand forward to participate in the operations against Vicksburg. Despite Grant's prompt compliance with this order,[34] his directive was delayed in reaching McClernand, and the Illinois-based general was not able to arrive at Memphis in time to join Sherman before he moved down the river. While Grant's own cavalry in western Tennessee was unable to trap the elusive Forrest and Grant was pondering the implications of his broken line of communication, his overland force received a second and more serious blow.

Concerned about the growing threat of Grant's advance from the north, Pemberton authorized Van Dorn to destroy Union supplies and disrupt the vital Mississippi Central Railroad on which Grant relied for his operations. On December 18, Van Dorn left Grenada at the head of a picked cavalry force of 3,500. His lightly-equipped force enhanced its ability to move rapidly by leaving the artillery behind. Only his three subordinate commanders knew the target of his raid. Three days of circuitous and deceptive marching, first to the east and then again back to the west, brought Van Dorn's raiding

party to within a few miles of Holly Springs early on the morning of December 20. *(See Atlas Map No. 19.)* His cavalrymen surprised the weaker Federal garrison and wasted no time putting the torch to the half-million-dollar stockpile of supplies that Grant had accumulated to support his continued advance.[35] His work done, Van Dorn led his raiding cavalrymen north, destroying as much of the railroad as he could before he turned south on the day before Christmas. Outnumbered Union cavalrymen hunted for him and tried to draw his column of weary troopers into a fight, but Van Dorn eluded his pursuers and returned to Grenada on December 28. Grant's operation had been seriously jeopardized. His stalled advance could no longer fulfill its vital mission of threatening Pemberton's forces from the north to divert forces from opposing Sherman's attack against Vicksburg. The Union commander considered abandoning the project altogether.

At Helena, Arkansas, Sherman received reports of the Holly Springs disaster on December 21. However, he was uncertain about how credible the reports were and how seriously Van Dorn's raid would impede Grant's progress.[36] In the absence of other instructions, Sherman pushed on toward Vicksburg. On December 26, three of his four divisions, numbering approximately 25,000, landed on the south bank of the Yazoo River. His troops spent the next two days reconnoitering and testing the Confederate defenses north of Vicksburg. Watching Sherman's activity with growing anxiety, Pemberton was relieved to learn of Grant's withdrawal north of the Tallahatchie. This withdrawal, necessitated by Grant's recent misfortunes, enabled Pemberton to move three brigades from Grenada and

Confederate Cavalry Raid of a Union Railroad Depot

Rear Admiral David D. Porter

middle Tennessee to Vicksburg. When Sherman assaulted the Confederate defenses at two points on December 29, Pemberton, who had built up his defending force to between 12,000 and 13,000 troops, repulsed the Federal attack. Sherman's summary of the attack in his report was brief and direct: "I reached Vicksburg at the time appointed, landed, assaulted, and failed."[37] He withdrew to Milliken's Bend, north of Vicksburg, and was soon joined by McClernand. Being the senior, McClernand took command of those forces in the vicinity of Vicksburg and soon worked out a plan with Sherman and Admiral Porter. Union forces would move up the Mississippi River, enter the Arkansas River, and reduce the Post of Arkansas, from which Confederate armed vessels challenged unarmed Federal steamboats on the Mississippi. *(See Atlas Map No. 19a.)* By January 11, 1863, the Post of Arkansas had surrendered to McClernand's vastly superior force and the firepower of Porter's gunboats.[38] But the Post of Arkansas was nowhere near the primary target of Grant's operation—Vicksburg. In a terse message to Halleck on the eleventh, Grant termed McClernand's diversion a "wild-goose chase," and laid the problem of divided command that had been created in Washington in Halleck's lap.[39]

President Lincoln and Secretary of War Stanton remained silent on the issue, leaving Halleck to choose between satisfying McClernand, who had requested independent command of the expedition, and backing Grant, in whom Halleck was showing increasing confidence. Halleck settled the issue on January 12 when he telegraphed Grant: "You are hereby authorized to relieve General McClernand from command of the expedition against Vicksburg, giving it to the next in rank or taking it yourself."[40] At this time, Grant showed keen sensitivity to the political pressures with which President Lincoln had to contend—pressures that operated beyond the narrow limits of military necessity. While Grant had already expressed his willingness to designate Sherman as commander of the expedition, the apparent rebuff to McClernand would undoubtedly send political ripples all the way back to Washington. Therefore, despite the fact that Halleck had authorized Grant to give command of the expedition "to the next in rank," Grant chose a more conciliatory course of action. Abandoning the overland operation, which had already been crippled by the raids of Forrest and Van Dorn, he prepared to move to the Vicksburg area to command the operation personally. Upon his arrival there, Grant quietly deactivated McClernand's "Army of the Mississippi," and reorganized his force into four corps,* as Washington authorities had directed in mid-December.[41] But McClernand was determined to fire off the last salvo. Objecting to his assignment to the command of a mere corps under Grant, McClernand appealed directly to President Lincoln, citing his victory at the Post of Arkansas as an uncomfortable challenge to the competence of the Regulars:

> I believe my success here is gall and wormwood to the clique of West Pointers who have been persecuting me for months. How can you expect success when men controlling the military destinies of the country are more chagrined at the success of your volunteer officers than the very enemy beaten by the latter in battle?[42]

Lincoln did not see fit to reply to McClernand's outburst, and, for the time being at least, Grant had mastered one opponent. While McClernand fumed, Grant could concentrate on the Confederate forces defending Vicksburg.

The Bayou Expeditions

The failure of Sherman's assault against Vicksburg on December 29 and the withdrawal of Grant's overland task force to Memphis during January of 1863 returned Grant to the

---

*The four corps were commanded by McClernand, Sherman, Hurlbut, and James B. McPherson.

point at which he had started a month and a half earlier. Now, having decided to travel down the river in late January to personally direct operations in the vicinity of Vicksburg, he committed himself to a new phase of his attempt to wrest the Confederate citadel from Pemberton's forces. Grant's campaign would depend increasingly on the waterways surrounding Vicksburg. The close working relationship between the Navy and ground forces that had begun with the capture of Forts Henry and Donelson in 1861 continued to form an important part of the war in the West. It could be no other way. One of the reasons that it worked was the growing mutual respect between Porter and Grant. Each recognized his dependence on the resources that the other had to offer, and each exhibited a refreshingly cooperative attitude toward producing a workable solution that would eventually open the Mississippi River to Federal use.

Soon after Grant arrived at Young's Point, which was located just above Vicksburg and on the other side of the river, he directed the initiation of work on three different projects, each of which offered a way to turn the flank of the Confederate forces defending the Mississippi strongpoint. Each also depended on the ability of Federal boats to navigate the waterways around Vicksburg. There was a new and compelling reason for prompt and positive action. The fall elections of 1862 had eroded Republican strength in both the House and the Senate. Fed by the apathy and discouragement resulting from Ambrose Burnside's disastrous defeat at Fredericksburg in December, the peace party in the North was gaining popularity.[43] The administration in Washington looked to Grant for a victorious campaign that would serve notice to Congress and the public that the North was capable of competing successfully with southern armies in the field.

At his new headquarters, Grant was so close to Vicksburg that he probably could view the work of the Confederate defenders as they strengthened their fortifications. Yet his army faced not only the great water barrier, but the interminable swamps, marshes, and inundated lowlands that strengthened the defense of Vicksburg in the north, east, and south. Dry land existed in some areas, sufficient to support the approach of Union troops once they reached it, but Grant had to find a way to reach it.

Grant explored the possibility of passing river transports loaded with troops safely by the batteries of Vicksburg in order to make a landing on the east side of the river, somewhere south of Vicksburg. Because the river flowed directly under the bluffs on which Vicksburg stood, he looked for alternate routes by which transports could move out of range of the strong Confederate batteries. Soon after his arrival in the vicinity of Vicksburg, Grant resumed the work that had been started and then abandoned the past summer on a canal across the tongue of land around which the river flowed, directly

**A Federal Transport Attempts
to Push Its Way Through Obstacles in the Swamps**

across from Vicksburg. *(See Atlas Map No. 19b.)* To Sherman's corps fell the task of widening and extending the canal—hard, wet, cold work that would take its toll in sickness and death.[44] Grant was probably influenced in his decision to pursue this project by the reminder from Halleck that President Lincoln, a midwesterner who was familiar with the Vicksburg area, took a keen interest in the work on the canal and was optimistic about its results.[45]

There were other possibilities in the area as well, and Grant had the manpower to test each of them. At the end of January, his departmental strength was approximately 103,000. Roughly 40,000 were available at Vicksburg. Another 15,000 remained at Memphis, ready to move south if needed. Part of the reason that the force remained at Memphis was that Grant simply had no place to encamp them in the vicinity of Vicksburg. Their presence would be not only wasted but counterproductive at his forward position until the time came when he could find a way to launch a major force across the river.

At the same time that Sherman's XV Corps was trying to create a canal out of the mud and water opposite Vicksburg, Grant decided to make a second attempt to bypass Vicksburg to the west by entering Lake Providence north of Vicksburg, on the other side of the river. *(See Atlas Map No. 19b.)* Using shallow draft transports, a force could follow the bayous and rivers south until it reached the Red River. The force could then proceed north again via the Mississippi River to a bridgehead on the east side of the river, below Vicksburg. It was an ambitious plan, and one about which Grant became increasingly enthusiastic. On January 30, prior to his journey up the river to see the proposed entrance to Lake Providence, Grant expressed his optimism in a message he sent to Porter, asking for the necessary light draft gunboats to accompany the expedition:

> . . . I learn that Lake Providence, which connects with Red River through Tensas Bayou, Washita and Black Rivers, is a wide and navigable way through.
>
> As some advantage may be gained by opening this, I have ordered a brigade of troops to be detailed for the purpose, and to be embarked as soon as possible.[46]

After his visit to Lake Providence, Grant wrote to Major General McPherson, the commander of XVII Corps, ordering additional support:

> Move one division of your command to this place with as little delay as practicable, and come with it yourself. One brigade of McArthur's division is now here, and the balance will be ordered up as soon as I return. This bids fair to be the most practicable route for turning Vicksburg.[47]

Down the river, Sherman shared his commander's optimism regarding his plan to use the Lake Providence route to bypass Vicksburg. Grant's most trusted lieutenant was also candid about the prospects of his own venture when he wrote Grant:

> I have hastily read the reports of the Lake Providence scheme. It is admirable and most worthy of determined prosecution. Cover up the design all you can, and it will fulfill all the conditions of the great problem. This little affair of ours here on Vicksburg Point is labor lost.[48]

Despite Sherman's pessimism, Grant was not yet ready to abandon the attempt to dredge a canal across Vicksburg Point. Frequent rains and the rising level of the Mississippi River created the most difficult conditions for digging in the soaked soil, but the work went on.

One other major project involving the waterways surrounding Vicksburg remained to be tried. Far to the north, a levee had been constructed a few years before the war to prevent the Mississippi River from entering Yazoo Pass, a waterway that linked up with the Tallahatchie River and, subsequently, with the Yazoo River, approaching Vicksburg from the north. *(See Atlas Map No. 19b.)* The levee, nearly 100 feet thick and 18 feet high, permitted the reclamation of large sections of

previously inundated land along the east side of the river, with the result that numerous cotton plantations prospered in the area during the late 1850s. Grant's plan was to break the levee, let the Mississippi River flow through, and open a route that would enable gunboats and transports to take a large task force of soldiers to the high ground north and east of Vicksburg. To superintend the task, Grant chose his chief topographical engineer, Lieutenant Colonel James H. Wilson, a recent graduate of West Point. On January 29, Wilson started for Helena, Arkansas to examine the levee and devise a rapid method of breaking it and clearing the inland water routes for the passage of the Navy's boats. Work started on the afternoon of February 2 with the placement of 50-pound explosive charges in the levee. Wilson's report to Grant's headquarters on February 4 could not help but encourage the general about the prospects of this latest venture:

> About 7 o'clock (3 February), after discharging a mine in the mouth of the cut, the water rushed. The channel was only about 5 feet at first, though the embankment was cut through in two places, with an interval of about 20 feet between them, the cut through which the water was first started being considerably the larger.
>
> By 11 p.m. the opening was 40 yards wide, and the water pouring through like nothing else I ever saw except Niagara Falls. Logs, trees, and great masses of earth were torn away with the greatest ease. The work is a perfect success.
>
> The pilots and the captain of the gunboat Forest Rose think it will not be safe to undertake to run through the Pass for four or five days, on account of the great rapidity and fall of the water. It will take several days to fill up the country so much as to slacken the current.[49]

By the morning of Wilson's writing, the Pass had been opened to a width of 75 or 80 yards, thereby creating a waterway that could easily accommodate the vessels that Grant proposed to use. Further exploration of the connected waterways on February 7 revealed a route suitable for passage of Federal boats for several miles inland; but the discovery of many trees, cut so as to fall into the stream beyond Moon Lake *(see Atlas Map No. 19b)* where the stream was no wider than 100 feet, substantiated the growing rumors that the Confederates were planning to challenge the Union task force.[50] Actually, advisers to General Pemberton had identified the Yazoo Pass approach as a potential soft spot in the defenses of Vicksburg fully two months before Grant decided to try the route.[51] The felling of trees to obstruct the channels of the narrow and twisted streams was only the beginning of the imaginative and determined activity of the Confederate defenders to thwart the Yazoo Pass expedition.

As Grant patiently awaited the outcome of the three schemes in progress, he turned his attention to other pressing problems that had arisen with the increase in the size and intensity of his penetration of Confederate territory. To ease the financial strain on plantation owners and businessmen in the trans-Mississippi area and to insure that citizens in areas formerly controlled by Confederate forces understood that the Federal Government was interested in their welfare, Washington directed the resumption of the cotton trade in the area over which Grant extended military control. While cotton trade with Confederates would not be tolerated, President Lincoln was persuaded by his advisers that a rapid resumption of normal trade in cotton would not only bring needed cotton into Federal commercial channels, but would also provide financial relief for those plantation owners and businessmen whose income depended upon the sale of cotton. For the soldiers who had to administer the policy, however, the cotton trade introduced a variety of problems. Because most Southern States and private individuals chose to withhold their cotton, a shortage of the commodity was created in the North. As prices rose rapidly, the resumption of cotton trade along the border between North and South offered a unique and extremely attractive opportunity for unscrupulous businessmen, who followed the armies closely. One trader, located with Grant at Oxford, Mississippi during the Union overland attempt against Vicksburg, tried to bribe the general:

> [He] paid 12,000 dollars for 1500 bales of cotton, contingent on his ability to move it to Columbus, Kentucky—where it would be worth 500,000 dollars to him. This trader told Grant that he himself would find the transportation; all he wanted from Grant was a permit. Grant refused to give it to him, and warned him that if the cotton came within his lines he could confiscate every bale of it for the government; whereupon the trader offered to cut the General in on the profits.[52]

As the pressure from Washington and the traders increased, Grant devised a comprehensive set of regulations aimed at preventing the money of the cotton speculators from traveling south into the Confederacy, where it would help to finance the South's war efforts. But the regulations were difficult to enforce as long as Washington encouraged the trade. Money that went south to buy cotton provided the Confederates with the means to purchase munitions—either from northern sources, in a trade that flourished alongside the unsettling cotton trade, or from foreign sources. Perhaps the most embarrassing event of the whole business of the cotton trade occurred in December of 1862, when Grant's own father nearly involved the general in issuing a permit for cotton trade to four partners of a Cincinnati firm, one of whom was Grant's father.[53]

An equally frustrating problem had been created by the growing host of slaves who viewed the advancing Union armies as liberators. Lacking everything except what they carried with them—and that was little enough—the "contrabands," as they were called, settled enthusiastically and optimistically in the vicinity of any Union troops that bivouacked or even halted. The contrabands strained the logistical capability of Grant's army, especially in the matters of food, clothing, and medical care. They also created a potentially explosive political dilemma, the solution of which could not fail to elicit criticism from the sector of the northern populace that was not altogether certain what its attitude toward the self-liberated slaves should be. Nor did the former slaves lack only the basic necessities for subsistence. They also lacked employment, a far more serious deficiency that could only lead to more trouble as idleness grew into apathy, restlessness, and discontent. Some found temporary employment working for private soldiers, while others were used by official sanction to perform chores around camps, thereby releasing soldiers for other duty. Grant sent as many north as he could, and even found an Ohio philanthropist who offered to move larger numbers to his state, with the Government paying the bill. The latter expedient was vetoed by the War Department, while the other solutions were merely piecemeal attempts to deal with a growing problem that threatened to obstruct the ability of Grant's forces to maneuver effectively and virtually ruled out any attempt to maintain a reasonable degree of security around Union camps.

Grant finally took a positive step toward a resolution of the contraband problem by adapting to it the same type of solution that he had already applied to so many problems and projects in the past. He describes his reasoning in his *Memoirs*:

> It was at this point, probably, where the first idea of a "Freedman's Bureau" took its origin. Orders of the government prohibited the expulsion of the negroes from the protection of the army, when they came in voluntarily. Humanity forbade allowing them to starve. With such an army of them, of all ages and both sexes, as had congregated about Grand Junction [November 1862], amounting to many thousands, it was impossible to advance. There was no special authority for feeding them unless they were employed as teamsters, cooks and pioneers with the army; but only able-bodied young men were suitable for such work. This labor would support but a very limited percentage of them. The plantations were all deserted; the cotton and corn were ripe: men, women and children above ten years of age could be employed in saving these crops. To do this work with contrabands, or to have it done, organization under a competent chief was necessary. On inquiring for such a man Chaplain (John) Eaton . . . was suggested.[54]

Although initially reluctant to undertake a task for which he had no preparation, Eaton soon found that Grant had given serious and thorough consideration to both the immediate and long-term solutions of the problem. With Grant's unwavering support, Eaton established contraband camps, borrowed assistants from troop units whose commanders resisted the diversion of their soldiers, and not only organized the labor force for useful work, but also established a fairly reasonable logistics system that permitted him to provide subsistence regularly for the helpless and homeless contrabands.

While the efforts to solve the cotton trading problem and to cope with the influx of thousands of contrabands were the most demanding of Grant's non-military administrative activities, they were by no means the only activities that forced Grant to look beyond the military aspects of his campaign. Deep in enemy country, he found himself to be more than merely the commander of Union troops. He was the extension of the civil arm of the Government as well as the senior military commander in the broadest sense of that term. It was not in Grant's nature to assume authority or presume to advise his Government in matters clearly outside the limits of his assigned command. On the other hand, Grant's capacity and sensitivity as a general can only be fully comprehended by understanding the willingness with which he accepted the amazing variety of complex social and political problems associated with his command, and the energy that he applied to solving those problems.

The focal point of Grant's attention remained the solution to the Vicksburg riddle, the major step in re-establishing Federal control of the Mississippi River. By March, decisions would have to be made regarding the practicability of two of the three attempts to turn the Confederate flank at Vicksburg. In early February, more than a week was spent dragging a small tugboat overland to Lake Providence in order to test that route for the feasibility of transporting a large number of troops to the Red River, south of Vicksburg. If the route could be used, Grant intended to cooperate with Banks in the reduction of Port Hudson, and then move against Vicksburg from the south. But McPherson had to report that the early optimism that he and Grant had shared was based on an inadequate appreciation of the poor trafficability of the route southward. The key to making the route passable was to reach Bayou Macon *(see Atlas Map No. 19b)*, after which the way was clear to the Mississippi River. That point, however, could not be reached. As the Mississippi River and adjacent waterways were swelled by the winter rains and the runoff from snow farther north, the water level steadily rose. In the vital link between Lake Providence and Bayou Macon, called Bayou Baxter, the rising water created extremely difficult working conditions. Cypress stumps, the bases of which were under as much as eight feet of water, were virtually impossible to remove and blocked the flooded bayou. Even if the bayou had been cleared, it is doubtful that Grant could have moved more than a fraction of the 20,000 troops envisioned in his original plan. Shallow draft steamboats less than 200 feet

long—the length was dictated by the sharp turns in the bayous—were hard to find, and Grant estimated that he needed 30 of them. Even with Halleck's aid in procuring the size and type of steamboat that Grant needed from other departments, the total fell short of what Grant required, and the supply of what was available trickled in slowly during the first week of March. Satisfied that he had made every effort to develop the Lake Providence route as a means of bypassing Vicksburg, Grant resigned himself to the impracticality of the venture and called off the project in the first half of March.[55]

Sherman fared no better with the ambitious canal project on Vicksburg Point. The same rising water level that contributed to the abandonment of the Lake Providence scheme increased the difficulties of Sherman's digging project. Nor was the rising water level the only obstacle that confronted Sherman. Adam Badeau, in his *Military History of Ulysses S. Grant,* outlines the situation that existed on the canal project after the troops and dredgeboats had struggled for two months to widen, deepen, and extend the canal:

> The work was tedious and difficult, and seemed interminable; and towards the last it became also dangerous, for the enemy, well aware how important it was to thwart this operation, threw shells all over the peninsula, and, as Grant had predicted, erected batteries which commanded the lower end of the canal. But, at last, there seemed some prospect of success; the dredge-boats worked to a charm; the laborers reached a sufficient depth in the soil; the wing was ready to connect with the main artery, and the undertaking was apparently all but completed; when, on the 8th of March, an additional and rapid rise in the river, and the consequent increase of pressure, caused the dam near the upper end of the canal to give way, and every attempt to keep the rush of water proved abortive.[56]

Attempts to repair the damage to the canal produced little cause for optimism. The increased number of batteries that the Confederates place on the east side of the Mississippi River, commanding the southern exit of the canal, convinced Grant that passage through the canal would be safe only for shallow draft boats moving under the protection of darkness. Sadly, on March 27, he abandoned work on the canal.[57]

Two projects aimed at bypassing Vicksburg on the west side of the river had failed. A frustrated Grant redoubled his efforts to force an approach to Vicksburg using the waterways north of the town and east of the river. The Yazoo Pass expedition gained increasing importance as it became the only remaining scheme that offered some chance of success. As if Grant needed further incentive, a message arrived from Halleck that was almost comical in light of the massive efforts Grant was making to capture the Confederate strongpoint. To Grant, Halleck telegraphed: ''General: There is a vacant major-generalcy in the Regular Army, and I am authorized to say that it will be given to the general in the field who first wins an important and decisive victory."[58] Identical messages were sent to "Fighting Joe" Hooker, who faced Lee in Virginia, and to Rosecrans in Tennessee.

The Yazoo Expedition

After Lieutenant Colonel James Wilson was able to break the levee across Yazoo Pass in early February and explore the first few lines leading to the Coldwater River, Grant issued orders to provide the required boats from Admiral Porter's squadron and 600 troops from Sherman's command.[59] Porter chose Lieutenant Commander Watson Smith to command the naval contingent of the expedition, an important post on which the success or failure of the venture depended. To Smith, Porter issued detailed instructions, a number of which deserve attention since they display Porter's grasp of some of the difficulties that lay ahead:

> Proceed carefully, and only in the daytime; 600 to 800 soldiers will be detached to accompany you, and you will take 100 on board each light-draft.
>
> .   .   .   .
>
> When you get to Tallahatchie, proceed with all dispatch to ascend it as far as the railroad crossing, and completely destroy the railroad bridge at that point, after which you will, if possible, cut the telegraph wires and proceed down the river to the mouth of the Yalabusha.
>
> When you get to the Yalabusha, you will proceed with all your force down the Yazoo River and endeavor to get into the Sunflower River, where, it is said, all the large (Confederate) steamers are stowed away.
>
> These you will not have time to capture; therefore you will destroy them . . .
>
> Obtain all the information you can in relation to ironclads, and destroy them if you can while they are on the stocks.
>
> If this duty is performed as I expect it to be, we will strike a terrible blow at the enemy, who do not anticipate an attack from such a quarter. But you must guard against surprise, and if overwhelmed run your vessels on the bank and set fire to them.
>
> Do not risk anything by encumbering yourself with prisoners, except officers, whom you must not parole.[60]

For two weeks, the soldiers and sailors labored to clear Confederate-placed obstructions from the portion of Yazoo Pass between Moon Lake and the Coldwater River. By February 10, the number of ground troops had grown to 1,000 as Brigadier General Cadwallader Washburn joined the expedition with two regiments. His troops found the work extremely slow and difficult, for the Confederates had cut down huge cottonwoods and sycamores along the bank so that they fell into the channel and had to be removed to permit passage of the vessels. Some of the trees measured four feet in diameter and weighed 35 waterlogged tons. Six-inch cables ordered by Wilson helped to move the larger trees, but the windlasses and winches on board the ships could only do so much. Hauling the trees onto the bank frequently required the combined strength of 250 to 400 men tugging on cables while standing in water waist or even chest deep.[61]

Finally, the pass was cleared on February 21. Commander Smith, whose seven tinclads and ironclads waited on the Mississippi River at the entrance to the pass, ordered his flotilla to move through to the open waters of the Coldwater River. Troops with 15 days' rations and 160 rounds of ammunition per man climbed aboard the 14 transports that were to carry the vanguard of the expedition.[62] Grant had designated Brigadier General Benjamin M. Prentiss to head the effort, and had ordered the dispatch of an additional division commanded by Brigadier General Leonard F. Ross to join the task force. Despite the fact that the pass had been cleared, the narrow, twisting nature of it dictated a slow rate of progress by the flotilla of warships and transports. Movement at night was impossible, and even in the daytime the pilots could rarely see more than 100 yards ahead or behind. The fact that the flotilla traveled the 12 miles from Moon Lake to the Coldwater River in three and a half days is irrefutable evidence of the extremely difficult conditions that the sailors faced. The rate of movement increased once the flotilla entered the Coldwater River, and by nightfall of March 5, Commander Smith was ready to enter the Tallahatchie.[63] However, the Confederates were not standing idle as the Federal expedition moved closer.

The report of the Federal activity in Yazoo Pass reached Pemberton in early February, while he was inspecting the defenses of Vicksburg. Confederate scouts and sympathetic citizens kept Major General William Loring, the commander at Jackson, Mississippi, informed of the progress of the Federal venture. By February 20, Pemberton had recognized the scale of Grant's operations. He chose to challenge the advance of the Federal flotilla on the Tallahatchie, but left to Loring the choice of the best spot to mount a defense. At about this time, Loring arrived at Greenwood, near the confluence of the Tallahatchie, Yalabusha, and Yazoo Rivers. *(See Atlas Map No. 19b.)* The Confederate commander approved the selection of the designated site as the best defensive position. Fort Pemberton was the name given to the area, which lay on a narrow piece of land only 500 yards across between the turns of the Tallahatchie and Yazoo Rivers. The choice was superb.

The site was nearly eight feet above the river—a rare occurrence in that area—and commanded both waterways, while also providing an excellent and dry location for artillery emplacements. Using cotton bales and earth, the Confederates set to work to strengthen the position and, by March 11, seven artillery pieces had been emplaced. The 32-pounder that the Confederates had manhandled into position was the main armament of the fort. When the approach of the Federal task force was imminent, Loring ordered that an unfinished blocking raft be swung into position, and sank the *Star of the West,* a captured Union steamer, in the Tallahatchie.[64]

The vital phase of the project to breach the defenses of Vicksburg from the north began on March 11. Rounding a bend in the river north of Fort Pemberton, the Union ironclad *Chillicothe* sighted the Confederate stronghold 800 yards ahead. In the half-hour exchange between the fort and the ironclad, the strength of the Confederate defensive works and the telling effect of the southerners' heavier guns persuaded Lieutenant Commander Watson Smith to withdraw. Later in the day, an effort to approach the Confederate fort by two Indiana regiments was turned back about three-quarters of a mile north of the fort, partially by Confederate skirmishers, but mainly by the inundated condition of the surrounding land. In the afternoon, three Federal warships tried to get close enough to the fort to destroy its artillery, but met with no success. Under the supervision of Colonel Wilson, two 30-pounder Parrott rifles were dismounted from warships and emplaced in a cotton-bale battery, 700 yards upstream from the Confederates' 32-pounder. However, the strength of the Confederate parapets withstood the fire of Wilson's improvised

**Confederate Heavy Artillery Mounted
in Fortifications Overlooking the Mississippi River**

battery, even as another duel between Fort Pemberton and two Federal ironclads on March 13 ended in another frustrating failure for the Union sailors.[65] After three days of strenuous but futile activity, exasperation led to dissension, accusations, and recriminations between the Federal Navy and Army leaders, bringing little credit to either contingent. Colonel Wilson joined General Ross in expressing disappointment at the perceived lack of energy with which the Navy prosecuted the attack on the fort. Late on the eighteenth, a disgusted Wilson fired off a note to Grant's adjutant, Lieutenant Colonel John A. Rawlins:

> I'm disgusted with 7, 9, 10, and 11-inch guns; to let one 6½-inch rifle stop our Navy. Bah! They ought to go up to 200 yards and "make a spoon or spoil a horn." They are to attack tomorrow, but may not do much. I have no hope of anything great, considering the course followed by the naval forces under direction of their able and efficient Acting Rear-Admiral, Commodore, Captain, Lieutenant-Commander Smith. One chance shot will do the work; we may not make it in a thousand. No more troops are needed here till Greenwood is taken. I think we have troops enough to whip all the rebels in this vicinity if we can only get by the fort. One good gunboat can do the work, and no doubt; the two here are no great shakes.
>
> We are stopped now certain. Ross has done all in his power to urge this thing forward. If what he suggested had been adopted, the ironclads would have been here fifteen days ago and found no battery of any importance. So much for speed.[66]

The frustrated Federals turned to other alternatives to reduce the stubborn Confederate resistance centered on Fort Pemberton. At Wilson's suggestion, General Ross sent word back to Helena, Arkansas to cut another breach in the levee, thus raising the level of water in the hope of forcing the Confederates to evacuate the Fort. But the effort produced an insufficient effect on the water level to threaten the Confederate position. From March 16 through March 20, Ross sent detachments of infantrymen in every direction in an attempt to find an approach to the fort, but the same flood of water that enabled the Federal flotilla to negotiate the bayous thwarted Federal efforts to find a dry avenue of approach to the fort. On March 18, a change of naval commanders—Watson Smith was relieved for medical reasons and replaced by Lieutenant Commander James Foster—produced a council of war at which the conferees concluded that further efforts were useless. Foster determined to return the naval forces to Helena, but General Ross persuaded him to remain at Fort Pemberton for at least a few days until Brigadier General Isaac F. Quinby could arrive with additional ground forces.[67]

While the Federal task force on the Tallahatchie sputtered and stalled, Grant explored yet another way to break the

Confederate obstruction that blocked his most promising approach to Vicksburg on the waterways. On March 16, he sent a message to McPherson explaining the difficulties of the task force that was stopped at Fort Pemberton, and describing the potential value of using Steele's Bayou, nearer Vicksburg, to send a force in behind Fort Pemberton. *(See Atlas Map No. 19b.)* Grant and Admiral Porter had just returned from a reconnaissance of the Steele's Bayou route, which would enable the passage of gunboats and transports into the Yazoo River. Grant's message to McPherson reveals that he was not only concerned about the need to break the obstruction at Fort Pemberton, but was also beginning to grow anxious about the vulnerability of the amphibious task force stationed near the fort. To McPherson, he wrote:

> If we can get our boats in the rear of them in time, it will so confuse the enemy as to save Ross' force. If they do not, I shall feel restless for his fate, until I know that Quinby has reached him.[68]

Sherman drew the assignment to test the route beginning at Steele's Bayou. His force, composed of his own troops and Porter's sailors, found themselves with the same chore that the task force had faced when it opened the Yazoo Pass: clearing obstructing trees from the treacherous bayous.[69]

Alerted to the expedition up Steele's Bayou, Pemberton used the time afforded by the slow Federal progress to construct a hasty defense. By March 21, the resourceful Confederates had blocked the exit from Deer Creek; Porter and Sherman were forced to report the failure of their expedition to Grant.[70] Nor was the progress of the task force facing Fort Pemberton any more encouraging. Renewed efforts by the Federal gunboats to reduce the fort and Quinby's further searching for a way to reach the fort with ground troops proved utterly futile. On March 28, Colonel Wilson returned to the stalled force with a message from Grant that terminated the expedition and ordering its withdrawal. Fortunately, with the exception of some harassment by sharpshooters along the riverbank, the Confederates under Loring did not seriously challenge the retreating Federal task force. Had Loring chosen to do so, he would have found the Union force extremely vulnerable, at least until it reached Moon Lake.[71]

A Fresh Initiative

Failure was not a new experience for Ulysses S. Grant. In 1854, the inability to reconcile the separation from his family in Illinois with his assignment in California had persuaded Grant to resign his commission and leave the Army. Each of the several enterprises that he undertook between his resignation from the Army and his return in 1861 fell short of success, and seemed to vindicate what his father had said when he returned from the Army: "West Point spoiled one of my boys for business. . . ."[72] To a few of his critics, the disappointing results of Grant's several attempts to turn Vicksburg and come to grips with Pemberton's army revived the apparition of "Grant the Failure."

Yet, curiously, the disappointments of the several abandoned ventures to reach Vicksburg and Pemberton's army failed to depress Grant. On the contrary, by late March of 1863, he had emerged as a confident, respected, and even optimistic troop leader who enjoyed the increasing respect of President Lincoln and Halleck. Perhaps the metamorphosis was linked to the strength of character and determination necessary to sustain the disappointments of the failures. Bruce Catton, one student of the generalship of Grant, describes the change in this way:

> The simple fact is that Grant was not quite the same person in the early spring of 1863 that he had been before. He had been growing, developing, finding himself, in the months since Halleck left for Washington. The change is evident through a study of his dispatches, reports and official correspondence. They become crisper, more solid, straight to the point, business-like; the impression gained by studying them is that of a man who has at last mastered the job of running an army, who no longer doubts either his own status or his own powers and who is moving ahead with full confidence . . . Nobody was quite ready to say that Grant was a great man; nobody, at the same time, failed to realize that when you touched this stoop-shouldered, unassuming little man you touched somebody very special.[73]

Grant's performance certainly did not enjoy universal approval, nor did it lack continued scrutiny and criticism. In the middle of February 1863, the editor of the *Cincinnati Gazette* sent to the Secretary of the Treasury, Salmon P. Chase, a letter from a correspondent who was following the army near Vicksburg:

> How is it that Grant who was behind at Ft. Henry, drunk at Donelson, surprised and whipped at Shiloh, and driven back from Oxford, Miss., is still in command? Gov. Chase, these things are true. Our noble army of the Mississippi is being *wasted* by the foolish, drunken, stupid Grant. He can't organize or control or fight an army. I have no personal feeling about it, but I know he is an ass.[74]

Bombarded by criticism of this sort, President Lincoln decided to send out a trusted agent to assess and report on Grant's abilities. Charles A. Dana, former managing editor of the *New York Tribune*, was dispatched by the War Department, presumably to investigate the system of pay in the western armies. However, this transparent cover was inadequate to conceal the real purpose of his visit—and the purpose was known to Grant and his staff before Dana arrived. Sent to spy on Grant, Dana was welcomed by the general into his inner circle over the protests of his staff, and rapidly became an ardent supporter of this "uncommon fellow," as Dana later called him. When he described Grant after the war, Dana was impressed with his modesty and honesty:

> Not a great man, except morally; not an original or brilliant man, but sincere, thoughtful, deep and gifted with courage that never faltered; when the time came to risk all, he went in like a simple-hearted, unaffected, unpretending hero, whom no ill omens could deject and no triumph unduly exalt.[75]

Unlike his colleague, Sherman, who was almost fanatical in his intolerance of newspaper correspondents, Grant cultivated a more accommodating relationship, the subtlety of which did not escape one newspaperman who wrote to an associate: "General Grant informs us correspondents that he will willingly facilitate us in obtaining all proper information. . . ." and then explained that the general was "not very communicative."[76] In late March and early April of 1863, Grant was equally uncommunicative about the next move that he contemplated in his unending effort to engage Pemberton's army.

After the war, Grant would concede—as some of his subordinates, notably Sherman, insisted at the time—that the best course for his army to follow led back up the river to Memphis and then down the Mississippi Central Railroad, along the same route he had originally chosen. Yet he could not use that route. With his army gathered around Milliken's Bend above Vicksburg, any major movement back up the river would appear to be an admission of defeat, something that neither the public nor the Government would view with favor. More specifically, it would be an open invitation to the high command to yield to Grant's critics and replace him with someone else. Grant was not yet ready to concede that he had exhausted every means of reaching the east side of the river in the vicinity of Vicksburg. Thus he again turned his attention to the possibility of moving his army south of Vicksburg, with the intent of either making a landing on the east side of the river at a point from which he could advance against Pemberton's army defending the Confederate stronghold, or moving south to cooperate with Banks in the reduction of Port Hudson. To move a major portion of his army across the Mississippi River south of Vicksburg, Grant needed the help of the Navy. Characteristically, Porter was willing, and offered his cheerful cooperation. However, he also offered a stern reminder that from Grant's next attempt to turn Vicksburg there would be no turning back. The slow speed of Porter's

boats would not prevent Porter from running past the Confederate batteries southward with the current, but the return trip against the current was an entirely different proposition. On March 29, he wrote to Grant:

> I am ready to cooperate with you in the matter of landing troops on the other side, but you must recollect that when these gunboats once go below we give up all hopes of ever getting them up again. If it is your intention to occupy Grand Gulf in force it will be necessary to have vessels there to protect the troops or quiet the fortifications now there. If I do send vessels below it will be the best vessels I have, and there will be nothing left to attack Haynes' Bluff, in case it should be deemed necessary to try it.[77]

After Porter had made extensive preparations to protect the boats against the Confederate shells by piling cotton bales around the vulnerable parts of the vessels, eight gunboats and three transports made the run past the Vicksburg batteries on the night of April 16. The expedition was a success; only one transport sank as a result of the hail of artillery shells that bombarded the eleven vessels. Another contingent of six transports repeated the dash past the batteries six nights later, with the loss of only one vessel.[78]

The Navy was unquestionably doing its part to support Grant's latest scheme for reaching Vicksburg, despite the fact that neither the naval nor ground elements in the Western Theater responded to any single commander. Each took its orders directly from the Navy Department and the War Department, respectively, in Washington. Grant's cooperative relationship with Porter, the commander of the Mississippi Squadron—and, on occasion, Farragut, commander of the Gulf Squadron—was a vital element in the success of joint operations on the western waterways. Because it worked so well, the authorities in Washington saw no reason to attempt to systematize what the western commanders had already developed on an *ad hoc* basis. While the view of the authorities in Washington is certainly understandable, it is clear that the improvised substitute for a sound organization depended too heavily on the fortunate personalities of the key commanders involved, a circumstance on which the War Department and the Navy Department would not always be able to rely in future combined land-sea operations.

The plan that Grant developed to turn the Vicksburg defenses from the south was not a hasty lunge of desperation that emerged from the frustrating failures to reach the east side of the Mississippi by other routes. Quite the contrary, it was a studied project that had matured quietly and privately in the mind of Grant, even as work moved forward on the several attempts along the bayous surrounding Vicksburg. It was a complex plan, full of risks, and it demanded the full range of Grant's ability as a general to manipulate the resources at his disposal. Grant's principal problem was to find a way to move his troops south of Vicksburg and on the west side of the Mississippi to a point from which they could cross the river well *below* Vicksburg. He therefore directed McClernand to reconnoiter an overland route from the major base of the army at Milliken's Bend to Hard Times, repairing the roads between the two points. *(See Atlas Map No. 19b.)* By the end of March, over two weeks before the first elements of Porter's fleet ran past the batteries of Vicksburg, McClernand had made great strides in his repair of the roads.[79] By April 16, when Porter's first boats began to pass the Vicksburg batteries, McClernand had reported sufficient progress in preparing the roads to permit the passage of troops and wagons. On May 1, Grant issued orders to McPherson's corps, concentrated in the area of Milliken's Bend, to follow the route prepared by McClernand's corps. Grant's target was Grand Gulf, on the eastern side of the river, but he spared no effort to divert Pemberton's attention—and, more importantly, available Confederate reserves—from that point. During the weeks preceding the actual crossing of the Mississippi River below Vicksburg, three separate diversionary operations served to confuse Pemberton and cause him to disperse his troop dispositions.

Early in April, the division commanded by Brigadier General Frederick Steele left Sherman's corps at Young's Point and moved up the river to Greenville. Moving inland to Deer Creek *(see Atlas Map No. 19b),* the division turned south along the creek to burn, destroy, or carry off the livestock and other means of subsistence upon which the Vicksburg defenders relied. Steele's expedition triggered the dispatch of a reinforced brigade from Vicksburg. More significantly, it occupied the attention of Major General Carter L. Stevenson, the commander at Vicksburg, and Pemberton, distracting them just at that time when Grant's troops and supply wagons were moving southward in a steady stream to Hard Times. The first of Grant's diversionary operations had served its purpose, and Steele was able to leave Greenville late in April and rejoin Sherman in time to participate in the main operation south of Vicksburg.[80]

Of Grant's four corps commanders, Hurlbut had the least glamorous role, defending the rear of Grant's army, wrestling with the daily chore of handling the fugitive slaves and cotton traders that gathered in the Memphis area, and superintending the heavy logistical requirements of Grant's operations down the river. Grant also called upon Hurlbut to launch the second of his diversionary operations, a pattern of cavalry raids that would strain Pemberton's already thin defenses. Hurlbut was prepared to put his plan into action by the end of March, but was unaware that Rosecrans, commanding the department to the east, had coincidentally developed a plan for parallel raids. Since the departure of Halleck, there had been no overall commander in the West. Grant was not aware of Rosecrans'

plans and, therefore, Hurlbut was equally uninformed. Fortunately, Rosecrans' plan depended on the cooperation of Brigadier General Grenville M. Dodge at Corinth. Through Dodge, who was under Hurlbut's command, Rosecrans and Hurlbut learned of each other's contemplated operations and worked to harmonize them. Essentially, the coordinated plan that emerged involved three thrusts to tie down Confederate forces in northern Alabama and Mississippi, followed by two cavalry raids to cut the Southern Railroad in southern Mississippi and the Western and Atlantic Railroad in northern Alabama.

The three initial thrusts successfully pinned Confederate forces in position. When the two cavalry raids were launched, the one in northern Alabama ended in failure; most of the troopers were captured by the resourceful Confederate cavalry commander, Nathan Bedford Forrest. The Mississippi portion of the plan, however, worked to perfection. Following Hurlbut's instructions, Colonel Benjamin H. Grierson, a school teacher turned cavalryman, led his 1,700 troopers southward from La Grange, Tennessee on April 17 to begin one of the most effective cavalry raids of the Civil War. On April 21, Grierson reached the vicinity of West Point, Mississippi, on the Mobile and Ohio Railroad. Closely pursued by Confederate cavalry, Grierson detached approximately one-third of his command, instructing Colonel Hatch, the commander, to destroy the railroad and then return to La Grange by whatever route he chose, luring the Confederate pursuers after him. The deception worked as the Confederate cavalry followed Hatch northward while Grierson continued southward with the remainder of his command. By April 24, Grierson and his saddlesore riders had reached Newton Station, where they cut the Southern Railroad line.

Hurlbut had given Grierson discretionary orders, permitting him to return by the route that he had followed to get to the railroad, or to either join Grant's forces at Grand Gulf or find some other way of linking up with Federal forces. Aware that he had already produced confusion in Confederate headquarters and caused several regiments and brigades to search the countryside for him, Grierson decided to capitalize on the deep penetration that he had already made and continue the disruption of Confederate defenses by proceeding farther southward. Weary, but proud of what they had accomplished, the blue-coated cavalry stayed in the saddle and moved on. As it turned out, Grant's forces had been unable to take Grand Gulf by the time that Grierson reached that area on April 27; nor could Grierson find evidence of a Union bridgehead on the east bank south of Grand Gulf. Successfully eluding his pursuers, Grierson moved south along the Mississippi Central Railroad, finally joining Banks' force at Baton Rouge, Louisiana on May 2. In 16 days, Grierson had covered over 600 miles through the backyard of the enemy, destroying enemy's attention from our movements south of Vicksburg, and not with any expectation of attacking.[82]

Sherman's reputation with the press was well known to Grant. His nearly fanatical intolerance led Sherman to view the correspondents who accompanied the army as nuisances at best and more often, he asserted, aids to the enemy in determining the future movements of Union troops. Grant knew that Sherman was sensitive to the scathing attacks that he had received at the hands of the press, some claiming he was insane, while others simply declared him unfit for command due to sheer incompetence. Perhaps Grant wanted to spare Sherman another episode of apparent failure in the newspapers by leaving to his lieutenant the choice of whether the demonstration ought to be made. Or perhaps he judged correctly what the reaction of his fiery subordinate would be. To Grant, Sherman replied the next day:

> I received your letter of the 27th last night. . . . We will make as strong a demonstration as possible. The troops will all understand the purpose, and will not be hurt by the repulse. The people of the country must find out the truth as they best can; it is none of their business. You are engaged in a hazardous enterprise, and, for good reasons, wish to divert attention; that is sufficient to me, and it shall be done. . . .[83]

On April 30 and May 1, Sherman had ten regiments and two artillery batteries on board transports escorted by gunboats, moving up the Yazoo River. The gunboats exchanged volleys with the Confederate batteries on Snyder's Bluff, a portion of the northern defenses of the town. General Stevenson, commander at Vicksburg, focused his attention on Sherman's demonstration during the crucial period when Grant was making last-minute preparations for the launching of McClernand's corps across the river, below Vicksburg. The most important result of Sherman's demonstration was that Stevenson withheld reinforcements from Brigadier General John S. Bowen, who commanded the troops in the immediate vicinity of the site where McClernand's corps would land. On April 28, Pemberton had ordered Stevenson to prepare a force of 5,000 men to rush to Bowen's aid if Grant's forces landed on the east side of the river. Underlining the effectiveness of Sherman's demonstration, communications between Stevenson and Pemberton clearly indicate that Stevenson considered the threat of Sherman's operations as serious as those being conducted by Grant in the vicinity of Grand Gulf.[84]

The unsuccessful attempt by Porter's gunboats to silence the well-protected Confederate guns at Grand Gulf on April 29 persuaded Grant to look elsewhere for a landing site for McClernand's corps. The fortunate disclosure to Grant by an escaped slave that a good road existed inland from Bruinsburg

Colonel Benjamin H. Grierson Conducts a Union Cavalry Raid, Diverting Confederate Forces From Opposing Grant's Crossing of the Mississippi River, April 1863

railroads and supplies as he went. But the more important result of his raid was the intense concern that it provoked at Pemberton's headquarters, where troops equal to a division in strength were diverted in a frantic and futile attempt to stop him.[81]

Sherman's corps, stationed in the area of Milliken's Bend, drew the assignment for Grant's third diversionary operation. His corps was scheduled to ultimately follow McPherson's corps down the road that had already taken McClernand's corps to Hard Times. On April 27, Grant suggested to him:

> If you think it advisable, you may make a reconnaissance of Haynes Bluff, taking as much force and as many steamers as you like . . . The effect of a heavy demonstration in that direction would be good so far as the enemy are concerned, but I am loath to order it, because it would be so hard to make our own troops understand that only a demonstration was intended, and our people at home would characterize it as a repulse. I, therefore, leave it to you whether to make such a demonstration. If made at all, I advise that you publish your order beforehand, stating that a reconnaissance in force was to be made for the purpose of calling off the

gave the general a good, alternate site. Early on the morning of April 30, transports under the protection of Porter's gunboats began making the crossing to Bruinsburg. After months of digging and cutting trees, Grant's soldiers were embarking on the last and most spectacular phase of the operation against Vicksburg. In his *Memoirs,* Grant attempted to recall his feelings on that day:

. . . I felt a degree of relief scarcely ever equalled since. Vicksburg was not yet taken it is true, nor were its defenders demoralized by any of our previous moves. I was now in the enemy's country, with a vast river and the stronghold of Vicksburg between me and my base of supplies. But I was on dry ground on the same side of the river with the enemy. All the campaigns, labors, hardships and exposures from the month of December previous to this time that had been made and endured, were for the accomplishment of this one object.[85]

Notes

[1]*The War of the Rebellion: A Compilation of the Official Records of the Union and Confederate Armies* (130 vols.; Washington, 1880–1901), Series I, X, Pt. 2, 105–106. (Hereinafter cited as *OR*. Unless otherwise indicated, all subsequent references to the *OR* are to Series I.) The citation *ORN* will be used to refer to the companion *Official Records of the Union and Confederate Navies During the War of the Rebellion*. (References to the *ORN* will also be to Series I, unless otherwise indicated.)

[2]Letter, Halleck to E.A. Hitchcock, April 18, 1862, cited in T.H. Williams, *Lincoln and His Generals* (New York, 1958), pp. 85–86.

[3]Ulysses S. Grant, *Personal Memoirs of U.S. Grant* (2 vols.; New York, 1885), I, 377.

[4]Grant, *Personal Memoirs*, I, 376.

[5]*OR*, X, Pt. 1, 773.

[6]William T. Sherman, *Memoirs of General William T. Sherman* (2 vols.; New York, 1875), I, 282.

[7]*OR*, XVII, Pt. 2, 656.

[8]*Ibid.*, 114.

[9]*Ibid.*, 136.

[10]*OR*, XVI, Pt. 2, 515–516.

[11]*Ibid.*, 863.

[12]*OR*, XVII, Pt. 2, 243.

[13]*Ibid.*, 250.

[14]*OR*, XVI, Pt. 2, 821.

[15]*Ibid.*, 876.

[16]Vincent J. Esposito (ed.), *The West Point Atlas of the American Wars* (2 vols.; New York, 1959), I, Map 83.

[17]*ORN*, XVIII, 195 (Message, Farragut to Welles); Shelby Foote, *The Civil War: A Narrative* (3 vols.; New York, 1958-1974), I, 357; Virgil Carrington Jones, *The Civil War At Sea* (3 vols.; New York, 1961), II, 61, 437.

[18]*ORN*, XVIII, 136, 367; Jones, *The Civil War At Sea*, II, 67, 71–72, 80–90.

[19]*ORN*, XVIII, 253; Jones, *The Civil War At Sea*, II, 72–73, 81–82.

[20]*ORN*, XVIII, 132, 142, 154, 158, 164, 182, 243, 255, 269, 361–365; Jones, *The Civil War At Sea*, II, 99–114; Richard S. West, Jr., *Mr. Lincoln's Navy* (New York, 1957), pp. 144–157.

[21]*OR*, Series IV, II, 281.

[22]*OR*, XV, 752; LII, Pt. 2, 324; West, *Mr. Lincoln's Navy*, pp. 177–193; *ORN*, XVIII, 473, 491, 492; Jones, *The Civil War At Sea*, II, 167–171.

[23]Kenneth P. Williams, *Lincoln Finds a General* (5 vols.; New York, 1949–1959), IV, 148 summarizes from "Grant's Letters to Elihu B. Washburne," *Journal of the Illinois State Historical Society*, XLV (1952), 257–261.

[24]*OR*, XVII, Pt. 2, 296.

[25]*Ibid.*, 297.

[26]*Ibid.*, Pt. 1, 466–467.

[27]*Ibid.*, Pt. 2, 347–348, 361–363, 366–367.

[28]K.P. Williams, *Lincoln Finds a General*, III, 19.

[29]*OR*, XVII, Pt. 2, 849–853. See also *Ibid.*, 332–334 (McClernand to Stanton, November 10, 1862); *Ibid.*, 334–335 (McClernand to Halleck, November 10, 1862); *Ibid.*, 375–376 (McClernand to Stanton, December 2, 1862).

[30]*Ibid.*, 282.

[31]*Ibid.*, 307–308.

[32]*Ibid.*, Pt. 1, 473–475. On December 9, 1862, Halleck agreed that Sherman would be the better choice to command the expedition.

[33]*Ibid.*, Pt. 2, 401, 415, 420.

[34]*Ibid.*, 425 (Grant to McClernand, December 18, 1862).

[35]*Ibid.*, Pt. 2, 1, 503.

[36]*Ibid.*, 604.

[37]*Ibid.*, 613.

[38]*OR*, XVII, Pt. 2, 552, 561–562.

[39]*Ibid.*, 553.

[40]*Ibid.*, 555.

[41]*Ibid.*, 432.

[42]*Ibid.*, 566.

[43]Bruce Catton, *Grant Moves South* (Boston, 1960), p. 370.

[44]*OR*, XXIV, Pt. 3, 9–10.

[45]Catton, *Grant Moves South*, p. 377.

[46]*OR*, XXIV, Pt. 3, 17.

[47]*Ibid.*, 33.

[48]*Ibid.*, 32 (Sherman to Grant, February 4, 1863).

[49]*Ibid.*, Pt. 1, 373.

[50]*Ibid.*, 374.

[51]*ORN*, XXIII, 709.

[52]Catton, *Grant Moves South*, p. 349.

[53]*Ibid.*, pp. 352–353.

[54]Grant, *Personal Memoirs*, I, 424–425.

[55]Catton, *Grant Moves South*, pp. 356–365.

[56]Adam Badeau, *Military History of Ulysses S. Grant* (3 vols.; New York, 1885), I, 166–168.

[57]*Ibid.*, 165–166.

[58]*OR*, XXIV, Pt. 3, 75.

[59]*OR*, XXIV, Pt. 1, 17; Pt. 3, 36; *ORN*, XXIV, 249–250.

[60]*ORN*, 224.

[61]Edwin C. Bearss, *Decision in Mississippi* (Jackson, Miss., 1962), pp. 153–158; *OR*, XXIV, Pt. 3, 38, 54, 56, 57; Pt. 1, 360–361, 374, 375, 376, 378, 388, 401, 402; *ORN*, XXIV, 251, 252–253, 255, 256.

[62]*OR*, XXIV, Pt. 3, 62.

[63]Bearss, *Decision in Mississippi*, pp. 172–175.

[64]*OR*, XXIV, Pt. 1, 415 (Loring's report of March 22). For a brief summary of Confederate efforts to halt the Federal advance on the Tallahatchie, see Bearss, *Decision in Mississippi*, pp. 161–170.

[65]*OR*, XXIV, Pt. 1, 379; *ORN*, XXIV, 247, 273–276.

[66]*OR*, XXIV, Pt. 1, 379.

[67]*Ibid.*, 385, 390, 392–393, 396, 397–398; *ORN*, XXIV, 280–282, 284.

[68]*OR*, XXIV, Pt. 3, 112.

[69]*Ibid.*, 112–113.

[70]*Ibid.*, 126, 127, 134–135. In *OR*, XXIV, Pt. 1, 23, Grant's letter to Halleck, March 27, 1863, anticipates failure of the expedition up Steele's Bayou even though it continued beyond that date.

[71]Bearss, *Decision in Mississippi*, pp. 204–207.

[72]Hamlin Garland, *Ulysses S. Grant: His Life and Character* (New York, 1898), p. 129. See also Lloyd Lewis, *Captain Sam Grant* (Boston, 1950), pp. 338–339.

[73]Catton, *Grant Moves South*, pp. 391–392, 393. For a more thorough analysis of the change that had occurred in Grant, see Catton's entire chapter, "The Man on the River," pp. 388–406. T. Harry Williams, *Lincoln and His Generals* (New York, 1958), pp. 226–232, 272–273, offers a view of the way Lincoln viewed Grant

during this period.

[74]Letter from the *Gazette's* editor, Murat Halstead, to Chase, February 19, 1863, cited in Catton, *Grant Moves South*, pp. 394–395.

[75]Charles A. Dana, *Recollections of the Civil War: With the Leaders at Washington and in the Field in the Sixties* (New York, 1902), pp. 61–62.

[76]T. Harry Williams, "The Military Leadership of North and South" in David Donald (ed.), *Why the North Won the Civil War* (Baton Rouge, La. 1960), p. 51.

[77]*ORN*, XXIV, 518.

[78]*Ibid.*, 552–554; *OR*, XXIV, Pt. I, 30–31.

[79]*OR*, XXIV, Pt. 3, 164, 170–171, 186, 188–189, 190, 194, 204–205 (Messages between Grant and McClernand).

[80]*Ibid.*, 186–187, 201–202; Pt. 1, 501–506.

[81]Badeau, *Military History of Ulysses S. Grant,* I, 188–189; *OR*, XXIV, Pt. 3, 202, 264, 276, and Pt. I, 523 (Hatch's report is on pp. 529–531); D. Alexander Brown, *Grierson's Raid* (Urbana, Ill., 1954), p. 223.

[82]*OR*, XXIV, Pt. 3, 240.

[83]*Ibid.*, Pt. 3, 242–243.

[84]*Ibid.*, 800–804, 806; *OR*, XXIV, Pt. I, 575–576. On April 28, Stevenson even suggested to Pemberton that the activity at Grand Gulf was "a feint to withdraw troops from a main attack here."

[85]Grant, *Personal Memoirs,* I, 480–481.

Pemberton's Defense   5

The preceding chapter reviewed the alternatives available to General Grant in his search for a way to reach Vicksburg, remove it from Confederate control, and open the Mississippi River to Federal traffic. An understanding of Grant's alternatives and the courses that he chose to follow from November 1862 through the end of April 1863 provides a useful background for an examination of the decisions made by Federal leaders in the Western Theater. Evaluating the campaign through the eyes of the Union commanders, however, can only provide a partial understanding of the Vicksburg Campaign. The Confederate situation, too, must be examined if the campaign is to be fully understood.

The situation facing the Confederate commander, Lieutenant General John C. Pemberton, upon whose shoulders rested the primary responsibility for resisting the relentless probes and advances of Grant, was strikingly different from the situation that dictated Grant's decisions. Grant was the attacker. To Pemberton fell the task of defending. The study of that defense is useful to the student of the Civil War, in that it had an impact on the entire course of the war. Moreover, the Vicksburg Campaign, examined from the southern vantage point, is useful in another way, for it offers a model of the Confederate strategy and conduct of the war in its entirety. The defense of Vicksburg is the defense of the Confederacy in microcosm. The multifarious influences that played a vital role in determining what Pemberton could do reflect the broader impact of the similar range of influences on the methodology and strategy of the Confederate Government in Richmond. A study of the Confederate defense of Vicksburg is therefore nothing less than a look through the keyhole of a door that exposes to our view the problems and competing requirements that plagued the Confederacy in 1862 and 1863. Pemberton's role in the Vicksburg saga is that of the defender, and finally the defeated; but a thorough study of his conduct of that campaign should help to reveal the complexities of the obstacles and frustrations that made Pemberton's task one of the most difficult—if not the most difficult—of any Confederate commander in the war.

Preparing the Defense

Dated September 30, 1862, the Secretary of War's order that assigned Pemberton to command in the West established the guidelines that would dictate his plans for the long months of the Vicksburg Campaign. That order included the following instructions:

> You will proceed to Jackson [Mississippi] and relieve General Van Dorn from the command of the district assigned to him by General Bragg, for the purpose of permitting him to command the forces ordered to advance into West Tennessee. You will turn your attention immediately to the defense of the States of Mississippi and Louisiana east of the Mississippi River, and consider the successful defense of those States as the first and chief object of your command. . . .

> Your military department will comprise the State of Mississippi and so much of Louisiana as lies east of the Mississippi River. Until further orders you will report directly to this Department.[1]

Pemberton's Initial Assessment

While the Secretary's order also authorized Pemberton to launch an attack against New Orleans if the opportunity presented itself, that mission remained of secondary importance. Pemberton found the arrangement of command a bit awkward and so informed the Adjutant General of the Confederate Army on October 9, pointing out that two of his subordinates, Major Generals Earl Van Dorn and Mansfield Lovell, were senior to him. The difficulty was soon resolved when the Confederate Senate, after due deliberation, confirmed the appointment of Pemberton to lieutenant general on October 14. Now he could concentrate on the more pressing matters that demanded his attention in Mississippi.[2]

It was a troubled command that Pemberton joined. Van Dorn was under a cloud of criticism and blame for the Confederate defeat at Corinth in early October at the hands of Major General William S. Rosecrans.* The month of October gave Pemberton a chance to acquaint himself with his new command, allowing him to spend a great deal of time on the road inspecting the territory that he was to defend. Reports concerning the steady flow of troops into Memphis—Major General John A. McClernand, it will be recalled, was recruiting in the Midwest—reached Pemberton. Other ominous reports from Van Dorn's cavalry stressed that not only had the quantity of Grant's cavalry increased, but also that the quality of its leadership was improving as Federal patrols pushed back Confederate cavalry in preparation for Grant's November advance. The concentration of two of Grant's corps around Grand Junction *(see Atlas Map No. 19a)* in the latter part of October, as well as the increased activity of his cavalry along the Mississippi Central Railroad, gave Pemberton a fairly clear picture of Federal intentions.[4] The decision that the Confederate commander faced was how best to oppose Grant's design.

Grant's advance progressed slowly, geared to the rate at which he could repair and use the Mississippi Central Railroad. On November 5, Pemberton still could not be certain of the extent of Grant's operations, and telegraphed Van Dorn at Holly Springs: "Unless it is positively certain that the enemy is advancing on you in full force, do not change your position yet. I doubt his intention to do so. I want you to keep all your available cavalry threatening him."[5] But by November 9, the pressure of Grant's advance forced Van Dorn to prepare to abandon Holly Springs. On that same day, Pemberton advised the authorities in Richmond of his decision to fall back to the Tallahatchie River and fortify a defensive position there.[6] *(See Atlas Map No. 19a.)* Pemberton, however, was not thinking only of defense. He expected Grant to try

*In November 1862, a Confederate court of inquiry cleared Van Dorn.[3]

Lieutenant General John C. Pemberton

to break his line with vigorous attacks; after the Federal force had expended its strength against the Confederate defenses, Pemberton planned to launch a counterattack.

An Unfortunate Division of Authority

The extent of Pemberton's authority in the West ended at the Mississippi River, a curious coincidence that paralleled the general extent of authority given Grant by the leaders in Washington. When Grant called upon the force at Helena, Arkansas to send a detachment across the Mississippi River in November to threaten Pemberton's position on the Tallahatchie, the cooperative spirit of Major General Cadwallader Washburn promptly produced the sortie that Grant desired. Pemberton, faced with a similar but more pressing need for reinforcement by troops in Arkansas under the command of Lieutenant General Theophilus H. Holmes, was disappointed when his repeated requests for help brought no troops. Holmes was concerned about the potential danger of increased activity from Federal forces in Arkansas and Missouri, as well as the distance of 300 miles that his troops would have to march in order to support Pemberton.[7] In fairness to Holmes, it should be remembered that the responsibility for failure to cooperate with Pemberton, who was outnumbered from the time that he took command, must be shared by the War Department in Richmond. Like Pemberton, Holmes was reporting directly to the Confederate Secretary of War. Holmes' expectation of an impending attack persuaded him to retain all of his forces for his own defense. In early December, Holmes reminded the War Department that his troops not only constituted the last line of resistance to a Federal swoop through Arkansas, but, by virtue of their presence, also bolstered the loyalty and confidence of the Arkansans. If a decision had to be made regarding the seriousness of the respective situations in Arkansas and Mississippi, that decision should have been made in Richmond.

Holmes' denial of Pemberton's request for troops highlights an issue that is of great importance in the study of military history. In this case, the extent of activity that Holmes feared in Arkansas never materialized, despite the fact that McClernand led his excursion up to the Post of Arkansas a few weeks later. What the historian sees after the fact and what the participant is aware of at the time are frequently two entirely different sets of circumstances. The student of history who judges the actions of a commander on the basis of information that the commander did not have at the time is being both foolish and unfair. In his one-volume study of the generalship of Sherman, the British historian Sir Basil H. Liddell Hart offers this caution to the analyst who is determined to evaluate the decisions of a commander:

> . . . the issue of any operation of war is decided not by what the situation actually is, but by what the rival commanders think it is. Historically and practically, it is far more important to discover what information they had, and the times at which it reached them, than to know the actual situation of the ''pieces.'' A battlefield is not a chessboard.[8]

The situation that Holmes saw may not have been as threatening as he perceived it to be, but it was sufficiently menacing to prevent him from sending troops out of his department.

Grant Increases the Pressure

Nor was the Confederate picture any brighter in the South. Indeed, Pemberton felt that the reports of the movements of those Federal forces under Major General Nathaniel P. Banks required an immediate visit to Port Hudson, Louisiana. Because this trip would prevent Pemberton from personally exploring the situation in northern Mississippi, the Confederate commander telegraphed Van Dorn, asking for an accurate evaluation of the Federal advance from the north.

Two weeks later, Pemberton still held the line of the Tallahatchie River, and was maintaining what he considered to be minimum garrisons at Port Hudson and Vicksburg. To Richmond, he sent a concise summary of his situation:

> It is evident . . . that another expedition is preparing against Port Hudson. This army [on the Tallahatchie River] does not exceed 24,000 effectives of all arms. Have sent to Vicksburg every man I can. The force there will not be over 4,500; Port Hudson about the same. Unless Holmes' army gets to Vicksburg at once I shall be compelled to withdraw this army to defend it. My forces are entirely inadequate.[9]

In the same message, Pemberton estimated that Grant commanded 60,000 men in the north. Actually, he was not far from the mark. In the two corps that Grant had on the Tallahatchie River, he had over 33,000 men. Sherman's wing at Memphis, part of which Grant would move to join his main force south of Holly Springs in a few days, could add another 21,000. In his entire department, Grant had over 70,000 troops by the end of November, and the total was growing daily.[10]

However, Grant did not accommodate Pemberton by attacking the well prepared Confederate defensive position on the Tallahatchie River. Instead, as mentioned above and described in the last chapter, a combined force of cavalry and infantry staged a sortie to threaten the left and rear of Pemberton's defensive position. The outnumbered Confederate force abandoned its defensive works on the Tallahatchie and fell back to occupy another line on the Yalabusha River, farther south. (*See Atlas Map No. 19b*). Even as he fell back to the next defensible river line, Pemberton recognized that another option was open to Grant: a simultaneous thrust down the Mississippi River. To Bragg, in eastern Tennessee, Pemberton wrote on November 30:

> I am compelled to fall back for the defense of Vicksburg. The effective force there does not exceed 4,000. General Holmes is doing nothing to assist me. The enemy is moving from 10,000 to 15,000 from Delta by mouth of Coldwater toward Grenada. Sherman with 20,000 is at Lumpkin's Hill, 12 miles in my front. Grant is moving also with the whole or part of his army, from 35,000 to 40,000 and will doubtless cross a large force at New Albany. Columbus, Miss., is not fortified. Within a few days a large expedition by the Mississippi River will move direct for Vicksburg for a combined and water attack. You see my situation; it is for you to decide how far you can help me. I am now moving my baggage to Yalabusha.[11]

Pemberton's message reveals the pressure that Grant's advance had brought to bear on the Confederate defenders. It signals not only the complexity of the Confederate defense in Mississippi, but also the simultaneous weight of the Federal advantage in troops and resources in all theaters. To understand why the Confederacy was unable to send Pemberton either the reinforcements he needed or the ammunition and arms of specific types that would become increasingly short of supply, it is necessary to pause momentarily and examine some of the fundamental difficulties that existed in the Confederacy in late 1862 and early 1863—difficulties that aggravated the hard-pressed Southern forces both in Mississippi and in other theaters.

Fundamental Weaknesses of the Confederacy

Like any other nation at war, the South was faced with the task of determining where and how it was to raise the extraordinary amount of money necessary to prosecute a war. Taxation never became a primary method of raising the money that the Confederate Treasury needed. The first comprehensive tax measure passed by the Confederate Congress was adopted on April 24, 1863–nearly two years after the war began—and, in one act of legislation, combined aspects of an internal revenue measure, a license tax, and an income tax. Because a provision of the Confederate constitution dictated that taxes be apportioned according to the population, the tax did not impose a levy on land or slaves. Evidently, this loophole provoked bitter criticism from the large number of middle- and low-income people who owned little or no land and had no slaves. A variety of other loopholes weakened the effectiveness of the tax measure, even though later legislation attempted to correct these deficiencies. But the inadequacy of Confederate taxation was perhaps best expressed by historian E. Merton Coulter, who concluded after careful study that the South realized "about one percent of its income from taxes."[12]

The most famous expedient to raise money for the Confederacy was adopted in 1863, when the Government solicited the help of a French financier. Erlanger raised millions for the Confederacy in return for Confederate bonds backed by the cotton crop. It was cotton speculation on the broadest scale, and for his risk, Erlanger was granted exorbitant margins for profit plus a healthy commission. Profits were tremendous.[13] Other loans, when added to the sum of the Erlanger loan, yielded about 39 percent of the total revenue of the Confederacy. The remaining revenue, after taxation and loans, came from the source that contributed the least to the stability of the Confederate economy—the printing press. While the issue of paper currency added about $1.5 billion to the circulation of money in the South, it also added fuel to the inflationary pressure that develops during any period

Military Supplies on a Civil War River Wharf

of sustained war. Because there was no thorough system of controls to keep prices in line—and probably a reluctance to use such controls—the leaders of the Confederate Government helplessly watched the gold value of Confederate notes drop from an index of 90 in 1861 to 82.7 in 1862, and then plummet to 29.0 in 1863. By 1865, the Confederate dollar was worth 1.7 cents.[14] Just a few months after the conclusion of the Vicksburg Campaign, a Confederate bureaucrat in Richmond took the time to record a few notes on prices that help to explain the plight of the Confederacy after only two years at war: butter was selling for $4 a pound, wood $38 a cord, coal $1.25 a bushel, and so forth.[15] Nor could the Confederate Government regain control of the runaway inflation. Only six months after these prices were noted, wood had risen to $50 a cord and butter to $15 a pound, while potatoes were $25 a bushel and a pair of chickens brought $30.[16]

While the flawed Confederate fiscal policy did not have a direct impact on the ability of Pemberton to defend Vicksburg and the Mississippi River, it did have a profound impact on the soldiers in Pemberton's army. Desertion was a problem that plagued Robert E. Lee and his Army of Northern Virginia by late 1862 and early 1863. It had its effect on Pemberton's army as well. Indeed, by the early part of 1863, nearly everyone suffered from the unchecked inflation that spread over the Confederacy. The families of soldiers were no exception, and without a man at home to help along, they often suffered more than others. It seemed incomprehensible to most southerners that an area with such obvious food resources should be suffering from food shortages, both at home and in the armies. The South's poor system of transportation was a part of the problem; its mismanagement of resources was another part. But the rising prices fed by inflation contributed a major share. One writer complained:

There is no doubt an ample sufficiency of Corn in this country for its consumption; but holders can't be moved to sell for less than the most exorbitant prices & many women & children are entirely without. Now just let this news reach our Soldiers in the Army whose families are thus oppressed, & I should not be surprised to hear any day that many of them had laid by their arms and marched off home.[17]

The news did reach the soldiers in the Army, and many of them did precisely what the writer feared: lay down their arms and return home. It was a cruel choice that the common soldier faced—not whether to desert or stay, but whether to desert his unit or desert his loved ones at home.

When the ardor that brought the first eager waves of volunteers subsided, the rising rate of desertion exacerbated the troop shortages reported by the various senior commanders in the field. The Confederacy then turned to conscription, a necessary act, but one that proved as unacceptable and vexatious to many southerners as runaway inflation. A particularly unfortunate provision of the conscription act prevented the drafting of the slaveholder or overseer of any household owning 20 slaves. (The number was later reduced to 15.) This provision, added to the general unpopularity of the conscription act, could only lend substance to the murmured complaint around campfires of a "rich man's war, poor man's fight." Desertion and resistance to the conscription act produced legal and social complications for the Confederate Government that went far beyond the subject of this study. However, the immediate effect on the Vicksburg Campaign was a shortage of troops across the Confederacy in the early part of 1863 that could not help but compound the problems that Pemberton faced. Considering the resourcefulness of Grant in exhausting every possible avenue to reach Vicksburg, Pemberton stretched his troops thin—too thin—so that he would be able to resist Grant's forces wherever they appeared next. Because his requests for reinforcements were rarely satisfied, Pemberton was required to man defensive positions that spanned almost two states with a force that never exceeded 50,000 men.

Confederate Cavalry Raids Help Forestall the Federal Overland Advance

Despite his handicaps, Pemberton was not yet ready to permit Grant's southward progress to proceed unchecked. The Confederate withdrawal to the Yalabusha River gave Grant an uncontested crossing over the Tallahatchie, which encouraged the Union commander to call Sherman forward from Memphis. Yet the road to Vicksburg was far from open. Pemberton spared no effort in turning the Yalabusha line into as strong a defensive position as the Tallahatchie had been. Meanwhile, Grant moved southward slowly and cautiously, insuring the maintenance of an open logistical artery, the Mississippi Central Railroad. The importance of the railroad to Grant's scheme was lost neither on Pemberton nor on the Confederate commander to the east, General Braxton Bragg. Both knew that Grant's supply line would become increasingly vulnerable as the Federal force advanced southward.

While there was relatively little Federal activity on his own front, Bragg was aware of the increasingly heavy pressure to which Pemberton was being subjected. He responded by dispatching the resourceful and imaginative Brigadier General Nathan Bedford Forrest to western Tennessee. His instructions to Forrest were simple: to create a diversion by operating in Grant's rear.[18] With a force of slightly over 2,000 men, Forrest crossed the Tennessee River on December 15, capturing Lexington, Tennessee and its garrison two days later. *(See Atlas Map No. 19a.)* An attack against Jackson was repulsed, but Forrest turned his brigade north to take Trenton, Humboldt, and Union City—all way stations along the vital Mobile and Ohio Railroad. Capturing towns or their garrisons was not the work for which Forrest had crossed the Tennessee River a few days earlier, but the captures produced the desired results. Forrest had no intention of holding the towns or the prisoners that he took. In most cases, he quickly paroled the prisoners—the most notable exception being a Union colonel who was kept for four days until he had exhausted his finances playing poker with his captors—but was careful to impress them with the idea that his force was much larger than it actually was. Dispatching couriers to the generals of imaginary subordinate commands was just one of the tricks that Forrest used to inflate the size of his force in the prisoners' eyes. The fruits of Forrest's bluff can be read in the reports exchanged by his Federal pursuers at the time. Influenced by the convincing stories of paroled prisoners, the reports contained estimates of Confederate troops that ranged from a conservative one of 3,000 to one of 10,000. The towns that Forrest captured were useful only as temporary bases of operations while his soldiers busily tore up railroad tracks and telegraph lines, exchanged their worn or outdated firearms for new Yankee models, and destroyed any stores or ammunition that they could neither use nor carry.

Despite the fact that Federal brigades were out scouring the countryside for the Confederate raiders, and at times nearly cornered Forrest's brigade, the shrewd cavalry commander managed to avoid a decisive engagement in all but one instance. Using the most deplorable roads and repairing unused bridges, Forrest eluded his pursuers repeatedly, or kept them at arm's length by the combination of his reputation and the inflated reports of his strength. Finally, on New Year's Day, 1863, Forrest returned to the Tennessee River, had his troops raise the flatboats that they had sunk after their first crossing, and moved the entire brigade across the freezing waters of the river in 12 hours.[19] In all, Forrest's raiders had destroyed nearly $1 million worth of Federal property; but, more importantly, they had created the diversion that Bragg had ordered. Troops totaling nearly 10 times the strength of Forrest's brigade had tried to trap his elusive force during the 15 days that he operated in western Tennessee. Nevertheless, he had acquired forage, food, weapons, and ammunition from Union depots, and had raised recruits from among sympathetic Tennesseans. Civil War cavalry raids are often criticized by historians for their unproductiveness compared with other missions the cavalry could have been performing at the time. Forrest's raid, however, was an exception to the general rule. It was so effective, in fact, that it played an important part in influencing Grant to change plans in early 1863. At this same time, another Confederate cavalry raid brought additional pressure to bear on the Federal forces disposed along the Mississippi Central Railroad axis.

Early in December, a few weeks after Pemberton and Bragg had reached a tentative agreement on the feasibility and desirability of Forrest's raid, the germ of a similar idea took root in the mind of Lieutenant Colonel John S. Griffith of the First Texas Brigade of Cavalry. After discussing his idea with several other officers in the brigade, Griffith sent a letter to Pemberton on December 5, 1862, outlining a bold departure from the existing pattern of Confederate cavalry employment in the Mississippi Theater of War. The scattered brigades of the Confederate cavalry generally adopted a defensive role in support of the infantry. No effort to combine the cavalry units throughout Pemberton's army and to employ the mounted arm in an offensive manner—capitalizing on its inherent mobility—was evident until late November or early December of 1862. It is not known who first had the idea to mass the mounted units, but Griffith was the first to articulate a precise concept for the offensive power of Pemberton's cavalry. And it was high time. When Griffith advanced his ideas to Pemberton, Grant had already forced Pemberton to abandon the Tallahatchie River and was rolling irresistibly forward. The effects of Forrest's advance into the Federal rear area were, of course, no more than a matter of conjecture at that time. Griffith suggested the use of 3,000 to 4,000 cavalrymen—approximately three brigades—commanded by the man whom Griffith and his fellow officers felt best qualified to lead the mobile strike force: Major General Earl Van Dorn.[20] Pemberton liked the concept and called for Griffith the next day in order to discuss it further, but the press of other matters delayed any action on Griffith's proposal for a week. On December 12, Pemberton directed Van Dorn to take

command of all cavalry in the vicinity of Grenada, launch a sweep around Grant's left flank, destroy the Federal depot at Holly Springs, and wreck as much of the Mississippi Central and the parallel Memphis and Charleston Railroads as he could manage.[21] The preparations for the cavalry raid included leaving the artillery and extraneous individual gear behind, thereby giving the column of 3,500 cavalrymen every advantage of mobility. Only the three brigade commanders—Griffith, William H. Jackson, and Robert McCulloch—knew the details of the projected raid and the targets of the mission.* The column that left Grenada on December 18 dodged patrols and eluded pursuers, destroying the depot at Holly Springs on December 20, striking north and tearing up parts of the Mississippi Central Railroad, and finally slipping back into Grenada on December 28, weary but satisfied with the results of the 12-day expedition.

Any attempt to measure the influence of Forrest's and Van Dorn's cavalry raids on Grant's subsequent decision to abandon his overland approach will lead to a subjective estimate at best. Undoubtedly, McClernand's eager assumption of control of operations in the Vicksburg area at the same time and his divergent expedition to the Post of Arkansas influenced Grant as well. Nevertheless, the importance of the mounted Confederate arm is unmistakable. Like Grierson's raid in support of Grant's river-crossing below Vicksburg a few months later, the two Confederate raids were classic examples of the use of cavalry as a small, highly mobile unit in an economy-of-force role. At the same time that the Confederate cavalrymen were raising serious doubts in Grant's mind about the wisdom of continuing his overland advance,[22] Sherman's attack at Chickasaw Bluffs (December 29) failed. December was an important and productive month for the Vicksburg defenders; during that month, Grant's forces were temporarily slowed, allowing Pemberton to evaluate the status of his defense throughout Mississippi and Louisiana.

A Weakness in Confederate Command

While the failure of Holmes to send reinforcements across the Mississippi was unsettling and disappointing to Pemberton, it was not the primary military problem undermining Confederate strategy in the Western Theater of War. The fundamental weakness involved an inadequate command arrangement devised for the war in the West. Parenthetically, it is instructive to note that the problems affecting strategic distribution of resources in the Western Theater paralleled a similar but broader problem that confronted the Confederate high

*Van Dorn's maneuver in Grant's rear, and the results it achieved, is detailed in Chapter 4.

command. It would be difficult to sustain the argument that a modern, integrated, efficient command system would have offered the South a good prospect for victory, especially in view of the other enormous deficiencies that were already becoming apparent by 1863. Nevertheless, the combination of faulty organization. and conflicting personalities had a weakening effect on Confederate strategy in the West from mid-1862 to mid-1863. The resultant confusion and conflicting requirements had disastrous results for John C. Pemberton, the man who most needed the unswerving support and cooperation of adjacent commanders and superiors.

Johnston's Role

When General Joseph E. Johnston was wounded on May 31, 1862 in the Battle of Seven Pines near Richmond, he was replaced by Robert E. Lee. After a long period of recuperation, Johnston reported himself ready for duty on November 12. Later that month, the Confederate Secretary of War, James A. Seddon, placed General Johnston in command of the departments of General Braxton Bragg, Lieutenant General E. Kirby Smith, and Lieutenant General Pemberton.[23] From the start, Johnston and President Jefferson Davis did not see eye to eye on how reinforcements, if needed, would be provided for Pemberton. Significantly, Holmes' command in Arkansas, totaling 20,000 to 25,000 troops, was not under Johnston's control. While President Davis and the Secretary of War urged Holmes to support Pemberton with troops if he could spare them, no orders to that effect were sent. Instead, the President felt that Johnston could reinforce Pemberton from the units under his control, specifically, Bragg's army in eastern Tennessee. Johnston's protests that those troops would have to travel twice as far as those of Holmes, and that Bragg still faced a sizable army under Rosecrans near Nashville, failed to impress the Confederate President. To complicate matters, Johnston never reconciled himself to the fact that he could perform a useful function by acting to coordinate western strategy and resources. He regretted that he commanded no troops directly. Years after the war, Johnston analyzed the futility of his command as he viewed it:

> Before Mr. Davis returned to Richmond [from Johnston's headquarters at Chattanooga] I represented to him that my command was a nominal one merely, and useless; because the great distance between the armies of Tennessee and Mississippi, and the fact that they had different objects and adversaries, made it impossible to combine their action; so there was no employment for me unless I should take command of one of the armies in an emergency, which, as each had its own general, was not intended or desirable. He replied that

the great distance of these departments from the seat of government made it necessary that there should be an officer near them with authority to transfer troops from one to the other in emergencies. I suggested that each was too weak for its object; and that neither, therefore, could be drawn upon to strengthen the other; and that the distance between them was so great as to make such temporary transfers impracticable. These objections were disregarded, however.[24]

The situation did not look promising for the provision of reinforcements for Pemberton. Early in December, President Davis overrode Johnson's objections and ordered Bragg to send Major General Carter L. Stevenson's 10,000-man division to Pemberton.[25] Dutifully, Johnston issued the order, although he opposed it.

Distribution of Forces and States Rights

The matter of strategic distribution of combat power was a symptom of a more profound weakness that grew more pronounced as the conflict wore on. Earlier in 1862, when success had marked the initial thrusts of Lee, Kirby Smith, and Bragg against three Union forces on the defensive in the Eastern and Western Theaters, the southern leadership in Richmond—and, significantly, in the state governments—had seen no need to determine what the defensive requirements of the Confederacy as a whole would be when the Federal armies stopped the southern penetrations and were able to resume offensive operations. When that situation emerged in late 1862, the southern leadership found itself handicapped by a strategy that demanded the defense of every part of Confederate territory. Whether or not the strategy was valid or supportable in view of the resources available to the Confederacy is not as significant as the more fundamental effect it had of pinning southern forces in widely separated parts of the Confederacy, thereby limiting if not removing the possibility of retaining strategic reserve forces.*

The disunity that threatened the development of an integrated Confederate defensive strategy grew from the stubborn reluctance of the Southern States to admit a subordination of regional interests to the national, or confederational, goal. In his biography of Lee, the distinguished historian Douglas Southall Freeman describes the weakness that plagued the formulation of southern defensive strategy from the second year of the war onward:

> The influences that were to thwart the efforts of the administration in later attempts to effect large-scale concentration were already operative [mid-1862] and had

---

*Strategic reserve forces are those forces that are withheld from action until they are needed to influence a battle that could decide the outcome of an individual campaign or an entire war.

to be taken into account. The Southern states were allies, not a united nation, and the conduct of military operations was subject to nearly all the difficulties, save that of language, that weaken most alliances. Would they have the larger vision now? Were the much-cherished states' rights, which were so potent a factor in leading the South to declare its independence, to prove an obstacle to the attainment of that independence?[26]

The Confederate States resisted the relinquishment of their sovereignty to the Government in Richmond in varying degrees. A substantial share of the resistance came from state political leaders. Two governors—Joseph E. Brown of Georgia and Zebulon Vance of North Carolina—were the most outspoken in their criticism of any expansion of central power in the Confederacy, and provided the most conspicuous examples of the opposition that Jefferson Davis faced. Brown was intensely loyal to the Confederate cause of independence, but jealously guarded what he considered to be state prerogatives. While he probably devoted as much sincere effort to the Confederate cause as any other governor in the early years of the war, and inspired a similar response in the people of his state, he also took steps to insure that Georgia would be able to defend herself. To that end, Brown supervised the raising of a substantial state war chest and the development of foundries. He also raised and maintained state troops called the "Georgia regular army." But as the war progressed, Brown's devotion to the southern cause noticeably cooled. He began to consider ways of negotiating a separate peace between Georgia and the United States, and was sufficiently confident of his own executive ability to consider himself a suitable successor to Jefferson Davis.[27]

The Governor of North Carolina, Zebulon Vance, was resolute and unswerving in his staunch support of the Confederate cause during the entire war, but that support did not discourage Vance's regular and spirited criticism of the policies generated in Richmond. The issues over which Vance differed with the Confederate authorities were typical of the issues that caused the most frequent squabbles between governors and the Central Government. Conscription stood near the top of the list, but it was followed closely by the collection of taxes, the matter of financial support for the war, and the provision of supplies for armies in the field.[28] In addition, the aloof, stiff personality of the Confederate President aggravated the already difficult relationships between the states and the Central Government.

In no way should the foregoing discussion be construed as a suggestion that President Lincoln did not have his share of headaches with strong-willed or sovereignty-conscious Union governors. Nor did the Government in Washington move with greater speed than the Confederacy to develop a more comprehensive overall strategy in the early part of the war. The

major difference—the one that made the task of the Confederate Government infinitely more difficult than that of its northern counterpart—was the growing shortage of the means with which to wage war.

Frustrating the Federal Initiatives

Pemberton welcomed the lull that followed Sherman's repulse at the bluffs north of Vicksburg in late December of 1862 and Grant's abandonment of the overland approach in January of 1863. Because he could not predict with certainty where Grant would strike next, he devoted his attention to strengthening the weakest sectors of his command in anticipation of renewed Federal efforts. The peculiarities of the terrain and the high water level that normally accompanied late winter and spring along the Mississippi favored his defense. Vicksburg itself stood on the most defensible terrain along the east side of the river between Memphis and Baton Rouge. Until Grant could reach the east side of the river, the Confederate stronghold atop 200-foot bluffs would be relatively invulnerable. The overland approaches to Vicksburg provided a most formidable obstacle to any attacker, restricting the movement of a ground force to what few roads and high ground were not inundated by the Confederates' most useful temporary ally, high water.[29] Having gained confidence from his success in beating back the first two Federal attempts to reach Vicksburg, Pemberton directed the redisposition of his limited forces into a series of strongpoints that were located along what he believed to be the most likely approaches that Grant would next try.

Pemberton's Disposition of Forces

Although Port Hudson remained the key to the defense of the Mississippi River south of Vicksburg, Pemberton could spare no additional troops to increase its strength. Because of the great distance and poor routes between Port Hudson and Pemberton's forces to the north, the 5,500 troops stationed at the fort would have to defend that location with little or no help. Stevenson's division, recently arrived from Bragg's army, was entrusted with the defense of Vicksburg itself. Brigadier General John S. Bowen was ordered south with three brigades to construct batteries and strengthen the defenses at Grand Gulf. His force formed the southern wing of Stevenson's Vicksburg-centered command. Correctly anticipating that Grant might attempt to exploit the waterways north of Vicksburg, Pemberton charged Major General William W. "Old Blizzards" Loring, a resolute and rugged Indian fighter, with the task of selecting and fortifying a defensive position that would halt any Federal advance using the navigable Yazoo River. Small

Confederate Fortifications at Port Hudson

detachments were dispatched to guard vital spots along the two important north-south railroads through Mississippi and Louisiana—the Mississippi Central and the Mobile and Ohio—while another small detachment remained to defend the Mississippi capital at Jackson, where Pemberton maintained his headquarters.[30] Pemberton lacked the combat power and naval resources necessary to attack the Federal forces that Grant was accumulating at Young's Point and Milliken's Bend across the river. Consequently, he was forced to devote his efforts to strengthening his defenses as rapidly as possible while awaiting Grant's next move. The wait was not long.

By January 10, 1863, Pemberton was convinced that Grant's and Sherman's first efforts had been turned back. Both elements of the Federal Army appeared to be withdrawing. The next day, Pemberton's adjutant reported the following dispositions of Confederate troops: at Grenada, 15,000; at Vicksburg, 18,000; at Port Hudson, 10,000; and at Columbus and Jackson, 1,800 each. On the sixteenth, Loring reported the movement of a substantial number of troop-filled Union transports down the Mississippi. Pemberton could only be dismayed by the fact that on January 17, Johnston planned to send 6,000 cavalry under Van Dorn out of Pemberton's department to assist Bragg by interfering with Rosecrans' communications.

Stevenson, commanding at Vicksburg, watched the size of the Federal force grow across the river. On January 23, he advised Pemberton that he suspected an attempt to assault Warrenton, below Vicksburg.[31] *(See Atlas Map No. 19b.)* Evidence that Grant would attempt to reopen the canal on Vicksburg Point, which Pemberton relayed to the War Department on January 24, caused him to add that a landing by Grant at Warrenton would force Pemberton to withdraw the force that he had at Grenada. On that same date, Pemberton estimated

Grant's force across from Vicksburg at 40,000—approximately the number that Pemberton had in his entire army throughout Mississippi and Louisiana.

On February 6, in response to a query from Johnston, Pemberton reported that he was unable to ascertain Grant's purpose at that time, despite the degree of activity across the river. Three days later, however, a message from a naval officer on the Yazoo River announced the Federal success in cutting the Yazoo Pass levee. Another message on February 12 disclosed the entry of transports into Moon Lake. By February 17, Pemberton concluded that the Federal activity above the Yazoo River was no mere feint, but a concerted effort to use that waterway to approach Vicksburg from the north. That same day he began to strip guns and men from Stevenson's command in order to strengthen the defenses in the vicinity of Yazoo City, even if it meant weakening the Vicksburg defenses.[32]

Defending the Yazoo Waterway System

Looking ahead to what the weight of the Federal forces in the area might do to his fragile defense, Pemberton included an ominous warning in his February 17 message to President Davis. He advised the President of the two Union attempts in progress—on the canal and down the Yazoo River—and requested from Davis his assistance in providing additional ammunition and subsistence supplies, suggesting that the stockpiling of such items be started immediately in anticipation of the unlikely but possible siege of Vicksburg by Federal forces.[33] Information received by Pemberton from the vicinity of Port Hudson on the twentieth was reassuring, however, for it indicated no evidence that Banks was coordinating an attack with Grant's efforts in the north, a possibility that Pemberton had foreseen but could do little to prevent.[34] Fortunately for the Confederates, that coordinated action of Grant and Banks never occurred. By February 21, Loring had reached the area of the Yazoo River near Greenwood and reported to Pemberton:

> . . . I Found that Major Merriwether had . . . acted promptly in his selection of a place where we may be enabled to construct suitable works for the defense of the river. He has chosen this point [later named "Fort Pemberton"], and vigorously commenced the erection of works which I trust, when completed, will do much toward preventing the passage down of the enemy.
>
> .   .   .   .
>
> The river here will also be obstructed with rafts . . . [but] will not be placed in position to obstruct the streams until the enemy's approach renders it absolutely necessary to do so.[35]

Loring knew that closing the streams prematurely could only hurt the Confederates, since Pemberton's commissary officer continued to draw a substantial amount of the army's subsistence supplies from the abundant resources of the plantations and farms north of Vicksburg. Once the Federal expedition controlled that area and its waterways, the loss of that important source of supplies would necessitate some belt tightening among the citizens of southern Mississippi, and in Pemberton's army as well.

Poor communications and muddy roads forced the Confederate commanders to rely heavily on couriers; but by February 24, both Loring and Pemberton were aware that the Federal transports had managed the difficult task of removing obstacles from and maneuvering through the torturous, twisting Yazoo Pass, and had reached the more open water of the Coldwater River. More ominous news followed from Loring on March 2, when he reported that gunboats mounting 24-pounders formed the vanguard of the flotilla.[36] Nor could Pemberton concentrate only on the growing threat of the expedition that Loring faced on the Tallahatchie. A report from the commander of Pemberton's scouts on March 3 indicated that a reliable source "who got it directly from high Federal military authorities" told of preparations to attack Vicksburg's upper and lower batteries with gunboats, possibly as a prelude to an amphibious assault. This report and others like it forced Pemberton to choose between sending additional reinforcements to Loring to resist the backwater approach and maintaining the troop strength of the Vicksburg defenses. The Confederate general decided in favor of Vicksburg, confidently advising Johnston on March 4 that the defensive works Loring was completing at Fort Pemberton could be adequately defended by the troops that Loring had available.[37]

Shortages of certain critical items continued to plague the Confederate defenders in Mississippi. On March 8, Loring reminded Pemberton that his success in stopping the enemy on the Tallahatchie would depend on the timely supply of additional artillery ammunition—especially the large-caliber variety needed to challenge the armor plate and improvised cotton-bale bulwarks of the Federal gunboats. "The only drawback," wrote Loring, "will be the want of ammunition."[38]

Information received from his scouts across the river gave Pemberton positive indications of Major General James B. McPherson's simultaneous effort to open a bypass on the west side of the river, using the Lake Providence route. Pemberton knew, however, that he had no way of checking that effort, and would have to content himself with watchful waiting. On the other hand, he could influence the progress of Sherman's corps as it dug the canal across Vicksburg Point. At first, the canal appeared to be a hopeless project, holding little chance for Federal success. But the addition of steam-driven dredges in February and the accelerated progress in widening and deepening the canal forced Pemberton to consider the possibility of Grant moving both the Federal fleet and troops through the canal and past Vicksburg unhindered. Growing apprehensive about the Federal progress directly across the river, Stevenson advised Pemberton on March 11 that he planned to establish a substantial battery at the water's edge in Warrenton to harass the canal builders and challenge any boats that might try to use the canal if completed.[39]

While he was visiting Mobile to inspect the defenses of that Alabama port, Johnston not only continued to observe the progress of the various projects that Grant vigorously pushed forward around Vicksburg, but also offered Pemberton some hope of help from the Confederate forces across the river. On March 15, he told Pemberton of his wish "to correspond with Lieutenant General [E. Kirby] Smith, to ascertain if any of his troops can operate against the enemy's forces which threaten you on the Mississippi, or if he can make a diversion. . . ."[40] Without command of the troops across the river, however, Johnston could only request a cooperative maneuver, and his requests remained unfilled.

The success that John C. Pemberton was having in fashioning a defense against Grant continued to encourage both the Mississippians and the authorities in Richmond. And well it should have. Pemberton's performance prompted a warm compliment from Johnston: "I have just read your letter [of 14 March]. . . . Your activity and vigor in defense of Mississippi must have secured for you the confidence of the people of the State; that of the Government you have previously won."[41] Bad weather and difficult working conditions produced by high water helped to force the final abandonment of both the scheme to open a water route through Lake Providence and Sherman's canal project. The only Confederate contributions to the defeat of the canal project were the batteries overlooking the canal's south end. Without a cooperative sortie from Confederate troops across the river, Pemberton's command could do little to influence the abandonment of McPheson's Lake Providence expedition. But the remarkable aspect of Pemberton's early efforts to defend his two-state section of the Confederacy is the resourcefulness with which he countered a more numerous and more mobile enemy. Admittedly, Pemberton would make some mistakes before the final fall of Vicksburg. But too often the drama of the final weeks of the Vicksburg Campaign obscures the expert Confederate defensive measures that were employed from late fall of 1862 until well into April 1863.

The best example of the measured economizing of Pemberton's combat power can be found in the defensive system built by Loring in the waterways north of Vicksburg. As the Federal expedition appeared to gather momentum in late February and March, Pemberton resisted overreacting to the pressure of frequent requests from Loring for reinforcements. At the same time, he carefully maintained troops for the defense of Vicksburg and readied contingents to repel possible landings by Grant elsewhere along the east side of the river. Moreover, the sizable detachment of troops remaining in the area of Memphis, ready to reinforce Grant before Vicksburg if Grant called for them, posed a constant threat of another overland advance, one for which Pemberton continued to prepare.

The extent of the Confederate preparations at Fort Pemberton was not apparent to the Federal attackers until March 10, when the lead elements of the Federal expedition joined forces at a point slightly over 30 miles north of the fort. The next day, the first attempt to reduce Fort Pemberton failed. Loring had already ordered that an improvised raft be swung into a blocking position across the stream and that the *Star of the West*, a captured Union steamer, be sunk as another obstacle to Federal passage. The most serious Federal efforts to reduce Fort Pemberton or to force Loring's men to abandon it by outflanking the position continued for approximately two weeks. By April 1, Loring's strength had gradually increased to 7,000 of all arms as Pemberton gathered small contingents of troops, including the Mississippi state militia, to send to Loring. In the meantime, Grant's decision to terminate what was rapidly becoming a dangerously exposed expedition ended the venture, and the Confederate north flank was again secure.[42]

Although the Confederates were reluctant to pursue the retreating Federal flotilla up the Tallahatchie, they almost bagged another task force that Grant had dispatched up Steele's Bayou to threaten Fort Pemberton from the rear and to reinforce Brigadier General Isaac F. Quinby's operation north of the fort. The Confederates anticipated this last move up Steele's Bayou as soon as Rear Admiral David D. Porter

ascended the waterway. They then hurried to block Deer Creek, the most restricted part of the water route, before the Federal flotilla could emerge into the navigable Yazoo River below Fort Pemberton. Poor communications among the Confederate commanders nearly exposed them to a breakthrough by Grant's dual pincers north and south of Fort Pemberton,[43] but the initiative of the local commander in blocking Deer Creek and deploying skirmishers along the water route flanking Porter's boats turned the tables on the Federal force. A hard-pressed Porter sent a message by courier to Sherman on March 19, explaining that his forward progress had been brought to a near halt, and urgently requesting that Sherman hurry forward with infantry to clear the Confederate sharpshooters from the flanks of his boats. Anyone appearing on the decks of Porter's boats soon became a casualty. How close the Confederates came to capturing Porter's fleet is underlined by Sherman's discovery of additional Confederate activity behind Porter's boats:

> It also happened that, at the instant of my arrival, a party of about four hundred rebels, armed and supplied with axes, had passed around the fleet and had got below it, intending in like manner to block the channel by the felling of trees, so as to cut off retreat. . . . I inquired of Admiral Porter what he proposed to do and he said he wanted to get out of that scrape as quickly as possible.[44]

With the help of Sherman's troops, Porter extricated his flotilla from the trap that the eager Confederates had prepared for him. The experience, however, ended any further hope of using Steele's Bayou and its connecting waterways to reach the Yazoo River and, ultimately, a position to the east of Vicksburg.

Confederate Uncertainty About Grant's Intentions

The gradual addition of militia from Mississippi and the arrival of a few brigades from the East brought Pemberton's strength to just under 50,000 by the end of March.[45] Every effort that Grant had initiated to date had been successfully thwarted. Nevertheless, Pemberton was concerned about his determined opponent's next move. Grant's directive to McClernand to open a usable road to Hard Times on the west side of the river produced increased activity that was not unnoticed by Confederate scouts, but Pemberton interpreted the effort as part of a demonstration.[46] The difficulty of Pemberton's task in attempting to separate fact from rumor is made understandable by the number of disparate reports that reached him on April 2. From a subordinate at Jackson, Pemberton received the suggestion, based on rumors from Memphis, that Grant, having failed in every undertaking to reach Vicksburg, was preparing to take his army into Tennessee to link up with Rosecrans for a combined operation. The dispatch of many empty transports down the river from Memphis added weight to this interpretation. (Actually, these transports were moving southward to join Porter's gunboats, which were to run past the Vicksburg batteries later in the month.) Another report offered the possibility of a renewed overland approach from Memphis, this time down the Mobile and Ohio Railroad instead of the Mississippi Central Railroad that Grant had used earlier. Either course of action was possible, and Pemberton was forced to consider each carefully. A message to Johnston at Tullahoma, near the headquarters of Bragg, confirms that Pemberton regarded a linkup of Grant and Rosecrans as a realistic Federal option. By April 6, Pemberton could report to Richmond his positive conviction that Grant had withdrawn the bulk of his troops from the bayou expeditions, ending that series of Federal attempts.[47]

Characteristically, the prospect of decreased pressure on Pemberton in early April inspired Jefferson Davis to look for a more useful employment of Pemberton's troops. "Under existing circumstances," Davis wrote on April 7, "what troops . . . can you send, for temporary service, to Tullahoma, with due regard to the safety of your position?"[48] Pemberton, however, was not as confident as the President about the permanence of Grant's withdrawal, and urged caution concerning the transfer of troops from his department:

> Latest official reports represent enemy as probably leaving Tallahatchie; also that he is landing in large force at Greenville (south of Memphis), moving down Deer Creek by land, and endeavoring to get through Hushpuckanaw into Sunflower River. It is said, in Memphis, Grant will also attack Vicksburg, in front, in a few days. Attempt on Port Hudson is abandoned for the present. I am moving a brigade from there farther north, but do not think it safe, under existing circumstances, to diminish force in this department.[49]

Repeatedly, Pemberton advised Johnston and authorities in Richmond that one of the primary reasons for his inability to discover Federal efforts more quickly and accurately stemmed from the small number of cavalrymen he had to perform the essential role of reconnaissance.[50] While he acknowledged the possibility of Grant's reinforcing Rosecrans during the next week, Pemberton was not ready to accept the increasingly prevalent view that Grant was abandoning efforts to capture Vicksburg or Port Hudson or both. By April 13, however, pressure on Pemberton from his superiors forced him to compromise. The secrecy with which Grant surrounded his next step in the effort to reach Vicksburg was beginning to pay dividends. Pemberton advised his quartermaster to provide transportation for the movement of 8,000 men to Bragg's

assistance at Tullahoma, Tennessee.[51] Reluctantly, the Confederate commander looked for ways to cover the absence of these troops from his overall defense, inquiring of the local commander at Port Hudson if he could release some of his troops for duty farther north, near Vicksburg.

Confederate Failure to Counter Grant's Turning Movement

By the middle of April, Pemberton was entering the crucial phase in the defense of Vicksburg. If Grant passed below Vicksburg, Pemberton calculated that Grant would be able to choose between two means of employing his army. One option would be to join Major General Nathaniel P. Banks and reduce Port Hudson in preparation for a drive against Vicksburg from the south. The other choice, Pemberton reasoned, was an attack against Vicksburg itself. Clearly, Grant had the combat power available for multiple thrusts against Vicksburg, but Pemberton judged that the main blow would fall on Grand Gulf, with possible secondary attacks against Vicksburg and the northern rim of the city's defenses. The accuracy of at least part of Pemberton's estimate was borne out by Grant's tentative selection of Grand Gulf for the landing of McClernand's corps, once Porter's gunboats had silenced the guns that the Confederates had mounted there. But Grant was working to confuse the issue of where he would attempt to penetrate the Vickburg defense, and whether the penetration would take place in one location or in a number of areas. His dispatch of Major General Frederick Steele's division to Greenville, above Vicksburg, forced Pemberton to look northward in the first two weeks of April. Despite Steele's reported withdrawal on April 11, after laying waste to the countryside, Stevenson, commanding at Vicksburg, chose to leave an additional brigade in that area to discourage what he believed to be a part of the overall plan to envelop Vicksburg.[52]

To the south, at Grand Gulf, General Bowen reassured Pemberton on April 12 that he could resist an attempted landing at that site. In addition, he had a small observation force across the river that was keeping track of McClernand's progress southward to Hard Times.[53]

Although Pemberton also prepared to challenge the anticipated passage of Porter's fleet past the batteries of Vicksburg, he was acutely aware that he had an insufficient number of heavy artillery weapons at Vicksburg to seriously damage a large number of boats under a determined commander. Nowhere within his department, nor within Johnston's command, could he hope to free the needed heavy artillery pieces. He therefore appealed to the Ordnance Department at Richmond, with disappointing results. On April 17, Pember-

A Four-Gun Confederate Battery, Typical of the Well-Protected Artillery Defending Vicksburg

ton exploded in a terse message to the Ordnance Chief: "The Brooke gun arrived here yesterday without a solitary projectile. Where am I to get them?"[54] To make matters worse, there was no bolt for the excellent, breech-loading artillery piece.[55] Assurances from Jefferson Davis that several of the requested weapons were on the way, with ammunition, could do little to assist the Confederate defenders in challenging the Federal fleet that Porter was soon to begin moving past Vicksburg.[56] The fact of the matter was that the Confederate Ordnance Department, under the capable direction of Colonel Josiah Gorgas, was simply unable to meet the demands of Pemberton as well as those of the other southern field forces. Nor was the overworked Confederate rail network able to efficiently transport what the Ordnance Department did have available. (Even the vital rail link between Jackson and Vicksburg was regularly out of service, and delayed the movements of troops and supplies while repairs were improvised.)

Finally, a part of Grant's overall scheme became sufficiently clear to enable the Confederates to set aside the assumption that the Federal command had abandoned further attempts to reach Vicksburg in favor of reinforcing Rosecrans. Early on the morning of April 17, Pemberton advised Johnston: "The following just received from Vicksburg: 'Eight boats passed the bend; one was burned, two apparently disabled, and five gone down. C.L. Stevenson.' Indications of an attack on Vicksburg are so strong, I am not warranted in sending any more troops from this department."[57] Both Johnston and Pemberton knew that Grant could do little with boats alone, except perhaps bombard the shoreline batteries. The troops that Grant was steadily marching to Hard Times constituted the most important element in the Federal task force. Therefore, Johnston urged Pemberton to contact Kirby Smith, who had been commanding the department across the river since February, suggesting that Smith "might cut off the enemy's supplies going to New Carthage."[58]

Once again, the implications of the critical weakness in the Confederate command structure and philosophy became obvious. Kirby Smith in Arkansas, like Holmes in Missouri earlier, found reasons, important and overriding in his view, to justify his unfortunate decision not to comply with the request for a cooperative attack of the vulnerable Federal supply line on the west side of the river. Any serious interruption of Grant's communications between Milliken's Bend and New Carthage or Hard Times would have, at the very least, upset the Federal timetable. Specifically, it would have forced the Federal forces to fight in another direction at a time when all of Grant's efforts were directed toward establishing a base from which he could launch an assault across a formidable water barrier.

The earlier decision of President Davis to make Johnston the theater commander for all Confederate activity between the Appalachian Mountains and the Mississippi River was a sound one—as far as it went. But the reluctance to extend Johnston's authority west beyond the river gave the Federal forces the ability to mount a major operation precisely along the boundary between the two Confederate zones of responsibility. Nor did the Confederate command in Richmond—President Davis, for all practical purposes—recognize that the decisions required to coordinate activities on the two sides of the river would therefore have to be made promptly in Richmond. Far away from Washington and Richmond, a major engagement was in progress as two armies fought for an objective that was of vital importance to the overall war effort. The events that took place during the important month of April 1863 show a sharp contrast between the attitudes of the Federal and Confederate presidents toward the conduct of the war. While Grant enjoyed a relatively flexible and broad authority, the South's awkward and patently inadequate command arrangement retarded rather than assisted the Confederate control of the Mississippi River. Even conceding the probable superiority of Grant's generalship over that of Pemberton, the command conditions under which each fought his part of the war in the West favored the Federal general.

The dilemma that Pemberton faced grew progressively worse as the Federal forces on the west side of the river moved closer to a successful river crossing. The inability to see through the cloud surrounding Grant's scheme is evident in the dispatch sent by Stevenson to Pemberton on April 17:

> Every movement of the enemy indicates that they are about to execute some plan. Until it is developed, I request that troops may be kept in reserve not farther than Jackson, to re-enforce this position (Vicksburg) if attacked on three sides. Reports from scouts and citizens on the upper river [are] that troops are moving down; none going up. . . .[59]

Erroneous rumors of other Federal activity continued to reach Pemberton and disturb his concentration on Grant's movements around Vicksburg. Nevertheless, each of these rumors had to be considered and evaluated in the context of potential courses of action available to the Federal forces. On April 18, a subordinate in northern Mississippi reported "reliable information of the enemy advancing along the two railroads in considerable force,"[60] a probable consequence of the initial covering operations designed by Stephen Hurlbut to prepare for Grierson's cavalry expedition through Mississippi. From Johnston, Pemberton learned of a "superior force from Corinth"[61] that had been sighted at Tuscumbia, Alabama. This report prompted Pemberton to direct his commander at Columbus, Mississippi to send all state and Confederate mounted troops in the north to Corinth. Pemberton sensed that his forces were being scattered too widely to repulse the main blow, wherever it fell. On April 20, he sought assistance from Johnston: "Can you not make a heavy demonstration with cavalry toward Abbeville [near Holly Springs] on Tallahatchie River, if only for 50 miles? The enemy is endeavoring to force a diversion of my troops to Northern Mississippi."[62]* On the same day, Pemberton received another report, this one factual, stating that the depth of the penetration of Grierson's fast-moving raiders was somewhere west of Columbus, Mississippi. From nearby Confederate garrisons, Pemberton dispatched regiments and brigades in an attempt to capture the Federal raiders. Nor did the rumors that part of Grant's force was being sent to reinforce Rosecrans die easily. Pemberton continued to receive reports from Confederate scouts of sizable bodies of troops—8,000 to 10,000 were reported on April 21—on their way to join Rosecrans.[63] No commander could expect to be more completely shrouded in what Clausewitz so accurately termed the "fog of war" than Pemberton was during the third week of April.

With Federal pressure mounting on every front, Pemberton continued to give priority to the immediate vicinity of Vicksburg, where he had pinpointed the majority of Grant's forces to be located. Another contingent of Porter's fleet ran the Vicksburg batteries on the night of April 22, reinforcing Pemberton's opinion that his resolute opponent planned a major operation south of Vicksburg. But where? As of April 28,

*Two days later, he repeated the request.

Grant's Transports Run the Vicksburg Batteries During the Night

Pemberton believed the preparations of McClernand's corps at Hard Times to be no more than a demonstration. He continued to feel that the defensive strength of Vicksburg itself precluded a frontal attack against the town. Pemberton focused his attention on Grand Gulf, the logical place for Grant to establish a bridgehead. Stevenson, at Vicksburg, disagreed, viewing the concentration below Vicksburg as a feint, and reiterating his opinion that Grant would make the main attack against Vicksburg and its northern defenses.[64] Despite Stevenson's repeated protests, Pemberton ordered him to retain a ready reserve of 5,000 to support Grand Gulf. The heavy attack against Grand Gulf on April 29 reinforced Pemberton's judgment of Grant's intended scheme, but the coincident disruption of the telegraph communications between his headquarters and points along the river denied Pemberton timely reports of events along the river on that date.[65] Transports loaded with troops added substance to the growing anticipation that a major Federal crossing was about to be launched. (The loaded transports were Sherman's, as he carried out his role of providing a demonstration against Chickasaw Bluffs and Hayne's Bluff on April 29–30.) Throughout the thirtieth, Pemberton still could not be certain where Grant's main effort would emerge, even as reports reached him at Jackson of the landing of Federal troops at Bruinsburg. Sherman's convincing demonstration kept Stevenson's attention so riveted on the northern defenses of Vicksburg that the latter erroneously reported to Pemberton the landing of the first of Sherman's lead regiments there on April 30.[66]

By May 1, the extent of Grant's landings in the vicinity of Bruinsburg cleared away any last doubts about the location of the main Federal effort. Grant's feeling of relief at establishing a sizable force across the river has already been mentioned, even though he recognized, as did Pemberton, that some of the heaviest fighting lay ahead. The gravity of the Confederate situation was summarized by Pemberton's brief message to Jefferson Davis on May 1:

A furious battle has been going on since daylight just below Port Gibson. . . . Bowen says he is outnumbered trebly; he has about 8,000. Enemy can cross all his army from Hard Times to Bruinsburg. . . . Large re-enforcements should be sent me from other departments. Enemy's movement threatens Jackson, and, if successful, cuts off Vicksburg and Port Hudson from the east. Am hurrying all re-enforcements I possibly can to Bowen. Enemy's success in passing our batteries has completely changed character of defense.[67]

Notes

[1] *The War of the Rebellion: A Compilation of the Official Records of the Union and Confederate Armies* (130 vols.; Washington, 1880–1901), Series I, XVII, Pt. 2, 716–717. (Hereinafter cited as *OR*. Unless otherwise indicated, all subsequent references to the *OR* are to Series I.)

[2] *Ibid.*, 724, 728.

[3] *OR*, XVII, Pt. 1, 414–459. Contains a complete account of the court of inquiry that was convened at Van Dorn's request. Pemberton accepted the findings of the court on November 28, 1862, setting aside all charges against Van Dorn.

[4] *OR*, XVII, Pt. 2, 734 (Van Dorn's message); Van Dorn transmitted more positive indications to Pemberton of the Federal advance on November 4.

[5] *Ibid.*, 742.

[6] *Ibid.*, 745.

[7] *OR*, XVII, Pt. 2, 737, 739, 752, 753, 757, 766, 771 (Pemberton's requests for help from Holmes); *Ibid.*, 782–784 (Holmes' arguments for retaining his troops in Arkansas).

[8] Sir Basil H. Liddell Hart, *Sherman: Soldier, Realist, American* (New York, 1958), p. viii.

[9] *OR*, XVIII, Pt. 2, 766.

[10] *Ibid.*, 311 (Grant's strength at the end of October). See *Ibid.*, 337–338, for his strength at the end of November.

[11] *Ibid.*, 771 (Pemberton to Bragg, November 30, 1862).

[12] E. Merton Coulter, *The Confederate States of America, 1861–1865* (Baton Rouge, La., 1950), p. 182.

[13] John C. Schwab, *The Confederate States of America, 1861–1865* (New York, 1901), p. 36.

[14] Richard C. Todd, *Confederate Finance* (Athens, Ga., 1954), p. 120; Schwab, *The Confederate States of America*, p. 172.

[15] Edward Younger (ed.), *Inside the Confederate Government* (New York, 1957), p. 108.

[16] John B. Jones, *A Rebel War Clerk's Diary at the Confederate States Capital* (2 vols.; Philadelphia, 1866), II, 212.

[17] Charles W. Ramsdell, *Behind the Lines in the Southern Confederacy* (Baton Rouge, La., 1944), p. 46.

[18] Robert Selph Henry, *"First With the Most" Forrest* (Indianapolis, 1944), pp. 107–108.

[19] *OR*, XVII, Pt. 1, 595–597 (Forrest's report). Only one of Forrest's subordinates—Dibrell—turned in a report after the raid. Also see Henry, *"First With the Most" Forrest*, pp. 108–121.

[20] Victor M. Rose, *Ross' Texas Brigade* (Louisville, 1881), p. 130.

[21] *Ibid.*, p. 84.

[22] Ulysses S. Grant, *Personal Memoirs of U.S. Grant* (2 vols.; New York, 1885), I, 432–438.

[23] Joseph E. Johnston, "Jefferson Davis and the Mississippi Campaign," in *Battles and Leaders of the Civil War*, ed. by Robert Underwood Johnson and Clarence Clough Buel (4 vols.; New York, 1884–1888), III, 473–474.

[24] *Ibid.*, 475.

[25] *OR*, XVII, Pt. 2, 800.

[26] Douglas Southall Freeman, *R.E. Lee: A Biography* (4 vols.; New York, 1934), II, 85.

[27] Louise Biles Hill, "Governor Brown and the Confederacy," *Georgia Historical Quarterly*, XXI (December, 1937), 371–373.

[28] Richard E. Yates, "Zebulon B. Vance as War Governor of North Carolina," *Journal of Southern History*, III (February, 1937), 59–60.

[29] Edwin C. Bearss, *Decision in Mississippi* (Jackson, Miss., 1962), pp. 144–147.

[30] An understanding of Pemberton's activities to strengthen his overall defense must be pieced together from several dispatches available in *OR*, XVII, 821–826, 828, 833. In addition, see Johnston, "Jefferson Davis and the Mississippi Campaign," p. 474, and John C. Pemberton, *Pemberton: Defender of Vicksburg* (Chapel Hill, N.C., 1942), pp. 73–77.

[31] *OR*, XVII, Pt. 2, 828, 830, 831, 833, 837, 838; XXIV, Pt. 3, 597, 599–600.

[32] *OR*, XXIV, Pt. 3, 618, 620, 623, 629, 630.

[33] *Ibid.*, 631–632.

[34] *Ibid.*, 636–637.

[35] *Ibid.*, 638.

[36] *Ibid.*, 642, 643–644, 649.

[37] *Ibid.*, 650, 652.

[38] *Ibid.*, 656–657.

[39] *Ibid.*, 662, 665–666.

[40] *Ibid.*, 670.

[41] *Ibid.*, 685.

[42] Francis Vinton Greene, *The Mississippi* (New York, 1882), pp. 91–108.

[43] *OR*, XXIV, Pt. 3, 686–687.

[44] William T. Sherman, *Memoirs of General William T. Sherman* (2 vols.; New York, 1875), I, 338.

[45] *OR*, XXIV, Pt. 3, 702.

[46] *Ibid.*, 709.

[47] *Ibid.*, 711, 712, 717.

[48] *Ibid.*, 719.

[49] *Ibid.*

[50] *Ibid.*, 769, 773, 789, 791, 797.

[51] *Ibid.*, 739.

[52] *Ibid.*, 735.

[53] *Ibid.*, 736, 743–744.

[54] *Ibid.*, 759.

[55] *Ibid.*, 766.

[56] *Ibid.*, 760, 773.

[57] *Ibid.*, 751.

[58] *OR*, XXIV, Pt. 3, 753.

[59] *Ibid.*, 756–757.

[60] *Ibid.*, 766.

[61] *Ibid.*, 767.

[62] *Ibid.*, 769.

[63] *Ibid.*, 773.

[64] *Ibid.*, 797, 800.

[65] *Ibid.*, 800, 801–902, 804.

[66] *Ibid.*, 805, 806.

[67] *Ibid.*, 807.

The Fall of Vicksburg

6

By May 1, 1863, after four months of feints, demonstrations, and frustrating attempts to penetrate the swamps, bayous, and woods around Vicksburg, Grant finally had a toehold on the east side of the Mississippi River. It had not been easy; but Pemberton's concentration of forces, made complicated and difficult by the Federal curtain of deception, had caused Grant's crossing to be less complex than it might have been. Then, evading the strength of the Confederate defenses, Grant hurried McClernand's corps ashore at Bruinsburg and followed it rapidly with McPherson's corps.

The last and most brilliant phase of the campaign to reduce Vicksburg and open the river was about to commence. A tribute to Grant's perseverance and initiative, it would prove to be one of the war's most extraordinary applications of the military art. More than that, for President Lincoln it would provide sustenance and a clear-cut victory at exactly the time that the Confederate eastern army was withdrawing from Gettysburg, chastened but still defiant. How Grant achieved the complete dominance of Pemberton is a tale of confidence, hard marching, and strategic genius.

Establishing the Bridgehead

As the Federal forces moved inland, Pemberton's southern flank was being turned. By 2:00 a.m. on May 1, the leading division of McClernand's corps had made first contact with Bowen's Confederate defenders eight miles inland from Bruinsburg, near Bayou Pierre. *(See Atlas Map No. 20.)* Initially, two Confederate brigades took up positions on a fork in the road near Port Gibson, greatly assisted by the terrain, which made an attack in force extremely difficult. Medium-sized but steep and broken hills alternated with deep ravines, and both were covered with dense undergrowth and cane. Although McClernand soon had his whole corps forward, he found it extremely difficult to deploy the corps so as to make

the full force of his advantage in combat power felt by the Confederate defenders. The object of the Confederate force was to delay the Union attackers, thus gaining time for reinforcements to arrive, and to deny the bridges over Bayou Pierre to the Federal spearhead. By noon, additional brigades and regiments had arrived piecemeal to strengthen the Confederate defense, bringing the total of Bowen's defenders to approximately 9,000—a force that was still substantially smaller than the force of 24,000 that Grant concentrated against them. As the weight of the lead elements of McPherson's corps joined McClernand, the brigade on the left of the Confederate defensive position gave way, but the brigade on the right held fast. At about 5:00 p.m., McPherson successfully attacked and turned the Confederate right just as the weight of McClernand's corps was becoming overpowering; the southern line crumbled, some elements falling back to the east, while the elements on the right flank retreated toward Grand Gulf. Giving way slowly and stubbornly, the Confederates managed to burn bridges over both branches of Bayou Pierre.

The victory near Port Gibson was a small but important one for the Union forces, as it gave them time to gather their strength in order to continue the penetration farther inland. Grant had not even had time to wait for his baggage or horses when he landed, but had borrowed a horse in order to join the battle outside of Port Gibson in the middle of the morning. When the Confederates withdrew from their position along Bayou Pierre, he first directed McPherson's corps to repair bridges, and then launched them northward in pursuit of the fleeing Confederates. By May 3, McPherson had driven the Confederates back across the Big Black River at Hankinson's Ferry. *(See Atlas Map No. 20.)* The speed of Grant's determined thrust inland payed handsome dividends, for McPherson's advance to Hankinson's Ferry threatened Grand Gulf, which was promptly evacuated by the Confederates. Having secured his bridgehead, Grant quickly moved his forward supply base to Grand Gulf. This base would also serve as the landing site for Sherman's corps, which was then moving down from north of Vicksburg after completing its successful demonstration against the northern rim of the defenses of Vicksburg.[1]

A Daring Decision

Grant now faced the first major decision since his landing on the east side of the river. Counting Sherman's corps, which had not yet crossed the river, Grant had at his disposal approximately 51,000 troops. In addition, 5,000 were at Helena, 33,000 were under Hurlbut in the vicinity of Memphis and Corinth, and another 8,000 were in western Tennessee and Kentucky. Between Hayne's Bluff and Jackson, Pemberton had scattered approximately 40,000 troops that could be concentrated against Grant in the vicinity of Vicksburg. Although Grant's base of operations was at Grand Gulf, his main supply base was far to the north at Memphis, and the movement of supplies to his forces south of Vicksburg had to come down the river past the batteries of Vicksburg. The utilization and maintenance of that supply line to the north would almost certainly entail the loss of ships, casualties, and interruptions in the arrival of supplies. The railroad between Jackson and Vicksburg gave Pemberton the ability to shift reinforcements rapidly between the two points. Indeed, reinforcements were already moving toward Jackson from the east, giving Pemberton the opportunity to force Grant to fight in two directions if he advanced against Vicksburg from his position near Grand Gulf. While Grant had the advantage of numbers, he was operating in the enemy's country with at best a tenuous supply capability. To further compound the Union problem, the terrain south and east of Vicksburg—which consisted of broken hills and ravines, and was almost entirely wooded and interlaced with streams and bayous—favored an excellent defense.

Weighing on Grant's mind was Halleck's earlier instruction to cooperate with Banks in his attack of Port Hudson to the south, a directive that initially caused Grant to consider sending a corps of 15,000 to assist Banks. The matter of reducing Port Hudson in cooperation with Banks had merit, for it would permit Grant to open a supply line to the south, unthreatened by the batteries of Vicksburg. Time, however, was the factor that would determine what Grant did next, and he was helped in his decision by information from Banks; that general, then wrapping up his most recent expedition up the Red River, indicated that he would not be able to join Grant's force in front of Port Hudson until May 10. Grant's explanation of his next move is described in his *Memoirs:*

> Up to this time my intention had been to secure Grand Gulf, as a base of supplies, detach McClernand's corps to Banks and co-operate with him in the reduction of Port Hudson. The news from Banks forced upon me a different plan of campaign from the one intended. To

> wait for his co-operation would have detained me at least a month. The reinforcements would not have reached ten thousand men after deducting casualties and necessary river guards at all high points close to the river for over three hundred miles. The enemy would have strengthened his position and been reinforced by more men than Banks could have brought. I therefore determined to move independently of Banks, cut loose from my base, destroy the rebel force in rear of Vicksburg and invest or capture the city.[2]

It was a daring plan, full of calculated risks. To add to the concern that Grant's plan would undoubtedly cause among the Union authorities in Washington, Major General Joseph Hooker was in the process of trying to turn Robert E. Lee out of his position on the Rappahannock River in an engagement that lasted from May 2 to May 6. The excellent plan that Hooker had devised would turn into a disaster in his hands, and certainly would not encourage the high command in Washington to accept what appeared to be an extremely risky operation south of Vicksburg. Grant anticipated a cautious reaction from Washington:

> I knew well that Halleck's caution would lead him to disapprove of this course; but it was the only one that gave any chance of success. The time it would take to communicate with Washington and get a reply would be so great that I could not be interfered with until it was demonstrated whether my plan was practicable. Even Sherman, who afterwards ignored bases of supplies other than what were afforded by the country while marching through four States of the Confederacy with an army more than twice as large as mine at this time, wrote me from Hankinson's Ferry, advising me of the impossibility of supplying our army over a single road. He urged me to "stop all troops till your army is partially supplied with wagons, and then act as quick as possible; for this road will be jammed, as sure as life." To this I replied: "I do not calculate upon the possibility of supplying the army with full rations from Grand Gulf. I know it will be impossible without constructing additional roads. What I do expect is to get up what rations of hard bread, coffee and salt we can, and make the country furnish the balance."[3]

An Indirect Approach

By moving quickly, rather than waiting for a buildup of supplies at a depot at Grand Gulf, Grant intended to strike at the rear of Vicksburg before the Confederates could assemble enough strength to halt him. At the same time, the fact that Grant did not expect to depend on a firm supply line of his own would bewilder Pemberton, who anticipated that Grant would move inland, supporting his force conventionally with a line of communication to a river base. In the campaign for Vicksburg, that assumption would cost Pemberton vital time—and, later, much more. Grant was justified in suspecting that the high command in Washington would not quickly sanction the course that he had charted for his forces east of the river. Later, in July, President Lincoln would confide in a personal letter to Grant that he considered Grant's course at this time the wrong one.[4] Halleck, predictably, did not withhold his doubts as long, advising Grant as soon as possible that the plan was too risky. Grant, he said, should return to Grand Gulf and cooperate with Banks.[5] But by the time that Grant received Halleck's message—several days later—it was too late to retrace his steps to the relative security of his base at Grand Gulf.

The supply train that would carry ammunition and basic supplies for Grant's army was an improvised and expedient collection. One author described the ammunition train as "a curious assemblage of fine carriages, farm wagons, long coupled wagons with racks for carrying cotton bales—every vehicle, indeed, that could be found on the plantations which had been used either for work or pleasure. These vehicles were a nondescript outfit, drawn by oxen and mules wearing plough harness, or straw collars and rope lines."[6] The arrangements for supply would continue to occupy an important place in Grant's planning until he could devise a more reliable system for his forces later in the campaign. Meanwhile, he had ordered Sherman to end his demonstration against Vicksburg as soon as McClernand's leading elements began crossing the Mississippi. Accordingly, by May 3, Grant was able to direct his trusted subordinate to organize a supply train of 120 vehicles, bring them across the river to Grand Gulf, and load them with enough rations to provide a five days' supply for Sherman's corps as well as a two days' supply for McPherson's and McClernand's corps. For the time being, at least, additional supplies would have to be collected from the countryside southeast of Vicksburg.

Having satisfied himself that the logistical arrangements for his army were progressing as well as circumstances would permit, Grant turned his attention to the next step of his campaign. From Hankinson's Ferry, Warrenton was only 12 miles away, while Vicksburg was another 10 or 12 miles farther north. The only major obstacle that lay between the Federal army and Vicksburg was the Big Black River. Information reached Grant, however, that Confederate forces had been sighted east and northeast of Vicksburg. Consequently, an advance toward Vicksburg—the logical route that the Confederates would expect him to take—would result in the concentration of all the troops that Pemberton could assemble near the river port to challenge his advance. At the same time, Grant was concerned over what the Confederate force at Jackson would do to his flank or rear if he turned his full

effort toward Vicksburg without delay. He therefore did not choose the conventional approach. Instead, his first target would be the Confederate reinforcements near Jackson. By attacking and defeating that force, Grant later could concentrate against Vicksburg without fear of being seriously challenged on his northern flank or in the rear. Moreover, once he had met and defeated—or at least dispersed—the forces at Jackson, he would be astride the Confederate line of communication that stretched from Jackson to Vicksburg. The Confederate stronghold would, in fact, be cut off. Grant's decisions to operate with minimal logistical support in the enemy's country and to strike first at Jackson were the boldest and most unorthodox aspects of his plan. Yet the success of his plan depended not nearly as much on its inherent audacity as it did on Grant's ability to accomplish the next phase of his operations before the outline of his plan became apparent to Pemberton and Johnston. Speed was the essence of Grant's scheme, and the urgency with which he pushed subordinates and staff alike energized the entire Union command.

Moving through broken and wooded terrain, Grant began his advance toward Jackson while remaining alert to the possibility of a Confederate advance against his left flank. Rather than attempting to cross the Big Black River, Grant used it as flank security, moving Sherman's and McClernand's corps along the south side of the river until they reached the railroad between Jackson and Vicksburg. McPherson was to advance through Rocky Springs and Utica toward Raymond. *(See Atlas Map No. 20.)* The movement began on May 7, with McPherson on the right, Sherman in the center, and McClernand on the left. Although he did not yet know what Johnston could do to reinforce Pemberton or how rapidly Pemberton could concentrate against him, Grant was determined to reduce the risk by keeping his three corps within supporting distance of one another.

McClernand's Corps Marches Through the Bogs

The Confederate Response

Pemberton had been deceived concerning both the location that Grant would use to gain a foothold on the east side of the river and the size of the force that Grant would place there. That error was just the beginning of several miscalculations that would plague the Confederate command during the subsequent two and a half weeks, giving Grant sufficient time to seal the fate of the Vicksburg forces. In fairness, however, considering the numerous attempts that had already occupied the attention of the Confederate defenders over the preceding four months, there was certainly room for skepticism concerning the legitimacy of Grant's latest expedition. Pemberton's first reaction, as described in the previous chapter, was to order Stevenson to reinforce Bowen in the vicinity of Grand Gulf and to request additional reinforcements from the War Department and Johnston. Although some of the reinforcements reached the area of Port Gibson in time to take part in the fighting there, they did not add enough strength to the defending forces to enable it to withstand the combined power of the corps of McClernand and McPherson.

Apparently, Jefferson Davis was not sufficiently confident of Pemberton's ability to entrust the conduct of future operations entirely to him. On May 9, the President ordered Johnston to leave Tullahoma immediately and move to Jackson, from which location Davis intended Johnston to direct operations in Mississippi personally.[7] It was the beginning of an awkward arrangement of Confederate command that would persist until the fall of Vicksburg. Even before Johnston arrived, he gave Pemberton orders on May 1 based on his first report from Pemberton concerning the Union activity against Grand Gulf. "If Grant's army lands on this side of the river," Johnston telegraphed, "the safety of Mississippi depends on beating it. For that object you should unite your whole force."[8] Sound advice, since any force attempting a river crossing or amphibious assault is normally most vulnerable when it is attempting to establish a bridgehead. Unfortunately, Johnston's advice conflicted with the instructions that Pemberton received a few days later from President Davis in Richmond, before Grant's forces left the area of Hankinson's Ferry:

> I am anxiously expecting intelligence of your further active operations. Want of transportation of supplies must compel the enemy to seek a junction with their fleet after a few days' absence from it. To hold both Vicksburg and Port Hudson is necessary to a connection with Trans-Mississippi. You may expect whatever it is in my power to do.[4]

For whatever reasons, Jefferson Davis apparently viewed Grant's operations as no more than a large raid that would soon have to reunite with river support.

In his report many months after the campaign, Pemberton indicated that he shared Davis' view, writing: "I had good reason . . . to believe that he [Grant] would be forced either to advance immediately upon Edwards Depot [Station] to give me battle . . . or to return at once to his base upon the Mississippi River."[10] It is evident that Grant's decision to operate with limited logistical support behind the enemy lines led Pemberton to misjudge where and how far Grant could take his forces. In the same report, Pemberton stated: "I was firmly convinced that the enemy's supplies must be very limited, as he moved with but few wagons, and his dependence upon those to be drawn from his distant base at Grand Gulf or Bayou Pierre very precarious."[11] The Confederate commander was primarily concerned with keeping the railroad line between Jackson and Vicksburg open and holding the line of the Big Black River, thus making it possible to fall on Grant's line of supply if the chance were offered. Consequently, on May 3, Pemberton grouped his command between Vicksburg and the right bank of the Big Black River, anticipating that Grant would move directly on Vicksburg if he intended to continue operations. As late as May 11, Pemberton was not certain that Grant's advance toward Raymond was a legitimate threat to Jackson. His instructions to Brigadier General John Gregg, whose brigade was on the way to Raymond, gave Gregg two options. If the force opposing him was too strong, he could fall back on Jackson. If, however, Grant's thrust toward Raymond was merely a move to gain maneuver room in order to turn against Pemberton and seize the Big Black River bridge at the Vicksburg and Jackson Railroad crossing, Gregg was to attack Grant's force in the rear or flank.[12] On the thirteenth, Pemberton started moving three divisions toward a defensive position about a mile south of Edward's Station. There, they would await the attack that Pemberton thought would momentarily come from Grant. The three divisions (Loring, Stevenson, and Bowen) were in position the next day. Grant, however, had no intention of inviting a battle with Pemberton until he had dealt with the force at Jackson.

By May 14, Johnston had arrived in Jackson, where he discovered that a Union force blocked the road between the two Confederate forces. He promptly wired the Confederate President in Richmond: "I am too late."[13] Grasping at once that the Confederate forces would have a better chance of opposing Grant if they were united, Johnston sent a message to Pemberton by courier:

> I have lately arrived, and learn that Major-General Sherman is between us, with four divisions, at Clinton. It

is important to re-establish communications, that you may be re-enforced. If practicable, come up on his rear at once. To beat such a detachment, would be of immense value. The troops here could co-operate. All the strength you can quickly assemble should be brought. Time is all-important.[14]

Pemberton gave Johnston's courier the distinct impression that he intended to obey the order as soon as he reached his forces. (He received the message at Bovina, 10 or 12 miles from his camp.) But when he reached his camp, Pemberton consulted with his commanders and decided that instead of launching a cooperative attack against Sherman's rear, he would follow a plan of his own design.[15] To Johnston, he wrote:

> I shall move as early to-morrow morning as practicable with a column of 17,000 men to Dillon's, situated on the main road leading from Raymond to Port Gibson, 7½ miles below Raymond and 9½ miles from Edward's Depot. The object is to cut enemy's communications and to force him to attack me, as I do not consider my force sufficient to justify an attack on enemy in position or to attempt to cut my way to Jackson.[16]

The message must have come as a blow to Johnston, who knew that he did not have an adequate force to withstand the combined strength of Grant's army for very long. Grant, in the meantime, had not been idle. The following section recounts the story of the Union advance that preceded Johnston's May 14 arrival in Jackson, Mississippi.

Splitting the Confederate Forces

After the halt to await the arrival of the bulk of Sherman's corps and the consolidation of supply services in the Grand Gulf area, the course that Grant should pursue was neither clear-cut nor obvious. He could not be certain where and in what strength the Confederates near Vicksburg and Jackson would attempt to oppose him. To reduce the possibility of being surprised by the enemy's emergence from an unexpected quarter, Grant gave special attention to the security of his army as it maneuvered in the area south of the Vicksburg and Jackson Railroad. Each segment of the next two weeks of campaigning would be important as Grant moved relentlessly toward his goal—Vicksburg. But until he could eliminate the threat of the Confederate forces near Jackson, his Army of the Tennessee would remain vulnerable to attacks from two directions. Therefore, the next phase of the campaign was crucial, not only to the overall success of the campaign, but to the survival of Grant's army in the enemy's territory.

A Rapid Advance

Despite his emphasis on speed, Grant's concurrent caution is evident in the steps that he took to guard against a surprise attack and to conceal his intentions from the Confederate commanders. When the march began from the vicinity of Hankinson's Ferry *(see Atlas Map No. 20)*, the Union corps moved eastward two abreast, with McClernand on the left, hugging the Big Black River, and McPherson on the right, advancing toward Raymond via Rocky Springs and Utica. Sherman's corps followed, initially using both roads; it had been charged by Grant to guard against a Confederate sortie over any of the numerous crossings along the Big Black River as McClernand's advance uncovered them. Maximum flexibility was the keynote of Grant's scheme of advance as his corps moved forward without encountering significant resistance through May 11.

When Grant reached Rocky Springs, he began to receive reports that Pemberton had concentrated his divisions in the vicinity of Edward's Station.[17] This information prompted Grant to change the relative positions of his corps and to modify his pattern of advance. Sherman's and McClernand's corps marched from Cayuga to Auburn together, at which point Sherman's corps took over as lead element of the left of Grant's army, and McClernand's corps struck a new course directly north from Auburn. Pemberton's gathering of strength near Edward's Station was perceived by Grant as a sign that his enemy planned to offer battle there; but the wily Grant had no intention of engaging the Confederate forces at a time or place of Pemberton's choosing. Nevertheless, keeping Pemberton in the vicinity of Edward's Station was essential to Grant's plan to attack the Confederate forces at Jackson, so McClernand's move northward served to reinforce Pemberton's misconception that his own army and Vicksburg were Grant's immediate targets.[18]

It is worthwhile to consider the relative degree of confidence that Grant had in the ability and judgment of his three corps commanders. McClernand remained the most troublesome of Grant's subordinates, and that fact may well have persuaded Grant to shift Sherman into a leading position so that his and McPherson's corps would carry the load of the fighting when they reached Jackson. Earlier, at Port Gibson, McClernand had been forced to delay his inland march for three hours while his commissary issued the necessary three days' rations, a task that could and should have been accomplished either on the boats or before loading. At the same time, McClernand's reaction to the appearance of Confederate defenders near Port Gibson brought from him no more imaginative tactics than headlong, frontal assaults—effective, but costly in manpower.[19] The implicit trust that Grant had in Sherman and

McPherson further explains his shifting of the corps. Grant rarely gave evidence of being a keen practitioner of lessons learned from military history, but his careful alignment of the most appropriate subordinate with each new mission is reminiscent of the techniques repeatedly employed by Napoleon Bonaparte during his campaigns.

By May 11, Grant was sufficiently satisfied with the progress of the advance all along his front to advise McPherson of his next intermediate objective. To that general, who had pushed past Utica *(see Atlas Map No. 20)*, he wrote:

> Move your command tonight to the next crossroads if there is water, and tomorrow with all activity into Raymond. At the latter place you will use your utmost exertions to secure all subsistence stores that may be there, as well as in the vicinity. We must fight the enemy before our rations fail, and we are equally bound to make our rations last as long as possible. Upon one occasion you made two days' rations last seven. You may have to do the same thing again.[20]

Ever mindful of the concern of his commanders for the status of major friendly units adjacent to their own, Grant added: "Sherman is now moving out on the Auburn and Raymond road, and will reach Fourteen-Mile Creek tonight. When you arrive at Raymond, he will be in close supporting distance."[21]

On that same day, Halleck was sending his message suggesting to Grant that he return to Grand Gulf so that he could cooperate with Banks from there, most likely in an attack on Port Hudson.[22] Earlier, Grant had received a message from Banks, urging Grant to send reinforcements in order to assist him on the Red River. In his reply, Grant had explained the extent of his operations in the interior of the country around Vicksburg and Jackson, pointing out that he was past the point at which he could easily extricate his force. Instead, he suggested to Banks the possibility of Banks' dispatch of reinforcements to *him*, near Vicksburg, citing rumors that had suggested the partial evacuation of Port Hudson.[23] (To a limited degree, Grant was right, since Pemberton had already removed some of the garrison from Port Hudson in early April in order to strengthen the Vicksburg defenders. As a matter of fact, the next troops that McPherson would meet, near Raymond, were from Port Hudson.) On the eleventh, Grant also dispatched a short message to Halleck, unaware as yet that the General-in-Chief had urged him to concentrate at Grand Gulf:

> My forces will be this evening as far advanced towards Jackson as Fourteen-Mile [C]reek, the left near the Black [R]iver, and extending in a line as nearly east and west as they can get without bringing on a battle. As I can communicate with Grand Gulf no more, except it becomes necessary to send a train with heavy escort, you may not hear from me again for several days.[24]

The Battle of Raymond

McPherson began moving toward Raymond soon after three o'clock on the morning of May 12. Soon his advance division began to encounter Confederate screening elements from Gregg's brigade. By 11:00 a.m., McPherson had met the main body, 5,000 strong, two miles southwest of Raymond. *(See Atlas Map No. 20.)* Each commander misjudged the size of the opposing force, and the resulting confusion was understandable. In actuality, McPherson's corps outnumbered Gregg's brigade—the only force that opposed its advance—3 to 1. Nevertheless, while Gregg thought that he was being attacked by a much smaller force, McPherson estimated that he had substantially more than a brigade opposing him. Gregg was undoubtedly influenced by his orders from Pemberton, which had suggested that the Union force he was engaging was merely a feint to draw attention away from the major Union effort in the vicinity of Edward's Station.[25]

Gregg opened the action with a vigorous attack against Major General John A. Logan's division, the lead element of McPherson's corps, stopping the Federal advance south of Fourteen Mile Creek. Still believing that he faced a much smaller force, Gregg shifted a regiment to the east, hoping to envelop the Federal right flank and rear while he pinned the force to his front in position on the road to Utica. The dust and smoke of the battle, as well as dense underbrush and woods, contributed to the confusion in the Federal ranks and prevented McPherson from gaining a clear picture of what was happening. As the Confederate secondary attack against his right flank developed, McPherson sent Stevenson's brigade to the right. From noon until approximately 1:30 p.m., the initiative remained with the Confederate force as McPherson struggled to overcome the tangle of difficult terrain and bring the weight of his corps to bear on the two-pronged Confederate attack. Finally, volleys from Stevenson's infantrymen halted the Confederate flanking attempt, even as Gregg was hurrying his last (reserve) regiment forward to reinforce the flanking maneuver. So far, the battle had not developed the way a contest between a corps and brigade should. Influenced more by the conditions of the terrain than by design, McPherson continued to feed regiments and brigades into the left and right of his line piecemeal until the Confederate attacks in both areas had been halted. The 3-to-1 advantage enjoyed by McPherson, as well as the superior and more numerous Federal artillery, now began to have its effect, and McPherson was able to launch a counterattack. But the individual bravery and spirited counterattacks that characterized the actions of the Confederate regiments combined to produce continued stiff resistance to the advance of McPherson's corps. Finally, in the late afternoon, McPherson succeeded in forcing the retreat of Gregg's right regiment. Without support on its flank, the left of the Confederate line was forced to retreat as well. Both elements moved back through Raymond toward Jackson.[26]

The Seizure of Jackson

The battle at Raymond cleared away the last sizable Confederate force that stood between Grant and the Mississippi capital. While McPherson was engaged with Gregg's brigade, Sherman's and McClernand's corps brushed aside Confederate skirmishers and crossed Fourteen Mile Creek. It is worth pausing for a moment to examine the method of the Union advance from the time that McClernand's troops first landed at Bruinsburg. Earlier, Grant's total available force was given as approximately 51,000. But not all of the troops were in the main striking force of his three corps. Security elements for his bases at Hard Times and Grand Gulf, as well as detachments used to guard crossing sites over creeks and rivers to his rear, reduced Grant's actual combat strength to roughly 33,000. The fact that Pemberton could count on approximately 40,000 troops, as well as regiments on the way to Jackson from the East, emphasizes that Grant was effectively outnumbered in the campaign area that included Vicksburg and Jackson. His success in the first two battles—at Port Gibson and Raymond—grew out of his ability to concentrate a superiority of combat power at each of these vital points while the Confederate forces remained dispersed. This situation would be duplicated as Grant closed in on Jackson. The fight at Raymond, followed by the withdrawal of Gregg to Jackson as well as rumors that additional Confederate troops were on the way to Jackson, confirmed in Grant's mind that his decision to concentrate first against that threat to his rear was correct.[27]

Retaining the flexibility that had marked his advance to Raymond, Grant shifted McPherson to the north. The corps commander was now ordered to proceed from Raymond to Clinton on the Vicksburg and Jackson Railroad, to destroy the railroad there, and to prevent any junction of the Confederate forces using that route. Sherman's and McClernand's corps moved into Raymond, where they encountered a sullen citizenry that only a day before had welcomed Gregg's brigade with enthusiastic cheers. Despite heavy rains that turned the roads into no more than muddy trails, Grant pushed his corps commanders relentlessly on May 13. Once his work was done at Clinton, McPherson moved on toward Jackson. From Raymond, Sherman advanced toward the same objective. McClernand, in reserve, placed divisions at Clinton, Raymond, and on the road behind Sherman, beyond Mississippi Springs. McClernand's task was two-fold: to protect against an attack from the rear, and to be prepared to reinforce either

McPherson or Sherman or both.[28] McPherson and Sherman communicated directly on the thirteenth and early on the next day to insure that they would arrive in front of Jackson at the same time. On May 14, early in the morning, Grant wired Halleck: "I will attack the State capital today."[29]

Despite the continuing rain, Grant was determined to attack Jackson before the Confederates had time to organize their defenses. Early on the morning of May 14, McPherson advised Sherman: "General Joe Johnston is in Jackson, and it is reported they have 20,000 men. I do not think there is that many, though they have collected considerable of a force. They have fortified on the different roads on this side of town, and are forming an abatis."[30] At about 9:00 a.m., McPherson's lead elements met the first Confederate pickets five miles out of town and drove them back. He pushed on until he encountered the main entrenched Confederate defense, two and a half miles outside the capital. In places, the roads over which McPherson pushed his weary infantrymen were under a foot of water. While the infantrymen pitched in to help move caissons, limbers, ambulances, and guns through the deepening mud, they could probably be heard cursing in disgust as mounted couriers and officers splashed by, drenching them with mud and water.[31]

In Jackson, Johnston had only 6,000 troops with which to oppose the approximately 25,000 men of the two advancing corps of Sherman in the south and McPherson in the north. The gap between Grant's two corps—one of nearly two miles' distance—might have caused a commander less confident than Grant to delay his attack until the situation had been corrected. But Grant, estimating that both wings of his army were strong enough to avoid defeat in detail, urged his corps commanders forward.[32] Grant's decision was justified, for Johnston soon recognized the hopelessness of his defensive stand and, at 3:00 a.m. on the morning of May 14, decided to evacuate Jackson. Gregg, with a minimal force, was left behind to delay the Federal corps long enough for Johnston to withdraw troops and supplies to the north. Performing his mission well, Gregg delayed the troops of both Sherman and McPherson until a report reached him at 2:00 p.m. that the last of the supply trains had cleared Jackson on the way to Canton. The rear guard pulled out to the north, and Grant could report to Halleck that the occupation of Jackson had been completed between 3:00 p.m. and 4:00 p.m. that afternoon.[33] In his message to Halleck the next day, Grant gave no indication that he was reducing the pressure on the enemy: "The enemy retreated north evidently with the design of joining the Vicksburg forces. I am concentrating my forces at Bolton, to cut them off, if possible."[34]

The Union soldiers were beginning to realize that they were part of an epoch-making campaign of the war. Hard marching and short rations seemed somehow less distasteful as they

gleefully read the Jackson newspapers of the day before declaring that "Yankee vandals would never pollute the streets
of Jackson."[35] What the soldiers did not realize was that the
relentless pushing of their commander was preventing many
casualties. Grant had no way of knowing when or how many
reinforcements were on the way to join Johnston. Actually,
in a few days, Johnston's 6,000 would grow to 15,000, as
troops were hurried to beleaguered Mississippi from the East.
Another 9,000 would be added a few days later.[36] For the
Union soldiers of the Army of the Tennessee, hard marching
and short rations were indeed a small price to pay for the
important advantage that Grant gained when he drove
Johnston's forces out of Jackson on May 14, before they could
be reinforced.

Closing on Vicksburg

Grant may have contemplated giving his troops a rest in
Jackson. Rations left behind by the Confederates would have
been a welcome change from the cold and often uncooked
variety his troops had consumed for the last two weeks;
moreover, it would appear that Johnston posed no immediate
threat, even if reinforced. But McPherson brought information
to Grant that set aside any thought he might have entertained
of resting the troops. When Johnston had sent instructions to
Pemberton to join him at Clinton, he had used the common
technique of dispatching the message via several couriers to
insure its delivery to Pemberton. One of the couriers promptly
delivered his copy to McPherson, who in turn informed Grant
of its contents on the afternoon of May 14. Grant, therefore,
actually had the message before Pemberton. The courier had
been thrown out of Memphis some time earlier with much
publicity attached to his role as a rebel sympathizer and outspoken critic of the Federal Administration. In fact, he was
an undercover Union agent, but the reputation generated by
the affair in Memphis had led Johnston to trust him as a
courier. The dispatch told Pemberton to move to Clinton and
strike Grant in the rear. Johnston would try to join forces with
him there.[37] On May 13, Johnston mistakenly identified
McPherson's corps at Clinton as being Sherman's; more importantly, Johnston, like Pemberton, thought that Grant's main
effort would be directed toward Vicksburg, and was therefore
under the impression that between them there was only an
isolated corps of the Federal army. Confusion was growing
in the Confederate headquarters. As described earlier, Pemberton chose to disregard Johnston's order to unite the two forces,
and attempted to strike Grant's line of communication instead.
Unaware of what Pemberton would do, Grant meanwhile assumed that he would obey Johnston's order.

Confederate Confusion

Rapidly, Grant issued orders to prevent the concentration of
the Confederate forces. Sherman would remain in Jackson
with two of his divisions and complete the destruction of
stores, manufacturing facilities, and railroads. The rear of
Grant's army became its head, as McClernand, gathering his
divisions at Raymond and Clinton, began to march westward.
Three roads, roughly parallel to each other, led into Edward's
Station from the east. *(See Atlas Map No. 21.)* McClernand's
corps used all three roads, with McPherson's corps following.
Above all, Grant wanted to find and fight Pemberton's army
before he could be reinforced by Johnston. To McClernand,
he wrote:

> It is evidently the design of the enemy to get north of
> us and cross the Black [R]iver and beat us into Vicks-
> burg. We must not allow them to do this. Turn all of
> your forces toward Bolton station and make all dispatch
> in getting there. Move troops by the most direct route
> from wherever they may be on receipt of this order.[38]

To Halleck, on the same day, May 15, Grant sent a message
explaining his inability to comply with Banks' recent request
to send troops south. In his message to Halleck, Grant stated
simply: "I could not lose the time."[39]

Pemberton's strike southward from Edward's Station to
threaten the Federal line of communication miscarried—
primarily because there was no substantial line of communication between Grant's army and Grand Gulf to strike. The
same rain that had drenched the Union forces on May 13 and
14 prevented Pemberton's rapid movement as his force
marched toward Raymond on the fifteenth. Baker's Creek,
which he had to cross, was so swollen that another delay
occurred while the Confederates constructed a bridge over its
deepening, turbulent waters. After his force had crossed the
creek, however, Pemberton received another directive from
Johnston early on the morning of May 16, advising him that
Johnston's force was north of Jackson at Canton, that reinforcements were on the way from the eastern armies, and that the
only way they could hope to stop Grant after his victory at
Jackson was to unite north of the Vicksburg and Jackson
Railroad.[40] This time, Pemberton decided to comply with
Johnston's order. He countermarched, turning the rear of his
column, including its wagon trains, into the head. Because
of the narrow road he was using and the absence of an alter-
native route, it was an awkward maneuver at best. Meanwhile,
Johnston, north of Jackson and anticipating a junction with
Pemberton if the latter could obey his orders, felt compelled
to move farther away temporarily because of the threat of
Sherman's corps moving north against him from Jackson.
(Actually, Sherman's troops were merely carrying out Grant's

orders to destroy all of the rail lines leading out of Jackson.)

The Confederate defense was in utter disarray. Because Grant was urging McPherson's and McClernand's corps westward with all possible speed, Pemberton would not be able to retrace his steps beyond the Vicksburg and Jackson Railroad before his lead elements were struck by the head of McClernand's corps. To make matters worse, Pemberton could not even unite all of his forces to meet Grant's attack. A day and a half earlier, when he had moved southeast to find Grant's line of communication, nearly 10,000 troops had been left behind to defend Vicksburg.[41]

The Battle of Champion's Hill

Fortunately for Pemberton, an excellent piece of defensive terrain was available, and he was not long in choosing it as a site for the deployment of his three divisions. Rising over a hundred feet above the surrounding countryside and cut by numerous gullies and ravines, Champion's Hill was covered with dense woods. Even though first contact between the Confederates and Brigadier General Andrew J. Smith's division of McClernand's corps occurred at 6:30 a.m. on May 16, hours passed before the advance Federal elements could deploy for an attack. Pemberton used that time to hurry his divisions into defensive positions, with Stevenson on the left, Loring on the right, and Bowen occupying the center. *(See inset, Atlas Map No. 21.)*

Because it had proved impossible for Grant to close up and mass McClernand's corps at Bolton, as originally planned, McClernand's leading division opened the battle when it met Confederate skirmishers on the road from Bolton to Edward's Station. When Brigadier General Alvin P. Hovey found the Confederate main body in position on the plateau of Champion's Hill, he immediately formed a line of battle. Pushing straight ahead, his infantry moved up the slope through the dense woods, capturing Confederate prisoners and guns, only to be driven back by the furious counterattack of Stevenson's division. The rest of McClernand's corps was not yet close enough to assist Hovey, but Major General John A. Logan of McPherson's corps soon brought his division into line on Hovey's right, and the pattern for the ensuing battle was set. Arriving on the battlefield with Logan's troops, McPherson quickly assumed control of the right side of the Federal line. McPherson's second division, commanded by Brigadier General Marcellus M. Crocker, moved into position to the left of

The Battle of Champion's Hill, May 16, 1863

Hovey. Despite repeated messages from Grant, the remainder of McClernand's corps played no substantial role in the early and middle part of the day's fighting. In Grant's opinion, the failure of McClernand to bring up his other divisions promptly and join in the battle was the factor that ultimately allowed Pemberton's army to escape.[42] McClernand was so convinced that the major share of the battle would be fought on the left, where he was located with the bulk of his corps, that he sent orders to Hovey to pull out of his position, where he was heavily engaged, in order to move to the left of the line! Grant, of course, countermanded the order.[43]

Grant was not the only commander who had difficulty getting his subordinate units into the fight. When Stevenson's division became fully committed against McPherson, Pemberton had to reinforce Stevenson with troops from Bowen's division and extend Bowen to the left to close the gap between the two divisions. The gap had opened as Stevenson steadily shifted to the left to prevent an envelopment of his flank by Logan's force. To strengthen the part of his front that was under heaviest attack, Pemberton ordered Loring to send at least a part of his division to reinforce Bowen and Stevenson. "Feeling assured that there was no important force in [Loring's] front," Pemberton wrote after the battle, "I dispatched several staff officers in rapid succession to Major-General Loring, ordering him to move all but one brigade . . . to the left as rapidly as possible."[44] Ironically, Loring, who faced McClernand, was convinced, like McClernand, that the major part of the day's battle would be fought in his sector. Pemberton continued in his report:

To the first of these messages, sent about 2 p.m., answer was returned by Major-General Loring that the enemy was in strong force in his front and endeavoring to flank him. Hearing no firing on the right, I repeated my orders to Major-General Loring, explained to him the condition of affairs on my left, and directed him to put his two left brigades into the fight as soon as possible. In the transmission of these various messages to and fro, over a distance of more than a mile, much valuable time was necessarily consumed. . . .[45]

By mid-afternoon, Stevenson was not only hard-pressed along his entire front, but also was in danger of being outflanked on his left by Logan. He therefore advised Pemberton that he could not hold out much longer against the increasing Union pressure. Pemberton went off in search of Loring himself, found one of his brigade commanders to the rear of Bowen's division, and hurriedly sent regiments to the most threatened sectors of the front.[46]

But the weight of the Federal attack—which had been renewed at about 1:00 p.m., after Stevenson's division had held it in check for well over two hours—caused Stevenson's force to begin to crumble. Even the shift of Bowen's division at 1:30 p.m. had brought only temporary relief. As the fresh Union division of Crocker reached the field and added its weight to the right of the line, McClernand finally responded to Grant's repeated messages and began to advance along both the Middle and Raymond Roads. The Federal division of Brigadier General Peter J. Osterhaus, on the Middle Road, presented the most serious threat to Pemberton, for it was attacking directly into Bowen's flank. *(See inset, Atlas Map No. 21.)* At about 5:00 p.m., Pemberton ordered the general retirement of his army from the field. Grant ordered two of McClernand's divisions to take up the pursuit, and as soon as McPherson's two divisions had refilled their cartridge boxes, he added them to the pursuit of Pemberton's demoralized army. The Confederate commander, however, was able to move his three divisions and his trains back to the Big Black River before nightfall brought an end to the Federal pursuit. It was a costly battle, characterized by the heaviest fighting that had occurred since Grant's crossing of the Mississippi River. Confederate casualties in killed, wounded, and missing totaled 3,524. Despite the fact that they were the attackers, Federal losses were only 2,441. But the most important result was described by Grant, who was still keeping one wary eye on Johnston:

We were now assured of our position between Johnston and Pemberton, without the possibility of a junction of their forces. Pemberton might indeed have made a night march to the Big Black, crossed the bridge there, and, by moving north on the west side, have eluded us, and finally returned to Johnston. But this would have given us Vicksburg. It would have been his proper move, however, and the one Johnston would have made had he been in Pemberton's place. In fact, it would have been in conformity with Johnston's orders to Pemberton.[47]

Crossing the Big Black River

Before daylight on May 17, Grant had McClernand's and McPherson's corps on the move to the west.* *(See Atlas Map No. 21.)* Upon reaching the Big Black River at about 8:00 a.m., the advance division of McClernand's corps found the

---

*Except for Major General Frank Blair's division, which had been convoying the army trains, the third corps in the Army of the Tennessee, commanded by Sherman, had not participated in the battle at Champion's Hill. Early on May 16, Grant had ordered Sherman to move the rest of his corps to Bolton. Promptly responding, Sherman closed his rear guard there at about 3:00 a.m. on the seventeenth. Shortly after daybreak, he was again on the march—to Bridgeport, a hamlet on the Big Black River that was about 11 miles north of the site where Grant expected to find Pemberton defending against the bulk of the Army of the Tennessee. Because Grant anticipated difficulty in crossing the Big Black in the face of the Confederate defenses, he had ordered Sherman and the bridge train under Blair to Bridgeport, expecting McClernand and McPherson to hold Pemberton in position while Sherman crossed the river.

Confederates in an entrenched position just to the east of the river. Pemberton had not originally intended to defend the east bank in strength, planning to station there only a rear guard to delay Grant and also hold open a line of retreat for Loring's division. Pemberton erroneously believed that Loring was still coming from the Champion's Hill area. In the confusion of the Confederate withdrawal on May 16 and the pressure exerted by Grant, however, the bridgehead had come to be occupied by a larger force than originally planned—and Loring's division never arrived. By laying planks on a railroad bridge and turning a steamer sideways in the river, Pemberton had provided two bridges by which his army could escape across the water if necessary. With his right anchored on Gin Lake and his left tied into the river, the Confederate commander occupied a position that was impossible to outflank. The morale in his army was low, however, following the dispiriting events of the past week, and Grant's army was ever increasing in both strength and confidence.

Battle was joined between the two armies shortly after McClernand deployed his divisions across the front and moved into position to assault the Confederate defenses. A Union brigade led by Brigadier General Mike Lawler first tested the strength of the Confederate left. Then, with the enormous and irrepressible Lawler leading it forward—the general had a reputation for hard fighting throughout Grant's army—the brigade charged across the cotton field into the deep, muddy bayou that protected the front of the Confederate line. Almost inexplicably caving in a section of the position on the left flank, Lawler's troops inspired other Federal regiments to join the attack, and soon the entire Confederate defense weakened and gave way. The rout was on. Pemberton's troops streamed over the two bridges across the Big Black River and only halted their pursuers by setting fire to the bridge and steamer.[48]

Sherman's XV Corps Crosses the Big Black River

Many of them did not manage to get back before the bridges were destroyed, however, and became prisoners. The action was over by 9:30 a.m. Using lumber from buildings in the vicinity, as well as logs and cotton bales, Union soldiers quickly set to work building three bridges, which, however, were not opened for crossing until the next morning. In the meantime, Grant rode north to join Sherman, whose troops finished building a ponton bridge by nightfall. The two generals sat together on a log, watching Sherman's corps cross the last obstacle standing between Grant and Vicksburg.[49] Ironically, Grant had again received a request to cooperate with Banks as his soldiers were breaking the Confederate defense at the Big Black River. Whether the request was from Halleck or Banks is unclear, but, in either case, Grant was too close to his prize to give serious consideration to such a major diversion of his force.[50]

The Capture of Vicksburg

At daybreak on the morning of May 18, Grant's army was again on the move, repeating a habit that had become ingrained during the previous two weeks. Four bridges were completed by the morning of that day, permitting all three corps to advance toward Vicksburg. By nightfall, they had reached the outer fortifications of Vicksburg. Sherman occupied the right, McPherson the center, and McClernand the left. *(See Atlas Map No. 22a.)* A gap existed south of McClernand's corps, but Pemberton made no attempt to extricate his battered army from Grant's closing trap. Early on May 19, Grant and Sherman joined the advance of Major General Frederick Steele's division, on Sherman's extreme right, as it moved to occupy and consolidate a position on Walnut Hills, north of Vicksburg. After having operated with an intermittent supply line for over two weeks, Grant was anxious to control the area north of Vicksburg and adjacent to the Yazoo River as rapidly as possible in order to re-establish a direct, reliable line of communication over which supplies could be sent from Memphis. It was a feeling shared by Grant's soldiers, for, as Grant relates in his *Memoirs:*

Most of the army had now been for three weeks with only five days' rations issued by the commissary. They had an abundance of food, however, but began to feel the want of bread. I remember that in passing around to the left of the line on the 21st, a soldier, recognizing me, said in rather a low voice, but yet so that I heard him, "Hard tack." In a moment the cry was taken up all along the line, "Hard tack! Hard tack!" I told the men nearest to me that we had been engaged ever since the arrival of troops in building a road over which to supply them everything they needed. The cry was in-

The Union Assault on Vicksburg, May 22, 1863

stantly changed to cheers. By the night of the 21st all the troops had full rations issued to them. The bread and coffee were highly appreciated.[51]

Storming the Fortress Ends in Failure

The resolute Union commander was not yet prepared to wait out the results of a lengthy siege of Vicksburg. On May 19, Grant decided to capitalize on what he believed to be the demoralized state of the Confederate defenders and attempt to carry their fortifications by assault. The attack commenced all along the Federal line at 2:00 p.m., producing some of the bloodiest fighting of the campaign. It also revealed that Grant's assessment of Confederate morale was in error. Probably the most stubborn defense was offered in the sector opposite Sherman's corps, where the intensity of the Confederate artillery and infantry fire was so great that Sherman did not believe he could withdraw his corps until dark. By the time they fell back, one of Sherman's battalions had lost over 40 percent of its men and could count 55 bullet holes in its battle flag.[52] The entire loss to Grant's three corps in killed, wounded, and missing amounted to over 900, compared with Confederate losses of about 250.

Even though the experience of the nineteenth should have told Grant that any attempt to carry the Confederate works by frontal assault would be costly and futile, the commander's

persistency led him to launch a second assault on May 22. Far heavier casualties resulted from the attacks by all three of Grant's corps in this second attempt, and part of the blame rests squarely on Grant's shoulders. Neither Sherman's nor McPherson's corps made any substantial headway after the attack began at 10:00 a.m. *(See Atlas Map No. 22a.)* While McClernand enjoyed better results in the morning hours and actually occupied some of the outer redoubts, McPherson and Sherman suspended their attacks. Grant received repeated requests by courier from McClernand: "I am hotly engaged with the enemy. He is massing on me from right and left. A vigorous blow by McPherson would make a diversion in my favor." Again, at about noon, McClernand stated: "We are hotly engaged with the enemy. We have part possession of two forts, and the stars and stripes are floating over them. A vigorous push ought to be made all along the line."[53] Although Grant tended to discredit the degree of success that McClernand reported, at 3:00 p.m., with McClernand still heavily engaged, he reluctantly ordered a renewal of the attack by McPherson and Sherman. As before, both were repulsed by the determined Confederate defenders. By 5:30 p.m., the Confederates on McClernand's front had driven his leading elements from the toeholds that they had won, and McPherson and Sherman had already suspended their afternoon attacks. At nightfall, McClernand withdrew the remainder of his corps, and the Federal army had no more to show for a full day's fighting than the sobering total of 3,199 killed, wounded, and missing.[54]

Curiously, although he distrusted McClernand's repeated and optimistic declarations of progress, undoubtedly because of his subordinate's demonstrated tendency to exaggerate in the past, Grant never left his position in the northern part of the Federal line to verify McClernand's reports. There was ample time for such an inspection. In addition, although a number of historians and contemporary critics cite McClernand's insistence on renewing the attack as the primary cause for the high casualty toll, at least one historian primarily attributes the failure to the unimaginative method with which Grant sought to break the Confederate defenses. Perhaps the victories of the preceding weeks had infused Grant with an unwarranted cockiness, atypical of his more frequent mode of generalship. The British historian J.F.C. Fuller commented on the excellent preparations for the attack by Grant's corps, laying the blame for the Federal failure on Grant's decision to attack along the entire front rather than against a specific point or points in the hope of achieving a breakthrough that could then be exploited with a ready reserve.[55] Regardless of the cause, the responsibility for the decision to attack on May 22, and at least partial responsibility for the failure of the attack, must be borne by Grant. Sadder and wiser as a result of his inability to crack the Confederate fortifications after two costly attempts, Grant settled down to regular siege operations.[56]

A Formal Siege Commences

Within the defenses of Vicksburg, Pemberton was not out of contact with Johnston. As a matter of fact, he continued to receive messages from Johnston throughout the siege that followed, primarily by means of bold line crossers who infiltrated the Federal siege lines at night.* Up to the time at which the Federal forces completed the investment of the Confederate stronghold, Johnston and Pemberton continued to dispute the course that Pemberton should follow. On May 18, soon after Pemberton's withdrawal into the Vicksburg fortifications, a message arrived from Johnston:

> If Haynes' Bluff is untenable, Vicksburg is of no value and cannot be held. If, therefore, you are invested in Vicksburg, you must ultimately surrender. Under such circumstances, instead of losing both troops and that place, we must, if possible, save the troops. If it is not too late, evacuate Vicksburg and its dependencies, and march to the northeast.[58]

*Besides encouragement from Johnston, the defenders of Vicksburg received another vital item—percussion caps for their rifled muskets. However, as many probably fell into Federal hands as reached the besieged southerners.[57]

Heavy Siege Cannon—A 96-Pound Parrott Gun

But Pemberton was not to be dissuaded from the opinion that he had formed regarding the value of Vicksburg, a point of view he was confident was shared by President Davis. When he wrote his report nearly a month after the fall of Vicksburg, he stoutly defended his decision with these words:

> The evacuation of Vicksburg! It meant the loss of the valuable stores and munitions of war collected for its defense; the fall of Port Hudson; the surrender of the Mississippi River, and the severance of the Confederacy. These were mighty interests, which, had I deemed the evacuation practicable in the sense in which I interpreted General Johnston's instructions, might well have made me hesitate to execute them. I believed it to be in my power to hold Vicksburg. I knew and appreciated the earnest desire of the Government and of the people that it should be held.[59]

Pemberton was apparently willing to assume the role of a passive defender, and leave to outside forces the task of breaking Grant's encirclement, for he added:

> With proper economy of subsistence and ordnance stores, I knew that I could stand a siege. I had a firm reliance on the desire of the President and of General Johnston to do all that could be done to raise a siege. I felt that every effort would be made, and I believed it would be successful.[60]

Pemberton's decision forced Grant into a siege that consumed over a month and a half. While time was important to the Union, the costs to the Confederacy were of much greater

**A Captured Confederate Artillery Park
After the Fall of Vicksburg**

consequence. Pemberton not only lost an army, but also 50,000 arms and other equipment that the Confederacy could ill spare.

Grant's intensive preparation for the siege included every means at his disposal to insure that the Confederate army neither escaped nor received help from a relief force. Standard siege works were constructed with as many as 13 approach trenches under construction at any given time. *(See Atlas Map No. 22b.)* Mining and countermining occupied both the besieged and the besieger, as the armies virtually went "underground." One Union mine, detonated on June 25, killed several Confederates engaged in countermining and opened a temporary breach in the Confederate line, but the result was not promising enough to justify an assault. On July 1, another mine was detonated, but produced results that were no more satisfactory. Despite the impatience of the Government in Washington, Grant was willing to outlast his enemy rather than resort to the type of operations that had proven so costly on May 19 and 22. So close grew the opposing trenches that hand grenades were regularly thrown and frequently thrown back before the crude devices detonated.

Outside the siege lines, Grant successfully parried Confederate efforts to aid Pemberton. Halleck sent reinforcements that swelled Grant's army to over 70,000, a force more than adequate to pen in Pemberton's 30,000 troops as well as to resist any attempt by Johnston's 30,000-man force to lift the siege. Active Federal reconnaissance by division-sized forces to the east and northeast kept Grant informed of Johnston's activity and denied the Confederate commander the opportun-

ity to surprise the Union forces in the rear. By June 22, Grant had received sufficient reinforcements to turn over the command of Sherman's corps to Steele and place Sherman in command of the 30,000 troops that were positioned from Hayne's Bluff to the Big Black River bridge. This force was charged with the mission of defending the rear of the besieging force. *(See Atlas Map No. 23.)* Halfhearted attempts by General Kirby Smith to come to Pemberton's aid from across the river were anticipated by Grant. Consequently, these attempts were thwarted by active patrolling and shelling by Porter's gunboats and by troops from Hurlbut's corps, which was still headquartered in Memphis. The latter drove back the only serious expedition by Smith's troops at Milliken's Bend on June 7.[61]

Early during the siege of the Confederate stronghold, Grant was forced to take a disciplinary action that improved command relations in his army. On May 30, the publicity-conscious McClernand issued a congratulatory order to his troops that subsequently found its way into the newspapers. Claiming that his own corps had played a major role in the operations to date, McClernand was less than generous—if not outright fallacious—in his remarks concerning the contributions of the other two corps. At least that was the way it appeared to McPherson and Sherman, who promptly sent indignant letters of protest to Grant on June 17. Weary of the constant difficulty caused by his incorrigible subordinate and stating, "I cannot afford to quarrel with a man whom I am obliged to command," Grant relieved McClernand of his command on June 18.[62]

Living Quarters of the Vicksburg Besiegers

Pemberton continued to receive dispatches from Johnston that were meant to be encouraging, holding out the hope of relief by Johnston's force. The last of these dispatches was dated July 3:

> I hope to attack the enemy in your front about the 7th, and your co-operation will be necessary. The manner and proper point for you to bring your garrison out must be determined by you from your superior knowledge of the ground and distribution of the enemy's forces. Our firing will show you where we are engaged.[63]

Even as Johnston was writing the message, however, Pemberton was already communicating with Grant about terms of surrender. On July 4, Vicksburg surrendered its garrison of approximately 30,000 men.[64] Port Hudson followed suit, capitulating to Banks on July 9, after the commander of the Confederate garrison there learned of the fate of Vicksburg.

Wasting no time in contemplation of the momentous victory, Grant launched Sherman at the head of an army of nearly 50,000 in pursuit of Johnston. *(See Atlas Map No. 23.)* When the Confederate commander withdrew into Jackson, hoping that Sherman would attack him there, Sherman chose to besiege Johnston and immediately began dispatching forces to encircle the town. Unwilling to lose another Confederate army, Johnston withdrew to the east. After a pursuit of 12 more miles, Grant re-called Sherman when it became evident that a continuation of the operation would be of little value at that time.[65]

The campaign was over. The Mississippi was open all the way to the Gulf, and the Confederacy was split.

Notes

[1]*The War of the Rebellion: A Compilation of the Official Records of the Union and Confederate Armies* (130 vols.; Washington, 1880–1901), Series I, XXIV, Pt. 1, 633–635, 661–662, 668–669. (Hereinafter cited as *OR*. Unless otherwise indicated, all subsequent references to the *OR* are to Series I.); Edwin C. Bearss, *Decision in Mississippi* (Jackson, Miss., 1962), pp. 211–218.

[2]Ulysses S. Grant, *Personal Memoirs of U.S. Grant* (2 vols.; New York, 1885), I, 491–492.

[3]*Ibid.*, p. 492.

[4]Roy Basler (ed.), *The Collected Works of Abraham Lincoln* (9 vols.; Rutgers, N.J., 1953), VI, 326.

[5]Adam Badeau, *Military History of Ulysses S. Grant* (3 vols.; New York, 1885), I, 234. Halleck's dispatch was dated May 11, 1863.

[6]W.C. Church, *Ulysses S. Grant and the Period of National Preservation and Reconstruction* (New York, 1897), p. 164.

[7]Joseph E. Johnston, "Jefferson Davis and the Mississippi Campaign," in *Battles and Leaders of the Civil War,* ed. by Robert Underwood Johnston and Clarence Clough Buel (4 vols.; New York, 1884–1888), III, 478. (Hereinafter cited as *B&L*).

[8]*OR*, XXIV, Pt. 3, 808.

[9]*OR*, XXIV, Pt. 1, 327.

[10]*Ibid.*

[11]*Ibid.*

[12]*Ibid.*, 324–325.

[13]Jefferson Davis, *The Rise and Fall of the Confederate Government* (2 vols.; New York, 1881), II, 404.

[14]*OR*, XXIV, Pt. 3, 870.

[15]Johnston, "Jefferson Davis and the Mississippi Campaign," in *B&L*, III, 479.

[16]*OR*, XXIV, Pt. 3, 876.

[17]Ulysses S. Grant, "The Vicksburg Campaign," in *B&L*, III, 498–503.

[18]Grant, *Personal Memoirs,* I, 499–501; *OR*, XXIV, Pt. 1, 259–260 (Pemberton's report).

[19]Badeau, *Military History of Ulysses S. Grant,* I, 205–210; Grant, *Personal Memoirs,* I, 484.

[20]*OR*, XXIV, Pt. 3, 297.

[21]*Ibid.*

[22]Grant, "The Vicksburg Campaign," in *B&L*, III, 515.

[23]*OR*, XXIV, Pt. 3, 281 (Message from Banks to Grant, May 8); 288–289 (Message from Grant to Banks, May 10); 298–299 (Message from Banks to Grant, May 12).

[24]*OR*, XXIV, Pt. 1, 35–36.

[25]*OR*, XXIV, Pt. 3, 855–856, 861, 862.

[26]*OR*, XXIV, Pt. 1, 736–739 (Gregg's report; reports of subordinates follow it); 704–705 (McPherson's report; reports of subordinates follow it).

[27]Grant, *Personal Memoirs,* I, 500–501.

[28]Grant, "The Vicksburg Campaign," in *B&L*, III, 504; *OR*, XXIV, Pt. 3, 305–308.

[29]*OR*, XXIV, Pt. 1, 36.

[30]*OR*, XXIV, Pt. 3, 309.

[31]Stephen E. Ambrose (ed.), *Struggle for Vicksburg* (Harrisburg, Pa., 1967), p. 22.

[32]Badeau, *Military History of Ulysses S. Grant,* I, 244–245.

[33]Grant, "The Vicksburg Campaign," in *B&L*, III, 505–507; Johnston, "Jefferson Davis and the Mississippi Campaign," in *B&L*, III, 478–479.

[34]*OR*, XXIV, Pt. 1, 36.

[35]Bruce Catton, *Grant Moves South* (Boston, 1960), p. 441, quoting from Jenkin Lloyd Jones, *An Artilleryman's Diary* (Madison, Wis., 1914).

[36]Johnston, "Jefferson Davis and the Mississippi Campaign," in *B&L*, III, 479; Catton, *Grant Moves South,* p. 440.

[37]*OR*, XXIV, Pt. 3, 808, 809; Grant, "The Vicksburg Campaign," in *B&L*, III, 507.

[38]Badeau, *Military History of Ulysses S. Grant,* I, 252.

[39]*Ibid.*, p. 654; *OR*, XXIV, Pt. 1, 36.

[40]*OR*, XXIV, Pt. 1, 262, 263; John C. Pemberton, *Pemberton: Defender of Vicksburg* (Chapel Hill, N.C., 1942), pp. 152–153.

[41]*OR*, XXIV, Pt. 1, 51–53 (Grant's report); 260–263 (Pemberton's report).

[42]*OR*, XXIV, Pt. 3, 317–319; Grant, "The Vicksburg Campaign," in *B&L*, III, 512–513.

[43]Grant, *Personal Memoirs,* I, 519.

[44]*OR*, XXIV, Pt. 1, 264 (Pemberton's report of August 2, 1863).

[45]*Ibid.*

[46]*Ibid.*, 264–265.

[47]Grant, "The Vicksburg Campaign," in *B&L*, III, 513.

[48]Badeau, *Military History of Ulysses S. Grant,* I, 277–278; *OR*, XXIV, Pt. 2, 138; Pemberton, *Pemberton: Defender of Vicksburg,* pp. 168–169.

[49]*OR*, XXIV, Pt. 3, 322; William T. Sherman, *Memoirs of General William T. Sherman* (2 vols.; New York, 1875), I, 324.

[50]Grant, *Personal Memoirs,* I, 524–526; Catton, *Grant Moves South,* pp. 447–448, 533–534.

[51]Grant, *Personal Memoirs,* I, 529–530.

[52]Ambrose, *Struggle for Vicksburg,* p. 49.

[53]Earl Schenk Miers, *The Web of Victory* (New York, 1955), p. 204.

[54]Thomas L. Livermore, *Numbers and Losses in the Civil War in America, 1861–1865* (Boston, 1901), p. 100.

[55]John F.C. Fuller, *The Generalship of Ulysses S. Grant* (New York, 1929), pp. 153–154; Grant, *Personal Memoirs,* I, 531.

[56]Grant, *Personal Memoirs,* I, 534.

[57]A.A. Hoehlung, *Vicksburg: 47 Days of Siege* (Englewood Cliffs, N.J., 1969), pp. 66, 74, 147, 172.

[58]*OR*, XXIV, Pt. 1, 272 (Pemberton's report of August 2, 1863).

[59]*Ibid.*

[60]*Ibid.*

[61]*OR*, XXIV, Pt. 1, 6–7 (Halleck's report); 54–69 (Grant's report); 271–281 (Pemberton's report); Hoehlung, *Vicksburg: 47 Days of Siege,* pp. 277–279; Sherman, *Memoirs,* I, 356–358; Badeau, *Military History of Ulysses S. Grant,* I, 352–379; Grant, *Personal Memoirs,* I, 532–555.

[62]*OR*, XXIV, Pt. 1, 102–104; Badeau, *Military History of Ulysses S. Grant,* I, 362–364. For McClernand's spirited and lengthy rebuttal written in September 1863, see *OR*, XXIV, Pt. 1, 169–186.

[63]*OR*, XXIV, Pt. 3, 987. See also 971–972, and Pt. 1, 280–281.

[64]*OR*, XXIV, Pt. 1, 6–7, 58–59, 283–285.

[65]Badeau, *Military History of Ulysses S. Grant,* I, 385, 393–397.

Lee on the Rappahannock: Fredericksburg and Chancellorsville

7

When Lee withdrew his bloodied and battle-weary troops to the south bank of the Potomac on September 19, 1862, McClellan only timidly probed the Confederate covering force. There was no aggressive pursuit, employing the fresh and preponderant Union forces. The Union commander had let a decisive victory slip through his fingers at the Battle of Antietam; now, as October gave way to November, he re-supplied the Army of the Potomac and reinforced it, but did not order it to attack Lee's much smaller force. Resting his army and wasting valuable time, McClellan rationalized his failures in a letter to his wife: "I have done all that can be asked in twice saving the country."[1]

While Halleck and McClellan argued over the telegraph wires about what the Army of the Potomac should do next, Lee's Army of Northern Virginia was being reorganized. Newly promoted to Lieutenant General, James Longstreet and Thomas J. "Stonewall" Jackson were named to command the I and II Corps, respectively. Stragglers were returned and new recruits were added to brigades of now famous divisions, such as those of Anderson, McLaws, A.P. Hill, and Early. By November, the Army of Northern Virginia numbered over 80,000.[2] Meanwhile, as the armies of McClellan and Lee each expectantly awaited an offensive enemy maneuver, Major General "Jeb" Stuart and about half of his cavalrymen raided Pennsylvania and rode completely around McClellan's army. Stuart's mission was to destroy a key railroad bridge north of Chambersburg. In this he failed, but he did manage to terrorize the citizenry of both Chambersburg and a sleepy little college town some 25 miles to the east, called Gettysburg.[3]

McClellan intended to march into Virginia and hold the passes through the Blue Ridge Mountains in anticipation of attacks by Jackson on his line of communication. By the end of the first week in November, Jackson and his corps were located in the vicinity of Winchester, in Jackson's beloved Shenandoah Valley. Longstreet was in the vicinity of Culpeper Court House. (See Atlas Map No. 24.) The Army of the Potomac had crossed its namesake on October 26, and by November 6 was concentrated roughly in the vicinity of Warrenton, with cavalry picketing the gaps of the Blue Ridge Mountains and extending southward to the Rappahannock. Although he would later argue to the contrary, as the end of the campaigning season neared, it appeared that McClellan had no real plan of attack or scheme of maneuver in mind. On November 7, Lincoln finally lost his patience. As a result, McClellan, one of the most popular generals in the Army, received a telegram from Secretary of War Edwin Stanton, relieving him of command.

A New Commander

McClellan turned command of the Army of the Potomac over to the general whose name was given to the tri-arched bridge over Antietam Creek. Ambrose E. Burnside and McClellan had been friends for years. But even his old friend remarked after Antietam that "[Burnside] is very slow; is not fit to command more than a regiment."[4] Those words must have burned in McClellan's memory as he relinquished command. What would this bewildered, chubby little man do to "his army"? What did the future hold for Burnside and the Army of the Potomac?

Why Lincoln should fire McClellan and appoint Burnside in his place was the question that seemed to be on everyone's mind. For one thing, McClellan had done nothing offensively with the army since Antietam. Lincoln told a visitor at the White House that he had "the slows." The commanding general also was talking with Lincoln's political opponents. Therefore, not only did the immensely popular McClellan

121

Major General Ambrose E. Burnside

lack aggressiveness as an army commander, but he also represented a political threat to Lincoln. Hooker was a possible choice, but he was a good friend of McClellan and thus also a potential political threat. Franklin was also a possibility; but he was a McClellan supporter, a little old, and had not shown any brilliance as a commander. That left Ambrose Burnside. Burnside had achieved some success on independent operations. He was neither as flamboyant as McClellan nor as conceited. And he did not represent a political threat. More important, in Lincoln's opinion, he had a great deal more potential than the others.

By November 9, the new commander had taken charge and was ready to propose a plan of action to the War Department. Burnside felt that if he remained in the Warrenton area, his communications would be threatened by Jackson. By shifting south towards Fredericksburg, he could establish a logistical base at Aquia Creek. The water route to Aquia Landing was secure, and there was a railroad running south from there to Falmouth. Once there, the army should have little trouble in forcing a crossing of the Rappahannock and capturing Fredericksburg. Besides the tactical importance of the town and its railroad and road net leading south towards Richmond, Burnside might have had a psychological reason for wanting to seize it. Fredericksburg was a colonial settlement to which many of the Virginia families traced their lineage. Among these were the Lees. In its conception, Burnside's plan was

as sound as those of his predecessors, and certainly more practical; but it was very complex in its timing, and success would depend greatly on an almost perfect execution of myriad details.

Burnside hoped to achieve tactical surprise by appearing to concentrate his force in the vicinity of Warrenton, when in fact he was concentrating at Aquia Creek and Falmouth. A rapid crossing of the Rappahannock River would put the Army of the Potomac on Lee's flank, thereby threatening Richmond and forcing Lee to react to Burnside's presence. Then, having the initiative, Burnside would attack the inferior and divided Confederate force—Jackson was still in the Valley—destroying the Army of Northern Virginia. While Burnside's plan offered promise, certain details would create trouble if poorly handled. To facilitate a rapid crossing of the water barrier at Fredericksburg, Burnside had requisitioned pontons, and asked that they be hurried forward to Falmouth. That request involved one of those important little details that would have to be attended to with care. As events turned out, it was not.

Lincoln approved Burnside's plan on November 14, and the next day the Army of the Potomac began its movement in the direction of Fredericksburg. *(See Atlas Map No. 24.)* Such a quick response on the part of the army was not ordinary. Perhaps Lincoln had found a commander who could both move with celerity and fight. The march went smoothly and well, and on November 17 the advance Federal units began closing into Falmouth, a mere 500 meters from the wharves of Fredericksburg. The town of Fredericksburg was held by a Confederate force the size of an infantry regiment. Major General Edwin V. Sumner wanted to conduct a hasty river crossing by fording the Rappahannock, but was refused permission. Burnside feared that Sumner's force would be stranded on the far side if the weather turned bad and the river rose; he preferred, instead, to cross his entire force on the ponton bridges that were due to arrive the next day.

Robert E. Lee suspected that the change in commanders would also bring a change in plans for the Army of the Potomac. Accordingly, on November 12 he sent a warning order* to Jackson to be prepared to join Longstreet, and advised Longstreet to be prepared to move toward the Rappahannock in the event that the Union forces shifted in that direction. Lee, however, was in a quandary of the type that confronts any commander faced with the difficult task of interpreting fragments of information about the enemy and arriving at a decision. For the next seven days, as Stuart's cavalry patrolled and gathered information, Lee mulled over Burnside's intentions, not completely convinced that Fredericksburg was his objective. Although he had earlier thought it would be more

---

*A commander uses a warning order to provide his subordinate with preliminary notice of a more detailed order that is to follow.

feasible to stand behind the North Anna River, by the nineteenth he had all of Longstreet's corps enroute to Fredericksburg, expecting to defend there. Perhaps hoping to use Jackson as a flank threat, however, he delayed directing that commander to join Longstreet for several more days.[5]

One of Ambrose Burnside's foibles was that once committed to an idea or plan, he had difficulty changing it. The pontons did not arrive on November 18, or on the following day either; in fact, because of an oversight in Washington, the pontons did not arrive until November 25. The week's delay completely changed the military situation. The tactical surprise and speed of execution that was such an important part of the plan of attack had been lost. If Burnside had been flexible in his execution, he could have marched upriver and crossed his entire force—or at least a large portion of it—on the eighteenth or nineteenth, and attacked a vastly inferior force. Longstreet's entire corps did not arrive at Fredericksburg until November 21. If Burnside had forced a crossing at Kelly's Ford, he might have caught the flank of Longstreet's corps in its march toward Fredericksburg, or at least secured the tactical advantage of interior lines by placing the Army of the Potomac between Longstreet at Fredericksburg and Jackson in the Valley. However, Burnside did nothing. By waiting for the pontons to arrive and for the railroad to Aquia Landing to be repaired and improved, he wasted valuable time. At one point, he considered conducting a crossing on November 26. As he only had enough pontons for one bridge, however, the plan was discarded as being too risky.

By November 30, Jackson and his corps had arrived, and Lee had placed the Army of Northern Virginia in a defensive position along the heights that ran parallel to the river on its western side. It was obvious to Lee that Burnside, if he were to do anything at all, would try to force a crossing of the Rappahannock either at Fredericksburg or south of the town, where an alluvial plain ran for about two kilometers from the river's edge to the bottom of some high ground. Behind Fredericksburg, Longstreet's I Corps occupied the high ground known as Marye's Heights. Longstreet's line ran south from Marye's Heights along a ridge to to an area where Jackson's II Corps was digging trenches. Jackson's corps was deployed in depth, while Longstreet had depth at Marye's Heights, but his line thinned farther south to the point where Pickett's and Hood's divisions were almost in a linear position. Major General Jubal A. Early's division was about 10 miles south of Fredericksburg at Skinker's Neck, and Major General Daniel Harvey Hill's division was approximately 10 miles farther downstream at Port Royal. Lee's army, therefore, was spread out over a front more than 20 miles long, with the largest part of the army in the vicinity of Fredericksburg and large detachments at likely crossing sites north and south of the town. (*Map 25a shows the dispositions thirteen days later; but*

except for Early's and D.H. Hill's divisions, those dispositions approximate Lee's initial position just described.) Because of the heights they occupied, the Confederate forces were able to keep the Federals under constant observation. Lee had a pretty good idea of Burnside's intentions, and any major movement of Union troops would either be observed by the Confederates or reported by rebel citizens on the eastern bank of the Rappahannock.

One of Burnside's methods of intelligence collection was much more sophisticated than those of Lee, although not nearly as effective. Professor T.S.C. Lowe used balloons for aerial observation of the enemy's movements, bivouacs, and dispositions. His balloonists reported to Burnside the disposition of Early's and Hill's divisions at Skinker's Neck and Port Royal, respectively.[6] (*See Atlas Map No. 24.*) This intelligence was accurate enough, but Burnside placed too much reliance on Lowe's men, who not only were marginally effective operating over wooded country, but also became favorite targets of enemy sharpshooters and artillerists. Moreover, Burnside failed to aggressively reconnoiter on the ground to more accurately ascertain the extent of Lee's position. As a result, although he had originally planned to cross the river at Skinker's Neck, Burnside apparently concluded that the Confederates were concentrated largely in the vicinity of Port Royal and Skinker's Neck, with their left flank thinning out toward Fredericksburg. He thus decided to make multiple crossings at and just downstream of the latter town—right into the teeth of Lee's defenses.

One of Professor T.S.C. Lowe's Balloons

To facilitate the command and control of the army, Burnside had reorganized it into Grand Divisions, each of which was composed of two or more corps. The Right Grand Division, under the command of Major General Edwin V. Sumner, consisted of Major General Darius N. Couch's II Corps and Brigadier General Orlando B. Willcox's IX Corps. The Center Grand Division, under Major General Joseph Hooker, was comprised of Brigadier General George Stoneman's III Corps and Major General Daniel Butterfield's V Corps. Major General William B. Franklin's Left Grand Division was made up of I Corps under Major General John Reynolds and the VI Corps of Major General Wiliam F. Smith. Initially, a Reserve Corps was formed, and probably should have been called the Reserve Grand Division, because it, too, consisted of two corps: the XI Corps, commanded by Major General Franz Sigel, and the XII Corps, under Major General Henry W. Slocum. Still on the march from the north, neither of the reserve corps would arrive at Fredericksburg in time to participate in the battle.

There were 312 artillery pieces in battalions and separate batteries scattered throughout that part of the army and its reserve at Fredericksburg. The artillery reserve was under the command of Brigadier General Henry J. Hunt. Brigadier General George D. Bayard was in command of the misused and misunderstood cavalry.

Facing the 117,000 Federals available for combat, Lee had 73,000 troops present for duty.[7] As the early December days passed, Lee's army dug and fortified, shifted artillery, cleaned weapons, and prepared to fight a defensive battle.

Fredericksburg

In a book published in 1846, Lieutenant Henry W. Halleck noted that "the passage of a river by main force, against an enterprising and active enemy on the opposite shore is always an operation of the greatest difficulty, and not infrequently accompanied with the most bloody results."* He could not have more accurately predicted the outcome of Burnside's deliberate crossing of the Rappahannock River.

Soldiers on both sides of the Rappahannock were aware that Burnside was going to make a deliberate river crossing at Fredericksburg. When Jackson's corps arrived on November 30, it became obvious that Burnside would have a difficult

time accomplishing his mission. However, Burnside knew that the crossing would have to be made, and made without further delay. On November 28, Lincoln had traveled to Aquia Creek to discuss the lack of action with Burnside. Although no minutes of the meeting were taken, we may assume that Burnside was given some firm advice about his mission, and that he was told to proceed as quickly as possible. We know that the meeeting was long, because Burnside accompanied the President back to Washington to continue their discussion.[8] Perhaps Lincoln, Halleck, and Burnside found some consolation in the fact that the Army of the Potomac was half again the size of Lee's army, that it was better equipped and supplied, and that its morale was high. Lee's men, however, more than made up for their lack of numbers in the defensive position they held—and Burnside did not have his entire army concentrated at Fredericksburg.

Terrain and Weather

There are some obstacles to the tactical movement of troops that may be described as "seasonal obstacles." At Fredericksburg, the seasonal obstacles were the canal north of the town and Hazel Run and Deep Run south of the town. *(See Atlas Map No. 25.)* If these water obstacles were covered by fire in the summer months, they could be crossed after the firepower was suppressed, or—if casualties were acceptable—under fire. All three obstacles were chest deep, and therefore fordable. In December 1862, however, the cold weather became a limiting factor in the crossing of these streams. The subfreezing temperatures that nipped at the ears and fingers of the soldiers meant that the army would suffer more casualties from frostbite and exposure in crossing those streams than it could accept.* Indeed, the casualties from the elements and enemy fire would virtually total 100 percent of the men making the crossing. Thus, the obstacles that in summer would have presented almost a pleasant diversion to the sweltering soldier in blue were now barriers that forbade his lateral movement on the enemy's front. The December weather, however, also offered a helping hand to Burnside's army. The bitter cold of the winter morning moving over the warmer water of the Rappahannock River created a thick fog. This natural blanket would conceal the engineers as they assembled their ponton bridges on the eastern side.

While the fog provided an advantage for Burnside's engineers by concealing them from the sight of the Confederates, the sound of the engineers' labors carried to the posts that had been established along the riverfront. Longstreet had sol-

*As a young officer, Halleck earned a reputation as one of the Army's more promising intellectuals. The excerpt printed here is from his *Elements of Military Art and Science* (New York, 1846), p. 356. Halleck resigned from the Army shortly after the publication of this book. Returning to the service upon the outbreak of the Civil War, he soon gained high rank. At the time of the Fredericksburg Campaign, Halleck was serving as General-in-Chief in Washington. Throughout his life, he remained a man of intellectual interests and tastes, if not always the most practical of leaders.

*In *Fiasco at Fredericksburg,* Vorin Whan refers to inch-thick ice and temperatures of 24° F.[9]

diers in the town, observing the Yankees during the day and listening to them at night. It was also not unusual for the common soldier to improve upon his individual logistics by swapping coffee for tobacco. The men who were assigned to these posts were usually involved in the forbidden practice of fraternizing with the enemy. Sometimes, hard intelligence came from the idle chatter. Besides his soldiers, James Longstreet also had several thousand eyes and ears working for him along his front; the citizens of Fredericksburg were watching and listening.

While Marye's Heights dominated the town of Fredericksburg, across the Rappahannock River there was another important ridge called Stafford Heights. *(See Atlas Map No. 25a.)* Here, the Union chief of artillery, Henry Hunt, had placed nearly 150 of his heaviest guns. Stafford Heights commanded the terrain on both sides of the Rappahannock River, giving the Union gunners a definite advantage in observation. However, their artillery had insufficient range to reach either the Confederate batteries on Marye's Heights or the stone wall at its base.

While Lee's army had less artillery than the Army of the Potomac, it had an advantage in the superior positioning of its guns. The batteries that bristled on Marye's Heights had been placed there by Longstreet's acting chief of artillery, Colonel E. Porter Alexander. The guns were placed in depth and in revetments for protection against the superior numbers of Union artillery pieces. When Longstreet inspected the artillery position in late November, Alexander remarked: "General, we cover that ground now so well that we will comb it as with a fine-tooth comb. A chicken could not live in that field when we open on it."[10] His prediction was to prove very accurate.

Below Alexander's guns, in the town of Fredericksburg—the ancestral home of Washington, Custis, and Lee—Brigadier General William Barksdale's men prepared for battle. Barksdale's brigade of 1,600 Mississippi riflemen moved into Fredericksburg with the mission of fortifying the riverfront to prevent Federal troops, principally the engineers, from building ponton bridges across the river. Barksdale had led his brigade at Antietam only a few months before. He was a lawyer by profession and a newspaper publisher by avocation. At the time of Mississippi's secession, William Barksdale had been a congressman in the United States House of Representatives; he promptly resigned and became a soldier in the militia of his state. Barksdale loved a fire fight,* and was brave beyond reason or necessity. He had fought in the Mexican War, and was idealized by his men as a fearless leader, a superb tactician, and a man who would volunteer his command for a difficult assignment. Preparing for battle, his

infantrymen cut loopholes in colonial buildings along the Rappahannock River and dug rifle pits in the black silt of its western bank. The Mississippians were the forward edge of Lee's defense.

Behind the town, at the base of Marye's Heights, was a sunken road running parallel to the hill. *(See Atlas Map No. 25a.)* On the eastern side of the sunken road was a stone wall three or four feet high. The road ran north-to-south for several hundred yards. Immediately behind the road rose Marye's Heights. In front of it was a clearing of several hundred feet, a ditch, and then the brick houses of Fredericksburg. A man standing in the road could easily see any movement on the field as far north as the canal and as far south as Hazel Run. He was also covered and concealed from enemy observation, and—if he rested his rifled musket on the stone wall—he could aim quite accurately. Farther behind him on the hill were rifle pits and trenches concealing more riflemen. Behind them and on top of the hill was the artillery, dug in, with guns aimed at the possible crossing sites. Brigadier General Thomas R.R. Cobb's brigade occupied the position behind the stone wall. Cobb was a good soldier and was well liked by his men. He kept them occupied and warm in the December cold, steadily improving the defensive position. If the Yankees attacked his position, Cobb was confident that his brigade could whip two or three times its number. He also knew that the enemy almost never did what you wanted him to do. Nevertheless, it would be clear to the Federal commander that to attack as strong a position as Cobb's would be suicidal.

Late on the evening of December 9, Burnside notified Halleck that the crossing would be made under the cover of darkness the next night. His complete ignorance of the true disposition of Lee's forces was revealed by his statement "that a large force of the enemy is now concentrated in the vicinity of Port Royal, its left resting near Fredericksburg, which we hope to turn." The commanding general sent the telegram in the clear, through the telegraph office at Aquia Creek. Halleck answered the next day, neither approving of nor disagreeing with the plan, but rebuking Burnside for his lack of security.[11]

Barksdale, Longstreet, and, in turn, Lee, knew of the intended crossing almost as soon as it began. The sounds of pontons creeking, bolts being tightened, planks being unloaded, and men cursing as they smashed fingers in their labors wafted across the icy Rappahannock. Burnside was finally coming.

Burnside's Bridges

Burnside's chief engineer issued a brief, clear order to his troops concerning the sites of the bridges that were to be constructed. Two would be built at Fredericksburg, one south

*A fire fight is an exchange of small arms fire.

of an old canalboat bridge, and three more below the mouth of Deep Run.[12] *(See Atlas Map No. 25a.)* It was the sound of construction at the northern bridges that Barksdale's riflemen heard the night of December 10. Although the darkness and fog initially shielded the Union engineers from Confederate fire, as construction continued and the bridges reached midstream, the engineers began to suffer casualties. The Mississippians were firing at sounds, and were enjoying some success. As the rising sun began to burn off the fog, the Confederate rifle fire became more deadly. At ranges of less than 100 yards, the unarmed and exposed pontoniers had little chance. They were continually driven back to the eastern side, and as many times surged back in an attempt to finish their work. By the middle of the morning, however, it was clear that the Union soldiers could not complete their work under the withering rifle fire being delivered by Barksdale's men. Although Longstreet's artillery could reach the bridges, it did not fire for fear of hitting the Mississippi riflemen or the town itself.

Something had to be done to rejuvenate the stalled operation. Barksdale's men had stopped the construction of the bridges with their accurate fire. Their positions in the houses and the rifle pits protected them from return fire. Help might

have come from another quarter had Burnside reacted promptly. By 9:00 a.m., two of the bridges in Franklin's area had been completed, and Confederate pickets across the river had been dispersed. In spite of the Deep Run and Hazel Run obstacles, determined infantry moving northward along the river might have hastened the construction of the bridges by defending against the Confederate riflemen. But no order was issued to this effect.

At 10:00 a.m., Hunt's artillery began to shell the town. Solid shot was used to knock down pre-Revolutionary brick walls and collapse the buildings in which the marksmen hid. Shells were interspersed with the solid shot. Soon, smoke from burning buildings mixed with the fog, further cloaking the Mississippians from the gaze of the Federal cannoneers. More than 9,000 artillery rounds fell on the hapless town. Although the fire and destruction in Fredericksburg was quite severe, it resulted in little more than the razing of the historic town; Barksdale's men maintained their position and continued to fire upon the pontoniers.[13] It was another of those cases, frequently noted in history, of determined, well dug-in defenders not being dislodged by fire alone.

Artillery continued to pound Fredericksburg well into the afternoon. At about 2:00 p.m., the Confederates along the

Union Engineers Attempt to Lay a Ponton Bridge Under the Cover of a Heavy Artillery Bombardment

**Federal Infantry and Artillery Are Rafted
Across the Rappahannock River**

river noticed boats loaded with Federal infantry leaving the eastern side. The blue-clad soldiers swung the balance against the riflemen from Mississippi. Ever so slowly, the sniper fire slackened, and the Rebel line backed away from the river. As the fire lessened, the engineers went back to work and the bridges were extended across the river to the bridgehead now held by the Federal infantry. By 4:30 p.m., Barksdale's men had dropped back several hundred yards. McLaws then sent an order to Barksdale to withdraw the brigade and abandon the town. Barksdale was a fighting general and wanted to stay and punish the Yankee infantry; the town had been shelled, and Barksdale was ready for battle. McLaws repeated the order, and Barksdale reluctantly complied.[14]

For more than 12 hours, the Mississippians had delayed Burnside's northern wing. The blue infantry now occupied the burning town, but they had yet to face the full strength of Lee's dug-in legions on the high ground west of the Rappahannock.

The Attack of the Union Left Wing

With the coming of dawn on December 12, fog hung heavily in the valley, allowing the Union troops to cross the completed bridges in relative safety. Lee had not determined exactly where the main attack would come, but it was obvious that it would be launched either at Fredericksburg or at the bridgehead south of Deep Run. At any rate, having been granted a respite by Burnside's reluctance to exploit Franklin's bridges

earlier, Lee's army spent the day preparing to repel the imminent attack. Positions were strengthened and reserves were brought closer to the Confederate lines. It was not until late in the afternoon, however, that Lee directed D.H. Hill and Early to move their divisions from the south to Fredericksburg.

Lee positioned himself and his staff on a hill near the center of his lines. (Today, this hill is known as Lee's Hill.) From here he could observe firsthand the battlefield to the north and south. His staff would be able to reach Longstreet and Jackson quickly, and any information that his subordinates needed to send him could easily be dispatched by messenger. By 1862, technical improvements were being made in military communications. Field telegraphs, heliographs, semaphores, and pyrotechnics were all being employed to send messages. In battle, however, the messenger, either on foot or on horseback, was still the most reliable means of communication. Lee had this in mind when he selected his location for the command post.

While Lee was making sure that all orders would be timely and clear during the battle, his counterpart in the Army of the Potomac was having trouble issuing clear and concise orders. On December 12, Ambrose Burnside issued only verbal orders for the Federal concentration, and these were vague and, in part, conflicting. Early the next morning, he followed these orders with a written one that was confusing at best. *(See Atlas Map No. 25a.)* The order directed Franklin to send one division to seize the high ground in the vicinity of Hamilton "if possible," while readying his entire command to move down the old Richmond Road. Sumner was to move a division or more westward to seize Marye's Heights. Burnside hoped that the seizure of the two points would compel Lee to evacuate the entire position. Clearly, Burnside still did not realize that he was attacking Lee's entire army. He remembered the troops located at Port Royal and Skinker's Neck, but was unaware that they had rejoined Lee's army the previous night. The idea of two grand divisions attacking two widely separated points—that is, not attacking in concert—was unworthy of a man with the Union commander's experience.

Burnside had not actively sought information concerning the enemy's strength, weaknesses, disposition, probable course of action, or anything else of any military value. The balloons were of little use in the heavy fog, but there was the cavalry, and it was capable of gathering the necessary intelligence on which to base a sound decision. From December 11 until December 15, Sumner's brigade of cavalry fed and groomed their horses and never even crossed the river. Although one of Franklin's brigades crossed the river, it did little else; unfortunately, its commander, Bayard, was killed by a shell fragment. Hooker's brigade of cavalry, under the command of Brigadier General William W. Averell, moved to the rear of Butterfield's corps and remained there for the duration of the campaign. Burnside simply assumed that the attack by the two infantry divisions would be successful, that the Grand Divisions would push aside the Confederates, and that there were few Confederates in front of him. He made these assumptions without knowing anything about the enemy's strength and disposition.

Major General George Gordon Meade's division was selected by Reynolds to lead the attack on the high ground in the vicinity of Hamilton (better known as Prospect Hill), a position held in depth and fortified by Jackson's II Corps. Meade's division would be followed and supported by the divisions of Brigadier General Abner Doubleday and Brigadier General John Gibbon. Each division was supported by a battery of artillery. Henry Hunt had consolidated the rest of the guns under the artillery reserve and personally placed them where they could best support the mission of the army. This resulted in 147 guns being placed on Stafford Heights, all of which were rifled and, supposedly, had the range to support Sumner's and Franklin's attacks on the Confederate positions. (Hunt would complain after the battle that the projectiles were not as accurate at long range as they should have been—indeed, some "shorts" did land among the Federal troops.[15]) The plan, therefore, required that Meade move across the plain toward the low hill that was his division's objective without either the advantage of cavalry for reconnaissance missions or the direct control of sufficient long-range artillery.

The Union attack began at about 8:30 a.m. on December 13. *(See Atlas Map No. 25a.)* Supported by Gibbon on the right and Doubleday on the left, Meade's leading brigades reached the Old Richmond Road, where they began receiving enfilading fire from Confederate artillery positioned to the south. The brigades of Meade, and then Gibbon, went on line parallel to the road as the rebel guns tore into their ranks from the flank.

While Meade's men had marched out of the mists along the Rappahannock that morning, Major John Pelham, with the horse artillery of Stuart's cavalry, had observed them from his position on Jackson's far right. Pelham conceived a seemingly foolhardy plan to take some guns and move forward of the Confederate lines to fire on the flank of the advancing Yankees. He decided to use two guns: a Blakely rifle and a trusty 12-pounder Napoleon. The dashing young artilleryman led his force swiftly toward the advancing blue infantry, reined in near a crossroad on the Old Richmond Road, and quickly unlimbererd his guns. Opening his cannonade with solid shot, Pelham quickly caused confusion in the Federal ranks.

Pelham's position was compromised with the first puff of white smoke from his guns. Union guns swung around to meet this unexpected threat from the flank. Pelham's only rifled piece, the Blakely, fired one shot that broke the axle of a Union gun, but then was immediately put out of action

itself by a battery volley. Pelham's cannoneers redoubled their efforts with the faster firing Napoleon smoothbore. Meade's attack slowed and then stopped.

From his vantage point on the hill in the center of his line, Lee watched Pelham and his courageous cannoneers. "It is glorious to see such courage in one so young," Lee remarked to his aides,[16] as the shot and shell ploughed the ground among the Rebel gunners. A messenger from Stuart finally convinced Pelham to return to his own lines. He was running out of ammunition, and had few men left to continue firing. So, amidst bursting shells from the Federal artillery, Pelham withdrew his section of artillery, leaving the soldiers in gray and blue with an indelible memory of his bravery.

As Pelham and his horse artillery made their escape, the fire of the Federal guns west of the river was directed toward the high ground that was the infantry's objective. The bombardment was severe. The fog that had covered the valley earlier in the morning had lifted, and the red earth of Virginia, which had been disturbed to create battleworks, was visible through the foliage. No matter how intense the fire from Federal batteries, Jackson had instructed his artillery not to fire, so as to conceal their positions until they could devastate the Union infantry. For more than an hour, the Union batteries bombarded the hill. Not receiving any rounds in return, save for those fired during Pelham's escapade, they assumed that the Confederate batteries were out of action. The order to advance again was sent to the infantry. First regimental and then brigade lines formed and moved forward. *(See Atlas Map No. 25a.)*

Closer and closer came the blue horde. Then came the command to fire—that moment for which the Confederate gunners had waited. The Napoleons sent their deadly missiles into the massed infantry. Once more, Pelham, this time reinforced with guns from Jackson's corps, opened fire on the flank. Again and again, powder and shot were rammed home. Again and again, lanyard and striker were inserted, and guns were aimed, fired, and rolled back into position. The Federal ranks began to disintegrate under the pounding of the Confederate batteries. Slowly—more slowly than they had advanced—the Union divisions fell back out of range. Considering the pounding these men had taken, the orderly withdrawal was a tribute to their spirit and courage. They had gained some ground, and that was not to be lost. "Just time for the artillery to come up, and then we'll give it another go,"[17] they thought.

A few minutes after noon, Meade began his advance again. Gibbon's division was on his right and slightly to the rear. Doubleday's division was now facing the left flank, to guard against Stuart's cavalry. This way, Meade could concentrate on the attack and not worry about his flanks. Even so, he had his reserve brigade face to the left just in case Stuart attacked. For almost an hour, the long thin lines of Reynolds'

I Corps pushed across the plain toward the railroad and then into the woods at the base of the low hills. Reynolds had told Meade to head for a wooded spit of land that jutted out onto the plain. This point had been chosen because it could be clearly seen by the subordinate commanders and the men. It would be easy for a company commander to point out the site, so that if the chain of command were disrupted by casualties, the private soldier could press on to the final objective.

Unfortunately for the Confederates, that particular part of the line had been left undefended, and was also on the boundary between the brigades of Lane and Archer of Major General Ambrose P. Hill's division. Although the swampy area was normally considered an obstacle to large-scale troop movements, the same cold air that had turned Hazel Run and the canal from summer diversions into major obstacles had brought fairly firm footing to the waterlogged terrain. Meade's infantrymen moved into the woods and started up the hill. They fired individually now, no longer resorting to the commanded volley fire* that had been used earlier, during the crossing of the plain. Almost before anyone knew what was happening, the Federal troops crashed into Brigadier General Maxcy Gregg's brigade, positioned in the second line of defense. Within an hour, Meade had captured approximately 3,000 prisoners.

While Meade was having success, Gibbon's division was held up at the tree line, and a gap began to develop between the two units. When the separation became apparent to the Confederates, Early launched a vicious counterattack against Meade and Gibbon.[18] The Union infantrymen abandoned the same wood line they had so gloriously assaulted a half an hour earlier and stumbled down the hill, out of the tree line, and onto the open plain, bolting toward the railroad. The cheering, yelling Rebels were close on their heels.

As the battered elements of the two divisions fell back across the plain with the Confederates in hot pursuit, Brigadier General David B. Birney's Union division formed a line on the Old Richmond Road, and then launched an attack. This saving attack caught the Confederates on the flanks and slowly drove them back. The battle on the southern flank was almost over. Jackson tried to counterattack later in the afternoon, but the massed artillery of the Federals broke up the operation before it could be launched. The sanguinary Jackson, wanting to destroy the Army of the Potomac, remarked, "I did not think that a little red earth would have frightened them. I am sorry that they are gone. I am sorry I fortified."[19] In Longstreet's sector, the Confederates were not sorry that they had fortified. There, one of the bitterest lessons of the Civil War was being taught in front of the stone wall.

A Field of Carnage

Farther north, Sumner's attack of Marye's Heights had been delayed by the fog. Led by Major General William H. French's division, it did not commence until 11:00 a.m.—almost three hours after Meade had begun his attack. As the Union infantrymen marched out of the rubble-strewn streets of Fredericksburg, they were channelized by the terrain. *(See Atlas Map No. 25a.)* The drainage ditch running from the canal north of the town to Hazel Run formed an obstacle that the troops were forced to cross by means of two narrow bridges. Once over the bridges, French's men had to traverse a field several hundred yards wide. Before the day was over, this field would become a scene of carnage.

The slaughter began while Sumner's divisions massed in the streets of Fredericksburg. This mass of blue was a target that Alexander's gunners could not resist. As the fog lifted and exposed the Federal divisions, Confederate artillery slammed volley after volley into their ranks.* Battered by the Confederates, the Union infantry looked up the streets at the two narrow bridges, the open field at the base of Marye's Heights, and a stone wall that concealed a sunken road. To hundreds of men, it would be the last thing they would ever see. Behind the wall, in the sunken road, Cobb's infantrymen prepared to wreak havoc. Rifled muskets, deadly accurate at several hundred yards, were leveled at belt-buckle height.

French's division poured over the bridges and onto the field. The water in the ditch was only chest deep, but was not realistically fordable because of the severe cold. Later that day, some men would try to ford the obstacle, only to die from exposure.[20] The first ranks from French's division deployed from column into line as they left the bridges. They ran forward toward the apparently low wall at the base of the hill, having no way of knowing that the wall was four feet high on the far side. With shells bursting above their heads and within their ranks, they charged across the gentle, undulating field. Then a line of orange flame appeared for an instant a few inches above the wall, soon disappearing in a cloud of white smoke. The sound of lead balls piercing flesh and smashing bone could be heard among the Federal infantry. Behind the wall, the men of Cobb's brigade reloaded before their enemy could recover from the initial shock. Caught in the open by the artillery on Marye's Heights and Cobb's riflemen behind the stone wall, French's men sought cover. Slight depressions were soon filled with infantrymen hugging the frozen ground for survival. Others found safety behind those already dead, and listened with horror to the thud of lead bullets striking their grisly parapets.

*Volley fire occurs when the troops of a unit fire their weapons in unison, usually on command.

*As noted earlier, Alexander's batteries on Marye's Heights could fire with impunity because Hunt's guns on Stafford Heights could not bring effective counterbattery fire against them.

After the Battle of Fredericksburg, Federal Dead Lie in Front of the Stone Wall at the Base of Marye's Heights

In rapid succession, French's division was followed by those of Major General Winfield S. Hancock, Major General Oliver O. Howard, and Brigadier General Samuel D. Sturgis. These Union soldiers bravely charged across the torn field already strewn with dead and wounded, only to suffer the same fate. One regimental commander, watching the fruitless attacks against the stone wall, noted that the regiments slowed down in the field to fire a volley before closing on the wall. He decided that his men would fix bayonets and charge without firing a volley.[21] They rushed across the field in line, leaping over their fallen comrades and yelling their lungs out—but they only got to within fifty yards of the wall before the assault sputtered out.

The Union attack was now stalled on both fronts. Although Franklin received at least one order to renew the attack, he remained inactive, and Burnside apparently acquiesced. Taking advantage of this situation, Lee moved Major General George Pickett's division and one brigade of Major General John B. Hood's division to Marye's Heights in time to help defend against the attack that Burnside renewed at about 3:30 p.m. *(See Atlas Map No. 25b.)* Despite Hooker's protests, this attack was made by two of his divisions. In all, on December 13, fourteen separate assaults were launched against the wall. All failed. Union casualties in front of the wall numbered almost 6,000.

All through the night of December 13, the moaning and cries of the wounded could be heard by soldiers on both sides. With the coming of dawn, the Union soldiers could see the bodies of their comrades lying on the field. They were stark white. Some of the Confederate soldiers had stripped the bodies during the night—warm clothing was scarce in the Army of Northern Virginia. Lee's men were not without compassion, however. On the morning of the fourteenth, one of them was unable to stand the cries of the wounded. Without a flag of truce, Sergeant Richard Kirkland of the 2nd South Carolina Volunteers leaped over the wall and began to give the Union wounded the water that they craved. Not a shot was fired, and when he finally went back over the wall to his regiment, Kirkland was cheered by the watching Federal soldiers.[22]

The Aftermath

Burnside wanted to renew the attack on December 14 and, in fact, had planned on leading the first assault against Marye's Heights himself.[23] His subordinates, however, dissuaded him from making such a futile and wasteful effort. During the afternoon, a truce was arranged and the dead were buried. The battle of Fredericksburg was over.

On the night of the fourteenth, the Army of the Potomac skillfully withdrew across the Rappahannock. Burnside removed all of his troops and supplies—down to the last foot of telegraph wire—and then pulled in the ponton bridges. When Lee awakened the next morning, he was surprised to learn that the Union forces were gone.

Back across the river, the Army of the Potomac nursed the wounds that had been sustained during another savage demonstration of the newly gained supremacy of the tactical defense. Once again—and more clearly than at Antietam—defenders who were dug in on defensible terrain had used rifled small arms and carefully directed artillery with deadly effect, decimating the attacking infantrymen who advanced in outmoded formations in the open. The carnage at Fredericksburg, particularly in the northern sector defended by Longstreet, illustrates the problem that the attacker faced during the entire war—how to close to and break through an enemy position that was sited behind field fortifications.

In the half century since the Napoleonic wars, technology had given the advantage to the defense. The rifled muzzle-loader gave infantrymen a weapon capable of keeping artillery beyond that close range from which it could bash holes in defenders' positions, and fortifications kept enemy small arms fire from being very effective. However, technology had not yet provided explosive shells that had reliable fuzes and ranges capable of enabling field artillery to suppress enemy batteries or mask fortifications at long distances. Under these circumstances, the infantry suffered appalling casualties while attempting to breach defensive positions of the Fredericksburg variety. Brute force and sheer weight of numbers were no longer enough, even if an army was willing to take the heavy casualties; tactics would have to change, as, indeed, they gradually did. But without technological assistance, tactical innovation alone could not solve the attacker's problem. That fact, too, became very clear. Longstreet, perhaps before Lee, saw how the tactical defense could be exploited in the right circumstances. Ultimately, Lee would use it with great success when he had no strategic alternative left. Even at Fredericksburg, however, an appreciation of the strength of his defensive position may well have influenced Lee to leave the initiative to his opponent after Burnside's bloody repulse.

Although Robert E. Lee had been furious at Burnside for destroying Fredericksburg, the Confederate general had allowed the defeated army to escape intact. Lee's critics properly have been hard in condemning his want of vigilance on the night of December 14. As for his failure to counterattack on the fourteenth, it is probable that, even though the early morning fog might have partly nullified the effectiveness of Hunt's guns, Lee feared the Federal artillery that had blunted Jackson's earlier effort. Equally important, Lee half expected Burnside to renew the attack; fighting solely on the defensive, the odds remained in Lee's favor. When Burnside failed to attack, the chagrined Lee remarked: "Had I divined that was to have been his only effort he would have had more of it."[24] Before too many more months elapsed, he would get another chance.

As 1862 came to a close, Lee's men continued to improve their positions in the hills above the Rappahannock River. In Longstreet's sector, the trenches and lunettes were extremely sophisticated. That general wanted his earthworks to be able to withstand an attack by multiple corps while being held by only one Confederate division.[25] Visiting him one day in January, Jackson was astonished by Longstreet's fortifications, and immediately began to prepare similar ones in his sector.

Meanwhile, on the Union side of the river there was indecision and discontent. Finally, on January 20, 1863, after consulting Washington, Burnside started his army north along the Rappahannock in an attempt to turn Lee's position on the left. As the ill-fated Union soldiers trudged along, a January thaw came. The frozen ground turned to mud under the feet, hooves, and wheels of the moving army. Cold rain pelted the soldiers, soaking them, their gear, and their bivouacs. Morale reached a new low. Burnside, now completely dispirited, sent the army into winter quarters. On January 25, Lincoln relieved him, Sumner, and Franklin, and placed Joseph Hooker in command of the Army of the Potomac. In the war against Lee's Army of Northern Virginia, a new phase was about to begin.

Major General Joseph Hooker

Chancellorsville

Hooker had not had an easy time of it during his military career. Graduating from West Point in 1837 barely in the upper half of his class, Hooker entered the artillery and served in Florida in the Seminole War. Like many of his contemporaries, he participated in the Mexican War, wherein he had a personal confrontation with Winfield Scott. In 1853, Hooker resigned and took up farming in California. With the coming of the Civil War in 1861, Hooker was one of the first to offer his military skills to his country. He was turned down repeatedly. Eventually, Lincoln had him appointed as a brigadier general of volunteers and commander of a brigade. The man had a very disagreeable personality and a reputation as an intriguer; he had never been popular with his West Point classmates. Moreover, because of his sharp tongue, caustic remarks, constant criticism (especially of his military superiors), and ruthless ambition for promotion and more prestigious military responsibilities, his contemporaries distrusted him. Yet for all his faults, Joe Hooker was also known as a man with great courage in battle, and had a reputation as a superb combat leader.[26] The question in the minds of many, however, was whether Hooker was the best man for the job.

Hooker's Reforms and Lee's Preparations

Low morale, desertions, a deteriorating administration, bad food, cold weather, and the need for a reorganization of the army were the initial problems facing Hooker in January 1863. To complicate matters, Halleck informed him that the administration in Washington wanted the army to take the offensive against Lee as soon as possible. Hooker interpreted "as soon as possible" to mean "as soon as practicable." He had an army to bring back from the brink of despair first, a fact Lincoln had appreciated when he warned Hooker:

> I much fear that the spirit which you have aided to infuse into the army, of criticizing their commander and withholding confidence from him, will now turn upon you. . . . Neither you nor Napoleon, if he were alive again, could get any good out of an army while such a spirit prevails in it.[27]

The ranking generals who had fought at Fredericksburg were gone, with the exception of Hooker. If Hooker had had any effect on the army's morale with his almost insubordinate actions and talk, it is ironic justice that he was called upon to solve a problem he may have helped cause.

Hooker was fortunate in that his newly appointed chief of staff had survived the shake up following the fiasco of Fredericksburg and the "Mud-March." Daniel Butterfield was a graduate of Union College and had been a merchant in New York City before the war. Upon the commencement of hostilities, he had enlisted, and soon was commissioned in the volunteers. Engaging in combat during the Peninsular Campaign of 1862, he was wounded. (In 1892, he was awarded the Medal of Honor for his actions at Gaines' Mill in 1862.) He commanded the V Corps at Fredericksburg, and was involved in the ill-fated attacks on Marye's Heights. Butterfield had also composed the bugle call known ever since as "Taps."[28] He and Hooker got along well right from the start. Hooker was the professional soldier, and Butterfield was the "organization man"; together, they were a good team and exactly what the Army of the Potomac needed.

Grand Divisions became a thing of the past when Hooker's reorganization began to take effect. The new Army of the Potomac would be comprised of seven corps of infantry, and the cavalry would be consolidated into an eighth corps. No longer would bits of the mounted arm be attached to brigades and divisions, a practice that usually caused the cavalry to be either ignored or improperly utilized in battle. Fredericksburg was a perfect example of the misuse of cavalry. Most infantry commanders to whom the cavalry were attached did not understand how the mounted arm was to be used or what missions the regiments were to be given.

Brigadier General George Stoneman took charge of the new Corps of Cavalry. His divisions were commanded by Brigadier General Alfred Pleasonton, Brigadier General William W. Averell, and Brigadier General David Gregg. The cavalry had never performed satisfactorily against Stuart's

horsemen, but now that the Union cavalrymen were being armed with the latest in breech-loading firearms (Sharps), it was hoped that they would make a better showing.

Another matter that demanded Hooker's attention was the gathering, evaluation, and dissemination of military intelligence. When Hooker assumed command, no intelligence section or agency existed. A contemporary critic noted:

> When General Hooker assumed command of the army there was not a record or document of any kind at headquarters of the army that gave any information at all in regard to the enemy. There was no means, no organization, and no apparent effort, to obtain such information. And we were almost as ignorant of the enemy in our immediate front as if they had been in China.[29]

Hooker appointed Colonel George H. Sharpe, a regimental commander, to head a "separate and special bureau" of Military Information. Placing the bureau under the Provost Marshal, he appointed Sharpe as Deputy Provost Marshal General.[30] Sharpe proved to be the ideal man for the job. A graduate of Rutgers and the Yale Law School, prior to the war he had practiced law and served with the diplomatic service until he entered the volunteer forces in New York.[31] His first action in organizing the Military Information Bureau was to select scouts from the cavalry and infantry who could survive on their own and make accurate observations and reports. Later he added some signalmen, because they were usually in a position to observe enemy movements.[32] Sharpe continued to use Lowe's balloons for observation, but he also used a goodly number of spies. (So did Longstreet and Jackson, although Lee had an aversion to the use of spies on moral grounds.)

In an effort to prevent Lee from easily obtaining information, Hooker also took action in the area of counterintelligence. Heretofore, the Confederates had only to get copies of the New York and Washington newspapers to learn of military strengths, intentions, sickness rates, morale, and movements. Hooker set about plugging some of the leaks that the press was exploiting. By the end of April, he had begun to control what reporters were writing by decreeing that correspondents must clear stories through his headquarters on pain of expulsion from the army area.[33] Hooker's organizational reforms in the overall intelligence area were well considered and effective; by the end of the war, his bureau had become an army-wide agency that coordinated all military intelligence activities. In reorganizing the artillery, however, Hooker erred.

In Henry Hunt, Hooker had a great artillery commander. Hunt had distinguished himself in the Mexican War as an artilleryman, and after the war had served on a board that established doctrine for the use of artillery. Nevertheless, Hooker removed Hunt from command of the artillery, and relegated him to an administrative role. In turn, he gave tactical control of the artillery batteries to the division and corps commanders. This shift in tactical control was disadvantageous for two reasons: first, in the absence of an overall commander, it became very difficult to mass the fires of the numerous batteries; second, because the high-level personnel often lacked artillery experience, the deployment of artillery frequently depended on junior battery commanders. Additionally, a generous promotion and transfer policy among artillery officers resulted in very few being left for the upcoming campaign season. In fact, by April, there were only 5 field grade officers left in the artillery to direct the 10,000 men and 412 guns in the Army of the Potomac.[34] With so few officers of all ranks, and with Hunt involved in the administration of the branch instead of remaining in control of the batteries, confusion and chaos were inevitable.

As April 1863 brought the promise of spring, Hooker's faith in himself knew no bounds. He also had faith in his army, "the finest army on the planet." In numbers, he had almost 135,000 men under his command, with another 125,000 in support between Washington, D.C. and North Carolina. The Army of the Potomac alone outnumbered Lee's force 2 to 1. In artillery, the ratio was even more in favor of the Union army, being almost 3 to 1.[35] Since Fredericksburg, several changes had been made in the commanders of the corps. (*Compare Atlas Maps No. 25 and No. 26.*) These corps also now had distinctive insignia, designed and issued at Butterfield's instigation. The revitalized Army of the Potomac was fit and anxious to take the field against Lee's Army of Northern Virginia, which, in turn, had been putting the winter months to equally good use.

On the morning of December 15, 1862, when Lee had awakened to find Burnside and his army gone, he knew that the Army of the Potomac would be back, with or without Burnside. The Battle of Fredericksburg had been won decisively by the Army of Northern Virginia, but not without irreplaceable losses. Brigadier General Thomas R.R. Cobb had died at the same stone wall where his men had killed thousands of Federal infantrymen. Maxcy Gregg, too, had died. There were also over 5,000 men who would have to be replaced, if possible. Moreover, Lee was worried about supplying his army. Regiments were forced to forage for food over a countryside that had long been depleted of sufficient foodstuff. Blankets, clothes, shoes, tentage, and horses were all in scarce supply. The situation was so serious that Lee informed the Secretary of War that he feared his men might have difficulty enduring the hardships of the approaching campaign.

There were some things in Lee's favor, however. He had

superb subordinates who had grown accustomed to his tactical schemes during the past year. Aggressive generals like Jackson, Early, A.P. Hill, and Stuart were a few of his most valuable assets. Lee knew that all of his commanders, from regimental to corps levels, were outstanding, and could be depended upon to execute any order received on the battlefield. He also had the advantage of interior lines. By utilizing Stuart's cavalry to gain early warning and develop the situation, he could react to a threat from Hooker's army by massing his forces at the critical point and time.

Once it was determined that Burnside would not resume hostilities following the "Mud March," the Army of Northern Virginia went into winter quarters on the site where it had fought the Battle of Fredericksburg. As noted earlier, the troops kept warm during the day by digging even more extensive and sophisticated entrenchments. Before they were done, the entrenchments stretched from the vicinity of Port Royal almost to Banks' Ford—nearly 22 miles.[36] Many of these positions were prepared in depth, with interconnecting communications trenches that were designed so that if the first line fell, the Confederates could drop back to the second line and continue to fight. If the attack came from a flank, the connecting communications trenches would become fighting trenches. Soldiers fighting in World War I would have found the trench system on the heights above Fredericksburg a familiar sight.

Besides improving their defensive positions, the Confederate soldiers were kept busy drilling and preparing for the spring campaign. On January 20, 1863, Jeb Stuart even held a review of his troops for Lee and Jackson.[37] New weapons captured from Federal troops were issued to the infantry, and the men were trained in their use. Some members of the II Corps were issued European rifles.[38] The weapons derived from these various sources enabled Jackson to replace over 10,000 muskets during the winter.[39] He also improved discipline and training in his corps, raising the men to a peak of military efficiency. Kyd Douglas, a company commander in Jackson's old brigade, noted that "everybody seemed to be working to get the army in effective condition and I may say here that it never was in better shape in discipline and morale than it was when the next campaign opened."[40]

During the winter respite from campaigning, Lee did some reorganizing of the artillery in his army. Separate batteries were consolidated into battalions of four batteries each, and the battalions were assigned to the corps. The corps chief of artillery had direct control of the battalions,[41] with a small reserve being maintained under the army chief of artillery, Brigadier General William N. Pendleton.

Lee was a little worried about his ability to repulse a strong attack in the vicinity of Fredericksburg. He had sent Longstreet with two of his divisions to Suffolk, far to the south, to gather supplies to sustain the army during the summer and to watch the Union IX Corps. The two divisions that Longstreet had left behind (McLaws and Anderson) were stretched rather thinly. In all, Lee had about 60,000 men to face more than twice that number. The situation was a familiar one—that of Lee facing a numerically superior, well equipped force with a poorly supplied, relatively small army comprised of stalwart fighters and outstanding combat leaders. It was very important, therefore, that Stuart's cavalry, covering both flanks, be able to give immediate warning of any advance by Hooker's army.[42]

Not unnaturally, these considerations weighed on Lee's mind on April 29, 1863, as he rode to confer with Jackson in response to a message brought by courier. Arriving at a vantage point above Fredericksburg, he joined Jackson, who was observing Union engineers assemble ponton bridges on the far side of the Rappahannock River. Lee watched for a while, decided it was a feint on Hooker's part, and then remarked to Jackson, "I think that if a real attempt is made to cross the river, it will be above Fredericksburg."[43] He decided to wait and see what Hooker was up to before making any commitments.

Hooker's Plan

Right up until the time of execution, Hooker was very secretive about his plans, refusing to discuss them in detail even with his staff. In answer to a message from the Union commander at Suffolk in which Hooker was advised of Longstreet's activities and asked for information about his plans, Hooker replied: "I have communicated to no one what my intentions are."[44] Even when he began implementing his grand plan, he declined to issue a general order, contenting himself instead with the issuance of individual letters of instruction, veiled in secrecy, to subordinate commanders. It appears, however, that initially he hoped to force Lee out of his position at Fredericksburg by sending the Union cavalry on a deep raid to attack the Confederate lines of communication; this accomplished, he would follow with the infantry, trapping Lee's army between the infantry and the cavalry.

Stoneman's cavalry, 10,000 strong, moved out on April 13, carrying double the basic load of ammunition for carbines and pistols and supported by a train of 275 wagons. The written order from Hooker to Stoneman reiterated an earlier admonition: "fight, fight, fight, bearing in mind that time is as valuable to the general as the Rebel carcasses."[45] Stoneman appeared to have several advantages—well equipped troops in good spirits, an enemy that remained unaware of his movements, and an intelligence document giving enemy strengths and locations. Stoneman made good progress toward the upper

Rappahannock fords—until it began to rain hard on the night of the fourteenth. (*These operations not shown on Atlas Maps.*) The rain continued steadily for three more days, and intermittently for the next two weeks. When Stoneman was unable to cross the river, Hooker's plan became unhinged.

Hooker's modified plan was better than the original scheme, and involved the entire army from the outset. (*See Atlas Map No. 26.*) Bold in concept, it required that the three corps of Slocum, Howard, and Meade make a turning movement by way of Kelly's Ford, while the three corps under Major General John Sedgwick stage a demonstration below Fredericksburg by crossing troops to hold Lee's attention. If Lee withdrew troops from the heights, Sedgwick was to attack and carry the position. (Major General Daniel E. Sickles' corps, although assigned to Sedgwick, was really more in reserve. As events developed, it actually moved in support of the turning force.) Couch's corps—less Gibbon's division, which was under Confederate observation—would take position at Banks' Ford, ready to support the main effort. The cavalry still had the mission of destroying Lee's line of communication.[46] It was an ambitious, aggressive, and daring plan. Hooker was going to divide his army in front of an enemy, but one that was obviously defensively oriented. The scope and sweep of the plan was almost European in its conception, involving maneuver on a grand scale, attacks on communications, the use of feints and demonstrations, an envelopment of the enemy's army, and exploitation of the cavalry's mobility and shock action. Perhaps the egotistical intriguer was really what the Army of the Potomac needed. Unlike his predecessors, Hooker appeared to be looking for a fight.

A Promising Beginning

The execution of Hooker's plan commenced auspiciously. On April 27, while George Stoneman and 10,000 horsemen waited for the swollen Rappahannock River to recede, the corps of George Meade, O.O. Howard, and Henry Slocum began winding their way up the Rappahannock. Using the terrain along the river's edge to screen their movement, the infantry columns worked their way north to the fords, undetected by the southerners across the river. On April 28, Couch's two divisions (French and Hancock), which had been so cruelly punished at Fredericksburg on December 13, moved to Banks' Ford, where they demonstrated. Farther upriver, roads to U.S. Ford were prepared for heavy traffic. Hooker had reduced the number of wagons needed to transport supplies by substituting 2,000 pack mules.[47] Men of the V Corps, XI Corps, and XII Corps crossed the receding Rappahannock River during the night of April 28. The next day, while Lee and Jackson watched engineers build bridges as part of the demonstration assigned to Sedgwick's VI Corps and Reynolds' I Corps at Fredericksburg, the three flanking corps crossed the Rapidan River. Meade moved across Ely's Ford, while the other two corps used the Germanna Ford. They were soon joined by Couch's II Corps, which crossed at U.S. Ford.[48] On April 30, Sickles was ordered to bring his III Corps to join Hooker and the maneuver force at a crossroads known as Chancellorsville.

Hooker had done it. He had outmaneuvered Robert E. Lee, and was now sitting on his flank and rear. His improved intelligence and counterintelligence programs had aided him in the brilliant accomplishment. The movement of the three corps of Meade, Howard, and Slocum was unknown to Lee. (Stuart had allowed Hooker's force to get between his and Lee's positions, thus necessitating a longer time to transmit information to Lee.) Sedgwick's demonstration was a failure in that Lee was not fooled, but the turning movement had nevertheless been made.

The counterintelligence effort to screen the movement of Stoneman's cavalry corps was very successful. False messages were allowed to fall into the hands of Stuart's patrols, and the Confederate general was convinced that the Federal cavalry was enroute to the Shenandoah Valley.[49] Stoneman's real mission was a modification of his original one. He was to move as quickly as possible to "strike and destroy the line of the Aquia and Richmond Railroad."[50] On April 30, the cavalry did finally cross the Rappahannock, meeting light resistance. Stoneman continued his ride around Lee. He did some damage to Lee's rear, but was mostly ignored by the Confederates for the rest of the campaign.[51] Averell got bogged down at Rapidan Station with 3,400 men against an imaginary foe. He was later relieved of command and replaced by Brigadier General Alfred Pleasonton.[52]

In an amazing reversal, once he had Stoneman running through the rear of Lee's army, his infantry corps concentrated at Chancellorsville, the crossing sites secured, and Sedgwick across the river at Fredericksburg, Hooker stopped and did nothing. *(See Atlas Map No. 26.)* Instead of pushing a little bit farther, uncovering Banks' Ford and getting out of the area known as the Wilderness, he halted and waited for Couch to close in and for Sickles' corps to move up from Fredericksburg. The troops were in high spirits because they had fooled the enemy. Hooker had beaten Lee at his own game. Even the generals were enthusiastic about their accomplishment. George Meade, the "Old Snapping Turtle," greeted Slocum at Chancellorsville:

> This is splendid, Slocum; hurrah for old Joe! We are on Lee's flank and he doesn't know it. You take the Plank Road toward Fredericksburg, and I will take the Pike, or vice versa, if you prefer, and we will get out of this Wilderness.[53]

But Slocum dashed Meade's hopes by showing him an order just received from Butterfield. The order had been issued at 2:15 p.m. on April 30:

> The General directs that no advance be made from Chancellorsville until the columns [II, III, V, XI and XII Corps] are concentrated. He expects to be at Chancellorsville tonight.[54]

The high spirits of the army began to dissipate in the dank and eerie gullies, ravines, and endless thickets of the Wilderness. The primary reason for the loss of morale was Hooker's hesitation at this crucial time. When he reached Chancellorsville, Hooker issued an order that he had written earlier in the day. In it, he severely criticized the Confederates and concluded by saying that the recently completed Union turning movement would cause Lee either to flee or to come forth and attack Hooker's force. There it was—Hooker's admission that he preferred to defend, thereby passively surrendering the initiative to Lee. All the fruits of the brilliant maneuver were to be relinquished at the first sign of Confederate aggressiveness. Subordinates did not miss the point, even though Hooker bombastically added, "God Almighty will not be able to prevent the destruction of the rebel army!"[55]

Initial Actions

Hooker had his first inkling of Lee's next move when Anderson's division appeared at Chancellorsville. *(See Atlas Map No. 26.)* As early as April 27, Stuart's patrol had warned Lee that a sizable group of Federal soldiers was moving up the Rappahannock. By the twenty-ninth, Lee felt that the Federals might be trying to outflank him. Accordingly, he decided to shift Anderson west towards the crossroads at Chancellorsville—just in case.[56] He also moved the three divisions on his right flank closer to Fredericksburg. Deciding that Chancellorsville was too far forward, Anderson pulled back to Tabernacle Church and began entrenching. If Hooker was trying to flank the Army of Northern Virginia, Lee wanted to know about it. Furthermore, he wanted to have some force capable of delaying Hooker long enough to enable Lee to react with the remainder of his army.

When Jackson awoke on April 30, he watched the Federal troops on Stafford Heights and to his immediate front. He was all soldier now—an aggressive, fierce, belligerent corps commander, eager to fight. Would Lee give him permission to attack? Maybe. Then Jackson received his orders: "Move at dawn tomorrow up to Anderson."[57] Jackson decided that Early's division would remain at Marye's Heights, reinforced by Barksdale's brigade of Mississippi riflemen. First, Hooker had divided his army in front of the enemy; now Lee was doing the same. The long winter was over; it was time to fight.

Jackson's usual foresight enabled him to have his troops on the march towards Chancellorsville shortly after midnight. Arriving at Anderson's position early on May 1, he informed that commander of his plan for an advance, and ordered him to join forces. There would be no entrenching for the II Corps.

Jackson's corps was moving into an area of Virginia (the Wilderness) that was sparsely populated. *(See Atlas Map No. 26.)* The ground was thickly wooded with scrub oaks, long needle pines, swamp maples, and ash, all entwined with grape vines, ivy, and holly. The gently undulating terrain was crisscrossed by shallow streams that were almost covered by the brush and trees. Movement through the thickets and along the streams or runs was almost impossible, and ground cover severely restricted the use of artillery and cavalry. There was, however, one piece of terrain that was open and a little higher than the rest; it was called Hazel Grove. *(See Atlas Map No. 27.)*

Maneuver through the Wilderness was to a large degree limited to the road net, and for such a desolate place, the net was more than adequate. The road that Jackson's corps moved along towards Chancellorsville was the Plank Road; it was covered with planks two inches thick and sixteen feet long nailed to two parallel logs buried in the ground. This gave the road a hard, level surface and a fairly good all-weather capability. The roadway was far from ideal, however; a number of planks were missing, broken, or so rotten that they broke through under the weight of a cannon or supply wagon.[58] Another major road was the Turnpike. In the swampy sections it was corduroyed and covered with gravel to a depth of three to four inches; like the Plank Road, it was sixteen feet wide. While not an all-weather road, the Turnpike was considered a high-speed avenue through the endless thickets and swampy bottoms of the region.

Ignoring both the difficulty of the terrain in the Wilderness and the advantage in time he had gained over Lee, Hooker dawdled, delaying his eastward advance until 11:00 a.m. on May 1. Having only Pleasonton's brigade of cavalry, which had difficulty penetrating Stuart's screen, Hooker's three columns moved somewhat blindly. *(See Atlas Map No. 27.)* At this same time, the two columns of Jackson and McLaws were moving on a collision course with the Federal forces.

Initial contact between the Union and Confederate forces was light and limited to pickets exchanging shots. Gradually, the situation developed. Major General George Sykes' division (Meade's V Corps) found McLaws' brigades moving up the Turnpike and drove them back. Sykes pressed his advantage until he found himself flanked, and then fell back and withdrew through Hancock's division, which held firmly on a slight ridge line. Slocum had similar success in halting Anderson's men. Both columns reported that they were in

good positions, having left the Wilderness and reached relatively clear terrain. In the meantime, with the bulk of his corps, Meade had continued to march. He now found himself unopposed and on the Confederate flank. Hooker had the upper hand. Holding an overall preponderance of numbers, he had massed his army (with the exception of the cavalry), forced Lee out of his fortifications overlooking the Rappahannock River, and fought him to a standstill clear of the Wilderness.

Then, just when everything was in his favor, Hooker lost his courage. Earlier, in the April 30 order released at Chancellorsville, he had shown signs of equivocation and hesitancy. Back at Fredericksburg and Banks' Ford, Professor Lowe's balloons had been active, observing Lee's shift of troops and the weakening of his position on Marye's Heights. The news that the largest part of Lee's force was moving toward Chancellorsville apparently unnerved Hooker. At about 2:00 p.m., he ordered his corps commanders to break contact and fall back to Chancellorsville. *(See Atlas Map No. 27.)* They were incredulous. Every advantage they had gained was to be given up. Couch wanted to hold the ridge line that Hancock had organized, and asked permission to stay in place; permission was refused. Then Hooker countermanded the retirement order—but it was too late. The Confederates had seized the ridge.

Meanwhile, Sedgwick's efforts had been stymied by a series of disparate, mishandled orders. A directive from Hooker told Sedgwick to demonstrate, but *not* to attack. Then Hooker changed his mind, ordering Sedgwick to attack if success seemed probable. Sedgwick, however, received the second message, ordering the attack, before the first, ordering the demonstration. Thus, Sedgwick, understandably confused and thinking that the later message was the final one, decided to make a demonstration. Hooker next canceled Sedgwick's instructions because it was too late to launch an attack. It was beginning to appear that Hooker planned to fight defensively with his right wing—the stronger one—while expecting Sedgwick to go on the offensive against well-entrenched troops. Most critical of all, however, was the fact that Hooker had surrendered the initiative to the always dangerous Lee. He would not regain it.[59]

From the Confederate viewpoint, the situation was equally vague, but leaders more determined than Hooker were in control. Jackson advanced up the Plank Road with the II Corps, while McLaws moved up the Turnpike. *(See Atlas Map No. 27.)* The latter had already contacted Federal skirmishers, as previously noted, but Jackson was disturbed because he had yet to make contact. He was also worried about his left flank. Then came the sounds of musket fire from Anderson's skirmishers. Although Jackson now knew that Hooker's army was to his front, he still fretted over the security of his flank.

"Press them," shouted Jackson. He knew that he might find superior numbers to his front—perhaps even a prepared defensive line—but he wanted to avoid blundering into a Federal army drawn up behind a prepared defensive position. As the soldiers of the II Corps pushed into the thickets along the Plank Road, Jackson, fearing an ambush, would halt them when a thicket appeared particularly dark or impenetrable. He would then have a battery of guns brought up, and throw shot and shell into the threatening location. Once it had been determined by his "reconnaissance-by-fire" that the enemy was not planning an ambush, his troops pressed on.[60] In this fashion, Jackson's men followed Slocum's corps back into the Wilderness. During the process, a messenger rode up to Jackson carrying word from Stuart that the cavalry had closed on the left flank and were in position to alleviate any worry that Jackson had about Hooker's attacking. Greatly relieved, Jackson sent word back to Stuart to "keep closed on Chancellorsville."[61]

While Hooker and Lee gathered their forces for the now inevitable pitched battle in the Wilderness, the small Confederate force left at Fredericksburg stiffened its defenses for whatever action Sedgwick might initiate. *(See Atlas Map No. 27.)* With a reinforced division and 45 guns, Early held the position against Sedgwick's total of 40,000 men.[62] Against these odds of 4 to 1, it was clear that the Confederates would have to make maximum use of the fortifications that had been so laboriously built by the I and II Corps.

A Bold Plan

As night fell on May 1, 1863, the leaders on both sides wondered what the enemy was planning. Jackson pondered Hooker's dispositions in the endless thickets of the Wilderness. Was there a way around Hooker's flank that would enable the II Corps to pounce on the Union rear? Were there roads other than those shown on the map made by Jedediah Hotchkiss? Jackson rode back along the road from Catherine Furnace to its junction with the Plank Road. There, he met Lee. The two generals went into the woods and sat down on a log. They discussed the day's events and wondered what had prompted Hooker's withdrawal to Chancellorsville. Jackson felt sure that Hooker's offensive was a disaster and that the Army of the Potomac would be in full retreat the next day. Lee was not at all sure that Hooker's plan had failed, or even if his main attack would be made at Chancellorsville.[63] While the two men talked, they were joined by Jeb Stuart. The cavalry commander was in an expansive mood, and announced that while Fitz Lee and his brigade were reconnoitering to the west, they had discovered that the Federal right appeared to be exposed.

Scouts earlier sent to the front to survey the Union lines had determined that the Federal infantry and artillery were behind field fortifications. Trees had been felled to bolster the hasty defenses; the Army of the Potomac was preparing to fight a defensive battle. Lee realized the futility of attacking a force that was not only superior to his in numbers but was also protected by breastworks; he also knew that time was important, and that Early's small force could not stop a determined assault by Sedgwick. Looking at the trackless woods pictured on the map, Lee made the decision to attack Hooker's flank. Jackson would lead the maneuvering force. Jackson was jubilant at the prospect of flanking Hooker; he quietly announced, "My troops will move at 4 o'clock.[64] Somehow, with Stuart screening the force, Jackson would find a way around Hooker's right flank. There must be a way through that tangle of vines and underbrush.

Jackson departed, moving deeper into the woods to get some sleep. Stretched out on the ground, he dozed until awakened by the cold. He found a small fire and tried to warm his chilled body. Chaplain Lacy joined the general at the fire. Jackson remembered that the minister had once tended his flock in the vicinity of Chancellorsville. Although Lacy knew of many little trails to the west, he was unsure about their capacity for carrying artillery. However, Lacy did know a Colonel Charles C. Wellford at Catherine Furnace who was quite familiar with the area and had a son who could guide them.[65] Jackson sent Lacy and Hotchkiss, Jackson's trusted topographer, off to Catherine Furnace to learn if a road existed that would permit the II Corps to slip around Hooker's right flank. After they left, Jackson was joined at the fire by Colonel Armistead L. Long. As Jackson sipped the coffee offered by Long, both heard a clattering sound. The noise had been caused by Jackson's sword; having been only propped against a tree, it had fallen to the ground. The general paid no attention, but Long thought the incident a bad omen.[66]

Lee, wanting to know Jackson's final plan, joined his lieutenant at the fire. Jackson told him about the reconnaissance mission on which he had dispatched Lacy and Hotchkiss. The two men were sitting on crates around the fire, trying to ward off the morning chill, when into the circle of flickering light came Jed Hotchkiss. He announced that there was a road, and also a man to guide them. *(See Atlas Map No. 28.)* Lee asked, "General Jackson, what do you propose to do?" Jackson pointed to the map and the road sketched in by Hotchkiss. "Go around here," he said. "What do you propose to make this movement with?" asked General Lee. "My whole corps," replied Jackson.[67]

Lee had already divided his army in the face of the enemy, and now his most trusted subordinate was telling him that the army was to be divided again, leaving Lee with only McLaws' and Anderson's divisions. Those two divisions were already

On the Night of May 1, 1863, Generals Lee and Jackson Discuss Strategy for the Battle of Chancellorsville

in contact on the right and center. Jackson would take 26,000 men and attack the open Union right flank, while Lee and two-thirds that number of troops tried to hold off Hooker's entire army. It was a very daring plan—one that could mean victory or destruction in detail, depending upon the Union reaction. The two soldiers knew what Lee's final decision would be. "Well, go on" stated Lee.[68] As May 2 dawned, "Stonewall" Jackson prepared his soldiers for the flank march to the west.

Storm in the West

By ordering his commanders to break contact and fall back on May 1, Hooker had lost the respect of his subordinates and revealed his own lack of confidence. Late in the afternoon of that day, he issued a directive ordering an immediate preparation of the position for defense. Perhaps he had been unduly swayed by the devastating result of Lee's defensive fighting at Fredericksburg; at any rate, he was no longer the bombastic boaster, and his nerve had been shaken. The directive con-

cluded: "The Major General commanding trusts that a suspension in the attack today will embolden the enemy to attack him."[69] The troops had been cutting trees for breastworks and abatis since they had fallen back to Chancellorsville. In anticipation of the defensive battle he now nervously expected, at around midnight Hooker had ordered Reynolds' I Corps to join the bulk of the army at Chancellorsville. The folly of failing to allow Meade to secure Banks' Ford earlier in the day would be revealed when Reynolds moved early on May 2 and, finding the ford in Confederate hands, was forced to use U.S. Ford. Lee had foreseen the importance of the crossing site and had dispatched Wilcox late the previous evening to secure the ford. *(See Atlas Map No. 28.)*

Early on the morning of May 2, as Hooker inspected the field fortifications in the immediate vicinity of the Chancellor House, he was heard to remark, "How strong, how strong!"[70] The only problem with fighting a defensive battle with an advantage in numbers of troops and superior artillery—all behind prepared works—is that one must be dealing with an enemy who is ignorant of the ways of war and who wants to die. Hooker would not find that enemy at Chancellorsville. While Hooker was checking his fieldworks, Jackson's column was on the march in an attempt to evade most of them.

On the morning of May 2, Brigadier General David Birney's division of Sickles' corps occupied the key terrain of Hazel Grove. From that vantage point, at about 8:00 a.m. Birney observed a large column of troops, with many wagons dispersed throughout the column, moving south, away from the front. He reported this to Sickles and Hooker, whose initial action was to warn Howard to advance his pickets and to pay attention to his right flank, as it appeared that the enemy was moving "to our right." However, Hooker did not personally visit Howard, and within four hours directed his commanders to load supplies for a movement the next morning. Within six hours, he ordered Sedgwick to attack Marye's Heights because "the enemy is fleeing." These actions leave some doubt as to Hooker's real conclusion. It would seem that by 5:00 p.m. he had reconfirmed in his own mind what he had been saying all along would happen when Lee encountered the Army of the Potomac.[71] It apparently never occurred to him that a strong and timely attack against Jackson's column—Meade's corps and most of Sickles' corps were not in contact with the enemy—might reap untold advantages.

The sight of Jackson's Corps marching across the front of one of the divisions of his III Corps was more than Sickles could stand. *(See Atlas Map No. 28.)* A politician temporarily turned soldier, Sickles was aggressive and impetuous, too much so sometimes. Now he badgered Hooker to let him attack, foreseeing an opportunity to hurt Lee's army badly and also believing that the Confederates were withdrawing. Around noon, he finally received permission to make a cautious, harassing advance. Using Birney's and Major General Amiel W. Whipple's division, Sickles turned it into a full-fledged attack. Ultimately, on Hooker's orders, Sickles also pulled in Brigadier General Francis Barlow's brigade of the XI Corps. Howard personally selected this brigade—his corps reserve—and went with it, a bare two hours before Jackson's onslaught. Sickles' sortie achieved inconsequential results, primarily because it came too late to do much more than nip at flank and rear guards and take a few prisoners. However, it did cause two of Jackson's brigades to reverse the direction of their march as a precaution to protect the column; consequently, neither of them was initially able to take part in Jackson's assault.[72]

It took Jackson's men about six and a half hours to cover 12 miles of road and reach a position on Hooker's right flank. Jackson's foot cavalry had done it again. Now the general faced a new challenge—deploying an infantry corps in that tangle of undergrowth and thickets. Even with the veterans of the II Corps moving as quickly as possible, it took over three hours to deploy properly. And then, only 6 of Jackson's

15 brigades were in position to participate in the initial attack and pursuit of Howard's corps. *(See Atlas Map No. 28.)* It was not until almost 6:00 p.m. that the following exchange took place between Jackson and a subordinate:

> Are you ready, General Rodes?
> Yes, sir.
> You can go forward, sir.[73]

With that simple command, Jackson unleashed a furious attack on Howard's unprepared XI Corps.

Without detracting from the boldness of the Lee-Jackson concept and the brilliance of its execution, the unprepared state of the XI Corps was as much a result of Union neglect as Confederate surprise. Warned by Hooker before noon, Howard replied that he was taking measures to ward off an attack from the west. His measures were, in fact, very inadequate, largely because Howard believed the woods to be practically impenetrable. At mid-afternoon, warnings came in from the pickets about the sizable body of troops forming for an attack. Nevertheless, both Howard and Hooker elected to downplay these reports.[74] The result of this breakdown in security was dramatically exploited by "Stonewall" Jackson. In *John Brown's Body*, Stephen Vincent Benet describes the attack:

> When the blue-coated unprepared ranks of Howard saw
> that storm, heralded by wild rabbits and frightened deer,
> burst on them yelling, out of the whispering woods,

Jackson's Attack on Howard's Corps, May 2, 1863

they could not face it. Some men died where they stood, the storm passed over the rest. It was Jackson's storm. It was his old trick of war, for the last time played.[75]

Wild-eyed deer, rabbits by the dozen, flushed partridges, and other frightened animals ran toward the east, out of the cover of the protecting thickets. The soldiers of the XI Corps who were right on the flank were startled by the panicked denizens of the Wilderness. A few moments passed; then the Union troops could hear the bugles ordering the brigades forward, followed by the chilling screams of thousands of rebel infantrymen. Panic began to grip the soldiers in blue who were about to be swept up in a gray and butternut wave. Now they could see the Confederate infantry through the trees. Thick lines of white smoke rose above the front ranks as the Rebels began to fire in volley. Those Federal troops who could reach their stacked weapons fired once, and then turned and filled the tracks left by the fleeing animals. For the next hour, units of Howard's XI Corps broke and fled in disorder and panic before the onrushing rebel horde. Pockets of Union resistance were overcome. Later, with the coming of darkness and the stiffening of Union ranks, Jackson's attack began to grind to a halt. He had reached a point just west of Fairview Hill. In the meantime, Lee had made limited attacks against the Union left.

At about 8:00 p.m., Jackson and a small party of mounted staff officers rode forward of the Confederate lines to reconnoiter the Federal positions. Jackson wanted to ascertain both the activities of the Union forces and the feasibility of continuing the attack that night. The small party rode close enough to hear Union soldiers yelling at each other and felling more trees with which to bolster their defenses. Jackson's aides were becoming increasingly alarmed at his exposing himself to so much danger, and finally convinced the general to return to his own lines. As the reconnaissance party approached a North Carolina unit that had been attacked by a battalion of Union cavalry earlier in the evening, a volley of musket fire blazed in the night. Jackson's horse, frightened by the fire, ran through the underbrush, out of control. Jackson tried to tighten her reins, but his left arm and right hand had been struck by bullets. One of his staff ran toward the Carolinians and shouted that they were firing on their own men. His shout was answered with another volley. A.P. Hill was finally able to convince the Confederates that they were firing on friendly forces. Jackson eventually controlled his horse, but with much pain. His arm, he knew, must have been broken.[76]

Dismounting with the help of his companions, Jackson, weak and in shock, stumbled back toward his lines with the support of two aides. Once inside the lines, he lay down near a tree until the corps surgeon could be summoned. Fearing a counterattack any moment, Hill went to lead his division. No

sooner did he arrive there than a Federal shelling began. A round exploded near Hill, wounding him in the legs. Ordinarily, with Jackson wounded, Hill would have taken command; but being wounded himself, Hill decided to advise Stuart of the situation and ask him to take temporary command of the II Corps. Stuart, replying almost immediately, expressed regret at the wounding of his good friend, Jackson, and agreed to take command of the troops.[77]

A litter had been brought to carry the Confederate leader to the rear. Jackson did not want his troops, especially the ones who had shot him, to know that he had been wounded. While the bearers were trekking through the dark tangles of the Wilderness, the Federal cannonade that had begun with the wounding of Hill was renewed. At times, Jackson's aides shielded his body with their own—he must be protected against any further injury. Although Jackson sustained no additional wounds, one of the bearers tripped on a vine, and Jackson was dropped on his wounded arm. It was a severe blow, and the pain was almost more than he could endure. After an eternity of suffering, the general was brought to a road and a waiting wagon. Jackson was loaded into the wagon for a bumpy and pain-racked ride back to a safe area where he could be cared for properly. Although not mortal, the wounds were serious.

Lee at His Best

If Hooker had taken the initiative on the morning of May 3, he might well have destroyed Lee's army in detail. The Confederates were divided into three parts: Early's force at Fredericksburg, Stuart's (Jackson's) force in the west, and Lee's force in the center. *(See Atlas Map No. 29.)* The three were not mutually supporting. If Hooker had kept his cavalry with the army instead of sending it on a raid, he might have been able to determine where the weak points in Lee's lines were. As it was, he had only Pleasonton's small force, and this he did not use very effectively. Even lacking cavalry, however, Hooker should have better appreciated the importance of the position that Sickles occupied at Hazel Grove on the morning of May 3. Not only was it important as a position for artillery, but it also provided the salient* point from which Hooker could freely attack either Stuart or Lee—and he had the fresh yet experienced I and V Corps available to launch the attack. The fact that upon visiting Sickles early that morning Hooker had ordered the III Corps pulled back to Fairview is just one

---

*A salient in a line of troops is a protrusion of the line of contact toward the enemy.

more indication of how completely Lee had gained a moral ascendancy in the contest of wills between the two men.

Not long after Sickles pulled his troops back, Stuart occupied Hazel Grove and immediately planted a 31-gun battery there. *(Compare Atlas Maps Nos. 28 and 29.)* Although the Confederate guns could not dominate the numerically comparable Union battery at Fairview, Stuart's gunners were able to rain very effective fire on the Federal infantry in support of the fierce assault that Lee's divisions and Jackson's avenging brigades soon mounted. After two hours of furious fighting, the Federal ammunition began to run low and the Confederate attacks slowly gained ground. Then a Confederate artillery round struck the pillar of the Chancellor House against which Hooker was leaning, knocking him unconscious. Up until then, he had been little more than a passive spectator of the raging battle. Upon being revived, Hooker summoned Couch, the next senior, but refused to relinquish command. Instead, at mid-morning, he directed Couch to move the army rearward, to a new position. *(See Atlas Map No. 30.)* A fierce fighter, Couch was crestfallen, but he obeyed. This enabled the Confederates to unite their two wings, and Lee, ever the aggressive leader, pushed his tired troops forward in an attempt to reap a greater victory.[78] At about this time, word reached him that Jackson's left arm had been amputated. The saddened Lee remarked, "General Jackson has lost his left arm, but I my right."[79]

Having ordered the withdrawal, Hooker was content to sit with his sizable force in a defensive posture while waiting for Sedgwick to carry out the demanding task he had given him. At 9:00 p.m. on May 2, Hooker had sent the VI Corps commander an order to attack Fredericksburg, capture everything in the town, and then move down the Turnpike and take Lee from behind. Accordingly, at dawn on the third, Sedgwick had attacked Early's strongly fortified position and had been repulsed three times. *(See Atlas Map No. 29.)* His fourth attack, however, was successful. Early then fought a delaying action along Telegraph Road while Wilcox and his brigade delayed along the Turnpike. *(See Atlas Map No. 30.)*

Upon being informed of Sedgwick's success, Lee reacted in predictable fashion, again showing the calculating, bold, and brilliant brand of generalship he had displayed during the past few days. He had correctly evaluated Hooker's worth as a leader. Without hesitation, Lee detached McLaws' division and hurried it eastward to stop Sedgwick, at the same time reluctantly canceling plans for another assault of Hooker's new position. Fighting each other to a standstill, McLaws and Sedgwick bivouacked that night on the battlefield near Salem Church.

During the night of May 3, the two opposing commanders considered courses of action and issued orders. While Butterfield tried to keep an increasingly skeptical President informed

as best he could,* Hooker lapsed into an increasingly passive and defensive attitude. More than ever, he seemed to envision Sedgwick's small force as the prime Union instrument of action.[80] A message dispatched to Sedgwick at about midnight—he received it on the morning of the fourth—informed the VI Corps commander that Hooker wanted Lee to attack the entrenched Army of the Potomac and that Sedgwick, while still expected to advance, had permission to withdraw via either Banks' Ford or Fredericksburg if his corps became endangered. (Foreseeing his possible isolation from Fredericksburg, Sedgwick had arranged with the army engineers the day before for the construction and securing of a ponton bridge at Scott's Ford.)

On the Confederate side, Lee continued to think offensively. Correctly gauging Hooker's defensive intentions, he decided to try to destroy Sedgwick and to *again* split his own forces. That night, he ordered Early to unite with McLaws. The next morning, he added Anderson's division and went to command the attack himself, leaving Stuart behind to contain Hooker. *(See Atlas Map No. 31.)* The Confederate deployment took considerable time, largely because of Sedgwick's skillful defensive alignment, which obstructed Confederate communications. When Lee was finally able to attack late in the afternoon of May 4, Sedgwick defended doggedly, withdrawing in good order during the night. Before dawn, he crossed the Rappahannock at Scott's Ford. Meanwhile, although outnumbering Stuart 3 to 1, Hooker made no effort to advance. Whether his injury was responsible for his passivity is not known; his lack of action is well documented, however.

Hooker had no fight left in him. At a council of war held on the night of May 5, he overrode the majority opinion of his corps commanders and elected to withdraw across the Rappahannock. *(See Atlas Map No. 32.)* Covered by Meade's V Corps, the crossing began during the night and continued unhampered early into the next morning.† The "finest army on the planet," led by "Fighting Joe" Hooker, who had boasted that he would have no mercy on Lee, would have to wait another day to force defeat upon Lee and the Army of Northern Virginia. Although Lee had completely dominated and defeated Hooker with his brilliance and daring, the Army of the Potomac was more humiliated than hurt. This is more evident today than it was in 1863, when the complex maneuvering and fighting that took place during the first week in May presented a bewildering mosaic to the onlooker. A diarist humorously noted:

---

*During most of the battle, Butterfield and several of the staff remained at Hooker's original Army Headquarters at Falmouth. Via telegraph, Hooker communicated with Sedgwick through Butterfield.

†Lee had planned an attack for early on May 6. As at Fredericksburg, he was taken completely by surprise by Hooker's evacuation and did not realize until well into the morning that the Union forces had left.

It would seem that Hooker has beaten Lee and that Lee has beaten Hooker; that we have taken Fredericksburg, and that the rebels have taken it also; that we have 4500 prisoners, and the rebels 5400; that Hooker has cut off Lee's retreat, and Lee cut off Sedgwick's retreat, and Sedgwick has cut off everybody's retreat generally, but has retreated himself although his retreat was cut off; that Longstreet has not left Suffolk at all, and again that he has never been there. In short, all is utter confusion. Everything seems to be everywhere, and everybody all over, and there is no getting at any truth.[81]

It was probably Jackson who first analyzed Hooker's disaster. While being carried from the field, he said:

It was, in the main, a good conception, sir; an excellent plan. But he should not have sent away his cavalry; that was his great blunder. It was that which enabled me to turn him, without his being aware of it, and to take him by his rear. Had he kept this cavalry with him, his plan would have been a very good one.[82]

Jackson was only partially correct about what had happened at Chancellorsville; for, if it had not been for Lee's courageous decision to split the army again in the face of a numerically superior foe, Hooker would not have been taken on the flank.

As it turned out, Hooker had contributed to his own downfall by showing utter ineptness as an army commander once his excellent plan required battlefield execution. Not only had he sent the cavalry away, but he also had not committed all the infantry corps. Lincoln had directed him to "put in" all his men, but he had failed to do this. His and Howard's haphazard security precautions, his failure to better coordinate the wings of the army, and his blunder in giving up Hazel Grove were important factors in his defeat. Perhaps most critical of all, his surrendering of the initiative not only cost him the confidence of his subordinates, but gave the daring Lee the opportunity to exploit the situation.

On the Confederate side, Lee had the complete confidence and trust of his commanders. He also used them very well. Undoubtedly, Lee's courage and daring had more than a little to do with Hooker's bumbling. Always outnumbered, the Confederate leader acted wisely on the available information, had the strength of conviction to take daring risks, and utilized interior lines brilliantly. Above all, he sought the initiative and, once having gained it, refused to relinquish it. Lee's battlefield brilliance was never more in evidence than during the Chancellorsville Campaign. He was truly at his best.

If casualties can be used as a scale to measure success in battle, Chancellorsville would almost be a draw. Lee lost approximately 13,000 men while the Army of the Potomac suffered almost 17,000 casualties.[83] Lee could not replace his losses, however, and Hooker could absorb his and still greatly outnumber the Army of Northern Virginia. One of Lee's losses, moreover, was irreplaceable. Jackson developed pneumonia and died on May 10. Lee had lost a staunch friend and the greatest of his lieutenants. He would sorely miss him during the Confederate invasion of Pennsylvania the following month.

Notes

[1]Vincent J. Esposito (ed.), *The West Point Atlas of American Wars* (2 vols; New York, 1959), I, 70.

[2]Esposito, *West Point Atlas,* I, 70; Vorin Whan, *Fiasco at Fredericksburg* (State College, Pa., 1961), p. 2; Edward J. Stackpole, *Drama on the Rappahannock* (Harrisburg, Pa., 1957), p. 278.

[3]*The War of the Rebellion: A Compilation of the Official Records of the Union and Confederate Armies* (130 vols.; Washington, 1880–1901), Series 1, XIX, Pt. 2, 28. (Hereinafter cited as *OR*. Unless otherwise indicated, all subsequent references to the *OR* are to Series I.)

[4]Whan, *Fiasco,* p. 16.

[5]Douglas Southall Freeman, *R.E. Lee: A Biography* (4 vols.; New York, 1934), II, 429–432; Kenneth P. Williams, *Lincoln Finds a General* (5 vols.; New York, 1949–1959), II, 510–515.

[6]Stackpole, *Drama,* pp. 44, 112.

[7]Gustavus J. Fiebeger, *Campaigns of the American Civil War* (West Point, 1914), p. 77; Stackpole, *Drama,* p. 277; Whan, *Fiasco,* pp. 1–2; K.P. Williams, *Lincoln Finds a General,* II, 526–528, 538.

[8]Stackpole, *Drama,* p. 102.

[9]*Ibid.,* p. 178; Whan, *Fiasco,* p. 37.

[10]Whan, *Fiasco,* p. 80.

[11]Stackpole, *Drama,* p. 121; *OR,* XXXI, 64.

[12]Fiebeger, *Campaigns,* p. 70; Stackpole, *Drama,* p. 122; Whan, *Fiasco,* p. 32.

[13]Douglas Southall Freeman, *Lee's Lieutenants: A Study in Command* (3 vols.; New York, 1942), II, 335–336; Stackpole, *Drama,* p. 136; Whan, *Fiasco,* p. 40.

[14]Freeman, *Lee's Lieutenants,* II, 336–337.

[15]Stackpole, *Drama,* pp. 160–161.

[16]Freeman, *Lee's Lieutenants,* II, 350.

[17]Stackpole, *Drama,* p. 180.

[18]Freeman, *Lee's Lieutenants,* II, 356; Stackpole, *Drama,* p. 190.

[19]Freeman, *Lee's Lieutenants,* II, 389.

[20]Stackpole, *Drama,* p. 226; Whan, *Fiasco,* pp. 100–101.

[21]Whan, *Fiasco,* p. 97.

[22]Freeman, *Lee's Lieutenants,* II, 378–379; Whan, *Fiasco,* p. 106.

[23]Stackpole, *Drama,* p. 230; Whan, *Fiasco,* p. 102.

[24]K.P. Williams, *Lincoln Finds a General,* II, 535; John F.C. Fuller, *Decisive Battles of the U.S.A.* (New York, 1942), p. 218; George F.R. Henderson, *The Civil War: A Soldier's View,* ed. by Jay Luvaas (Chicago, 1958), pp. 95–98, 109–110. Quotation is from Freeman, *R.E. Lee,* II, 473.

[25]Freeman, *R.E. Lee,* II, 480–481.

[26]Mark M. Boatner, *The Civil War Dictionary* (New York, 1959), p. 409.

[27]Joseph P. Cullen, ''The Battle of Chancellorsville,'' *Civil War Times Illustrated,* VII, No. 2 (1963), 4.

[28]Boatner, *Civil War Dictionary,* p. 409.

[29]John Bigelow, *The Campaign of Chancellorsville* (New Haven, Conn., 1910), p. 47; Edward J. Stackpole, *Chancellorsville: Lee's Greatest Battle* (Harrisburg, Pa., 1958), p. 15. Quotation is from Bigelow.

[30]Bigelow, *Campaign,* p. 47; Stackpole, *Chancellorsville,* p. 16.

[31]Boatner, *Civil War Dictionary,* p. 735.

[32]Stackpole, *Chancellorsville,* p. 39.

[33]*Ibid.,* p. 20.

[34]*Ibid.,* p. 28.

[35]Bigelow, *Campaign,* pp. 499–504.

[36]Freeman, *R.E. Lee,* II, 480–481; Stackpole, *Chancellorsville,* p. 64.

[37]Henry K. Douglas, *I Rode With Stonewall* (Chapel Hill, N.C., 1940), p. 206.

[38]*Ibid.*

[39]Stackpole, *Chancellorsville,* p. 67.

[40]Douglas, *I Rode,* p. 206.

[41]Stackpole, *Chancellorsville,* pp. 69–70.

[42]*Ibid.,* p. 76.

[43]Cullen, ''Chancellorsville,'' p. 8.

[44]*OR,* XL, 256.

[45]Cullen, ''Chancellorsville,'' p. 7.

[46]K.P. Williams, *Lincoln Finds a General,* II, 568–570; Esposito, *West Point Atlas,* I, 84.

[47]Bigelow, *Campaign,* pp. 173, 176; Cullen, ''Chancellorsville,'' p. 8.

[48]*Ibid.,* pp. 186–187, 191–193, 8.

[49]Stackpole, *Chancellorsville,* p. 110.

[50]Bigelow, *Campaign,* p. 188; Stackpole, *Chancellorsville,* p. 109.

[51]Stackpole, *Chancellorsville,* p. 112.

[52]*Ibid.*

[53]*Ibid.,* p. 145.

[54]*OR,* XL, 305.

[55]Stackpole, *Chancellorsville,* p. 147.

[56]Frank E. Vandiver, *Mighty Stonewall* (New York, 1957), p. 456.

[57]*Ibid.,* p. 457.

[58]Stackpole, *Chancellorsville,* pp. 100–101.

[59]K.P. Williams, *Lincoln Finds a General,* II, 580–582.

[60]Vandiver, *Mighty Stonewall,* p. 460.

[61]*Ibid.,* p. 459.

[62]*Ibid.*

[63]*Ibid.,* p. 463.

[64]*Ibid.,* p. 465.

[65]*Ibid.,* p. 466.

[66]*Ibid.*

[67]*Ibid.,* pp. 466–467.

[68]Vandiver, *Mighty Stonewall,* p. 468.

[69]*OR,* XL, 328.

[70]Stackpole, *Chancellorsville,* p. 219.

[71]*Ibid.,* p. 210; Bigelow, *Campaign,* pp. 276–277, 289; *OR,* XL, 363.

[72]Stackpole, *Chancellorsville,* pp. 216–217; K.P. Williams, *Lincoln Finds a General,* II, 586–587.

[73]Vandiver, *Mighty Stonewall,* p. 474.

[74]Bigelow, *Campaign,* pp. 279, 286, 288; *OR,* XXXIX, 628–630 (Howard's report of the campaign).

[75]Stephen Vincent Benet, *John Brown's Body* (New York, 1973), p. 279.

[76]Vandiver, *Mighty Stonewall,* p. 479.

[77]*Ibid.,* p. 480.

[78]Stackpole, *Chancellorsville,* p. 298; K.P. Williams, *Lincoln Finds a General,* II, 593–595.

[79]Vandiver, *Mighty Stonewall,* p. 492.

[80]*OR,* XL, 377–399; K.P. Williams, *Lincoln Finds a General,* II, 598.

[81]Morgan Dix, *Memoirs of Adam John Dix* (2 vols.; New York, 1883), II, 57.

[82]Fiebeger, *Campaigns,* pp. 154–155.

[83]Esposito, *West Point Atlas,* I, 91.

Gettysburg

8

After Robert E. Lee's brilliant victory at Chancellorsville, a few Confederate leaders hoped that the battlefield success would be followed by a diplomatic triumph. A year earlier, when Lee had marched north to give battle at Antietam, many influential southerners had held the same hope. Since that bloody but indecisive fight, however, the South's relations with England and France had worsened. In the intervening year, Europeans had grown more opposed to the idea of recognizing the Confederacy as a sovereign state. Moreover, Richmond's decision to withhold cotton from European markets had not served to pressure the European powers either to look more favorably on southern aspirations or to dispute the Union blockade of the Confederacy. By mid-1863, it was the opinion of many southern leaders that no help would be received from Europe. The South could not achieve independence through international recognition; independence could be gained only through military victory.

At Vicksburg, on one of its borders, the Confederacy was rapidly approaching a crisis. Two days after Major General Joseph Hooker withdrew the Army of the Potomac across the Rappahannock River, Major General Ulysses S. Grant began to move his forces from Grand Gulf toward Jackson, Mississippi. Living off the land on the eastern side of the Mississippi River, Grant's army was close to achieving a decisive victory. Jefferson Davis ordered General Joseph E. Johnston to take charge of all Confederate forces in Mississippi in order to mount a unified effort. But this was only a stopgap measure, not a solution. Vicksburg needed additional help.

Only in the East did conditions appear to favor the Confederacy. Lee's splendid maneuvers in the Chancellorsville Campaign had added to his reputation of unequaled excellence. The Army of Northern Virginia appeared to be an invincible instrument of Lee's will. The return of Lieutenant General James Longstreet's corps to northern Virginia after the battle would enable the army to operate with renewed strength and vigor. It was now time for the Confederate leaders to decide

whether the East or the West would be the scene of the principal Confederate effort.

The Confederate Decision to Invade the North

Prior to the Battle of Chancellorsville, Davis had tried to establish the relative importance of the Eastern and Western Theaters. While the threat to Vicksburg could not be overlooked, the growing strength of Hooker's Army of the Potomac made the situation in Virginia equally grave. From mid-March to mid-April, Davis and Lee continued to exchange ideas on Confederate strategy. Davis was particularly worried about a report that the Federal IX Corps under Major General Ambrose E. Burnside had been transferred from the East to the West. *(See Atlas Map No. 33.)* An additional threat was posed by the presence of Major General William S. Rosecrans' Army of the Cumberland in front of General Braxton Bragg's army at Murfreesboro, Tennessee.* It appeared that the Union was about to mount a major effort in the West, and that the Confederacy should respond by similarly reinforcing its western armies.

Lee disagreed with Davis' argument that the Confederacy should reinforce the West in response to Union initiatives. He believed that the North could shift troops from theater to theater much more easily than the South. If this was the case, the South should not shift forces to counter northern transfers, because the Confederacy always would be behind in its response. Instead, the Confederate Army should take advantage of a Federal weakness when Union troops were shipped out of an area. The correct Confederate response, then, would be an attack in the weakened sector. In the present situation, Johnston should consolidate his forces in the West to meet

*The operations around Murfreesboro are discussed in Chapter 9.

145

the Federal threat, and Lee should mount an attack to take advantage of Burnside's transfer. By April 18, however, the crisis that had prompted the strategy discussions had ended without a decision. Burnside's force failed to materialize as a threat, and Rosecrans showed no signs either of being reinforced or of advancing into central Tennessee. But the basis for Lee's ideas on strategy had been formed.[1]

Robert E. Lee made two assumptions about the military operations that might take place during 1863. First, he believed that the intense summer heat in the lower south and the resultant illnesses would prevent active campaigning in that area during June, July, and August. Consequently, after May, the Federals would be incapable of taking any action against Fort Sumter, South Carolina. Confederate troops would have to man only the water batteries against naval attacks, and the remaining soldiers could be withdrawn to reinforce other areas. In addition, the threat to Vicksburg would diminish as the summer months advanced. This meant that Virginia should become the focal point of Confederate attention.[2]

Lee's second assumption was that Virginia was of primary military importance. That state was important because the main Union thrust in 1863 would be there. Even after the heavy Federal losses at Chancellorsville, Lee felt that he was outnumbered 3 to 1. Hooker's strength continued to build, and therefore the Army of Northern Virginia needed reinforcements. On May 9, however, Secretary of War James A. Seddon suggested that Lee send Major General George E. Pickett's division of Longstreet's corps to reinforce Major General John C. Pemberton in Mississippi. Lee's response was quick and predictable: ". . . it becomes a question between Virginia and the Mississippi," Lee wrote to the Secretary of War.[3] Reiterating his opinion that campaigning was impossible in Mississippi during the summer, Lee noted that Pickett would arrive in the West at about the same time that active operations there would cease. Thus, not only would Lee lose the use of Pickett's valuable division, but Pemberton would have no use for the division.[4] The Confederate general appealed to President Davis:

> I judge from the tone of the Northern papers that it is the intention of the administration at Washington to reenforce the army of General Hooker. . . . It would seem, therefore, that Virginia is to be the theater of action, and this army, if possible, ought to be strengthened.[5]

It appeared to Lee that a choice between Mississippi and Virginia had to be made, and that Virginia was the proper selection.

Lee's counterproposal to a reinforcement of the West was made without a real understanding of the situation there.

Although he was offering advice on overall Confederate strategy, he was speaking with the voice of a local commander. He saw the West as an area whose value was confined to the support of operations in the East. When the West needed help, he felt that each commander should do the best he could with the resources available. When the East appeared threatened, on the other hand, he asked for reinforcements from other armies—as had happened in September and December 1862, when he sought assistance from Bragg's army. Also, Lee did not seem to understand that Union forces in the West were active on two fronts. He saw only the operations along the Mississippi River as presenting a danger to the Confederacy, completely overlooking the deadly Federal line of operations that extended from Nashville, through Chattanooga, towards Atlanta. This lack of a clear picture of the overall Confederate military situation resulted in a proposal that was narrow in outlook and limited in scope.[6]

From the fourteenth to the seventeenth of May, Lee met with Davis and the Confederate Cabinet. He restated his position that with the limited resources available to the South, the government could support only one major operation: either in the East or in the West. Lee argued strongly that the Army of Northern Virginia must mount a second invasion of the North. Seddon, the original proponent of reinforcing Pemberton, quickly acquiesced. The choice seemed obvious. Either reinforce a winner (Robert E. Lee) or send troops to men of questionable ability (John C. Pemberton and Joseph E. Johnston). With the withdrawal of Seddon's support for western reinforcement, the rest of the Cabinet, with the exception of the Postmaster General, voted for Lee's plan.

This abrupt end to plans for a western campaign occurred as a result of Lee's reasonable and compelling arguments.[7] An invasion of the North would defend Richmond, for, by seizing the initiative and moving northward, Lee would force Hooker to follow, and thus prevent a possible siege of the Confederate capital. Moving the Union Army away from the Rappahannock River would offer great advantages. After their next defeat, the Federals would not be able to hide behind the river's excellent defensive network. A great victory on northern soil also could force the Federals to withdraw troops from the South Atlantic coastline, and perhaps draw troops from the West. Moreover, a victory would encourage the northern peace movement, and possibly change Lincoln's attitude toward negotiations. Great Britain and France also might have to alter their feelings about Confederate independence and conclude that a new nation in North America had been created. Finally, and probably most important, provisions would be plentiful in the North. Feeding the Army of Northern Virginia was one of Lee's most pressing problems. By moving into the rich Cumberland Valley of Pennsylvania, Lee would find a solution to a difficult supply task. Afterwards, he could

Major General James Longstreet

stockpile the accumulated supplies in Virginia. It is no wonder that these arguments had such a strong impact on the Confederate Cabinet.[8]

The Cabinet's decision to adopt Lee's plan led to a compromise in implementation. Lee's army was not reinforced in the way that he had requested. Instead, all of the available troops in South Carolina and Tennessee were sent to Vicksburg. But Lee's army was strengthened by the return of Longstreet's corps from its operations in southeastern Virginia. Stronger now than he had been at Chancellorsville, Lee was prepared to strike. Longstreet's return, however, posed an unusual problem.

While passing through Richmond on his way back to the Army of Northern Virginia, Longstreet had stopped in the Confederate capital to discuss strategy with the Secretary of War. Longstreet had devised a plan to rectify the situation in the West. He believed that the Federal army that was most vulnerable to destruction was Rosecrans' army at Murfreesboro, Tennessee. *(See Atlas Map No. 33.)* He suggested that Johnston's army at Jackson, Mississippi move towards Rosecrans from one direction while Longstreet led two divisions towards Rosecrans from the opposite direction. Once Rosecrans' force was destroyed, Johnston and Longstreet could advance towards Cincinnati, Ohio. Grant would thus be forced to move his army and counter the Confederate advance in the direction of the Ohio River. Vicksburg would be saved.

Seddon rejected the plan. He felt that Grant would retreat from Vicksburg only after he had been defeated. But the

damage was done. Thinking himself a strategist whose advice had been considered by the highest levels of government, Longstreet arrived at Lee's headquarters on May 18.[9]

Longstreet told Lee of his interview with the Secretary of War and advanced the same plan to Lee that he had proposed to Seddon. Upon hearing of Lee's plan for a second invasion of the North, however, Longstreet dropped his idea. But an argument developed over how the invasion should be conducted. Apparently influenced by the excellent results obtained by his defensive stand at Fredericksburg, Longstreet urged that once contact had been established with the Union army on northern soil, the Confederates should go on the defensive. A strategic penetration followed by a tactical defensive was a rather novel idea, and Longstreet left the meeting with the impression that Lee had accepted the concept. This was unfortunate, because Lee did not intend to adopt Longstreet's philosophy.[10]

Longstreet's return gave Lee the opportunity to accomplish a long-overdue task. He wanted to refine the organization of the Army of Northern Virginia, a combat instrument that had remained essentially unchanged since its inception. Each of its infantry corps was too large and unwieldy for one man to manage. "Stonewall" Jackson's death enabled Lee to reduce the size of each existing corps and create an additional corps without hurting anyone's feelings. The additional experience that had been gained in the last month convinced Lee that there were now qualified men available to fill the new positions. Lieutenant General Richard S. Ewell assumed command of Jackson's old unit, the II Corps. The newly created III Corps was given to Lieutenant General Ambrose P. Hill. The new corps organization required the appointment of two new division commanders. Major General Henry Heth received one appointment, and Major General William Dorsey Pender the other.

The artillery, too, was reorganized. First, the reserve that previously had been controlled at army level was divided up among the three corps. Second, the cavalry division under Major General J.E.B. Stuart was enlarged by the addition of a brigade from southwest Virginia under Brigadier General A.G. Jenkins and a brigade from western Virginia under Brigadier General John D. Imboden.

Both this vast reorganization and the losses suffered at Chancellorsville would have an impact on Lee's conduct of the invasion of the North. Two of the three corps commanders were new to their positions, while five of the nine division commanders were new to their level of command. Moreover, only twenty-five of the thirty-seven brigadier generals had some experience at that rank, six brigades had new leaders, and another six were under the command of colonels.[11]

The problems of a new organization were combined with several potential dangers. One was that while Lee marched north, Hooker might capture Richmond. Hooker also might successfully counter Lee's move to turn his right flank and, in turn, cut Lee's line of communication. Not the least of the problems was the lack of a clear-cut, concrete military objective for the Army of Northern Virginia. The Confederate Cabinet believed that Lee was going to "threaten" Washington, Baltimore, and Philadelphia. One of Lee's aides was under the impression that Philadelphia was not an objective, but rather that a great battle was to be fought west of the Susquehanna River. One of Lee's division commanders said that the commanding general had told him that the capture of Philadelphia was a key objective of the entire campaign. Regardless of the final objective, however, it was clear that the Confederates were going to fill their stomachs with the food available on the northern farmland. It was also clear that Chancellorsville had proven that the Army of Northern Virginia could do just about anything that Lee asked,[12] There were obstacles in Lee's path, but they were not insurmountable.

The Road to Gettysburg

If Lee's victory at Chancellorsville had made a great impact on Confederate thinking, it had also stirred action in Union quarters. On May 7, President Abraham Lincoln and Major General Henry W. Halleck, the General-in-Chief, visited Hooker's headquarters in the field. Lincoln was particularly concerned about the morale of the Army of the Potomac, fearing that the recent defeat might have destroyed all of the esprit de corps that Hooker had so painstakingly built. The President thought that another southward advance in the near future could restore some of the army's confidence, and thus suggested this option to Hooker when he arrived in the field. After placing the blame for his defeat at Chancellorsville on the XI Corps, Hooker told Lincoln that he expected to continue to operate along the same line as before. Satisfied that Hooker and the Army of the Potomac were in a reasonable state of readiness, Lincoln and Halleck returned to Washington.[13]

Within a week, Hooker informed Lincoln that his army was prepared for a new offensive. He set the date for May 14. Alarmed that the Army of the Potomac's move might be premature, Lincoln hurriedly summoned Hooker to the capital for a conference. He explained to the commanding general that additional time might be needed to restore the army's combat effectiveness, and that Hooker should conduct only those operations that would keep the Army of Northern Virginia out of "mischief." Feints, demonstrations, and "occasional cavalry raids" might be all that was necessary. Convinced of the need for wariness, Hooker returned to his army and patiently watched for the enemy's next move.[14]

Lee's Movement and Stuart's Embarrassment

Hooker did not have long to wait. Lee began moving his units early on the morning of June 3. Leaving A.P. Hill's III Corps to hold the attention of the Federals at Fredericksburg, Lee sent Longstreet's and Ewell's corps westward toward the Shenandoah Valley. *(See Atlas Map No. 34a; Confederate movements on June 3-19 are now shown.)* Once again, this area of rich farmland would serve as an invasion route into the North. Marching 15 miles on the first day, the Army of Northern Virginia intended to slip past Hooker's right flank before the Federal commander realized what was happening.[15]

On the same day that Ewell's corps left its position along the Rappahannock River, Major General J.E.B. Stuart held a grand review of his heavily reinforced cavalry division. It was a fabulous display of the cavalry's strength. A former Confederate secretary of war, George W. Randolph, was the reviewing officer; everyone watched with pride as the cavalry executed a mock charge, and the horse artillery fired blanks to repulse an imaginary enemy attack. The pomp and pageantry lacked only one thing—the admiring eye of Robert E. Lee.

Lee, who had been making last-minute preparations for the invasion of Pennsylvania, was unable to attend the review. But the proud Stuart wanted the commanding general to see the abilities of his horsemen, so a second review was held for Lee's benefit on June 8. At the conclusion of the exhibition, Lee congratulated Stuart and issued the cavalryman his instructions for the invasion. Stuart was to cross the Rappahannock early the next morning and cover the right flanks of Longstreet

Major General Alfred Pleasonton (*seated*) and His Staff

and Ewell as they moved northward. Stuart ordered his men to prepare for an early move on the ninth. With all of their baggage packed for a quick departure, the cavalry settled down for the night.[16]

Before they could move out the following morning, however, Stuart's troopers were surprised by the sound of gunfire coming from the direction of Beverly Ford. During the time that Stuart had been showing off to Lee, Major General Alfred Pleasonton's Federal cavalry corps had been preparing for an attack. Directed by Hooker to strike the Confederate forces believed to be assembled in the vicinity of Culpeper, Pleasonton had forced a crossing at Beverly Ford and rapidly dispersed Stuart's pickets. Surprised and almost captured by the impetuosity of the Union attack, Stuart's horse artillery fled to the rear.

After stablizing his lines in the vicinity of his headquarters on Fleetwood Hill, Stuart received reports that a second Federal column had crossed downstream and seized Brandy Station in his rear. Responding to this crisis, Stuart sent two brigades to the area. The enemy advance from this new direction, however, carried Fleetwood Hill, and the battle swayed back and forth as mounted column crashed into mounted column. After sending an aide to Longstreet to ask for reinforcements, Stuart received the necessary infantry aid and drove the attackers back across the river. The largest cavalry clash ever to take place on the North American Continent had almost resulted in a disaster for the Confederate cavalrymen.[17]

The Battle of Brandy Station had important repercussions. Upon his return from the action, Pleasonton reported to Hooker that he had stopped Stuart, who had been about to embark on another one of his famous cavalry raids. This report left Hooker with the impression that any future shift in southern forces would be in support of a Confederate cavalry raid. More important, though, the Union cavalrymen felt that they had proven themselves to be the equals of their southern counterparts. No longer did the blue ranks view Stuart's men as being qualitatively superior to the Federal cavalry. Brandy Station had shown Stuart to be fallible and the southern cavalry to be beatable. As a result of the battle, Stuart had also lost the services of one of his brigade commanders. Robert E. Lee's son, Brigadier General William H.F. Lee, was severely wounded in the leg, and became incapacitated for the coming campaign.* But Stuart lost more than the services of a valuable general; he lost the support of some of his admirers in the South. The *Richmond Examiner* published a particularly scathing editorial that criticized Stuart not only for his unpreparedness for the Federal attack, but also for his meaningless grand reviews:

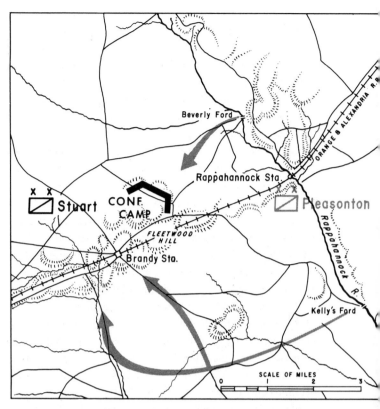

Union Attack on Brandy Station, June 9, 1863

. . . this puffed up cavalry of the Army of Northern Virginia has been surprised . . . and such repeated accidents can be regarded as nothing but the necessary consequences of negligence and bad management. If the war was a tournament, invented and supported for the pleasure of a few vain and weak-headed officers, these disasters might be dismissed with compassion. But the country pays dearly for the blunders. . . .[19]

Stuart was stung by the comments, and realized that he would have to accomplish a great deal in the approaching campaign to restore his reputation.

The brief clash at Brandy Station had no impact on Lee's timetable for the invasion of Pennsylvania. Longstreet and Ewell moved quickly forward toward the Shenandoah and Cumberland Valleys. A.P. Hill maintained a close watch at Fredericksburg, and when Hooker conducted a reconnaissance in force† with Major General John Sedgwick's VI Corps on June 5, Hill presented a picture that convinced the Union commander of the Confederates' continuing presence along the river. Lee then saw a chance to confuse Hooker further by conducting a feint toward Washington. After asking Davis that troops from North and South Carolina be organized under the command of General P.G.T. Beauregard, Lee added that

---

*During his convalescence, Lee was captured in a Union raid and remained in a prison camp until March 1864.[18]

†A reconnaissance in force is an operation intended to test the enemy's strength and disposition.

Beauregard's forces should then move to Culpeper and threaten Washington. Not only would this feint confuse Hooker, he argued, but it would also remove the pressure that the Federal forces on the Peninsula were exerting against Richmond.[20]

Operations on the Peninsula had bothered Lee since late May. His concern was intense, because the invasion of Pennsylvania was designed to remove pressure from Richmond, not expose it to sudden attack. Two Federal corps commanded by Major General John A. Dix were operating in the vicinity of Williamsburg, Yorktown, and Norfolk. *(See Atlas Map No. 33.)* Although Dix felt that his force of 32,668 men was too small to accomplish much, he tried to complete the tasks assigned to him by Halleck. The General-in-Chief wanted Dix to "threaten" Richmond, destroy several bridges north of the Confederate capital, and tie down a large enemy force. Later, Dix would be criticized because he did not accomplish more, but he did burn two bridges and tear up some railroad tracks north of the city. He also sent out a cavalry raid that netted 35 army wagons, 700 horses and mules, and 100 prisoners, including W.H.F. Lee, who was recuperating from the wound that he had received at Brandy Station. Dix's operations clearly demonstrated that Richmond would be vulnerable as long as Lee remained in Pennsylvania. Davis, therefore, rejected Lee's plan for a feint toward Washington under Beauregard's command, arguing that there were simply no forces available to support the operation.[21] Too many Federal troops were operating on too many fronts for Davis to strip all Confederate commands to reinforce Lee.

Hooker Vacillates

Even without Lee's proposed feint toward Washington, Hooker was having great difficulty discerning southern intentions. Pleasonton's action at Brandy Station had provided information indicating that the Confederate cavalry had been preparing for a major move at the time of the Federal strike. Sedgwick's attack on June 5 seemed to indicate that Lee's main force was stationary in its positions near Fredericksburg. When these two bits of information were put together, it seemed as though the Confederates were ready to mount only a large raid into Maryland. Yet Hooker received reports that Hood's and Pickett's divisions had rejoined the Army of Northern Virginia. With these reinforcements, Lee could easily mount an invasion similar to the one he had conducted in September 1862.

Hooker's dilemma grew as he tried to decide how to counter either a cavalry raid or a major invasion by Lee's entire army. First, he felt that in either case, the Union forces in the vicinity of Harper's Ferry would be vulnerable and therefore should be withdrawn. Second, if Lee tried another invasion, Hooker believed that the Army of the Potomac should lunge southward

and destroy Lee's rear guard. On June 5, he suggested this course of action to Lincoln.[22]

Lincoln rejected Hooker's suggestion because he felt that, since a defender had so many advantages, Hooker's lunge would turn into a stalemate while Lee marched unhampered northward. It was a case of the old question of proper objectives. Halleck offered some ideas to Hooker in a letter that immediately followed Lincoln's answer, including the recommendation that Hooker attack Lee's march column if the southern commander attempted another invasion. In a quandary, Hooker remained in his positions for an additional five days, trying to reach a decision. Finally, on June 9, he wrote the President that a major raid by the Confederate army seemed to be the most likely enemy course of action. Hooker insisted that, while a large portion of Lee's army was absent from his front, he should march in and seize the enemy's capital:

> If left to operate from my own judgment, with my present information, I do not hesitate to say that I should adopt this course as being the most speedy and certain mode of giving the rebellion a mortal blow. I desire that you will give it your reflection.[23]

Lincoln did not take long to reflect. He fired off a letter to Hooker that reiterated the instructions that Hooker had been given the previous January: "If you had Richmond invested to-day [sic], you would not be able to take it in twenty days.... I think Lee's army, and not Richmond, is your sure objective point."[24] Lincoln added sound advice by telling Hooker to take advantage of his central position and operate against Lee's army on interior lines.

By June 11, there was speculation in the Army of the Potomac that Lee was off on a second invasion of the North. This was confirmed on the following day when Ewell's corps surrounded Major General Robert H. Milroy's command of 6,900 men in the vicinity of Winchester. *(See Atlas Map No. 33.)* Milroy contemplated a defensive stand, decided against it when he realized the magnitude of the force opposing him, and evacuated his positions. Unfortunately for the hapless Federals, Ewell was prepared for Milroy's retreat and ambushed the Union column as it marched north. On the fifteenth, the remnants of Milroy's command filtered into Harper's Ferry. *(Action not shown on map.)* As Hooker became more fully aware that Lee was shifting infantry in a northwesterly direction, he began to fear that Lee's intention was to cut the Orange and Alexandria Railroad—the Army of the Potomac's principal line of communication. *(See Atlas Map No. 34a.)* Accordingly, on June 13 he decided to counter Lee's turning movement by concentrating his army in the vicinity of Centreville to protect its supply line.[25]

In May, Hooker had flanked Lee's army; in June, the commanders' roles were reversed as Lee moved his army to a threatening position on the Union flank. The Army of Northern Virginia had been on the move for over a week before Hooker decided to respond with a shift of his own forces. Although it is easy to criticize Hooker for his delay, it should be remembered that Lee had masked his movements with great skill. The southern commander carefully deployed his forces to confuse his opponent. In addition, the Blue Ridge Mountains offered an excellent screen behind which Lee could shift his army. Moreover, Stuart's cavalry aggressively defended the passes into the Shenandoah Valley, making it extremely difficult for the Federals to gather information. Although Hooker's initial response was slow, his hesitation was warranted by the situation that he faced. Once on the move, however, the commander of the Army of the Potomac displayed the same caution that had earmarked his earlier conduct—he appeared to be satisfied with simply making the troop movement.

Once again, Lincoln felt obligated to remind Hooker that Lee's army was the proper objective. Remembering that his earlier advice had gone unheeded, he rephrased his guidance in terms that a hunter could understand: "If the head of Lee's army is at Martinsburg and the tail of it . . . between Fredericksburg and Chancellorsville, the animal must be very slim somewhere. Could you not break him?"[26] Hooker, however, had no taste for hunting, and refused to act until he could be absolutely certain about the dispositions of the Army of Northern Virginia. Fearing that he would be ridiculed if he acted too quickly and missed the main body of Lee's army, Hooker made no major moves from June 17 to June 24. Instead, he consolidated his positions around Centreville and awaited the outcome of the cavalry probes that he had ordered Pleasonton to make.[27]

Virtually unopposed, Lee led his forces northward. *(See Atlas Map No. 34a.)* Upon the withdrawal of Hooker's army from the vicinity of Fredericksburg, Lee moved A.P. Hill into the Shenandoah Valley. He then ordered Ewell forward in the direction of Harrisburg to test Pennsylvania's defenses. Longstreet, still in the Valley, remained stationary to reinforce the Confederate cavalry screen. When Stuart's screen held against the Federal pressure, Hill crossed the Potomac River on the twenty-fourth, and Longstreet began crossing on the following day. With his units spread over a wide front, Lee took advantage of the absence of enemy pressure. Methodically, the Army of Northern Virginia gathered supplies from the Pennsylvania countryside. Several communities were forced to pay cash ransoms, but Lee kept a firm hand on the conduct of his men; Confederate money or receipts were issued in return for everything taken. A principal part of Lee's mission was being ably accomplished.

Pleasonton's efforts to gather information remained futile. Stuart's cavalry effectively blocked every attempt that the northern cavalryman made to penetrate the enemy's screen and locate the Army of Northern Virginia. Slowly, however, information began to filter in from Major General Darius N. Couch's headquarters in Pennsylvania.* With some apprehension, Couch watched the approach of Lee's army into Pennsylvania. He did not have any regular troops under his command, and the New York and Pennsylvania militia, called up in response to Lee's invasion, arrived slowly and had little training. Couch's real value was the focal point he provided for the collection of intelligence. Several agencies in Pennsylvania had been hurriedly organized to report on the movements of the Confederate army. Two were formed by the Pennsylvania Railroad, and one was put together by a private citizen. These three groups provided a great deal of useful information to Couch, who in turn kept the commander of the Army of the Potomac informed.[28]

The news about Lee did not embolden Hooker. Rather, he became convinced that his army was outnumbered by the Army of Northern Virginia. On June 23, he visited Washington and talked to Lincoln, Stanton, and Halleck. The details of the meeting are not known, but the defense of Harper's Ferry was discussed. Halleck wanted it held, and Hooker did not. The commander of the Army of the Potomac thought that it was exposed and would fall easily to the Confederates. He also felt that the Union forces there would be a valuable addition to his army in the field. When Lincoln supported Halleck's idea that the position should be held, Hooker left the capital without a promise of the reinforcements that he earnestly felt he needed. Persisting in this belief, he sent his chief of staff, Major General Daniel Butterfield, to Washington to demand that the capital's defenses be stripped to furnish troops for the field. Again, Hooker's request was denied. Halleck already had sent 25,000 veteran troops to bolster the Army of the Potomac, and additional forces simply did not exist. Finally, on June 25, Hooker began to move his army northward across the Potomac River.[29] *(Movements not shown on map.)*

Apparently, Hooker intended to strike at Lee's line of communication. Although he did not state that this was the purpose of the move, his dispositions and the movements of his corps seem to indicate that intention. Lee's supply line, however, was not particularly vulnerable to attack. His army was living off the land in Pennsylvania. The only items that had to be moved by supply wagon were war stores, such as ammunition. Until the Army of Northern Virginia became involved in a pitched battle, Lee's line of communication was virtually nonexistent. In fact, most of the items moving through the

---

*Couch had commanded the II Corps at Chancellorsville in May 1863. Completely disgusted by Hooker's performance in that battle, he had asked to be relieved. His request was approved, and he was subsequently placed in command of the Department of the Susquehanna, with headquarters in Harrisburg, Pennsylvania.

Harper's Ferry

Shenandoah Valley were heading southward toward Richmond, rather than northward toward Lee's army. A decision made in Washington, however, would prevent Hooker from trying to sever Lee's almost nonexistent supply line.

As the army crossed the Potomac, Hooker reopened his arguments for abandoning Harper's Ferry and re-calling its garrison to join the Army of the Potomac. Twice, Halleck turned down the new requests. Hooker began to feel that he was confronted by an intolerable situation: he was forced to defend the widely separated points of Washington and Harper's Ferry, and an enemy army that he believed outnumbered his was operating somewhere in his rear. Accordingly, he telegraphed the General-in-Chief: ''I beg to be understood, respectfully, but firmly, that I am unable to comply with this condition with the means at my disposal, and earnestly request that I may at once be relieved. . . .''[30] To his surprise, Hooker found that his latest request was approved immediately. Lincoln, having looked for an opportunity to replace Hooker since late May, authorized the General-in-Chief to send a courier to the Army of the Potomac with orders appointing a new commander.

In contrast to Lee's maneuvers, Hooker's performance had been lackluster. At first cautious by necessity, Hooker continued to perform in a dull and plodding fashion when the situation required aggressiveness. It appears that he may have been overcome with doubts similar to the ones that had plagued him in the Chancellorsville Campaign. He may also have been reluctant to fight the man who had humiliated him in May. His brief attempts at maneuver were not directed at clear objectives. Finally, he was indecisive, and his vacillations permitted the initiative to pass to Lee, allowing him to

move into Pennsylvania unmolested. Hooker's replacement would have to gain control of the situation promptly.[31]

At about 3:00 a.m. on June 28, Major General George G. Meade was awakened by an officer from Washington. The courier told the V Corps commander that he brought trouble. Quickly, Meade searched his mind for the memory of a misdeed that would require a summons from Washington. Finding nothing of note, Meade replied that his conscience was clear. The messenger handed the general a communication from the War Department. Meade opened the letter and found that indeed there was trouble—Hooker had been relieved from command of the Army of the Potomac, and he was Hooker's replacement.[32]

A New Commander

Lincoln had chosen Meade as the new commander in consultation with Stanton, but not Halleck. He had considered several others for the position before finally choosing Meade. Late in May, Lincoln had offered the command to Darius Couch, who then was still the senior corps commander in the Army of the Potomac. In the process of resigning as corps commander, Couch declined, but he recommended that Lincoln consider either Major General John F. Reynolds, the I Corps commander, or Meade. Hearing that he was being mentioned in connection with command of the Army, Reynolds traveled to Washington to remove his name from consideration.* By default, then, Meade was the only nominee.[33]

Meade's military service record was good. An 1835 graduate of West Point, he resigned in 1836 after serving briefly in the Seminole War. He reentered the army in 1842 as a topographical engineer, and was brevetted for the performance of a daring reconnaissance in the Battle of Monterey during the Mexican War. After the war, he served along the Florida coast and the Delaware Bay, surveying and building lighthouses. When the Civil War broke out, Meade was appointed Brigadier General of Pennsylvania volunteers. In 1862, he was badly wounded in the Battle of Glendale during the Peninsular Campaign. His wartime experience included command at every level from brigade through corps. As a corps commander at Chancellorsville, Meade had voted that the Army of the Potomac remain south of the Rappahannock River and attack Lee's army.[34]

George G. Meade brought an element of humility to the post of commanding general that had been missing in most of his predecessors. Instead of issuing a bombastic assumption-of-command order, Meade simply stated that he had ''no

---

*Although it is not exactly clear why Reynolds did not want to be appointed, it appears that he was afraid Washington would interfere too much with his command.

Major General George Gordon Meade

promises or pledges to make.'' He did not consider himself a Napoleon, and his friends knew that he preferred others to think of him as a professional, clearheaded soldier. He was known to act decisively and vigorously once he had studied the terrain over which he must fight and had gained an appreciation of the dispositions of friendly and enemy troop units. In short, he was an experienced combat leader.[35]

With his appointment order, Meade received instructions from Halleck. Promising not to issue detailed orders that would interfere with Meade's command prerogatives, Halleck directed the new commander of the Army of the Potomac to keep the Confederates away from Washington and Baltimore. In addition, Meade must keep in mind that his army was ''the army of operation against the invading forces of the rebels.'' Halleck also gave Meade the authority to appoint or relieve subordinates as he preferred.[36]

Meade acted on this last element of his directive first. He knew that it was important to find a chief of staff with whom he would be comfortable. Hooker's chief of staff, Butterfield, was adequate, but it was customary for a commander to appoint his own chief of staff. Butterfield was also known to harbor some resentment toward Meade because of an earlier

question concerning the command of the V Corps; Butterfield had been in line to take the job, but Meade was appointed instead because of seniority. For these reasons, Meade asked Major General Andrew A. Humphreys, a division commander in the III Corps, to be his chief of staff. Humphreys declined, pleading that he preferred a frontline command. Next, Meade turned to the chief engineer of the Army of the Potomac, Brigadier General Gouverneur K. Warren, and asked him to take the post. Warren begged off, saying that, as it was mid-campaign, Meade needed to keep as many people as possible in the same positions—including his chief of staff and his chief engineer. Having been turned down twice, Meade accepted Warren's sound advice.[37]

Meades appointment as commanding general was the final step in a major shakeup of the Army of the Potomac. On May 12, Hooker had reorganized the army's artillery. Artillery batteries were grouped into brigades, and each artillery brigade was assigned to an infantry corps. This was a departure from the previous arrangement, wherein individual batteries had been assigned to infantry divisions. The new organization gave the corps commander greater firepower and allowed him to position his artillery units according to the tactical situation. The Artillery Reserve for the army also was changed; it was increased from 12 to 21 batteries, thus giving the commanding general a greater ability to influence the action by moving his artillery resources to threatened areas. Commanders within the army also had been rearranged. On May 22, Major General Winfield Scott Hancock assumed command of the II Corps. He was the second new corps commander appointed within a month—Major General Oliver O. Howard had taken command of the XI Corps in April—and his designation was followed by the assignment of Major General George Sykes to the command of Meade's old corps on June 28. Finally, the commanding general of the cavalry corps was relatively new to his job; Major General Alfred Pleasonton had assumed command on May 22. Like the Army of Northern Virginia, the Army of the Potomac was testing a new organization as it headed toward Gettysburg. The only difference was that in the Federal army, the army commander also had been changed, and he was the newest to his job of anyone in either force.[38]

The Armies Maneuver Toward Contact

Changing commanders in the middle of a campaign can be dangerous, but Meade's appointment seemed to have a beneficial effect on the army. Hooker had made many mistakes and many enemies, so Meade's designation helped morale. The army seemed to move with new confidence. Meade's confidence, on the other hand, was not great. Generally, he had been uninformed about Hooker's orders, plans, and intentions.

Combined with his ignorance about Lee's army, this lack of information forced Meade to be cautious. His caution, though, was not of the same type that had debilitated Hooker. Meade knew that he had to advance and fight Lee; he just did not want to fight on terrain that would be to Lee's advantage.[39]

Meade decided to abandon Hooker's plan to move toward Lee's line of communication. He felt that the best course of action would be to advance northward, keeping Lee's army to his west. In this way he could cover Washington and Baltimore. If Lee made a move in the direction of either city, Meade would attack. If Lee tried to cross the Susquehanna River and was foiled in the attempt, Meade, again, would attack. Clearly, he intended to fight Lee wherever events seemed to lead him.

Meade set the march objectives for each corps, forcing a blistering pace on the men. With only sketchy information about the location of Lee's forces, Meade kept his corps within supporting distance of one another as they moved north toward Frederick, Maryland. *(See Atlas Map No. 34b.)* No matter which corps struck Lee's army first, Meade could bring the weight of his army to bear in a short period of time. After reaching Frederick, Meade continued pushing the Army of the Potomac toward Pennsylvania. Because his span of control* was too great for efficiency—he was trying to supervise the movements of seven infantry corps—he gave the I Corps commander, Reynolds, direction of one wing of the army. With three infantry corps (I, III, and XI) and one cavalry division under his control, Reynolds directed almost half of Meade's total strength. Since Reynolds' wing was closest to the enemy, Meade's allocation of combat power was justified.[40]

Reynolds moved his forces past Emmitsburg, Maryland northward into Pennsylvania. Although he was still unsure of the location of the Army of Northern Virginia, on June 30, Meade informed him that Lee probably would concentrate his army in the vicinity of Gettysburg. Reports that Lee's forces were located at York, Chambersburg, and Cashtown seemed to indicate that the existing road net would support a concentration of Lee's army at this small Pennsylvania farm town. Accordingly, Reynolds sent two of the cavalry brigades from Brigadier General John Buford's cavalry division forward to Gettysburg to search out the enemy and prevent a surprise Confederate thrust southward.[41]

Meade was not the only commanding general who was uncertain about the location of his opponent. Robert E. Lee was unsure about the movements of the Army of the Potomac. Lee's problem stemmed from a misunderstanding with his senior cavalry commander, "Jeb" Stuart, who had been out of touch with Lee since June 25. Without Stuart's ability to

*As a term, "span of control" refers to the number of subordinates a person directs.

Major General "Jeb" Stuart

gather good intelligence, Lee was in a position to which he was unaccustomed—he did not know what the Federals were doing.

Stuart had successfully screened the right flank of the Army of Northern Virginia while it passed down the Shenandoah Valley. When A.P. Hill withdrew from Fredericksburg and joined the rest of the army, Stuart's original mission ended. On June 21, Stuart informed Lee that the Army of the Potomac still had not moved from its positions around Centreville. Satisfied that Hooker's army posed no grave danger to the southern forces, Stuart proposed a plan that he thought would refurbish his reputation, which had been tarnished at Brandy Station. The cavalryman requested permission to take three brigades of cavalry and cross the Potomac River *east* of the Federal army. Once across the river, Stuart would ride around the Union forces and rejoin the main army in the north, thus duplicating the daring feat he had accomplished in the previous year on the Peninsula when he rode around McClellan's army.

With some reservations, Lee approved Stuart's plan. He wanted Stuart to judge whether he could pass around Hooker's army "without hindrance." If this was not possible, Lee expected him to withdraw to the west side of the mountains and move with the main army. In either case, the commanding general wanted Stuart to ''move on and feel the right of Ewell's troops, collecting information, provisions, & c.'' In a final note, Lee added that Stuart was to leave instructions with the two cavalry brigades remaining at the rear of the main army. These units were to post pickets at the passes into the Shenandoah Valley, and when the Federals withdrew from their front, they were to form a rear guard for the main body. Lee did not tell Stuart to keep him informed of the enemy's movements, and Stuart did not tell the cavalry commanders remaining with the army to do so.[42] Both Lee and Stuart appear to have assumed that Hooker would strike at Lee's extended line of communication. It was a tempting target for the Federal commander—and, apparently, Hooker did intend to sever it. As instructed, the two Confederate brigade commanders ordered the cavalry deployed to protect Lee's supply line; thus, Lee was supposed to know when the Union countermove occurred. As already noted, though, Meade did not move against Lee's line of communication. Instead, he advanced to intercept Lee's army, and the Confederate cavalry lost contact with the enemy.

At 1:00 a.m. on June 25, Stuart broke camp and headed east. *(See Atlas Map No. 34b.)* He took with him his three best brigade commanders: Brigadier General Wade Hampton, Brigadier General Fitzhugh Lee, and Colonel J.R. Chambliss. At dawn, he passed through the Bull Run Mountains. Five miles farther on, he stumbled into Hancock's II Corps. Stuart deployed, fired some artillery, and withdrew when Hancock started to attack. This brush with Hancock not only caused a delay, but also forced Stuart to ride farther east than he had originally intended. Nevertheless, by 3:00 a.m. on June 28, Stuart's entire force was in Maryland, east of the Army of the Potomac. Near Rockville, the raiders ran into a Federal supply train and captured 125 enemy wagons. Remembering Lee's order to gather provisions, Stuart decided to take the wagons with him. This caused a second dangerous delay in his progress. Without the wagons, the Confederate cavalrymen could cover 40 miles each day; with the wagons, Stuart's best daily ride would be only 25 miles.[43]

Having lost touch with Lee's army, Stuart headed north into Pennsylvania to find the right flank of Ewell's corps. On June 30, his column reached Hanover, where he briefly clashed with some Federal cavalry. At this point, he was only eleven miles east of Gettysburg and, had he shifted his force to the west, he might have encountered the bulk of Lee's army. Instead, believing that he would find Ewell's corps near York, Stuart changed the direction of his march to the northeast. Six miles outside of York, however, he learned that the Confederate troops located at York had marched westward the day before. Turning northwest toward Carlisle, Stuart sent couriers off in search of Lee's headquarters.[44]

By June 30, Lee had gathered most of his army together

Harrison, the Confederate Spy Who Reported Meade's Movements to Longstreet on June 28, 1863

in the vicinity of Chambersburg-Cashtown-Heidlersburg. *(Positions not shown on map.)* The Army of Northern Virginia had been enjoying the free use of the Pennsylvania countryside when on June 28, a Confederate spy reported to Longstreet that the Union army was in Maryland. When Longstreet forwarded this information to the commanding general, along with the notice that Hooker had been replaced by Meade, Lee's reaction was one of great surprise. He had expected his cavalry to report when the Union forces started to follow his army. At once, he ordered Ewell's corps to return from York, and assembled Longstreet's and Hill's corps on the road between Chambersburg and Gettysburg. Thus, by the evening of June 30, 43,000 Confederate infantry had concentrated within a few miles of Gettysburg. Lee sought to learn more about the Army of the Potomac, but his best source of information was riding toward Carlisle.

Late on July 1, Stuart arrived at Carlisle and prepared to launch an assault on the town. About then, two of the couriers who had ridden off to find Lee returned and told Stuart that the commanding general wanted him at Gettysburg. Stuart fired his artillery at some militia, burned the cavalry barracks located in the town, and headed for Gettysburg, 30 miles away. At noon on the following day, with his tired troopers strung out on the roads behind him, Stuart walked into Lee's headquarters. Lee looked up. ''Well, General Stuart,'' he exclaimed, ''you are here at last!''[45]

Because Stuart's operations forced Lee into a meeting en-

Brigadier General John Buford

gagement at Gettysburg, Stuart's fateful ride has evoked much historical controversy. Historians have tried to affix responsibility for the failure of the Confederate cavalry during the period prior to the battle. The blame can be shared by Lee and Stuart. On the one hand, Lee did not give clear instructions to Stuart. He did not say precisely what Stuart's mission was to be in the campaign. Nor did he use the four brigades of cavalry with the main body effectively. On the other hand, Stuart seemed to be more concerned with his own reputation than with the proper use of his cavalry. Additionally, he took the most resourceful commanders with him, instead of leaving the most qualified officers with the army. Also, although he was not able to move "without hindrance" because of his contact with Hancock's corps at the outset, he continued his raid. The impact of Stuart's ride can be overemphasized, but it is clear that Lee needed Stuart from June 28 to June 30. Stuart's unusual ability to find the correct information, to evaluate it in a way that would assist Lee, and to forward it to the commanding general promptly, was missing during the critical period immediately preceding the battle, thus enabling Meade to suprise Lee. There was sufficient cavalry with the main army; Lee simply did not have Stuart to direct it properly. Federal General Henry Hunt's analysis of Stuart's ride probably is the best summation that has been made of the whole affair: "It is a good lesson on cavalry raids around armies, a thing easily done but of no particular use."[46]

While Lee was assembling his army, Reynolds was pushing his forces in the direction of Gettysburg. On June 30, Buford, in the van with two brigades of cavalry, clashed with a Confederate infantry regiment near the town. The Confederates withdrew to the west, followed by Buford, who dismounted his cavalrymen on the high ground that guarded the roads leading toward the enemy. *(See Atlas Map No. 35a.)* He spread out his pickets, and sent a dispatch to Reynolds that outlined his estimate of the situation. Buford thought that Hill's corps was at Cashtown and that Longstreet was marching to join him. Ewell's position was not known, but it appeared that his corps was approaching from the directions of Carlisle and York.[47] Reynolds analyzed this information and decided to order his part of the army to rest for the night. Nervous anticipation combined with grim determination ran through the army; as one Union general wrote to his commander on the eve of the battle, everyone felt that "we must and will fight to the end."[48]

The Battle of Gettysburg

At Cashtown on the evening of June 30, Major General Henry Heth listened to a report from Brigadier General Johnston J. Pettigrew. On orders from Heth, Pettigrew had marched to Gettysburg that morning to secure some shoes that had been reported to be in the town. Pettigrew related that when he approached Gettysburg, he had encountered a Union cavalry force. Not wanting to bring on a general engagement without permission, Pettigrew had withdrawn to Cashtown. While Heth listened to his brigade commander's tale, A.P. Hill rode up and joined the group. Hill remarked that the cavalry force probably represented only an outpost. Heth agreed, and asked permission to return to Gettysburg on the following day and get the shoes. Hill replied, "Do so."[49]

The First Day

At about 5:00 a.m. on July 1, Heth left Cashtown with four brigades of infantry. When he reached some hills overlooking Willoughby Run, he directed his artillery to fire into the edge of the woods to their front. Receiving no reply from the direction of the woods, Heth's division continued marching toward Gettysburg. At about 8:00 a.m., his infantry ran into Buford's dismounted cavalry on McPherson's Ridge. *(See Atlas Map No. 35a.)* The Federal skirmish line brought the gray column to a halt. Heth pushed the attack, apparently expecting to find only a small reconnaissance force opposing him. Although sent only after shoes, Heth knew that a few Union prisoners would be a handsome prize to present to Hill in the evening.[50] Buford's men returned the Confederate fire and maneuvered to block the enemy's approach. The cavalrymen put up a stiff fight, stopping the two brigades that Heth had on line. With support from only six artillery pieces, however, Buford needed additional help. He sent dispatches to Meade, Reynolds, and Pleasonton, telling them that a battle was developing.

Buford's message—indeed, his earlier decision to defend on McPherson's Ridge—had the effect of committing Meade to fight at Gettysburg. Reynolds received the note while in the line of march toward Gettysburg. He pondered its implications in light of his instructions from Meade. Meade had seemed unsure of where to concentrate his army. He felt that if the Confederates were east of Gettysburg, the town probably would not be a good place to bring on a battle; if Lee's army was west of the town, however, Gettysburg might be a good place to fight—but Meade did not know enough about the area to make a judgment. He had asked for Reynolds' advice. Meanwhile, he had ordered most elements of the army to close up. The best advice Reynolds could give was that I Corps, temporarily under the command of Major General Abner Doubleday, should speed its approach toward Gettysburg. The battle had begun.

During Reynolds' ride through Gettysburg, he found Buford observing the battle from the cupola of the Lutheran Theological Seminary on the western edge of town. Together, the two generals rode forward. Buford seemed concerned; it looked as if Lee's entire army was being thrown against his two brigades. Reynolds asked him if the cavalry could hold until I Corps arrived. Buford thought that they could, and Reynolds ordered Doubleday to bring his corps up to support Buford. At about 10:00 a.m., Major General James S. Wadsworth's division arrived, followed shortly by Brigadier General John C. Robison's division. Buford's cavalry withdrew, and the infantrymen took their place on McPherson's Ridge. Wadsworth's veteran division included the famous ''Iron Brigade'';* these men were anxious to get at Heth's troops. The battle raged back and forth as attack met counterattack. Two of Heth's brigades suffered greatly, and Brigadier General James J. Archer fell into Federal hands. The Union I Corps seemed to be having a great deal of success. Reynolds urged his men forward into McPherson's Woods to continue to drive

Major General John F. Reynolds

the Confederates back. When he turned to the rear to see if any more troops were arriving, he was struck behind the right ear with a musket ball. He was dead within a minute.[51]

Reynolds' death created a temporary crisis on the battlefield. In the rear, however, several Union generals were trying to bring additional weight to bear against the Confederates at Gettysburg. Howard's XI Corps was moving along the Emmitsburg Road toward town when a staff officer arrived from Reynolds. Following the officer's instructions, Howard halted his corps near a peach orchard *(see Atlas Map No. 35a)* and rode forward with his staff to view the terrain. First, he stopped at the north end of Cemetery Ridge. Having decided that it was an excellent defensive position, he then rode into town to get a better idea of the fighting already underway. In the town, Howard was notified that Reynolds was dead, and that he was the senior officer on the field. With only nine years of military service, Howard suddenly had a responsibility that exceeded his experience. He ordered his corps forward.

At about 11:20 a.m., another of Reynolds' couriers arrived at Meade's headquarters. The messenger reported that Reynolds was determined to contest every inch of ground, and was prepared to barricade the streets of Gettysburg should the need arise. Satisfied with Reynolds' decision, Meade sent a letter to Halleck, informing the General-in-Chief that he was ready to receive an attack by Lee's army. Almost in passing, he also mentioned that a defensive position had been selected along Pipe Creek in Maryland. *(See Atlas Map No. 34b.)* This line of defense would cover Washington quite well.

---

*The Iron Brigade was perhaps the most famous unit in the Army of the Potomac—and for good reason. Formed of regiments of volunteers from Wisconsin and Indiana in 1861, it was trained by a demanding soldier, Brigadier General John Gibbon, and fought its initial actions under his command. To provide a sense of esprit to the brigade, Gibbon outfitted the men in black felt hats and white gaiters. Hence, the force was originally called the ''Black Hat Brigade.'' In its baptism of fire, the Black Hats suffered 30 percent casualties as they fought Jackson's corps to a standstill at Second Bull Run. At South Mountain (Antietam), the brigade got its second nickname when McClellan admiringly observed that the unit must be made of iron. On the first day of the battle at Gettysburg, the Black Hats fought superbly, initially decimating Archer's brigade and then withstanding attacks by an overwhelming number of Confederates; in all, the brigade lost two-thirds of its 1,800 men in the fighting.

Meade had already begun to sense, however, that the clash of arms in Gettysburg had made any thought of fighting the battle at Pipe Creek academic. The gravity of the situation became more apparent when another courier arrived from Gettysburg at 1:00 p.m. to inform Meade of Reynolds' death. Turning to his chief engineer, Meade told Warren to ride to the battlefield and gain an understanding of what was happening. Soon afterward, Meade met Hancock, his II Corps commander, and told him to ride to Gettysburg and take charge of affairs. If the area was not suitable for defense, Hancock must find a position that was. If it was satisfactory, the Army of the Potomac would reinforce the site quickly. Meanwhile, Meade would remain in his headquarters at Taneytown and await Hancock's report.[52]

Pressure continued to build against I Corps on McPherson's Ridge. *(See Atlas Map No. 35b.)* Ewell's corps, moving to the sound of the guns, was beginning to appear on the roads from Carlisle and Heidlersburg. Buford sent a brigade of cavalry to Oak Hill to watch the Federal right and to prevent a junction of Ewell's and Hill's corps. At about the same time that Meade learned of Reynolds' death, the Union XI Corps arrived on the field. Buford informed Howard of Ewell's approach, and the XI Corps commander told Major General Daniel E. Sickles and Major General Henry W. Slocum to bring the III and XII Corps forward. The urgency of the situation was obvious in Howard's request: "General Reynolds is killed. For God's sake, come up—Howard."[53] Rapidly, the two corps pushed toward the front.

Howard's earlier reconnaissance with his staff had convinced him that it was crucial to hold Cemetery Hill, on the north end of Cemetery Ridge. Dominating the approaches from Gettysburg, Cemetery Hill was an obvious place to build a defensive position if the Union effort north of the town failed. Howard therefore placed Brigadier General Adolph von Steinwehr's division on the hill and sent his remaining two divisions forward to extend Doubleday's right flank. Howard's foresight was fortunate, because the efforts of the I and XI Corps failed. Outnumbered, outflanked, and outgunned, the XI Corps' front began to give way. Sometime after 3:00 p.m., Howard ordered both the I and XI Corps to retire through the town and to assume a new defensive line. In the beginning, the withdrawal was orderly, but in the streets of the town, the units became mixed and the pace of the retreat quickened. By the time the men reached Steinwehr's position on Cemetery Hill, although they were not panic-stricken, they were moving energetically to the rear.

Steinwehr's division had a calming influence on the retreating columns. More important, Winfield Scott Hancock's coolheaded handling of the situation created order out of virtual chaos. Soon after Howard had issued the retreat order, Hancock arrived and took command of the field. The II Corps commander placed Doubleday's withdrawing corps on Steinwehr's left and ordered the two remaining divisions of the XI Corps into the line to support Steinwehr. *(See Atlas Map No. 36a.)* Realizing that Culp's Hill on the right flank was also key terrain and that the XI Corps was incapable of defending it, Hancock directed Doubleday to split his corps and send one division to organize a position on the Union right. The Federals emplaced artillery and began to construct breastworks.[54]

Across the open fields opposite the Union left, Robert E. Lee watched Howard's retreating soldiers climb Cemetery Hill. The time seemed right for Ewell to continue to press the attack and drive the Federals southward, away from Gettysburg. Lee sent an aide to Ewell to tell the II Corps commander to push the enemy. Ewell was directed "to carry the hill occupied by the enemy, if he found it practicable, but to avoid a general engagement until the arrival of the other divisions of the army. . . . " So Ewell hesitated. He wanted Major General Edward Johnson's division to be present before he attacked the heights. The troops on the field were exhausted from the day's fighting, and Ewell could not move enough artillery into position to properly cover an assault. Johnson's division would help to offset these shortcomings. Several men on Ewell's staff were shocked by Ewell's hesitancy. They thought that "Stonewall" Jackson, Ewell's predecessor, would have driven the enemy right off the hill, with or without either Johnson or the artillery. But Ewell waited, and the Federals built. When the van of Johnson's division arrived, Ewell ordered it to halt. He had just received reports that a Union column had been spotted marching along the York Pike, opposite the Confederate left flank. By the time the report had been proven false and Johnson was in position to attack, it was 8:00 p.m.—too late to launch an assault in daylight. Ewell directed his corps to rest for the night.[55]

While Lee waited for Ewell's attack of Cemetery Hill, Longstreet rode up and joined the commanding general. Lee told his "war horse" that their forces must have run into the entire Army of the Potomac. He mentioned that Ewell had been ordered to seize Cemetery Hill, and added that if Meade remained on the field the following day, he was going to attack. A serious argument broke out between the two generals. Recalling what he thought Lee's promise had been prior to the opening of the campaign, Longstreet urged Lee to slip around Meade's left flank and position his forces between the enemy and Washington. This would force Meade to try to dislodge the Confederate army. Since all the advantages rested with the defender, Lee would thus produce another brilliant victory like Fredericksburg. Longstreet's argument fell on deaf ears. Lee repeated that he would attack Meade on the next day if the Army of the Potomac remained on the field. The discussion ended.

The Second Day

Lee wanted his attack to start as early as possible on July 2. He planned to exploit success and have Ewell make the main attack against the Federal right. When he rode to Ewell's headquarters in the evening to outline his plan, however, Lee encountered more opposition. While Ewell listened and nodded in agreement, Major Generals Jubal A. Early and Robert E. Rodes, two of Ewell's division commanders, argued against the plan. They felt that the enemy right was too strong and that Cemetery Hill was unassailable. Faced with men who had detailed knowledge of the enemy situation, Lee changed his mind and told Ewell to make an attack in support of Longstreet, who would assault the Union left. Lee directed Ewell to start his attack when he heard Longstreet's guns. But thinking better of the plan after he had returned to his headquarters later that night, Lee told Ewell to cancel his plans for an attack and move his corps around to support the Confederate right.[56]

Lee was concerned about the length of his line. *(See Atlas Map No. 36b.)* Meade, his defensive position shaped like an inverted fishhook, occupied a central position. Only three miles separated the right and left extremities of his line. Lee, on the other hand, was operating on an exterior line, and his soldiers had to travel nine miles to get from one flank to the other. By moving Ewell to the right, Lee would shorten the distance between his flanks and neutralize Meade's advantage of interior lines.

When Ewell received Lee's order to shift his troops right, he again balked. Riding over to Lee's headquarters, Ewell dismounted and argued in favor of an attack against the Federal right. A brief reconnaissance had shown him that Culp's Hill was vulnerable to attack. Once on that hill, the Confederates could command the Union position on Cemetery Hill. Lee again changed his plans, this time telling Ewell to seize Culp's Hill on the following day.

During the night, a Federal dispatch fell into Confederate hands. The dispatch indicated that the Union XII Corps already was present on the field and that the V Corps was enroute, its line of march appearing to lead directly into Ewell's left flank.* Before he could ask for a change in plans, Ewell received a new directive from Lee: the Confederate II Corps was to assault Culp's Hill when the sound of Longstreet's guns indicated that the attack against the enemy left had started. Ewell was "to make a diversion in their favor, to be converted into a real attack if an opportunity offered."[57]

During the night, Longstreet's corps hurried toward Gettysburg. Delayed on the morning of July 1 by the passage of a part of Ewell's corps near Greenwood, most of the I Corps

*It was an incorrect assumption. The V Corps arrived on the field farther south.

joined the main army at about midnight. On the morning of July 2, Lee, Longstreet, Hill, Heth, and Hood sat beneath a tree on Seminary Ridge and discussed plans for the day's attack. Lee told Longstreet that he wanted the I Corps to lead the main attack up the Emmitsburg Road with two divisions. Longstreet again objected, but Lee repeated his instructions. By this time, the lead elements of Longstreet's corps had arrived from their bivouac site of the previous night. Some of the men had only been able to get two hours sleep, but most were ready for the day's activities. They were ordered to stack arms and rest while the commanders reviewed the situation, conducted a reconnaissance, and selected a suitable site for their attack.

From the Confederate position along Seminary Ridge, it appeared that the Federal line on Cemetery Ridge did not extend very far south along the ridge line. Some heights along the Emmitsburg Road appeared to be suitable for the emplacement of artillery in support of an infantry assault up the road toward the enemy flank near Cemetery Hill. Lee sent a reconnaissance party around to the right to verify that the enemy line did not extend southward toward Little Round Top. Lee's staff officers went to the crest of Little Round Top; looking through the trees below, they could not see any Federal troops on Cemetery Ridge. They returned and confirmed Lee's suspicion that the Union left was exposed to attack. Unfortunately for the Confederates, the reconnaissance party had taken a quick look at the enemy lines during the time when the Federals were in the process of shifting troops. In fact, the Union lines did extend south along Cemetery Ridge. Lee therefore had a complete misunderstanding of Meade's position.[58]

Throughout the previous night, the Army of the Potomac had been gathering on the hills south of Gettysburg. The XII Corps arrived, one division going to defend Little Round Top while the remaining troops marched to the right flank at Culp's Hill. When the III Corps arrived, it moved to positions on Cemetery Ridge, linking Little Round Top to the rest of the line. *(Position not shown on map.)* The V Corps was held in reserve behind Cemetery Ridge. When the II Corps appeared early on July 2 and took up positions between the I and III Corps, six of Meade's seven corps were present; the final corps, the VI, would arrive in the afternoon. Meade, who had been on the field since midnight of July 1, finally had most of his 85,500 men present. Lee, with approximately 75,000 soldiers, was facing a formidable line that stretched from Culp's Hill, around Cemetery Hill, southward along Cemetery Ridge, and finally to the Round Tops—two hills that dominated the whole Federal line. Just before Lee's staff officers had mounted Little Round Top early in the morning, the division from the XII Corps, which had been defending the hill since the previous night, had moved off to rejoin its parent unit on the right. The III Corps, which was to extend to the left and protect the Round Tops, had not yet been able to comply with Meade's orders. The Confederates had seen a weakness in the Union position, but the weakness was only temporary.[59]

Sickles' tardiness in complying with Meade's instructions to cover the hills on the left was not his worst mistake of the day. Upon reaching his assigned position on Cemetery Ridge, that impetuous commander looked toward the Confederate lines and decided that his corps was not in the best location. Trees and boulders covered both the ground that he was to occupy and the area to his front. Moreover, the ground to his front seemed slightly higher. From there, Confederate artillery might be able to command his lines. Sickles rode to Meade's headquarters to request permission to move about a mile forward. Meade was not adamant in his rejection of Sickles' proposal, preferring to explain the importance of the entire Federal position to his corps commander. Sickles believed that Meade's answer gave him sufficient latitude to do what he thought was best. Sickles then asked Meade to permit the Army of the Potomac's artillery chief, Brigadier General Henry Hunt, to return with him to his corps and advise him on the proper positioning of his artillery. Granted permission, Sickles took Hunt with him to his corps' position on Cemetery Ridge and tried to convince Hunt that the III Corps should move forward to the higher ground. Hunt refused to be trapped into giving an answer. Just then, Hunt heard artillery fire to the right. As he rode off to determine its cause, he told Sickles that any change in the III Corps position would have to be approved by Meade. Sickles, sensing that a crisis was approaching on his own front, sent some skirmishers into the woods to find out what the Confederates were doing. Twenty minutes later, they reported enemy movement toward the south. Thinking that he had to act promptly to prevent the high ground from falling into enemy hands, Sickles moved his corps forward. Back on Cemetery Ridge, Hancock, whose corps was on Sickles' right, was astounded by the move. One of his division commanders suggested that perhaps Meade had ordered a general advance and that Hancock's corps had missed the order.[60]

Sickles had advanced the III Corps into a salient. *(See Atlas Map No. 36b.)* This extended his line to a length far greater than could be adequately defended by one corps. Also, the shape of Sickles' line would expose it to both Confederate fire and attacks from three directions. Furthermore, not only had Sickles disobeyed his orders to occupy Cemetery Ridge, but he had also left Little Round Top undefended.

At 3:00 p.m., with his corps already positioned in the salient, Sickles arrived at Meade's headquarters on the Taneytown Road. Meade had summoned all of his corps commanders for a council of war. Earlier, Sickles had asked permission to miss the meeting, but Meade ordered him to attend.

Major General Daniel E. Sickles

As Sickles dismounted, Meade walked out of the door to his headquarters and told Sickles to return to his corps. Heavy artillery fire could be heard in the direction of the Union left. Sickles remounted and rode quickly back to his men. Behind him, Meade mounted his horse, and he and Warren rode to ascertain the situation on the III Corps' front. When they reached Cemetery Ridge, Meade's chief engineer said, "Here is where our line should be." Hearing the Confederate cannon fire to the front, Meade replied, "It is too late now," and rode in the direction of the fire. Warren, wanting to get a better view of the terrain, rode to the crest of Little Round Top.[61]

When Warren reached the top of the hill, he could see that the position was undefended, the left flank was exposed, and the Confederates were ready to attack. Quickly, he rode to the bottom of the hill and sent a message to Meade, requesting that a division be sent to defend the critical position on the left. In order to determine whether the hill was in immediate danger, Warren directed a nearby artillery battery to fire into the woods at the base of the hill toward the Confederate lines. Sunlight flashed off musket barrels as soldiers at the edge of the woods scrambled for cover. The situation was critical! Noticing a blue column of infantry apparently marching to reinforce Sickles, Warren rode over to request help. When he reached the unit, he discovered that it was a regiment from the brigade that he had earlier commanded. As he started to explain the army's plight to the regimental commander, Warren saw his younger brother, Edgar, approaching. Edgar Warren was an aide to Brigadier General Stephen H. Weed, commander of a brigade in the V Corps. The army's chief engineer received promises that the entire brigade would send help. Next, Warren directed an artillery battery and the brigade's lead regiment to move to the top of the hill. He then rode to see the V Corps commander and secure additional reinforcements. The ensuing fight for Little Round Top was a close contest. Federals ran up one side of the hill as Confederates ran up the other. *(Action not shown on map.)* The fight ended with the Army of the Potomac holding the position.[62] Warren had taken action in time.

Meade arrived at Sickles' headquarters just as the III Corps' pickets were being driven in by the Confederate attack. Meade's calm attitude was surprising, considering his reputation for irascibility. He simply said to Sickles, ''General, I am afraid you are too far out.'' Sickles, after disagreeing, added, ''However, I will withdraw if you wish, sir.'' ''I think it is too late,'' Meade replied. ''The enemy will not allow you. If you need more artillery, call on the Reserve. The Fifth Corps and a division of Hancock's will support you.'' Just then, Meade's horse bolted at the sound of a cannon shot, and the commanding general rode away to hurry reinforcements forward in support of the III Corps.[63]

After many delays, Longstreet had finally commenced the artillery preparation for his attack against Sickles. Although he thought that the attack was poorly timed and had been aimed in the wrong direction, he was determined to follow the letter, if not the spirit, of Lee's instructions. His division commander on the far right, Major General John B. Hood, recommended that the right wing of the attack be extended around the Round Tops. Longstreet replied that Lee's orders were to attack up the Emmitsburg Road, and that everyone would obey the orders of the commanding general. Nevertheless, Hood extended his lines to the right to include Little Round Top, and his near success against Warren on that hill was proof that the Federal line of battle was vulnerable. After a one-hour cannonade, Longstreet attacked, supported by Major General Richard Anderson's division of Hill's corps. *(See Atlas Map No. 36b.)*

Although the position that Sickles selected gave many advantages to the Confederates, the fight for the Peach Orchard and the Wheatfield lasted almost four hours. Before being seriously wounded, Sickles skillfully plugged the holes in his lines almost as quickly as they developed. The appearance of

Confederate Troops Attack Cemetery Ridge, July 2, 1863

the V Corps on Sickles left bought time for the Federals and prevented a complete disaster. Hancock, too, sent a division, and it bolstered the right of the III Corps. But the Confederates had too many advantages; the position in the Peach Orchard gradually gave way. Stubborn Union resistance continued as the ground in the Wheatfield was contested. Finally, it too became an untenable position. The III Corps broke and fled. The Confederates followed close on the heels of the retreating northerners, but as they approached Cemetery Ridge, fresh Federal troops appeared. Major General John Sedgwick's VI Corps had arrived on the field, and Meade had immediately sent it to the left to act as a reserve force. *(Movement not shown on map.)* When the remnants of the III Corps began streaming back through the lines, Sedgwick counterattacked in conjunction with a brigade from the V Corps, and the Confederates were stopped cold. Parts of the XII Corps also had been sent to the left to help restore the position, and the sight of all these Union troops waiting on Cemetery Ridge was too much for Longstreet's and Anderson's troops. After a bitter fight, it appeared to the Confederates that they had only pierced the outer lines of the Union defenses. *(See Atlas Map No. 37a.)* With darkness approaching, Longstreet halted the attack and consolidated his position in the Peach Orchard.[64]

On the northern end of the line, Lieutenant General Richard S. Ewell had finally heard the sound of Longstreet's guns at 4:00 p.m. Charged by Lee to create a diversion for Longstreet's attack, Ewell ordered his artillerymen to open fire on the Federal positions on Cemetery and Culp's Hills. The artillery duel that followed was one-sided, as the terrain prevented Ewell's gunners from getting most of their cannon into action. The Union artillery on Cemetery Hill clearly had the advantage. Nevertheless, Ewell decided to attack with his infantry during the waning minutes of daylight. On the far left, Johnson's division pushed up Culp's Hill. The Confederates easily occupied some entrenchments that had been abandoned by the XII Corps when it moved off to the Union left to help save the situation there. As Johnson continued his advance, Howard and Wadsworth rushed units to support the lone XII Corps brigade that had been left behind to hold the hill. Johnson's division received the full fury of the Federal counterattack. With his men caught in the thick woods and hampered by the stone cliffs on the face of Culp's Hill, the Confederate commander decided to call off the night attack and wait for daylight to renew the assault.

On Johnson's right, Major General Jubal Early's division fared little better. *(See Atlas Map No. 37a.)* Two of his brigades assaulted the enemy on Cemetery Hill and initially made good progress. Seeing that his men had, in some places, reached the enemy's artillery positions, Early rode to his right to ask Major General R.E. Rodes to launch a supporting attack.

When Early approached, Rodes was just getting his last units into line. He said that he had been unable to obtain support from Major General William D. Pender's division (under the command of Brigadier General James H. Lane) of Hill's corps on his right. Nevertheless, he would attack if Early thought it advisable. Just then, Early received word that his own two brigades had been ejected from the Union line; consequently, he told Rodes to cancel the attack. Effective Union artillery fire, reinforcements from Hancock's corps, and darkness had ruined Ewell's uncoordinated attack on Cemetery and Culp's Hills. The major fighting on July 2 was over.[65]

Although not in good humor over the execution of his plans for the day's fighting, Lee felt that he had reason to be confident of eventual success. Casualties had been heavy on both sides; three general officers in the Confederate ranks were dead or dying, but four general officers in the Union army had fallen. (Sixty-five percent of Meade's total losses during the three days of fighting occurred on the second day.) Longstreet had driven the enemy from the field in front of Cemetery Ridge, and, on his left, a brigade from Anderson's division had actually reached the crest of the ridge. On the far left, Johnson's division had been partially successful; it held positions well forward on Culp's Hill. The Army of Northern Virginia had met stiff opposition; in keeping with its finest traditions, however, Lee believed that it again had shown that it could beat the Army of the Potomac.[66]

The Third Day

After the fighting ceased on July 2, Meade assembled his principal commanders at his headquarters in the Leister House. It was a warm night, and 12 general officers, a bed, a table, and a couple of chairs had been crowded into the small 10- by 12-foot front room. Tired out from the day's fighting, Warren went to sleep in a corner of the stuffy enclosure. The opening discussion was very informal, and Major General John Newton, acting commander of the I Corps, mentioned that he thought Gettysburg was not the right place to fight a battle. The general course of the discussion, however, seemed to indicate that the site of the battle already had been chosen and that the best course of action was to stand and fight. When the talk turned to this last subject, Meade's chief of staff posed three questions. He wanted to know how many commanders wished the army to retreat, how many wished to stand and fight on the defensive, and how many supported an attack. Having secretly prepared a contingency plan for the army's retreat, Butterfield was particularly concerned about the first question. The general consensus was that the army should remain in its present position and wait for Lee to attack. Meade concluded the meeting with the comment,

Union Troops Prepare for Battle on Culp's Hill, July 3, 1863

"Such then, is the decision." As the officers filed out of the room, Meade stopped Brigadier General John Gibbon, a division commander in Hancock's corps, and said, "If Lee attacks tomorrow, it will be in *your front*. He has made attacks on both our flanks and failed and if he concludes to try it again, it will be on our center."[67] Thoughtfully, Gibbon returned to his position on Cemetery Ridge.

Right after daylight on July 3, events seemed to refute Meade's analysis. On the slopes of Culp's Hill, Johnson pushed his brigades forward in an effort to take the remainder of the hill. *(See Atlas Map No. 37b.)* As on the previous day, he was forced to make the attack without adequate artillery support. However, instead of meeting only one brigade, as he had on July 2, Johnson found that the entire XII Corps had returned to occupy its old positions. The fighting was furious, but the conclusion was foregone. Johnson lost the foothold that he had gained the day before, and the XII Corps recaptured its former positions. The Federal right was secure.

Almost exactly as Meade had predicted, Lee thought that he had solved the problem posed by the Federal defense. Major General George E. Pickett's division had not yet participated in the fighting, and it was ready for battle. Stuart's cavalry also had arrived on the field. Pickett's fresh troops could strike the enemy center while Stuart attacked the enemy from the rear. Caught between the jaws of a vise, the Federal center would collapse, and the field would be won. Lee rode

to Longstreet's headquarters to issue his final instructions.

When Longstreet heard Lee's plan, he told the commanding general that an attack across a mile-wide open field could not succeed. Lee said that Longstreet's other two divisions would be held back to protect the right flank while Pickett made his attack. Moreover, in the north, seven brigades from Hill's corps would lengthen Pickett's line and strengthen the attack. Longstreet asked Lee how many men would make the attack, and Lee said that 15,000 would take part. Longstreet retorted that "the fifteen thousand men who could make [a] successful assault over that field" could never be found. Ignoring Longstreet's protests, Lee directed him to organize the attack.[68]

Colonel E. Porter Alexander, Longstreet's artillery commander, organized the artillery for the pre-assault bombardment. He positioned 172 guns along the front of the attacking force. A clump of trees on the right center of the Federal lines had been designated the assault objective. Alexander was ordered to position himself so that he could see the effect of his fire on the area that was in the vicinity of these trees. When he thought that his guns had paved the way for Pickett's advance, he was to give the signal. Confidently, Alexander finished his preparations. Then, however, he received a note from Longstreet that startled him. Longstreet wanted Alexander to determine whether the attack should be made after he had surveyed the damage caused by his artillery. Alexander quickly replied that he could not evaluate the effect of his

Cemetery Ridge After Pickett's Charge, July 3, 1863

fire to that degree of accuracy. He added that if a course of action other than Pickett's charge was available, its feasibility should be explored. Alexander began to have an uneasy feeling.[69]

When Alexander's guns opened fire at 1:00 p.m., Brigadier General John Gibbon was with his Federal soldiers on Cemetery Ridge. Although the ferocity of the cannonade impressed him, he was not sure that it was the prelude to an attack. Most of the enemy rounds seemed to be passing over the heads of his troops, and he thought that the Confederates had something in mind besides softening up his position for an infantry attack. Alexander's fire was not only high, but also was rapidly consuming the available ammunition. The Confederate artilleryman had decided that if his fire did not have much effect within 30 minutes, he would suspend the attack and save ammunition. At 1:25 p.m., Alexander suddenly noticed the Federals withdrawing some artillery from a spot near the clump of trees. In addition, he thought that he detected a slackening in the Union artillery fire.* Quickly he sent a note to Pickett, telling him that the time for the attack had arrived. Pickett went to Longstreet for the final release. Longstreet, still disgusted by the whole concept, would not answer his division commander; he simply nodded his head. Pickett ordered his brigades forward.[70]

To observers on both sides of the field, Pickett's charge was impressive. *(See Atlas Map No. 37b.)* The care with which the Confederates kept their troops aligned and the heroism they displayed as they marched across the open field were inspiring. But the Federal fire was equally impressive. Artil-

lery on Cemetery Hill and Little Round Top raked Pickett's lines with a withering crossfire. The cannoneers worked feverishly as they switched from shell to canister. Great holes were torn in the Confederate lines and the musket fire was devastating, but the men kept coming. They swarmed over the stone wall in front of the clump of trees on Cemetery Ridge. Union regiments rushed to plug the hole. Suddenly, the attack ceased; the remnants of Pickett's charge staggered back across the field. Once again, modern weapons had demonstrated the futility of an infantry assault across an open field.

To the east of Pickett's charge, Stuart's cavalry attack also was checked, as Union cavalrymen showed that they were a worthy adjunct to the infantry on Cemetery Ridge.

Finally, a battle had occurred in which the Army of Northern Virginia could not do everything Lee asked. All of the planning, marching, and fighting had come to nothing. Hampered by a new organization, reluctant commanders, and a poor tactical plan, Lee could not beat the Army of the Potomac. Opposite him, Meade had taken full advantage of the terrain, his commanders, and his army's firepower. The battle of Gettysburg was over.

A Critique

From start to finish, Gettysburg marked a low point in Lee's career. The decision to invade the North had been ill advised and based on faulty assumptions. While a strategy to mount an invasion in the East, protect central Tennessee near Chattanooga, and defend Vicksburg in Mississippi was admirable in concept, it was clearly beyond the South's limited capabilities. Lee's idea that the hot summer weather would free sufficient troops to accomplish all of the Confederacy's military

---

*The Union chief of artillery, Brigadier General Henry Hunt, had ordered his batteries to stop firing and conserve ammunition.

objectives did not take into account the North's determination to win. Lee also failed to establish a decisive, obtainable goal for his invasion. These shortcomings, combined with the new organization that had been imposed on the Confederate Army, provided a poor foundation for a risky adventure.

Lee's march northward demonstrated much of his ability as a careful planner and resourceful commander, but it also exposed a fatal flaw—he tended to underestimate his opponent. He made excellent use of terrain, moving through the Shenandoah and Cumberland Valleys, and he exploited the moral ascendency that he had achieved over Hooker. But he lost contact with the Union army and did not realize the seriousness of the situation until Longstreet's spy reported that the Federals were north of the Potomac River. His poor use of the four brigades of cavalry that accompanied him and his mistake of allowing Stuart to galavant across the Pennsylvania countryside precipitated a battle that was not at the time or place of his choosing. He was forced to fight a meeting engagement with an army that outnumbered his own.

Once in battle, Lee was convinced that the Army of Northern Virginia could win by attacking. Chancellorsville appeared to be his model for victory, while Fredericksburg was locked somewhere in the recesses of his mind. His men attacked fruitlessly for three long days. Even after July 1, other alternatives existed. He could have withdrawn southward—taking all the supplies that he had gathered without loss—and accomplished most of his campaign objectives. The one critical objective that would then have gone unfulfilled was the gaining of a decisive victory on northern soil. The question of whether or not this was a worthwhile objective is a moot point. It is well to remember, however, that in 1863, European diplomatic recognition of the Confederate States of America probably would have come only after the North had ceased its efforts to subdue the South. As long as the North continued to fight, England and France were determined to remain uncommitted on the issue of southern independence. But how could the South force the North to cease fighting? The answer apparently did not lie in the defeat of Union armies; for two years, the North had shown that major defeats would not halt its efforts to achieve a reunion with the rebellious states. Nor did it seem realistic to believe that the South could exhaust the North, considering the relative material resources of the two sides. Only by skillfully applying a defensive strategy could the South possibly have been able to approach exhausting the North. Lee, however, advocated an offensive strategy. He wanted to win the war by winning a decisive battle. He was not yet willing to try to make time an ally of the South.

Finally, Lee's style of leadership did not work with the men he had under him at Gettysburg. With Jackson, Lee could suggest and recommend; but with Ewell, he needed to be precise and demanding. With Jackson, Lee could reason and

persuade; but with Longstreet, he needed to be firm and exacting. Hesitancy, indecision, and performance that bordered on immaturity characterized many of the command relationships that existed in the Army of Northern Virginia on those first three days of July. As a result of these shortcomings, Lee wasted the one resource that could not be replaced by blockade-running and home industry—manpower. The advance into Pennsylvania reduced the strength of the Army of Northern Virginia by 22,638 officers and men.[71]

The Pursuit

When the survivors of Pickett's attack disappeared into the trees on Seminary Ridge, Meade did not counterattack. His army was disorganized, his units were mixed, and his men were exhausted. Additionally, most of Lee's army was intact, and the Confederate artillery stood menacingly in the position that it had occupied prior to Pickett's charge. Consequently, Meade ordered his army to relax in light of the severe test it had faced for the past three days.

Lee, also, gave his men a brief rest. Then, in a driving rainstorm on July 4, he ordered his army to retreat. Withdrawing through Cashtown and Fairfield, the Army of Northern Virginia headed back through the Cumberland Valley. When it reached the Potomac River at Williamsport, it discovered its path of retreat blocked. The only ponton bridge over the river had been destroyed by a Federal cavalry detachment. Heavy rains had swelled the river, and the fords were impassable. With its back to the river, the army appeared to be in grave danger.

Meade slowly followed Lee's army. *(See Atlas Map No. 38a.)* Perhaps influenced by his original instructions to cover Washington and Baltimore and to operate against the "invading forces of the rebels," Meade acted as though his mission had already been accomplished. He seemed to be escorting Lee's army out of the North, and—as Lincoln later remarked—he resembled an old woman trying to shoo her geese across a creek.[72] Advancing southward, his leading units caught up with Lee's army at Williamsport on July 10. *(See Atlas Map No. 38b.)* Methodically, he began to organize his army for an attack; but on the night of July 13, Lee safely crossed the Potomac into Virginia.

Lincoln and Stanton were furious over Meade's failure to destroy Lee's army when it was trapped against the river. But George G. Meade had done something that none of his predecessors had done: he had beaten Robert E. Lee and the Army of Northern Virginia. In Confederate eyes, the significance of this accomplishment must have been great when considered in conjunction with Grant's crushing victory at Vicksburg on the same date.

Notes

[1]Archer Jones, *Confederate Strategy From Shiloh to Vicksburg* (Baton Rouge, 1961), pp. 200–204; *The War of the Rebellion: A Compilation of the Official Records of the Union and Confederate Armies* (130 vols.; Washington, 1880–1901), Series I, XXV, Pt. 2, 703. (Hereinafter cited as *OR*. Unless otherwise indicated, all subsequent references to the *OR* are to Series I.)

[2]*OR*, XXV, Pt. 2, 752, 726, 782.

[3]*Ibid.*, 790.

[4]Clifford Dowdey and Louis H. Manarin (eds.), *Wartime Papers of R.E. Lee* (Boston, 1961), p. 482.

[5]*OR*, XXV, Pt. 2, 791.

[6]Jones, *Confederate Strategy*, p. 239; Dowdey and Manarin, *Papers of R.E. Lee*, pp. 293, 353; Thomas L. Connelly and Archer Jones, *The Politics of Command* (Baton Rouge, 1973), pp. 38–39.

[7]Douglas Southall Freeman, *R.E. Lee: A Biography* (4 vols.; New York, 1934), III, 19; Jones, *Confederate Strategy*, p. 215; John H. Reagan, *Memoirs With Special Reference to Secession and the Civil War* (New York, 1906), p. 121.

[8]Armistead L. Long, *Memoirs of Robert E. Lee* (New York, 1886), p. 267; Dowdey and Manarin, *Papers of R.E. Lee*, p. 508; Peter J. Parish, *The American Civil War* (New York, 1975), p. 280; Freeman, *R.E. Lee*, III, pp. 18–19; J. William Jones (ed.), "Letter From Henry Heth to the Secretary of the Society, June, 1877," in *Southern Historical Society Papers* (45 vols.; Richmond, 1876–1920), IV, 153.

[9]Jones, *Confederate Strategy*, p. 238; James Longstreet, *From Manassas to Appomattox: Memoirs of the Civil War in America* (Philadelphia, 1896), p. 327.

[10]Freeman, *R.E. Lee*, III, 20–21.

[11]*OR*, XXV, Pt. 2, 810; Dowdey and Manarin, *Papers of R.E. Lee*, p. 490; Freeman, *R.E. Lee*, III, 14; *OR*, XXV, Pt. 2, 840; *Ibid.*, XXVII, Pt. 2, 283–291; Douglas Southall Freeman, *Lee's Lieutenants: A Study in Command* (3 vols.; New York, 1942), II, 712.

[12]"Letter from Henry Heth," in *Southern Historical Society Papers*, IV, 153, 160; Freeman, *R.E. Lee*, III, 22–24; Long, *Memoirs of Lee*, pp. 268–269; Reagan, *Memoirs*, pp. 121–122.

[13]*OR*, XXV, Pt. 2, 438.

[14]*Ibid.*, 473; T. Harry Williams, *Lincoln and His Generals* (New York, 1952), pp. 245–246.

[15]Dowdey and Manarin, *Papers of R.E. Lee*, pp. 501–503; Henry K. Douglas, *I Rode With Stonewall* (Chapel Hill, N.C., 1940), p. 241.

[16]Freeman, *Lee's Lieutenants*, III, 2–5; Henry B. McClellan, *The Life and Campaigns of Major General J.E.B. Stuart* (Boston, 1885), p. 261.

[17]John W. Thomason, *Jeb Stuart* (New York, 1930), p. 401; *OR*, XXVII, Pt. 1, 27–28; Freeman, *Lee's Lieutenants*, III, 8–13.

[18]*OR*, XXVII, Pt. 1, 904; McClellan, *Campaigns of Stuart*, p. 294; Thomason, *Jeb Stuart*, p. 408.

[19]Freeman, *Lee's Lieutenants*, III, 19.

[20]*OR*, XXVII, Pt. 3, 924–925.

[21]Dowdey and Manarin, *Papers of R.E. Lee*, p. 496; *OR*, XVIII, 733; *Ibid.*, XXVII, Pt. 1, 18–19, 77.

[22]*OR*, XXVII, Pt. 1, 30.

[23]*Ibid.*, 31–32, 35.

[24]*Ibid.*, 35; see also, *Ibid.*, XXV, Pt. 2, 12–13.

[25]George Meade (ed.), *The Life and Letters of George Gordon Meade* (2 vols.; New York, 1913), I, 385; *OR*, XXVII, Pt. 2, 44;

[26]*OR*, XXVII, Pt. 1, 39.

[27]*Ibid.*, p. 40.

[28]Kenneth P. Williams, *Lincoln Finds a General* (5 vols.; New York, 1949–1959), II, 668–669; Edwin B. Coddington, *The Gettysburg Campaign* (New York, 1968), pp. 139–140.

[29]T. Harry Williams, *Lincoln and His Generals*, p. 258; K.P. Williams, *Lincoln Finds a General*, II, pp. 641–642.

[30]Coddington, *Gettysburg Campaign*, pp. 186–189; *OR*, XXVII, Pt. 1, 58, 60.

[31]T. Harry Williams, *Lincoln and His Generals*, pp. 247, 252.

[32]Meade, *Life and Letters of Meade*, II, 11.

[33]T. Harry Williams, *Lincoln and His Generals*, pp. 259, 247; Meade, *Life and Letters of Meade*, I, 373; Edward J. Nichols, *Toward Gettysburg: A Biography of General John F. Reynolds* (University Park, Pa., 1956), pp. 220–223.

[34]Freeman Cleaves, *Meade of Gettysburg* (Norman, Okla., 1960).

[35]*OR*, XXVII, Pt. 3, 374; George R. Agassiz (ed.), *Meade's Headquarters, 1863–1865; Letters of Colonel Theodore Lyman* (Boston, 1922), p. 25.

[36]*OR*, XXVII, Pt. 1, 61.

[37]W.A. Swanberg, *Sickles the Incredible* (New York, 1956), pp. 197–200; Emerson G. Taylor, *Gouverneur Kemble Warren* (New York, 1932), pp. 119–120.

[38]*OR*, XXV, Pt. 2, 471–472; Frederick H. Dyer, *A Compendium of the War of the Rebellion* (3 vols.; New York, 1959), I, 287, 301, 318, 323.

[39]*OR*, XXVII, Pt. 3, 374; Meade, *Life and Letters of Meade*, I, 389.

[40]Cleaves, *Meade of Gettysburg*, p. 130; *OR*, XXVII, Pt. 1, 61, 65; Nichols, *Toward Gettysburg*, p. 194.

[41]*OR*, XXVII, Pt. 3, 415–420.

[42]Thomason, *Jeb Stuart*, pp. 421–424; *OR*, XXVII, Pt. 3, 923, 927–928.

[43]Thomason, *Jeb Stuart*, pp. 428–440; K.P. Williams, *Lincoln Finds a General*, II, 659; Coddington, *Gettysburg Campaign*, p. 205.

[44]Thomason, *Jeb Stuart*, pp. 434–436.

[45]*Ibid.*, 436–440.

[46]Coddington, *Gettysburg Campaign*, p. 205.

[47]*OR*, XXVII, Pt. 1, 69; Nichols, *Toward Gettysburg*, p. 196.

[48]*OR*, XXVII, Pt. 3, 379.

[49]James L. Morrison, Jr. (ed.), *The Memoirs of Henry Heth* (Westport, Conn., 1974), p. 173.

[50]*Ibid.*, p. 174; Coddington, *Gettysburg Campaign*, pp. 273–274.

[51]*OR*, XXVII, Pt. 3, 460–461; Nichols, *Toward Gettysburg*, pp. 200–202, 205.

[52]Cleaves, *Meade of Gettysburg*, pp. 134–136; *OR*, XXVII, Pt. 1, 70–71; Taylor, *Gouverneur Kemble Warren*, pp. 123–124; Oliver O. Howard, *Autobiography of Oliver Otis Howard* (2 vols.; New York, 1908), I, 409–413.

[53]Swanberg, *Sickles the Incredible*, pp. 202–203.

[54]Howard, *Autobiography*, I, 413–418; Coddington, *Gettysburg Campaign*, pp. 294–297.

[55]*OR*, XXVII, Pt. 2, 318, 445; Douglas, *I Rode With Stonewall*, p. 247; Jubal A. Early, *Autobiographical Sketch and Narrative of the War Between the States* (Philadelphia, 1912), p. 270.

[56]Longstreet, *From Manassas to Appomattox*, p. 358; *OR*, XXVII,

Pt. 2, 446.

⁵⁷*OR*, XXVII, Pt. 2, 446.

⁵⁸John B. Hood, *Advance and Retreat* (New Orleans, 1880), p. 56; Coddington, *Gettysburg Campaign*, pp. 371–373.

⁵⁹Coddington, *Gettysburg Campaign*, pp. 244–250.

⁶⁰Swanberg, *Sickles the Incredible*, pp. 208–211; Meade, *Life and Letters of Meade*, II, 70–71, 74.

⁶¹Taylor, *Gouverneur Kemble Warren*, pp. 122–123.

⁶²*Ibid.*, pp. 128–130.

⁶³Swanberg, *Sickles the Incredible*, p. 212.

⁶⁴Hood, *Advance and Retreat*, pp. 57–59; Coddington, *Gettysburg Campaign*, pp. 386–410.

⁶⁵Edward J. Stackpole, *They Met at Gettysburg* (Harrisburg, Pa., 1956), pp. 214–215; Early, *Autobiographical Sketch*, p. 274; Coddington, *Gettysburg Campaign*, pp. 439–440.

⁶⁶Douglas, *I Rode With Stonewall*, p. 249; Stackpole, *They Met at Gettysburg*, p. 216.

⁶⁷John Gibbon, *Personal Recollections of the Civil War* (New York, 1928), pp. 140–142, 145; *OR*, XXVII, Pt. 1, 73.

⁶⁸Early, *Autobiographical Sketch*, p. 275; Longstreet, *From Manassas to Appomattox*, pp. 386–387.

⁶⁹E. Porter Alexander, with introduction and notes by T. Harry Williams, *Military Memoirs of a Confederate* (Bloomington, Ind., 1962), pp. 418–421.

⁷⁰Gibbon, *Personal Recollections*, pp. 147–149; Alexander, *Memoirs of a Confederate*, pp. 422–423.

⁷¹Thomas L. Livermore, *Numbers and Losses in the Civil War in America, 1861–1865* (Boston, 1901), p. 103.

⁷²T. Harry Williams, *Lincoln and His Generals*, p. 288.

Grant and the West   9

As Grant was tightening the noose around Vicksburg and Hooker was following Lee northward into Pennsylvania, a third Federal army commenced an offensive movement in central Tennessee. Following the inconclusive Battle of Stones River in December 1862, Major General William S. Rosecrans had kept the Army of the Cumberland in the vicinity of Murfreesboro, Tennessee, pending the arrival of the spring campaigning season. By finally ordering his army to advance on June 24, 1863, Rosecrans compounded the Confederacy's already difficult situation.

In June of 1863, the principal Federal armies were exerting pressure on three fronts. While Lee held the initiative for the moment in the East, the authorities in Richmond nevertheless kept minimal troops in other areas in order to provide resources for his second invasion of the North. With the Army of the Potomac reacting aggressively to Lee's thrust, the outcome was likely to be costly, even if Lee won the battle that was sure to come. Regarding Mississippi, even the most optimistic southerner could find little in the Vicksburg situation to buoy his hopes; Grant's stranglehold on the Confederate fortress was too strong. Rosecrans' southward advance put an additional strain on the scant resources and limited number of troops available to the Confederacy. (See Atlas Map No. 39.)

In this predicament, the South could only obtain relief if its generals proved to be forceful and maneuvered skillfully. Perhaps Braxton Bragg, commander of the South's Army of Tennessee, could save the situation in middle Tennessee and spark a Confederate rejuvenation. During the six months remaining in 1863, the Confederate general would strive for such success—first against Rosecrans, and then against Grant, who assumed direction of Union operations in the West shortly after his victory at Vicksburg.

The Middle Tennessee Campaign

In the early weeks of 1863, the future looked decidedly bleak for Bragg and his army. Although the Battle of Stones River

was a standoff, afterwards, Bragg had opted to withdraw his troops to the Duck River. This move, which amounted to a dispirited retreat from the battlefield, increased the demoralization that already existed in the army. It also contributed to the growing dissatisfaction of Bragg's corps commanders with his leadership. Lieutenant General William J. Hardee, probably Bragg's best corps commander, felt compelled to tell the commanding general that the corps commanders were "unanimous in the opinion that a change in the command of this army is necessary."[1] The cause of the defeat at Murfreesboro was being laid at the feet of Bragg. Lieutenant General Leonidas Polk, another of Bragg's corps commanders, wrote to the Confederate President and expressed a similar opinion. Polk recommended that Bragg, a good organizer and disciplinarian, be transferred to Richmond to assist Jefferson Davis, and that General Joseph E. Johnston be sent to assume command of the Army of Tennessee. Largely as a result of Johnston's advice, Bragg was not relieved of command. In spite of this decision, however, the dissension in the high command of the Army of Tennessee remained.[2]

Bragg's selection of the Duck River as a principal defensive line was based on two considerations. First, he was concerned about feeding his army. Although well clothed and armed, the army was short of most foodstuffs, particularly beef. However, while the area between Columbia and McMinnville could fulfill many of the requirements for food and fodder, the soldiers still had a difficult hand-to-mouth existence. For example, during one two-week period before the Middle Tennessee Campaign began in June, the army was over 400,000 rations short. The situation was exacerbated by few wagons, an inadequate number of horses and mules, and Confederate policy, which sent most of the contents of the Atlanta depots northward to Lee's army. Shortages thus forced the army to disperse over a wide front in order to increase its foraging territory.[3]

Bragg's second reason for selecting the Duck River line was based on the terrain. A high ridge line north of the Duck

Major General Braxton Bragg

Confederate cavalry operations; the poor relationship between Bragg's cavalry commanders also hampered the quest for information about the Federals.

Throughout most of the spring, Major General Earl Van Dorn commanded the cavalry covering Bragg's left, while that on the right was under the command of Major General Joseph Wheeler. Van Dorn, however, could not get along with his subordinate, Brigadier General Nathan Bedford Forrest. Largely due to professional jealousy, they were on the verge of challenging each other to a duel in April. In addition, Forrest did not like Wheeler. The two had served together during a February raid on Fort Donelson that achieved poor results and led to ill feelings between the two cavalrymen. Thereafter, Forrest had transferred from Wheeler's command, swearing that he would never again work with Wheeler. Wheeler, in turn, could not get along with his subordinate, Brigadier General John H. Morgan, who had a penchant for independent operations. In May, Van Dorn was killed, and his troops were transferred back to Mississippi. Forrest took command of the remaining cavalry on the Confederate left. Although Van Dorn's death eased the friction between Bragg's senior horsemen, when Rosecrans opened the campaign in June, the commanders of the two wings of the Confederate cavalry were barely on speaking terms.[4]

River offered ample protection to the dispersed army. Four gaps ran through the ridge: Guy's Gap, Bellbuckle Gap, Liberty Gap, and Hoover's Gap. An attacker approaching the main Confederate defensive works at Tullahoma from the north would be canalized by these four openings through the Duck River Ridge. *(See Atlas Map No. 39.)* Thus, although Bragg's army was dispersed over a wide area, it was protected by the topography of the region.

Confederate Confusion and Indecision

Beyond the Duck River ridge, Bragg's cavalry tried to learn about Rosecrans' plans for moving his army. Although the Federals had been relatively inactive since the Battle of Stones River, few Confederates expected this inactivity to continue beyond the spring of 1863. The Confederate cavalry, however, was having great difficulty gathering information about the enemy. Many troopers were mounted on broken-down farm horses, as the local supply of adequate horses had been exhausted.* Nor were inferior horses the only hindrance to

Joseph Wheeler

*Since each cavalryman in the Confederate Army was required to furnish his own mount, most soldiers with a preference for the cavalry purchased any available horse to avoid service in the infantry.

The cavalry's poor reconnaissance work was a result of both the discord among the commanders and the poor capabilities of the horsemen. Conflicting information was transmitted to Bragg as the cavalry attempted to discern Rosecrans' intentions. Every possibility—from a Union evacuation of Murfreesboro to Union preparations for an early offensive—was reported as fact. The situation was further clouded when part of the Army of the Cumberland advanced through the gaps in the ridge north of the Duck River on April 20, pushed the Confederates back, and then abruptly retreated. Without question, Bragg lacked meaningful information about the capabilities and objectives of Rosecrans' army.[5]

As a result of his poor understanding of the tactical situation, Bragg was unable to produce a clear-cut defensive strategy. Prior to April, he had intended Polk to strike eastward from Shelbyville when Rosecrans advanced southward toward Tullahoma and Chattanooga. *(See Atlas Map No. 39.)* But Bragg was not sure where to prepare the main defensive position that would fix the Federals in place while Polk struck their exposed flank. In March, he had ruled out Tullahoma because the Yankees could move eastward around Tullahoma and approach Chattanooga from a more northerly direction. By June, however, Tullahoma, astride the main rail line paralleling the Union axis of advance toward Chattanooga, had been selected as the chief Confederate defensive position. Hardee would stop the Federals there, and Polk would execute the offensive portion of Bragg's defensive-offensive strategy. Unfortunately for the Army of Tennessee, neither Hardee nor Polk had a clear understanding of Bragg's plan.[6]

Tactically, the terrain seemed to favor a Union advance around the Confederate left. An advance in this direction would avoid the Duck River ridge and prevent the heavy losses that the Federal troops might incur while trying to force the gaps. Strategically, however, an advance around the Confederate right would be more plausible, as it would bring the Federals closer to Chattanooga. By April, the Confederates were convinced that Rosecrans would make his main effort on the right.[7]

On the right, the Confederate defenses were very weak—partly due to Hardee's ignorance of Bragg's overall plan. Hardee was also uncertain about Tullahoma; it appeared to him that the defenses there would be vulnerable to a turning movement. In addition, he had too few forces to defend all of the approaches to Manchester and Tullahoma. Finally, ill feelings between Hardee and Bragg were so great by June that "communications had simply broken down" between the two generals.[8]

Federal Plans

Unlike Bragg, Rosecrans knew the weaknesses in the troop

Major General William S. Rosecrans

dispositions of his enemy. Both his reconnaissance in force in April and the active operations conducted by his cavalry had given him an accurate picture of the Army of Tennessee. Equipped with this information, he was determined to trap Bragg's army and seize Chattanooga. Prior to the opening of the campaign, however, Rosecrans also intended to be fully prepared for any unforeseen circumstances. This gave rise to a series of letters that was reminiscent of McClellan and Lincoln's 1862 correspondence.[9]

The authorities in Washington wanted Rosecrans to commence active campaigning promptly. Lincoln and Stanton were afraid that the Confederates might detach a portion of Bragg's army and send it to reinforce the armies opposing Grant at Vicksburg. It was imperative that Rosecrans maintain pressure against Bragg in order to prevent a tipping of the balance in Mississippi. Rosecrans' interpretation of events, however, was different. He felt that the Army of the Cumberland should not risk a decisive battle until Grant had reached a decision at Vicksburg. Rosecrans apparently reasoned that if the siege in Mississippi failed and the Army of the Cumberland lost a battle at about the same time, a great national crisis would occur. Although it was difficult to dispute Rosecrans' logic, it seemed to the authorities in Washington that the siege at Vicksburg would fail only if Bragg were permitted to reinforce either General J.E. Johnston or Lieutenant General John C. Pemberton. Rosecrans' chief of staff, Brigadier General James A. Garfield, advised his commander on June 12 that "The Government and the War Department believe that the army ought to move upon the enemy; the army desires it, and the country is anxiously hoping for it . . . I believe an immediate advance of all our available forces is advisable, and under the providence of God will be successful.''[10] Finally persuaded that the time was right for an attack, Rosecrans briefed his commanders on the evening of June 23.[11]

The commander of the Army of the Cumberland wanted Bragg to believe that the main Federal advance would be launched against the Confederate left flank. Because of this element of deception, Rosecrans maintained the strictest secrecy about his campaign plan. Widespread knowledge of the plan might compromise its success. Therefore, when Rosecrans' commanders gathered on the evening of June 23, they heard the plan for the first time. Each commander was then given a written order that covered only his portion of the operation. Rosecrans wanted to insure that the Confederates would react only to his army's movements, and not to a captured master plan.[12]

Rosecrans' plan was complex. In order to create the impression of a large westward movement around the Confederate left, Major General Gordon S. Granger's Reserve Corps was to move to Shelbyville by way of Salem. *(See Atlas Map No. 39.)* Preceded by aggressive cavalry actions, Granger was to appear to be making the main attack. As a supporting attack for Granger's corps in this overall deception plan, cavalry and infantry would move through Woodbury, around the Confederate right. While Bragg was reacting to the apparent principal threat to his left, Major General Alexander McCook was to advance through Liberty Gap, Major General George H. Thomas was to move through Hoover's Gap, and Major General Thomas L. Crittenden was to march his corps to Bradyville, where it would become the general reserve. Rosecrans hoped that these maneuvers would confuse the Confederate commanders. The result could be the neutralization of the defenses of the Duck River ridge and the turning of the Confederate position at Tullahoma.[13]

Union Deception and Maneuver

Wheeler's cavalry responded exactly as Rosecrans wanted. On June 22, Wheeler began shifting his units from the right toward Shelbyville. Large Union forces had been reported moving in that direction. These reports were seemingly confirmed on June 23, when Federal cavalry advanced from Eagleville toward Shelbyville. Wheeler continued to shift his forces, and, by June 24, only a single brigade of Confederate cavalry covered the front that extended from Liberty Gap to Hoover's Gap. *(Movements not shown on map.)* Moreover, only one Confederate regiment guarded Hoover's Gap.

When the three Federal corps designated to make the major effort began their move on June 24, the weather took a turn for the worse. Heavy and unseasonable rains that lasted for 17 days transformed the dirt roads into quagmires. Thus, supplies were toilsome to move, food was hard to cook, and troops were difficult to inspire.

The strengths of the opposing forces were about equal. Although Rosecrans was outnumbered in cavalry, 13,962 to 6,806, he had the larger army, 50,017 to 46,665. But generalship rather than numbers would be the deciding factor in the campaign.[14]

Federal Troops Drag Artillery Along the Muddy Mountain Roads

Rapid execution marked the opening stages of Rosecrans' drive. By the night of June 24, elements of Thomas' corps had seized Hoover's Gap, and McCook's corps was in possession of Liberty Gap. Granger, conducting the feint toward the Confederate left, had reached Christiana.

Hardee reacted accordingly. On the twenty-fifth, he shifted his forces from the Manchester Pike to Wartrace. *(Movement not shown on map; Hardee's corps originally guarded Bellbuckle, Liberty, and Hoover's Gaps before moving to Wartrace.)* Apparently, he felt that the main Yankee threat would materialize at either Guy's Gap or Liberty Gap. By consolidating his corps at Wartrace, Hardee hoped to avoid an enemy penetration of his position.

Hardee's movements, of course, opened up the Confederate right flank. By June 26, the lead elements of Thomas' corps were only six miles from Manchester. Nevertheless, Bragg was convinced that the main Union effort was being made through Liberty Gap, and therefore ordered Polk eastward to strike the right of the Federals near the gap. Late in the afternoon, however, Bragg countermanded Polk's orders. Now convinced that the best course of action was to defend from prepared positions, he ordered the Army of Tennessee to consolidate at Tullahoma. *(See Atlas Map No. 39.)* Within four days, Bragg's entire Duck River defense line had been turned, and the terrain advantage of the Duck River ridge had been lost. The army was retreating toward its final defensive position.[15]

Rosecrans, also, was certain that the decisive battle should take place at Tullahoma. It no longer appeared possible to cut Bragg's line of communication. After seizing the gaps, the Army of the Cumberland had moved more slowly than anticipated, being hindered by foul weather and excess baggage. Unable to trap the enemy, Rosecrans hoped to destroy him in battle.[16]

Unhappily for the Army of Tennessee, a disagreement among its leaders again broke out. While Bragg wanted to defend at Tullahoma, Polk—and later Hardee—argued against this course of action. A Union raid against Decherd on June 28 convinced them that their supply line to Chattanooga had been cut. They therefore urged withdrawal from the seemingly vulnerable position at Tullahoma.

On June 30, Bragg prepared to defend his position in Tullahoma. He now realized that he had been misled into believing that the Federal army was advancing on Shelbyville when actually it had massed at Manchester. His army's position was difficult, but not impossible. The dispute with his corps commanders, however, produced doubts about the Tullahoma position. Finally, on the evening of the thirtieth, Bragg ordered the army to withdraw to the Elk River. *(Movement not shown on map.)*

As a defensive line, the Elk River ranked very poorly.

Although the rains had swelled the river, and the only crossing sites were provided by the bridges, a vagary of the weather could make the temporarily impassable barrier fordable at many places. Realizing this, Bragg ordered the position abandoned on July 2. After briefly considering stands at Decherd and Cowan, he finally decided to cross the Tennessee River and consolidate at his base in Chattanooga. Middle Tennessee had been lost to the Confederacy.[17]

A Critique

In addition to losing middle Tennessee, Bragg failed to slow the Federal advance behind him. The Nashville and Chattanooga Railroad remained relatively intact. After three minor bridges along the route were repaired in July, the Army of the Cumberland had a principal supply route that extended all the way to the Tennessee River. Bragg also failed to keep a firm hand on his subordinates. On July 2, he had directed Brigadier General John H. Morgan to lead a cavalry raid into Kentucky. Although Morgan had been told to restrict his operations to Kentucky and to remain south of the Ohio River, his force was finally captured by Federal cavalry north of that river, near the Pennsylvania border.

Bragg's poor relationship with his subordinates was one of the major factors that contributed to the loss of middle Tennessee. Toward the end of June, the disputes between Bragg, Polk, and Hardee led to a situation that disabled the command structure of the Army of Tennessee. These personality clashes, combined with Bragg's poor health, finally forced him to admit that he was "utterly broken down."[18] Indecisive, he produced neither a clear strategic plan nor inspirational leadership. As a result, Bragg was outgeneraled.

Rosecrans, also, demonstrated some faults in the campaign. Many of his orders were unclear and imprecise. Granger, leading the move toward Shelbyville, mistakenly retraced his steps to Murfreesboro after reaching the objective of the feint. *(Movement not shown on map.)* Because Rosecrans' instructions had not been clear, Granger would not have been available if battle had been joined at Tullahoma.[19] Rosecrans also seemed to have a problem with his supply lines. Naturally, the unexpected rainfall aggravated the situation, but his army was overloaded with impedimenta. Nonetheless, the capture of middle Tennessee and 1,634 Confederates at a loss of 83 Federals killed and 473 wounded was noteworthy.[20] Coming at the same time as the great victories at Vicksburg and Gettysburg, Rosecrans' triumph was well received in Washington.

The Fall of Chattanooga

On July 4, Rosecrans ordered a halt to the pursuit of Bragg's army. The hard marching and deteriorating supply situation demanded that the Army of the Cumberland refit and reorganize. Its left rested on McMinnville, while the right flank was anchored on Winchester. In Winchester, Rosecrans established his headquarters and began issuing the orders that would restore the army's state of readiness. *(See Atlas Map No. 40.)* First, the railroads needed to be repaired. The lines to Murfreesboro, Stevenson, and Tracy City were reopened. Second, supplies had to be accumulated. Rosecrans wanted to have enough rations on hand to feed the army for 25 days. Ammunition, of course, was essential; sufficient stores were secured to fight two major battles. A strategic prize as valuable as Chattanooga could not be won without extensive marching and hard fighting.[21]

The Importance and Natural Strength of Chattanooga

Chattanooga was the center of an expansive rail network. To the northeast, the East Tennessee and Georgia Railroad connected Chattanooga with Knoxville, Tennessee—an important area of pro-Union sentiment—and Lynchburg, Virginia. To the northwest, the Nashville and Chattanooga Railroad provided the principal link with central Tennessee, a good food-producing area. The rail lines also tied Chattanooga to northern Alabama and—via the Western and Atlantic Railroad—to Atlanta. This last rail line was extremely important. It led not only to the critical Confederate quartermaster, commissary, and ordnance depots in Atlanta, but also to the munitions and iron centers of central Georgia. Chattanooga was the gateway to the interior of Georgia and the heartland of the South. Both northern and southern leaders understood its strategic importance. In addition, both recognized that the terrain surrounding it favored the defender.

Chattanooga was dominated on three sides by high mountains. *(See Atlas Map No. 40.)* To the north, Walden's Ridge overlooked the meandering Tennessee River as it threaded its way past Chattanooga. Raccoon and Sand Mountains guarded the avenues of approach from the west, while Lookout Mountain loomed high overhead on the southern side of the city. Heavy forests offered excellent concealment in most places. An attacker would need a brilliant plan to overcome this difficult terrain.

If Rosecrans attempted another turning movement, he would be taking a great risk. An advance around Bragg's strategic flank through either Stevenson or Bridgeport would expose the Federal line of communication to a countermove. An attempt to strike Bragg's supply line to Atlanta would force Rosecrans to extend his own line for over 90 miles, across four mountain ranges and a major river obstacle. The mountains surrounding Chattanooga not only represented major obstructions to an attacker, but also provided excellent

Chattanooga As Seen From the Tip of Lookout Mountain

observation points for a clever defender.

Braxton Bragg, however, did not view the mountains and ridges as a protective barrier. Instead, he saw them as a screen that shielded the Army of the Cumberland from view. Indeed, he compared himself to a man helpless in a house full of rat holes:

> It is said to be easy to defend a mountainous country, but mountains hide your foe from you, while they are full of gaps through which he can pounce upon you at any time. A mountain. is like the wall of a house full of rat holes. The rat lies hidden at his hole, ready to pop out when no one is watching. Who can tell what lies hidden behind that hole.[22]

In reality, Bragg had voiced the solution to his problem. The key was the "watching." Like the man who needs a cat to help him to find out which holes the rats will use, Bragg needed his cavalry to discover which gaps Rosecrans would choose as a means of infiltration.

Confederate Problems and Plans

While Bragg was content to wait for the Federals behind the mountains of Tennessee and Georgia, Leonidas Polk was not. Bragg's corps commander wrote a letter to Jefferson Davis in which he proposed a plan to regain control of central Tennessee. Polk felt that the forces remaining under Johnston should be sent to Chattanooga to reinforce the Army of Tennessee. He argued that the combined force could then crush Rosecrans and advance into Kentucky. Furthermore, the northward advance might turn Grant's position at Vicksburg and force the Union to evacuate its forward positions along the Mississippi River. Routes to the trans-Mississippi West could be reopened. Unfortunately, the proposal had many of the dream-like qualities of earlier Confederate schemes. Moreover, the combination of Johnston's and Bragg's armies would not form a force of overwhelming numbers. Johnston could spare a force of only 9,000—hardly enough to help Bragg impose a devastating defeat on the Army of the Cumberland. Perhaps Polk's plan was only another subtle effort to have Bragg superseded by Johnston. In any event, it was quietly shelved.[23]

Both Bragg's health and his relationship with his subordinates remained at a low ebb. In July, the quarrelsome D.H. Hill replaced Hardee. Hill found Bragg ''gloomy and despondent. He had grown prematurely old . . . and showed much nervousness. His relations with his next in command [General Polk] and with some others of his subordinates were known not to be pleasant. His many retreats, too, had alienated the rank and file from him. . . .''[24] Bragg's health continued to decline. Feeling that the constant campaigning and the frequent altercations with his subordinates had contributed to his deteriorating physical condition, he hoped for a period of rest. The threatening posture of Rosecrans' army, however, prevented him from leaving the Army of Tennessee.[25]

Bragg's defensive plan was based on the security of Chattanooga. A defensive network of trenches was constructed around the city. Forrest and Wheeler posted their cavalry units along the Tennessee River in order to provide early warning of any Yankee approach. At Bridgeport *(see Atlas Map No. 40)*, Bragg stationed a brigade of infantry. It occupied a bridgehead on the north side of the river that could, if necessary, facilitate an advance into central Tennessee. For the most part, however, the north bank of the river was in Rosecrans' hands. Until the Union army appeared at the river's edge, Bragg would remain ignorant of Federal movements.

Bragg's intelligence service, the Coleman Scouts, tried to keep its commander informed of Union activities. With the loss of middle Tennessee, however, it was difficult to obtain information from those spies situated in the vicinity of Nashville. Moreover, 120 miles of backwoods road separated the Scouts from Bragg. Since reliable intelligence was scarce, the commander of the Army of Tennessee was forced to depend on his cavalry—cavalry that was positioned on the wrong side of the river for aggressive patrolling.[26]

Union Plans and Initial Movements

As he readied his army for the coming campaign, Rosecrans received a barrage of correspondence from Washington, accusing him of a lack of aggressiveness. Late in July, Halleck informed Rosecrans that ''The patience of the authorities here has been completely exhausted, and if I had not repeatedly promised to urge you forward, and begged for delay, you would have been removed from the command.''[27] In a series of telegrams, Halleck continued to browbeat Rosecrans throughout late July and early August. At one point, he ordered Rosecrans to report the daily movement of each corps until each had crossed the Tennessee River. At other times, Halleck issued peremptory orders, stating that the Army of the Cumberland must move immediately. Undaunted, Rosecrans continued to build up supplies and wait for an opportune moment to execute his plan.[28]

Once again, Rosecrans intended to rely heavily on deception—this time to convince Bragg that his right flank was being turned. He hoped that two conditions would help to make this maneuver plausible to the Confederates. First, Major General Ambrose E. Burnside, commanding an independent corps, had been ordered by Halleck to march into eastern Tennessee and position his force at Knoxville. *(Off map, to the north.)* This movement would take place at the same time that Rosecrans began operations. Rosecrans trusted that the Confederates would expect the Army of the Cumberland to advance to the north of Chattanooga in order to link its left flank with Burnside's corps. Second, as both commanders knew, the terrain favored a move around the Confederate right. Once across the Tennessee River, Rosecrans could maneuver in relatively open country, where there were few obstacles to impede his approach to the Western and Atlantic Railroad, Bragg's lifeline to Atlanta. Confronted by this evidence, seemingly so preponderant, Bragg watched his right—and Rosecrans prepared to turn his left.

In good spirits, the Army of the Cumberland began its move on August 16. *(See Atlas Map No. 40.)* Crittenden's corps moved toward the Sequatchie River Valley. Simultaneously, Thomas' corps took a direct route to the Tennessee River, and McCook moved his corps toward Bellefonte and Stevenson. North of Chattanooga, a cavalry detachment from Crittenden's corps conducted demonstrations to confuse Bragg.[29]

While these moves were befuddling Bragg, Confederate leaders focused on events around Chattanooga. In the previous campaign, Rosecrans had been fortunate. His operations had been mounted concurrently with those of the two other principal Federal armies—one in the East (Gettysburg), and the other in the West (Vicksburg). Now, however, only the Army of the Cumberland was actively campaigning. With no Federal pressure being exerted at any other points, Chattanooga was the center of Confederate attention.

Grant had been aware of the danger of allowing Rosecrans to operate alone. After the fall of Vicksburg, he had recommended that an operation be mounted against Mobile,

Alabama. This would tie down Confederate forces, and, once the city had fallen, would enable the Union army to operate against Bragg's flank and rear. It would be difficult for the Confederates to mass their forces against both his and Rosecrans' army. The concurrent pressure on two fronts would be too much for the South to bear, and the way would be open for a move into Georgia. Unfortunately for Rosecrans, Grant's plan was not adopted, leaving the Army of the Cumberland to operate in isolation.[30]

Deception helped Rosecrans avoid a rapid Confederate reaction to his early initiatives. Groups of Union soldiers appeared at every ford across the Tennessee River throughout an area that extended 70 miles north of Chattanooga. Two or three artillery batteries moved continuously through clearings that were visible from the Confederate side of the river. Loud hammering seemed to indicate the construction of boats and pontons in preparation for a river crossing.* Numerous tents were pitched along Walden's Ridge. At dusk, buglers sounded the evening calls; at night, fires appeared along the crest of the ridge. Directly across the river from Chattanooga, two regiments of infantry and a battery of artillery appeared. On the twenty-first, the battery opened fire on the city, sinking one small boat and causing great consternation. It seemed clear to the Confederates that Rosecrans was making his move north of their defensive positions.[31]

Bragg's Reaction

Confederate surprise on August 21 appeared to be complete. The lack of reliable information about the Federals combined with the sudden shelling of Chattanooga caused one corps commander to remark that he "was most painfully impressed with the feeling that it was to be a hap-hazard campaign on our part."[32] Immediately, Bragg withdrew the brigade of infantry positioned west of the river at Bridgeport (*see Atlas Map No. 40*), and sent an urgent call to Johnston for reinforcements. After learning from Major General Simon B. Buckner that Burnside was moving into east Tennessee, Bragg was certain that the report of large Union forces moving across Walden's Ridge was accurate. Although some Federals had been seen southwest of Chattanooga, most of the information seemed to point toward a combined effort by Burnside and Rosecrans north of the city. With this in mind, Bragg ordered Buckner to withdraw to Loudon in the direction of the Army of Tennessee. (*Buckner's final position at Loudon is shown on map.*) Bragg wished to insure that Buckner's corps would not be isolated by a Federal crossing of the Tennessee River.[33]

*Hidden in the trees, Union soldiers hammered on empty barrels and threw wood chips and freshly cut timber into the river.

It appears that Bragg had completely lost track of Rosecrans' army during late August. With only 500 cavalrymen guarding the crossing points west of Chattanooga, it is not surprising that he could not predict the location of the Federal main attack. Both Bragg and his corp commanders believed that the Confederate right was in danger of being turned. Indications of the true situation emerged on August 31, when a citizen of Stevenson, Alabama reported that a large Federal force was crossing the river at Caperton's Ferry. Wheeler's cavalry confirmed the report on September 1. Bragg, at last, was aware of the nature of the deception. Yet he waited until September 5 to order Wheeler to "drive in the enemy's pickets, and assail him so as to develop his designs, strength, and position."[34] By then it was too late to defend the river; the last detachments and the trains of the Army of the Cumberland had cleared the river on the fourth.[35]

Rosecrans made a wide sweep around the Confederate left, trying to cut Bragg's line of communication. (*Movements not shown on map.*) McCook's corps had the longest distance to travel. It marched toward a pass over Lookout Mountain that was 40 miles from Chattanooga. Thomas' corps, the center of mass of the turning movement, drove toward Steven's Gap, only 20 miles from the city. Crittenden's corps, crossing at Bridgeport, moved parallel to the south bank of the river and headed for Chattanooga. Granger remained north of the river, guarding the railroads, depots, and other points that might be vulnerable to an enemy counterattack. Rosecrans was taking a great risk. His units were spread over a front of 40 miles, and because of the mountainous terrain, no corps was in supporting distance of another. Nevertheless, the risk seemed to be paying a dividend.

Realizing that again he had been outwitted, Bragg was indecisive. During the early days of September, he was torn between a last-ditch stand at Chattanooga and a retreat to Rome, Georgia. It appeared that Rosecrans' move around the left was directed toward Rome. Chattanooga, of course, had excellent defensive positions already prepared. Faced with this dilemma, Bragg finally acted on September 7. He ordered Confederate troops to evacuate Chattanooga and head for Rome. Buckner was directed to bring his corps from east Tennessee and to join the army as it marched toward Rome. Without a fight, Chattanooga was abandoned.[36]

It appeared to Rosecrans that the Army of Tennessee was in the midst of a precipitant withdrawal toward Rome. Throwing caution to the wind, he ordered a rapid pursuit of the Confederates. His already scattered corps were dispersed further: McCook was ordered to seize Summerville, Thomas was directed to secure LaFayette, and Crittenden was instructed to occupy Chattanooga and maintain pressure against the rear of the retreating Confederates. At about the same time that Rosecrans ordered his army to pursue, Bragg suddenly recognized the weaknesses of the Union dispositions. He ordered a counterattack.[37]

Bragg wanted to strike at the center of the Army of the Cumberland. Major General James S. Negley's division from Thomas' corps was alone and exposed in the vicinity of McLemore's Cove. *(See Atlas Map No. 41a.)* The commander of the Army of Tennessee sent Major General Thomas C. Hindman's division south through the cove to strike the vulnerable Federals in the rear. At the same time, Major General Patrick R. Cleburne's division of Hill's corps was directed to hit the Federals in front. Negley's division seemed to be easy prey. But Hindman was not the right man for the mission. He advanced cautiously through McLemore's Cove, measuring each step carefully to insure the protection of his own line of retreat. He watched attentively, afraid that he might be trapped by an unseen enemy waiting to pounce on his solitary division. Finally, Buckner's corps was dispatched in support of Hindman in order to speed the advance. After two days, however, Hindman still was two and a half miles from his objective. Thus, by the night of September 11, Negley was back at Steven's Gap, safely reunited with the XIV Corps. The Army of Tennessee had missed an excellent opportunity.

Although disappointed and furious about Hindman's performance, Bragg still thought he saw an opportunity to defeat Rosecrans in detail. His attention now turned to his right, where Crittenden's corps was advancing southward from Chattanooga. At 3:00 a.m. on September 12, Bragg ordered Polk to move north and attack the enemy.[38] Hindman's division and William H.T. Walker's corps were sent in support. *(See Atlas Map No. 41b.)* Now it was Polk's turn to fail to meet the expectations of his commander. Fearing that his force was too small, Polk awaited the arrival of additional troops, and refused to attack at the hour specified by Bragg. When he finally attacked the objective designated by Bragg, he found that the Federals had retreated. *(Movement not shown on map.)* Disgusted by the performance of his subordinates, Bragg concentrated the army at LaFayette, and for the next four days brooded about his army's impotence.[39]

Preliminaries to Chickamauga

Bragg's brief flurry of activity as he tried to strike Negley's division in McLemore's Cove warned Rosecrans that his army might be in trouble. The unexpected move was a hint that Bragg's retreat could have been a cleverly constructed ruse. Polk's abortive move against Crittenden on the twelfth again suggested that the Army of Tennessee was not in headlong retreat. Rosecrans hastily began to concentrate his scattered corps. He briefly considered an attack on LaFayette by his soon-to-be reunited army, but by the time McCook had

marched his corps into McLemore's Cove, Bragg was again attempting to envelop the Union left.[40]

Although Bragg apparently intended to interpose his army between the Union force and Chattanooga, he neglected to specify the Rossville-LaFayette road as an objective, thereby failing to provide for the blocking of Rosecrans' route of withdrawal to Chattanooga. Instead, he issued orders early on September 18 "to turn the [enemy's] left . . . and sweep up the Chickamauga [Creek]."[41] The units that were designated to execute these vague orders were not in position to move immediately. After a short advance toward their attack positions, they ran into enemy cavalry that offered strong resistance. *(Movements not shown on map.)* Time was also lost when columns from different divisions became mixed on the roads leading to the crossing sites over the Chickamauga. In addition, Bragg was still unaware of the exact locations of the enemy forces. He thought that Crittenden's left rested on Lee and Gordon's Mills, when actually it extended much farther north. Imprecise orders, faulty intelligence, defective troop dispositions, and poor timing produced another stillborn plan. A coordinated attack could not be launched until September 19.

In analyzing the fall of Chattanooga and the subsequent ineffective maneuvering, Lieutenant General D.H. Hill later heavily criticized Bragg. Hill felt that there were two problems with Bragg's generalship: "first, lack of knowledge of the situation; second, lack of personal supervision of the execution of his orders."[42] Certainly, this is an accurate appraisal. Bragg missed important opportunities to destroy his opponent's army in detail.

Rosecrans' actions also were faulty. Throughout the campaign, his army courted disaster. Although he captured Chattanooga without a fight, he risked the piecemeal destruction of his force. Initially, Bragg's failures contributed considerably to Rosecrans' surprisingly easy successes. Now, however, the Army of the Cumberland faced a formidable enemy force.

The Battle of Chickamauga

All through the night of September 18, Rosecrans continued to gather his forces and to shift the center of mass of the army toward his left. He was concerned about the Confederate movements during the previous day. It seemed obvious that an attempt was being made to envelop his left. By moving his units northward, he hoped to prevent Bragg from positioning his forces between the Army of the Cumberland and Rossville. *(See Atlas Map No. 42a.)*

Surprisingly, Bragg did not issue additional instructions to his army for operations on September 19. Apparently, he saw no reason to amplify the orders he had disseminated on the previous day. Although warned by Polk that Federal troops had been moving northward throughout the night, Bragg persisted in his belief that the Union left lay near Lee and Gordon's Mills. In reality, instead of being in position to "sweep [Rosecrans' army] up the Chickamauga [Creek]," Bragg's army was directly east of the Union leftmost corps, which was commanded by Thomas.

The First Day

When it was reported to Thomas on the morning of September 19 that an isolated Confederate brigade was in position to his front, he ordered Brigadier General John M. Brannan's division to attack the rebel unit. With his order, Thomas initiated the Battle of Chickamauga. The fighting commenced at about 10:00 a.m. Brannan soon needed help; the brigade turned out to be two Confederate divisions. A seesaw fight developed, as both sides reinforced the units that had originally clashed.

The strengths of the two armies were about equal. Bragg's force numbered about 66,326, and the Army of the Cumberland totaled approximately 53,919. Bragg, however, concentrated his troops on his northern (right) flank, thus giving his army a preponderance of strength in that area. His massing of combat power to the north also gave Bragg the initiative, forcing Rosecrans to shift forces to support Thomas. Division after division marched north. Each fresh Confederate drive on the nineteenth met stubborn Federal resistance. *(Movements and attacks not shown on map.)* Bragg then shifted his forces to the center. In the afternoon, a brief Confederate success near Alexander's Bridge was blocked at 4:30 p.m. by a Union counterattack near the Widow Glenn's. With the seesaw battle continuing until darkness, the first day of fighting along Chickamauga Creek produced no decision. As night fell, uneasiness permeated the field; a second day of fighting would be required to settle the issue.[43]

Throughout the night of the nineteenth, the Federals built breastworks to protect their positions. Bragg, in turn, restructured his army. He hoped that the new organization might produce a more coordinated effort that would dislodge Rosecrans. Dividing his army into wings, Bragg placed Leonidas Polk in charge of the right wing and gave command of the left wing to Lieutenant General James Longstreet, who was expected to arrive on the field sometime during the night. Longstreet's arrival would be the culmination of a long and difficult attempt by the Confederacy to take advantage of its central position.

Reinforcements from the East

While Polk's earlier scheme to reinforce Bragg's army with troops from Johnston's army had not been adopted because Johnston could not spare the men, a similar proposal had been made more recently. Involving eastern units, it was destined to become the Confederacy's only successful attempt to take advantage of its central position. In June 1863, General P.G.T. Beauregard had proposed that elements of Lee's army be sent to reinforce the Army of Tennessee. Noting that Lee might spare 30,000 soldiers, Beauregard argued that, at the very least, Longstreet's corps should be available. After all, he reasoned, that corps had not been present when Lee won his great victory over Hooker at Chancellorsville. Obviously, Lee should be able to defend Virginia while Longstreet went west to help Bragg strike a decisive blow against Rosecrans' army.

About this same time, Longstreet advanced a similar concept. Lee's "war horse" spoke to the Confederate Secretary of War and proposed that his corps be sent to reinforce the Army of Tennessee. Again, the possible consequences of a crushing defeat of Rosecrans' army were emphasized: Grant's line along the Mississippi would be turned, and Kentucky and Tennessee would be open for reoccupation. Even though Longstreet felt that "our best opportunity for great results is in Tennessee," he might have had more in mind than the destruction of the Army of the Cumberland; the command of the new force was very attractive.[44]

The command of the heavily reinforced army in the West was offered to Lee, probably because of his record of achievement. He turned it down, pleading lack of knowledge of the situation in the West. Longstreet felt no such humility. On September 5 he wrote Lee: "If my corps cannot go west, I think that we might accomplish something by giving me . . . [three] brigades, and putting me in General Bragg's place. . . . We would surely make no great risk in such a change and we might gain a great deal."[45] Lee had refused overall command; Longstreet had requested it. Nevertheless, Bragg retained it.

On September 8, the lead elements of Longstreet's corps passed through Richmond enroute to the West. Major General John B. Hood's division headed the parade as it meandered through the South. The loss of Chattanooga forced Longstreet's corps to travel through the Carolinas and Georgia in order to reach Bragg's army near LaFayette. *(See Atlas Map No. 2.)* Poor rail lines, inadequate rolling stock, and a wide variety of rail gauges prevented Longstreet's movement from being either rapid or concentrated. Hood's division began arriving at Ringgold on the afternoon of September 18, but only five of Longstreet's nine brigades arrived in time for the battle. Nevertheless, a lesson on the utility of railroads was being demonstrated. Longstreet's arrival spelled disaster for his old West Point roommate, William S. Rosecrans.

Rosecrans was aware that the Army of Tennessee was

being reinforced. On September 15, Halleck had warned him that three divisions from Lee's army were being sent to Bragg. On the eighteenth, the commander of the Army of the Cumberland believed that Lee's reinforcements were already in Atlanta. A strong defensive seemed to be the best course of action in the face of Bragg's newly acquired strength. On the evening of the first day of the Battle of Chickamauga, Rosecrans assembled his generals for a council of war. He told them of his plan to remain on the defensive. Thomas was to hold the left side of the line, and McCook was instructed to hold the right. Crittenden's corps was placed in reserve behind the junction of McCook's and Thomas' corps; Granger was to remain in general reserve on the Rossville-Ringgold Road.[46]

The Critical Day

As on the first day, the area occupied by Thomas' corps was the scene of the initial fighting on September 2. *(See Atlas Map No. 42b.)* Bragg adhered to his original plan of trying to sweep the Union forces to the left. Once again, however, his orders were incorrectly issued and inadequately executed. He envisioned a coordinated attack commencing on the right. Following this, each division would launch a separate attack along the line to the left. Obviously, it was vital for the unit on the extreme right to begin the attack at the time designated by Bragg—specifically, at daylight. But Polk, the wing commander, wanted to insure that all units were in their proper positions before the first attack commenced. Through a series of errors that included misdirected couriers, misunderstood orders, and Bragg's failure to supervise the plan's implementation personally, the attack on Thomas' corps did not start until approximately 9:00 a.m.

Longstreet was even less prepared to participate in the attack early on September 20. He had arrived on the field late at night on the nineteenth. Irritated that no one from Bragg's staff had met him in order to guide him to the commanding general's headquarters, Longstreet finally found Bragg at about midnight, at which point he received a briefing on the situation. Bragg told Longstreet that he had been given command of the left wing. In addition, he informed him of the plan to force the Yankees into McLemore's Cove. Naturally, Longstreet was not well acquainted with the terrain because he had never seen it in daylight. Moreover, except for the men in his own five brigades, Longstreet had never worked with any of the officers under his command. Deciding that it was too dark to reconnoiter his lines and too late to gain undying loyalty from his new subordinates, Longstreet went to bed. Early in the morning, he began the difficult task of gaining control of his new command.[48]

By 11:00 a.m., Longstreet was prepared to commence the attack. In a note to Bragg, he recommended that he be permitted to attack before the units on his immediate right began to move forward. Before he received a reply, Longstreet was surprised to see one of his divisions start the assault, seemingly without orders. His consternation undoubtedly increased when he learned that Bragg had ordered the division forward. A staff officer informed him that the commanding general was angry that the attacks on the right had been late, and that, accordingly, Bragg had sent an officer to tell each division commander on the left to attack at once. Immediately, Longstreet issued orders to the rest of his subordinates to begin the attack. Although expecting to strike strong resistance on the Federal right center, Longstreet's lead division commander encountered only scattered resistance. There was a gap in the Union lines, and most of Longstreet's troops were able to pass through it. Rosecrans had made a serious error.[48] *(See Atlas Map No. 42b.)*

Rosecrans' error had its origin in an event that had occurred much earlier in the morning. In his continuing effort to reinforce Thomas, Rosecrans had ordered Negley's division to move from the right center of the line to the left, where Thomas was strengthening his position and extending his line. However, while checking his units during the morning, Rosecrans found that Negley had not yet started to move. Rosecrans, realizing that the Confederate attack would be launched at any moment, was angered by Negley's tardiness. When questioned, Negley replied that he couldn't leave the line because Brigadier General Thomas J. Wood's division of McCook's corps had not arrived to replace his unit. Hurriedly, Rosecrans rode to Wood's headquarters and rebuked him in the presence of Wood's staff: "What is the meaning of this, sir? You have disobeyed my specific orders. By your damnable negligence you are endangering the safety of the entire army, and, by God, I will not tolerate it. Move your division at once, as I have instructed, or the consequences will not be pleasant for yourself."[49] Suffering under the reprimand, Wood hastily moved his division forward to replace Negley's unit, and Negley moved to reinforce the left. *(Movements not shown on map.)* Although there was no immediate harmful consequence, damage, in fact, had been done; Wood was ready to obey—without question—any order issued by the commanding general.

At about 11:00 a.m., Wood received an order from Rosecrans' staff that should have been questioned: "The general commanding directs that you close up on Reynolds as fast as possible, and support him."[50] In order to execute the instructions, Wood would have to pull out of the line, pass to the rear of Brigadier General John M. Brannan's division, which was on his left, and approach Major General Joseph J. Reynolds' unit from the rear. *(See Atlas Map No. 42b.)*

McCook, present when the order arrived, promised Wood that he would send units to plug the hole created by Wood's departure.

Rosecrans' order to Wood was issued out of ignorance of the situation. He did not intend for Wood to withdraw from the line. During the morning, Thomas had sent aides to Rosecrans' headquarters to request additional reinforcements. The two aides who rode along the line in order to reach Rosecrans thought that they detected a gap in the Federal line. As each passed Reynolds' unit, they came upon an open field that did not seem to be covered by any Federals. On the opposite side of the field, they came in contact with Wood's men. Thus, there appeared to be a hole that was flanked by Wood's and Reynolds' divisions, but not protected in the rear. Instead of checking the edge of the woods on the western side of the open field, the staff officers rode to Rosecrans' headquarters, submitted Thomas' request for reinforcements, and reported that "Brannan's division was out of line, and that Reynolds' right was exposed."[51] Brannan was not out of line, and Reynolds' right was not exposed; but Rosecrans, assuming that the information was correct, issued the fateful order that forced Wood to withdraw from the front. Immersed in "the fog of war," Rosecrans created a gap in his line.

At 11:30 a.m., Longstreet's men poured through the hole. *(See Atlas Map No. 42b.)* They struck the rear of Wood's division as it was organizing into a march column and preparing to move northward. One brigade fled before the onslaught. Wood then re-formed the remainder of his division, shifting it to face southward. Outflanked, and with Confederates to their rear, Brigadier Generals Philip H. Sheridan's and Jefferson C. Davis' divisions raced for McFarland's Gap. Longstreet rapidly took advantage of the situation and, instead of turning to the left as Bragg originally intended, turned to the right, trying to roll up the entire Yankee line. When Federal resistance stiffened in the vicinity of Snodgrass' Hill, Longstreet asked Bragg for help. He thought that the situation dictated a transfer of forces from Polk's wing to his command. This added combat power would exploit success, and perhaps complete the destruction of the Union army.

Bragg did not reinforce Longstreet. He felt that the attacks by the right wing had been repulsed so severely that the troops would not be able to continue the fight. At 3:00 p.m., he left the battlefield and returned to his headquarters near Reed's Bridge. The sound of heavy fighting due west of his position continued throughout the afternoon. It was not obvious to him that his enemy had been beaten badly. In fact, even Longstreet was not sure of the magnitude of his victory, because Thomas' corps was tenaciously resisting every effort to dislodge it from its precarious position. The Union general would not admit defeat.[52] *(Action not shown on map.)*

On this afternoon, Thomas earned his title of "The Rock

Major General George H. Thomas

of Chickamauga." At first, he was not aware that the right side of the line had disappeared. He simply continued a stout defense of the left. By about 2:00 p.m., he was certain that his reinforced corps was the focal point of Bragg's attack. Refusing his right flank,* he tenaciously held his threatened position. Plugging gaps as they opened and readjusting the lines as new threats appeared, "he issued orders to restore the line in the quiet conversational tone that politeness prescribes for a ladies' drawing-room. It was the discipline of a lifetime concentrated on a moment."[53] Thomas' inspirational leadership was aided by the unexpected arrival of reinforcements from the north. Granger's corps was marching to the sound of the guns.

Granger's Reserve Corps had watched most of the battle from a distance. By 11:00 a.m., Granger recognized that Thomas needed help and, without instructions from Rosecrans, Granger ordered his men south. *(See Atlas Map No. 42b.)* Although he struck Forrest's covering force along the way, Granger brushed them aside after a brief action. Hurrying forward, his corps reached Thomas in time to save the XIV Corps from probable destruction. Further assisted by the unanticipated appearance of a brigade that had been tending to its wounded in the rear, the left held.[54]

---

*When a force has positioned its flank against an obstruction, such as an unfordable river, and has thus protected itself from assault by significant numbers, the force is said to have refused a flank.

In the meantime, Rosecrans had traveled to Chattanooga. He had been present behind the right wing when Longstreet's attack passed through the gap left by Wood. Caught up in the retreat of his army, Rosecrans withdrew with most of his staff. Upon reaching a fork that was formed by a road that led to Chattanooga and a road that led to Thomas' corps, Rosecrans told his chief of staff to ride for the city and organize a defense while he determined the status of Thomas' corps. Rosecrans' chief of staff argued that the commanding general was better able to organize a defense of a city than he. A brief argument ensued. Garfield finally convinced Rosecrans that the commander's proper place was in Chattanooga. At about 4:00 p.m., Garfield reached Thomas and informed him of the magnitude of the disaster on the right. He also advised Thomas that Rosecrans had authorized a withdrawal if necessary.

Facing mounting pressure on three sides, Thomas was forced to withdraw an hour and a half later. Pulling the least heavily engaged units from the line first, he moved his corps back through McFarland's Gap. Marching north to Rossville, by midnight Thomas had skillfully fortified the important mountain pass. *(Movement not shown on map.)* The roads to Chattanooga were closed to a Confederate attack.[55]

The Battle of Chickamauga provides some excellent examples of good and bad generalship. Certainly, Thomas' stout defense demonstrated clear thinking and grim determination in the face of great adversity. Granger's decision to move to the sound of the guns was a key element in the avoidance of a total Federal disaster. Longstreet also showed excellent judgment when he deviated from Bragg's plan and tried to exploit success as best as possible. But failings in the leadership of both armies also were very evident. Rosecrans' and Bragg's absence from the battlefield at the end of the second day's fighting illustrates flaws in leadership. In addition, the heavy casualties—11,413 Union killed or wounded and 14,674 Confederate killed or wounded—testifies that the fighting, although it produced only mediocre results, was hard. Rosecrans' army was safe in Chattanooga, and Bragg had not been able to undermine Federal control of Tennessee. Paradoxically, although Chickamauga was a Confederate victory, a decision reached after the battle further eroded the morale of the Army of Tennessee.[56]

The Aftermath

Bragg initially felt that he could retake Chattanooga without a fight. Early reports from Forrest's cavalry indicated that Rosecrans was evacuating the city. Accordingly, on September 22, Bragg ordered Wheeler and Forrest to cut the Union line of retreat from Chattanooga. On the twenty-third, however, Bragg personally viewed the Federal activity in the city, and saw that troops were firmly established in the old Confederate

defenses. An attack would be difficult. On September 27, Bragg learned that the strength of his own army consisted of only 36,000 infantry. More discouraging news followed the next day when he discovered that two corps of the Army of the Potomac were enroute to the Army of the Cumberland. If Bragg were not already sufficiently discouraged, Johnston delivered another blow when he informed him that two corps from Grant's army also were on the way to Chattanooga. Clearly, Rosecrans' army was not defenseless, and its strength was building rapidly.

Bragg's army was in no condition to conduct a sustained campaign. Even before the Battle of Chickamauga, the Army of Tennessee had been on half rations. The movement of Longstreet's corps from Virginia had required most of the railroad rolling stock, so that there was little available to ameliorate the supply situation. In addition, Longstreet's corps did not bring any wagons or livestock because of the shortage of rail cars; all of the corps' subsistence had to come from the meager resources available to the Army of Tennessee. In short, Bragg felt that his army would not be able to assault the Army of the Cumberland in the Chattanooga defenses.[57]

Bragg's failure to conduct an immediate pursuit after the battle brought a quick response from his corps commanders. On September 26, Longstreet, Hill, and Polk held a conference to discuss what needed to "be done in view of the palpable weakness and mismanagement manifested in the conduct of the military operations of this army."[58] The meeting resulted in letters being sent to the President and to the Secretary of War asking that Bragg be replaced by Robert E. Lee. Jefferson Davis was forced to visit the army in early October in order to smooth over the obvious difficulties.

As a result of the meeting, President Davis gave Bragg his unqualified support. Polk was relieved of command of his corps, and D.H. Hill also was removed from command. Hindman was "suspended" from command of his division and sent to Atlanta. The anti-Bragg faction had been removed, but at the cost of crippling the morale of the leadership of the army.[59]

Another outcome of the battle focused on the issue of interior lines. Prior to the battle, the Confederate Government had decided to shift troops from one theater to another in order to concentrate a preponderant force. Longstreet's reinforcement of Bragg, however, was poorly handled, partly as a result of poor staff work and partly as a result of overtaxed support facilities. Four of Longstreet's nine brigades and all of his artillery failed to arrive in time for the battle, and the logistical support elements of the corps could not be moved at all.

The Union, however, handled such tasks with apparent ease. The Federal response to Rosecrans' loss at Chickamauga was both rapid and massive. Two corps of the Army of the

Potomac were shifted to reinforce the Army of the Cumberland. In an impressive display of logistical superiority, 25,000 men, 10 batteries of artillery and their horses, and 100 cars of baggage moved over 1,200 miles in 11 days. The Confederate advantage of central position was offset by superior Union lateral communications. Although the South would continue to debate the issue of interior lines, the North obviously possessed them.

From a northern viewpoint, perhaps the most significant consequence of the Battle of Chickamauga was the wholesale reshuffling of the command structure in the West. The leadership of the Army of the Cumberland was altered significantly. Major General George H. Thomas replaced Rosecrans as commanding general. McCook and Crittenden, who had joined Rosecrans in headlong flight from the battlefield, were removed from command of the XX and XXI Corps, respectively. The two corps were consolidated and placed under Gordon Granger, the general who had marched to the sound of the guns and helped Thomas prevent a total disaster on September 20. The most significant charge of all, however, was the elevation of Grant to a position of greater responsibility.

The Opening of the Gateway

On October 9, Major General Ulysses S. Grant received a message at Vicksburg, Mississippi. The Secretary of War wanted Grant to go to Cairo, Illinois—the nearest telegraphic link between Vicksburg and Washington. Grant and his staff left the same day.

In Cairo, Grant was instructed to go to Louisville, Kentucky to meet an official from the War Department. In order to reach Louisville, Grant had to proceed by rail via Indianapolis. When Grant's train reached Indianapolis, it was met by a special train from Washington. An important visitor transferred to Grant's train—Secretary of War Edwin M. Stanton wanted to discuss the western armies.

Having never met Grant, Stanton voiced some general amenities before he stated the purpose of the meeting. It had been decided that unity of command needed to be achieved in the West, and that Grant was the right man to command the new centralized structure. The Departments of the Ohio, the Cumberland, and the Tennessee were to be consolidated into the Military Division of the Mississippi. Grant was to be the commanding general of the organization; he would be in charge of all units between the Allegheny Mountains and the Mississippi River (with the exception of troops in Louisiana). As a final note, Grant was told that he could choose who was to command the Army of the Cumberland: either Rosecrans or Thomas. Grant chose Major General George H. Thomas.[60]

The Opening of a Federal Supply Line

Obviously, the most critical point in Grant's new command was Chattanooga. After spending an additional day discussing events in the West with the Secretary of War, Grant left to visit Thomas' threatened army. Enroute to Chattanooga, he stopped in Stevenson, Alabama, where he met Rosecrans. *(See Atlas Map No. 43.)* Having quietly turned over the command of his army to Thomas, Rosecrans was enroute to his new command in Missouri. He briefed Grant on conditions in Chattanooga and outlined some plans that had been formulated to improve the situation. Grant was rather surprised by Rosecrans' briefing; the plans appeared to be quite good. But, as Grant later remarked, "My only wonder was that he had not carried them out."[61] That night, Grant left Stevenson; on October 23, he arrived in Chattanooga.

Grant's trip to Chattanooga was an excellent introduction to the grim realities facing the Army of the Cumberland. To reach his destination, he was forced to follow the army's supply route, starting from its base at Bridgeport. From Bridgeport, Grant traveled northeast to Jasper. His route then followed the Sequatchie River Valley for 20 miles before turning southeast across Walden's Ridge into the city. Grant learned that it took 10 days for a supply wagon to travel one way along this tortuous path. *(See Atlas Map No. 43.)* He was also astonished to discover that 10,000 horses and mules had already died trying to carry supplies to Thomas' hungry soldiers. When he assumed command, Thomas had made a seemingly heroic vow that he would hold Chattanooga until he starved. To Grant, this now appeared to have been more than an idle boast. Starvation was a strong possibility, and Grant knew that the opening of a secure supply line was his first priority.[62]

The vulnerability of the Army of the Cumberland's line of communication had been demonstrated early in October. On September 29, Braxton Bragg had ordered Wheeler to take two reinforced cavalry divisions and cut the Union supply line through the Sequatchie Valley. On October 1, Wheeler crossed the Tennessee River and passed through the Federal cavalry force that screened the northern flank. His raid, which penetrated to the Union rear area, created an uproar. *(Wheeler's route shown on Atlas Map No. 43.)* Yankee cavalry followed in close pursuit. Destroying 800 enemy supply wagons, Wheeler proved that the Army of the Cumberland's hold on Chattanooga was tenuous. Rosecrans responded by examining alternate means of supply.

On the day that he was relieved of his command, Rosecrans directed his chief engineer, Brigadier General William F. Smith, to devise a way of establishing an alternate supply route. The best method of moving supplies to Chattanooga from Bridgeport seemed to be by water. However, as Confederate positions on Raccoon Mountain and Lookout Mountain dominated the Tennessee River approaches, Smith was convinced that the opening of a new supply route could only be achieved through surprise. If the Federals attempted an overland march eastward along the south bank of the river to Chattanooga, they would be exposed to an attack against their flank. If they tried a move westward from Chattanooga, they would be forced to conduct a river crossing operation beneath the towering heights that overlooked the river at Brown's Ferry. The Confederates would probably then seal off the bridgehead, and the operation would be doomed. On the day after he was assigned the task of developing a plan, Smith proposed that a combination of these two concepts be used.[63]

Smith suggested that a crossing at Brown's Ferry be made at the same time that a large Federal force crossed the river at Bridgeport and advanced eastward. The Confederates might be able to mass sufficient forces to counter one move, but they would not be able to stop both operations. If they attacked one force, the other Union force would be immediately available for a counterattack. Bragg would then be compelled to make a decision: he could either strip his siege lines and risk a decisive battle on his left, or continue with the siege and allow Thomas the use of a new supply route. Smith's plan combined speed with surprise. On October 24, Grant ordered that it be executed.

As a result of careful planning, the Union operation to open a new supply line went smoothly. Before sunrise on October 27, a waterborne assault force from Chattanooga seized a bridgehead at Brown's Ferry. *(See Atlas Map No. 44a.)* A weak Confederate counterattack was easily repulsed, and two Union brigades soon reinforced the position. In the meantime, Major General Joseph Hooker crossed the river at Bridgeport with his two corps from the Army of the Potomac and advanced eastward. By 3:00 p.m., Hooker's men held Wauhatchie. Cautiously, the two corps continued to advance, expecting an attack by Longstreet's corps. Encountering only light resistance, they moved to within a mile of Brown's Ferry and camped for the night. The line from Bridgeport to Chattanooga was open.

That afternoon, Longstreet and Bragg decided to launch an attack. Its object was to sever the Federal line to Bridgeport. However, the Confederate failure to make adequate preparations for a night attack—one of the most difficult of all military operations—had disastrous results. In the dark, the Rebels were at first unable to find the location of Hooker's rear guard. *(Movements not shown on map.)* After midnight, they stumbled into the Yankees at Wauhatchie. Hooker's rapid reinforcement of his covering force ended the contest. The Confederates broke off the attack, and the new Federal supply route—the "cracker line"—was secure.[64]

Having established a line into Chattanooga, Grant gathered

Supplies Are Loaded for the "Cracker Line"

his resources and began to build up his stock of supplies. He collected as much railroad rolling stock as possible in order to keep the supplies moving out of Nashville. In addition, a railroad line that had been heavily damaged by war was rebuilt, giving the army access to northern Alabama. *(See Atlas Map No. 43.)* This provided Grant with two routes between Nashville and Stevenson and greatly improved the flow of supplies into Chattanooga. Once sufficient stores had been established, Grant wanted to move against Bragg's army.[65]

Confederate Haggling

Bragg continued to have problems with his subordinates. In a letter to Jefferson Davis, he blamed Longstreet for the Federal success that resulted in the opening of the "cracker line." He asked the Confederate President to return to the army for another visit. Perhaps Bragg hoped to rid himself of Longstreet in the same manner that he had eliminated Hill, Polk, and Hindman from his command. In any event, Davis recommended a plan that produced the same effect; he suggested that Longstreet's corps be sent to attack Burnside's force near Knoxville.

Bragg liked the idea. Burnside's defeat would force Grant to detach part of his force and counter the threat in east Tennessee. It also would remove Longstreet, whose feelings about Bragg had been expressed in his attempt to have Bragg removed in September. Bragg wanted Longstreet's men to march against Burnside, swiftly defeat him, and then prepare either to return to Chattanooga or to move into Kentucky and cut the Federal line of communication to Tennessee. He felt that "something worth while [sic] could be effected by the operation."[66]

The Railroad Near Murfreesboro Undergoes Repairs

Longstreet did not like the project. He knew that his force was not large enough to achieve a quick victory over Burnside. Nevertheless, the project would enable him to get away from a general whom he felt was incompetent. After voicing his dissatisfaction with the scheme, he gathered his troops and, on November 5, set out for Knoxville. His force included 12,000 infantry, as well as 5,000 cavalry under the command of Wheeler; thus, Bragg's army was reduced by almost 25 percent.

Union Plans

Longstreet's departure provided Grant with a great opportunity. He ordered Thomas to attack the northern end of Missionary Ridge as soon as possible. *(See Atlas Map No. 44a.)* This would not only take advantage of the weakening of Bragg's army, but would remove the pressure from Burnside. Bragg would be forced to re-call Longstreet from east Tennessee when his right was threatened by an envelopment. Thomas' response, however, changed Grant's views about an attack. The Army of the Cumberland was still incapable of an offensive because of supply shortages. The few emaciated horses left in the army could not pull the artillery needed to support the attack. Grant would not have sufficient combat power until Major General William T. Sherman arrived with reinforcements.[67]

Sherman had been moving toward Chattanooga since late September, marching along the line of the Memphis and Charleston Railroad, which had been badly torn up by the war.

He had been ordered east from Mississippi in response to the reinforcement of Bragg's army by Longstreet. His move, however, had been slow. Since the railroad was a principal supply route, Sherman had been ordered to repair it as he marched. Because of this time-consuming task, Sherman was still 200 miles from Chattanooga when Grant arrived on October 23. On the twenty-fourth, Grant wired Sherman to "drop everything" and push forward to Stevenson.[68]

When Sherman's command reached Bridgeport on November 13, he went ahead to Chattanooga. At this point, Grant, accompanied by Sherman, most of the other principal commanders, and his chief engineer, conducted a reconnaissance of the Confederate positions. The Federal generals discovered that a force which crossed to the north bank of the Tennessee River at Brown's Ferry would be screened from the view of the Confederates by the mountains. Thus, Sherman's Army of the Tennessee would approach in full view of the Confederates and, when opposite Chattanooga, could disappear from sight. Sherman might then gain surprise, either by suddenly appearing at Knoxville and attacking Longstreet or by appearing at the mouth of the Chickamauga Creek and enveloping Bragg's right flank.

Satisfied with his knowledge of Bragg's dispositions, Grant announced his plan of attack on November 18. *(See Atlas Map No. 44b.)* At daylight on the twenty-first, Sherman was to cross the Tennessee River, envelop Bragg's right, and push the Confederate flank toward Tunnel Hill. Thomas was to move eastward from Chattanooga. When Sherman's men reached Tunnel Hill, Thomas' troops were to link up with the Army of the Tennessee, and the two armies were to complete the destruction of the Confederate right. In the meantime, Hooker's soldiers were to move into Lookout Creek valley and pin the Confederates in their positions on the left. Major General O.O. Howard's XI Corps was designated the general reserve.[68]

Grant's plan was simple but promising. It exploited the North's superior numbers—56,359 Federals to 46,165 Confederates—by preventing Bragg from reinforcing endangered parts of his line. The appearance of Hooker's and Thomas' formidable forces on the Confederate left and center would prohibit Bragg from taking units from these sections of his front. When Sherman appeared unexpectedly on the Confederate right, Bragg would be in a quandary—he would have to stop Sherman's five divisions without weakening the units facing Hooker and Thomas. Thus, Sherman's attack was a key element in the plan.

Preliminary Operations

Sherman's approach march to his attack position went badly. Having anticipated Grant's plan to position his army on the

Union left, Sherman had begun moving his troops on November 17. On the twentieth, it started raining, and the roads deteriorated rapidly. On November 21, the date set for the attack, Sherman's men were still struggling in the rain, trying to reach their crossing point over the Tennessee River.

Nevertheless, Sherman's move had a beneficial effect. As had been anticipated, when Sherman's men disappeared behind the mountains north of Chattanooga, Bragg had to guess Sherman's objective. He assumed that the Federals were enroute to east Tennessee to try to aid Burnside, now besieged in Knoxville. Accordingly, Bragg dispatched two divisions to assist Longstreet. On the twenty-third, however, he re-called one of the divisions—Thomas had attacked the center of his position and seized part of his lines.[70]

Grant had changed his plans. On November 22, he received information that Bragg might be about to effect a withdrawal. Sherman's delay had postponed the time set for the attack, and now it appeared that Bragg might escape unscathed. Because it was essential that Bragg be fixed in his positions until Sherman was ready to attack, Grant ordered Thomas to assault the enemy's center in front of Missionary Ridge.

At about noon on November 23, Thomas marched his army out of Chattanooga and formed it into a line of battle. Most of the Confederate army along the heights surrounding Chattanooga could see the Army of the Cumberland as it drew up its lines in an impressive display of pageantry and strength. At precisely 2:00 p.m., the parade formation swept forward, drove the Confederates back, and seized a line along Orchard Knob and Indian Hill. *(See Atlas Map No. 43b.)* Grant's army had flexed its muscles, and the show of strength had made an impression on the defenders. On the following day, the spectators on Missionary Ridge watched another exhibition of might by the Union army.

As Sherman's corps was still crossing the river, Thomas felt that it was an opportune moment to press the Confederate left and stop Bragg from shifting forces to oppose Sherman's crossing. In response to Thomas' urgings, Grant ordered Thomas to commit Hooker's force earlier than had been planned. The move was intended to be a demonstration to fix the Confederates, but when Hooker moved forward at 4:00 a.m. on November 24, he discovered that the Confederate positions were weak. The ensuing Battle of Lookout Mountain became known as "the battle above the clouds." *(See Atlas Map No. 44b.)* Fog and rain hid most of the battle from the view of the blue-clad audience in the valley and the gray-clad spectators on Missionary Ridge. When the clouds parted momentarily, onlookers were afforded a brief glimpse of the battle. By nightfall, word spread that a second Confederate position had fallen to Grant's army. In confirmation, when the sun rose on the morning of the twenty-fifth, the Stars and Stripes was seen flying from the crest of Lookout Mountain.[71]

While Hooker had been enveloping the Confederate left, Sherman had been pushing his troops across the river opposite Bragg's right. Ashamed of his army's slow movement, Sherman hurried his soldiers into attack positions as soon as they crossed the Tennessee. He was shocked, however, to discover that the terrain was quite different from what he had expected. When he had made his reconnaissance from the north side of the river with Grant, he thought that he had seen Missionary Ridge rising at a uniform rate until it reached Tunnel Hill. This hill appeared to be the most likely location for the Confederate defenses. But when he arrived at the northern end of Missionary Ridge, Sherman learned that the ridge did not rise uniformly. There were several smaller hills that had to be crossed before he could reach the main ridge line. As the Confederates were defending these smaller hills, it would be a hard fight before Sherman's men could reach Tunnel Hill. Late in the afternoon of November 24, Sherman organized his men for the difficult assault.[72]

Bragg felt that the most vulnerable part of his line was located on Tunnel Hill. Thomas' seizure of Orchard Knob, combined with Sherman's sudden appearance on the banks of the Tennessee, convinced Bragg that his northern flank was in serious danger. He was in the process of reinforcing his right when Hooker struck the Lookout Mountain position. To Bragg, however, it still seemed that the right was the most threatened point; even as the Battle of Lookout Mountain raged throughout the twenty-fourth, Sherman continued to build the strength of his force.

The Crucial Day of the Battle

On the evening of November 24, Bragg met with his corps commanders, Lieutenant General William J. Hardee and Major General John C. Breckinridge, to discuss plans. Hardee advised retreat; Breckinridge urged a stand. Bragg, deciding that there was not sufficient time to plan a withdrawal under enemy pressure, sided with Breckinridge. He then gave Breckinridge the command of three divisions and told him to hold the left. Hardee received four divisions, and was instructed to hold the endangered right. Since Missionary Ridge seemed virtually impregnable, Breckinridge defended over two-thirds of the front with the smaller force. Hardee massed his troops around Tunnel Hill.

Grant distributed his force in a similar fashion. He still envisioned Sherman sweeping south and linking up with Thomas at Tunnel Hill. Thus, Sherman was given the preponderance of strength and the mission to crush a well-entrenched enemy. Hooker was to move forward and strike the Confederate left.

Entrenched and determined, Hardee withstood Sherman's strong attacks on November 25. *(See Atlas Map No. 44c.)*

Major General William J. Hardee

Repeatedly, the Federals attacked; repeatedly, the Confederates repulsed them. The fighting was continuous throughout most of the day, but Sherman's men could not crack Hardee's defenses. Even after Grant sent Howard's corps to Sherman's aid, there was no success; the position was too strong, and the Confederates were too resolute. Late in the afternoon, Sherman abandoned the attack and awaited additional instructions. Hardee, satisfied that his corps was safe, rode to the left to see how Breckinridge was doing. When he passed Benjamin F. Cheatham's division, Hardee discovered that Breckinridge's corps was gone.[73]

It has been called "the miracle of Missionary Ridge." Breckinridge's "impregnable" position had been carried by a frontal assault that had not been ordered by either Grant or Thomas. The soldiers of the Army of the Cumberland had risen to the occasion, driven the Confederates from their positions, and sent them fleeing into Georgia. The result of an unusual set of circumstances, it has caused a vast amount of discussion and analysis.

The "miracle" commenced at about 2:00 p.m. Grant told Thomas to attack the Confederate center in order to relieve Sherman of some pressure. Thomas passed the word to Major General Gordon S. Granger, his center corps commander, "to make a demonstration upon the works of the enemy . . . at the base of Mission Ridge [*sic*]."[74] Granger passed these

instructions to his division commanders, and between 3:00 p.m. and 4:00 p.m., the assault commenced. The Federals easily took the Confederate rifle pits at the base of Missionary Ridge. Once there, however, they found that they were in trouble. At their starting point on Orchard Knob, the Yankees had been out of enemy artillery range. At the base of the ridge, however, they were exposed to the murderous fire of Confederate guns. It became a question of retreating to safety, standing and dying, or attacking to eliminate the Confederate artillery. The troops chose the last course of action. *(See Atlas Map No. 44d.)* Spurred on by their regimental and brigade commanders, the men in the Army of the Cumberland raced to the top of Missionary Ridge, causing the defenders to break and flee.[75]

There were a number of factors contributing to the Confederate flight. The defenders on Missionary Ridge had watched most of the events of the last three days from front row seats. They had witnessed the fall of Orchard Knob on November 23; they had seen Lookout Mountain seized on the following day; they had seen Hooker march off to their left and out of their view on the twenty-fifth; they had heard the heavy firing surrounding Sherman's assaults on the right; they had heard the firing on their left when Hooker reappeared and attacked the southern end of the ridge. Moreover, they knew that their position was not strong; each man was seven to eight feet from his neighbor, and few fortifications had been constructed on top of the ridge before November 23. Finally, a gap existed between Bates' and Anderson's divisions in the center of the line. As a result, a general feeling of uneasiness existed among the defenders of Missionary Ridge. When the long lines of blue coats swept across the plain below and started up the ridge, it was too much. Breckinridge's corps departed.[76]

There was no Union cavalry pursuit after the battle for Missionary Ridge. The dearth of forage on the southern side of the Tennessee had forced the cavalry to remain north of the river throughout the campaign. Sheridan's division, however, initially pursued the Confederates. At Ringgold, Georgia, Cleburne's division fought a stout rear-guard action on November 27 that stopped Hooker's corps and allowed the Confederates to continue their retreat to Dalton. Two days later, Braxton Bragg asked to be relieved from his command; the next day, Jefferson Davis obliged him by ordering him to turn over the command of the army to Hardee.

The Aftermath

Although Confederate casualties were smaller in number than those suffered at Chickamauga, the strength of the Army of Tennessee had been sapped. The 6,500 killed, wounded, and missing were of little importance when compared with the devastating blow that had been delivered to the morale of the survivors. Braxton Bragg had experienced his last defeat as a commanding general. Moreover, the remainder of the army knew that the gateway to the South was open and that they were the last defenders of the heartland.[77]

Bragg's final defeat was the result of a series of errors. The decision to send Longstreet to eastern Tennessee was ill-advised. It robbed Bragg of a sizable force and a competent corps commander. Moreover, Longstreet's campaign continued to draw men from Bragg's meager forces. On the eve of battle, Bragg sent an additional division to assist Longstreet—it was neither present to help Bragg save Missionary Ridge nor able to assist Longstreet's operation, which ended in failure. The organization of the siege lines around Chattanooga was faulty. The line stretching from Lookout Mountain to Chickamauga Creek was too long for the forces that were available. Bragg overestimated the natural strength of Missionary Ridge and positioned too many troops in the rifle pits at its base. The fortifications on the crest of the ridge were constructed both too late and in the wrong location; instead of placing the main line of defense along the military crest, the defenders placed their hopes in a line dug on the topographical crest.* In addition, Missionary Ridge was a difficult position on which to employ a reserve.[78] The steep reverse slope prevented the Confederates from reinforcing threatened portions of the line more quickly than the Federals, who had the initiative.

All of the errors that led to Bragg's defeat probably can be traced to the history of the Army of Tennessee. Bragg's army was not a defensive army. Most of its battles—from Perryville to Chickamauga—had been fought while on the offensive. Its commanders were not accustomed to preparing defenses and reacting to Union moves. Instead, they were used to holding the initiative and forcing the enemy to react. This offensive orientation, when combined with Bragg's indecisiveness and argumentative attitude, produced a force destined

to have difficulty when opposed by a general who was able to exploit his superior numbers.

Weight of numbers was certainly part of the reason for Grant's success at Chattanooga. Although the plan to open the "cracker line" was not his, when presented with a good plan, Grant placed its execution in the hands of a competent subordinate and wholeheartedly supported him with large forces. The plan to break the siege of Chattanooga was his, but it did not work the way he originally intended. As the events developed on the battlefield, he modified the plan, placed vast resources in the hands of competent subordinates, and exerted unrelenting pressure on the Confederates. To someone looking back with the advantage of hindsight, the Union army's success seems to have been the result of superior numbers and skillful subordinates. As one participant remarked, however:

> You have no conception of the changes in the army when Grant came. He opened up the cracker line and got a steamer through. We began to see things move. We felt that everything came from a plan. He came into the army quietly, no splendor, no airs, no staff. . . . He began the campaign the moment he reached the field.[79]

Ulysses S. Grant was in charge, dominating all aspects of the situation.

The year of 1863 had been a critical one in the War of the States. It had been a good year for the Federals. For the Confederates, however, the year had been far from satisfactory. Begun on a high note with Lee's brilliant victory at Chancellorsville, it ended on a low note with Bragg's resounding defeat at Chattanooga. While the North continued to refine its command structure, the South continued to look for a good commander for its western army. In the South, the future looked bleak, indeed. The trans-Mississippi West had been severed from the Confederacy and was gone forever. Tennessee had fallen, and a massive Federal army already was in Georgia. In the North, though, the future was beginning to look brighter. The size of the area under the control of the Federal Government at the end of 1863 was ample proof that the tide had turned.

---

*The topographical crest is the highest point on a hill. The military crest is the point—usually lower than the topographical crest and nearer to the enemy—from which the defender has better observation and fields of fire.

Notes

[1]Nathaniel C. Hughes, *General William J. Hardee: Old Reliable* (Baton Rouge, 1965), p. 148.

[2]*The War of the Rebellion: A Compilation of the Official Records of the Union and Confederate Armies* (130 vols; Washington, 1880–1901), Series I, XX, Pt. 2, 698–699. (Hereinafter cited as *OR*. Unless otherwise indicated, all subsequent references to the *OR* are to Series I.)

[3]Kenneth P. Williams, *Lincoln Finds a General* (5 vols; New York, 1949–1959), V, 208; Thomas L. Connelly, *Autumn of Glory: the Army of Tennessee, 1862–1865* (Baton Rouge, 1971), p. 114.

[4]Connelly, *Autumn of Glory*, pp. 123–125.

[5]*OR*, XXIII, Pt. 2, 703–704, 707, 715, 784–785; *Ibid.*, Pt. 1, 267–270.

[6]Connelly, *Autumn of Glory*, p. 117.

[7]K.P. Williams, *Lincoln Finds a General*, V, 229.

[8]*OR*, XXIII, Pt. 2, 617–618, 862; Connelly, *Autumn of Glory*, p. 119.

[9]William M. Lamers,*The Edge of Glory: A Biography of General William S. Rosecrans, USA* (New York, 1961), p. 277.

[10]*OR*, XXIII, Pt. 2, 424.

[11]K.P. Williams, *Lincoln Finds a General*, V, 210–211, 216.

[12]*Ibid.*, 217–218.

[13]*OR*, XXIII, Pt. 1, 405.

[14]Lamers, *Rosecrans*, p. 279; Gilbert C. Kniffin, "Maneuvering Bragg Out of Tennessee," in *Battles and Leaders of the Civil War*, ed. by Robert Underwood Johnson and Clarence Clough Buel (4 vols.; New York, 1884–1888), III, 635–636 (Hereinafter cited as *B&L*.)

[15]K.P. Williams, *Lincoln Finds a General,* V, 221–226; Connelly, *Autumn of Glory*, p. 128; *OR*, XXIII, Pt. 1, 583, 618; *Ibid.*, Pt. 2, 896.

[16]K.P. Williams, *Lincoln Finds a General*, V, 236.

[17]Connelly, *Autumn of Glory*, p. 130; Hughes, *Hardee*, p. 157; *OR*, XXIII, Pt. 1, 583–584.

[18]Arthur H. Noll, *Doctor Quintard, Chaplain C.S.A. and Second Bishop of Tennessee: Being His Story of the War* (Sewanee, Tenn., 1905), p. 87; Connelly, *Autumn of Glory*, p. 134.

[19]K.P. Williams, *Lincoln Finds a General*, V, 232–233.

[20]Lamers, *Rosecrans*, p. 289.

[21]H.V. Boynton, "The Chickamauga Campaign," in *Papers of the Military Historical Society of Massachusetts, Campaigns in Kentucky and Tennessee Including the Battle of Chickamauga, 1862–1865* (Boston, 1904), pp. 324–327.

[22]D.H. Hill, "Chickamauga–The Great Battle of the West," in *B&L*, III, 641.

[23]*OR*, XXIII, Pt. 2, 932–933.

[24]Hill, "Chickamauga," in *B&L*, III, 639.

[25]Don C. Seitz, *Braxton Bragg: General of the Confederacy* (Columbia, S.C., 1924), p. 323.

[26]Connelly, *Autumn of Glory*, pp. 162–164.

[27]*OR*, XXIII, Pt. 2, 552.

[28]*Ibid.*, 553, 555–556.

[29]Robert S. Herr, *Episodes of the Civil War, Nine Campaigns in Nine States* (San Francisco, 1890), p. 139.

[30]Ulysses S. Grant, *Personal Memoirs of U.S. Grant* (2 Vols.; New York, 1885), I, 579.

[31]John B. Turchin, *Chickamauga* (Chicago, 1888), p. 25.

[32]Hill, "Chickamauga" in *B&L*, III, 640; *OR*, XXX, Pt. 2, 136.

[33]K.P. Williams, *Lincoln Finds a General*, V, 243; Joseph H. Parks, *General Leonidas Polk, CSA.* (Baton Rouge, 1962), p. 322; Connelly, *Autumn of Glory*, pp. 166–168; *OR*, XXX, Pt. 4, 526.

[34]*OR*, XXX, Pt. 4, 602.

[35]Turchin, *Chickamauga*, p. 27.

[36]*OR*, XXX, Pt. 1, 852; Herr, *Episodes of the Civil War*, p. 140.

[37]Connelly, *Autumn of Glory*, pp. 171–175.

[38]*OR*, XXX, Pt. 3, 483, 488, 492.

[39]*OR*, XXX, Pt. 1, 247, 327; Connelly, *Autumn of Glory*, p. 187; Parks, *Polk*, p. 330.

[40]K.P. Williams, *Lincoln Finds a General*, V, 250; *OR*, XXX, Pt. 1, 485–487.

[41]*OR*, XXX, Pt. 2, 451.

[42]Hill, "Chickamauga" in *B&L*, III, 641.

[43]*OR*, XXX, Pt. 1, 55–56, 250–251; Glenn Tucker, *Chickamauga: Bloody Battle in the West* (Indianapolis, 1961), p. 128; Thomas L. Livermore, *Numbers and Losses in the Civil War in America, 1861–1865* (Boston, 1901), pp. 105–106.

[44]*OR*, XXIII, Pt. 2, 838; James Longstreet, *From Manassas to Appomattox: Memoirs of the Civil War in America* (Philadelphia, 1895), p. 435.

[45]*OR*, XXIX, Pt. 2, 699, 701.

[46]John B. Jones, *A Rebel War Clerk's Diary at the Confederate States Capital* (2 vols.; Philadelphia, 1866), II, 51; *OR*, XXX, Pt. 3, 644; Lamers, *Rosecrans*, p. 321; *OR*, XXX, Pt. 1, 57. 211–216.

[47]*OR*, XXX, Pt. 2, 198; Connelly, *Autumn of Glory*, pp. 220–221, 211–216.

[48]*OR*, XXX, Pt. 2, 288, 364.

[49]Tucker, *Chickamauga*, pp. 205–207.

[50]*OR*, XXX, Pt. 1, 635.

[51]Turchin, *Chickamauga*,. p. 112.

[52]*OR*, XXX, Pt. 2, 289.

[53]K.P. Williams, *Lincoln Finds a General*, V, 260; Wilbur D. Thomas, *General George H. Thomas: The Indomitable Warrior* (New York, 1964), p. 392.

[54]*OR*, XXX, Pt. 1, 430; Arba N. Waterman, "The Battle of Chickamauga," in MOLLUS, *Military Essays and Recollections* (4 vols.; Chicago, 1891–1899), I, 244.

[55]Tucker, *Chickamauga*, p. 312; Boynton, "The Chickamauga Campaign," in *Campaigns in Kentucky and Tennessee*, p. 371.

[56]Livermore, *Numbers and Losses*, pp. 105–106.

[57]Connelly, *Autumn of Glory*, pp. 230–233.

[58]*OR*, XXX, Pt. 2, 67.

[59]Parks, *Polk*, p. 344.

[60]Ulysses S. Grant, "Chattanooga," in *B&L*, III, 681–682.

[61]Thomas B. Van Horne, *History of the Army of Cumberland: Its Organization, Campaigns, and Battles* (Cincinnati, 1875), p. 394; Grant, *Personal Memoirs*, II, 28.

[62]Charles A. Dana, *Recollections of the Civil War: With the Leaders at Washington and in the Field in the Sixties* (New York, 1898), p. 129; *OR*, XXXI, Pt. 2, 29; Grant, *Personal Memoirs*, II, 26–27.

[63]Van Horne, *Army of the Cumberland*, pp. 387–392; William F. Smith, *The Relief of the Army of the Cumberland and the Opening of the Short Line of Communication Between Chattanooga, Tenn., and Bridgeport, Ala. in October 1863* (Washington, 1891) p. 18.

[64]Van Horne, *Army of the Cumberland*, pp. 397–401; Connelly, *Autumn of Glory*, pp. 255–261.

[65]*OR*, XXXI, Pt. 3, 26; Grant, ''Chattanooga,'' in *B&L*, III, 692.

[66]*OR*, LII, Pt. 2, 556; Longstreet, *Manassas to Appomattox*, p. 481; Seitz, *Bragg*, p. 392.

[67]*OR*, XXXI, Pt. 3, 216.

[68]*Ibid.*, Pt. 1, 713.

[69]Van Horne, *Army of the Cumberland*, pp. 410–411.

[70]Livermore, *Numbers and Losses*, pp. 107–108; Connelly, *Autumn of Glory*, p. 272.

[71]*OR*, XXXI, Pt. 2, 33, 106; Van Horne, *Army of the Cumberland*, p. 424.

[72]Lloyd Lewis, *Sherman, Fighting Prophet* (New York, 1932), pp. 318–319.

[73]Connelly, *Autumn of Glory*, pp. 273, 275; Van Horne, *Army of the Cumberland*, pp. 424–429.

[74]*OR*, XXXI, Pt. 2, 132.

[75]*Ibid.*, 258, 264, 281, 301.

[76]Connelly, *Autumn of Glory*, p. 273; Roy K. Flint, ''The Battle of Missionary Ridge'' (Unpublished Master's Thesis, University of Alabama, 1960), pp. 174–176.

[77]*OR*, XXXI, Pt. 2, 682.

[78]Grant, *Personal Memoirs*, II, 85; Flint, ''Missionary Ridge,'' pp. 200–201.

[79]Bruce Catton, *Grant Takes Command* (Boston, 1969), p. 56.

Prelude to Victory: 10
A New Commanding
General

With the advent of 1864, the Confederacy faced an alarming strategic situation. Although Richmond appeared to be secure under the protection of Robert E. Lee's Army of Northern Virginia, the Western Theater was in a shambles. Ulysses S. Grant's armies were poised menacingly in northwest Georgia, and there was little hope that the trans-Mississippi West could be regained. *(See Atlas Map No. 45.)* The strategic dilemma that had confronted Jefferson Davis since the beginning of the war continued to exist. With so few material resources available to the South, he needed to defend all areas against Federal encroachments. While the Confederate ordnance chief, Colonel Josiah Gorgas, had successfully scattered Confederate industries throughout the South so that the loss of any one particular area would not be disastrous, a defense of all areas was still required in order to prevent the loss of the dispersed industrial and agricultural sites. The stark fact remained that the Confederate Army was not large enough to stop every inroad being made by the Federal Army.

In the East, no major fighting had taken place since the Battle of Gettysburg in July of the previous year. Although the commander of the Army of the Potomac, Major General George G. Meade, had conducted two campaigns in the fall, both had indecisive results. *(Movements not shown on map.)*

In October, Lee outflanked Meade's position along the Rapidan River. Meade thereupon hurriedly withdrew his army northward across the Rappahannock River, and the contending armies marched toward Centreville. Arriving at Broad Run, Lee's III Corps commander, Lieutenant General Ambrose P. Hill, thought that he had been granted the opportunity of a lifetime—apparently, the Federal III Corps was in the process of crossing the stream without adequate security. Hill, the general who had committed Lee to battle at Gettysburg, ordered his troops forward. Unfortunately for Hill's men, they were not attacking the Union rear guard; in fact, they were blundering into the center of the Army of the Potomac. The Federal II Corps suddenly appeared on Hill's flank, inflicting

heavy losses on his corps; two Confederate brigades were badly smashed. Lee withdrew his army southward.

In late November, Meade moved southward and readied his men for battle in front of Lee's army along Mine Run. Although it was bitterly cold, Meade hoped that an attack could be successfully launched. Remembering the lesson of Gettysburg, he carefully deployed his troops in a manner that would allow them to overcome the inherent strength of the defender. He also placed the main attack against Lee's flank under the command of the man who had saved the army on the second day of Gettysburg, Major General Gouverneur Kemble Warren. Having assured Meade that he could successfully carry Lee's flank, Warren changed his mind after the pre-assault artillery bombardment had commenced. Reluctantly, the commanding general accepted Warren's recommendation that the attack be canceled, and the Army of the Potomac marched despondently northward to winter quarters.

Winter also ended operations in the West in 1863. The much-heralded victory at Missionary Ridge had climaxed a year of successful campaigning along the Mississippi River and in the State of Tennessee. It was clear that one man had been responsible for the successes on both of these fronts. Major General Ulysses S. Grant was the man of the hour.

Organizing for Victory

While Meade had been competing with Grant for honors as the North's foremost general, his failure at Mine Run tipped the scale in favor of Grant. As early as December, Congress began deliberating on the best way to reward Grant for his victories. In the United States Army, the rank of lieutenant general had been held on a permanent basis only by George Washington.* This seemed a fitting tribute to bestow upon

---

*Winfield Scott had also been promoted to lieutenant general, but he held that rank on the basis of a brevet promotion.

Lieutenant General Ulysses S. Grant

the man who had done so much to advance the North's war effort. The Senate, however, could not decide whether it was appropriate to name Grant in the bill that revived the rank. Feeling that naming Grant in the law would impinge on the President's powers as Commander-in-Chief, Congress finally passed a law that simply stated that the officer ''commissioned as lieutenant general, shall be authorized, under the direction of the President, to command the armies of the United States.''[1]

New Union Titles

The elevation of Grant to the rank of lieutenant general necessitated a change in the process used to select the General-in-Chief. In the past, Lincoln had been authorized to appoint a General-in-Chief from the many officers who held the rank of major general. Now, however, there was a single, senior general officer. If he failed, it would be difficult to replace him with a man of lower rank. Nevertheless, on March 2, 1864, Lincoln named Grant to the post, and the die was cast.

Obviously, Grant did not fulfill the nation's earlier dream of a Napoleon who would end the war in one lightning campaign. Instead, he was viewed as ''a steadfast, pertinacious commander, one who faithfully represented the practical, patient, persevering genius of the North.''[2] Grant brought to the position of General-in-Chief an attitude that was far different from that of his predecessor, Major General Henry W. Halleck. Halleck had viewed his post as that of an adviser to the Secretary of War and to the President. Grant did not see it in that light. He had been appointed ''Commanding General of the Armies of the United States,'' and he intended to perform his job as a commander, not an adviser. He would not pepper his subordinate with suggestions, recommendations, or advice on military doctrine. Instead, he would issue orders and expect full compliance. He would command the armies of the United States, informing only the President and the Secretary of War of his actions. He was not a Napoleon, but he would take charge of the Federal armies.

Halleck was not shunted aside and sent away to some distant post to be forgotten. He was too valuable for that. He understood the bureaucracy in Washington, and he had dealt with the War Department bureaus for almost two years. Efficient high-level administration of the Army had been his most successful contribution. Moreover, he understood the political climate in the capital, and although sometimes known as an intriguer, he frequently could overcome political obstacles and attain the desired goal. His service to the President and the Secretary of War also had been valuable, even though it had fallen short of their expectations. For these reasons, Halleck was named Chief of Staff of the Army, and was assigned to act under the direction of the Secretary of War and the Commanding General.[3]

As it turned out, Halleck's appointment was fortunate. He acted as a link between Grant and his civilian superiors in Washington. Because of his experience in dealing with Lincoln and Stanton, Halleck was able to translate many of Grant's ideas and orders into terms that the President and the Secretary of War could appreciate. In addition, he served as a valuable link between Grant and the War Department bureaus. Grant did not have to squeeze support out of the sometimes obstinate bureau chiefs; he simply told Halleck his needs, and Halleck supplied the necessary supervision to insure complete compliance. Although Halleck was known by the same title as the modern-day Chief of Staff, his authority and responsibilities were of a lesser nature. Nevertheless, Halleck performed many of the advisory and supervisory functions that occupy the attention of a modern Chief of Staff. He was a definite asset to the North's command structure in 1864.[4]

Grant's Selection of Key Subordinates

As soon as Halleck was notified that Grant had been promoted to the rank of lieutenant general, he ordered the western commander to report to Washington. Grant tried to be unobtrusive, but his attempt at quiet modesty was quickly lost in the widespread attention he received upon his arrival. Uneasy in the public eye, Grant met the President and Secretary of War on the evening of March 8, and on the following day received his commission as lieutenant general. The new commander then escaped the attention of the Washington press by taking a train to Brandy Station to visit the Army of the Potomac on the following day.

Unacquainted with the Army of the Potomac, Grant wanted to see the North's principal eastern army and to interview Meade. Although he admired Meade's victory at Gettysburg, he was not sure that the army was in the best hands. In the latter part of the previous year, he had thought that Major General William F. Smith would be well suited to the post. (Smith was the architect of the plan that opened the ''cracker line'' at Chattanooga in October 1863.) In spite of this preconception, Grant changed his mind during his conversation with Meade.

There was definite tension in the air during the first meeting between the two men. Neither had seen the other since the Mexican War. Meade knew that Grant's recent appointment reflected an attitude of favoritism towards the western armies and their commanders. Almost before Grant could open his mouth at the meeting, Meade said that he expected that Grant would want to replace him. Meade added that he thought that this would be fine, and that Sherman probably would be an excellent successor. Grant was truly taken aback by this opening statement. He had not come to relieve Meade on this visit, even though the command of the army really had not been settled in his own mind. Perhaps before he actually was prepared to make a decision. Grant reassured Meade that the command of the Army of the Potomac was not in question. The discussion quickly turned to other matters.

In the long run, Grant's quick reassurance to Meade probably was for the best. Obviously, Meade knew the Army of the Potomac better than any western general, and although he had not lived up to everyone's expectations, he still was the only general to have defeated Lee's Army of Northern Virginia. Furthermore, Grant's appointment already had created some resentment in the eastern army. Several generals felt that the western forces were experiencing great success only because they did not have to face the South's best army under its ablest general. If Grant had brought a second general east to take command of the army, the "outsider" might have had great difficulty gaining the loyalty of his subordinates.* Moreover, a new commander coming from the West undoubtedly would have brought his own staff with him. It would have taken the new staff time to grow familiar with the eastern army and its systems—and, with the campaigning season rapidly approaching, time was scarce. Finally, stripping the West of all of its best generals might have a debilitating effect on future Union efforts there. Clearly, Grant's decision to retain Meade in command was logical and sound.[5]

Grant spent only a day with the Army of the Potomac, leaving on March 11 for Nashville and a meeting with Major General William T. Sherman. He needed to turn over the command of the Military Division of the Mississippi to Sherman. He also wanted to discuss the coming campaign, and to decide where his headquarters should be established. He already had concluded that Washington was not the place for him. The capital's political atmosphere, the reputation of the War Department for interfering in the General-in-Chief's duties, and the social responsibilities of residence in the capital had convinced him that he could never accept an appointment that would force him to stay in Washington.[6]

Sherman reinforced many of Grant's misgivings about establishing headquarters in the East. He told Grant that the western armies enjoyed an excellent reputation for good reason—the West was where the war was being won. Moreover, Grant knew most of the senior officers in the West, while most of the generals in the East were strangers to him. But Grant was aware of other factors—factors that favored his presence in the East. Political interference in the affairs of a general who served in the East was a problem; if Grant stayed in the West, Meade would continue to be forced to contend with the hindrance. Grant's presence in the East might remove many of

the political burdens from Meade's shoulders.* Also, the administrative and logistical supervisory apparatus for the support of all of the armies was in Washington. Finally, Grant had been openly challenged when he had visited the East. Several of Grant's ideas on campaign strategy had been greeted with the derisive remark, "Wait until you meet Bobby Lee." Despite Sherman's objections, Grant decided, at least temporarily, to establish his headquarters with the Army of the Potomac.[7]

The Shaping of Union Strategy

Having made the decision to stay in the East, Grant next turned the discussion to matters of grand strategy. For the next several days, he and Sherman broadly outlined the strategic concepts that would be employed in 1864. Grant had been troubled by the lack of coordination that seemed to exist between the various Federal armies. To him, they looked "like a balky team, no two ever pulling together, enabling the enemy to use to great advantage his interior lines. . . ."[8] Determined to correct this, he told Sherman that the western army must move in concert with the eastern army. He also wanted Sherman to fully utilize some of the military talent that had been ignored during the early war years. Too many generals had been shelved for political rather than military reasons, and Grant wanted talented officers to be reinstated in the Army. Although the attempt did not work in some cases—George B. McClellan chose to run for the Presidency, and Don Carlos Buell flatly rejected the offer because he felt that he was qualified for more than the proposed post—Grant clearly wanted the best men serving in the right positions. By the end of March, Grant was back in the East, and had established his "Headquarters in the Field" at Culpeper, Virginia.

During Grant's brief absence, Meade had reorganized the Army of the Potomac. The Gettysburg Campaign had convinced him that the army's organization was too unwieldy. During the battle, he had tried to gain better control of his seven corps by organizing his units into wings. But this was only a temporary measure. The situation had improved somewhat when two corps were sent West to reinforce Rosecrans' army after September's Battle of Chickamauga. Because the remaining five corps still required an excessive span of control for one man, Meade organized his army into three corps in March 1864. The old I and III Corps were deactivated, and the regiments were distributed among the II, V, and VI Corps.

Earlier, the Army of the Potomac's strength had been in-

*The Army of the Potomac, already torn apart by the rivalry of the "Hooker men" and the "McClellan men," might have been faced with an intolerable situation by the addition of the "Western men."

*Meade, for example, was making frequent trips to Washington at this time to testify before the Joint Congressional Committee on the Conduct of the War. He was trying to defeat politically motivated attacks against him—attacks that accused him of urging a retreat at Gettysburg.

creased by the addition of the IX Corps under Major General Ambrose E. Burnside. Burnside's presence, however, created a difficult situation for Grant. Meade had served as a corps commander under Burnside at Fredericksburg, and Grant thought it best that Meade's earlier commander not be placed under a former subordinate. Accordingly, Grant used the IX Corps as a strategic reserve, positioning it at Annapolis, Maryland and placing it under his own control. With the army's organization set and its strength fixed, Grant could now consider the strategic alternatives and issue his instructions for the war's final campaign.[9]

Commencing in late November 1863 and continuing for almost three months, Grant and Halleck had exchanged views on possible Federal strategy. Initially, Grant restricted his thinking to the Western Theater, again advancing a proposal that he had previously made while at Vicksburg—that is, to move a Union army down the Mississippi River and capture Mobile, Alabama, and then advance inland against Montgomery and Selma. Following several exchanges of correspondence, however, Grant came to understand that Lincoln—and necessarily Halleck—were more interested in eastern Tennessee and the Chattanooga area than in Mobile.* Somewhat peevishly, if diplomatically, the western commander then suggested that the best way to get Longstreet out of Tennessee was to have Meade take the offensive against Lee. Finally, in an important January 8 letter, Halleck invited Grant to submit his views on strategy for *all* the theaters of war.†

Grant's reply to Halleck's invitation was in two parts, neither of which, as it turned out, was particularly well received. In his letter of January 15, Grant continued to advocate the Mobile offensive, but now complemented it with a second thrust from Chattanooga into Georgia. While the two armies would operate independently in terms of command arrangements, they were to be part of a common strategic design.

The second part of Grant's reply to Halleck was contained in a January 19 letter. Probably prepared hurriedly, it did not reflect the western general's usual mature approach to strategy. Grant saw another march on Richmond as being an exercise in futility. Instead, he proposed that an army of 60,000 men sail down the Atlantic coast and move inland to seize Raleigh, North Carolina. Once in Raleigh, the Federal army could destroy the main north-south railroads that supplied the more

northerly Confederate armies. Lee would then be forced to evacuate Virginia in order to restore the Confederate capital's communications with the Confederacy. Grant saw other advantages springing out of such an operation. Areas that had been spared the ravages of the contesting forces would now feel the full brunt of the war. This would not only enable the Federal army to live more easily off the countryside, but, when the North Carolina soldiers realized that their homes were being threatened, might increase the number of desertions from the Confederate army. The seizure of Raleigh would also allow the liberation of many slaves who were indirectly aiding the South's war efforts. Furthermore, Wilmington, North Carolina, an important seaport for blockade-runners, would be cut off from the interior. Because of the South's warm climate, operations could be started earlier in North Carolina. Finally, the campaign would force the Army of Northern Virginia to fight on unfamiliar terrain of the North's choosing.[10]

Halleck's reply, undoubtedly influenced by Lincoln's views, found fault with the westerner's ideas. The General-in-Chief thought that the Chattanooga-Mobile scheme was too ambitious, considering the number of troops available; it also might endanger eastern Tennessee. Regarding Grant's proposal for a North Carolina expedition, Halleck did not think that the North had 60,000 troops who could be spared to open a new line of operations. More important, he felt that Grant had identified the wrong objectives. Seizing Raleigh—or even Richmond—would offer nothing as long as Lee's army remained intact. While the Federals were concentrating their efforts against these southern cities, Lee could easily march northward and seize important northern cities. Union operations on the seacoast would collapse as the Federals scrambled to organize sufficient troops to eject Lee from the North. "We have given too much attention to cutting the toe nails of our enemy instead of grasping his throat," Halleck philosophized. "Our main efforts in the next campaign should unquestionably be made against the armies of Lee and Johnston," he advised Grant.[11]

Making the destruction of Lee's army an objective was not a new idea. Lincoln had suggested this concept to Halleck during the previous year. Again displaying a remarkable ability to understand strategic concepts that even his generals sometimes failed to grasp, the President told the General-in-Chief that it did not make any sense to him for the Federal army to beat Lee back over a series of entrenched lines, only to end up confronting the Army of Northern Virginia as it lay safe inside a fortified city. If Lee's army could not be destroyed in the open field, Lincoln reasoned, it certainly was not going to be annihilated while fighting from the forts around Richmond. "Since [the Peninsular Campaign] I have constantly desired the Army of the Potomac to make Lee's army,

*The President was ever conscious of the strong pro-Union sentiment in eastern Tennessee. Accordingly, he was both frustrated and a little concerned over Longstreet's presence in an area near the Tennessee-Virginia border—a location from which he could threaten Knoxville. Likewise, Lincoln worried that the Confederates would advance to and through Chattanooga if Grant were to weaken the Union position there in order to move a sizable force to Mobile.

†By this time, Congress and the press were talking about Grant being made lieutenant general and assuming a position of greater responsibility. Accordingly, Halleck was naturally interested in Grant's overall views—as was Lincoln.

and not Richmond, its objective point," stated the President. Apparently, Halleck liked Lincoln's idea, for he reiterated it to the future Commanding General when he advised Grant of the imprudence of an expedition into North Carolina.[12]

Now, in April 1864, as Grant reviewed Union options and arrived at a final judgment, his strategic concept reflected the influence of Lincoln and Halleck. To Sherman, Grant issued clear and simple instructions. "You I propose to move against Johnston's army, to break it up and to get into the interior of the enemy's country as far as you can, inflicting all the damage you can against their war resources."[13] *(See Atlas Map No. 45.)* It was up to Sherman to devise a plan that would break up the Army of Tennessee. Similarly, he was expected to define enemy "war resources" and decide how best to damage them. Grant knew Sherman, and therefore knew that the western general operated best when given a free hand. Sherman had never disappointed his commander in the past—nor would he in the future.

Completing his concept of operations for the West, Grant instructed Major General Nathaniel P. Banks to mount an expedition from New Orleans. In early March, Banks had started a campaign aimed at the capture of Shreveport, Louisiana. *(Operation not shown on map.)* Grant wanted this expedition concluded as early as possible so that Banks could participate in the great coordinated offensive that would compress the Confederacy into an ever-shrinking area. Now realizing the soundness of Halleck's earlier statement about the paucity of Federal troops, Grant ordered Banks to strip all of his commands so that 25,000 to 30,000 soldiers would be available for a joint army-navy expedition against Mobile. Banks was directed to abandon Texas—except for 4,000 troops that were to guard the Rio Grande River—and leave the minimum number of troops along the Mississippi. Mobile, Alabama would be the site of the Union's secondary effort in the West.[14]

Grant next turned to operations in the East. He was convinced that a faulty philosophy had been followed throughout the war. It seemed ridiculous to possess a vast material advantage over an opponent and then fail to use it. Although great campaigns had been launched, each one had ended without achieving a decisive advantage over the Confederate opposition. More important, each campaign had been followed by a period of inactivity. This had permitted the Confederacy to marshal its meager resources and build up its armies to an acceptable fighting strength. By failing to maintain continuous pressure, the North had failed to wear down the southern armies. Rather, the Confederates—and particularly the Army of Northern Virginia—had gained useful battlefield experience. Grant was determined to change this by applying continuous pressure against the Confederacy, with Lee's army

being subjected to the greatest application of force. He saw Sherman's and Banks' armies as forming the right wing of a giant Union effort; Meade's Army of the Potomac would operate at the center of the effort, and Major General Benjamin F. Butler's Army of the James would be the left wing. *(See Atlas Map No. 45.)*

Grant instructed Butler to move from his present position at Fort Monroe, Virginia and seize and fortify City Point. From there, Grant wanted him to advance along the south side of the James River, all the while focusing on Richmond as the final objective. The Commanding General, however, told Butler that he did not know what Butler's final movements should be. Certainly, he did not expect the general to seize Richmond with a force of only 20,000 men. Indeed, he wanted Butler to be aware that close cooperation between the Army of the James and the Army of the Potomac was a key part of the plan. "Then, should the enemy be forced into his intrenchments in Richmond, the Army of the Potomac would follow and . . . the two armies would become a unit," Grant told Butler.[15]

Grant gave the toughest assignment to Meade: "Lee's army will be your objective point. Wherever Lee goes, there you will go also."[16] So far, the Army of the Potomac *had* shadowed

Major General Benjamin F. Butler

Lee's movements; nevertheless, the Army of Northern Virginia appeared as strong as ever. Lincoln's and Halleck's ideas had been translated into a direct order to the commander of the Army of the Potomac. The enemy's army was the objective. The implications of that mission, however, had not been explored. What did it mean—to fight Lee continuously? Few generals, if any, realized the difficulty of trying to destroy an enemy army with mid-nineteenth century weapons. Meade's campaign would be bloody.

A final touch to the plan was added by Grant's orders to Major General Franz Sigel. Sigel commanded the Department of West Virginia, and Grant wanted him to mount an operation in the Shenandoah Valley. This would serve two purposes. First, Sigel would occupy the enemy's attention and force the Confederates to divert troops in defense of the Shenandoah's resources. Second, Sigel would help the total effort by destroying the enemy's war resources in the Valley. Although Sigel's operation was clearly a secondary effort, it provided the final part of a plan that sought to eliminate Richmond's local resources with a Shenandoah army, isolate the capital with Butler's army, and grind down Lee's force with Meade's army.[17]

Grant was not completely convinced that Lee's army could be destroyed in the open field. His instructions to Butler revealed his belief that Lee would end up in Richmond, with the Army of the James and the Army of the Potomac joining forces for a final siege. After all, the Vicksburg Campaign had ended similarly, and there was no reason to believe that the Confederates thought Richmond less valuable than Vicksburg. Accordingly, on April 15, Grant told Meade's artillery chief to prepare a siege train and to have the siege guns and materiel ready to move by water. The Navy was asked to be prepared to furnish some ironclads to protect the Army along the James River, and an army engineer was ordered to secure enough pontons to cross the James River. Grant's plan was now complete.[18]

It is instructive to note the principles emphasized in Grant's national military strategy for 1864. First, his belief that all Federal armies must operate in concert so as to bring overwhelming pressure to bear was clearly evident. In his instructions to his commanders, Grant said that all armies would move at the same time; he felt that late April was the earliest possible date to start campaigning. Second, Grant's recognition of the need to impair the Confederacy's ability to fight was obvious. Besides telling Meade and Sherman to destroy the enemy's means of waging war—namely, Lee's and Johnston's armies—Grant told Sigel and Sherman to ruin the Confederacy's "war resources." These two concepts, when combined, could result in only one thing—attrition. Once the Confederate States had been physically worn out, the war would be over. Fortunately for the North, Meade shared Grant's views on the destruction of Lee's army; he just had

not been able to devise a way of doing so without incurring unacceptable losses.

Meade's Preparations for an Advance

Meade plunged headlong into the task of preparing for the coming campaign. He ordered special marksmanship training for his soldiers, and he cut down on the army's baggage by reducing the number of wagons authorized to move each regiment's stores.* He also tried to find a solution to the problem of expiring enlistments.[19]

For the most part, the War Department did not replace the losses of existing regiments. Instead, new regiments were formed from the men flowing into the ranks as volunteers or draftees. From 1864 onward, the Army felt the result of this policy. In the late spring of 1864, the men who had enlisted in 1861 reached the end of their three-year service obligation. Since most regiments were constituted of men who had enlisted at about the same time, whole units could disappear when individual obligations were fulfilled. Both Meade and Grant understood the magnitude of the problem. They not only foresaw that entire regiments might march home in the middle of the campaign, but also that the fighting efficiency of these same regiments would be impaired prior to the legal end of their service. Soldiers would become cautious when they neared the end of their enlistment, and this caution could infect an entire regiment. Units that once comprised the most dependable part of the line no longer could be counted on to meet the same high standards. Meade called on these units to avoid dishonoring the excellent reputation that they had painstakingly built up, while Grant, taking a more practical approach, called on Halleck to strip Washington's defenses and get more troops into the field. Heavy artillery units were converted into infantry and sent to the Army of the Potomac. Other units in the northwest that had enjoyed the quiet of homefront garrison duty also were ordered to swell the ranks of the armies in the field. By utilizing such means, Grant made the maximum amount of combat power available to his field commanders.[20]

Although heavy rains in April prevented an early start of the campaign, the roads had dried out sufficiently by the twenty-seventh to enable Grant to set the date of the advance. Sigel was ordered to begin moving on May 2, while everyone else was directed to start two days later. Instructions filtered down to Meade's corps and division commanders on the second. The plan called for the Army of the Potomac to slip around Lee's right flank and try to move through the Wilderness. As this tangled mass of forest growth had been the scene

---

*By western standards, this was still an exorbitant amount.

of Major General Joseph Hooker's failure in May 1863, Grant and Meade seemed to be inviting disaster. The Army of the Potomac, however, needed to stay somewhere between Lee's army and Washington, and had to move near its waterborne supplies. The route that would allow Meade to meet both these requirements was guarded by the Wilderness and by Robert E. Lee.[21]

Confederate Difficulties

Lee's army had remained in winter quarters near Mine Run since Meade's abortive campaign in November 1863. *(See Atlas Map No. 46.)* Lee was perplexed by the situation confronting the Confederacy. The South needed to maintain the initiative and prevent the North from gaining the upper hand. But the Confederacy was rapidly running out of men and supplies. Something needed to be done that would wrest the initiative from the North without consuming either supplies or men. Longstreet suggested that his corps, wintering in east Tennessee, move in conjunction with a force under General P.G.T. Beauregard. (Beauregard's army would be formed by troops presently defending South Carolina.) The Beauregard-Longstreet task force would strike out for Louisville, Kentucky. This threat to Sherman's line of communication would force the North to evacuate Tennessee. Once Sherman was gone, General Joseph E. Johnston's army at Dalton, Georgia could advance northward and join Beauregard and Longstreet somewhere along the Ohio River.

In a very disappointing interview with Jefferson Davis and General Braxton Bragg, Davis' new senior military adviser, Lee and Longstreet submitted the plan. Quietly, they listened as Bragg made an alternate proposal. He wanted Longstreet and Johnston to combine their armies in the vicinity of the headwaters of the Little Tennessee River near Knoxville and advance against Sherman's base at Nashville. Clearly at an impasse, the President and his senior generals left the meeting knowing that neither plan would be carried out. The final compromise consisted of a watch-and-wait attitude.

By late April, Lee suspected that Grant would try a three-pronged offensive against his army and Richmond, but he was powerless to do anything about it. He must wait for the Federals to strike the first blow. In anticipation of that blow, Longstreet's corps was re-called to join the main army.[22]

The Road to Richmond

Promptly at midnight on May 3, Major General Philip H. Sheridan and two divisions of cavalry started moving to the south. Brought east by Grant to take command of the Cavalry Corps of the Army of the Potomac, Sheridan preceded the

infantry columns as they headed for the ponton bridges that had been secretly built across the Rapidan River.

Both Grant and Meade hoped that they could cross the river and advance through the Wilderness before Lee could launch a counterstroke. *(See Atlas Map No. 46.)* While several of his staff officers made some flippant remarks about Lee's army, Grant, although confident of success, was not as quick to prejudge an untested opponent. His immediate concern was to get Meade's army through the Wilderness. Unfortunately for the Federals, Meade's efforts to trim the Army's logistical tail had not been completely successful; over 4,000 supply wagons jolted along the twisted roads, following the army. The Army of the Potomac could not clear the heavily wooded area in one day because the wagon train needed to be protected. As a result, on the afternoon of May 4, the combat elements stopped in the Wilderness and waited for the arrival of the tail.[23]

Lee saw his opportunity and moved accordingly. Longstreet, coming from a distance of 42 miles, still was not present, but Lee hoped to strike Meade's troops in the Wilderness. The Federal force's numerical superiority in men and guns would be partially offset by the heavy, entangling undergrowth, and Lee knew that he had to take advantage of this. Advancing in two columns, the Army of Northern Virginia proceeded cautiously. Lee did not want to incur a general engagement before Longstreet arrived.

The Wilderness Campaign

Still not sure that the entire Army of the Potomac was involved in the move to his front, Lee halted his army for the night, west of the thick forest. After spending an uneventful night in bivouac, the Army of Northern Virginia resumed its cautious advance. Shortly, the word was passed back that there were Federals on the roads ahead.[24]

Meade's advance also was cautious. As his trains still had not completed the crossing of the river, exposing them to a Confederate attack would be foolhardy. Still, Meade was sure that he outnumbered the Confederates 118,769 to 83,000.* Therefore, he ordered his three corps to deploy on a line facing westward. In the meantime, Grant ordered the IX Corps to protect Meade's line of communication north of the Rapidan River.

At 5:00 a.m. on May 5, Meade began to implement his plan to turn his corps to the west. This was the critical day in the opening stages of the campaign. If the Confederates attacked, the Army of the Potomac would have to fight in the Wilderness. If there was no attack, however, Meade would

---

*In fact, Meade overestimated Confederate strength by about 22,000.

have time to advantageously position his army between Lee and Richmond, on terrain that would exploit the North's superior numbers. At 7:15 a.m., Meade received a dispatch from Major General Gouverneur Kemble Warren, the V Corps commander, informing him that a sizable force of Confederate infantry was on the Orange Turnpike, two miles west of the Wilderness Tavern. *(See Atlas Map No. 46.)* Meade ordered Warren to attack.[25]

While Meade wanted Warren to develop the situation,† he also wanted his army closed up in case Lee had already launched his main attack. Accordingly, he told his II Corps commander, Major General Winfield Scott Hancock, that Warren had found part of the enemy's force and that Hancock should halt so that the army would not be further dispersed. With the immediate situation under control, Meade sent a staff officer to tell Grant that a battle was developing. Grant, back at the Rapidan River awaiting the arrival of Burnside's IX Corps, read Meade's note: "I have directed Genl. Warren to attack them at once with his whole force." Concurring with Meade's actions, Grant expressed his own offensive inclination in a note to Meade: "If an opportunity presents itself for pitching into a part of Lee's army, do so without giving time for disposition."[26]

Because a third of his army was still missing, Lee was conservative in his response to the initial contact. Nevertheless, his determination was just as strong as Grant's. He sent Lieutenant General Richard S. Ewell's corps forward on the Orange Turnpike and Lieutenant General Ambrose P. Hill's corps forward on the Orange Plank Road. While neither commander was to bring on a general engagement until Longstreet arrived, each also was committed to preventing the Federals from making an escape. The Battle of the Wilderness rapidly got underway.

Warren's initial assault was very successful, and the Confederates fled before the furious attack. Driven for almost a mile, they finally regrouped and stopped the Union advance. Increasingly, the heavy timber and dense undergrowth made it exceedingly difficult to keep the advancing lines of men straight. Visibility was extremely limited, and the thick smoke created by the musket volleys concealed the assailants. The opposing lines were very close to each other, and at the regimental level, an ambush was the prevailing form of defense. It was a "blind and bloody hunt to the death, in bewildering thickets, rather than a battle."[27]

While not interfering with Meade's conduct of operations, Grant was not idle. He ordered elements of Burnside's IX Corps forward to join the battle. The narrow roads, however, restricted Burnside's movement, and because his command

was some distance from the battlefield, it took time for his troops to be brought into position.* In the interim, Grant sat on the ground at his headquarters, smoked his pipe, and whittled on a piece of wood. He seemed to realize that this battle could probably best be settled by the corps commanders.

On the Union left, Meade was tightening the line. He ordered Hancock to sideslip his II Corps northwest and tie in with the left of Warren's corps. *(See Atlas Map No. 46.)* Until Hancock arrived, however, the gap on Warren's left needed to be filled. Meade consequently shifted a division from Major General John Sedgwick's VI Corps around to the Union left. The confusion among units created by the Wilderness was aggravated by Meade's instructions, which mixed units from different corps. At about 2:00 p.m., Hancock's corps began to arrive. Although that general was directed to attack immediately, he needed an additional two hours to organize his command. Two more Federal attacks were then launched without success.[28]

On May 6, the fighting continued to be of a confused nature in the heavy undergrowth. On this day, however, Lee seized the initiative. Shortly after daybreak, Longstreet's corps arrived on the field. With his army finally consolidated, Lee was now able to put into motion his own plan. First, he sent Longstreet around the Union left to try to envelop Hancock's corps. *(Attack not shown on map.)* The move was reminiscent of "Stonewall" Jackson's flank march at Chancellorsville the year before. Longstreet's men fell on the unsuspecting Federals and began to roll up Hancock's flank. The similarity did not end there, however. During a lull, Longstreet was wounded by his own men while organizing his troops to exploit their initial success. He fell from his horse, wounded by a ball that had passed through his throat and lodged in his right shoulder. Fortunately for the Confederacy, it was not a mortal wound; but Longstreet's services were to be lost for several months.

Lee then tried to attack the opposite flank. Brigadier General John B. Gordon had discovered that the Federal right was unguarded. *(Gordon's move not shown on map.)* Unable to convince his division commander that a flanking assault should be launched, Gordon finally received permission from Lee to make the attack. But it was late in the day, and darkness prevented Gordon from following up his initial success against Sedgwick's corps.[29]

On the opposite side of the lines, Grant and Meade reviewed the day's activities. They realized that there was not much to show for their efforts. After their orders had been sent out during the day, there had been little for them to do. Most of the time, they either sat or lay on the ground, waiting for reports from the front. They studied their maps and discussed the

---

†When forces seek to learn more about enemy dispositions and intentions, they are said to develop the situation.

*Burnside's corps did not reach a position from which it could exert sufficient pressure to influence the course of the battle until about noon the next day (May 6).

II Corps Prior to Longstreet's Attack, May 6, 1864

chances for success. But the Wilderness was not a good battle-
ground. There just was not enough room to maneuver infantry
or employ artillery. Grant, however, had learned the first part
of a lesson that would not be completely understood for some
time. He remarked to Meade that in the West, the Confederates
would have retreated after a battle like the Wilderness. Robert
E. Lee was, indeed, a different kind of opponent.

Grant Moves South

On the morning of May 7, Union skirmishers moved forward
and found that the Confederates had withdrawn into trenches.
Convinced that attacking an entrenched enemy was a costly
business, Grant hoped that Lee's men would come out of their
works and engage in battle. When the southerners remained
in their protected positions, the Commanding General decided
to try a new approach. He directed Meade to prepare his army
for a night march around the Confederate right flank. Perhaps
Lee could be cut off from Richmond with a surprise move.
The quiet that prevailed over the Union lines, however, already
had alerted Lee that something was afoot. Meade's army had
not been badly hurt during the previous two days of fighting,
and all of Lee's counterattacks had been stymied. These inconsequential results of the fighting, coupled with the apparent
lack of Union activity, led Lee to assume that the Yankees

**Generals Meade and Grant Discuss
the Battle of the Wilderness**

were going to begin another move.[30] Surprise would not be achieved when the Federals slipped away.

After dark, Warren's and Sedgwick's men withdrew from their positions and passed behind Hancock's corps. In front of the moving column, Grant and Meade rode with their staffs. The generals were astonished by the reaction of the troops. Word had circulated that the army was moving on to Richmond. In the past, battles similar to the one just concluded had resulted in the withdrawal and refitting of the army for a new offensive. But this time there would be no withdrawal. Instead of running like a beaten dog back across the Rapidan River, the Army of the Potomac moved forward like a victorious legion. The troops were overjoyed. Brandishing burning pine knots, they cheered Grant and Meade as they rode past. A new chapter was being written in the army's history.

Unfortunately, the joy was short-lived. Cavalry units clogged the roads and the head of the column went astray in the darkness. Valuable time was lost as the infantry waited for the roads to be cleared. Finally, at 11:00 p.m., the cavalry moved off the road and allowed the foot soldiers to pass. To their front, Spotsylvania Court House stood at a key crossroads. Situated on routes that led around Lee's flank, its occupation by the Federals would signify that Meade had outflanked Lee. *(See Atlas Map No. 46.)* The Army of Northern Virginia, however, arrived at the crossroads first.[31]

A heated discussion developed between Meade and Sheridan as a result of Lee's timely arrival at Spotsylvania Court House. During the night march, Meade had come upon one of Sheridan's cavalry divisions. The division commander had not received any instructions from Sheridan. Meade therefore issued orders to all of Sheridan's cavalry divisions and hurried on his way. Sheridan, however, had already issued orders; they just had not arrived when Meade found the waiting cavalrymen. As a result, Sheridan rode to Meade's headquarters on the following day and told his commander that since Meade was issuing orders to his cavalry divisions, Sheridan was not going to send any more directives as a corps commander. Old arguments were reopened in the ensuing discussion, and Sheridan vowed that he could "whip" Major General "Jeb" Stuart and his Confederate cavalry if Meade would only let him do his job. Meade stormed off to the Commanding General to tell him about his argument with Sheridan. When Grant heard Sheridan's comment about Stuart, however, he directed Meade to allow Sheridan to make good his boast. Within the hour, Meade issued the necessary order, and Sheridan rode out toward Richmond the next morning. His raid would result in the death of Stuart.[32]

The Battle of Spotsylvania

Duplicating his performance in the Wilderness, Lee fought the Army of the Potomac to a standstill at Spotsylvania. Try as they might, the Federals could neither roll up Lee's flanks nor break through his firmly entrenched Confederates. On May 10, however, one Federal attack impressed both Grant and Meade.*

Brigadier General Emory Upton commanded a brigade in the VI Corps. He had a reputation for being a good tactician. At Rappahannock Station in the previous November, he had been responsible for the capture of almost two complete Confederate brigades. Sound tactical planning, decisive leadership, and courageous execution had been the hallmarks of Upton's earlier success. Now, on May 10 at Spotsylvania, he was called upon to use his tactical abilities and repeat his earlier feat.

Civil War tactics had come a long way since the early days of the war, when green troops had tried to accomplish Napoleonic maneuvers. By 1864, regiments could be depended upon to perform in conformity with contemporary tactical manuals. Although the training and actions of the individual soldier had not changed much during the war, several innovations in the employment of bodies of troops had occurred. Units normally were deployed for battle in two ranks. Together, the two ranks were called a line. Each line was an assault wave designed to maximize the shock effect of a bayonet attack. A rank of skirmishers protected the front, and the increased use of rifled weapons increased the value of the skirmishers. Moreover, since each infantryman was now also a rifleman, a commander no longer had to rely on hand-picked groups to make up his skirmish line. Instead, he could increase the strength of his skirmish line simply by ordering regular infantry units forward. Large numbers of skirmishers armed with rifles, however, were not seen as the solution to the tactical impasse created by the tremendous firepower of the defenders. It was felt that a skirmish line was too flimsy, and would break and flee when confronted by a line of infantrymen wielding bayonets. As Upton's tactical manual later stated, ". . . to insure victory, a line or lines of battle must ever be at hand to support or receive the attack."[33]

Once the pre-assault artillery bombardment had ended, it was the job of the infantry to carry the defender's position with a bayonet assault. At Rappahannock Station in November, Upton had forced his men to rely on the shock effect of their assault lines by refusing to allow them to insert firing caps in their muskets. Thus prevented from firing, his soldiers rushed across the field and into the Confederate position before the defenders could muster sufficient firepower. Upton reasoned that an attacker who stopped to fire during the assault not only would inflict few casualties on the protected defender,

---

*The impression was so strong on Grant that after the war, he directed Emory Upton, the commander of the attack, to rewrite the Army's manual on tactics.

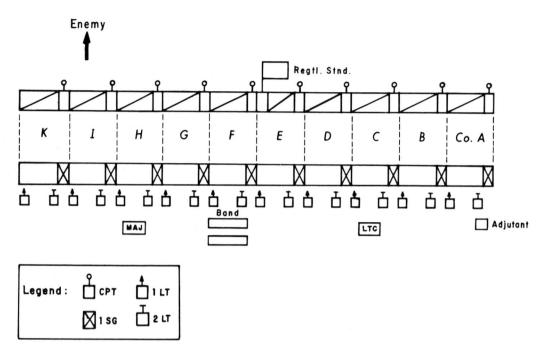

Regiment Formed Into Line of Battle, 1864

but also would needlessly expose himself to the defender's fire.*

Besides the elimination of firing during the attack, other innovations had been made. One was the attack by successive lines of infantry. Once the assaulting infantry began to feel the devastating effect of the defender's fire, the individual soldier tended to automatically extend the line laterally by placing more space between himself and the soldiers on his right and left. This gave the appearance of an attack by lines of skirmishers rather than lines of infantry. Once the defender's position had been reached, however, the conduct of the attack was the same as that of a conventional attack. Each successive line of infantry crashed into the defender, mixed with the already-engaged line in front, and gradually built up enough mass to break the defender's line—or lost so many soldiers during the assault that the attack failed. Some generals also experimented with attacking in rushes. The infantry lines dashed from position to position, taking advantage of any cover and concealment that could be found along the way. The final result, however, remained the same—either the defeat in detail of each attacking line, or the achievement of a breakthrough resulting from the mass created by successive attacking lines.[34]

Gradually, over the years, a tactical formula had been developed that promised success in the attack. According to the formula, infantry were expected to: advance quickly to avoid

exposure to long-range enemy fire; open ranks enough to prevent the formation of a target, but stay close enough so that sufficient mass could be created at the objective; keep the interval between lines sufficiently great to permit flexibility, but not so great as to allow defeat in detail to occur (this could be anywhere from 3 to 300 yards); and take advantage of cover and concealment enroute to the objective. All halts were prearranged, since the rudimentary communications systems did not permit a flexible response to verbal orders from the unit commander. If the formula seemed simple, its execution was not. Nevertheless, on May 10, Emory Upton again succeeded where others had failed.

In short, Upton treated each of the four lines of his attacking brigade as a separate unit. Each line had a different objective, and all contributed to the accomplishment of the brigade's mission. The first line was directed to break the enemy's front and then to turn to the flanks to deliver enfilading fire on the rest of the Confederate line. The second line was to occupy the Confederate trenches, fire to the front, and wait for any counterattack. The third line was to lie down behind the second and act as a reserve. The fourth was to wait at the line of departure, providing support when it was needed.

Upton took the existing organization and formulated a plan that took advantage of its strengths while exploiting the weaknesses in the Confederate positions. As a result, his attack was initially successful. *(See Atlas Map No. 46.)* However, although he penetrated the southern lines, he then waited vainly for support. In the end, Upton was forced to retreat, and Lee's army still blocked the road to Richmond. While

*Although Upton's reasoning was supported by seasoned commanders, the curious lack of bayonet wounds throughout the war seems to indicate that the assault depended less on the bayonet than on pure shock action.

Major General Emory Upton

Upton had not found the solution to the tactical impasse,* it was clear that an imaginative commander, who understood the resources that were available, could succeed.[35]

Throughout May 11, Meade prepared for a major attack against a large salient in the Confederate lines. Upton's attack on the tenth had been aimed at a portion of this salient that was called "the Mule Shoe." It was important that the attack be swift and violent. Shortly after Union artillery opened fire at 4:20 a.m. on May 12, Meade's infantry swarmed over the Confederate defenders. Hancock, whose II Corps led the main attack, had massed his 20,000 men on a very narrow front. Each line of battle was separated by only "several paces." This dense crowd suddenly appeared out of the early morning fog that shrouded the area between the opposing armies. In addition, the Confederates had been caught in the process of moving their artillery. The center of their line caved in, and there were blue coats everywhere. Swiftly, two Confederate generals, two thousand soldiers, and twenty guns were rounded up and sent to the Federal rear. As the attackers pressed on, however, they struck a second line of defense. Everything came to a halt.

It appeared that if pressure could be brought to bear against another portion of the Confederate line, the initial Union success might result in a quick victory. Consequently, Warren's V Corps was ordered to attack. When Warren could not get

*Upton admitted in his report that he had achieved the penetration because of superior numbers.

an assault organized, despite repeated instructions to do so, Meade disgustedly sent a dispatch to Grant explaining the problem. Quickly, Grant replied: "If Warren fails to attack promptly, send [Major General Andrew A.] Humphreys to command his corps, and relieve him."[36] Meade hurried to Hancock's headquarters, leaving his chief of staff, Humphreys, in charge of pushing reinforcements forward. Grant, also, was at the front urging the troops into the fray. Warren's corps was parceled out among the other corps, and all four corps finally were committed. But it was to no avail. The momentum had been lost, and the attacks faltered. By midnight, fighting had ceased between the exhausted armies.

More Futile Union Maneuvering Ends at the North Anna

There were several more Federal attempts to break the Confederate lines at Spotsylvania, but each ended in a severe repulse. Lee's army was firmly entrenched, and its position was virtually impregnable. Grant, however, believed that if he could catch the Army of Northern Virginia outside of its trenches, the Army of the Potomac could destroy it. He decided to try to force Lee to make a premature attack, and to this end directed Meade to send the II Corps alone toward Richmond. The Confederates might think that the corps was isolated and move out of their trenches to strike Hancock's men. The remaining three Union corps could then smash Lee before he had a chance to fortify his positions.

When Meade tried the plan on May 19, the Confederates again stymied the Union efforts. Thinking that the Federals might be trying to move around the Confederate right, Lee ordered Ewell's corps to attack the Federal right. Hopefully, Ewell would find out if the enemy was leaving. Ewell's attack struck at about the same time that Hancock was commencing his movement in furtherance of Grant's plan. The resulting meeting engagement between Ewell and Hancock created confusion on both sides, and the outcome was meaningless; it was a fitting conclusion to the stalemate at Spotsylvania.

A quick review of the campaign to date convinced Grant and Meade of two things. First, Grant felt that he had too much artillery. On the road, it encumbered his army and lengthened his march column. In battle, all of the guns could not be employed effectively because of the dense forests. Second, the fighting had been very costly. All told, the Wilderness and Spotsylvania battles had cost the Federals between 32,000 and 36,000 casualties. (Confederate losses, on the other hand, numbered between 16,700 and 21,400.) To solve the first problem, Grant sent one hundred artillery pieces back to Washington. To replace previous losses and reduce the incidence of future ones, he urged Halleck to keep reinforcements coming forward, and decided to abandon his attacks at Spotsylvania.[37]

Grant now directed Meade to begin a series of flanking movements. Each move was designed to interpose the Army of the Potomac between Lee's army and Richmond. Aware of the need to keep Meade away from Richmond, Lee successfully countered each Union attempt.

When the Federals left Spotsylvania on the evening of May 21, Lee anticipated the move and skillfully maneuvered his army to block the approaches to Richmond. Arriving at the North Anna River on May 22, the Confederates watched the enemy arrive on the following day. Although Meade believed that the southern position was too strong to attack, Grant decided to try an assault. Lee had deployed his army so that the center of his line rested on the river and the flanks were turned back. *(See Atlas Map No. 46.)* Thus, in deciding to test Lee's strength, Grant was forced to divide Meade's army: the Union right and left flanks were located south of the North Anna River, while the center of the Army of the Potomac was north of the river. Possessing both central position and superior lateral communications, the Army of Northern Virginia had interior lines. It used them to good effect. Each Union attack was easily repulsed. Although he had originally thought that Meade's army was in an advantageous position, Grant now changed his mind. On the evening of May 26, he again shifted the Army of the Potomac to the left.

Grant Continues to Move South

Grant was extremely confident. On May 26, he told Halleck that "Lee's army is really whipped." Adding that "our success over Lee's army is already insured," Grant could see that the Confederate army was becoming exhausted. Be that as it may, Meade did not share Grant's confidence. He told one of his aides, "I am afraid the rebellion cannot be crushed this summer." Meade's appraisal was closer to reality. The Army of the Potomac crossed the next major terrain obstacle, the Pamunkey River, unopposed. When it reached Totopotomoy Creek, however, the Army of Northern Virginia stood waiting. *(See Atlas Map No. 47.)* Lee had again won the race.[38]

Grant did not even bother to test the strength of the Confederate position. Again, he told Meade to shift the Army of the Potomac to the left. He also sent for reinforcements, and on May 30 he notified Meade that the Army of the Potomac would be augmented by Brigadier General William F. Smith's XVIII Corps, which had previously been a part of Butler's Army of the James.

Butler's initial advance up the James River on May 5 had met little enemy opposition. Moving his troops by water to City Point and Bermuda Hundred southeast of Richmond, Butler seemed to have gained the advantage through surprise. Once ashore, however, he did not press his advantage. Instead, he built a defensive network to protect his beachhead. On

May 12, he moved out of his impregnable defenses and began the advance that should have taken place a week earlier. Moving slowly towards Richmond, Butler finally ran into a Confederate force under General P.G.T. Beauregard. Beauregard, who had been feverishly scraping together an army since Butler's landing, attacked on May 16, while Butler was still trying to decide whether or not he should take the initiative. After the Federals withdrew to their fine defenses at Bermuda Hundred, Beauregard built trenches to seal them in. *(See Atlas Map No. 47.)* The threat created by the Army of the James had disappeared abruptly. The demise of this part of Grant's plan, along with Sigel's defeat in the Shenandoah Valley on May 15, placed the full weight of responsibility for the eastern campaign on the Army of the Potomac. Accustomed to this responsibility, Meade gladly accepted the assistance provided by Smith's XVIII Corps.[39]

The Battle of Cold Harbor

Grant's next move to the left brought Union and Confederate cavalry crashing together on the road near Cold Harbor. Hurriedly, each of the opposing commanders rushed infantry reinforcements to the point of contact. Major General Horatio G. Wright's VI Corps—Sedgwick had been killed by a sniper at Spotsylvania—arrived in time to prevent an early Confederate success. By 6:00 p.m. on June 1, Smith's corps—which had been delayed by faulty orders that assigned it an incorrect route of march—was in position on the VI Corps' right, prepared to assault. Swiftly, the two Union corps fell on the waiting Confederate infantry, and the defender's lines were driven back, stretched, and finally broken. But the impetus was gone from the attack, and the Confederates gradually stabilized their front. By nightfall, the two armies were exhausted, and the soldiers built the inevitable earthworks.

Meade was in good spirits. He thought that the Confederate position was vulnerable; if a little more weight were added to the attack, Cold Harbor might become the scene of a great triumph. Hancock and Warren were directed to hurry their corps forward to participate in the assault. But Hancock's men had to march all night, so that by the time they were in position at 7:30 a.m. on June 2, they were worn out. Hoping that a brief rest would rejuvenate the men of the II Corps, Meade postponed the attack until late afternoon. At 2:00 p.m., however, Grant told Meade to wait until the following morning. All final preparations should be made on June 2 and "a good nights rest given the men preparatory to an assault at, say 4:30 A.M. in the morning," Grant wrote.[40]

It is strange that no Federal general seemed to be in a hurry to launch the attack. True, the troops were weary from the continuous campaigning, but this was no excuse to pause. For the past 28 days, Lee had availed himself of every oppor-

Federal Attack at Cold Harbor, June 3, 1864

tunity to entrench his troops, and each assault on the entrenched Confederates had ended with the same result—a swift repulse. The third of June would be no exception.

During the night, rain fell, providing some relief from the oppressive heat. At 4:30 a.m., the blue ranks stepped out onto the ground that separated the two armies. *(See Atlas Map No. 47.)* Suddenly, the horizon seemed to light up with a wall of flame. The Confederates poured a devastating fire onto the attackers. "It was not war," one Confederate general wrote, "it was murder." In less than an hour, 7,000 Federal soldiers became casualties. Hastily, lines were dug at the point where the attack stalled. For the next several days, the soldiers nervously watched their opponents, who sometimes were less than 50 yards away. This was the last of Grant's fearful frontal assaults.[41]

An Interlude in the Valley and a Model River Crossing

On June 13, Lee sent the II Corps under Lieutenant General Jubal A. Early to the Shenandoah Valley. After having been saved by Sigel's repulse at New Market on May 15, the area had again become endangered when Sigel's replacement, Major General David Hunter, regained the initiative. Although it was risky for Lee to reduce his own forces so close to Richmond, something had to be done to retrieve the situation in the Valley. Early marched northward through the Shenandoah, threw Hunter into headlong retreat, and then marched southeastward towards Washington. *(Movement not shown on map.)* Within sight of the Federal capital, Early withdrew his corps after receiving information that the enemy's defense had been strengthened by the addition of the VI Corps. Although Early slipped back across the Potomac, the damage

had been done; the authorities in Washington again feared for the capital's safety. Undaunted by the concern in Washington, Grant again looked to Meade's left.[42]

After nine days of watching the enemy at Cold Harbor, Grant again moved the Army of the Potomac. Having run out of room to maneuver between Lee and Richmond, he now chose Petersburg, an important rail center, as the objective. Leaving the V Corps to screen the march, Meade sent his army southeast to the James River near Charles City Courthouse. *(See Atlas Map No. 47.)* Crossing the river on an immense ponton bridge over a period of three days, beginning on June 14, the army moved westward towards Petersburg. The Army of Northern Virginia was nowhere to be seen.

Finally, Meade had stolen a march on Lee. Unable to regain contact with the Federal army, the southern commander had been anxiously awaiting reports that would definitely establish its position. Beauregard, still guarding the approaches to Petersburg, now sent Lee information indicating that a large Union force had crossed to the south bank of the James. Lee, however, was reluctant to act prematurely, and early on the evening of June 15, Smith's XVIII Corps carried Petersburg's outer defenses. Before Smith's success could be exploited, Lee reacted decisively. Several vicious Union assaults were launched on June 18 *(see Atlas Map No. 47)*, but Petersburg and Richmond remained safely in Confederate hands. Grant therefore ordered siege lines to be opened around the cities.

Just as Lincoln had feared, Robert E. Lee had been forced back over a series of entrenched lines to the fortified line of Richmond and Petersburg. Just as Grant had predicted, however, Meade's and Butler's armies had Lee's men locked up tight. The losses on both sides had been tremendous. Federal casualties were in excess of 64,000 men; Confederate casualties numbered somewhere near 30,000. The real difference, however, was in the reinforcements both sides received. While Meade's army had 40,000 replacements added to its ranks, the Confederacy could add only 24,000 men to Lee's army. The war of attrition and started.[43]

The Road to Atlanta

In accordance with Grant's plan, Sherman moved his armies forward on the same day that Meade moved. On the one hand, Sherman's problem was a bit easier than Meade's. He faced an army that was neither as strong nor as confident as the Army of Northern Virginia. The Army of Tennessee only had 43,887 men to face Sherman's 110,123; moreover, it was still trying to recover from the disgrace at Missionary Ridge. On the other hand, Sherman's adversary was fighting in terrain that clearly favored the defender. Numerous mountain ranges and rivers protected the approaches to the interior of Georgia. On the whole, Sherman's problem was every bit as difficult as that faced by the eastern armies.

Like Grant, Sherman was controlling the movements of several armies. His subordinates were experienced combat leaders who had demonstrated great ability in the past. Major General George H. Thomas commanded the Army of the Cumberland, which consisted of three corps. Thomas' army was by far the largest of Sherman's three armies. In fact, his army was larger than the Confederate Army of Tennessee. Major General James B. McPherson commanded the Federal Army of the Tennessee. Although it also consisted of three corps, its strength was about half that of Thomas' army. Major General John M. Schofield commanded the last army, the Army of the Ohio. The smallest of the three armies, it consisted of only one infantry corps and a single cavalry division. All told, the three armies constituted a formidable force, and, unlike Grant, Sherman kept his armies operating together from the start of the campaign.[44]

Dalton to Cassville

On May 4, Sherman moved out against General Joseph E. Johnston's Army of Tennessee, which was in position northwest of Dalton. The Confederate army was firmly established along the heights known as Rocky Face Ridge. *(See Atlas Map No. 48.)* Sherman sent his largest army, commanded by Thomas, directly against the defenders. Thomas launched several frontal assaults, driving in the Confederate outposts and fixing Johnston in place. Meanwhile, Schofield advanced from the north and McPherson slipped around Johnston's left. When McPherson notified Sherman that he was only five miles from Resaca, it appeared that Johnston's entire army had been trapped. Pleased with McPherson's march, later in

the day, Sherman was disappointed to learn that McPherson had withdrawn to Snake Creek Gap. Johnston had narrowly avoided disaster.[45]

Joseph E. Johnston had assumed command of the Army of Tennessee in late December 1863. He had not, however, been the Confederacy's first choice. Following the defeat at Chattanooga, Bragg had been relieved of command of the Army of Tennessee and replaced by William J. Hardee, one of his subordinate corps commanders. But Hardee did not want any part of commanding the entire army. An excellent corps commander, he was satisfied with that role. Perhaps he lacked the confidence necessary to command an army. Whatever the reason, Hardee declined the offer of permanent command, and the Confederate Government looked elsewhere for the right man.

President Jefferson Davis turned first to Robert E. Lee. Again, Lee was asked to go West to turn the tide; again, Lee turned down the opportunity. Without taking permanent command, Lee did not think that he could solve too many of the western army's problems. Possibly acting on Lee's advice, Davis then turned to Joseph E. Johnston, a commander who had not enjoyed the President's confidence in the past. Johnston took the appointment, and almost at once discovered

General Joseph E. Johnston

that there were serious differences of opinion between the authorities in Richmond and himself.

Davis wanted the Army of Tennessee to go on the offensive, but Johnston refused. Johnston's reluctance should not have been a surprise. During his brief tenure as commander of the army, Hardee had advised the Confederate Government that "in our present condition it is necessary to avoid a general engagement. . . ." Davis and Bragg, both of whom had unrealistic expectations concerning Johnston's situation, were doomed to be disappointed, for on May 4, Sherman seized the initiative. Frantically, Johnston called for reinforcements, even personally appealing to Lieutenant General Leonidas Polk for help. Unselfishly, Polk responded by moving his force—three infantry divisions and one cavalry division—to reinforce Johnston.[46]

It was a division of Polk's Army of Mississippi that blocked McPherson's approach from Snake Creek Gap. Though temporarily saved from total disaster, Johnston realized that his Dalton position had been made untenable by McPherson's flank march. Accordingly, on May 12, he ordered his corps commanders, Lieutenant Generals John B. Hood and William J. Hardee, to withdraw their men to Resaca. Sherman had missed an excellent chance to trap the Confederates, but he had turned Johnston out of a good defensive position.[47]

Sherman was shifting the rest of his force in the direction of McPherson's army *(movement not shown on map)* when Johnston pulled back. As had been the case in Virginia, the Federal race around the Confederate flank was close, but ended in favor of the southern forces. *(See Atlas Map No. 48.)* The remainder of Polk's army closed with Johnston's main army, and the Confederates consolidated their position around Resaca. Polk's arrival increased the Confederate strength by 50 percent, making Johnston's already excellent defensive position even stronger.

Sherman attacked the Confederate left, and Johnston countered with a blow against Sherman's left. Neither attack made much progress, but Johnston thought he detected a weakness in the Union left. To exploit the weakness, he ordered an attack to be made on the fifteenth. Then, however, he received information from his cavalry that forced him to cancel his plan. The Confederate horsemen reported that two Union divisions had been sighted crossing a ponton bridge in the vicinity of Calhoun. Anxiously, Johnston sent Major General William H.T. Walker's infantry division southward to investigate. *(Movement not shown on map.)* In the afternoon, Johnston received Walker's report: there was no Federal threat in the vicinity of Calhoun. Johnston quickly ordered Hood to conduct the planned attack on the Union left. Hood had just started his men forward when Johnston received a second report from Walker: the Yankees had already crossed the river at Lay's Ferry. With his position at Resaca now untenable,

Johnston canceled Hood's attack, gathered his army, and marched unhappily southward towards Adairsville. Again, Sherman had turned the Confederates out of a good position without incurring heavy losses.[48]

Johnston's campaign strategy seems to have been to wear down Sherman's armies with small engagements, while awaiting a propitious time to launch a strong counteroffensive. The decreased strength of the Union army, which Johnston expected to result both from the losses incurred in these engagements and Sherman's siphoning off of troops to guard his lengthening line of communication, would eventually give Johnston the opportunity to strike with advantage. As his army marched into its positions near Cassville, Johnston thought that the right time for just such a counterblow had arrived.

Johnston thought that when Sherman pursued the retreating Confederates from Adairsville, the Union forces, divided in half, would follow the two roads leading southward. This might present Johnston with an opportunity to defeat Sherman's armies in detail. Accordingly, he directed Hardee and Polk to cover the two main roads, while Hood was ordered to position himself northeast of Cassville. When the enemy moved to attack Polk, Hood was to fall on their rear.

Unfortunately for the Confederates, Johnston's plan went awry. Although the Federals did just what Johnston wanted them to do, Hood did not. When it came time for Hood to launch his attack against the unsuspecting Union flank, one of Hood's staff officers reported an enemy force in the rear. *(See Atlas Map No. 48.)* Hood quickly changed the alignment of his corps to protect himself, and sent a force off to investigate the report. By the time Hood learned that he had been misinformed—the Federal force was relatively small—the two main Union columns were within supporting distance of each other. Once more unhappy at having missed an excellent opportunity, Johnston canceled Hood's attack and moved his army south of Cassville.[49]

Cassville to Kenesaw Mountain

Great controversy surrounds Johnston's subsequent instructions to his corps commanders. It appears that the Confederate commander wanted to remain north of the Etowah River. Polk and Hood, on the other hand, urged a retreat across the river.* They felt that Federal artillery, positioned on higher ground, could dominate Johnston's proposed position. At a meeting attended by the three generals, Johnston finally acquiesced to the demands of his two subordinates. As the meeting was breaking up, Hardee arrived and supported Johnston's original point of view. The commanding general's mind was made up, however, and he directed a retreat across the river.[50]

---

*After the war, Hood denied that he had made this recommendation. Polk had been killed, and so could not give his version of the events.

With the river now between his army and the Federals, Johnston was worried about Sherman's ability to move unseen around one of the Confederate flanks. Accordingly, on May 22, he sent Major General Joseph Wheeler and most of his cavalry around the Confederate northeastern flank to discover what the Federals were doing and to strike Sherman's supply line. *(Movement not shown on map.)* Although Wheeler captured 80 supply wagons near Cassville on May 24, his raid had no impact on Sherman's supply situation, because the Union commander had cut loose from his line of communication on May 23.

In yet another attempt to outflank the Confederates, Sherman sent his armies cross-country toward the Dallas-New Hope Church area. Johnston responded by shifting his army to the same area. At New Hope Church, Thomas' lead corps ran into a Confederate corps. After a three-hour fight, the only thing that the Federals could claim was 1,665 Union killed and wounded. When the two armies began probing the strength of each other's flanks, they were found to be unassailable. Moreover, because of the strength of the position, there was little likelihood that a frontal assault could succeed. By now, it had become common practice for an army to construct field fortifications as soon as it halted from the march. First, rifle pits were dug to protect the skirmish line. From 100 to 300 meters behind the rifle pits, the defenders built the first line of breastworks. These were constructed with logs so that only the eyes of the defenders were visible to the attackers. Two to three lines of breastworks were thrown up. Then, if time permitted, the first line of works was provided with further protection in the form of a deep ditch backed with sharpened stakes and *chevaux-de-frise.** Underbrush from the region was collected and added to the front so that an attacker would have great difficulty pushing his way through the tan-

---

**Chevaux-de-frise are obstacles that are constructed of six- to eight-foot-long timbers from which pointed stakes or spikes protrude.

Confederate Entrenchments in a Thicket at New Hope Church

gled mass of deadfall. Once in place, these works were virtually impossible to seize by a frontal assault.[51]

During the following weeks, the two forces extended their trenches eastward toward the Western and Atlantic Railroad. *(Movement not shown on map.)* At one point (June 14), Polk was trying to decide whether or not to adjust his lines when he was hit in the chest with an artillery round. His death was a reminder of the constant danger facing every man in each army. Although the casualty rates were not as high as those being incurred in Virginia, the losses were substantial. Still, Sherman felt that he needed to maintain the pressure on Johnston, both to prevent Johnston from reinforcing Lee and to keep his own soldiers confident in the face of the enemy trenches. With this last point in mind, he decided to launch a frontal assault against Johnston's position on Kenesaw Mountain.

Since the end of May, Sherman—the attacker—had lost fewer soldiers than his opponent. This was a curious reversal of the typical Civil War campaign; it was almost a law that the attacker would lose more soldiers than the defender. It was also a testimonal to Sherman's generalship. At Kenesaw Mountain on June 27, however, Sherman quickly learned that he could not be careless about his assaults. *(See Atlas Map No. 48.)* Without even making a dent in the Confederate lines, he lost over 3,000 men. In contrast, Johnston suffered only 450 casualties.[52]

Confederate Concern and Johnston's Relief

Rebuffed and chastened, Sherman returned to his old style of maneuver and began to probe Johnston's left flank. Abandoning his positions on Kenesaw Mountain, Johnston retreated through Marietta and stopped at the Chattahoochee River. Because he had earlier envisioned an eventual retreat to the river, an engineer officer had been assigned to supervise the construction of extensive breastworks there. Johnston reasoned that the natural strength of this line would permit him to hold Sherman in position with a fraction of his army while the remainder struck a blow against Sherman's flank or rear. Sherman, however, did not permit his army to be "fixed." Instead, he sent part of his force upriver to outflank the Confederate position.

The Union commander decided to cross the Chattahoochee at the mouth of Soap Creek. *(See Atlas Map No. 48.)* Even though there was only a small Confederate force to oppose the crossing, Sherman wanted to use secrecy to gain surprise. The Army of the Ohio was designated to make the main crossing. During daylight on July 8, Schofield sent one of his infantry divisions into concealed positions along the river's edge. The troops controlling the ponton train that was to

Lieutenant General Leonidas Polk

support the crossing then moved up Soap Creek and launched their craft out of sight of the Confederate defenders. One regiment was to cross in the pontons while the remainder of the brigade ran to the river's edge and delivered volleys of musket fire to keep the Confederates back. A second brigade was ordered upriver about a half mile, where it was to cross on a fish dam. At 3:30 p.m., the signal was given, and all parts of the plan were implemented without error. The Confederate outpost was only able to fire a single round from its solitary artillery piece before fleeing southward to spread the alarm that the Federals had crossed the river. Although he still had the opportunity to reinforce his northern flank and crush the bridgehead, Johnston vacillated and finally decided to withdraw his army to Peachtree Creek, just north of Atlanta.[53]

Johnston's abandonment of the Chattahoochee line was the final step of his defense of the Confederate heartland. The Confederate Government in Richmond had watched with alarm as Johnston evacuated position after position. To Jefferson Davis, in particular, it seemed that if Johnston was unable to stop Sherman in the mountains northwest of Marietta, he certainly would not be able to hold his foe in the more flat terrain near Atlanta—the center of the Confederate heartland and a key industrial site. The city was being threatened, and Johnston appeared powerless to save it. Davis tried to keep abreast of Johnston's plans, but the information that was sent from Georgia was sketchy. The only thing that Johnston could tell the President was that Sherman had overpowering strength, and because the Federals were cautious in their advance, there just had not been an opportunity to deliver a

Lieutenant General John B. Hood

telling blow. Accordingly, Davis sent his military adviser, General Braxton Bragg, to assess the situation. In his report to the President, Bragg belittled Johnston's policy of retreat and wrote glowingly of Hood's desire for aggressive action.* Davis gave Johnston one last chance and asked the general to outline his plans. Johnston's reply was not what the Confederate President was seeking: "As the enemy has double our number, we must be on the defensive. My plan of operation must, therefore, depend upon that of the enemy. It is mainly to watch for an opportunity to fight to advantage."[54]

As Davis felt that Johnston would still be "looking for an opportunity" while he was in the process of evacuating Atlanta, he directed the Adjutant General to relieve Johnston and appoint the aggressive Hood in his place. On July 17, Johnston received the news; on the following day, he relinquished command. In his acidly worded reply, he questioned

---

*Bragg's poor opinion of Johnston was the same as Johnston's opinion of Bragg (and Davis). To a congressional delegation, also sent to Atlanta to investigate the situation, Johnston said, "Yes, I know Mr. Davis thinks he can do a great many things other men would hesitate to attempt. For instance, he tried to do what God failed to do. He tried to make a soldier of Braxton Bragg, and you know the result. It couldn't be done."

Hood's abilities: "Confident language by a Military Commander is not usually regarded as evidence of competency."[55]

Hood's Defense of Atlanta

By July 18, Sherman had moved his entire force across the Chattahoochee. His immediate objective was the cutting of all of the rail lines leading into Atlanta. The city would fall as soon as its life lines had been severed. Moving north of the city, Sherman began a wide sweep designed to seize Decatur and cut the Georgia Railroad in the east. Living up to his reputation, Hood at once assumed the offensive, attacking the Federal force on July 20. *(See Atlas Map No. 49a.)* Sherman had maneuvered his armies in such a way as to allow Peachtree Creek to divide them. As a result, Hood believed that he had an excellent chance to defeat Thomas in detail. The southern prong of Hood's attack was delayed, however, while the Confederate right flank was being secured against McPherson's approach from Decatur. This permitted Thomas to cross the creek and prepare for Hood's assault. By the time the attack started, the Federals were ready. The dismal Confederate failure cost Hood 2,500 casualties.

On the following day, Hood devised a second counterattack plan. By withdrawing his army into the defensive works close to Atlanta, Hood freed Hardee's corps to launch an attack against McPherson's flank. *(See Atlas Map No. 49b.)* In what has been called the Battle of Atlanta, Hardee made an attempt to outflank the enemy. Having searched for but been unable to find the open flank of the Union line, Hardee finally launched his attack, only to run into a Federal division that had recently arrived after tearing up the railroad near Decatur. The cost was 8,000 Confederates killed and wounded, including the death of a division commander. On the other side, although the casualties were lighter—3,700—Major General James B. McPherson was killed in an encounter with some Confederate infantry.

Thinking that Hood had expended his offensive power, Sherman now began another flanking maneuver. He sent Major General Oliver O. Howard, McPherson's replacement, and the Army of the Tennessee around the western side of Atlanta. Howard's army was marching southward, intending to cut Atlanta's last rail link, when Hood launched his third attack. *(See Atlas Map No. 49c.)* Near Ezra Church on July 28, Major General Stephen D. Lee, now leading Cheatham's old corps, assaulted Howard's marching columns. Although unable to entrench, the Federals were able to throw up some hasty breastworks. These were enough to make the difference. The Confederates managed to protect the railroad from immediate destruction, but it cost them another 2,500 casualties.[56]

Hood's three attacks had exhausted the Army of Tennessee, and also had taught Sherman to use caution. The three Union

Sherman's Men Destroy Rail Lines in the Center of Atlanta

The Battle of Atlanta

armies now settled down to a siege of the city. The objective remained the same—to cut Atlanta's rail lines—but the method had changed. The slow, painstaking process of siege-craft would take time. To insure success, Sherman used all of the tools of war. Not only were the lines of contravallation dug with great care, but the heavy siege artillery was hauled up. A bombardment of the city began soon afterward.

Neither commander, however, had given up hope of waging mobile warfare. On the same day that Howard moved toward Ezra Church, Sherman sent three divisions of cavalry deep into the Confederate rear. *(See Atlas Map No. 49c.)* Hood responded by sending Major General Joseph Wheeler's cavalry corps in pursuit. In a brilliant display of generalship, Wheeler managed to defeat each of the Union divisions in detail and return to Atlanta relatively unscathed. Knowing that his army could not withstand the effects of a siege for long, Hood then sent Wheeler on a raid against Sherman's line of communication. *(Movement not shown on map.)* The Union commander, however, had taken great care to insure that the major rail bridges in his rear were well protected. Although Wheeler's raid penetrated deep into the Union rear, it had little influence on the operations around Atlanta.

Sherman continued to shift his line to the right, aiming for the Atlanta and West Point and the Macon and Western Railroads. Hood, in turn, carefully extended his own lines to keep the supplies moving freely into the city. Nonetheless, it was

only a question of time before the weight of numbers would decide the outcome. Finally, on August 26, Sherman felt that his position was secure enough to free most of his force from its supply lines and strike out against Hood's remaining rail links. *(See Atlas Map No. 49d.)* Leaving Major General Henry W. Slocum's corps behind to guard the bridge over the Chattahoochee River, Sherman sent the remainder of his force toward the section of the rail line between Rough-and-Ready and Jonesboro. Unaware of the overwhelming strength of Sherman's turning movement, Hood sent Hardee's corps southward to block it. On August 31, Hardee attacked; and on September 1, he in turn was attacked. The situation was hopeless; Hardee retreated to Lovejoy's Station. Late on September 2, with the last rail line firmly in Federal hands, Hood abandoned Atlanta and moved the remainder of his army to join Hardee at Lovejoy's. On September 3, just before dawn, while he was accompanying the forces pursuing Hardee, Sherman received the news from Slocum that Atlanta was in Federal hands. Deciding to abandon his pursuit of the Confederates and to give his armies a much needed rest, Sherman ordered a withdrawal to Atlanta. His message to Halleck was electrifying: ''Atlanta is ours, and fairly won.''[57] Sherman's victory served as a tonic to the people of the North, infusing them with hope after the months of frustrating stalemate in Virginia and Georgia. It also deflated the Democrats and buoyed Lincoln's re-election campaign.

Atlanta's Defenses (Shown After Federal Capture)

A comparison of Sherman's Atlanta Campaign and Grant's Richmond Campaign provides some instructive insights into Civil War generalship. Each force had to travel roughly the same straight-line distance and fight with relatively the same numerical superiority over the Confederates. But Sherman took his objective in less time and with fewer casualties. As of July 1, Grant's campaign had cost approximately 64,000 casualties, as opposed to 30,000 Confederate casualties. Sherman, startlingly enough, suffered fewer casualties than the Confederates—31,700 Federals versus 34,900 Confederates. Moreover, he managed to do this on terrain that clearly favored the defender.

Sherman's success can partially be explained by the simple fact of geography. He had to be careful about protecting his line of communication, but he did not have to protect the Federal capital. Even with Grant present to remove some of the political pressure, the Army of the Potomac could not move in a direction that the Government thought would "uncover" Washington. This prevented Grant from making the wide, sweeping maneuvers that Sherman so often was able to accomplish. The major difference between the results of the two campaigns, however, can be attributed to Robert E. Lee. Lee knew that he had to fight, and he often sought battle on terms that were unacceptable to Johnston. Lee was confident of his subordinates. He knew that they could give as good as they could take. Johnston, on the other hand, did not have the same confidence in his subordinates. Except for the victory at the First Battle of Bull Run, he had a mediocre reputation and was continuing a line of dreary defeats. Because he did not have faith in his army, he demanded that every detail be precisely correct before he would attack Sherman. Conversely, Sherman was supremely confident in his army's abilities. He had achieved a moral ascendency over Johnston —and Hood—that Meade had not attained over Lee. All of these factors contributed to a victory that was "fairly won."

Meanwhile, in Virginia, the grim siege of Richmond and Petersburg continued to grind on.

Notes

[1] U.S. Congress, *Congressional Globe*, 38th Congress, 1st Session, part 1, 586–594, 789–798.

[2] William Swinton, *Campaigns of the Army of the Potomac* (New York, 1866), p. 404.

[3] *The War of the Rebellion: A Compilation of the Official Records of the Union and Confederate Armies* (130 vols.; Washington, 1880–1901), Series I, XXXII, Pt. 2, 408; Pt. 3, 58. (Hereinafter cited as *OR*. Unless otherwise indicated, all subsequent references to the *OR* are to Series I.)

[4] T. Harry Williams, *Lincoln and His Genrals* (New York, 1952), pp. 301–302.

[5] Edgar T. Welles (ed.), *The Diary of Gideon Welles* (3 vols.; Boston, 1911), I, 538–539; Horace Porter, *Campaigning With Grant* (New York, 1897), pp. 19–21; Ulysses S. Grant, *Personal Memoirs of U.S. Grant* (2 vols.; New York, 1885), II, 117; Bruce Catton, *Never Call Retreat* (New York, 1971), p. 286.

[6] *OR*, XXXII, Pt. 3, 18; Porter, *Campaigning With Grant*, p. 22.

[7] Adam Badeau, *Military History of Ulysses S. Grant* (3 vols.; New York, 1885), II, 12, 23; *OR*, XXXII, Pt. 3, 83; Grenville M. Dodge, *Personal Recollections of President Abraham Lincoln, General Ulysses S. Grant and General William T. Sherman* (Iowa, 1914), pp. 69–70.

[8] Grant, *Personal Memoirs*, II, 555.

[9] William T. Sherman, *Memoirs of General William T. Sherman* (2 vols.; New York, 1875), II, 6–7; *OR*, XXXIII, 638–639; Badeau, *Military History of U.S. Grant*, II, 42–43, 88–89.

[10] *OR*, XXXI, Pt. 2, 72–73; XXXI, Pt. 3, 349–350, 458; XXXII, Pt. 2, 40–42, 100–101; XXXIII, 394–395.

[11] *OR*, XXXII, Pt. 2, 126–127, 412–413 (quotation).

[12] *Ibid.*, XXIX, Pt. 2, 207–208 (quotation); Williams, *Lincoln and His Generals*, pp. 295–297.

[13] *OR*, XXXII, Pt. 3, 246.

[14] *Ibid.*, XXXIV, Pt. 1, 11.

[15] Badeau, *Military History of U.S. Grant*, II, 10; Grant, *Personal Memoirs*, II, 127; *OR*, XXXIII, 795.

[16] Grant to Meade, April 9, 1864, in Historical Society of Pennsylvania, The George G. Meade Collection, Box 3. (Hereinafter cited as Meade Collection.)

[17] *OR*, XXXIII, 874.

[18] *Ibid.*, 904, 889; Welles, *Diary*, II, 6; Andrew A. Humphreys, *The Virginia Campaign of '64 and '65* (New York, 1883), p. 9.

[19] George R. Agassiz (ed.), *Meade's Headquarters, 1863–1865; Letters of Colonel Theodore Lyman* (Boston, 1922), pp. 79–80; *OR*, XXXIII, 907–908, 889–890, 919–922.

[20] Allen Nevins (ed.), *A Diary of Battle: The Personal Journals of Colonel Charles S. Wainwright* (New York, 1962), p. 344; Humphreys, *Virginia Campaign*, p. 283; *OR*, XXXIII, 879.

[21] Grant, *Personal Memoirs*, II, 140; *OR*, XXXIII, 997, 1009, 1017; John Gibbon, *Personal Recollections of the Civil War* (New York, 1928), p. 211.

[22] James Longstreet, *From Manassas to Appomattox: Memoirs of the Civil War in America* (Philadelphia, 1896), pp. 543–546; *OR*, XXXIII, 1282–1283; Douglas Southall Freeman, *R.E. Lee: A Biography* (4 vols.; New York, 1934), III, 266.

[23] Humphreys, *Virginia Campaign*, pp. 18–19; Agassiz, *Meade's Headquarters*, p. 87.

[24] Douglas Southall Freeman, *Lee's Lieutenants: A Study in Command* (3 vols.; New York, 1942), III, 346–349.

[25] Handwritten note by Meade estimating Confederate strength, in Meade Collection, Box 3; Humphreys, *Virginia Campaign*, pp. 14, 17, 23.

[26] Meade to Grant, dated 7:30 a.m., May 5, 1864, in National Archives, Record Group 108, Box 84; *OR*, XXXVI, Pt. 2, 403.

[27] Henry Steele Commager (ed.), *The Blue and the Gray* (Indianapolis, 1950), p. 979.

[28] Agassiz, *Meade's Headquarters*, p. 91; Grant, *Personal Memoirs*, II, 194.

[29] John B. Gordon, *Reminiscences of the Civil War* (New York, 1903), pp. 244–250; E.M. Law, "From the Wilderness to Cold Harbor," in *Battles and Leaders of the Civil War*, ed. by Robert Underwood Johnson and Clarence Clough Buel (4 vols.; New York, 1884–1888), IV, 126. (Hereinafter cited as *B&L*).

[30] Agassiz, *Meade's Headquarters*, p. 102; *OR*, XXXII, Pt. 2, 481; Freeman, *Lee's Lieutenants*, III, 375.

[31] William B. Rawle, et al., *History of the Third Pennsylvania Cavalry* (Philadelphia, 1905), pp. 421–422; David S. Sparks (ed.), *Inside Lincoln's Army: The Diary of Marsena Rudolph Patrick, Provost Marshal General, Army of the Potomac* (New York, 1964), pp. 369–370.

[32] Philip H. Sheridan, *Personal Memoirs of P.H. Sheridan* (2 vols.; New York, 1888), I, 368–369; Porter, *Campaigning With Grant*, pp. 84–85.

[33] John F.C. Fuller, "The Place of the American Civil War in the Evolution of War," *The Army Quarterly*, XXVI (1933), 324–325; Emory Upton, *Infantry Tactics: Double and Single Rank Adapted to American Topography and Improved Fire-Arms* (Westport, 1968), p. viii; John K. Mahon, "Civil War Infantry Assault Tactics," *Military Affairs*, XXIV (Summer, 1961), 59.

[34] Neill Malcolm (ed.), *The Science of War: A Collection of Essays and Lectures 1892–1903 by the Late Colonel G.F.R. Henderson, B.C.* (London, 1905), pp. 263–264; Arthur L. Wagner, *Organization and Tactics* (Kansas City, 1906), p. 265.

[35] *OR*, XXXVI, Pt. 1, 667–668.

[36] *OR*, XXXVI, Pt. 1, 358–359; Freeman, *Lee's Lieutenants*, III, 400–404; *OR*, XXXVI, Pt. 2, 654.

[37] Grant to Meade, May 18, 1864, in Library of Congress, Presidents' Papers Series, The Ulysses S. Grant Papers, Series 5, XLV, 143 (hereinafter cited as Grant Papers); Freeman, *Lee's Lieutenants*, III, 439–441; Charles A. Dana, *Recollections of the Civil War: With the Leaders at Washington and in the Field in the Sixties* (New York, 1898), p. 199.

[38] *OR*, XXXVI, Pt. 3, 114; Isaac R. Pennypacker, *General Meade* (New York, 1901), p. 301; *OR*, XXXVI, Pt. 3, 206; Agassiz, *Meade's Headquarters*, p. 118.

[39] Grant to Meade, May 30, 1864, in Grant Papers, Series 5, XLV, 168; Elbridge J. Copp, *Reminiscences of the War of the Rebellion, 1861–1865* (Nashua, N.H., 1911), pp. 347, 371; Bruce Catton, *Grant Takes Command* (Boston, 1969), p. 247.

[40] Porter, *Campaigning With Grant*, p. 165; Freeman, *Lee's Lieutenants*, III, 507; Grant to Meade, June 2, 1864, in National Archives, RG 108, Letters Sent, I, 174.

[41] E.M. Law, "Cold Harbor," in *B&L*, IV, 141.

[42] Frank E. Vandiver, *Jubal's Raid: General Early's Famous Attack on Washington in 1864* (New York, 1960), pp. 1–19; Humphreys, *Virginia Campaign*, p. 246; Grant, *Personal Memoirs*, II, 305.

[43] Catton, *Grant Takes Command*, p. 303; Freeman, *R.E. Lee*, III,

446, 459.

[44]*OR*, XXXVII, Pt. 1, 89–117.

[45]Jacob D. Cox, *Atlanta* (New York, 1882), pp. 36–37.

[46]Nathaniel C. Hughes, Jr., *General William J. Hardee: Old Reliable* (Baton Rouge, 1965), pp. 184–187; *OR*, XXXI, Pt. 3, 792, 843.

[47]Thomas L. Connelly, *Autumn of Glory: The Army of Tennessee, 1862–1865* (Baton Rouge, 1971), pp. 341–342.

[48]*OR*, XXXVIII, Pt. 3, 615.

[49]*Ibid.*, Joseph E. Johnston, *Narrative of Military Operations, Directed During the Late War Between the States* (New York, 1874), pp. 320–322.

[50]Connelly, *Autumn of Glory*, pp. 349–354.

[51]*OR*, XXXVIII, Pt. 3, 947–948; Johnston, *Narrative*, p. 325; Connelly, *Autumn of Glory*, p. 355; Stephen F. Fleharty, *Our Regiment: A History of the 102nd Illinois Infantry Volunteers* (Chicago, 1865), pp. 85–86.

[52]Hartwell Osborn, "Sherman's Atlanta Campaign," in *Western Reserve University Bulletin*, XIV, No. 6 (Cleveland, 1911), p. 128; Lloyd Lewis, *Sherman, Fighting Prophet* (New York, 1932), pp. 374–376; *OR*, XXXII, Pt. 3, 409; Connelly, *Autumn of Glory*, pp. 393–399.

[53]Johnston, *Narrative*, pp. 346–347; Cox, *Atlanta*, pp. 137–140.

[54]Jefferson Davis, *The Rise and Fall of the Confederate Government* (2 vols.; New York, 1881), II, 557; *OR*, XXXVIII, Pt. 5, 869, 883, XXXIX, Pt. 2, 713–714.

[55]General Samuel Cooper to Johnston, July 17, and Johnston to Cooper, July 18, 1864, in Joseph E. Johnston Papers, Special Collections, United States Military Academy Library, West Point, N.Y.

[56]Connelly, *Autumn of Glory*, pp. 439–444; *OR*, XXXVIII, Pt. 3, 369.

[57]Sherman, *Memoirs*, II, 96–101, 105–109; Lewis, *Sherman, Fighting Prophet*, p. 403; Connelly, *Autumn of Glory*, p. 458; *OR*, XXXVIII, Pt. 5, 777.

Attrition and War's End 11

The pattern of the final operations in the two major theaters of war was established during the summer of 1864. In the East, maneuver room was restricted, and Lee's tenacious defense further hampered Grant's ability to fight a war of movement. In the West, however, Sherman faced a lesser foe than Lee, and had the resources to maneuver freely across the spacious terrain of the Confederate heartland. Union victory and war's end would come in both theaters in 1865, and the already established pattern would dictate how the Federal armies would win those victories.

Following the Union failure to break through the Confederate defenses south of Petersburg in June 1864, the war in Virginia settled into a stalemate. Penned into a small area and no longer able to maneuver, Lee was committed to the defense of Richmond and was powerless to break the deadlock. Although enjoying a preponderance of numbers, Grant's two armies lacked sufficient combat power to crush the Confederates, who stood defiantly behind strong fortifications. Given these conditions, the only alternative available to the Union was to initiate a siege along classic lines. The process would be methodical and tiresome, and it would entail daily losses in the trenches that could only be discouraging, particularly in light of the heavy casualties already incurred along the road to Richmond. Moreover, sieges are slow to bring results, a fact that would dishearten many in the war-weary North. Grant's ever-tightening siege lines, however, would ultimately drive Lee to the point of capitulation.

The situation in Georgia offered more hope to Federal leadership. Although it had appeared in August that a stalemate similar to that in Virginia was developing, Sherman's seizure of Atlanta had lifted northern spirits and enhanced Republican prospects in the coming national election. Moreover, regardless of how one assesses its political importance, Atlanta had a clearly recognized strategic value. The South could ill afford to lose either the city's industry or its rail center. Controlling this strategically located city, Sherman was in a position to

move deeper into Confederate territory and inflict damage that would be disastrous to the South's war effort. At the same time, he faced a difficult choice because he had not yet accomplished the mission that Grant had assigned him—to break up the Confederate Army of Tennessee. Hood's army—badly crippled, to be sure—was still in the field. Sherman could either follow the elusive Hood or pursue a different strategic objective that might bring Hood to battle. Neither course of action, however, offered much hope for an early accomplishment of the mission. Sherman's final decision would be daring, and, in the end, would be decisive in its contribution to the winning of the war.

The Death of an Army

Sherman spent three weeks in Atlanta, refitting his armies and trying to formulate an effective strategic plan. With the supply line to Tennessee firmly established, trains arrived daily in Atlanta to fill the army's haversacks. During the respite, Sherman received two unofficial visitors from the South—former members of the United States Congress—who described the desolation that existed in Georgia. The war had not only taken a heavy toll on the land, but had severely affected the attitudes of the people. Sherman asked his guests to carry a message to the Governor of Georgia: only by withdrawing Georgia troops from Confederate service could the Governor avoid having his entire state take on the appearance so gloomily described by the two men. Although Governor Joseph C. Brown did not heed the warning, it was a portent of things to come.[1]

An Ambitious Confederate Plan

Meanwhile, Sherman lost the initiative to his Confederate opponent. The aggressive Hood was determined not to stand by idly while the Federals sat happily in Atlanta. Almost as soon as he had consolidated his army at Lovejoy's Station, Hood began thinking about a strike at Sherman's line of communication. On September 19, he shifted his army westward to Palmetto, and three days later he sent a dispatch to Richmond, outlining his plan. Hood contemplated crossing the Chattahoochee River, forming a line of battle southwest of Marietta, and cutting Sherman's rail link with Chattanooga. (*See Atlas Map No. 50.*) This would force Sherman either to attack Hood on terrain that favored the Confederates or to move south to establish a supply line to the Gulf. In the latter case, Hood vowed to "fall upon" Sherman's rear. In the former instance, he would defeat the Federals.

On September 25, while on a good will tour of the South, President Davis visited Hood's headquarters and held a long discussion with his western commander.[2] The Confederate President found that the personality clashes which had been characteristic of the Army of Tennessee since Braxton Bragg's assumption of command had not abated. Hood verbally attacked his corps commander, Lieutenant General William J. Hardee, blaming him for the army's failure to stop Sherman. Later, in a private conversation with the President, Hardee, in turn, accused Hood of "unjust, ungenerous, and unmanly" conduct. Again, Davis was being asked to solve a problem that should never have existed. Satisfied that he understood the situation within the western army, Davis continued his tour of the South. On September 27, he wired Hood instructions that ordered Hardee to a new command in South Carolina. A short time later, Davis allegedly strengthened the command structure in the West by forming a new organization, the Military Division of the West, and placing General P.G.T. Beauregard in command.[3]

Beauregard's appointment served many purposes, not all of which were military. Davis silenced many of Hood's congressional critics by focusing their attention on the flashy Beauregard. In addition, the appointment of Beauregard drew support from those congressmen who thought that general should be given a greater role in the war effort. It also kept Davis from having to reappoint General Joseph E. Johnston. In actuality, however, although Beauregard's new position gave an outward appearance of being important, it amounted to little more than an advisory job. He continually entered into the events that followed, but he was never able to exercise the influence that his appointment should have allowed him.

Beauregard's hollow appointment, Hardee's transfer, and Davis' tacit approval of Hood's plan, gave the commander of the Army of Tennessee free rein. Accordingly, without delay, Hood put into motion the plan he had discussed with the President. On September 29, the Army of Tennessee crossed the Chattahoochee and headed north for the Western and Atlantic Railroad. (*See Atlas Map No. 50.*) A cavalry clash near Marietta

on October 1 (*action not shown on map*) sent Hood's army marching farther north toward Allatoona. Sherman started in pursuit of Hood's men on October 3, but one of Hood's divisions reached Allatoona first. There, although the Federal defenders managed to hold out until reinforcements arrived, the Confederates ripped up the railroad between Acworth (just south of Allatoona) and Big Shanty. Heading away from the railroad, Hood's men first turned west and then north to drive for the Coosa River and the Western and Atlantic Railroad at Resaca.

By October 8, Hood had changed his plan. Sherman's supply line continued to be an inviting target, but Hood wanted to deepen his turning movement. It still appeared that the original concept was valid; Sherman was being drawn away from the South's interior. By going deeper, Hood might be able to pull the Federal army all the way back to the Tennessee River. Hood realized that Sherman might tire of the game and move south, but he felt that in that case, he could surprise the Federal forces and successfully attack their rear. Meanwhile, he continued to maneuver against Sherman's line of communication, taking care, however, to avoid battle with Sherman's numerically superior force. On October 13, the day that his troops overwhelmed a small Union garrison at Dalton, Hood received reliable information that Sherman was following and had reached Resaca. Promptly, he moved westward, halting briefly in the vicinity of LaFayette. Then, abiding by his October 8 plan, which envisioned a westward move if Sherman followed, Hood headed southwest towards Gadsden, Alabama, arriving there on the twentieth. (*See Atlas Map No. 50.*) On the next day, the commander of the Military Division of the West arrived at Hood's headquarters.[4]

Hood outlined his new plan to Beauregard, his nominal superior. Hood's success at avoiding battle and at inflicting damage on Sherman's line of communication had made it clear that the Federal rear was vulnerable. The commander of the Army of Tennessee now proposed that his army cross the Tennessee River and invade Tennessee. Hood saw Sherman's base at Nashville as a rich strategic prize, worthy of his army's efforts. Once Nashville had been taken, the Confederate army could move into Kentucky. If unopposed by a sizable Union force, it then could cross the mountains to the east, joining Lee's army at Richmond. Beauregard was not the right man to question the strength of Hood's plan. Too often in the past, he had been an advocate of a Confederate advance to the Ohio River. Now, when presented with a similar plan, he had no strong objections. Persuaded by the notion that the alternative of a Confederate withdrawal southward might be the final blow to the army's morale, he ordered Hood to put his plan into motion. From then on, Beauregard exercised no meaningful influence on the operations of Hood's army.[5]

The Federal Supply Depot at Nashville–One of Hood's Objectives

On October 22, the Army of Tennessee left for Guntersville, where Hood hoped to cross the Tennessee River, preparatory to launching his invasion of Tennessee. At that town, he also expected to link up with Major General Nathan Bedford Forrest's cavalry. Forrest was to replace Major General Joseph Wheeler's cavalry corps, which Beauregard had directed to remain south of the river. When Hood reached Guntersville, however, he learned that Forrest would be unable to join him there. Accordingly, he turned west, hoping to rendezvous with Forrest at Decatur and then cross the river. When the Federal garrison at Decatur appeared too strong to be overwhelmed quickly, the Army of Tennessee was forced to march farther west. (*See Atlas Map No. 50.*) Upon arriving at Courtland, Hood discovered that the nearby crossing site could not support the movement of a large army, and therefore headed farther downriver, reaching Tuscumbia on October 31. Hood then spent three difficult weeks building up his army's supplies and awaiting the arrival of Forrest. Finally, Forrest's command rode in on November 16. Now, however, heavy rains intervened to prevent the Confederate wagons from crossing the river. Four days later, on the twentieth, Confederate preparations were complete, and the river waters had fallen sufficiently to permit a crossing. With 38,000 men, Hood marched northward into central Tennessee.[6]

Sherman Contemplates a Daring Strategy

It may seem strange that Sherman did not attempt to destroy Hood's army during the three weeks that it lingered at Tuscumbia. Several considerations influenced his actions at this time, and therefore help explain his inactivity. Admiral David Farragut's capture of Mobile, Alabama and Sherman's seizure of Atlanta, Georgia had accomplished two of the goals in Grant's strategic plan for 1864. Although Hood's army was still on the loose, two of the territorial objectives that Grant considered essential were now in Federal hands. He had suggested to Sherman that Augusta, another important industrial center, might be a suitable target for Sherman's men once Hood had been eliminated as a threat. Sherman felt differently. Having pursued Hood for several weeks without accomplishing anything worthwhile, Sherman decided that it would be impossible to protect his line of communication from the far-ranging forces of Hood and the Confederate cavalry. Instead, Sherman proposed that he destroy the railroad from Chattanooga to Atlanta, cut loose from his supply lines, and march across Georgia to Savannah. This would cripple the South's military resources, demonstrate the Confederate Army's inability to protect the population, and take the war to the people. It was a plan radically different from any that Grant had yet considered.[7]

Sherman had been considering the concept of a march across Georgia since 1862. In a letter that he had written home that year, he stated that the only way to win the war was to reconquer the South using the techniques that the Army had been employing for years to defeat the Indians. The destruction of Indian villages had been the key, and Sherman believed that a similar idea was the key to Union victory.

"War is upon us; none can deny it," he again declared in a letter to Major General Henry W. Halleck in 1863. The South had decided to go to war, and Sherman felt that the North should continue to fight "till those who appealed to it are sick and tired of it. . . . I would not coax them or even meet them half way, but make them so sick of war that generations would pass before they would again appeal to it."[8] His February 1864 campaign to wipe out guerrilla activity in Meridian, Mississippi had been designed to achieve just such a goal. He realized that he was earning the undying hatred of many people, but, as he explained when he later ordered Atlanta to be evacuated: "If the people raise a howl against my barbarity and cruelty, I will answer that war is war and not popularity-seeking."[9] Finally, he had learned that it was possible for a large army to live off the land. Cutting loose from his supply line and marching to Savannah was not as risky as it seemed. It had worked for Grant in the Vicksburg Campaign, and Sherman had tried it successfully when he "dropped everything" to come to Thomas' aid at Chattanooga in October 1863.

Grant did not react very favorably toward Sherman's proposal. He still felt that Hood's army was the proper objective for the western armies. Sherman quickly reassured Grant that Hood would not be forgotten. On September 29, he had sent Major General George H. Thomas, "The Rock of Chickamauga," back to Nashville to organize a defense of the Federal rear. The IV and XXIII Corps had been dispatched to bolster Thomas' forces, and additional troops were being gathered from many of the western garrisons. Reluctantly accepting Sherman's arguments, on October 11, Grant had told him to conduct his march to the seacoast.

Much to Sherman's disgust, Hood's army then intervened. At the time that Grant was putting his initial approval on Sherman's plan, Hood was closing on Resaca and Dalton. As noted above, Sherman was forced to follow. "Damn him, if he will go to the Ohio River, I'll give him the rations," Sherman exclaimed. "Let him go north, my business is down South."[10] Reluctantly following Hood's army, Sherman finally found the needed lull in the pursuit when Hood settled down for his three-week stay at Tuscumbia. On November 2, Sherman received Grant's final approval. He now had the authority to start "the march, and make Georgia howl."[11]

Hood's Advance to Franklin, Tennessee

Hood was not sure about the location of Sherman's forces. Until mid-November, he received many reports indicating that Sherman was continuing to follow the Army of Tennessee. By the time he had crossed the Tennessee River, however, it was clear that Sherman had broken contact, and that control of central Tennessee would be decided by a confrontation between his own army and Thomas' makeshift force.

Hood marched his men northeast toward Columbia *(See Atlas Map No. 50)*, where they could cross the Duck River. Major General John M. Schofield, stationed at Pulaski with two Union corps, could see that his position was being turned, as Hood's direction of march was taking him to a point between Schofield's and Thomas' forces. He therefore abandoned his position and headed northward to the Duck River line. Early on November 29, Schofield received a dispatch from his cavalry commander, Major General James H. Wilson, which indicated that the Duck River position had also been turned. Forrest's Confederate cavalry column was north of the river, and Hood was laying ponton bridges to permit the southern infantry to follow close behind. *(See Atlas Map No. 51a.)* Schofield responded by sending an infantry division to a blocking position at Spring Hill, where it could protect the line of retreat to Franklin, if Wilson's report proved correct. Hood, meanwhile, was trying to reach Nashville ahead of Schofield. Unconcerned about Schofield's fleeing troops, he wanted the much richer prize at Nashville. Once his main infantry force crashed into Schofield's blocking force at Spring Hill, however, he changed his mind. Schofield's force could be destroyed and thereby eliminated as a reinforcement for Thomas, who could then be leisurely attacked at Nashville.

Realizing his own predicament, Schofield hurried his troops northward past Spring Hill. Under heavy Confederate attack, the division guarding the road managed to hold its position throughout November 29. Hood's men, on the other hand, were intent on destroying the Federal defense and not on cutting the Columbia-Franklin road. Late that night, Schofield's men finally marched out of the danger that had nearly consumed them.

Hood was infuriated by Schofield's escape. The road should have been blocked during the night, and the Federals should have been destroyed. Much of the blame for the Confederate failure must be placed on Hood's shoulders, however, for he had assumed that Schofield's rear guard at Columbia was heavily engaged with Lieutenant General Stephen D. Lee's Confederate corps. This was not the case; the Federals had been able to break contact in the darkness. Also, Hood had failed to ride forward and survey the Confederate position at Spring Hill. This would have given him an accurate picture of the true situation—that is, that the road was unguarded. Finally, he had ignored two reports, made during the night, indicating that the Federals were marching along the road to Franklin without opposition. One report, sent by a division commander, stated that the enemy was using the road at 5:00 p.m. on the twenty-ninth. The second report, sent as the result of an observation by a private soldier at 2:00 a.m. on November 30, reiterated that the road was open. Obviously, Schofield was taking advantage of the opportunity to use it. Although the fault was largely his, Hood was angered by Schofield's flight. Unfortunately for the Army of Tennessee, it would bear the brunt of Hood's rage.[12]

As soon as Hood realized that Schofield had escaped, he sent his army in pursuit. Arriving at Franklin in the early morning hours of the thirtieth, Schofield found his path blocked. The bridge over the Harpeth River was badly damaged, and his own pontons had been destroyed in the retreat from Columbia. Quickly, he set his engineers to work, hoping to repair the bridge in time to move his supply wagons across the river before Hood could seize them. As the remainder of his army filed in from its retreat past Spring Hill, he ordered it into positions south of the town. The soldiers immediately went to work constructing earthworks and organizing a defensive position. By the time Hood's army appeared on the Columbia Pike, both flanks of the Federal line rested on the river. One Federal division was posted well forward on the Pike, its mission being to discern Hood's intentions. *(See Atlas Map No. 51b.)*

Hood's intentions were not difficult to ascertain. It is quite possible that he had become emotionally distraught during the past several days. In any event, he was determined to prove his army's mettle. Unfortunately, before he had a chance to organize his force properly or to test the Union defenses, Hood ordered his army to attack. Forrest protested. He had found a crossing site upriver; reinforced by an infantry division, Hood's cavalry commander thought that he could slip into a blocking position to Schofield's rear and trap him. In addition, most of Lee's artillery was still absent. Nevertheless, Hood overrode his subordinate's objections and directed his men to attack immediately.[13]

The Confederate attack was initially successful. The Union covering force on the Columbia Pike tarried too long, and was overwhelmed before it could disengage. A mixture of fleeing Federals and attacking Confederates arrived at the main defensive line at about the same time. Afraid to shoot into the midst of their retreating comrades, the men in the main line held their fire too long. Moreover, before the effect of their sporadic fire could be felt, they were overwhelmed by the Confederate attack. Their flight left a gap in Schofield's lines.

Just behind the point of impact, a lone Federal brigade waited in reserve. *(See Atlas Map No. 51b.)* As soon as the hole in the frontline materialized, the Union commander sent his brigade forward to plug it. Although Hood's initial assault had promised great results, it now foundered. Caught in a death trap, Confederate soldiers huddled in the ditches of the Union defenses, afraid to move forward or to go back. Re-

peatedly, the remaining Confederates attacked, with the assaults continuing until well after nightfall. Schofield's men held firm; by 9:00 p.m., the exhausted Confederates had stopped their futile assaults.

Hood's army had suffered horribly. Out of 16,000 infantrymen employed, 6,252 were casualties. Of these, 1,750 were killed—more deaths than the Federals had incurred at Fredericksburg, Chancellorsville, Chickamauga, Shiloh, or Stones River. Confederate general officers particularly suffered, 12 of them being killed, wounded, or captured. The future effectiveness of the Army of Tennessee was clearly in doubt.[14]

Without Confederate interference, Schofield withdrew his troops from Franklin and marched towards Nashville. Apparently, the sharp repulse on the afternoon of the thirtieth had convinced the Confederates to keep a safe distance. All through the night, the blue column toiled northward. On the morning of December 1, it reached Nashville and the safety of Thomas' army. Now it was up to Hood to decide the next course of action.

The Battle of Nashville

Hood felt that he had gained a victory at Franklin. After all, the enemy had retreated, leaving the Confederates in control of the battlefield. He therefore decided to follow Schofield northward and form a defensive line opposite Thomas' army at Nashville. It is not clear why Hood chose this unusual plan, particularly after he had learned of the casualties his army had suffered at Franklin. After the war, he claimed that he was expecting reinforcements to arrive from the trans-Mississippi West. He also hoped that by assuming a defensive posture at Nashville he would force Thomas to attack. Once Thomas had been repulsed, Hood's army could follow on the heels of the retreating Federals and take Nashville. Both of these ideas sounded very fine when Hood recounted them in his memoirs years later. As events transpired, however, there was little likelihood of his either receiving reinforcements or repulsing Thomas. Both were pipe dreams of the worst sort.[15]

Once at Nashville, Hood divided his forces. On December 5, he sent Forrest with two cavalry divisions and three infantry brigades to Murfreesboro. Again, Hood's motive for this move is not clear. He suggested to Forrest on the eighth that the Federals might evacuate Murfreesboro if pushed. This seems a bit absurd, as the Union garrison there outnumbered Forrest's force. Regardless of Hood's intent, Forrest's absence left Hood with only 23,200 men to organize a defense. In Nashville, Thomas waited with over 49,700 soldiers.

Thomas was under great pressure to attack Hood and eliminate the Army of Tennessee. As long as Hood was free, the Federals would be compelled to keep the Mississippi River strongly garrisoned. Grant wanted these troops transferred to

Sherman as soon as possible. But Thomas would not be coerced into attacking before he was ready. First, he wanted to wait until Wilson's cavalrymen were properly mounted (several thousand men had been unable to accompany Wilson to Columbia because of the lack of horses). Second, unusually cold weather had set in on December 8. Below freezing temperatures were followed by ice storms. Convinced that any attacks launched in this severe weather would result in needless Union casualties, Thomas waited for warmer temperatures and the inevitable December thaw that would permit him to attack. Twice, Grant threatened Thomas with relief. The second time, Grant ordered Thomas to turn over his command to Schofield. But Schofield did not want to attack across the icy fields either, so the Federals continued to wait. Finally, Grant ordered Major General John A. Logan to go to Nashville and, if Thomas had not yet attacked, to take command of Thomas' forces. Nevertheless, by December 15, Grant still had received no word from Nashville. Boarding a boat at City Point, Virginia, Grant set sail for Washington, where he could catch a train to take him to the lethargic western army. As he got off the boat at the capital, however, Grant was greeted by heartwarming news. Thomas had crushed Hood's army on the fifteenth.[16]

Thomas had carefully planned the defense of Nashville, utilizing the trenches that had surrounded Nashville since its capture in 1862. *(See Atlas Map No. 57a.)* On the last day of November, Union ranks were swelled by the addition of Major General A.J. Smith's XVI Corps. Another 5,200 men arrived on December 2, having been drawn from Sherman's rear area troops at Chattanooga. Thomas even stripped his own supply and headquarters units to insure that the maximum number of infantrymen would be committed to the battle. On the right, he placed Smith's Corps, with its right flank anchored on the Cumberland River. Next in the line was the IV Corps, now commanded by Brigadier General Thomas J. Wood.* The XXIII Corps, under Schofield, was on Wood's left, and Schofield's left was extended to the river by the addition of Major General James B. Steedman's provisional division from Chattanooga. All of these units were located on a series of hills that guarded Nashville to the west and south. Thomas' flanks were further protected by a flotilla of gunboats that patrolled the river above and below the city. It would be difficult for an enemy flanking force to maintain a line of operations through this protective screen.

Because Hood did not have sufficient troops to encircle the Federal forces completely, he had a much more difficult time arranging his lines. Moreover, Hood's men had been forced to build their fortifications during the adverse weather that

*The previous commander, Major General David S. Stanley, had been wounded during the counterattack by the reserve brigade at Franklin.

The Interior of a Federal Fort at Nashville

had started in the early days of the month. Major General Benjamin F. Cheatham fixed the right flank of his corps on a deep cut of the Nashville and Chattanooga Railroad. *(See Atlas Map No. 52a.)* Almost a mile of open ground lay between Cheatham's flank and the Cumberland River. Lee's Corps occupied the center of the Confederate line along a series of low hills. Lieutenant General Alexander P. Stewart, his corps holding the left of the Confederate line, refused his open flank and arranged his forces so that his line of battle paralleled the Hillsboro Pike. Four miles of open terrain lay between Stewart's left and the river. Brigadier General James R. Chalmer's cavalry division was assigned the task of screening the gap.[17]

Thomas planned to make his main attack against this exposed flank. Wood's IV Corps and Smith's XVI Corps were to mount the principal assault against Hood's left, while Steedman's division created a diversion opposite Hood's right. Thomas' main attack was extended by the cavalry of Wilson, who was ordered to form his men on Smith's flank. Thomas had sufficient troops to permit him to retain Schofield's entire corps as a reserve. This corps was placed in the rear of the IV Corps.

Under the cover of a heavy fog, Steedman's diversionary force advanced at 6:00 a.m. on December 15. At about 8:00 a.m., his men struck Cheatham's flank. Hood's attention immediately was shifted to the right. Because Smith and Wilson took much longer to get into position than originally anticipated, their attack against Stewart did not get underway until about noon. This delay gave the Federals ample time to get properly organized for the assault. When they finally struck, they carried the southern line and continued to drive the Confederates across the Hillsboro Pike. Hood responded by ordering a division of Cheatham's Corps to hurry to the left and restore the crumbling flank. But Thomas had massed too much power on Hood's left. In quick succession, Schofield's corps was committed on Smith's right, Wood crushed the salient in the center of Stewart's line, and the Confederates fled to the rear. *(See Atlas Map No. 52a.)*

Ultimately, darkness halted the Federal exploitation. Not wanting to risk a night attack, the methodical Thomas carefully arranged his units for an attack on the next day. Satisfied with his army's performance, he sent a telegram to Halleck:

> I attacked the enemy's left this morning and drove it from the river . . . a distance about eight miles. Have captured General Chalmer's headquarters and train, and a second train of about 20 wagons, with between 800 and 1,000 prisoners and 16 pieces of artillery.[18]

Thomas had taken his time, and the Union high command had been worried. But the delay had been worthwhile.

The fighting on the next day was anticlimactic. Hood held grimly to the lines that his men had occupied at the conclusion of their retreat of the previous night. *(See Atlas Map No. 52b.)* Few options remained open to the Army of Tennessee. A retreat from the field might create panic, with the result being wholesale desertions. Furthermore, the demoralized columns might be cut to pieces by Thomas' pursuing hordes. By remaining in position, Hood insured the integrity of his army for at least one more night. When dawn broke, Thomas ordered his army forward to occupy positions facing the new Confederate line.

By noon, the Federals were in their attack positions. Wood and Steedman opened the assault on the right. *(Attack not shown on map.)* Again, Thomas planned to divert attention to the Confederate right while the main attack crushed the enemy left. As was anticipated, the attack on the right stalled quickly, but the principal assault got started at about 4:00 p.m. *(See Atlas Map No. 52b.)* Under pressure from three sides, Cheatham's Corps broke and fled. At about the same time, Wood again attacked, and Stewart's corps broke. Once more, nightfall prevented a complete disintegration of the Confederate army. Now, however, Hood had no options. He ordered his army to retreat to Franklin.

Confederate casualties in the battle are impossible to determine. Although Hood later claimed that his losses were small, the Federals captured 4,500 prisoners and 53 artillery pieces. The impact of the battle on the Confederate army can perhaps best be determined by analyzing the strength of each infantry division in Lee's corps. The average authorized strength of each brigade in the division was 5,000; after the battle, the average strength was 777 men. Federal casualties were 3,057, of which less than 400 were killed. Although Confederate losses may have been comparatively light for a two-day battle, Nashville marked the end of the Army of Tennessee as an effective fighting force.[19]

Following the battle, Forrest commanded the rear guard. On December 25, the remnants of the army crossed the Tennessee River at Florence. Beauregard and the Confederate War Department did not learn of the disaster until January 14, 1865, when Beauregard arrived at Tupelo, Mississippi to assess the state of the army. On the previous day, Hood had sent a cryptic telegram to Richmond. It stated simply, "I respectfully request to be relieved from the command of this army."[20] Beauregard found the reason for the telegram at Tupelo. There, the once proud army awaited new instructions. Its units were subsequently dispersed throughout the South to guard those areas being threatened by Federal columns. Although approximately 15,000 men went to Georgia and the Carolinas to assist Beauregard in organizing a defense against Sherman's invaders, the army's real history lay behind it.

A Critique

After the Battle of Nashville, Thomas posted major units at strategic locations throughout south central Tennessee and northern Alabama. Although he wanted to go into winter quarters, he was ordered to continue to apply pressure against the South. Therefore, he sent Wood and the IV Corps to Huntsville, Alabama, while Schofield's, Smith's, and Wilson's commands moved to Eastport, Mississippi. Already, Thomas' army was beginning to look like an army of occupation.

At first glance, Hood's campaign into Tennessee appears to have been the act of a desperate man. Moreover, some historians have suggested that Hood was mentally unbalanced after Schofield's successful evasion of disaster at Spring Hill.[21] A closer examination of the strategic situation following the evacuation of Atlanta, however, reveals that there were few alternatives available to the Army of Tennessee. Sherman had both the initiative and an overwhelming advantage in men and materiel. His position in Atlanta's defenses was virtually impregnable. Only by attacking Sherman's line of communication could Hood hope to forestall a Federal march into the South's interior. When he moved against the Western and Atlantic Railroad, Hood believed that his plan was working. For all intents and purposes, it was. Hood, however, could not prolong the maneuver indefinitely. At some point, he had to either accept battle with Sherman's numerically superior column or drive deeper into the Federal rear. Hood's experiences in battle around Atlanta seemed to indicate that the former course of action was not justifiable. This left him with the alternative of a march on Nashville.

That is not to say that the final stage of Hood's campaign was the product of clear thinking. Once Sherman had broken off the pursuit and Schofield had avoided the trap at Columbia, Hood should have reevaluated the problem. His idea of defeating Thomas, capturing Nashville, marching to the Ohio River, and eventually joining Lee's army at Richmond does not appear to have been based upon sound logic. He could not even negotiate the first obstacle, let alone embark on a raid deep into Union territory. Sherman's army posed the gravest danger to the South, and Hood needed to be guided by the seriousness of that threat. His strategy was too tenuous and too indirect to be of any consequence.

Sherman's strategy, on the other hand, demonstrated a sound reasoning power that has caused some military historians to rank the Union general as a genius. He knew that the size of his force enabled him to divide his armies in the face of the enemy. Thomas' assembled forces could easily deal with Hood while Sherman pursued another objective. The commander of the Military Division of the Mississippi realized that the breadbasket of the South was vulnerable to attack. He also understood that an attack against the southern homefront might change Confederate attitudes about a fight to the death. At the very least, it would demonstrate that the Confederate Army was no longer able to protect southern territory. As Sherman mentioned to Grant, the march to the sea "may not be war, but rather statesmanship. . . ."[22] He was determined to destroy the South's ability and desire to make war.

Sherman's March Across Georgia

Prior to beginning his march from Atlanta to Savannah, Sherman literally burned his bridges behind him. On November 12, the large railroad bridge at Allatoona was torn down, and the rails between the Etowah River and Atlanta were ripped up. Once Sherman had departed, it would be difficult for Hood's army to slip back into Atlanta and restore the city's former importance. The public buildings in Atlanta were destroyed, and all of the factories in Rome, Georgia also were burned. By the fourteenth, Sherman's forces—approximately 62,000 officers and men—were concentrated in Atlanta; on the following day, they departed for Savannah.

Sherman's columns encountered little resistance as they left Atlanta. Having organized his army into wings, Sherman sent his men in two directions, threatening both Macon and Augusta. *(See Atlas Map No. 53.)* His real objective, Milledgeville, the state capital *(not shown on map)*, was thus kept secret until he was ready to concentrate his forces there. On November 23, Sherman rode down the streets of the Georgia capital as his army moved relentlessly forward across the state. Macon, Millen, and Lumpkin's Station fell easily, and on December 10 the Federals arrived before Savannah. As Sherman expected a battle there, he prepared his army accordingly. Lieutenant General William J. Hardee, who commanded the Confederate forces at Savannah, rejected Sherman's note that demanded surrender of the southern forces. Nevertheless, Hardee saw no future in a battle against Sherman, and he quietly slipped his field artillery and infantry across the Savannah River on the night of December 20. On the following day, Sherman's men occupied the city. *(See Atlas Map No. 53.)* Sherman's note to Lincoln described his joy: "I beg to present you as a Christmas-gift the city of Savannah, with one hundred and fifty heavy guns and plenty of ammunition, also about twenty-five thousand bales of cotton."[23]

After a brief stay in the Georgia city, Sherman's divisions moved northward into the Carolinas. On the North Carolina coast, Schofield landed with two Federal corps. *(See Atlas Map No. 53.)* He then marched inland to Goldsboro, where it had been decided to establish a base for Sherman's approach-

Atlanta's Railroad Roundhouse Is Burned Prior to Sherman's Departure for Savannah

Part of the Ruins That Sherman Left in Savannah When He Marched Northward

ing army. Feverishly, the Confederates tried to scrape together a force to prevent a total dismemberment of the South's heartland. On February 23, General Joseph E. Johnston again was appointed to command the western forces.

Johnston's appointment was one of a series of dying gasps of the doomed Confederate Government. Earlier in the month, Lee had finally been appointed General-in-Chief. His appointment was followed in March by the passage of a law that permitted slaves to serve in the Confederate Army. Too late to make any difference, one third of the population of the South now was available to the Army. In March, also, the Government decided that it needed a new national flag. A red bar was added to the border of the "Stainless Banner," making the flag less likely to be mistaken for a surrender flag. Surrender, however, was rapidly approaching.

Another Federal column began moving in March. Over 13,400 cavalrymen under Major General James H. Wilson left their camps along the Tennessee River near Eastport and rode through Alabama. After finally eliminating Forrest's cavalry as a serious threat, they moved on to capture Selma and Montgomery. *(See Atlas Map No. 53.)* Heading eastward, they then seized Columbus and Macon, Georgia. On May 10, they finally ended their raid with the capture of Jefferson Davis near Irwinsville. *(The march from Macon to Irwinsville is not shown on map.)* By then, though, the major fighting had already ceased.

In battles at Averysboro and Bentonville, Johnston tried to stop the passage of Sherman's army. *(See Atlas Map No. 53.)* It was clear that the Federals were marching north to link up with Grant's armies at Richmond and Petersburg. Johnston's

attempts were useless, however, and when he learned that Lee had surrendered the Army of Northern Virginia at Appomattox, he asked Sherman for an armistice. On April 26, 1865, Johnston surrendered his army near Raleigh, North Carolina.[24]

The Defeat of Lee

In contrast to the war of movement in the West, the war in Virginia was static. The Army of Northern Virginia, the Army of the Potomac, and the Army of the James were tied together by the siege lines that surrounded the cities of Richmond and Petersburg. From the time Meade had failed to capture Petersburg on June 18, 1864, the armies had been frantically digging trenches. The problem that confronted Grant's combined armies was similar to the problem that Sherman faced at Atlanta. The railroads that led into the cities needed to be cut. With these supply lines severed, the Confederate position would become untenable, and Grant again could fight Lee in the open field.

Breastworks and Railroads

The responsibility for directing the siege was divided geographically between the two Federal armies. Generally, Major General Benjamin F. Butler's Army of the James besieged Richmond, and Major General George G. Meade's Army of the Potomac manned the siege lines around Petersburg. In order to oversee the operations of both armies, Grant established his headquarters in a central location (City Point), at the confluence of the Appomattox and James Rivers. *(See Atlas Map No. 54a.)*

Both sides built enormous works to protect their positions. Redoubts, redans, demilunes, and batteries were connected by a system of trenches and rifle pits. Abatis and *chevaux-de-frise* protected the front of each contestant's lines. Rifle and artillery fires were planned so that they interlaced and formed a curtain through which men could pass only with great difficulty. Forts were constructed at obvious weak points. The soldiers were vigilant, constantly alert for the slightest movement in the enemy's lines. It was a monotonous, dull, and dangerous job, but it was one that finally put to use the knowledge that had been gained by some officers during their training at West Point.[25]

Cadet instruction, which emphasized military engineering, had not always seemed to be of practical use to a commander trying to maneuver his army in an area such as the Wilderness. But the siege techniques and principles governing the construction of field fortifications that were taught at West Point were used on a small scale throughout the war. For instance, Major

Federal Soldiers in the Trenches Around Petersburg

General George B. McClellan's siege of Yorktown, Virginia in 1862 had employed these techniques. Other effective sieges were conducted over much longer periods of time. Major General Quincy A. Gillmore, for example, had laid siege to Fort Sumter for most of the summer of 1864. He also had been responsible for the construction of the siege batteries that had battered Fort Pulaski into submission in April 1862. These smaller efforts had provided the Federals with valuable experience—experience that they were able to apply during the operations against the Confederate capital that started in June 1864.

Included in the Federal plan for the siege of the Richmond-Petersburg area was the construction of a railroad. This was essential, as rail transportation continued to be the only reliable means of moving the supplies needed to support the mass armies of 1864. Soon, a line operated by the United States Military Railroad was constructed between the armies' base at City Point and the trenches surrounding the city. By July 7, trains were running regularly.[26]

On June 21, Grant began his first move to cut the railroad lines leading into Petersburg. The II and VI Corps were ordered westward to seize the Weldon Railroad. Grant hoped that this attack would lay the groundwork for a subsequent march to the Southside Railroad. The move was planned as a simple leftward extension of the existing line of battle. In order to get into position, however, the two corps were forced to make a wide sweep south and then west.

While the two Union corps were moving through a heavily wooded area on the opposite side of the Jerusalem Plank Road, the Confederates struck. *(Action not shown on map.)* Lee had sent Lieutenant General A.P. Hill's corps to protect the Weldon Railroad. Hill's men happened to pass between the Federal II and VI Corps while they were moving through the woods. Quick to exploit their advantage, the Confederates

attacked. The Union advance quickly fell apart, and the northern generals scrambled to restore their lines. Although the Union corps managed to re-establish their position, over 1,700 prisoners were taken by Hill's troops.

Major General James H. Wilson had been directed to mount a cavalry raid in conjunction with the attack by the II and VI Corps on the Weldon Railroad. Wilson's objectives were the two remaining Confederate railroads. One, the Southside, led out of Petersburg; the other, the Richmond and Danville, connected the Confederate capital with southwest Virginia. Wilson took about 5,500 men with him and, swinging south of Petersburg, struck the Southside Railroad about 14 miles west of Petersburg. Systematically, he ripped up approximately 30 miles of the line, and then headed north for the Richmond and Danville Railroad. Here, too, he successfully destroyed a good portion of the line before being forced to flee.

As soon as Wilson's move was discovered, Confederate cavalry rode out in close pursuit. Although the southern horsemen were not able to prevent the temporary destruction of the rail lines, they did drive off the Federal troopers. Meade, now concerned for Wilson's safety, sent Sheridan with the remainder of the cavalry to rescue the raiders. Wilson escaped, however, without help from Sheridan. From this experience, Grant and Meade learned the same lesson that Sherman would discover during the siege of Atlanta—cavalry could not effectively sever the railroads. Soon after Wilson's departure, trains again were running regularly into the southern cities. Only by planting an infantry force firmly astride the railroad could the flow of supplies be stemmed.[27]

The Petersburg Crater

While Union troops continued to dig and improve trenches pending the adoption of new means for breaking the deadlock,

**The 48th Pennsylvania Volunteer Infantry Regiment Mines
the Confederate Works Near Petersburg, July 1864**

Grant's headquarters started receiving suggestions from inventors who felt that modern technology could bring a quick end to the siege. Most of the suggestions were unrealistic, even outlandish. One engineer, for example, recommended that the besiegers construct a wall around Richmond that was higher than the tallest building in the city. The enclosure could then be filled with water pumped from the James River. Accompanying his plan with detailed drawings and elaborate calculations, the inventor promised that Grant could "drown out the garrison and people like rats in a cage."[28]

Other ideas were not quite as farfetched. One suggestion came from Lieutenant Colonel Henry Pleasants, commander of the 48th Pennsylvania Volunteer Infantry Regiment, a unit largely composed of Pennsylvania coal miners. Pleasants thought that it would be possible to tunnel under the Confederate positions. The tunnel could be filled with gunpowder that would be detonated to create a breach in the Confederate line. An infantry assault launched immediately after the explosion might achieve a significant breakthrough.

When Pleasants approached his corps commander, Major General Ambrose E. Burnside, with the plan, Burnside thought that the scheme had possibilities and ordered Pleasants to implement his concept. On June 25, work commenced. Meanwhile, Burnside had informed Meade of Pleasants' idea, and Meade began examining the possibility of following the explosion of the mine with an assault by three infantry corps. But there was also a great deal of skepticism about the plan. Meade and Grant sent engineers to inspect the area of the proposed detonation. They reported that the operation did not have much chance of succeeding. The section of the Confederate works designated to be blown up was covered by enfilad-

ing fire from other parts of the southern lines; therefore, a Union infantry assault could turn into a costly affair. Immediately to the rear of this area, a hill overlooked the lines. Undoubtedly, the enemy had taken advantage of the terrain and built a second line of defense on the ridge. Furthermore, it had become obvious that the Confederates suspected that a tunnel was being constructed. Southern pickets would call across the lines and laughingly ask how the tunnel was progressing. As the Federal mine approached the defender's lines, several Confederate countermines were sunk. When these exploratory efforts did not intersect the tunnel, the Confederates stopped countermining. Nevertheless, in light of the situation, Union success was far from being assured.[29]

After overcoming all obstacles, the men of the 48th Pennsylvania completed the tunnel on July 23. Because Grant did not want the mine to be used immediately, however, the gunpowder was set aside for later use. Still believing that the mine should be detonated only as a last resort, the Commanding General asked Meade for his analysis of the operation. Meade answered that he did not have any doubts that the mine could be exploded successfully. But the ridge behind the enemy's front was still a puzzle. Meade had examined the ground, and could not detect a second line of defense on the hill. The Confederates were not stupid, however, so they must have earthworks on the crest that were too well disguised to be seen from the Union lines. Meade concluded that although Lee's men could easily be forced out of their first line of defense by the mine's explosion and the subsequent infantry assault, the concealed second line probably could not be carried. However, he was prepared to attack if ordered to do so.[30]

While Grant authorized Meade to have the mine charged with gunpowder, he did not set the date for exploding the charge. First, he wanted to try another plan. Major General Winfield S. Hancock's II Corps and two divisions of cavalry were ordered north across the James River. Grant hoped that they might surprise the Confederates southeast of Richmond. Just after dark on July 26, Hancock's command crossed the Appomattox River. *(See Atlas Map No. 54a)*. The route they followed was marked by fires that Butler's men had set to serve as guiding beacons. Crossing the James at Deep Bottom, Hancock launched an attack on the morning of the twenty-seventh.

Initially, the II Corps made some progress, capturing four Confederate guns. Driving the enemy hard, the Federals advanced until they struck a more formidable line located along the banks of a creek. The Confederates had excellent fields of fire—in some places, the terrain was open for almost 1,000 meters—and thus forced Hancock to try a new approach. During the night of July 27, he directed Major General Philip H. Sheridan to use his two divisions of cavalry to turn the enemy out of their position. When dawn broke, however,

Sheridan discovered that the maneuver would be impossible. The Confederates, now heavily reinforced, were moving to turn the cavalry's flank. *(Movement not shown on map.)* Fighting a defensive battle for the next two days, Hancock carefully withdrew across the James River; on the night of the twenty-ninth, he rejoined the Army of the Potomac at Petersburg.[31]

Hancock's operation, however, was not a complete failure. Although he had been unable to mount a surprise attack on Richmond, he had caused Lee to reinforce his army north of the James River. As a result, the forces confronting Meade at Petersburg had been weakened. This created a favorable opportunity to explode the mine in front of Burnside's IX Corps. Grant wanted Hancock's corps to dash back south and support the attack after the mine was detonated. But when Hancock indicated that his corps would not be able to respond as quickly as Grant had hoped, July 30 was set as the date for the great experiment.

A deception operation was mounted to try to mask the location of Burnside's assault. It was hoped that the Confederates still believed that the Federals were reinforcing Hancock's attack north of the James. To support this notion, Sheridan covered the bridge across the river with hay and secretly crossed a cavalry division to the south bank during the night of the twenty-eighth. After daylight the next morning—and in full view of the watching Confederates—the same cavalry division marched, dismounted, across the bridge. Hopefully, the southerners would think that the Federals were reinforcing the position at Deep Bottom with infantry.

Other details were also carefully worked out. Burnside selected a division of black soldiers to lead the assault after the explosion. Because these men had not taken part in the continuous fighting that Burnside's corps had faced since crossing the Rappahannock River in May, the division—rested, and near its authorized strength—would make an excellent spearhead for the assault. Moreover, these troops had carefully rehearsed their role in the operation: following the explosion, they were to advance across the field, bypass the hole left in the ground by the explosion, flank the remaining sections of the Confederate line, and advance to seize the hill behind the enemy's front.

Then, inexplicably, Meade refused to endorse the division Burnside had chosen to lead the assault. While Burnside had touted the freshness of the troops, Meade claimed that the men's inexperience would make them undependable under fire. He made it clear that he wanted Burnside's best troops in the van.

Burnside was thunderstruck. There were just 12 hours left before the attack was to commence. Unable to convince Meade to change his mind, Burnside gathered his three remaining division commanders together and had them draw straws to see who would lead the attack. Brigadier General James H. Ledlie "won."[32]

Meade talked with each of Burnside's division commanders on the evening of July 29. He emphasized that the ridge behind the Confederate trenches was the key to the entire operation. The division commanders must make every effort to seize the crest before the enemy had a chance to react. The surprise of the exploding mine and the ferocity of the assault should provide the soldiers with sufficient time to win the hill. Additionally, the men must avoid crowding around the crater that would be created by the explosion. Convinced that Burnside's commanders knew what needed to be done, Meade returned to his headquarters to draw up his final orders.

Meade's plan was simple. Hancock's corps, just returned from its attack across the James, would take up the positions now occupied by Major General Edward Ord's XVIII Corps. *(See Atlas Map No.54.)* This would free Ord's men to cover the flank of the IX Corps, which was to make the main attack. From its position on the other flank of Burnside's troops, the V Corps would launch a supporting attack. Thus, the security of both flanks of the IX Corps would be insured. Sheridan was directed to attack Petersburg from the south and, if possible, from the west. As soon as the mine exploded, every available artillery piece would open fire and cover the advance of the infantry. Burnside was directed to prepare exits in his parapets—they were over eight feet high in some places—and to clear the abatis from his front so that the advancing troops would not be hindered as they moved toward the enemy trenches. Meade concluded his order with a call for cooperation between all of the commanders. After obtaining Grant's approval of the order, Meade went to bed "not sanguine of success."[33]

Early on the morning of July 30, Grant and Meade met at the IX Corps headquarters. Burnside had gone forward to watch the assault. At 3:30 a.m., the time designated for the detonation, the mine remained silent. With some trepidation, a soldier crawled into the tunnel to find out what had gone wrong. He discovered that the fuse had burned out at a splice. After relighting the fuse, he hurried to the rear. The mine exploded at 4:45 a.m.

It was a "dull sounding explosion, like a heavy gun, far away."[34] The sky was filled with men, cannon, and debris. Instead of a tidal wave of blue coats sweeping forward to exploit the advantage, however, the IX Corps advanced in driblets. Surprised by the force of the explosion, the men hesitated momentarily. Then they began scrambling over the edge of their parapets and picking their way through the abatis that protected their front. Because the positions had not been prepared in accordance with Meade's instructions, the attack was disorganized from the start.

When the advancing troops reached the crater, they stopped to peer in. Some soldiers went down into the hole * and started to dig up the Confederate guns buried by the explosion. Others helped some of the enemy wounded, but most began milling around in confusion. The hill behind the Confederate lines was silent. The ridge that Meade had puzzled over was empty—the Confederates did not have a second line of defense! Without orders, however, the Union troops remained around, and in, the crater. Quickly, the defenders recovered from their initial shock and began firing at the blue-clad mob in their midst. The crater then became a shelter for the Federal soldiers, and any hope for success disappeared into the hole in the ground. Someone needed to take charge.[35]

The senior Union commanders knew that something had gone wrong. Burnside and all of his division commanders, safe within their own lines, tried to get the assault restarted. At a little after 8:00 a.m., Brigadier General Edward Ferrero's black division from the IX Corps was moved forward, followed by an attack by part of the XVIII Corps. The additional troops only added more bodies to the traffic jam around the crater. At 9:15 a.m., another brigade was funneled into the confused crowd. Meade and Grant tried to find out what was happening. Dispatch riders rushed back and forth. Meade demanded to know the ''whole truth'' about the success of the attack.

Burnside's pride had been hurt. It appeared that Meade was accusing him of lying. He fired off a message to Meade: ''Were it not insubordinate I would say that the latter remark [concerning the ''whole truth''] of your note was unofficerlike and ungentlemanly.''[36]

While the generals argued, the Confederates counterattacked. Disorganized and demoralized, the Federals beat a hasty retreat through a withering fire. The Battle of the Crater was over—but the dispute was just starting. On August 1, Grant wired Meade and asked him if he knew the reason for the failure of the July 30 assault. It looked to him as though the best chance for breaking through the Confederate lines had just passed. Meade answered by stating that the IX Corps commander had failed to keep him properly informed of the progress of the battle. Furthermore, Burnside had been insubordinate, accusing Meade of ''unofficerlike and ungentlemanly'' conduct. For these reasons, the commander of the Army of the Potomac asked that Burnside be relieved from command of the IX Corps.

Without affixing any blame, Grant ordered that Burnside take a leave of absence and directed that Major General John G. Parke assume command of the IX Corps. Moreover, Grant appointed a court of inquiry to investigate the events of July 30. After 17 days of testimony, the court decided that the

*The crater measured 120 feet by 50 feet and was 25 feet deep.

blame for the failure was shared by many officers. Burnside had failed to completely follow Meade's orders; Ledlie had failed to exercise personal command of his division and, in fact, had hidden in a bombproof and drunk rum during part of the battle; Ferrero was blamed for not accompanying his troops during the attack, and two brigade commanders were similarly criticized. As a final note, the court mentioned that Meade should have appointed one officer to oversee the whole operation, since he was not present to direct it personally.[37]

The court's criticisms were responsible indictments of the Army of the Potomac's actions. The one thread that ran through all of the charges was that no senior officers had been present at the scene of battle. At the one place where high-level leadership was required, there were no high-level leaders. Consequently, the Federal units had turned into a mob. Despite the initial shock of the explosion, the Confederates had regained their composure, their organizational effectiveness, and their reputation for decisive action. They had won again.

Sheridan Devastates the Valley

Despite the Union's disheartening failure on the Petersburg front, the eastern Union forces finally achieved success on another front. Lieutenant General Jubal Early had created great consternation in mid-June when his Confederate corps advanced northward through the Shenandoah Valley and suddenly appeared in front of Washington. Early's raid had forced Grant to detach the VI Corps from its parent command in the Richmond area and send it to defend the capital. Although Major General Horatio G. Wright's men arrived in time to prevent a complete embarrassment of the Union leadership, Wright was unable to capture Early's force. The most important reason for the failure to catch Early's isolated corps was the Federal departmental organization in the area of Early's operations. The Confederates were maneuvering across the boundaries of four different Union departments: the Susquehanna, the Middle, the West Virginia, and the Washington. Grant was the only officer who was senior enough to coordinate the efforts of the departmental commanders. The Commanding General, however, was involved in the operations against Lee's army in the vicinity of Richmond and Petersburg.

In order to achieve unity of command, Grant recommended that the four departments be placed under the direction of one man, and that his command be called the Middle Military Division. Grant further recommended that Meade be given the new post.[38] Grant's organizational proposal was acceptable, but Meade's appointment was not. Lincoln rejected Meade's name because of the political situation. The radical Republicans were demanding the removal of Meade as commander of the Army of the Potomac. Although Lincoln had successfully resisted their efforts to date, if Meade was now reassigned as commander of the new Middle Military Division, the radical Republicans would appear to have gained a victory. Lincoln and Grant began discussing other men who might fill the post. Finally, they settled on a compromise candidate: Major General Philip H. Sheridan.

Sheridan was a good choice, as he was prepared to adopt the policy that Grant wanted pursued in the Valley. The Commanding General not only was concerned about eliminating Early's corps as a threat, but also wanted the Shenandoah Valley destroyed as a supply base for Richmond and as a route of invasion into Maryland. Used twice by Lee and once by Early, the Valley permitted an invader both to live off the land during passage and to debouch into the vulnerable areas of Maryland, Pennsylvania, and Virginia. During the initial pursuit of Early from Washington, Grant had mentioned that the pursuers should "eat out Virginia clear and clean as far as they go, so that crows flying over it for the balance of this season will have to carry their provender with them."[39] Unfortunately for the Federals, the man conducting that pursuit, Major General David Hunter, was not competent enough to accomplish the task. He embarked on a house-burning expedition that did nothing but incite the wrath of the civilian population. Moreover, his army was defeated in a counterattack by Early at Kernstown on July 24. Once more on the loose, Early sent a column into Pennsylvania, and on July 30, his troops burned Chambersburg in retaliation. The situation again was critical. Clearly, Sheridan would have to do a great deal of work before the threat would be eliminated.[40]

On August 6, Sheridan arrived to take command of his new organization. Four days after his arrival, he started southward. *(See Atlas Map No. 56.)* Expecting reinforcements from the Richmond-Petersburg defenses, Early fell back toward Strasburg. Taking up the pursuit, Sheridan reached Cedar Creek on August 12, and two days later learned that a sizable force had been detached from Lee's army and was heading for the Valley. Unsure of the Confederate strength and the terrain over which he was operating, Sheridan withdrew to Winchester. On the way back, the Federals destroyed all of the wheat and hay that they could find. Sheridan, however, was not satisfied with his position at Winchester. Continuing to withdraw northward, he finally stopped at Harper's Ferry. Early tried to catch the retreating Union column, but Sheridan had too great a head start. Nevertheless, it looked as if Sheridan was having as much trouble in the Valley as had his predecessors.

However, there were some significant differences between Sheridan and those who had previously commanded Valley operations. Sheridan was able to convince Grant that his retreat had been conducted for sound military reasons, and not because he had been beaten or even because he had lost his

courage. Thus, he was retained in command. Another difference, of course, was Sheridan's concentration on the Valley's agricultural resources. During his retreat, he had destroyed as much grain as possible, and his men had driven off a large number of cattle. There needed to be much more to the campaign, however, than simply an attack on Confederate resources. Thus, Sheridan's army was strengthened to improve his chances of gaining a victory over Early's reinforced corps. These reinforcements included the VI and XIX Corps, the Army of West Virginia (consisting of two infantry divisions), and a cavalry corps composed of three mounted divisions. Sheridan's Army of the Shenandoah now had a strength of 41,295 officers and men. Outnumbering Early's force of 18,911 by more than 2 to 1, Sheridan did not tarry in putting his enlarged force to good use.[41]

During the night of September 18, the Army of the Shenandoah moved south against Early's force, which was concentrated at Winchester. *(See Atlas Map No. 57.)* Contact was established at 5:00 a.m. on the nineteenth, and in the day-long battle that followed, Sheridan handed the Confederates a resounding defeat. The Battle of Winchester marked a final turning point in the war in the Valley; never would the Confederates regain their pre-eminence in the area. Early tried to halt the tide at Fisher's Hill, but on September 22, Sheridan again triumphed. *(See Atlas Map No. 57.)* Driven in panic for almost four miles, the Confederates finally restored some semblance of order and withdrew through New Market.

Upon hearing of the victories in the Valley, Grant urged Sheridan forward. He envisioned the army in the Valley continuing the pursuit and then crossing the mountains to destroy the railroads near Charlottesville. This would further reduce the supplies reaching the Confederates at Richmond and Petersburg. He also directed Sheridan to finish the crop destruction begun earlier and to carry off all of the livestock and liberate the slaves. "We want the Shenandoah Valley to remain a barren waste," Grant wrote.[42]

The Army of the Shenandoah was better able to handle the second mission than the first. It went to work on the farms with a vengeance. Finding that he had outrun his own supplies, however, Sheridan could not completely carry out Grant's instructions. A movement across the mountains would be prohibitive because there was not enough transportation to support his army over that extended distance. He recommended to the Commanding General that once the crops had been destroyed, the Army of the Shenandoah should be broken up and the units sent to wherever they could do the most good. Grant accepted the suggestion.[43] The recommendation proved to be a bit premature, however.

Operations in the Valley were not over. On October 19, Early, again reinforced, launched a surprise attack against Sheridan's reduced-strength army at Cedar Creek. *(Action not shown on map.)* The final result, however, was really not in question. The Federals could afford to keep more troops in the Valley than the Confederates were able to muster. Under Sheridan's able leadership, the Army of the Shenandoah won again, and the fate of the Shenandoah Valley was sealed. The remnants of Early's force now were nothing more than an annoyance. Sheridan's aggressiveness and unrelenting war on Confederate resources had paid dividends and permanently eliminated the Valley as a source of Union embarrassment.

Thrust and Parry Without Decision

On the main front in the East, the drudgery of siege warfare continued unabated from August 1864 to March 1865. In August, Grant once again mounted an operation against Petersburg's railroads. *(See Atlas Map No. 54b.)* Warren's V Corps attacked the Weldon and held it north of Globe Tavern. Lieutenant General A.P. Hill's corps counterattacked, driving the Federals southward and away from Petersburg, but the Union soldiers managed to retain their hold in the vicinity of the Tavern. On August 25, a more serious setback occurred when the Confederates attacked Hancock's II Corps near Ream's Station. *(Action not shown on map.)* Over 2,000 Federal soldiers were taken prisoner as Hancock's men fled in panic before the furious assault. Additionally, the Confederates managed to bypass the roadblock established by Warren. After supplies had been transferred from railcars to wagons at a point 20 miles south of Petersburg, the wagons proceeded along backroads around the Union left. Still, the Confederate supply situation was critical.[44] Major General Wade Hampton brought relief on September 17, however, when he mounted a raid around the Federal western flank and succeeded in capturing over 2,400 head of cattle, which disappeared quickly into the stomachs of Lee's hungry men.

Toward the end of the month, Meade responded to the Confederate initiative with another drive toward the railroads. He ran into a strong Confederate force near Peeble's Farm. From September 29 to October 2, the battle raged back and forth. When it was over, the Federal line was three miles longer than before. Again, at the end of October, the Army of the Potomac moved west to sever Petersburg's life lines. *(See Atlas Map No. 55a.)* Although on October 27 the Union army was prevented from severing the Boydton Plank Road near Burgess Mill, the constant pressure continued. During the three-day period beginning on February 5, the Federals fought another battle to seize the Boydton Plank Road. Although unable to hold the road for more than two days, the Union army now occupied trenches that extended for more than 37 miles. Lee's lines were stretched thin, and with the advent of spring, Grant hoped to deliver the final blow to the

Sheridan and His Key Commanders (*Left to Right:* Merritt, Sheridan, Crook, Forsyth, and Custer)

Army of Northern Virginia.[45] In this effort, he would receive help from an unexpected source.

Grant had directed Sheridan to move out of the Valley, proceed southward, and join Sherman's army, which was now in the Carolinas. When Sheridan reached the James River near Lynchburg, however, he found that he could not cross. Heavy rains had fallen throughout most of the winter, and the river was swollen. In addition, the Confederates had destroyed all of the bridges in the area. Deciding that his best move would be to join Grant's forces, Sheridan notified the Commanding General of his change in plans. As Grant did not question Sheridan's judgment, the cavalry from the Valley joined the armies in front of Petersburg on March 27.

Grant had decided to wait for the arrival of Sheridan's force before opening the spring campaign. Not only did he want the additional combat power that Sheridan would bring, but he also wanted to delay the war of movement in order to insure the destruction of Lee's army. Convinced that Lee would evacuate the Richmond-Petersburg defenses and try to move south to join Johnston's army, Grant needed more time to extend the left of the Army of the Potomac to the west, thus cutting Lee off from any good routes leading south. On March 24, Grant issued the order that was designed to prevent the joining of Lee's and Johnston's armies.[46]

Two corps from the Army of the Potomac were to leave the trenches of Petersburg and move west to Dinwiddie Court House on March 29. *(See Atlas Map No. 55b.)* Ord and three infantry divisions were to follow close behind. Sheridan, under the direct control of the Commanding General, was ordered to move his cavalry west of Petersburg and Richmond; he was to sever the last two rail lines leading into the cities. Effectively sealed off from his supplies and partially blocked from moving south, Lee would then be forced to flee west. At the same time, Grant hoped that Lee would leave his trenches and attack the Union forces. The two corps from Meade's army were bait. Hopefully, Lee would strip his trenches and move most of his force out to ambush the shifting column of Federals. With minimum strength in the Confederate trenches, Grant felt that he could overpower the remaining defenders. Grant told the corps and division commanders not to wait for orders; as soon as it became evident that the defenses had been weakened, they were to attack.[47]

In the meantime, Lee had already decided to attack. His lines were stretched too thin. By attacking a weak point in the Federal lines, he hoped to force Grant to shorten his lines. If a permanent rupture in the Union lines around Petersburg could be made, Meade would have to withdraw his left to prevent it from being isolated. This would buy time for Lee, who, as Grant had guessed, was considering the possibility of moving south to join Johnston. The entire plan was based on the assumption that Meade would simply withdraw his left to restore his lines. When Lee attacked on March 25, however, he found that this assumption was incorrect. *(Confederate attack not shown on map.)*

The Confederates achieved total surprise. Union Fort Stedman, the site chosen for the attack, fell easily to the early morning assault. Fanning out into the Federal rear, the Confederates tried to exploit their victory and destroy the enemy's lateral communications. The extent of the gamble, however, was quickly evident. Without having to ask Meade for help, the IX Corps commander easily contained the attack with some assistance from the V Corps. The rupture was sealed off, and Fort Stedman was retaken; 2,300 Confederate soldiers were captured in the exchange. Lee's last effort to regain the initiative had failed in the face of the overwhelming numbers opposing him.[48] Grant's plan to shift his forces to the west could now be implemented.

Five Forks

On the morning of March 29, Warren's V Corps, Humphreys' II Corps, elements of Ord's Army of the James, and Sheridan's cavalry began moving to the Union left.* *(See Atlas Map No. 55b.)* At the end of the first day's march, it began to rain,

ending the several days of dry weather that had improved the routes of march. Quickly, the roads turned to mud and the muck oozed over the shoes of the marching infantry. The teams of horses and artillery bogged down in the quagmire. Grant and Meade discussed suspending the operation until the weather turned more favorable. Sheridan, however, strongly urged Grant to continue the march. After much deliberation, Grant decided to proceed with the operation.

On the morning of the thirty-first, Confederates from Lieutenant General Richard Anderson's IV Corps† attacked Grant's vanguard under Warren. Lee had directed Anderson to attack in order to maintain a link between the Petersburg defenses and another Confederate force located near Five Forks. This second force, under Major General George E. Pickett, consisted of two infantry divisions and a cavalry corps. Pickett's men occupied a blocking position at Five Forks. This was a key location. As long as Lee held it, his escape routes to the west would remain open; if it fell, Lee's position would become more tenuous. When the Federal move to the west was detected, Lee reacted by ordering Anderson to counterattack.[49] *(See Atlas Map No. 55b.)*

Anderson's men struck while Warren's corps was still organized into a march column. The leading Union division fell back through the second division, and both units fled in confusion. Meade ordered Humphreys to support Warren. With this added help, the Confederates were pushed back to their original position by late afternoon. Nevertheless, more trouble lay ahead for the troops implementing Grant's plan. Sheridan's men ran into Pickett's blocking position near Five Forks and were repulsed. Again, the Federals retreated. Sheridan finally managed to stabilize his lines in the vicinity of Dinwiddie Court House.

When Meade heard of Sheridan's plight, he turned to Warren for help. The V Corps, having contained Anderson's attack, was close enough to support the Union position at Dinwiddie. Meade ordered Warren to send a brigade to Sheridan, but Grant, learning about Sheridan's setback, suggested to Meade that an entire division be sent to help the cavalryman. Meade countered with the proposal that the complete V Corps be sent in support. Grant agreed, and Warren was directed to move rapidly to help Sheridan. Although he knew that speed was essential, Warren carefully organized his march columns. Undoubtedly, he remembered the embarrassment caused by Andeson's attack, and was in no hurry to repeat the same mistake. His advance also was briefly frustrated by a destroyed bridge along his route. After rebuilding the structure, the V

---

*Hancock, the former commander of the II Corps, had been replaced by Meade's chief of staff, Major General Andrew A. Humphreys, in November 1864. Hancock's Gettysburg wound was bothering him, and he was offered the chance to go to the rear to recruit a new corps. He accepted. The troublesome Major General Benjamin F. Butler finally had been eased out of command of the Army of the James in January. Ord had replaced him.

†The IV Corps had been formed during the winter months. Anderson had commanded the I Corps while Longstreet was recuperating from the wound he received in the Wilderness. When Longstreet returned to duty, Lee formed a new corps and gave it to Anderson. This permitted Anderson to retain the rank of lieutenant general that had been given to him during his tenure as temporary commander of the I Corps.

Corps moved forward and joined Sheridan's force on the morning of April 1. *(See Atlas Map No. 55b.)*

Sheridan was in a bad temper. He had been expecting Warren's men since the previous night. Grant had assured him that the V Corps would arrive by midnight. Thus, when one of Grant's aides arrived to tell Sheridan that he could relieve Warren if he thought that it was necessary, Sheridan's anger became channeled toward a specific end. A successful fight at Five Forks and the capture of several thousand prisoners did not assuage his anger. When the battle was over and Warren sent an aide to Sheridan to report the V Corps' success, the aide was shocked by Sheridan's explosion: "Tell General Warren, I say, by God, he was not at the front. That's all I've got to say to him!"[50] He then handed the aide an order addressed to Warren that relieved him from command.

Warren's relief was a severe blow to the V Corps commander, who spent most of the rest of his life trying to redeem his good name. A formal court of inquiry was finally convened in 1881, and Warren's performance at the Battle of Five Forks was examined in detail. In its findings, the court could discover little fault with Warren's actions. In 1865, however, Warren was in no position to defend his actions. In 1863, he had ruined the Mine Run Campaign by deciding at the last minute that he could not attack. In the Wilderness, Meade's headquarters had noted that Warren was not performing well as a corps commander. At Spotsylvania, Grant had seen that Warren was unable to coordinate the efforts of his corps, and had told Meade to relieve Warren if the trouble continued. In the operations near Petersburg on June 17, 1864, Warren had been slow to get his attack started. Four days later, Meade had prepared a letter to Grant's chief of staff, requesting that Warren be relieved of command. Although Meade finally decided not to submit the request, by the time of the Battle of Five Forks, there were no more chances remaining for Warren.[51]

The Final Days

Sheridan's victory at Five Forks gave Grant the confidence he needed. Reasoning that Lee's army must be too extended to protect Petersburg, he ordered Meade to have the VI and IX Corps assault the trenches. Later that evening, however, he had second thoughts. Perhaps Lee still had enough combat power to protect the city. When he discussed this possibility with Meade, the commander of the Army of the Potomac assured Grant that the time for direct action had finally arrived. To add weight to his argument, Meade sent the Commanding General a copy of Wright's answer to the attack order: "The Corps will go in solid, and I am sure will make the fur fly. . . . If the corps does half as well as I expect we will

have broken through the rebel lines fifteen minutes from the word 'go'."[52] This was all the reassurance that Grant needed. He directed the frontal assault to commence on the following morning, April 2.

At the sound of a signal gun fired from Fort Fisher at 4:30 a.m., the blue columns moved forward in the early morning darkness. *(Federal attack not shown on map.)* The VI and IX Corps quickly swept aside the Confederate first line of defense, but Parke's IX Corps met heavier resistance in a second line. Wright, on the other hand, did not meet a second line, and continued to advance. Meade ordered Parke's reserves to support the VI Corps' success, and then told Humphreys to move the II Corps forward. It was all over in a short time; the majority of Wright's casualties occurred within the first 15 minutes of the fighting. Lee's position at Petersburg was untenable.

Realizing that the situation was hopeless, Lee notified the Confederate President that he was going to evacuate Richmond and Petersburg during the night of April 2. With barely 30,000 men left in the Army of Northern Virginia, Lee hoped to escape westward to avoid Grant's trap, and then turn southward to join Johnston's army. By midnight, the army had successfully cleared the cities and begun to thread its way along the banks of the Appomattox River. *(See Atlas Map No. 58.)* Behind it, the Federals could almost smell the final victory.[53]

Essentially, the classic Union pursuit was conducted along two roads that paralleled the Appomattox River. In the van of the northern column, Sheridan moved with his cavalry and the V Corps. Behind them, Meade rode with the II and VI Corps. Along the southern route, Ord's divisions from the Army of the James and Parke's IX Corps maintained a rapid pace. *(See Atlas Map No. 58.)* In order to move south to join Johnston, Lee would have to avoid both columns. The Confederates' most likely escape route was along the Richmond and Danville Railroad, which was blocked as a direct consequence of Grant's skill in directing the movements of his three independent commanders—Meade, Sheridan, and Ord.

Beginning his advance early, Meade pushed his men hard to reach the railroad ahead of Lee. Sheridan and the V Corps already were in position along the tracks, southwest of Amelia Court House. At 2:00 p.m. on April 5, Meade reached Sheridan's headquarters. Quickly, the II and VI Corps were placed beside Sheridan's waiting troopers. Meade, certain that the Confederates were to his front, planned to attack on the morning of the sixth. Lee, however, had learned that the Richmond and Danville Railroad was blocked; consequently, he turned his column west at Amelia Court House. *(See Atlas Map No. 58.)* Shortly thereafter, he again turned south, only to learn that although he had avoided Sheridan and Meade, the second column under Ord stood between him and Johnston. The noose was tightening: Lee's army had Ord and Parke to its front, while Meade, having learned of Lee's new route, was exerting pressure on the Confederate rear guard.

As a result of the confusion and disorder that accompanied Lee's desperate flight westward, his army had been split into two groups. In order to clear the road for the infantry, the supply wagons had been diverted to a different route. Not realizing that the trains were following a new road, the rear guard followed the wagons instead of the main body. In close pursuit, Humphreys moved his II Corps after the trains, while Sheridan and Wright, on the trail of the main body, moved in for the kill. Along Sayler's Creek, they found their quarry. *(See Atlas Map No. 58.)* Sheridan attacked from the south and Wright moved in from the east. The Confederates counterattacked, but it was a useless gesture. Sheridan estimated that he had captured 6 general officers and approximately 9,500 other prisoners. Upon learning of the disaster, Lee realized that his fighting strength had been cut in half.[54]

Operations on the seventh followed the pattern of a disorderly retreat and an aggressive pursuit. Lee knew that his only chance to escape depended on crossing to the north bank of the Appomattox River. Having crossed the river, he could burn the bridges behind him and march to Lynchburg, where he would be able to feed and rest his weary troops. The Federals knew that they must not let Lee destroy the bridges. Humphreys' corps followed Lee's army closely enough to prevent the loss of one bridge, but when Wright tried to cross at Farmville, he discovered that the bridge there had been destroyed. *(See Atlas Map No. 57.)* That night, Grant sent Lee a letter:

> The result of the last week must convince you of the hopelessness of further resistance. . . . I feel that it is so, and regard it as my duty to shift from myself the responsibility of any further effusion of blood by asking of you the surrender of that portion of the C.S. Army known as the Army of Northern Virginia.[55]

Apparently, Lee did not immediately share Grant's views. After asking what terms the Federal Government would offer, he pushed the remnants of his army toward Lynchburg. Throughout April 8, the Confederates marched rapidly; to their rear, however, Humphreys' II Corps marched equally fast. South of Lee's column, Sheridan and Ord approached Appomattox Court House. *(See Atlas Map No. 58.)* One of Sheridan's division commanders, Major General George A. Custer, captured a supply train at Appomattox Station. With the ring closing around the Army of Northern Virginia, Lee realized that few alternatives remained.

The correspondence between Lee and Grant continued. In response to Lee's request for surrender terms, Grant replied that he did not have the authority to offer specific conditions. His main object was to convince the Confederates to lay down their arms. When Lee read this last dispatch, he decided that the time had come for an interview. He asked Grant to meet him and, in a later dispatch, requested that the firing be

The McLean House, With Members of the Family Sitting on the Porch

stopped until the meeting had taken place. The Army of the Potomac was forming a line of battle for the final assault, and Lee wanted to avoid more bloodshed.[56]

Although Grant had agreed to an interview with Lee, Meade did not realize that a meeting was going to take place. He was with the II Corps, while Grant was with Sheridan's column. Meade had his first hint that something was afoot when a white flag appeared in the Confederate lines. Humphreys, suspecting a ruse, ordered his corps to receive the flag and then to push their skirmishers forward. Meade, also, was not sure of the sincerity of the request for a cease-fire. He was about to order a general attack when a member of Sheridan's staff rode out from the Confederate line. Meade learned that Lee and Grant were meeting at Appomattox Court House.[57]

The meeting at the McLean House in Appomattox was a quiet affair. Officers on both sides realized the significance of the occasion; there were few outbursts. Lee, having rejected an appeal by some of his subordinates that the Confederates switch to guerrilla warfare, was resplendent in his finest uniform. Grant, spattered with mud and wearing no sidearms,

quietly wrote out the only terms that he could offer: the Army of Northern Virginia must lay down its arms and park its artillery; the officers could keep their weapons and their horses, but all other implements of war now belonged to the United States Government. When this was accomplished, the Confederates could "return to their homes, not to be disturbed by United States authority so long as they observe their paroles and the laws in force where they may reside."[58] Lee accepted the terms.

For all intents and purposes, the war was over. As mentioned previously, Lee's surrender prompted Johnston to act similarly at Raleigh, North Carolina. Although Jefferson Davis and a few of his governmental servants continued their flight across Georgia, they were captured by Federal cavalrymen near Irwinsville.

While the war of bullets had ended, the war of words had just begun. Countless authors started to analyze the causes of the war and the reasons for the Confederate defeat. Myths and legends grew, while heroes and villains were singled out. In the midst of all of the colorful arguments about who was

© National Geographic Society

Lee and Grant Come to Terms at the McLean House in Appomattox (*Left to Right:* Lee, Marshall, Sheridan, Babcock, Porter, Ord, Grant, Williams, Bowers, Parker, and Custer)

the greatest general and which were the pivotal battles, however, some valuable military lessons were identified.

Observers from many European armies had come to America to view the war, to learn the appropriate lessons, and to return home with some pertinent conclusions. The ideas about waging war that they took home, however, were soon overshadowed by the lessons that observers thought they saw illustrated in the Franco-Prussian War of 1870–1871. The world's great military thinkers focused their attention on the Prussian way of war, while the American Civil War slipped into the background. Perhaps, though, the British were able to use some of the information they gained on the use of volunteer armies. In addition, France's interest in the organization and administration of the Union Army may have influenced some thinkers in that country. The Prussians, too, may

have learned something from the way American railroads were maintained and repaired during the war. For the most part, however, the American Civil War did not influence the development of European military doctrine.[59]

Years later, the tragedy of World War I revealed some similarities between the Civil War's tactical and technological lessons and the sobering military developments that produced the deadlock on the Western Front. Once again, armies saw demonstrated the ascendency of the rifle bullet, the futility of the bayonet assault, the superiority of the defense, the use of field fortifications and trench warfare, the failure of the mounted cavalry attack, and the stalemate induced by technological change. In 1865, however, there was only one obvious conclusion—the United States had achieved national unity by the force of arms. It remained for the people to heal the scars.

Notes

[1]William T. Sherman, *Memoirs of General William T. Sherman* (2 vols.; New York, 1875), II, 137–140.

[2]John B. Hood, *Advance and Retreat* (New Orleans, 1880), pp. 252–253; *The War of the Rebellion: A Compilation of the Official Records of the Union and Confederate Armies* (130 vols.; Washington, 1890–1901), Series I, XXXIX, Pt. 2, 862. (Hereinafter cited as *OR*. Unless otherwise indicated, all subsequent references to the *OR* are to Series I.)

[3]*OR*, XXXIX, Pt. 2, 832; Nathaniel C. Hughes, *General William J. Hardee: Old Reliable* (Baton Rouge, 1965), pp. 247–248.

[4]T. Harry Williams, *P.G.T. Beauregard: Napoleon in Gray* (Baton Rouge, 1955), pp. 241–242; *OR*, XXXIX, Pt. 3, 804–805.

[5]Thomas L. Connelly, *Autumn of Glory: The Army of Tennessee, 1862–1865* (Baton Rouge, 1971), pp. 481–483; Williams, *Beauregard*, pp. 243–244

[6]Hood, *Advance and Retreat*, p. 270; Stanley F. Horn, *The Army of Tennessee* (New York, 1941), pp. 380–382.

[7]*OR*, XXXIX, Pt. 3, 3, 162; Lloyd Lewis, *Sherman, Fighting Prophet* (New York, 1932), p. 425; Sherman, *Memoirs*, II, 166.

[8]Shelby Foote, *The Civil War: A Narrative* (3 vols.; New York, 1958–1974), III, 318; *OR*, XXX, Pt. 3, 698.

[9]*OR*, XXXVIII, Pt. 5, 794.

[10]*Ibid.*, XXXIX, Pt. 3, 202; Lewis, *Sherman*, p. 430.

[11]*OR*, XXXIX, Pt. 3, 162, 594.

[12]*Ibid.*, 882–883, 887, 891, 904, 917–918; Jacob D. Cox, *The Battle of Franklin* (New York, 1897), pp. 9–11, 26; Connelly, *Autumn of Glory*, pp. 491–492, 500–501.

[13]Paul E. Steiner, *Medical-Military Portraits of Union and Confederate Generals* (Philadelphia, 1968), pp. 225, 228; Stanley F. Horn, *The Decisive Battle of Nashville* (Baton Rouge, 1956), p. 19.

[14]Connelly, *Autumn of Glory*, pp. 502–506; Cox, *Battle of Franklin*, p. 15; *OR*, XLV, Pt. 2, 643–644.

[15]Hood, *Advance and Retreat*, pp., 299–300.

[16]Horn, *Battle of Nashville*, pp. 69–70; Thomas L. Livermore, *Numbers and Losses in the Civil War in America, 1861–1865* (Boston, 1901), pp. 132–133; *OR*, XLV, Pt. 1, 115–116, 143, 180, 195.

[17]Jacob D. Cox, *The March to the Sea: Franklin and Nashville* (New York, 1882), p. 104; Horn, *Battle of Nashville*, pp. 34–35.

[18]Cox, *March to the Sea*, pp. 107–112; Horn, *Battle of Nashville*, pp. 76–77; *OR*, XLV, Pt. 2, 194.

[19]Cox, *March to the Sea*, pp. 126–127; *OR*, XLV, Pt. 2, 799; Pt. 1, 728.

[20]Connelly, *Autumn of Glory*, pp. 512–514; *OR*, XLV, Pt. 2, 781; Cox, *March to the Sea*, pp. 126, 129.

[21]Connelly, *Autumn of Glory*, p. 502.

[22]*OR*, XXXIX, Pt. 3, 660.

[23]Sherman, *Memoirs*, II, 176–177, 231; Cox, *March to the Sea*, pp. 21–24; Earl S. Miers, *The General Who Marched to Hell* (New York, 1951), pp. 271–272.

[24]E. Merton Coulter, *The Confederate State of America, 1861–1865* (Baton Rouge, 1950), pp. 268, 119; James P. Jones, *Yankee Blitzkrieg* (Athens, Ga., 1976), pp. 172–175.

[25]Regis De Trobriand, *Four Years With the Army of the Potomac* (Boston, 1889), p. 626.

[26]Thomas Weber, *The Northern Railroads in the Civil War* (New York, 1952), p. 171.

[27]Andrew A. Humphreys, *The Virginia Campaign of '64 and '65* (New York, 1883), pp. 227–229; *OR*, XL, Pt. 1, 326–327; Philip H. Sheridan, *Personal Memoirs of P.H. Sheridan* (2 vols.; New York, 1888), I, 438–439, 444.

[28]Horace Porter, *Campaigning With Grant* (Bloomington, Ind., 1961), p. 372.

[29]*OR*, XL, Pt. 2, 600, 285; Allen Nevins (ed.), *A Diary of Battle: The Personal Journals of Colonel Charles S. Wainwright* (New York, 1962), p. 439.

[30]*OR*, XL, Pt. 3, 424–425.

[31]*Ibid.*, Pt. 1, 308–311.

[32]Sheridan, *Memoirs*, I, 450; *OR*, XL, Pt. 1, 46, 59–61.

[33]Humphreys, *Virginia Campaign*, p. 254; David S. Sparks (ed.), *Inside Lincoln's Army: The Diary of Marsena Rudolph Patrick, Provost Marshal General, Army of the Potomac* (New York, 1964), p. 404; Meade to his corps commanders, July 29, 1864, in National Archives, Record Group 108, Box 85; George Meade (ed.), *The Life and Letters of George Gordon Meade* (2 vols.; New York, 1913), II, 217.

[34]George R. Agassiz (ed.), *Meade's Headquarters, 1863–1865: Letters of Colonel Theodore Lyman* (Boston, 1922), p. 198.

[35]Nevins, *Journals of Colonel Wainwright*, p. 449; Adam Badeau, *Military History of Ulysses S. Grant* (3 vols.; New York, 1885), II, 483–484.

[36]Agassiz, *Meade's Headquarters*, pp. 199–201; *OR*, XL, Pt. 3, 600.

[37]*OR*, XL, Pt. 1, 119, 128–129.

[38]*OR*, XXXVII, Pt. 2, 433.

[39]Sparks, *Inside Lincoln's Army*, pp. 409–410; Freeman Cleaves, *Meade of Gettysburg* (Norman, Okla., 1960), p. 285; *OR*, XXXVII, Pt. 2, 301.

[40]Edward H. Phillips, *The Shenandoah Valley in 1864: An Episode in the History of Warfare* (Charleston, 1965), pp. 12–14; Jubal A. Early, *Autobiographical Sketch and Narrative of the War Between the States* (Philadelphia, 1912), pp. 399–405.

[41]George T. Stevens, *Three Years in the Sixth Corps* (Albany, 1866), p. 387; Livermore, *Numbers and Losses*, p. 127; George E. Pond, *The Shenandoah Valley in 1864* (New York, 1883), pp. 120–128; *OR*, XLIII, Pt. 1, 792.

[42]*OR*, XLIII, Pt. 2, 177, 202.

[43]*Ibid.*, 163, 210, 249.

[44]Badeau, *Military History of U.S. Grant*, II, 514–522; Francis A. Walker, *History of the Second Army Corps in the Army of the Potomac* (New York, 1891), pp. 601–602.

[45]Porter, *Campaigning With Grant*, pp. 209–212; letter, General Meade to Mrs. Meade, October 27, 1864, in Historical Society of Pennsylvania, The George G. Meade Collection, Box 6. (Hereinafter cited as Meade Collection.)

[46]Sheridan, *Memoirs*, II, 124–125; Jesse G. Cramer (ed.), *Letters of Ulysses S. Grant to his Father and his Youngest Sister, 1857–1878* (New York, 1912), pp. 106–107; Humphreys, *Virginia Campaign*, p. 316.

[47]Grant to Meade, March 24, 1865, in Meade Collection, Box 3.

[48]Armistead L. Long, *Memoirs of Robert E. Lee* (New York, 1886), pp. 404–405; John B. Gordon, *Reminiscences of the Civil War* (New York, 1903), p. 403; Douglas Southall Freeman, *Lee's Lieutenants: A Study in Command* (3 vols.; New York, 1942), III, 648–650.

[49]Sheridan, *Memoirs*, II, 145; Freeman, *Lee's Lieutenants*, III, 664–665; Agassiz, *Meade's Headquarters*, pp. 331–332.

[50]*OR*, XLVI, Pt. 3, 338, 340–342, 363, 420; Porter, *Campaigning With Grant*, p. 435; Emerson G. Taylor, *Gouverneur Kemble Warren* (New York, 1932), p. 222.

[51]Taylor, *Warren*, pp. 224–226, 241–247; Agassiz, *Meade's Headquarters*, p. 110; *OR*, XXXVI, Pt. 2, 654; Meade to Rawlins, June 21, 1864, in Meade Collection, Box 3.

[52]*OR*, XLVI, Pt. 3, 397–399, 407, 423, 456–457.

[53]Agassiz, *Meade's Headquarters*, p. 333; Stevens, *Three Years in the Sixth Corps*, p. 434; Long, *Memoirs of Lee*, pp. 409–410.

[54]Cleaves, *Meade of Gettysburg*, pp. 324–325; Freeman, *Lee's Lieutenants*, III, 707; Sheridan, *Memoirs*, II, 185–186.

[55]Bruce Catton, *Grant Takes Command* (Boston, 1969), p. 455; Humphreys, *Virginia Campaign*, p. 387; *OR*, XLVI, Pt. 3, 619.

[56]*OR*, XLVI, Pt. 3, 619, 664.

[57]Agassiz, *Meade's Headquarters*, p. 356–357.

[58]*OR*, XLVI, Pt. 3, 665–666.

[59]Jay Luvaas, *The Military Legacy of the Civil War: The European Inheritance* (Chicago, 1959), pp. 226–227.

Selected Bibliography

General

Alexander, E. Porter. *Military Memoirs of a Confederate*. Bloomington, Ind., 1962. Includes excellent descriptions of the use of Confederate artillery as well as firsthand accounts of the important battles.

Basler, Roy (ed.). *The Collected Works of Abraham Lincoln*. 9 vols. Rutgers, 1953. Contains letters and speeches that are annotated by the editor.

Benet, Stephen Vincent. *John Brown's Body*. New York, 1973. An epic of the war.

Boatner, Mark M. *The Civil War Dictionary*. New York, 1959. A good ready reference on a myriad of Civil War topics.

Brodie, Bernard and Fawn Brodie. *From Crossbow to H-Bomb*. Bloomington, Ind., 1973. A classic work on the history of the technology of warfare.

Catton, Bruce. *Never Call Retreat*. New York, 1971. The second volume of Catton's trilogy on the Civil War.

Church, W.C. *Ulysses S. Grant and the Period of National Preservation and Reconstruction*. New York, 1897. Heavily biased in favor of Grant.

Commager, Henry Steele (ed.). *The Blue and the Gray*. Indianapolis, 1950. A good collection of contemporary writings by participants on both sides.

Connelly, Thomas L. *Autumn of Glory: The Army of Tennessee, 1862–1865*. Baton Rouge, La., 1971. Very critical, well-researched analysis of the South's central army.

Connelly, Thomas L. and Archer Jones. *The Politics of Command*. Baton Rouge, La., 1973. Helps to explain the antagonism between the eastern and western Confederate generals.

Copp, Elbridge J. *Reminiscences of the War of the Rebellion, 1861–1865*. Nashua, N.H., 1911. An acid attack on slavery and secession.

Coulter, E. Merton. *The Confederate States of America, 1861–1865*. Baton Rouge, La., 1950. The best study done on the non-military aspects of the Confederacy.

Cramer, Jesse G. (ed.). *Letters of Ulysses S. Grant to his Father and his Youngest Sister, 1857–1878*. New York, 1912. A very sparse collection of Grant's letters.

Dana, Charles A. *Recollections of the Civil War: With the Leaders at Washington and in the Field in the Sixties*. New York, 1898. Sent as a War Department agent to spy on Grant, Dana became an unbridled Grant convert.

Davis, Jefferson. *The Rise and Fall of the Confederate Government*. 2 vols. New York, 1881. This work seeks to explain the validity of secession and the defeat of the Confederacy.

Donald, David (ed.). *Why the North Won the Civil War*. Baton Rouge, La., 1960. An excellent collection of articles analyzing the reasons for the Confederate defeat.

Dyer, Frederick H. *A Compendium of the War of the Rebellion*. 3 vols. New York, 1959. A complete order of battle of the Federal Army.

Early, Jubal A. *Autobiographical Sketch and Narrative of the War Between the States*. Philadelphia, 1912. Good account of one Confederate division commander's view of the war. Adulatory of Lee.

Eaton, Clement. *A History of the Southern Confederacy*. New York, 1965. A good, concise, one-volume history of the Confederacy.

Fleharty, Stephen F. *Our Regiment: A History of the 102nd Illinois Infantry Volunteers*. Chicago, 1865. Good description of service in Sherman's army.

Foote, Shelby. *The Civil War: A Narrative*. 3 vols. New York, 1958–1974. An undocumented but exciting narrative of the war.

Freeman, Douglas Southall. *Lee's Lieutenants: A Study in Command*. 3 vols. New York, 1942. The classic work on the Army of Northern Virginia.

Henderson, George F.R. *The Civil War: A Soldier's View*. Ed. Jay Luvaas. Chicago, 1958. A British soldier's view of the war; full of perceptive insights.

Jones, Archer. *Confederate Strategy From Shiloh to Vicksburg*. Baton Rouge, La., 1961. The classic on Confederate strategy.

Jones, John B. *A Rebel War Clerk's Diary at the Confederate States Capital*. 2 vols. Philadelphia, 1866. One of the most frequently cited sources of information on life in the Confederate capital.

Livermore, Thomas L. *Numbers and Losses in the Civil War in America, 1861–1865*. Boston, 1901. A ready reference on battle losses.

Long, E.B. and Barbara Long. *The Civil War Day by Day: An Almanac, 1861–1865*. New York, 1971. A highly useful, accurate, and detailed reference.

Luvaas, Jay. *The Military Legacy of the Civil War: The European Inheritance*. Chicago, 1959. A well-researched analysis of the lessons learned by European observers of the war.

Malcolm, Neill (ed.). *The Science of War: A Collection of Essays and*

Lectures 1892–1903 by the Late Colonel G.F.R. Henderson, B.C. London, 1905. Contains an interesting comparison of the armies involved in the American Civil War and the Franco-Prussian War.

Meade, George (ed.). *The Life and Letters of George Gordon Meade.* 2 vols. New York, 1913. Many of Meade's letters to his wife give excellent insights into his relations with other generals.

Nevins, Allen (ed.). *The War for the Union.* 4 vols. New York, 1959–1971. Part of an eight-volume series, these books provide a sociopolitical account of the war. Weak on operational detail.

Official Records of the Union and Confederate Navies in the War of the Rebellion. 30 vols. Washington, D.C., 1894–1927. An exhaustive compilation of Civil War correspondence.

Paris, Comte de. *History of the Civil War in America.* Philadelphia, 1875. An excellent account of this French nobleman's service with the Union Army.

Parish, Peter J. *The American Civil War.* New York, 1975. This well-researched text, presenting a European's view of the Civil War, ranks with the best.

Ramsdell, Charles W. *Behind the Lines in the Southern Confederacy.* Baton Rouge, La., 1944. A discussion of the homefront that does not go deeply below the surface.

Randall, James G. and David Donald. *The Civil War and Reconstruction.* Boston, 1961. The best single volume on the social, economic, and political history of the war.

Reagan, John H. *Memoirs With Special Reference to Secession and the Civil War.* New York, 1906. The Postmaster General of the Confederacy tells his story.

Regimental History Committee. *History of the Third Pennsylvania Cavalry.* Philadelphia, 1905. One of the countless regimental histories that has some excellent anecdotes on the life of a soldier.

Rose, Victor M. *Ross' Texas Brigade.* Louisville, 1881. Some random thoughts on service in the Confederate Army.

Schwab, John C. *The Confederate States of America, 1861–1865: A Financial and Industrial History of the South During the Civil War.* New York, 1901. An authoritative work that remains outstanding in the field of economic history.

Shannon, Fred A. *The Organization and Administration of the Union Army, 1861–1865.* 2 vols. Cleveland, 1928. An excellent account of how the Federal armies were raised, equipped, and trained.

Stevens, George T. *Three Years in the Sixth Corps.* Albany, N.Y., 1866. A journalist's excellent account of life in the Army of the Potomac.

Todd, Richard C. *Confederate Finance.* Athens, Ga., 1954. A good description of Confederate financial policies and hardships.

Vandiver, Frank E. *Their Tattered Flags: The Epic of the Confederacy.* New York, 1970. A factual and stirring account of the South's gallant but futile effort to fight a successful modern war. Includes operational military and political history.

War of the Rebellion: A Compilation of the Official Records of the Union and Confederate Armies. Washington, 1880–1901. 130 volumes of Civil War correspondence, poorly indexed but well organized. Still the primary source for new interpretations.

Weber, Thomas. *The Northern Railroads in the Civil War.* New York, 1952. An outstanding account of the strength of the Federals' railroad system.

Battles and Campaigns

Agassiz, George R. (ed.). *Meade's Headquarters, 1863–1865: Letters*

of Colonel Theodore Lyman. Boston, 1922. Interesting collection of letters by one of Meade's aides.

Ambrose, Stephen E. (ed.). *Struggle for Vicksburg.* Harrisburg, Pa., 1967. A reprint of a special issue of *Civil War Times Illustrated.*

Bearss, Edwin C. *Decision in Mississippi.* Jackson, Miss., 1962. Highly detailed study of Vicksburg with the conclusion that Champion's Hill was the war's turning point.

Bigelow, John. *The Campaign of Chancellorsville.* New Haven, Conn., 1910. An outstanding study of the strategy and tactics of the campaign.

Brown, D. Alexander. *Grierson's Raid.* Urbana, Ill., 1954. A complete study of the raid and its impact.

Carter, Samuel. *The Final Fortress: The Campaign for Vicksburg, 1862–1863.* New York, 1980. The most recent account of a pivotal campaign. Carefully researched.

Coddington, Edwin B. *The Gettysburg Campaign.* New York, 1968. The best study of the campaign to date.

Cox, Jacob D. *Atlanta.* New York, 1882. A Federal division commander's excellent description of the Atlanta Campaign.

————. *The Battle of Franklin.* New York, 1897. Very detailed description of the battle. Complimentary to Schofield.

————. *The March to the Sea: Franklin and Nashville.* New York, 1882. A very balanced description of the Federal armies in the western campaigns.

Douglas, Henry K. *I Rode With Stonewall.* Chapel Hill, N.C., 1940. A biased but well-written account of service in the Stonewall Brigade.

Esposito, Vincent J. (ed.). *The West Point Atlas of American Wars.* 2 vols. New York, 1959. Volume I contains a detailed operational history of the war with excellent maps.

Fieberger, Gustavus J. *Campaigns of the American Civil War.* West Point, N.Y., 1914. A straightforward account of the major campaigns.

Force, Manning F. *From Fort Henry to Corinth.* New York, 1882. A Federal division commander's colorless account of the early campaigns in the West.

Herr, Robert S. *Episodes of the Civil War, Nine Campaigns in Nine States.* San Francisco, 1890. A long-winded narrative by a Union corporal.

Horn, Stanley. *The Decisive Battle of Nashville.* Baton Rouge, La., 1956. A good study of the campaign. Probably overstates the battle's significance.

Humphreys, Andrew A. *The Virginia Campaign of '64 and '65.* New York, 1883. A well-balanced account of the campaign by Meade's chief of staff.

Johnson, Robert Underwood and Clarence Clough Buel (eds.). *Battles and Leaders of the Civil War.* New York, 1884–1888. A comprehensive collection of articles by the war's participants. Marred by considerable after-the-fact commentary.

Johnston, Joseph E. *Narrative of Military Operations, Directed During the Late War Between the States.* New York, 1874. Johnston's personal war against Jefferson Davis is continued in this work.

Jones, James P. *Yankee Blitzkrieg.* Athens, Ga., 1976. A well-documented account of Wilson's 1865 raid through Alabama and Georgia.

Jones, Virgil C. *The Civil War at Sea.* New York, 1961. An average but readable account of the naval forces.

Miers, Earl Schenk. *The Web of Victory.* New York, 1955. A brief examination of Vicksburg.

Military Historical Society of Massachusetts. *Campaigns in Kentucky and Tennessee Including the Battle of Chickamauga, 1862–1865.* Boston, 1904. One volume of an extensive, well-balanced series on Civl War campaigns, written by participants.

MOLLUS, *Military Essays and Recollections.* 4 vols. Chicago, 1891–1899. The Military Order of the Loyal Legion of the United States has compiled many excellent battle accounts based on regional interests.

Monaghan, Jay. *Civil War on the Western Border, 1854–1865.* Boston, 1955. A useful account of the little-known campaigns west of the Mississippi River.

Phillips, Edward H. *The Shenandoah Valley in 1864: An Episode in the History of Warfare.* Charleston, 1965. An attack against barn burning.

Pond, George E. *The Shenandoah Valley in 1864.* New York, 1883. An early account of Sheridan's operations.

Rich, Joseph W. *The Battle of Shiloh.* Iowa City, 1911. A brief description of the battle, this book lacks depth of analysis.

Smith, William F. *The Relief of the Army of the Cumberland and the Opening of the Short Line of Communication Between Chattanooga, Tenn., and Bridgeport, Ala., in October 1863.* Washington, 1891. One of Smith's attempts to prove that he was the unsung hero of the war.

Sommers, Richard J. *Richmond Redeemed: The Siege at Petersburg.* New York, 1981. This work rivals Bigelow's *Chancellorsville* as the model of a campaign study. Detailed and well-written.

Stackpole, Edward J. *Chancellorsville: Lee's Greatest Battle.* Harrisburg, Pa., 1958. An average account of Hooker's blunders.

———. *They Met at Gettysburg.* Harrisburg, Pa., 1956. Although somewhat confusingly organized, this is a readable account.

Swinton, William. *Campaigns of the Army of the Potomac.* New York, 1866. Fairly reliable narrative by a news correspondent.

Tucker, Glenn. *Chickamauga: Bloody Battle in the West.* Indianapolis, 1961. Although largely undocumented, this is still an excellent source.

Turchin, John B. *Chickamauga.* Chicago, 1888. A former Russian officer tells about the battle as he saw it in the Federal Army.

Van Horne, Thomas B. *History of the Army of the Cumberland: Its Organization, Campaigns, and Battles.* Cincinnati, 1875. A biased account of George H. Thomas and the Army of the Cumberland.

Vandiver, Frank E. *Jubal's Raid: General Early's Famous Attack on Washington in 1864.* New York, 1960. A fast-moving, well-documented story of Early's offensive.

———. *Mighty Stonewall.* New York, 1957. A well-written, well-researched biography of one of the South's leading generals.

Whan, Vorin. *Fiasco at Fredericksburg.* State College, Pa., 1961. An outstanding study of the Federal command in the Fredericksburg Campaign.

Williams, Kenneth P. *Lincoln Finds a General: A Military Study of the Civil War.* 5 vols. New York, 1949–1959. A critical analysis of operations from the beginning of the war until mid-1863. Written from the Union viewpoint, these volumes are detailed and factual.

Williams, T. Harry. *Lincoln and His Generals.* New York, 1952. A good study of Lincoln's influence on the military campaigns of the war.

Personalities

Badeau, Adam. *Military History of Ulysses S. Grant.* 3 vols. New York, 1885. A contemporary analysis of Grant's generalship by his military secretary.

Catton, Bruce. *Grant Moves South.* Boston, 1960. This work is part of the excellent trilogy on U.S. Grant, begun earlier by Lloyd Lewis.

———. *Grant Takes Command.* Boston, 1969. Also part of the trilogy on Grant, this volume is largely an account of the final year of the war in the East.

———. *U.S. Grant and the American Military Tradition.* New York, 1954. A brief analysis of Grant's impact on the Civil War and his subsequent failures.

Cleaves, Freeman. *Meade of Gettysburg.* Norman, Okla., 1960. A biography that is very biased in favor of Meade.

Connelly, Thomas L. *The Marble Man: Robert E. Lee and His Image in American Society.* New York, 1977. A critical biography that is less admiring of the Confederate general than most accounts.

Dodge, Grenville M. *Personal Recollections of President Abraham Lincoln, General Ulysses S. Grant and General William T. Sherman.* Iowa, 1914. How one Union general viewed the great men around him.

Dowdey, Clifford and Louis H. Manarin (eds.). *Wartime Papers of R.E. Lee.* Boston, 1961. An excellent collection of Lee's papers, containing valuable editorial notes.

Freeman, Douglas Southall. *R.E. Lee: A Biography.* New York, 1934. 4 vols. Excellent biography by a master biographer.

Fuller, John F.C. *The Generalship of Ulysses S. Grant.* New York, 1929. A thorough study that concludes that Grant was a master strategist. Biased in Grant's favor.

Gibbon, John. *Personal Recollections of the Civil War.* New York, 1928. Interesting account by a Federal division commander in the Army of the Potomac who was present for most of the major battles.

Gordon, John B. *Reminiscences of the Civil War.* New York, 1903. An extremely interesting memoir by a southern brigadier. Full of exciting tales.

Grant, Ulysses S. *Personal Memoirs of U.S. Grant.* 2 vols. New York, 1885. Among the best of the Civil War memoirs.

Henderson, George F.R. *Stonewall Jackson and the American Civil War.* 2 vols. New York, 1904. Biased in favor of Jackson, this work has gone through numerous reprints because of its popularity.

Henry, Robert Selph. *"First with the Most" Forrest.* Indianapolis, 1944. Although Henry finds little wrong with Forrest, this is a good account of the general's exploits.

Hood, John B. *Advance and Retreat.* New Orleans, 1880. An unconvincing defense of General Hood's actions.

Howard, Oliver O. *Autobiography of Oliver Otis Howard.* 2 vols. New York, 1908. A well-written memoir that is overly self-justifying in places.

Hughes, Nathaniel C. *General William J. Hardee: Old Reliable.* Baton Rouge, La., 1965. A well-researched study of a good tactician.

Lamers, William M. *The Edge of Glory: A Biography of General William S. Rosecrans, USA.* New York, 1961. A thorough account of an underrated general.

Lewis, Lloyd. *Captain Sam Grant.* Boston, 1950. The prewar story of Grant.

———. *Sherman, Fighting Prophet.* New York, 1932. Undocumented but well-researched biography that uses many of Sherman's own words to tell the story.

Liddell Hart, Basil H. *Sherman: Soldier, Realist, American.* New

York, 1950. An Englishman's view of Sherman's military genius.

Long, Armistead L. *Memoirs of Robert E. Lee*. New York, 1886. Lee's story told by one of his aides.

Longstreet, James. *From Manassas to Appomattox: Memoirs of the Civil War in America*. Philadelphia, 1896. A stout defense of Longstreet's wartime record, influenced by the southern attacks against him after the war.

McClellan, George B. *McClellan's Own Story*. New York, 1887. The reasons why others would not let him win the war.

McClellan, Henry B. *The Life and Campaigns of Major General J.E.B. Stuart*. Boston, 1885. A popular biography of a colorful cavalryman.

Morrison, James L., Jr. (ed.). *The Memoirs of Henry Heth*. Westport, Conn., 1974. Although Heth is brief on the Civil War, he details many interesting conversations with Lee.

Nevins, Allen (ed.). *A Diary of Battle: The Personal Journals of Colonel Charles S. Wainwright*. New York, 1962. The II Corps artilleryman provides many helpful insights into the relationships between the generals of the Army of the Potomac.

Nichols, Edward J. *Toward Gettysburg: A Biography of General John F. Reynolds*. University Park, Pa., 1956. A well-researched account of one of the Union's more able generals.

Parks, Joseph H. *General Leonidas Polk, CSA*. Baton Rouge, La., 1962. The military career of the Episcopal bishop turned general.

Pemberton, John C. III. *Pemberton: Defender of Vicksburg*. Chapel Hill, N.C., 1942. The general's grandson defends his ancestor's decisions.

Pennypacker, Isaac R. *General Meade*. New York, 1901. An undocumented biography. Very biased in favor of Meade.

Seitz, Don C. *Braxton Bragg: General of the Confederacy*. Columbia, S.C., 1924. Bragg's biographer is not enamored with the general.

Sheridan, Philip H. *Personal Memoirs of P.H. Sheridan*. 2 vols. New York, 1888. A glowing account of the general's Civil War exploits.

Sherman, William T. *Memoirs of General William T. Sherman*. 2 vols. New York, 1875. A straightforward account that spares no feelings.

Sparks, David S. (ed.). *Inside Lincoln's Army: The Diary of Marsena Rudolph Patrick, Provost Marshal General, Army of the Potomac*. New York, 1964. Patrick's bluntness is obvious in his diary. Excellent analysis of personalities in the Army of the Potomac.

Steiner, Paul E. *Medical-Military Portraits of Union and Confederate Generals*. Philadelphia, 1968. Some interesting psychological profiles of leading Civil War generals.

Swanberg, W.A. *Sickles the Incredible*. New York, 1956. A well-written account of a truly incredible man.

Taylor, Emerson G. *Gouverneur Kemble Warren*. New York, 1932. A biography of a cautious general; biased in favor of Warren.

Thomas, Wilbur D. *General George H. Thomas: The Indomitable Warrior*. New York, 1964. Very biased in favor of Thomas, but well-researched.

Thomason, John W. *Jeb Stuart*. New York, 1930. Another glowing biography of the ''cavalier.''

Welles, Edgar T. (ed.). *The Diary of Gideon Welles*. Boston, 1911. 3 vols. The Secretary of the Navy's thoughts on service in Lincoln's Cabinet.

Williams, T. Harry. *P.G.T. Beauregard: Napoleon in Gray*. Baton Rouge, La., 1955. An excellent biography of the man who wanted to be Napoleon.

Index

The abbreviations C.S.A. (Confederate States of America) and U.S.A. (United States of America) have been used to indicate the political allegiance of each of the participants in the Civil War.